Economics and Contemporary Issues

EIGHTH EDITION

RONALD L. MOOMAW
Oklahoma State University

KENT W. OLSON
Oklahoma State University

MICHAEL APPLEGATE
Oklahoma State University

BILL McLEAN
Oklahoma State University

SOUTH-WESTERN
CENGAGE Learning™

Australia • Brazil • Canada • Mexico • Singapore • Spain • United Kingdom • United States

Economics & Contemporary Issues, Eighth Edition
Ronald L. Moomaw, Kent W. Olson, Michael Applegate, and Bill McLean

Vice President of Editorial, Business: Jack W. Calhoun

Editor-in-Chief: Joe Sabatino

Acquisitions Editor: Steven Scoble

Supervising Developmental Editor: Jennifer E. Thomas

Associate Marketing Manager: Betty Jung

Content Project Management: Pre-Press PMG

Production Technology Analyst: Emily Gross

Media Editor: Deepak Kumar

Manufacturing Buyer: Sandee Milewski

Production Service: Pre-Press PMG

Copyeditor: James Reidel

Compositor: Pre-Press PMG

Senior Art Director: Michelle Kunkler

Cover Designer: Rokusek Design

Cover Image: ©Shutterstock

Library of Congress Control Number: 2009925654

ISBN-13: 978-0-324-82786-6

ISBN-10: 0-324-82786-5

South-Western Cengage Learning
5191 Natorp Boulevard
Mason, OH 45040
USA

Cengage Learning products are represented in Canada by Nelson Education, Ltd.

Printed in the United States of America
1 2 3 4 5 6 7 8 12 11 10 09

Brief Contents

Brief Contents

Contents

Preface

Economics and Contemporary Issues takes an issues approach to introductory economics. This makes for a user-friendly textbook that illustrates how economics helps students make sense of their world. The economy affects us personally and socially. An understanding of the way it works is crucial in personal planning and in making political and social decisions.

This book examines major issues, such as education, health care, Social Security, unemployment, inflation, the budget deficit, and international trade. It answers questions such as: Is education a good investment? Are we spending too much on health care? What causes inflation? Are we headed for a federal budget disaster? What are the benefits and costs of international trade? It also examines social and political phenomena that have continued importance in the twenty-first century—the collapse of Communism and central planning, the role of government in a modern economy, crime and drugs, poverty, and the failure of some economies to grow.

This textbook maximizes the advantages of the issues approach by examining issues that interest students, while developing core economic principles that provide penetrating insights and a basis for lifelong learning. An economic analysis of contemporary issues will often challenge students' deeply held beliefs about how the world works. Such challenges, combined with the analytical framework provided by economic theory, make this textbook ideal in a curriculum emphasizing critical thinking.

Students who use this textbook will develop an increased interest in economics, seeing it as important in understanding issues that affect them personally, as well as in understanding today's headlines. Experience has shown that students often continue their study of economics as a result of using this book.

THE INTENDED AUDIENCES

One audience for this textbook is students enrolled in the growing number of one-term issues courses offered by economics departments, often as general education courses. This book contains enough economic theory, however, for the traditional one-term survey course in economics. It is also appropriate for use as a supplement in traditional two-semester principles courses, or as a text for the economics part of social science survey courses. If the instructor adds other readings (and ample references are provided on the text's Web site), it can also be used as a core text in an upper-division issues or capstone course.

A BALANCED TREATMENT OF MICROECONOMICS AND MACROECONOMICS

The analysis of macroeconomic issues is often slighted in issues books, but not in this one. Seven of the 18 chapters cover macroeconomic issues, including national income accounting, unemployment, inflation, the federal deficit and debt, the balance of payments and trade deficits, and economic growth. The microeconomic aspects of agriculture, monopoly power, health care, crime, pollution, education, Social Security, and poverty are also examined.

A Basic Theory Core

Both the micro- and macroeconomic parts of this book use a small number of understandable, yet powerful, economic concepts and models.

In the microeconomics chapters, supply and demand and marginal analysis are used extensively. Models of competitive and monopolized markets are developed. The distinctions between social and private benefits and costs are used to analyze market and government failures. Measures of consumers' and producers' surpluses are used to illustrate efficiency gains and losses.

The basic macroeconomics tool is the model of aggregate supply and aggregate demand. Use of this versatile model enables beginning students to understand the forces that determine output, employment, the price level, and the effects of alternative fiscal and monetary policies, such as proposed changes in taxes and the Federal Reserve discount rate.

Up-to-Date, Comprehensive Background Information on Each Issue

Our experience shows that most beginning students know very little about economic history, data, and institutions. An issues course must fill this void by providing the information necessary for understanding the nature and significance of the problems addressed.

Essential information can be provided by both the instructor and the textbook. Although there is no perfect substitute for an instructor who seeks new information and provides it to students, this book simplifies the instructor's quest by providing current and comprehensive background information on each issue, and references to additional resources.

Flexibility in the Sequencing of Topics and Issues

This book is structured so that microeconomic principles (and issues) are examined before macroeconomic principles are introduced. Macroeconomic principles and issues can be studied first, however, because they have been designed to be independent of the microeconomics chapters. Instructors who prefer to teach macroeconomics first, following an introduction to the market system, can do so by assigning Chapters 1 and 2 and then going to Chapter 13.

Chapters 1 and 2 provide the foundation for Chapters 3 through 12. Chapter 13 provides the foundation for Chapters 14 through 17. A one-term principles survey course could include Chapters 1 through 5, 13 through 17, and other selected chapters to fit the instructor's interests.

An Emphasis on Globalization

Chapter 1 examines economic growth from an international perspective, and the last two chapters analyze international trade and finance. Today, however, most issues have a global dimension, and the book reflects this. In most chapters, students will find an "International Perspective" feature or a section dealing with an international dimension of the issue.

NEW TO THIS EDITION

Economic problems and issues change rapidly, requiring frequent updating of data and information. For the seventh edition of *Economics and Contemporary Issues*, we have literally gone back to the drawing board in over half of the chapters to produce a new edition that is truly different from its predecessors. Of course, we have at the same time done the standard things expected in a revision: updating all the data, tables, and figures; clarifying explanations; and including more examples and illustrations.

The boxed material that complements the main text by providing additional "Insights" and "International Perspectives" has also been revised and expanded. The most extensive change here is the addition of new "Insight" boxes in seven chapters that use basic economics to examine the effects of Hurricanes Katrina and Rita, and the manner in which the market system and government authorities responded to the crisis that ensued.

The number of references to Web sites has been greatly expanded, reflecting the growing importance of the World Wide Web as a source of current, comprehensive, and readily accessible information on the issues addressed in this book.

The power of the Internet has been multiplied again in this edition by providing text adopters with access to InfoTrac® College Edition, a database of over a million articles. Keywords to help the reader search this database effectively are provided in the margins of the text.

Chapter 1 Economic Growth: An Introduction to Scarcity and Choice. We begin the text with an analysis of economic growth, arguably the most important economic and social phenomenon of the last 200 years. The title reflects the fact that even rapidly growing economies are not relieved of the necessity to choose among alternative uses of scarce resources. The relationships among growth, scarcity, and choice are illustrated in the usual manner with the production possibilities curve. However, this model is also used in this edition to illuminate choices that the typical college student must make.

Chapter 2 An Introduction to Economic Systems and the Workings of the Price System. This chapter has two primary purposes: (1) to explain how market systems work and (2) to examine the experiences of formerly planned economies in their quest to transition to market systems. This edition continues to stress the importance of property rights and honesty in the transition process. The "International Perspective" on China is revised to account for the Land Ownership Law of 1998. A new section on "Comparative Advantage and Specialization" has been added, along with an "Insight" on Wal-Mart and FEMA that discusses how decentralization has advantages over centralization in disaster relief.

Chapter 4 Efficiency in Resource Allocation: How Much Do We Have? How Much Do We Want? It continues to use the concept of welfare gains and losses to illustrate the losses from market failures and government policies and regulations. It also continues to emphasize the trade-offs among efficiency, equity, and growth.

Chapter 5 Market Power: Does It Help or Hurt the Economy? This analysis of the economics of market power starts by developing the standard monopoly model. The model is then modified as appropriate and applied to the OPEC oil cartel and to the gasoline market. The section "Market Power and Economic Growth" from the Seventh Edition is revised. It encompasses both technological improvements and efficiency improvements. The chapter also has a new "Insight": Rita, Katrina, and Refineries: Economic and Political Rent Seeking.

Chapter 6 Air Pollution: Balancing Benefits and Costs. This chapter is essentially unchanged from the Seventh Edition. The economist's perspective on the pollution problem is examined with one supply-demand diagram that illustrates and quantifies the efficiency losses from pollution. This diagram is also used to illustrate how Coase's theorem works. Data are presented on the progress made in reducing air pollution under the Clean Air Act, and there is a section on the benefits and costs of the Clean Air Act. The section on pollution taxes and emissions uses an example that illustrates the cost savings possible with these approaches.

Chapter 7 Health Care: How Much? For Whom? This is a revised and updated chapter that addresses the principal problems of the U.S. health care system and issues related to reforming that system. The principal problems are: (1) the rising share of GDP devoted to health care; (2) the growing number of uninsured individuals; and (3) wasteful spending. We raise the issue of how much health care the U.S. can afford and examine several ways of rationally limiting expenditures.

Chapter 8 Crime and Drugs: A Modern Dilemma. This chapter continues to highlight the economic approach to crime. Cost benefit analysis using comparing marginal cost and marginal benefit to determine the optimal level of crime control as well as the equimarginal principle is center to the analysis used in this chapter. The relative merits of drug treatment versus conducting a war on drugs are also considered from an economic perspective.

Chapter 9 College Education: Is It Worth the Cost? This chapter remains built around a numerical example of the benefits and costs to a typical college graduate from investing in a college education. The determination of the rate of return from investing in a college education is revised to allow for: (1) the fact that the typical college student spends more than four years (4.57) completing a bachelor's degree; (2) the probability that a student will drop out each year (4 percent per year) after enrolling; and (3) the probability of completion within six years (58 percent). These revisions reduce the rate of return to both the student and society, but investing in a college education remains an attractive alternative from both perspectives.

Chapter 10 Educational Reform: The Role of Incentives and Choice. The purpose of this chapter remains that of demonstrating how economics can illuminate the debate on reforming U.S. elementary and secondary education. The chapter now has a discussion of No Child Left Behind (NCLB), and the analysis of government policy has been revamped to compare accountability (NCLB) and consumer choice.

Chapter 11 Poverty: New Approaches to an Old Problem. The analysis of the issues raised in this chapter depends heavily on the use of data on poverty measures and programs. All the data, figures, and tables have been revised to reflect the latest available information. Time series diagrams are used extensively to illustrate trends in the official poverty rate, the poverty rates of selected groups, the pre-transfer poverty rate, the anti-poverty effectiveness of government transfers, and the relationship of poverty and unemployment. The sections on childcare assistance and medical protection for individuals making the transition from TANF to work have been kept and the final section continues to focus on efforts to develop a more effective system of child support.

Chapter 12 Tracking and Explaining the Macroeconomy. This chapter focuses on measuring output and prices and developing the model of aggregate supply and aggregate demand.

Chapter 13 Unemployment: The Legacy of Recession, Technological Change, and Free Choice. This chapter has remained essentially unchanged. The relationship between full employment and the natural rate of unemployment is carefully explained and illustrated. The chapter distinguishes between active and passive macroeconomic policy. There is an "Insight" on the effects of Hurricanes Katrina and Rita on the economy. This material can be used to explain the links among unemployment, government actions to combat unemployment, and the degree of wage flexibility. It can also be used to more fully explain the economics of the minimum wage (developed in this chapter) and the causes of poverty (Chapter 11).

Chapter 14 Inflation: A Monetary Phenomenon. This chapter continues to analyze inflation using both the equation of exchange and the aggregate demand–aggregate supply model. There is a discussion of the relationship among monopolies, oil markets, and inflation. A new "Insight"—When Is an Increase in the CPI Not Inflation?—captures the effect of Hurricanes Katrina and Rita on inflation.

Chapter 15 Sustained Budget Deficits: Is This Any Way to Run a Government? The prospect of large and growing budget deficits is one of the most serious problems facing the U.S. economy. Recognition of the growing importance of this issue makes this the most thoroughly revised chapter in the text. It has been completely rewritten to focus on the causes and macroeconomic consequences of projected chronic budget deficits and expanding debt. It explains why they are not sustainable and examines alternative means of solving the problem.

Chapter 16 Social Security: Leading Issues and Approaches to Reform. The long-run deficit in Social Security is one the principal causes of the projected long-run federal budget deficit; hence, the new location of this chapter. The chapter retains much of the material explaining Social Security benefits from the Seventh Edition. Virtually a third of the material is new, however, including a discussion of reform plans proposed to fix the existing system and to supplement the system with individual accounts.

Chapter 17 International Trade: Beneficial, but Controversial. This chapter continues to explain and illustrate the bases for international trade, the net benefits of trade, controversial aspects of free trade, and the welfare costs of popular cures, such as tariffs and quotas.

Chapter 18 Financing Trade and the Trade Deficit. This chapter has been revised and reorganized to explain how exchange rates are determined and how trade deficits are financed. Then we examine three issues: the effects of growing U.S. foreign indebtedness, the case for and against the regulation of exchange rates, and the case for and against the regulation of international capital flows.

FEATURES

Economics and Contemporary Issues has several features that are important in an issues-oriented text:

- Effective aids to self-learning
- A balanced treatment of microeconomics and macroeconomics
- A basic theory core
- Up-to-date, comprehensive background information on each issue
- Flexibility in the sequencing of topics and issues
- An emphasis on globalization

Effective Aids to Self-Learning

The first route to self-learning is a clear, concise exposition of basic concepts. Beginning students readily understand *Economics and Contemporary Issues*. Every sentence has been written with them in mind.

To understand economics, students must master its basic vocabulary. To facilitate this, key terms are highlighted when they first appear and defined in three places: the body of the text, the margin, and the glossary. In addition, each chapter ends with a list of the key terms introduced in the chapter as a reminder to the reader.

To help students master the standard tools of economic analysis, there is a judicious use of graphs and tables that are carefully explained both in their accompanying captions and in the text narrative. The initial graphs are constructed from accompanying data to help the beginner master this important tool of economic analysis.

"Insights" and "International Perspective" features are provided to supplement text material and to illustrate the broad applicability of economics. For instance, there are several "Insights" relating to the effects of and responses to the 2005 hurricanes. Another "Insight" discusses the well-known coffeehouses in the Netherlands, and one asks whether the college that a student attends makes a difference in future earnings.

Self-testing is an essential component of self-learning. Each chapter contains review questions (with answers in the Instructor's Manual), and a carefully constructed Study Guide is available. Each chapter provides a summary of important points.

Most of today's students are computer-literate and familiar with the Internet as a source of information. This text helps the student (and instructor) tap this resource by providing a number of references to helpful Web sites. In addition, this edition provides text adopters with access to InfoTrac®, a database of over a million articles. Keywords to help the reader search this database effectively are provided in the margin of the text.

SUPPLEMENTARY MATERIALS

- Student Companion Web Site. Located at http://www.cengage.com/economics/moomaw, this site provides access to Online Quizzes, Key Terms, and Definitions, and much more.
- Economic Applications include EconNews, EconDebates, and EconData features to deepen understanding of theoretical concepts through hands-on exploration and analysis of the latest economic news stories, policy debates, and data. Organized by topic and continually updated, EconApps are easy to integrate into the classroom.
- InfoTrac® College Edition is a fully searchable online university library containing complete articles and their images. Its database allows access to hundreds of scholarly and popular publications—all reliable sources—including magazines, journals, encyclopedias, and newsletters.

If an access card came with this book, you can start using many of these resources right away by following the directions on the card. Get started today at http://infotrac.cengage.com

- *The Study Guide* contains for each chapter a list of objectives, review of key terms, quantitative problems, true/false, multiple-choice, and fill-in questions.
- *The Instructor's Manual and Test Bank* provides instructors with a useful tool in planning their course and preparing exams. The Instructor's Manual includes chapter overviews, teaching objectives, key terms, teaching suggestions, additional references, detailed lecture outlines, and answers to Review Questions. The Test Bank provides a variety of exam questions and problems in true/false, multiple-choice, and essay and discussion formats. Chapters also include Critical Thinking Multiple Choice Questions. Both are available—password-protected—to instructors on the text's Web site.

- *ExamView Computerized Testing Software* contains all the questions in the printed test bank. This program is an easy-to-use test creation software compatible with Microsoft Windows. Instructors can add or edit questions, instructions, and answers, and select questions by previewing them on the screen, selecting them randomly, or selecting them by number. Instructors can also create and administer quizzes online, whether over the Internet, a local area network (LAN), or a wide area network (WAN).

ACKNOWLEDGEMENTS

We did not produce this book alone and we greatly appreciate the contributions of users, colleagues, reviewers, students, and the editorial team at South-Western Cengage Learning. We appreciate all comments that we receive and rely on them as we make revisions. Please let us know how we can improve our book.

Many of the changes in this edition were made in response to the careful reviews and thoughtful suggestions of the following:

C. Alan Burns (Lee University)
Kenny Christianson (Binghamton University)
Laura Ebert (Marist College)
Ann Eike (University of Kentucky)
Fred Englander (Fairleigh Dickinson University)
Daniel Kou (Orange Coast College)
Holly Lippke Fretwell (Montana State University)
R. C. Gamble (Fort Hays State University)
Demetrios Giannaros (University of Hartford)
Randall G. Holcombe (Florida State University)
James C. McBrearty (University of Arizona)
Donald C. Rudow (University of Georgia)
Allen Sanderson (University of Chicago)
D. Eric Schansberg (Indiana University)
Rick Zuber (University of North Carolina–Charlotte)

We are grateful for their help, as well as that of the reviewers of previous editions:

Ugur Aker (Hiram College)
Michael Applegate (Oklahoma State University)
Michael W. Babcock (Kansas State University)
John P. Blair (Wright State University)
Gale Blalock (University of Evansville)
Eric Brooks (Orange County Community College)
Hyung C. Chung (University of Bridgeport)
Bruce Domazlicky (Southeast Missouri State University)
Pauline Fox (Southeast Missouri State University)
James R. Frederick (Pembroke State University)

Neil Garston	(California State University–Los Angeles)
Daphne T. Greenwood	(University of Colorado–Colorado Springs)
Robert B. Harris	(Indiana University–Purdue University at Indianapolis)
Emily Hoffman	(Western Michigan University)
Randall Holcombe	(Florida State University)
Joseph Horton	(University of Central Arkansas)
Philip J. Lane	(Fairfield University)
Christopher Lingle	(Loyola University–New Orleans)
John P. Manzer	(Indiana University-Purdue University–Ft. Wayne)
Melanie Marks	(Longwood College)
Doug McNeil	(McNeese State University)
John Merrifield	(University of Texas–San Antonio)
George Murphy	(University of California–Los Angeles)
Steven Petty	(College of the Ozarks)
John Pisciotta	(Baylor University)
Fred J. Ruppel	(Eastern Kentucky University)
John Scott	(Northeast Louisiana University)
Larry Sechrest	(University of Texas–Arlington)
Edwin A. Sexton	(Virginia Military Institute)
Alden Smith	(Anne Arundel Community College)
Paula Smith	(University of Central Oklahoma)
Steve Smith	(Rose State College)
Gary L. Stone	(Winthrop University)
Barbara Street	(Chaminade University–Honolulu)
Charles Stull	(Western Michigan University)
Rebecca Summary	(Southeast Missouri State University)
Manjuri Talukdar	(Northern Illinois University)
Millicent Taylor	(University of Southern Colorado)
Ranbir Varma	(Long Island University)

We also gratefully acknowledge the guidance, support, and encouragement provided by the South-Western Cengage Learning team, including Jennifer Thomas, Katie Yanos, Steven Scoble, Michelle Kunkler, Jennifer Ziegler, Betty Jung, and Jared Sterzer. They have greatly facilitated the development of this edition. We certainly could not have done it so quickly—or so well—without them.

Ronald L. Moomaw
Kent W. Olson
Micheal Applegate
William McLean

About the Authors

Ronald L. Moomaw is an Associate Professor of Economics at Oklahoma State University. He also serves as Associate Editor for the *Journal of Regional Science* and Assistant Editor for *Journal of Economics.* In addition to this book, Dr. Moomaw has authored or co-authored many articles appearing in journals, such as *Quarterly Journal of Economics, Southern Economic Journal, Journal of Urban Economics, Regional Science and Urban Economics, Journal of Regional Science, Urban Studies, Land Economics, Annals of Regional Science,* and *Review of Regional Studies.* His current research interests include efficiency in secondary education, economic growth of states, and local unemployment differentials. Dr. Moomaw has served as principal investigator on projects funded by the U.S. Department of Commerce and U.S. Information Agency. He also served on the faculty of the University of British Columbia and University of Virginia, as Senior Research Associate for The Urban Institute, and as an economist at the U.S. Department of Commerce. He is currently on leave at the University of Bonn.

Kent W. Olson is a Professor of Economics at Oklahoma State University. He has co-authored two textbooks and has written numerous articles that have appeared in *Land Economics, National Tax Journal, Social Science Quarterly, Journal of Business and Economics,* and *American Journal of Economics and Sociology.* His research interests include Social Security reform, health care reform, federal budget issues, and educational finance. Dr. Olson has served on the faculty of Occidental College, Arizona State University, Indiana University/Purdue University at Indianapolis, and United States International University. He is a member of the Western Economic Association, Southwest Economic Association and is listed in *Who's Who in American Men and Women of Science.*

BillMcLean has taught a variety of economics courses during the past thirteen years. His experience includes instructing both at the college and high school levels where he has taught Advanced Placement (AP) Microeconomics and Macroeconomics, Principles of Microeconomics, Intermediate Macroeconomics as well as Money and Banking. He is a reader for the National AP Economics Exam. His primary research covers economic education and economic teaching pedagogies. He earned his B.A. in Business Administration from Columbus State University and M.B.A from Florida Institute of Technology. He also holds a M.A. in National Security and Strategic Studies from the Naval War College. He is currently completing a Ph.D. in Economics at Oklahoma State University.

MikeApplegate is a Professor of Economics at Oklahoma State University. He has published in the area of quantitative policy analysis and has worked as an analyst in Panama, Guatemala, Dominican Republic, Nicaragua, and Zambia where he lived two years. His current research interest is using computable general equilibrium models for policy analysis. He has directed numerous dissertations using these models applied to various countries in Africa and the Middle East. He has taught at the undergraduate and graduate levels for over thirty-four years. He earned his B.A. in economics at Brigham Young University and his Ph.D. in economics at Iowa State University.

To the Student

Welcome to *Economics and Contemporary Issues*. This book will teach you how the American economy works and how economic incentives and institutions are related to important social problems. In the process of learning these things, you will sharpen your critical thinking skills.

The issues and problems you will study command the attention of concerned citizens and policy makers. Many of them will continue to be important long after you have finished this book; some will, hopefully, fade away. The principles you learn here, however, will help you to understand new problems and issues as they appear.

In examining each issue, we develop and apply the principles essential for understanding its economic dimensions, and then evaluate current and alternative approaches to dealing with it. The first step is the province of positive economics; the second is the focus of normative economics. Positive economics explains and predicts economic phenomena; normative economics selects social goals and evaluates policy alternatives according to how well they achieve these goals. This approach reflects the dual purpose of economics: To discover how the world works and to determine how it can be improved.

The basic normative questions posed throughout this book are whether government action is necessary to solve social problems and, if so, what policies should be adopted. For example, the chapter on air pollution considers whether curbing pollution—a social goal—can be accomplished efficiently by the private sector alone, and concludes that it cannot. Existing regulations and proposed policies are then evaluated to determine which of them are most likely to improve the situation. We use a similar approach in examining the other issues. We hope the net result will be a greater appreciation of the strengths and weaknesses of both the private and public sectors of the economy.

To achieve lasting benefits from economics, and to do well in your course, plan to go beyond merely memorizing this material. Learn, in addition, how to apply the principles and models developed in the text. We have attempted to write clearly and concisely so that you will understand the important principles. You will greatly enhance your ability to apply these principles, however, by answering the questions at the end of each chapter and by working through the Study Guide that Kenny Christianson of Binghamton University has written to help you master the material.

Finally, no single text can provide all of the information that pertains to the issues that we address. You can learn much more by examining the Web sites that we suggest throughout the text, by exploring recent articles using the InfoTrac® subscription that accompanies your purchase of this text, and by accessing the book's Web site at http://www.cengage.com/economics/moomaw.

CHAPTER 1

Economic Growth: An Introduction to Scarcity and Choice

OUTLINE

Two truly important documents of the past millennium that provided a basis for economic growth appeared in 1776. Thomas Jefferson's *Declaration of Independence* and Adam Smith's *Wealth of Nations* established guidelines for the growth of political and economic freedom during the next two centuries. These masterpieces emerged from ideas associated with the great artistic, political, and religious renewals that awakened Europe beginning early in the millennium. The values of the Declaration of Independence, as implemented and developed in the United States Constitution and Abraham Lincoln's Gettysburg Address, are beacons of political and economic freedom. As we shall see, these freedoms promote economic prosperity. Drawing from the same awakening, Adam Smith, the pioneering British economist, explained that an economy organized by markets and emphasizing economic freedom promotes the wealth of nations more effectively than one organized by a government plan.

Understanding how individuals interacting in an economy create prosperity has attracted many people to study economics because they know that understanding it is the key to improving the human condition. For instance, Alfred Marshall, another eminent British economist, was drawn to study economics by his concerns about poverty, saying, "[I] visited the poorest quarters of several cities and walked through one street after another, looking at the faces of the poorest people. Next, I resolved to make as thorough study as I could of Political Economy."[1] Marshall's "thorough study" resulted in his *Principles of Economics,* an unusual book in two ways. First, it was the dominant economics textbook for several decades at the beginning of the twentieth century, and it still exerts influence. Second, much of its analysis was based on Marshall's own contributions to economics as a discipline. Understanding economics because of its importance for the general welfare continues to fascinate economists. Nobel Prize–winning economist Robert Lucas of the University of Chicago noted the influence on his career of economic growth's ability to extinguish poverty. "Once I started thinking about economic growth," he said, "I could think of little else."

Economic growth has transformed life in industrialized countries. The material standard of living in the United States, for instance, is incomprehensibly higher for the average citizen than it was in 1776. Measures of health, education, life span, and material goods show vast improvement. The rich and famous 200 years ago enjoyed a consumption level of goods and services vastly superior to that of the average person in most dimensions—health, diet, entertainment, housing, education, and so on. Abraham Lincoln's early childhood in a small, windowless cabin with few books and little time for schooling contrasted sharply with the luxurious lifestyle enjoyed by Thomas Jefferson's children at Monticello.

[1]As cited in William Breit and Roger Ransom, *The Academic Scribblers,* rev ed. (Fort Worth, TX: Dryden, 1982), 20.

Because of a sustained economic revolution, most people in the United States have a material standard of living that far surpasses that enjoyed by the wealthy 200 years ago.

This revolution shows the fantastic ability of compound growth to raise living standards. *Gross domestic product* (GDP) is one measure of an economy's total output or production of goods and services.[2] Consequently, one measure of the standard of living is GDP per capita (person). Since 1820, GDP per capita in the United States has increased more than 24 times, although the growth rate was just 1.7 percent per year. Per capita GDP in 1990 dollars rose from $1,250 per person to over $30,000. The growth rate in Japan during this period was higher, 1.9 percent per year. This seemingly small difference was big enough to increase GDP per capita in Japan 33 times. In 1820, GDP per capita in the United States was about twice that of Japan; by the early 1990s it was just 20 percent greater. Big oaks grow from small acorns. By 2007 the U.S. advantage had grown to almost 36 percent because Japanese growth stagnated at about 1 percent per year and U.S. growth was about 2 percent.

Understanding the sources of persistent economic growth is crucial. Why does one country's output grow at 1.5 to 2 percent a year over long periods while another country's output grows at less than 0.5 percent a year or even shrinks? People in the first country prosper and in the second country struggle. From 1820 to 2007, Japan went from low-income status with GDP per capita 1.3 times that of India to advanced status with per capita GDP 7 times that of India. One country becomes a high-income country, and the other country remains low income.[3]

We hope that these short case studies, which show economic growth's power and potential to reduce world poverty, provide more than enough reason to start our journey in economics with economic growth. Jumping directly into this topic, we will use some concepts that are more thoroughly explained in later chapters. You'll acquaint yourself with these concepts here, and as we go through the course, you'll grasp them more completely. Initially, we look at several countries' economic growth from 1960 to 2007, emphasizing three points.

1. Economic growth in the high-income countries slowed after 1972, but it picked up in the United States in the 1990s.
2. GDP per capita in some countries may be catching up to that in the United States.
3. Some countries are experiencing significant economic growth, but others appear trapped at low growth rates.

We will discuss the sources of growth in the U.S. context and then expand the discussion to include other countries that have experienced significant economic growth and those that have failed to do so.

RECENT GROWTH EXPERIENCES

As seen in Figure 1.1A, since 1960 the United States has had a substantially lower per capita GDP growth rate than China, Korea, and Japan, and a lower rate than India and France. Its growth rate is slightly higher than that of Brazil and significantly higher than

[2]The GDP concept is developed in Chapter 12. For now, we can view it simply as an output measure. We've adjusted GDP for any general rise in prices, inflation. Because of this adjustment, all the measures are measures of real activity.

[3]Computed from data in Angus Maddison, *The World Economy: A Millennial Perspective* (Paris: Development Center—OECD, 2001) and Groningen Growth and Development Centre and The Conference Board, Total Economy Database, January 2009, http://www.conference-board/economics, August 2005, http://www.ggdc.net

INTERNATIONAL PERSPECTIVE

China: Economic Growth and Poverty

About 400 million Chinese escaped absolute poverty over a 20-year period beginning in 1981.[a] Absolute poverty is defined as a situation in which people lack the minimum necessary food, clothing, and shelter to survive and live a healthy life. It uses an income of $1 per day as the poverty line. Adjusted for inflation, per capita GDP more than tripled from 1978 to 2003. Using the 1990 price level, GDP increased from about $1,000 per person to about $4,500 per person.[b]

To put this change in perspective, 400 million people escaping poverty is greater than the entire population of the United States and almost equal to the population of the European Union. People in China had much more to eat, were much better clothed, and had many more of life's other necessities in 2004 than in 1978. In the early 1980s refrigerators, washing machines, and color televisions were luxuries owned only by the elite. By the early 2000s the appliances were commonplace. Every 100 families had 90 washing machines, 73 refrigerators, and 100 color televisions. From 1981 to 2004, egg consumption per person doubled in the cities and almost quadrupled in the countryside. Poultry consumption quadrupled and grain and vegetable consumption fell. The growth in GDP per capita expanded the opportunities for Chinese citizens in incredible ways.[c]

Adam Smith, Robert Lucas, and Alfred Marshall had it right. Prosperity is heavily influenced by political economy. Rapid economic growth is the only way that this huge number of people could escape poverty. The rest of the current chapter analyzes economic growth, and Chapter 2 considers why some economies prosper and others do not.

[a]Martin Ravallion, "Pessimistic on Poverty?" *The Economist*, April 7, 2004.

[b]Groningen Growth and Development Centre and The Conference Board, Total Economy Database, August 2005, http://www.ggdc.net

[c]See China Economic and Agricultural Data, Economic Research Service, U.S. Department of Agriculture, http://www.ers.usda.gov

Argentina's rate.[4] The United States' 2.2 percent growth rate, however, is greater than its 1.7 percent growth rate from 1820 to 1998, a rate that propelled its citizens to their current living standards. Japan's 3.8 percent growth rate and the Republic of Korea's 5.9 percent rate show that higher growth rates are possible. The Korean growth rate doubles GDP per capita in about 12 years, compared with a 36-year doubling time for the United States.[5]

If output per person doubled every 12 years in Korea and every 36 years in the United States, Korea would soon surpass the United States. France and India, on the other hand, grew slightly faster than the United States. India sustained this growth rate over 40 years. But it would have to grow at that rate for about 100 more years to reach Korea's current level of GDP per capita, and it would fail to overtake any of the countries in Figure 1.1A.

Figure 1.1B shows the growth rates for these countries for three periods: 1960–1973, 1973–1990, and 1990–2007, allowing us to consider changes in growth rates. For instance, five countries—the United States, Japan, Brazil, France, and Argentina—had significant decreases in their growth rates after 1972. This experience, shared with most industrialized countries, caused much concern about economic stagnation. Looking at the period since 1990, the United States compares favorably with Japan, Brazil, France,

[4]These countries provide a variety of experiences to compare with that of the United States. Japan's economy stagnated in the 1990s, but its overall performance from after World War II to the present has been exceptional. Korea's economy experienced a serious setback in the late 1990s but has since recovered. The data underlying Figures 1 and 2 are from Groningen Growth and Development Centre and The Conference Board, Total Economy Database, August 2005, http://www.ggdc.net

[5]A useful rule of arithmetic is that the doubling time for something growing at a compound rate can be approximated by dividing the rate into 72. For example, if an investment is earning compound interest of 8 percent, it will double in nine years.

Figure 1.1A **Annual Growth Rates of Real GDP per Capita: 1960–2007**
Since 1960, GDP per capita in China, Japan, and South Korea has grown much faster than in the United States, India, Brazil, France, and Argentina.

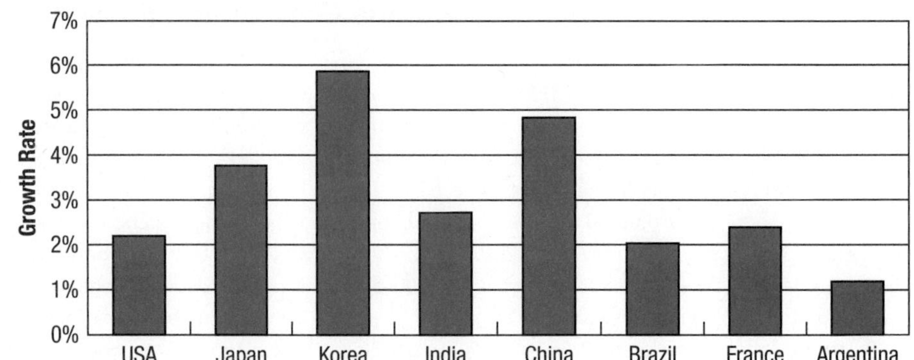

Source: The Conference Board, Total Economy Database, January 2009, http://www.conference-board.org/economics

Figure 1.1B **Growth Rates: 1960–1973, 1973–1990, and 1990–2007**
After 1972, growth rates of GDP per capita were high in South Korea, increased in China and India, and fell in the other countries in the figure.

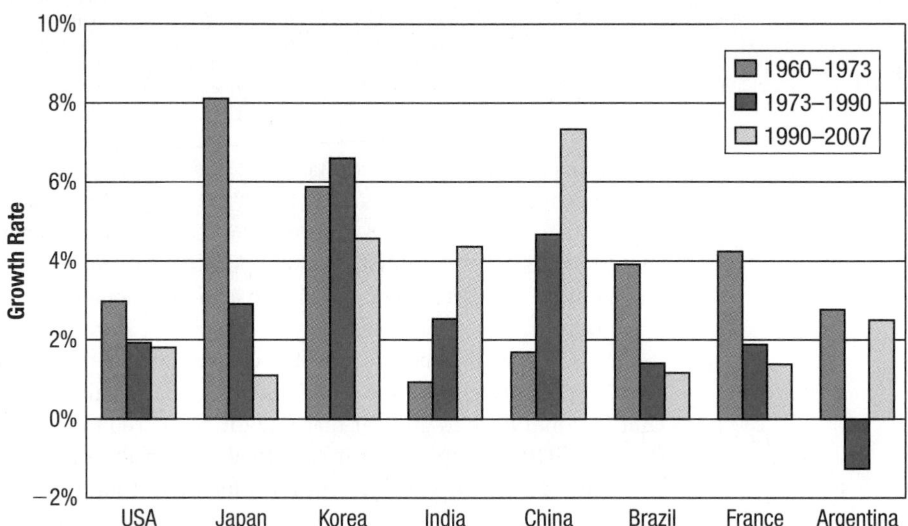

Source: The Conference Board, Total Economy Database, January 2009, http://www.conference-board.org/economics

and Argentina. This figure shows the stark alternatives facing other high-income countries: will their growth continue at or above their historical rates as in the United States or will it decelerate to low levels as in France and Japan?

Lower-income countries provide similar conflicting examples. Argentina's and Brazil's growth rates have fallen substantially since 1972, but India and China have enjoyed successive increases in their growth rates. Although Korea's performance declined after 1990, much of this decline was due to what appears to have been a temporary downturn in the late 1990s; its per capita GDP growth has accelerated since 1999 (not shown in the figure).

Can a poor country catch up with the advanced countries? Japan and India were at similar levels of development in 1820. Japan grew 0.3 percentage point faster than the United States during the next 170 years and achieved development similar to that of the United States by 1990. India grew 0.6 percentage point slower than the United States and remained a low-income country. Had India averaged a 1.9 percentage growth rather than a 1.1 percent rate, it would have joined Japan in the high-income world. The prospect of gradually becoming a high-income country over a 200-year span, however, gives little hope to current generations. Fortunately, the Japanese experience shows that the process need not take 200 years. In fact, partly because of World War II, the United States' average income advantage compared to Japan's grew until about 1950. In 1820, U.S. per capita GDP was twice that of Japan's; by 1950 it was five times greater. By the 1960s, as Figure 1.2A shows, Japan's GDP per capita was overtaking that of the United States. With its rapid growth rate, by 1990 Japan's GDP per capita was within about $4,000 of that of the United States. If the trends of the 1980s had continued, Japan would—as could be seen by extending the lines in the figure—be close to overtaking the United States.

Keywords: *economic growth and developing countries*

Access InfoTrac at http://infotrac.cengage.com

The Japanese experience in closing the gap is not unique; other East Asian countries, such as Korea, also have experienced rapid growth. The figure shows that Korea was closing the relative gap with the United States in the 1960s. In 1960, Korea's per capita GDP was about one-tenth that of the United States; by 2007 it was more than three fifths. Japan's economy has stagnated since 1990. With growth continuing and perhaps accelerating in the United States, the U.S. advantage has grown. Moreover, the Japanese experience in falling behind the United States since 1990 is not unique. Consider France. From 1950 to about 1980, France was overtaking the United States in GDP per capita. Beginning in early 1980, however, the figure shows the U.S. advantage over France increasing in both relative and absolute terms.

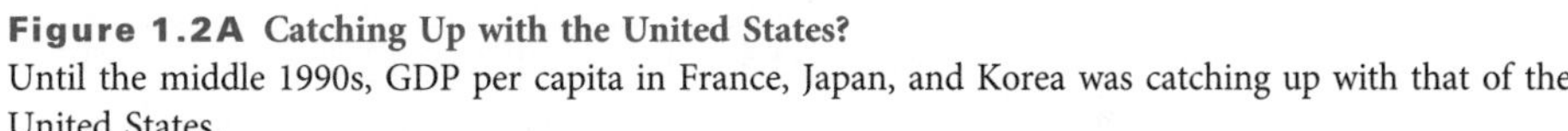
Figure 1.2A **Catching Up with the United States?**
Until the middle 1990s, GDP per capita in France, Japan, and Korea was catching up with that of the United States.

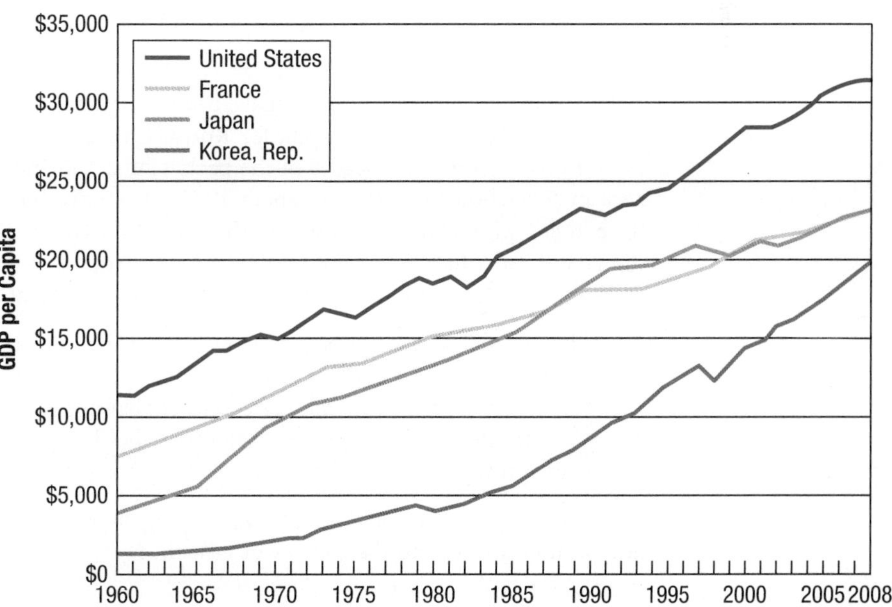

Source: The Conference Board, Total Economy Database, January 2009, http://www.conference-board.org/economics

Figure 1.2B Lower-Income Countries Converging?
China and India show a steady increase in per capita GDP, which could become like Korea's. Argentina and Brazil have erratic paths of per capita GDP.

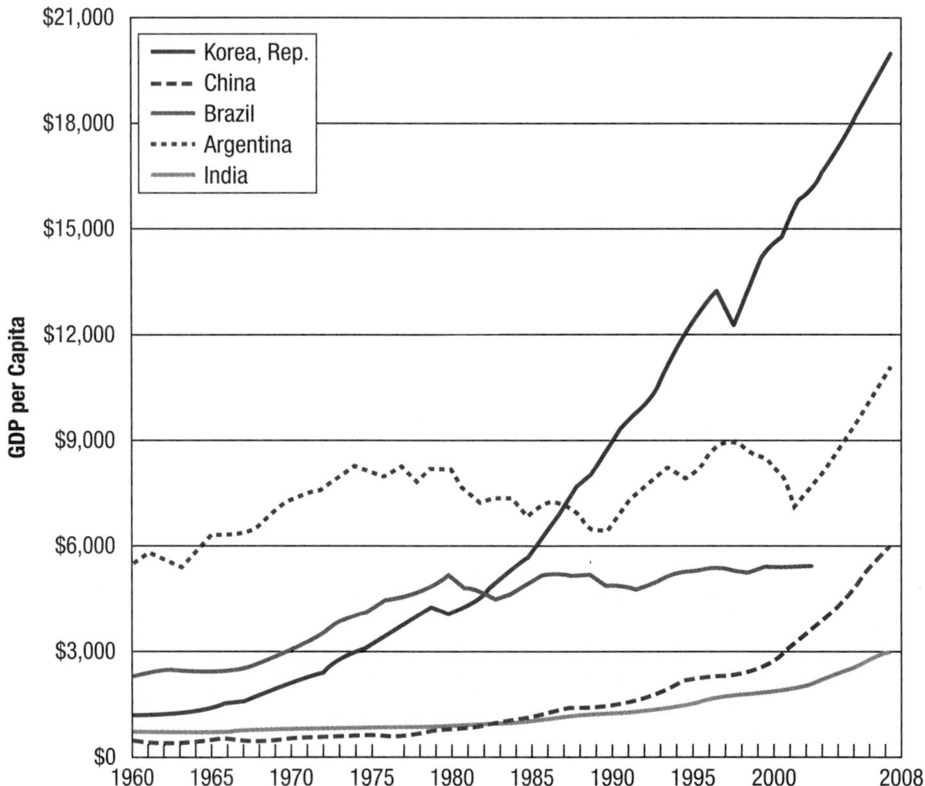

Source: The Conference Board, Total Economy Database, January 2009, http://www.conference-board.org/economics

Unfortunately, not all countries have been successful at economic growth since 1960. Figure 1.2B shows GDP per capita for Korea, China, Brazil, Argentina, and India since 1960. Korea is clearly the leader of the pack. China and India remained about neck and neck in stagnation from 1960 to about 1978. They have both shown remarkable growth since then, with China growing much faster. Moreover, since about the mid-1970s, China and India have been closing the gap with Argentina and Brazil.

In this overview of recent growth in selected countries, at least three questions arise.

1. What are the sources of economic growth in the United States and what are the prospects?
2. What are the similarities among countries that are successful in growth?
3. What are the similarities among countries that have failed to achieve steady economic growth?

These are big questions, and we can only touch on some of the factors involved.[6] In the next section, we turn to the sources of growth.

[6]Comprehensive answers to these questions are controversial, and beyond the scope of this chapter.

SOURCES OF ECONOMIC GROWTH

Keyword: *sources of economic growth*

Access InfoTrac at http://infotrac.cengage.com

Understanding economic growth requires us to consider society's production possibilities. Economic growth occurs when an economy produces more goods and services, a greater GDP, as time goes by. This section develops the production possibilities curve and then applies it to economic growth. We start with production possibilities for the individual. Then, we apply it to the entire economy.

Production Possibilities for the Individual College Student

As teachers and students, we are engaged in various economic activities. As a student, you are using your time and other resources for learning and for enjoying your life on a day-to-day basis. Your other resources consist of your native talents, the knowledge and talents that you have acquired through education and life experiences, books and equipment that you own or have access to, and your willingness and ability to make decisions with foresight. The fundamental situation that you face is that your time and native talents are limited. Your objective is to use your time, talent, and acquired resources in the most useful way.

It is reasonable to assume that decisions that you make as a student will influence your lifetime income. As discussed in Chapter 9, if you decide to complete your bachelor's degree, you can expect, on average to earn about a million dollars more over your lifetime than if you were to go to work directly after high school. Just how much more you will earn will depend upon choices that you make and circumstances that you face. The evidence presented in Chapter 9 suggests that taking more challenging courses within your chosen field and earning higher grades will probably pay off with higher earnings in the future. With a fixed amount of time and other resources, however, the more time that you devote to your academic work, the less time you will have for other kinds of activity. Many career development experts will assure you that participation in campus activities, public service, and social organizations is also important in preparing for a career. It is also important for your self-development to have leisure time and enjoyable leisure activities. Suppose that you can use your time to further your career opportunities or to live for the moment. Another way to describe this is that you can use your time to invest in your future—for your personal economic growth—or to live for the moment—for your present consumption.

The fact that your time is limited means that if you decide to take a few days off from school to attend some student activity off campus, say, a mock political convention, you do it at a cost. With only the two choices, investing or consuming, the cost of choosing the consumption activity is the value of what you would have learned had you stayed on campus. More specifically, if you choose to work additional hours in a job that is providing wages but no useful experience, the cost of that job is the value of what you would learned had you devoted that time to investing—study, campus leadership, or whatever.

As a college student, you are engaged in a delicate balancing act in which you are trying to take advantage of various opportunities affecting both your present and your future, all the while faced with limited time. Because of the limited time the cost of investing is the value of the consumption that you give up because of working less or socializing less. But it goes both ways. The cost of consumption—working so that you can pay your car insurance—is the value of the investment that you must give up.

Opportunity cost– The value of the best alternative sacrificed when a choice is made.

This idea of cost as being the value of what you give up is powerful. In general, whenever a choice is made many things are given up. The **opportunity cost** of the choice is the value of the *best* alternative given up. Many times, the value of what could be done with the time that is given up is the biggest part of the opportunity cost. As you will see, the opportunity cost of college includes both a time cost and a money cost. The time cost is the income that you could have earned if you were working rather than being in school. The money cost consists mostly of tuition, fees, and books. The opportunity cost includes both the time and money cost, with the time cost on average being the largest part of the opportunity cost.

Going to a college football game can be an expensive outing. The game takes four hours and the ticket might cost $50. If a business professor or engineering professor goes to the game, he or she might be giving up four hours of consulting income at $600 an hour. The opportunity cost of the game then is $2,450. Alternatively, a student may pay $50 instead of going to a two-hour movie for $10 and studying for two hours. The opportunity cost of the game is then $40 plus the value of what would have been learned.

The individual college student uses her resources—time, native ability, acquired learning, equipment—to produce more human capital and consumption goods. In some ways, the most important resource that she has is her decision-making ability with regard to the choice of investing versus consuming and with regard to the choice of activities that are most beneficial in terms of investing. The purpose of the investing is to produce more human capital, which means that choices must be made about major, about elective courses, about leadership activities, and about public service. In addition to the choice of the types of courses and activities, she must decide how much time to devote to courses and how much to activities. It is complicated because the courses and the activities probably both have a mixture of consumption and investment benefits. These choices are very similar to the decisions that people have to make when they decide to start a business or to develop a new way of doing business or to introduce a new product. They involve decisions about the organization of time and about taking risk. In the next section, we discuss how the choices made by students and the resource constraints that they face are similar to the choices made for an entire economy and the resource constraints that it faces.

Production Possibilities for the Economy

An axiom of economics is that the resources required to produce goods and services are scarce relative to people's aggregate wants for goods and services. The primary resources are labor, land, capital, and entrepreneurship:

Labor–
All physical and mental abilities used by people in production.

Land–
Resources found in nature, such as land, water, forests, mineral deposits, and air.

Physical capital–
Man-made, durable items used in the production process, such as factories, equipment, dams, and transportation systems.

Human capital–
The knowledge and skills embodied in people, as used in the production process.

- **Labor** includes the time, efforts, and services of people in the production of goods and services. For a college student, labor is the use of time for production of desired outcomes.
- **Land** includes all natural resources and raw materials, such as agricultural land and silicon, and for the student land is natural talents.
- **Physical capital** consists of durable produced goods, such as factories, industrial equipment, highways, and airports, that are used to produce goods and services. The use of a computer by a college student is the use of physical capital.
- **Human capital** has characteristics of both labor and capital. It consists of the acquired knowledge and skills embodied in people and applied to the production of goods and services. Like physical capital, it is a produced resource. It is produced through education, on-the-job experience, and other life experiences. For the student existing human capital is the education and training that he has at a particular point in his college career. It is also one of the products that he produces. An essential characteristic of capital is that resources, otherwise available for producing consumption goods and services, are used to produce it. For the production of physical capital, the resources might be labor, land, human capital, and physical capital such as a building, a car, and a computer. For human capital, they might be "land"

(natural ability), labor (that of the teacher and the student), human capital (again that of the teacher and the student), and physical capital (buildings, computers, and video equipment).

Entrepreneurship– The ability to see how other resources might be combined in producing a profitable good or service and the willingness to risk organizing a business to do so.

- **Entrepreneurship** is the ability to use the other four resources in a business or other activity to produce goods and services that might be sold at a profit, and the willingness to take the chance that the experiment—the business or the education—might fail. It involves foresight and the willingness to take a risk. For the business, the entrepreneur (the undertaker) is the founder of the business; for education, the student is the undertaker.

Finally, *technology* can be thought of as recipes that show how to use the resources to produce goods and services. People require food. In a world of *scarcity,* to produce more food, we must produce less of something else. Producing less of something else, say clothes, releases resources to produce the extra food. Every economic system must choose what goods and services to produce, how to produce these goods and services, and to whom to distribute them. These choices largely determine the growth rate of GDP per capita.

Suppose for simplicity that the choice is between just two alternatives: cars and food. Table 1.1 introduces a useful way to analyze this choice. The economy is assumed to produce only cars and food. We assume that all resources (land, labor, and capital) are fully employed and that the best technology is used. If all resources are used for food production, no cars can be produced and, we assume, 100 million bushels of food is the most possible. Now suppose that we decide to produce 100 thousand cars, which would require that we take resources from food production and use them for car production. Obviously, to produce the cars implies that we can't produce as much food—we have taken resources away from food production. If we produce 100,000 cars, the table, by assumption, shows that 95 million bushels is the most food that can be produced. Consequently, to produce the first 100,000 cars requires resources that could have produced 5 million bushels of food. The opportunity cost of the cars is the value of what is given up to produce them: the value of 5 more million bushels of food, given that you have 95 million bushels. Each combination of cars and food in the table can be produced only if all resources are used with the best technology. Consequently, each combination represents an appropriate use of resources. The best choice from all these combinations depends upon the preferences of the people in the economy.

A diagram makes it easier to understand. Let's summarize the information by plotting it on the chart included with Table 1.1, which you may want to reproduce in your notebook. The horizontal axis measures thousands of cars per year and the vertical axis measures food production in millions of bushels per year. Start by finding one of the points, say, D. To do so, go to the point on the horizontal axis that represents 300 thousand cars and draw a vertical dashed line to the top of the chart. According to the table, if 300 thousand cars are produced, the most food that can be produced is 70 million bushels. Draw a horizontal dashed line from 70 (on the vertical axis) to the right edge of the chart. The intersection of these two dashed lines is point D, representing 300 thousand cars and 70 million bushels. Plot the other points from the table in the same way and connect them with a smooth curve. In your diagram Point A shows the maximum amount of food that can be produced per year—100 million bushels—if all resources are used for food production and the best methods of producing food are used. The curve in your diagram, which you can compare with Figure 1.3, is a **production possibilities curve.** It shows the maximum combinations of the goods or services that can be produced using available resources. A maximum combination is the largest quantity that can be produced of one good for a given quantity of the other good. Each combination on AG assumes full employment of labor, capital, and land and the use

Production possibilities curve– A curve showing the maximum combinations of two goods or services that can be produced by an economy when resources are fully used and the best technology is applied.

TABLE 1.1 HYPOTHETICAL DATA FOR PRODUCTION ANALYSIS

	NUMBER OF CARS PER YEAR (THOUSANDS)	BUSHELS OF FOOD PER YEAR (MILLIONS)
A	0	100
B	100	95
C	200	85
D	300	70
E	400	50
F	500	25
G	575	0

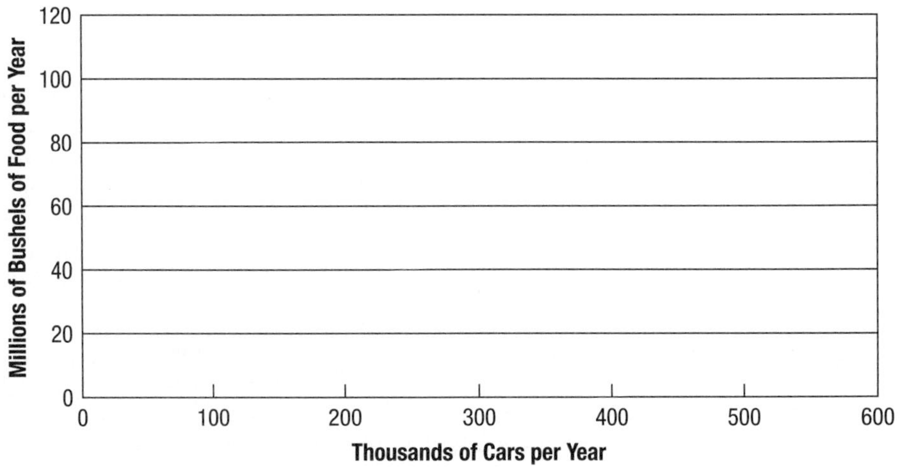

We assume that (1) the economy produces only cars and food, (2) all resources (land, labor, and capital) are fully employed, and (3) the best technology is used. If all resources are devoted to food production, no cars can be produced. This economy can produce 100 million bushels of food—combination A. If, for example, it chose to produce combination B—100 thousand cars and 95 million bushels of food—resources that could have produced 5 million bushels of food must be transferred to car production. The opportunity cost of the cars is what was given up to produce them: the value of 5 million bushels of food.

Best technology– The technology that requires the fewest resources to produce a given combination of goods and services.

Marginal cost– The opportunity cost of producing an additional unit of a good.

of the **best technology**—the technology that requires the fewest resources to produce a given combination of goods and services: in this case, cars and food.

The intervals on the horizontal axis associated with successive moves down the curve from A to B, C, D, E, and F correspond to equal increases in car production: each interval equals 100 thousand cars. The corresponding vertical intervals measure the reduction in food production for each increase in car production. An examination of Figure 1.3 shows that for successive equal increases in car production the corresponding decrease in food production gets larger. An equal increase in car production requires that more food be given up; the **marginal cost** of a car increases as more cars are produced.

Marginal cost increases as resources are transferred out of food production and into the production of cars because resources that are particularly suited to food production must be converted to a use, car production, for which they are less well suited. At first,

Figure 1.3 The Production Possibilities Curve Applied to the Choice Between Food and Cars
The economy is assumed to produce only food and cars. Along the production possibilities curve, marked by points A to G, resources are used fully and the best technology is applied. The combinations of food and cars, A to G, are the largest possible combinations. Starting at point A, production of food must decrease by 5 million bushels (from 100 million to 95 million) to produce the first 100,000 cars. Production of the next 100,000 cars requires giving up 10 million more bushels of food. The value of food given up with each move down the curve is the marginal cost of cars, which increases with each successive increase in car production.

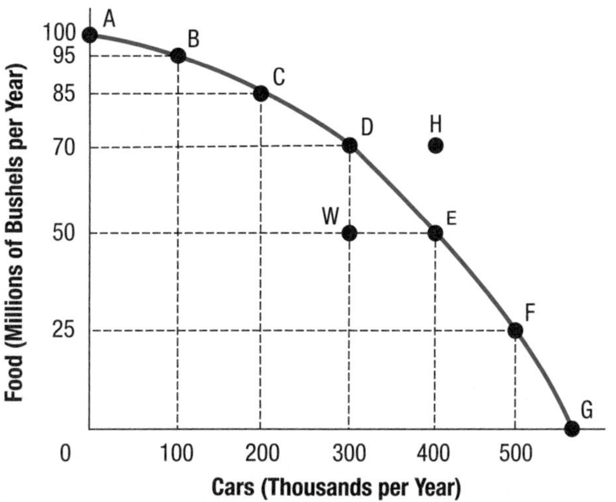

the types of land, labor, and capital that are better suited to car production than to food production will go to expanding car production. Thus, relatively little food production is sacrificed. Eventually, however, car production can be expanded only by taking more fertile cropland, more skilled farm labor, farmers who are especially good at farming, factories that are better suited for making farm implements than cars, scientists who are better at creating fertilizers and pesticides than at developing new methods of combustion, and engineers and construction workers who are better at designing and building farm structures than designing cars. Thus, equal increases in car production require ever-increasing sacrifices of food production. Marginal cost also increases for equal increases in car production because the value of a bushel of food increases as more cars and less food are produced. Why? Suppose at combination B (100 thousand cars, 95 million bushels of food) people are well fed. No one places a high value on one more or one less unit of food. Now consider combination F (500 thousand cars, 25 million bushels). People will now pay more for an additional unit of food because they are not as well fed. As more cars are produced, the marginal cost increases for two reasons:

- More food has to be sacrificed for one more car, and
- The value of the food that is sacrificed is greater.

The economy can also be at a point like W inside the production possibilities curve, producing 300 thousand cars and 50 million bushels of food. If so, the economy is operating with waste or inefficiency. Either resources are unemployed or the best technology is not being used. To see the inefficiency or waste, note that the economy could move to point E, making 100 thousand more cars without giving up any food, getting something—more cars—for nothing. (Note that a move to D, E, or any point on DE has to be an improvement because there is more of at least one good without any reduction in the other good.) The move is made by using previously unemployed resources or switching to best technology.

Scarcity–
The common situation for all economies, in which aggregate wants exceed the economy's ability to meet them because of limited resources.

Point H, a combination of 400 thousand cars and 70 million bushels of food, is outside the curve. Unlike W or any point on the curve, H cannot be reached, given the available resources and technology. It illustrates **scarcity**, the common situation of all economies. Scarcity occurs because with finite resources and a given technology, it is impossible to produce more of everything. Nevertheless, in the aggregate people want more. Unlimited wants and limited resources result in scarcity.

In a given year an economy is limited to points on (or inside) its production possibilities curve. If, for a given amount of one good, people want more of another good than is possible to produce, *scarcity exists and choices must be made.* The production possibilities curve shows that for 70 million bushels of food, the maximum numbers of cars that can be produced is 300 thousand. If everyone wants to have the same amount of food and someone wants one more car, scarcity exists. As previously mentioned, economists believe that scarcity—and, therefore, the necessity of choice—is the human condition. To reach point H, the economy must grow. It can grow if best technology improves or the economy acquires more resources: labor, land, capital, and entrepreneurship. The labor, land, and entrepreneurship available to an economy are not influenced much by day-to-day economic decisions. Thus, economic decisions that increase growth are those made by entrepreneurs that increase capital and/or improve technology.

The Best Combination of Goods and Services: Consumption Versus Growth

The best combination of goods and services is the one that fulfills wants as completely as possible. Figure 1.4, which assumes that the economy produces capital goods (tractors) and consumption goods (popcorn) helps clarify what this requires. In the figure, a move down the curve results in an increase in the number of tractors (capital goods) produced at the expense of a reduction in the amount of popcorn (consumption goods) produced. The opportunity cost of the tractors is the value of the popcorn not produced.

Figure 1.4 Production Possibilities and Economic Growth
An economy's output can increase if its production possibilities curve shifts to the right, as illustrated by the shift from P_0P_0 to P_1P_1. It can be caused by resource accumulation or technological improvement. Efficiency improvement, a move from W to P_0P_0, can also result in economic growth.

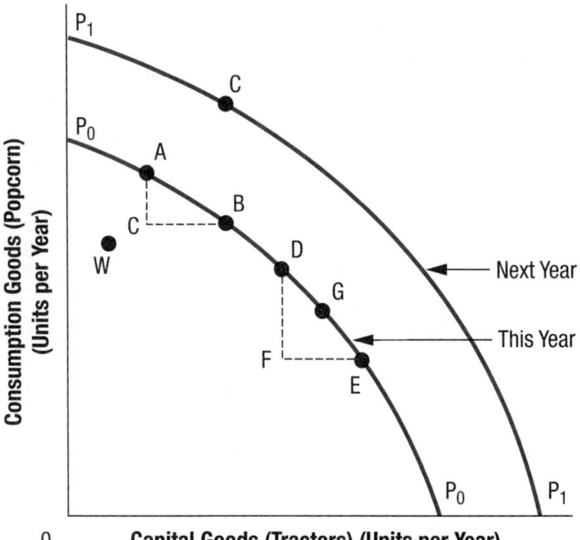

Marginal benefit– The satisfaction value received from consumption of an additional unit of a good or service.

For instance, suppose that at A it is necessary to sacrifice 1,000 bushels of popcorn to produce another tractor. The marginal cost of the tractor is the value of the 1,000 bushels of popcorn. What is the **marginal benefit?** In this example, the marginal benefit of the tractor is the value of the increased popcorn that can be produced in the future because more capital equipment—tractors—will be available in the future. It decreases as more and more tractors are produced because the benefit of the tractors is future popcorn consumption. But as more tractors are produced, more popcorn is produced in the future, but its value falls because the more popcorn you have the less one more box is worth to you.

It pays to move down the production possibilities curve from A to B and so on—producing more capital goods by sacrificing the production of consumption goods this year—so long as the marginal benefit of increased consumption goods in the future is greater than the marginal cost of a reduction in consumption goods today. Marginal benefit decreases as we move down the curve, and we shall see that the marginal cost increases.

The move from A to B and the move from D to E increase tractor production by the same amount. Inspection of the figure shows, however, that the sacrifice of present popcorn production is greater with the second move. As discussed, some resources are more suited to the production of one type of good; others are more suited to another type. As land, labor, and capital are transferred from the production of consumption goods to capital goods, the first increments transferred will be those with the greatest advantage in producing capital goods. As the process continues, the resources will have smaller and smaller advantages in producing capital goods. Because it takes more resources to produce another unit of the capital good, greater amounts of the consumption good are sacrificed to increase capital good production. Marginal cost also increases because of the reduction in the quantity of consumption goods; with fewer consumption goods, the value of the last unit sacrificed of the consumption good increases. As people give up more popcorn, they become hungrier and hungrier and place a higher value on a little more popcorn. As capital good production increases, more units of the consumption good are sacrificed and the value of present consumption goods increases.

This analysis identifies, in principle, the best combination of consumption and capital goods to produce. So long as the marginal benefit of an additional unit of the capital good is greater than the marginal cost, it increases net benefit (benefit – cost) to produce more capital goods. The value of future consumption gained is greater than the value of the present consumption lost. At some combination, marginal benefit just equals marginal cost; this is the best combination. This analysis shows why more growth is not always better: more growth requires a reduction in present consumption.

Resource Accumulation, Technological Improvement, and Efficiency Improvement

Technological improvement– An improvement in best technology that allows more output with a given amount of resources.

Long-term economic growth occurs if an economy increases its capacity to produce GDP—increases its production possibilities. An economy's production possibilities increase if it accumulates more resources: land, labor, and capital. Labor and capital have greater potential for expansion than land, so we will restrict attention to labor and capital growth. Production possibilities also grow if the best technology improves. **Technological improvement** means that the same amount of goods and services can be produced with less labor and capital, or equivalently that more goods and services can be produced with the same quantity of labor and capital. Finally, economic growth

Efficiency improvement– A change from less than the best to the best technology, which allows more output to be produced with the same resources.

occurs if an economy moves from using less than the best technology to using better or the best technology. This process, called **efficiency improvement**, also allows more output with a given amount of resources. Economic growth is possible, if

1. More resources are accumulated.
2. Technology improves.
3. Efficiency improves.

Figure 1.4 explains the three sources of economic growth in terms of production possibilities curves. In this analysis the economy produces two goods, a capital good and a consumption good, with two resources, labor and capital. This year's production possibilities curve, P_0P_0, shows the combinations of consumption and capital goods that can be produced if the economy has full employment of its labor and capital and uses the best technology. For instance, it could produce a combination represented by A, which emphasizes the production of consumption goods relative to capital goods. The only ways that this economy could grow, so that it has the potential to produce more of both goods in the next year, would be for it to have more labor and capital resources or for it to experience technological improvement. Thus, resource accumulation or technological improvement could cause the production possibilities curve to shift to P_1P_1, next year.

Resource Accumulation. Resource accumulation consists of increases in the labor force or in the stock of physical or human capital available to the economy. Population growth is the major source of labor force growth. GDP has to grow faster than population for the average standard of living, GDP per capita, to improve. Population (labor force) growth, with capital and technology fixed, will result in successively smaller increases in GDP. Although labor force growth causes GDP to grow, it will not cause GDP to grow fast enough to increase living standards. Capital accumulation, on the other hand, can increase living standards because the use of more capital permits an increase in GDP without any increase in the use of labor. Capital accumulation may consist of producing more capital equipment (physical capital) or increasing education and training levels (human capital).

Unfortunately, investment in physical and human capital is not free. Suppose that this year the economy is producing at A in Figure 1.4. For a given rate of technological improvement and labor force growth, assume that capital goods production at A, added to this year's capital stock, is just enough to push next year's production possibilities curve to P_1P_1. Now suppose that people believe that this growth is too slow. The only way to have more growth in this circumstance is to increase the production of physical and human capital: to move from A to, say, point B. To have more growth, which increases consumption in the future, it is necessary to sacrifice consumption goods today. Greater economic growth is not necessarily desirable because it means sacrificing in the present for the future.

Technological Improvement and Efficiency Improvement. Another source of economic growth is technological improvement. Improvements in best technology shift the production possibilities curve: P_0P_0 to P_1P_1 in Figure 1.4. Accordingly, more of both goods can be produced with the same amount of resources. A movement from A to C could occur because of scientific and engineering advances. Examples of advances in science that have expanded production possibilities are numerous. The basic discoveries related to DNA have resulted in improved plant varieties and new drugs. The development of transistors and semiconductors revolutionized calculation and communication. The introduction of the videocassette recorder and player and the DVD has transformed the entertainment industry.

Keywords: *economic growth and institution*

Access InfoTrac at http://infotrac.cengage.com

New economic institutions, which are sometimes created by entrepreneurs, are another source of technological improvement. Henry Ford's profitable development of assembly-line (mass) production, Sam Walton's profitable creation of a new way of retailing, and Eiji Toyoda's profitable introduction of flexible manufacturing (the Toyota production system) are all examples of technological improvement that go beyond what we typically think of as science and engineering advances. E-commerce has transformed the way some people shop. Residents of small towns, including college towns, can obtain goods quickly without leaving their homes. Suppose, in the past, a student or professor would make a 150-mile trip twice a year, especially to buy books. The cost of access to the books each time would be the cost of driving a car 150 miles, say $45, and the value of the driving time, say $60. E-commerce based on new technology and new economic institutions could save this individual up to $105 per trip.

Efficiency improvements are another source of economic growth and are, in some ways, similar to technological improvements. Improvements in efficiency lead to greater output from a given amount of inputs, but they do not shift the production possibilities curve. For instance, an economy may be operating inside its production possibilities curve, at a point such as W in Figure 1.4. Failure to use the best available technology is one source of inefficiency. Elimination of such inefficiencies allows the economy to move closer to the production possibilities curve. Such a change means that greater output is obtained from a given amount of resources. (Remember that the production possibilities curve assumes that the amounts of labor and capital are fixed.)

Growth based on technological or efficiency improvements can cost much less than growth based on capital accumulation. Technological improvements can occur as a by-product of investment in human and physical capital. A higher level of education or greater use of capital equipment can lead to scientific discoveries, to discoveries of new ways of doing old tasks, and to new ways of organizing economic activity (for example, E-commerce). Similarly, as educational levels increase, and as firms compete more with firms from other parts of the country and of the world, we may learn about and borrow state-of-the-art production techniques; efficiency will improve. Growth caused by such factors might not require much sacrifice of present consumption. Although not free, sometimes such growth can be close to it. Nevertheless, achieving growth through technological improvement or efficiency improvement is uncertain, and it can be costly because efforts to generate technological or efficiency improvements may fail.

PRODUCTIVITY GROWTH: WHAT CAN WE EXPECT IN THE "NEW ECONOMY"?

Capital intensity– The ratio of capital to labor in production, or units of capital per unit of labor.

Technical progress– Technological and efficiency improvements combined.

To understand what has happened to productivity growth, we must understand its components. The growth of labor productivity can be divided into one part caused by the growth of capital (human and physical) relative to labor and another part caused by technological and efficiency improvements. Human capital accumulation contributes to growth because it means that workers have greater education and experience. Physical capital accumulation contributes to growth because it means that workers have more capital to work with—more equipment. From this point on, we refer to the growth of human and physical capital relative to labor as growth in **capital intensity** and to technological and efficiency improvements as **technical progress.** In Figure 1.5 the height of each bar shows that output per hour (labor productivity) in the private business sector grew at 3.3, 1.5, and 2.3 percent per year during the periods 1960–1973, 1973–1990, and

Figure 1.5 U.S. Productivity Growth and Its Components, 1960–2007
The figure provides information about the private business sector. Each bar represents a particular time period. The height of the first bar set shows labor productivity growth in the first period. The two segments of the bars show the contributions of technical progress and capital intensity to the productivity growth. Moving from the first time period to the second, we see the slowdown in productivity growth. Notice the sharp decline in the contribution of technical progress. Notice also that in the first period technical progress accounts for more than half of the productivity growth, and that in the second period it accounts for much less than half. Movement to the third and fourth bars shows the gradual increase in productivity growth and the contribution of technical progress.

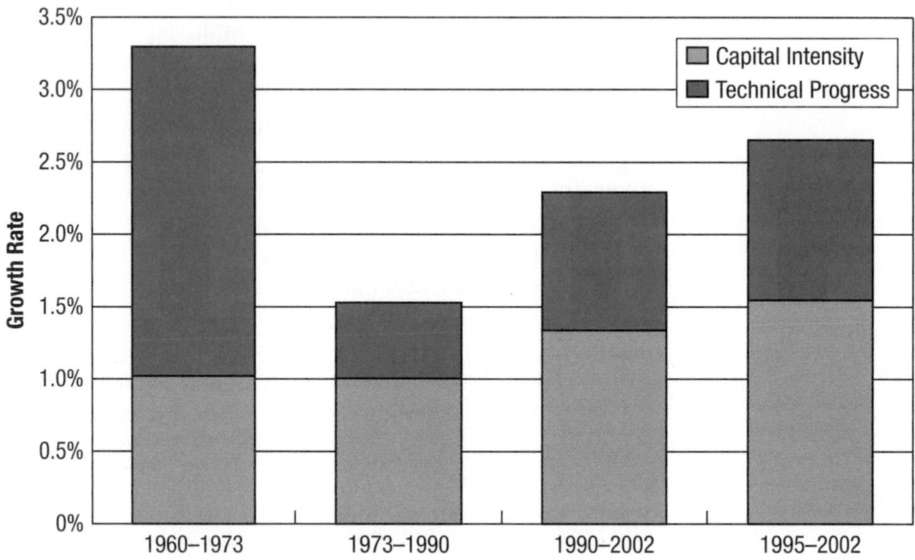

Source: Computed from U.S. Department of Labor data at http://stats.bls.gov

ADDITIONAL INSIGHT

The Cost of Hurricanes

Hurricanes Katrina and Rita imposed incredible personal costs on the residents of the United States Gulf Coast, including the loss of irreplaceable possessions—pictures, heirlooms, homes—injuries, displacement, and death. In addition to the physical and psychological costs, they imposed huge economic costs. Some of these economic costs are direct and relatively easy to measure. People lost working time and firms lost production time; the income and production lost because of disrupted electricity, temporary closing of firms, and relocation of people cannot be replaced. Nevertheless, for most people and firms the lost income and production are transitory. Private insurance, government insurance, other government programs, and charitable activities will help many people overcome these transitory losses. In some ways these losses are similar to the losses experienced by people when the economy is operating at less than full employment, that is, when it is in a recession.

Another cost that is easily seen, but perhaps difficult to fully appreciate, is the loss of capital stock. We see the destroyed cars, houses, commercial buildings, factories, roads, and bridges. This destruction is the destruction of one of the economy's resources—physical capital. The U.S. Congressional Budget Office estimates a loss of capital stock on the order of $70 to $130 billion. The value of the housing capital lost is somewhere between $17 and $33 billion. Consumer durable goods lost amounted from $5 to $9 billion. The midpoints of the estimates of the capital losses of the energy sector, other parts of the private business sector, and governments are $25 billion, $24 billion, and $19 billion respectively.[a]

If we consider a production possibilities curve for the economy, we can visualize the losses. Referring to Figure 1.4, the destruction of the capital stock would move the production possibilities curve from P_1P_1 back to P_0P_0. If the curve is at P_1P_1 and the economy goes into a period of unemployment and operates say at D, current production would be less than would be possible in normal circumstances. There would be a transitory loss in output because of unemployed resources. This use of the production possibilities analysis shows why there are transitory losses in production and employment when flooding prevents people from getting to work or electricity outages make it impossible to operate machinery. When the waters recede and the electricity is restored, the economy moves quickly back to P_1P_1.

When the capital stock is destroyed, however, the result is different. Now the maximum production has been reduced. Receding waters do not allow a destroyed business to reopen or allow a family to return to a destroyed house or apartment. It is not possible for the economy to return to its original production possibilities curve because resources have been destroyed. For the economy to reach its original position, P_1P_1, the production of consumption goods must be cut back and the production of capital goods increased. Rebuilding a bridge or rebuilding a home will create jobs and income for workers and revenues and sales for construction firms and materials suppliers, but it does not create net new output. The opportunity cost of the rebuilding is the value of consumption goods that must be given up. The benefit, of course, is the new bridge or home, but this is not a net benefit. It is simply replacing something that previously existed.

[a]See Douglas Holtz-Eakin, "Macroeconomic and Budgetary Effects of Hurricanes Katrina and Rita," Statement before the Committee on the Budget U.S. House of Representatives, October 6, 2005. http://www.cbo.gov/ftpdocs/66xx/doc6684/10-06-Hurricanes.pdf

1990–2002, respectively. The fourth bar (1995–2007) shows the acceleration growth after 1995 to 2.7 percent.[7]

The bottom part of each bar gives the contribution of increased capital intensity, which was about 1 percentage point per year in each period. A more experienced and better educated labor force, increases in human capital intensity, added from 0.2 to 0.4 percentage point to productivity growth over these periods, with the remainder due to increases in physical capital intensity. Technical progress, the top part of the bar, contributed the remainder: 2.3, 0.5, and 1.0 percentage point(s). From 1995 on, however, the importance of increases in human and physical capital increased.[8]

Keywords: *economic growth and new economy*

Access InfoTrac at http://infotrac.cengage.com

Figure 1.5 provides a visual description of the levels and changes in labor productivity's growth rate and that of its components. The heights of the bars trace a lazy J-shape—labor productivity first falls dramatically reflecting the growth slowdown that began in the 1970s and then rises tantalizingly suggesting that rapid growth may be emerging. Comparing the two components of productivity growth—technical progress and capital intensity—we see that the contributions of capital increase slightly from one period to the next, with a definite increase apparent from 1995–2000. Technical progress, on the other hand, makes a substantial contribution to the first period's productivity, a contribution that falls substantially in the 1973–1990 period. It then gets larger in the final period, with an extra boost after 1995. The decline in labor productivity growth and its subsequent recovery has largely reflected the behavior of technical progress with a small contribution from increases in capital intensity.

[7]To analyze long-run productivity growth, it is necessary to study long time periods so that short-run variations are minimized. Therefore, rather than examining decades, we examine 1960–1973, 1973–1990, 1990–2002, and 1995–2007.

[8]Calculations based on data from the U.S. Department of Labor at http://stats.bls.gov. You may want to visit the Multifactor Productivity Home Page at the Bureau of Labor Statistics, U.S. Department of Labor.

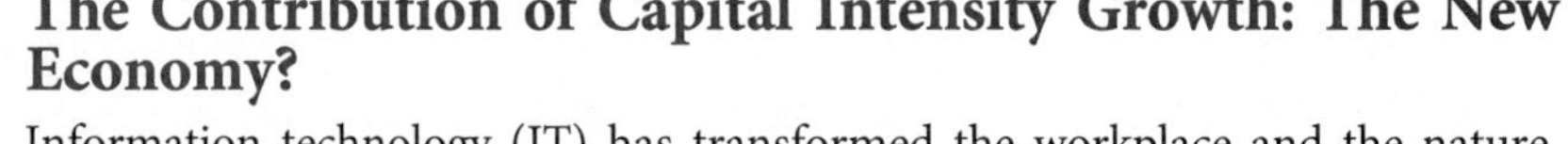

The Contribution of Capital Intensity Growth: The New Economy?

Information technology (IT) has transformed the workplace and the nature of work in the U.S. economy. This transformation rests on achievements of the semiconductor industry. Moore's Law predicted (in 1965) that the number of transistors per chip would double every 1.5 to 2 years. Accompanying this essentially correct prediction, semiconductor prices (logic and memory chips) plummeted by 40 to 50 percent a year. Combined with the breathtaking developments in communications technology and associated price decreases, the sharp semiconductor price decreases stimulated an acceleration of investment in IT assets. IT assets, in effect, were substituted for other types of capital assets and for labor across the economy's broad spectrum. The use of IT capital services (computers, software, and communications equipment) grew at almost 20 percent per year from 1995 to 1999, almost doubling the rate of the previous 5 years. Non-IT capital services grew at about 3 percent a year and labor services grew at about 2 percent. The growth rates imply that labor works with more non-IT capital and substantially more IT capital than in did in 1990 or even 1995. As Figure 1.5 shows, the growth of capital intensity makes an additional contribution to productivity after 1995. Expert economists conclude that an increasing and now large portion of the capital intensity effect on productivity is tied to increases in capital services from IT assets. In addition to the increased growth due to changes in capital intensity, labor productivity has grown faster in the 1990s because of the contribution of technical progress.[9]

INFOTRAC
College Edition

Keywords: *economic growth and information technology*

Access InfoTrac at
http://infotrac.cengage.com

The Contribution of Technical Progress: The New Economy?

Changes in labor productivity growth caused by fluctuations in technical progress limited our prosperity from the 1970s through the early part of the 1990s and may have enhanced it since then. What caused this fall and rise depicted in Figure 1.5?

It is ironic that in the 1970s and 1980s, a period of rapid scientific advances, technical progress all but disappeared from the U.S. economy. At first, this appears inexplicable, but it reminds us that technical engineering and scientific advances, by themselves, are not sufficient to create a dynamic economy. The former Soviet Union had world-class scientists and engineers, but technical progress was exceedingly slow because the Soviet economy did not (could not?) incorporate their discoveries into economic growth. Remember also that technical progress is more than scientific and engineering advances; technical progress is anything that increases output from a fixed amount of resources. Improved or new products based on research and development, greater efficiency in the economy, or improved management techniques might cause it. Numerous explanations for the slowdown have been advanced,[10] including the possibility that

INFOTRAC
College Edition

Keywords: *economic growth and OECD*

Access InfoTrac at
http://infotrac.cengage.com

- the inflation, unemployment, petroleum price increases, and price controls of the 1970s affected the economy's efficiency and caused management to focus on short-term results
- increased error in measuring productivity caused the measured growth to be less than the actual growth
- U.S. business firms by the early 1970s had incorporated much of the new knowledge about products and production developed before and during World War II into their established procedures.

---

[9]See Dale Jorgenson, "U.S. Economic Growth in the Information Age." *Issues in Science and Technology* 18, no. 1 (Fall 2001): 42–51.

[10]"William E. Cullison, "The U.S. Productivity Slowdown: What the Experts Say," *Federal Reserve Bank of Richmond Economic Quarterly* (July/August 1989): 10–21. This article provides an excellent review of discussion about the productivity slowdown. A more recent look at the issue is Roy H. Webb, "National Productivity Statistics," *Federal Reserve Bank of Richmond Economic Quarterly* (Winter 1998): 45–64.

The science and engineering advances of the 1960s and 1970s would have their greatest impacts in the information technology sectors, and just like earlier innovations—electricity, the telephone, the internal combustion engine, and assembly line techniques—did not have large immediate effects on the economy. By the 1970s, however, the previous innovations that had been reorganizing the economy since the turn of the twentieth century had had their dramatic impacts. We now know that major U.S. industries, such as automobiles, steel, and transportation, had peaked based on the available technologies. Firms and managers had prospered with the existing technologies; they naturally were suspicious of new technologies. IBM, for instance, did not anticipate the opportunities presented by desktop computing and did respond in ways that allowed it to maintain its preeminent position in computing. Similarly, the Big Three American automobile companies (Chrysler, Ford, and General Motors) were slow in adopting new production technologies more appropriate for the economy of the 1980s. Competitive pressure forced IBM and the Big Three to change. The competitive pressure came from the entrepreneurs who created Apple, Intel, and Microsoft on the one hand and the entrepreneurs who build a new Japanese automobile industry on the other. As the new firms and new technologies forced changes, these U.S. industrial titans suffered significant losses.

Creative destruction– Economic progress where the introduction of new technologies forces old ones out.

Although it was not obvious at the time, by the mid-1980s the IT revolution probably had begun a new wave of **creative destruction**, introducing new technologies and firms and eliminating old ones. These new technologies—new knowledge—will have their impacts over a long time period. Evidence is accumulating that the acceleration of technical progress of the mid-1990s will result in rapid productivity growth for an extended period.

The productivity acceleration of the late 1990s, according to a study by McKinsey Global Institute (MGI), was not broad-based; indeed, it could be credited to six sectors of the economy responsible for only about 30 percent of total output.[11] Some of these sectors are expected—industrial machinery and equipment (primarily computer manufacturing), electronics (primarily semiconductors), and telecommunications—and others—retail, wholesale, and securities brokerage—are surprises. They contributed to aggregate productivity growth in two ways: their productivity accelerated and/or the sectors were high-productivity sectors whose share of the overall economy increased.

Productivity in the semiconductor industry increased rapidly as Intel introduced chips at a faster pace. According to MGI, Advanced Micro Devices' competitive pressure pushed Intel to the faster pace. The computer industry's large productivity acceleration resulted from innovations in the input industries—disks, modems, microprocessors—that provided the computer industry with higher-quality inputs at lower prices. Again entrepreneurs and new firms created competition among suppliers that resulted in the lower prices to the computer assemblers, who in turn, prompted by competition, passed the improvements on to consumers through lower prices. In addition, more complex operating systems and more sophisticated applications lead to consumer's demand for high-performance computers, where productivity gains are magnified. Advances in IT have also stimulated productivity growth in the mobile phone segment of the telecommunications industry.

The acceleration of productivity growth in the above industries and their larger shares of the economy account for about the same increase in productivity as is attributed to the retail sector (basically Wal-Mart). Wal-Mart's productivity increase, its growing share of the market, and the pressure that it exerts on competitors are important sources of aggregate productivity growth. IT plays a role in Wal-Mart's competitive success, but the "big box" approach to retailing, along with supply management and innovative

[11]McKinsey Global Institute, *U.S. Productivity Growth 1995–2000* (Washington, D.C.: McKinsey Global Institute, 2001).

management techniques, are also key. (Incidentally, E-commerce had little to do with the productivity increase in retailing.) The wholesale sector provided a boost to productivity slightly larger than the retail sector. Again, IT facilitates the improvements, but the big boost comes from warehouse automation.

Outside the semiconductor, computer assembly, and mobile phone sectors, the "new economy" has had a dramatic and decisive effect on productivity growth only in the securities industry. Online stock trading jumped to about 40 percent of all retail stock trades, from a base of about zero in 1995. It is only here that the Internet has been absolutely necessary for the advances to take place.

Have the technological advances in the IT sector and the buildup in IT assets been responsible for the productivity acceleration? Certainly, they have played a role. As others have noted, much of the productivity acceleration is found in IT manufacturing and telecommunications. IT investment has facilitated advances in retailing and wholesaling, although competitive pressures have also been important. IT may result in continuing radical transformations such as those found in the securities sector. But other sectors, such as the retail banking and hotels, have invested heavily in IT and are not realizing productivity benefits. Whether or not we are in a new period of rapid economic growth due to advancing productivity related to IT investments is still to be determined. The prospects are encouraging, but the existence of the new technology is not sufficient to guarantee the results. Entrepreneurs, managers, and consumers must have incentives to make appropriate choices, and government must provide an economic environment that promotes efficiency.

INTERNATIONAL PERSPECTIVE

Economic Freedom and Economic Growth in Developing Countries

At the beginning of this chapter, we implied that the level and growth of living standards are likely to be higher in economies based on economic freedom rather than centralized government planning. In particular, we suggested that the values of the Declaration of Independence and *Wealth of Nations* promote economic prosperity. Some people turn this argument on its head. Some critics argue that economic and political freedom are luxuries that only prosperous economies can afford, in short, that prosperity causes economic and political freedom, rather than the other way around.

James D. Gwartney, Robert A. Lawson, and others have developed an economic freedom index available at the Fraser Institute Web site, *Economic Freedom of the World.* Studies by Gwartney and colleagues based on these data and other studies using similar freedom indices show a strong correlation between economic freedom and prosperity. These correlations, however, do not prove that economic freedom causes prosperity.

To understand what causes what, Gwartney and Lawson, in *Economic Reform Today,* examined their index for developing or low-income countries and identified the 12 (top 10 with ties) countries that had the greatest increase in economic freedom from 1975 to 1990. They were Chile, Jamaica, Malaysia, Turkey, Pakistan, Egypt, Portugal, Mauritius, Singapore, Costa Rica, Indonesia, and Thailand. They also identified those developing countries with the greatest decrease in economic freedom: Panama, Morocco, Algeria, Tanzania, Zambia, Congo, Venezuela, Honduras, Iran, Somalia, and Nicaragua. If economic freedom promotes prosperity, one can reasonably expect developing countries with increases in freedom to experience more growth in a later period than developing countries with decreases in freedom. Consequently, Gwartney and colleagues examined growth rates of these same countries in a later period (1985–1994). The countries with the biggest increases in economic freedom showed an average of 4 percent annual growth in real per capita GDP. Real per capita GDP fell at 1.2 percent per year in the countries with the greatest decreases in economic freedom. Thus, increases in economic freedom were followed by higher growth rates in a later period. Although other explanations are possible, this relationship between growth of economic freedom and growth of per capita GDP is consistent with the proposition that well-functioning market economies promote economic growth.[a] Using more recent data and different statistical techniques, Julio H. Cole has found that both economic freedom and increases in economic freedom are associated with more rapid economic growth.[b]

Greater appreciation for these results requires some discussion of the index. Gwartney and colleagues argue that low taxes, secure property rights, free markets, free trade, and price and monetary stability promote growth. The 12 countries that achieved the faster growth rates had several factors in common. They improved their inflation performance, and 11 of the 12 now allow their citizens to hold foreign currency accounts, making the domestic inflation less harmful. International trade became more important, and its importance (approximately) doubled for countries such as Malaysia, Turkey, and Thailand. Finally, 11 of the 12 countries reduced their highest marginal income tax rates to below 50 percent. The highest marginal tax rate, in Portugal, went from 82 percent to 40 percent. Malaysia's dropped from 50 percent to 34 percent. Gwartney and colleagues concluded that the economic success of Hong Kong and other countries that have well-functioning market economies is "powerful evidence concerning the potency of economic freedom and a market economy as an engine of growth and development."[c]

[a] James Gwartney and Robert Lawson, "Economic Freedom and the Growth of Emerging Markets," *Economic Reform Today* 2 (1996), online at http://www.cipe.org

[b] Julio H. Cole, "The Contribution of Economic Freedom to World Economic Growth, 1980–99," *Cato Journal* 23 (Fall 2003), 189–98.

[c] Gwartney and Lawson, "Economic Freedom."

Summary

Economic growth has raised citizens of the United States, Canada, Japan, and countries of Western Europe to living standards unimaginable just 100 years ago. Per capita income continues to grow in these economies, although at a slower rate than just after World War II. Several other countries, particularly in East Asia, experienced rapid growth beginning in the 1960s and 1970s that has transformed their economies.

The production possibilities curve for an individual or an economy helps to explain the sources of economic growth. The individual college student, for instance, has her or his ability, labor, decision-making ability, human and physical capital. He or she must allocate resources (particularly, own-labor time) between consumption goods and investment in education—human capital. The student's production possibilities are limited, implying scarcity and opportunity cost. Production possibilities for the economy show that for a fixed amount of resources (land, labor, human capital, physical capital, and entrepreneurship) and a given technology, an economy has a menu of efficient combinations of output. In particular, it can produce more consumption goods and fewer capital goods, or the reverse. If the country wants more rapid growth, it can increase the production of capital goods at the expense of consumption goods. It can sacrifice present consumption for the increased future consumption that increased investment in capital goods allows. The economy can also grow through technical progress: technological and efficiency improvements.

From the end of World War II until the early 1970s, rapid labor productivity growth fed by technical progress allowed compensation per hour to grow rapidly in the United States and other industrial countries. From 1973 to the early 1990s, the growth rates of labor productivity, compensation, and technical progress fell substantially. The twenty-first century, with increased competition and the coming of age of technologies, may be the beginning of a new spurt in productivity growth due to technical progress. We shall see.

Higher-income countries that have closed the gap with the United States have effective market economies: private property rights, flexible prices, a stable price level, appropriate incentives, and a stable legal system. Lower-income countries that are growing rapidly share these characteristics. Nevertheless, a great variety of economic policies exist in countries that have had sustained economic growth. In addition to promoting education and developing appropriate infrastructure, some countries have applied tariffs and other subsidies to some of their industries. Other countries have remained more hands-off. Few, if any, of the countries that have sustained economic growth for long periods have used a comprehensive central plan.

Key Terms

Opportunity cost
Labor
Land
Physical capital
Human capital
Entrepreneurship
Production possibilities curve
Best technology
Marginal cost
Scarcity
Marginal benefit
Technological improvement
Efficiency improvement
Capital intensity
Technical progress
Creative destruction

Review Questions

1. Compare the economic growth of Japan, Korea, and the United States since 1960.
2. Define the following terms:
   a. production possibilities curve
   b. technological improvement
   c. efficiency improvement
3. Is a faster rate of economic growth always desirable? Explain carefully using the production possibilities curve.
4. Use the accompanying graph to answer questions a through d.

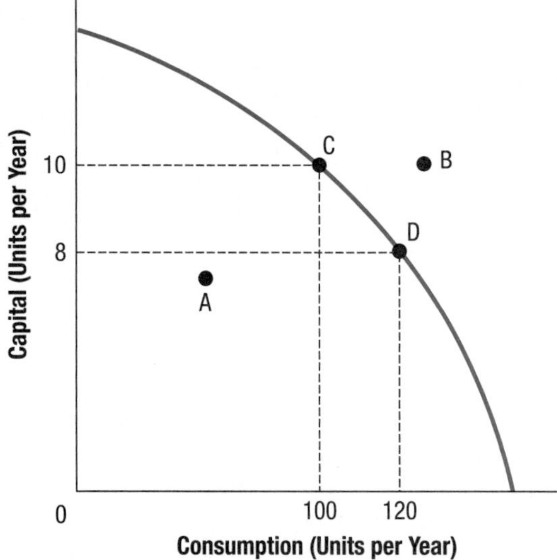

   a. What point would represent a combination of goods and services that cannot be produced with the economy's given resources and technology?
   b. What point would represent a combination of goods and services that might be produced if the economy were experiencing unemployment? What else could cause the economy to be at that point?
   c. Suppose the economy is currently producing at point C and would like to have the consumption goods represented by point D. What must be given up to obtain the increased consumption goods?
   d. Suppose the economy is at point D. What might be done to increase the chances of being at B next year? What are other ways to reach B?
5. The Black Death (the plague) killed one-third of the European population in a relatively short time in the fourteenth century. How would a pandemic that killed a significant percentage of an economy's population affect the production possibilities curve for that economy? How would this differ from the effect of the destruction of a similar percentage of the capital stock? (Hint: See the box on the cost of hurricanes.)
6. Do you know an entrepreneur? What is the role of the entrepreneur is promoting productivity growth. Do you think that most entrepreneurs are successful? Why or why not?
7. What caused the slowdown in labor productivity growth in the United States after 1973?
8. Explain the sources of the increased productivity growth in the United States in the 1990s after 1995.
9. "Productivity growth in Japan is greater than productivity growth in the United States because its workers are more productive." Is this statement true or false? Defend your answer.
10. What factors explain why labor productivity in Japan and Western Europe has grown faster than in the United States?
11. According to the box titled "Economic Freedom and Economic Growth in Developing Countries," countries with more economic freedom have higher levels of per capita income. Does this prove that economic freedom causes prosperity? Defend your answer. The box also states that

countries with increased economic freedom subsequently experience faster economic growth. Does this give you any more information about economic freedom and economic growth? Explain.

12. Discuss one advantage and one disadvantage that developing countries share as they try to encourage economic growth. What policies have proven successful in promoting economic growth?

13. Go to the Web site Economic News Online http://www.swcollege.com/bef/econ_news.html and choose the Equilibrium category under Fundamentals and choose an EconNews story that interests you. Read the full summary and answer the questions posed.

Web Sites

- *The World Bank.*
  The World Bank is an international agency focused on economic growth and development throughout the world. Its Global Development Network Growth Database is only one of its many data sets available online. Working papers and policy papers are also available—**http://www.worldbank.org**
- *The International Monetary Fund.*
  The IMF is another international agency dealing with economies throughout the world. Its quarterly periodical, *Finance and Development,* often contains material that is of interest to and accessible to students. It too has working papers, policy papers, and data—**http://www.imf.org**
- *The E. F. Schumacher Society.*
  E. F. Schumacher was the author of *Small Is Beautiful: Economics as if People Mattered* (New York: HarperCollins, 1989), which was first published in 1973. Not everyone agrees that economic growth is desirable. A visit to this site will give you leads to this position—**http://www.schumachersociety.org**
- *Free the World.*
  The Web site for the *Economic Freedom of the World* publications and data—**http://www.freetheworld.com**
- *Freedom House.*
  The Web site for indices of economic and political freedom—**http://www.freedomhouse.org**

CHAPTER 2

An Introduction to Economic Systems and the Workings of the Price System

OUTLINE

Market Economic Systems: An Introductory Look
What Does an Economic System Do? It Coordinates
The Price System as Coordinator
Comparative Systems: An Introductory Sketch
Transitions to a Market Economy: Some Experiences

Keywords: *Soviet Union and economic aspects*

Access InfoTrac at http://infotrac.cengage.com

Keyword: *central planning*

Access InfoTrac at http://infotrac.cengage.com

In the late 1950s, Nikita Khrushchev, General Secretary of the Communist Party of the Soviet Union, vowed to Western Europe and the United States: "We will bury you." It was of little comfort that he meant to do so economically. According to the relevant Soviet Economic Plan, by 1980 Soviet industrial production would be greater than the combined production of the capitalist countries, including the United States. Although the threat—or promise—now appears absurd, at that time many commentators in the West expressed serious concern about Soviet economic power.

After World War II, many observers, including policy makers in various parts of the world, considered centrally planned *(command) economic systems* superior to *market economic systems.* From this perspective, the Great Depression of the 1930s, in which market economies experienced extreme economic distress, foretold future economic troubles. Those who considered a command economy superior made several claims: little unemployment; reduced inequality; and the ability to redirect resources from uses deemed unimportant to uses that promote economic growth and military power. In this view, the economic problem was how to accumulate sufficient industrial capacity to become a modern economy.

A complete comparison of the structures of a command economy and a market economy requires extensive discussion, beyond our scope. Our short discussion, however, will help you understand the differences between the two systems. In a command economy a central plan details the amounts of various goods and services to produce. It sets targets for consumer goods and investment goods. For instance, the plan might call for building apartments in various parts of the country and building a steel mill. It would, of course, have to establish targets for many other activities. Planners in the former Soviet Union set prices and determined production for more than 500,000 different items. The planners had to consider numerous factors, including;

- what products people desired
- what products and actions the government desired
- how to produce various products
- who would receive the products
- how to move the inputs and finished products

If more apartments were to be built, the planners would have to decide what size to build, what types of construction to use, where to build them, and who would live in them. They would have to ensure that construction materials, kitchen appliances, furniture, and numerous other resources and products would be available. Moreover, the kitchen appliances would have to fit into the apartments' kitchens. The planners would not provide variety in terms of the apartments' size, layout, and style because this would complicate the planning problem. As a result, apartments in the Soviet Union were drab, gray, monolithic, and made from the same pattern.

In a market economy the same factors—what, how, and for whom—must be resolved, but without central planners. Instead, the market solution results from millions of independent decisions made by individuals. Each individual considers the opportunities available and the costs of different actions and decides to do those things that will make her or him better off. Would you expect the planned system to be organized and the market system to be chaotic? Many do! In fact, market economies do a much better job than command economies of delivering the right stuff to the right place at the right time. Imagine the numerous goods and services used in any large city every day. The astonishing fact is that people who are willing to pay the market price can buy almost any good that can be produced and shipped, usually without delay.

Although both command and market systems faced the same economic problem, as the last half of the 20th century unfolded, market economies increasingly outperformed command economies. Before World War II, East Germany probably had a slight economic edge over West Germany. Just a few years after the war, however, the West German market economy was providing its residents a better standard of living than was the East German planned economy. By 1990, West German per capita income was almost quadruple that of East Germany, which is certainly one of the reasons that the Berlin Wall fell. Comparisons of Communist North Korea to South Korea and Communist China to Hong Kong give the same result. After World War II, people in the non-Communist countries surged ahead of those in comparable Communist countries even if they started from similar economic and cultural bases.

From the end of World War II to the 1980s, the command economies (the Soviet Union and other Communist states) and the market economies (the United States and allied states) challenged each other's economic performance. The competition ended with the collapse of the centrally planned systems in the former Soviet bloc. Many of these countries with failed economies have tried to create market economies from the wreckage of their planned ones; some have succeeded. The collapse of Soviet Communism was a defining event of the 20th century; the successful transformation of these command economies to market economies is a central hope of the 21st. According to *The Economist*, "Across the whole region [Central and Eastern Europe and countries formed from the Soviet Union], the possibility and desirability of creating capitalism has now been accepted, even by the laggards." The most decisive reason "has surely been a simple recognition of the superiority of capitalism as an economic system."[1]

Because market (capitalist) economies have evolved without anyone actually deciding to create them—like Topsy, "they just grew"—it is sometimes difficult to understand their essential features. We can't see the trees for the forest. The process of abandoning a command economy—central planning—and creating a market economy provides a laboratory for the study of these features. This chapter uses that laboratory to discuss two fundamental questions: What are the essential characteristics of a market economy system, and why do market systems perform better than command systems? To make the discussion concrete, some of the experiences of former command economies—the transition economies—are examined.

MARKET ECONOMIC SYSTEMS: AN INTRODUCTORY LOOK

The changes countries make in trying to establish a market economic system imply much about the system's essential features: private ownership, market exchanges, and

[1]"After Communism," *The Economist* 27 (December 3, 1994).

market incentives. These countries have established a legal system consistent with *private ownership* of most business operations—particularly agriculture, manufacturing, retailing, wholesaling, and business and personal services. They also allow individuals to undertake voluntary economic transactions *(market exchanges)*—that is, they allow individuals' decisions about buying and selling goods and services to establish market prices that coordinate economic plans. Finally, they use market rewards and penalties as *incentives*: Economically successful people benefit from the wealth they create, and unsuccessful people suffer the consequences of deficiencies in wealth creation.

Relative price– The price of one good in terms of another good. It measures what must be given up to obtain a good.

Knowing the price of a good helps people decide if they want to purchase it. The relative price is the pertinent price when buying or selling. A **relative price**, the price of one good in terms of another good, measures what we must give up to purchase an item. It is an exchange value and measures opportunity cost. As we will see, relative prices and their changes summarize and convey a lot of information that individuals find extremely useful in their economic decision making. For instance, if a concert ticket is priced at $80, an individual sacrifices the best alternative use of the $80 to attend the concert. The $80 could be used to buy eight movie tickets at $10 per movie or four DVDs at $20 per DVD. Let's assume that José, a college student, has decided to spend $80 on one of these three alternatives. He then chooses the concert over purchasing four DVDs or going to eight movies. The relative price of the concert is four DVDs, or eight movies, or $80. The opportunity cost of the concert is the value of José's preferred alternative, which we assume is four DVDs. In deciding between the concert and the DVDs, José compares the expected benefit of owning the DVDs to the expected benefit of the concert. If prices change little over time, people become aware of relative prices as measures of exchange values—what they must give up of one thing to obtain another. This information greatly simplifies their decision making. Of course, when price changes, it signals that exchange values have changed.

The information conveyed by a change in market price, say, of concerts, depends upon what happens to prices of other products. Consider three examples. First, suppose that the concert ticket price doubles to $160 and that all other prices stay the same. This price increase might occur if the band becomes more popular. At $160, the sacrifice for a concert ticket would be eight DVDs. The price increase therefore signals that a greater sacrifice—at least the value of eight DVDs—is required to attend a concert. As a result, fewer people choose the concert. The price change provides the appropriate signal to consumers, telling them that attending the concert now requires a greater sacrifice of other items.

If the average of all prices is increasing over time, then prices might be unreliable indicators of sacrificed alternatives. For the second example, suppose that a year later the concert price doubles to $160, that all other prices double, and that José's entertainment budget also doubles—to $160. (If prices continue to rise, this is an example of *inflation*, a continuous increase in the average of all prices over time. Inflation is analyzed in Chapter 14.) José still has the choice of one concert, four DVDs, or eight movies. Because the cost of the concert in terms of DVDs and movies remains the same—four DVDs or eight movies—he still chooses the concert. If all prices change in the same proportion, relative prices and exchange values and opportunity costs do not change. Thus a steady rate of inflation might not seriously damage the usefulness of the price system in summarizing and conveying information.

Often, however, inflation accelerates and decelerates over time and has different effects on prices in different sectors of the economy. After some point, as inflation increases, it becomes more erratic. Erratic inflation prevents people from using past decisions and information as a reliable guide to future decisions. Suppose, for the third example, that the price of movie tickets remains at $10, the price of concert tickets is

$160 rather than $80, the price of DVDs goes up by a factor of four to $80, and his budget becomes $160. Relative to concert tickets, DVDs are now more expensive and movies less expensive. José now has to recompute the exchange values, to rethink relative prices. The cost of a concert ticket is now either two DVDs or 16 movies. José might now choose to go to 16 movies. Because of the change in relative prices, José forgoes the concert and purchases the movie tickets. As erratic inflation continues, people must evaluate their alternatives in detail each time they consider a purchase, increasing the cost of information captured from prices. A stable average price level, on the other hand, makes historical prices and exchange values an excellent source of information and thus reduces decision-making costs.

In addition, a well-functioning market system requires that individuals trust other individuals with whom they deal. A major step in this direction is the establishment of a clear and understandable legal system creating private property rights. The system must create all types of ownership structures: proprietorships, partnerships, and corporations. Besides property law, the legal system must include contract, criminal, tort, and other types of law. Many problems must be dealt with; they include, among others, fraud, theft, counterfeiting, misrepresentation of a product's attributes, and failure to mention safety problems. These laws encourage economic transactions by making the terms of the agreement less ambiguous and more binding. For the legal system to be most effective in promoting prosperity, however, people must generally accept, obey, and understand the laws. The laws must be easy to understand and be consistently enforced. If not, more government resources must be devoted to law enforcement, and people will devote more personal resources to protecting their persons and their property and to understanding and evading laws and regulations. A market economic system thus becomes less effective because resources are devoted to nonproductive activities, such as tax avoidance and evasion.

No legal system can regulate all situations in which honesty is an important stimulus for good economic performance. Besides formal rules of conduct based on a system of justice, well-functioning economic systems also require informal rules. People must be able to rely on each other's word. For example, suppose that when you asked other people the time of a meeting, some gave you the correct time but others did not. It is hard to imagine a law requiring that we tell each other the correct time. If we cannot rely on an honest answer, however, our lives become terribly inconvenient.

If you have ever bought or sold a used car, you understand the importance of honesty and trust. Suppose you are in the market to buy a used car. You see the exact car that you want in the classified advertisements; you also see one for sale in the used car lot of a new-car dealer. If you buy the car from the private seller through the classifieds, you will pay a lower price than you would pay the dealer. Moreover, the private seller will receive a better price for his used car than if he sold it to a dealer. It's a win-win situation. Yet, even though they might secure a better price in a private one-on-one transaction, many people decide to go through a dealer. Various reasons exist for using the dealer, but one of the important ones is that the dealer must be concerned about the effect of transactions on her reputation. She has an economic incentive to be honest, because her good reputation is valuable. On the other hand, if two people are mutually trustworthy, perhaps friends or family, they may bypass the dealer and both parties receive a better price. Of course, misunderstandings associated with business transactions might doom friendships and create family feuds.

To summarize some of the characteristics of a successful market system, we expand on the list in Table 2.1.

TABLE 2.1 CHARACTERISTICS OF A SUCCESSFUL MARKET SYSTEM

1.	A system of private property and property rights defined, established, and protected by law (**private ownership**).
2.	Flexible prices that fluctuate in response to individuals' voluntary decisions and exchanges (**market exchange**).
3.	Market **incentives** that are generated by a price system whose rewards and penalties motivate decision makers.
4.	Reasonably **stable prices** and a well-functioning **monetary system** that facilitates voluntary exchange.
5.	A culture with a **climate of trust** and in which a well-constructed and well-enforced legal system is broadly obeyed.

- First, a successful market system is one with a system of private property and property rights defined, established, and protected by law. Furthermore, private property must constitute a significant portion of the economy.
- Second, a successful market system has flexible prices that fluctuate in response to individuals' voluntary decisions and exchanges. Markets and flexible prices allow the economy to be organized based on voluntary decisions and exchanges. Given private property, individuals decide what to produce and consume based on their personal interests and opportunities. They also make career and production decisions based on their interests, opportunities, and talents and in light of what other people will pay for their labor or their products. Having decided what to produce or where to sell their labor, people exchange what they produce or what they earn for goods and services produced by other people. A market economy eases these voluntary exchanges by establishing prices for goods and services that allow individuals to purchase from others rather than directly exchanging what they produce.
- Third, in a successful market economy incentives are generated by a price system whose rewards and penalties motivate decision makers. In such a system, people make careful decisions and exchanges because they are responsible for the consequences. They keep the rewards and bear the costs, giving them incentive to be careful.
- Fourth, a successful market economy has a reasonably stable price level and a well-functioning monetary system that facilitates voluntary exchange. A well-functioning monetary system makes it unnecessary for people to trade bread for wine; they can sell bread for money and use the money to buy wine. For example, the use of money and prices allows college professors to teach without the bother of students paying them with house painting, babysitting, house cleaning, farm products, or whatever students and their families produce. As you well know, students pay colleges money; colleges in turn pay the professors, who buy what they want and can afford. With a stable monetary system and little inflation, prices generate information that simplifies voluntary exchange between individuals; they inform and motivate people in their economic decision making.
- Finally, a market system works best with a legal system that is broadly obeyed, and a culture that generates a climate of trust and respect for the legal and political systems. For this to occur, the legal and judicial systems must clearly and simply define and enforce the economy and society's rules. Moreover, people must generally behave in a mutually trustworthy manner.

INTERNATIONAL PERSPECTIVE

What Happened in China?

In the Chapter 1 box, "China: Economic Growth and Poverty," we briefly described how economic growth in China since 1978 has lifted more than 400 million people from absolute poverty and raised the standard of living of hundreds of millions of others who had been on the brink of absolute poverty. Now let's discuss one simple reason this occurred and some limitations to future growth.

According to *The Economist* and many other sources, China's initial growth and poverty reduction stemmed from changes in the agricultural sector of the economy. In particular, farmers were given responsibility for a certain parcel of land and given the rights to earn additional income based on the crops they produced. Prices of agricultural products were allowed to rise. Previously, farmers worked in collective farms and their incomes were not tied to their work effort. In short, the introduction of market incentives and flexible prices stimulated economic growth. From 1978 to 1984, rural incomes grew by 14 percent a year.

In the 1990s, policy makers recognized that the relatively slow growth in rural income and agricultural productivity after the mid-1980s was related to the limited rights that farmers had to the use of particular plots of land. The land was (and is) collectively owned, and the collective—a village or a cooperative society—could and did assign it to other uses and users. The farmers had assurance of the income from the crops they grew in a particular year, but they did not have assurance that they would be farming the same land year after year. Consequently, farmers did not have much incentive to make improvements in the land that would pay off in the future because they did not have secure rights to use the land indefinitely or to sell it and capture the value of the improvements in the selling price. In such circumstances, farmers were unwilling to make investments whose payoffs might be in the distant future.

In recognition of this problem, the Land Management Law of 1998 provided for the allocation of use rights to particular parcels of land for 30 years. This agricultural land is still collectively owned and the right to use it is not as secure as it would be with ownership by an individual farmer. Nevertheless, with this greater security farmers are more willing to invest in the land. But farmers do not have the right to sell the land that they use. Because they are unable to sell the land or to transfer it to heirs, they cannot be sure that they will reap the rewards of investments that would build the long-term fertility and productivity of the land. The greatest incentive for long-term investment in any resource exists when the individual decision maker has both use rights and the right to sell and keep the income from the sale of the resource. This restriction on the private ownership of land means that Chinese agriculture is unlikely to be the most productive it can be. Moreover, this lack of ownership also makes the development of a land rental market difficult, which limits farmers' flexibility. In addition, the farmers cannot use the land as collateral for loans, and they are reluctant to consider nonfarm employment because this could result in losing their use rights to the land.

Source: Suggested by "The Long March to Capitalism," *The Economist* 344 (November 13, 1997): 23–26. For the effects of the 1998 law, see Bryan Lohman, "Changes in Labor, Land, and Credit Markets Lead China's Farmers on the Path Toward Modernization," in Hsu Hsin-Hui and Fred Gale, *China: Agriculture in Transition, Agriculture and Trade Report No. WRS012* (November 2001), 9–12.

WHAT DOES AN ECONOMIC SYSTEM DO? IT COORDINATES

An economic system consists of a set of economic, political, social, and other rules. Given the rules, people make choices that, taken together, determine five interrelated economic outcomes: (1) the methods of production; (2) the quantities of various goods and services produced in an economy; (3) who receives the goods and services; (4) the overall stability of the economy and whether it produces at its capacity; and (5) the economy's growth. The remainder of this section discusses these concepts.

The Methods of Production. How will business firms produce? Will automobile producers, for example, make extensive use of robots, or will they move from assembly line production to team production? How-to-produce questions are among the easier ones that an economic system deals with, because they are partly answered by engineering considerations.

The Quantities of Various Goods and Services Produced in an Economy. How much and what types of food, clothing, and various other products should be produced? Reasonable answers depend on the talents and desires of the 300 million people and 150 million workers in the U.S. economy. What goods and services are they adept at producing? What goods and services do they wish to consume? The questions are difficult because people do not wish to consume everything they are good at producing, and are not good at producing everything they want to consume.

Who Receives the Goods and Services? The distribution of goods and services also raises difficult issues. To achieve a high level of economic output, people must be rewarded for what they produce so that they have incentive to continue and perhaps to increase their production. Compassion or justice, however, requires that those who cannot produce an adequate amount be taken care of in some way. The contradiction between the distribution of material goods as incentives and their distribution for compassion is troubling. People in most societies are unwilling to accept a distribution of goods and services based entirely on what one produces because some people would not obtain enough to survive. As a result, many people voluntarily give goods and services to the less fortunate (charity) and support government's mandatory redistribution (welfare).

The Overall Stability of the Economy and Whether it Produces at its Capacity. Periods of high unemployment or rapid inflation disrupt an economic system. When people are unemployed, their potential production is lost and can never be recovered. As discussed above, rapid inflation makes it harder for an economic system to operate. Because an unregulated market system may be subject to recurring episodes of unemployment and inflation, many economists believe that governments must promote economic stability.

The Economy's Growth. Economic growth in the United States and other industrial countries slowed in the past quarter century. Although the previous chapter suggests that the U.S. growth rate may have taken off at the turn of the century, parts of Western Europe and Japan are still experiencing slow economic growth. Therefore, the relationship between economic growth and economic policy remains on the front burner for high-income countries and remains a fundamental issue for those who would alleviate world poverty. Promotion of economic growth is complex and controversial. As discussed in Chapter 1, economic growth requires sacrificing in the present to provide for the future, making growth a feature of the conflict between generations.

This book introduces you to a market economic system, particularly the U.S. system, and its performance. Although the five economic outcomes listed above are interrelated and difficult to discuss in isolation, different parts of the book emphasize different outcomes. Economic growth was discussed in Chapter 1. Chapters 3 through 10 explore aspects of what goods to produce. Chapters 11 and 16 focus on distribution: poverty and Social Security. Chapters 12 through 15 deal with unemployment, inflation, and other issues related to the overall economy. Finally, Chapters 17 and 18 examine the international economy.

All these issues involve the central problem of coordination. We next examine why coordination is so complex in a modern economy. After identifying what an economic system must do—*coordinate*—we discuss how a market economic system does its job. Later, we compare market and centrally planned (command) economic systems.

The Division and Specialization of Labor

As early as 1776, when Adam Smith published his trail-breaking treatise in economics, *The Wealth of Nations*, economists recognized the importance of the division of labor. By the division of labor, Smith meant (1) the specialization of labor in a particular production process—today, that might be the person in a service station who specializes in changing oil—and (2) the specialization of firms in a few activities, such as the automobile service station that does only mufflers. Division of labor implies specialization of economic activity.

Smith argued that the division and specialization of labor gave "modern" economies a tremendous wealth advantage over "traditional" subsistence economies. He illustrated the division of labor in a firm by describing the specialized tasks of workers who produced straight pins. One worker "draws out the wire, another straights it, a third cuts it, a fourth points it, a fifth grinds it at the top for receiving the head; … and the important business of making a pin, is divided into about eighteen distinct operations, which in some manufactories are all performed by distinct hands."[2] Smith estimated that, in factories with extensive division of labor, the daily production of pins per worker might be 4,800 times the production of a single worker who did all the tasks.

Although you might think that producing a textbook involves no extensive division of labor, both types of specialization are important. The production of this book used the services of tens of thousands of specialized people and specialized business firms—the many economists who have researched the topics; the editors, publishers, and printers; the loggers and manufacturing employees who produced the paper; the people who invented and produced the computer hardware and software; and so on. The enormous availability of books today would have been unimaginable to monks in the Middle Ages, who manufactured books by hand, copying and beautifully illustrating manuscripts. Dramatically increased division of labor, along with new technology, has made books incredibly inexpensive today compared to their cost in the Middle Ages.

Smith's insights about the advantages of the division and specialization of labor remain relevant. He discussed three ways that specialization increases the output of goods and services.

First, specialization allows people to become highly skilled in particular tasks. Today we would say that specialized workers become more skilled through higher education, vocational training, and on-the-job training focused on a narrow speciality.

Second, specialization reduces the time wasted as people shift from one task to another. Smith referred to the time wasted by subsistence farmers, who did several jobs in a short time. Time-management experts currently make a similar point. They recommend that workers complete one task—for example, respond to their e-mail—before they switch to another task. By reserving large blocks of time for each task, people avoid losing time because of (1) mental shifting of gears, (2) putting materials away, (3) locating new materials, and so on. The fewer tasks an individual does—that is, the greater the specialization—the more time saved.

Third, Smith observed that specialized workers produced many inventions and innovations in the early Industrial Revolution; because they concentrated on just a few tasks, these workers would find better ways to do them. Some inventions and innovations today come from people who specialize in invention, itself an example of greater division

[2]Adam Smith, *An Inquiry into the Nature and Causes of the Wealth of Nations* (Oxford: Clarendon Press, 1979; repr. Indianapolis: Liberty Press, 1981), bk. I, ch. 1, p. 15.

of labor. Still, specialization aids innovation because a simple task is easier to automate than a complex one. Furthermore, just as in Adam Smith's day, contemporary workers invent and innovate in a search for new and better ways of doing their jobs. As we do our jobs, we gain knowledge. Often that knowledge is tacit—knowledge that we can use but can't explain easily to others. For instance, an expert at video games cannot use a lecture or a book to teach someone else to play the game equally well. If winning a particular game were important, an expert would choose to play the game herself rather than use a lecture or book to teach a beginner, even if the beginner had substantially better hand-to-eye coordination. Other people must learn by doing, just as the expert did. Because we cannot easily transfer tacit knowledge to others, the people who have it can make the best use of it themselves. Workers doing their jobs develop tacit knowledge that employers can unleash if they provide an appropriate work environment. Given the opportunity and the incentive, workers use tacit knowledge to develop new procedures and products that create wealth for their employers, for themselves, and for final users.

Greater division and specialization of labor are not unmixed blessings. The monk responsible for producing a beautiful manuscript had a great feeling of accomplishment. He could see the product of his labor. With increased specialization, many workers cannot see their accomplishments. Work that requires repetitive, monotonous actions leads to worker discontent. Economic systems must balance promoting division of labor with ways of avoiding the negative results of overspecialization.

Specialization based on division of labor and comparative advantage is an integral part of any economy.[3] If we specialize, however, we produce more of few things than we want to use and we produce nothing else. To obtain the many other goods and services that we want, we must trade, which means the consumption and production of vast numbers of specialized people must be coordinated.

Comparative Advantage and Specialization

Although Adam Smith knew that specialization leads to greater skills and greater production, he did not completely appreciate its power. He recognized that some people have an absolute advantage over other people in producing certain products and thus would be likely to specialize in those products. But what about a person with an absolute advantage in everything? What should she specialize in, if anything? David Ricardo, a British economist, raised and answered this question in his 1817 *Principles of Political Economy and Taxation.*

Absolute advantage– The advantage that an individual has if he can produce a good at lower cost than another individual.

Suppose that Sara has an absolute advantage over Jeff in producing the economy's two goods—pizzas and shirts. She has an **absolute advantage** because she can produce more of either product with her time and resources than Jeff can. She can produce either 10 pizzas or 10 shirts per week, compared to six or three, respectively, by Jeff. Sara can also produce seven pizzas and three shirts, four pizzas and six shirts, or various other combinations as given in Table 2.2. (Jeff also can produce different combinations as given in the table). With an absolute disadvantage in both goods, it might seem that Jeff would have to rely on his own production of pizza and shirts for survival. Why would Sara bother with getting anything from Jeff? Ricardo's remarkable insight is that both Sara and Jeff can gain by specializing.

To understand, consider Sara's production possibility schedule in Table 2.2. The production possibility schedule shows the maximum number of pizzas that she can produce, if she devotes all of her time to pizza production—10 pizzas per week. Similarly, it shows that as an alternative, she could produce 10 shirts. Furthermore, the schedule shows the

---

[3]Comparative advantage as a basis for international trade is further developed in Chapter 17.

TABLE 2.2 PRODUCTION POSSIBILITIES: TWO PRODUCERS

SARA		JEFF	
PIZZAS PER WEEK	SHIRTS PER WEEK	PIZZAS PER WEEK	SHIRTS PER WEEK
10	0	6	0
9	1	5	0.5
8	2	4	1
7	3	3	1.5
6	4	2	2
5	5	1	2.5
4	6	0	3
3	7		
2	8		
1	9		
0	10		

This table shows production possibilities schedules for Sara and Jeff. Sara's schedule shows that she can produce 10 pizzas or 10 shirts if she devotes all her effort to one or the other. Jeff can produce either six pizzas or three shirts. Sara has an absolute advantage in producing both products. Jeff, however, has a comparative advantage in shirts. Sara's comparative advantage is in pizza.

maximum number of pizzas that she can produce for any quantity of shirts; each combination on the schedule is efficient, meaning that the only way to produce more pizza is to produce fewer shirts and vice versa. By definition, the production possibilities schedule shows all of the efficient combinations of the two goods that she can produce; it shows all of the efficient alternatives. Suppose that rather than producing 10 pizzas, she chooses the alternative of seven pizzas and three shirts. By choosing this alternative, she gives up three pizzas to get three shirts. The cost of the alternative is what she gives up to obtain it—three pizzas. The opportunity cost, the value of the best alternative given up to take the action, is three pizzas. From the perspective of economics, opportunity cost is the only relevant cost. Sometimes it is convenient to consider opportunity cost on a per-unit basis. For Sara, the opportunity cost of one shirt is one pizza. For Jeff it is larger; to get one shirt he must give up two pizzas.

Suppose, however, that we go up rather than down the production possibilities schedules. If Sara is producing 10 shirts, she must give up one shirt to get one pizza. The opportunity cost to Sara of a pizza is one shirt. If Jeff is producing three shirts, he gets one pizza by giving 0.5 shirt. Perhaps surprisingly, Jeff's opportunity cost of one pizza, 0.5 shirt, is less than Sara's.

Let's review Sara's opportunity costs. She must give up one pizza to get one shirt, and she must give up one shirt to get one pizza. Her opportunity cost of a pizza is a shirt and vice versa. Recall that Jeff's opportunity cost for a shirt is two pizzas and his opportunity cost for a pizza is 0.5 shirt. In this light Sara has a cost advantage, a comparative advantage, in producing shirts, but Jeff has a comparative advantage in producing pizzas. A **comparative advantage** exists, by definition, if one person can produce an item at a lower opportunity cost than another person. Although Sara has an absolute advantage in producing both items, she has a comparative advantage in only one. Another way to understand her comparative advantage is to observe that she can produce two-thirds more pizza than Jeff, but she can produce more than three times the shirts.

Comparative advantage– The advantage that an individual has if she can produce a good at lower opportunity cost than another individual.

To see why they would specialize, suppose that Sara is producing and consuming six shirts and four pizzas per week and Jeff two shirts and two pizzas. Assuming a two-person economy, total production is eight shirts and six pizzas. If they specialize according to their competitive advantages, however, Sara produces 10 shirts and Jeff produces six pizzas. Total production in the economy has increased by two shirts without sacrificing any pizza. By specializing, Sara and Jeff have the same quantity of one good and more of the other good available for consumption. The gain from specialization, however, cannot be realized unless trade takes place. If not, Sara will be hungry and Jeff will be cold. Both parties can and will gain by specializing and trading. If Jeff, for instance, found that he did not gain, he would not specialize and trade. If both parties are informed, voluntary exchange must benefit both parties.

One possible outcome would be for Jeff to give Sara four pizzas in return for three shirts. Jeff would then have three shirts and two pizzas. Without specialization and trade, he would have two shirts and two pizzas. Specialization and trade have improved his position because he has an extra shirt and the same quantity of pizza. Sara is also better off. After specialization and trade, she has seven shirts and four pizzas. She has also gained a shirt. They both gain, even though Sara has an absolute advantage in producing both products. Specialization can increase the production (wealth) of an economy, if different people have different opportunity costs for producing products. The great diversity of talents, education, and interests ensures that opportunity costs differ and that everybody has comparative advantage. Specialization based on comparative advantage and division of labor is an integral part of any economy. It implies the necessity of trade, which means that any society has to have a way to coordinate the activities of vast numbers of *specialized* people.

Economic Coordination and the Market System

The coordination of economic activity through prices in a market system relies on *voluntary exchange* between two people. Its appeal rests on a simple idea: It occurs only if each person expects to benefit from the exchange. For the exchange to be truly voluntary, both parties must:

1. *Be responsible individuals who can make rational decisions*: An exchange between an adult and a child may not be voluntary because the child is unable to form opinions about the relative values of the items exchanged.
2. *Have reasonable access to information*: Suppose Sam, a doctor, knows that an expensive treatment that cures baldness for some people will not help Eric. Eric has no way of getting this information. If Sam convinces Eric to pay $3,000 for the treatment, the exchange is hardly voluntary.
3. *Have reasonable alternatives to the exchange*: Suppose Chris's one talent is playing the electric bass. He has applied for a job with Kate's band, which is his only place of employment. Chris is in a perilous position. If he has no other way to earn income, any agreement that Chris makes to work for Kate may not be voluntary. Fortunately, we face few situations that offer no alternatives for essential products. (We will discuss monopolies, in which buyers have limited alternatives, in Chapter 5.)

A major exception to the purely beneficial effects of voluntary exchange arises if a third party is negatively and involuntarily affected. Suppose Chris obtains the job with Kate's orchestra, but must practice at home five hours a day. If Sara and his other neighbors can hear his practicing, it could cause them involuntary harm. Such involuntary harm is an example of an *external cost*. If such effects are important in particular exchanges, the harm experienced by third parties must be considered along with the advantages gained by the trading parties. A real example is air pollution. Producers and consumers of paper benefit from their voluntary exchanges, but a paper mill's air pollution may harm people who live in its vicinity.

THE PRICE SYSTEM AS COORDINATOR

One of any society's most important tasks is to ensure that the quantity produced of any good (such as apartments) is the quantity that consumers purchase. If more apartments are produced than consumers demand, resources are wasted that could produce something else. If fewer apartments are produced than consumers demand, they will be dissatisfied. In this case, too much of something else is being produced and again resources are wasted. In *competitive markets*, which are markets with many buyers and sellers, the interaction of demand and supply determines the quantity of the good produced. This section discusses demand and supply using the market for apartments as a familiar example.

Demand

Consider the market for apartments of a given size and quality in, say, Gotham City. Gotham has a population of 5 million, income is $16,000 per person, and the price of a standard owner-occupied house is $90,000. Assume that population, income, and the house price are three of the four factors that affect how many apartments people want to rent. The fourth factor is apartment rental price. How many apartments will people plan to rent at different rental prices, holding income, population, and house price constant?

Quantity demanded– The quantity of a good that consumers plan to buy at each possible price, holding constant other factors that affect demand.

To answer, we develop a *demand schedule* for apartments that shows the consumers' **quantity demanded** of apartments per month at each possible price. The demand schedule exists for given values of *income, population, house price*, and *other variables*. If any of the values—other than apartment rent—changes, *the demand schedule changes*. If the price of an apartment is $500 a month, Table 2.3 shows that Gothamites demand 400,000 apartments. If the price were $450 a month, they would want 475,000 apartments. Thus, if the price falls from $500 to $450, the quantity demanded of apartments increases from 400,000 to 475,000.

Demand curve– A curve (line) showing the quantity demanded of a good for each possible price, holding constant other factors that affect demand.

We can summarize the demand schedule in a diagram. Because we use diagrams throughout this book, we have included a chart at the bottom of Table 2.3 for you to practice working with graphs. If you like, transfer the chart to a separate sheet of paper. Note that your graph will have price (rent) per apartment per month on the vertical axis in $100 increments and the number of apartments per month on the horizontal axis in increments of 100,000. Assume that all apartments are of equal size and quality. To draw the **demand curve**, a visual representation of the demand schedule, choose a point from the demand schedule and locate it in your figure. (Note that the demand "curve" can be a straight line.) For instance, at point E in Table 2.3, the price is $300 and the quantity demanded is 700,000. Find $300 on the vertical axis of your diagram and draw a horizontal dashed line at that price all the way across the diagram. Now find 700,000 on the horizontal axis and draw a vertical dashed line from there to the top. The intersection of the two dashed lines is point E on the demand curve. Find another point, maybe B, in the same way. Because data are chosen to trace out a straight line, the two points can be connected to give the demand curve.

Suppose now that the market price is $400. Draw a horizontal dashed line from $400 to the demand curve; at the intersection draw a vertical dashed line to the horizontal axis. The point where the dashed line hits the axis gives the quantity demanded of

TABLE 2.3 DEMAND SCHEDULE FOR APARTMENTS IN GOTHAM CITY

	PRICE (MONTHLY RENT PER APARTMENT)	QUANTITY (APARTMENTS PER MONTH)
A	$500	400,000
B	450	475,000
C	400	550,000
D	350	625,000
E	300	700,000
F	250	775,000
G	200	850,000

The demand schedule shows the quantity demanded of apartments at each price. For instance, if the price is $500 a month, the quantity demanded is 400,000 apartments per month. At a lower price of $450, the quantity demanded would be greater: 475,000 apartments. The demand schedule exists for a given income, population, and price of a house.

Demand price– The price at which consumers will just buy the exact quantity on the market. It is the maximum price that anyone will pay for the last unit.

Law of demand– As the price of some good changes with other factors constant, the quantity demanded for that good changes in the opposite direction.

apartments: 550,000. So the demand curve gives the quantity that consumers plan to buy, at each alternative price, assuming the other demand factors remain constant. Of course, only one price can exist at any particular time.

For another perspective on the demand curve, suppose 400,000 apartments are on the market. The **demand price** is the price at which consumers will buy exactly that quantity, the price at which the market would clear. To find it, draw a vertical dashed line from the horizontal axis (start at 400,000) to the demand curve and draw a horizontal dashed line to the vertical axis. The demand price for 400,000 apartments per month is $500 per month. The demand price has an important interpretation. Some consumer will rent the last apartment, the 400,000th, if the actual price is $500 per month. If the actual price were slightly higher, $501 per month, no one would rent the last apartment. It is not worth $501. In other words, the 400,000th apartment is worth at least $500, but no more than $500; thus, it is worth exactly $500. The demand price shows the maximum price that some consumer will pay for the last unit.

The demand-price concept helps us to understand the **law of demand**, which is that the quantity demanded of any good is negatively related to its price, holding constant other variables such as population, consumer income, consumer preferences, and the prices of other goods. Figure 2.1, which like your plot is based on Table 2.3, shows that a lower price—$300 rather than $400—results in a larger quantity demanded. Equivalently, the more apartments consumers rent, the lower the value consumers place on the last unit rented—the lower the demand price. Therefore, if consumers are to buy more, price must drop. Price must drop because the value of one more unit is less than the value of the previous one. Why? In the market for apartments, the demand price falls because the first apartments are rented by people who place the greatest value on them. If the price is $500, the only people willing to rent apartments are those who value them at a minimum of $500. To persuade more people to rent apartments, people who value them at less than $500 must want to rent them. But that happens only if the price is less than $500.

This will make sense if you think in terms of an individual consumer. Perhaps yourself. For instance, as you consume additional scoops of ice cream per day, what happens to your demand price? How much satisfaction does the fourth scoop of ice cream in a day provide compared to the first scoop? Most of us get more satisfaction from the first scoop than from the second, and so on. Because of this diminishing satisfaction, our top price for each additional scoop falls as the number we have already consumed rises. As quantity increases, demand price falls, implying that your demand curve for ice cream has a negative slope. Likewise, the market demand curve, which is made up of all of the individual demand curves, would have a negative slope.

Figure 2.1 Demand Curve for Apartments in Gotham City
The demand curve shows the quantity demanded of apartments per month at each alternative price. Only one price can exist at a time, so only one quantity demanded can exist in a particular month. The demand curve is plotted from the demand schedule in Table 2.3. At point E, price is $300 per apartment per month and quantity demanded is 700,000 apartments per month. Put this and other points in the diagram and connect them to reveal the demand curve. If the market price is $400, the demand curve says that the quantity demanded is 550,000 apartments. Or if 400,000 apartments are on the market, the demand price, the price at which 400,000 apartments could just be filled, is $500.

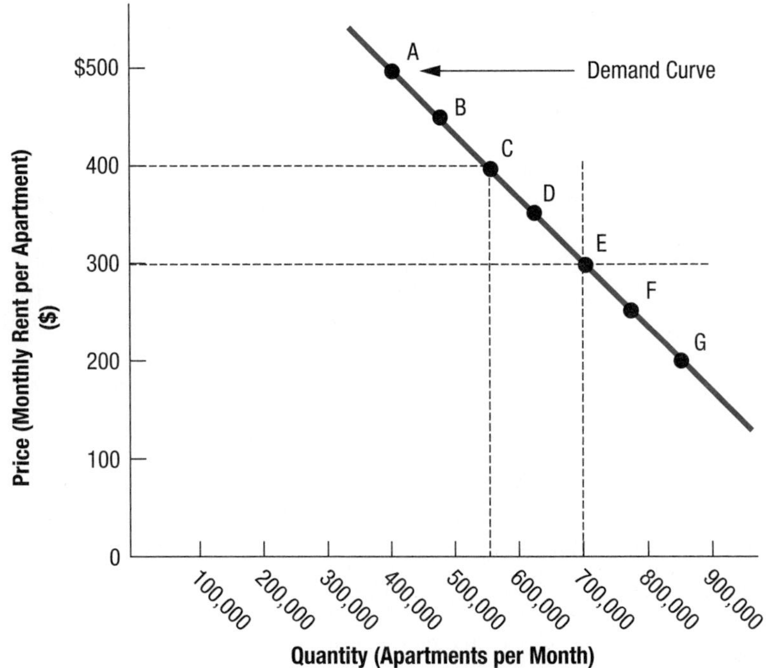

The demand schedule, quantity demanded, the demand curve, demand price, and the law of demand help us to understand one side of a market. To understand market coordination, however, it is also necessary to understand the other side—the supply side.

Supply

To understand the supply of apartments in Gotham City, suppose that construction technology and the prices of land, construction materials, and labor are fixed. Suppose also that the alternatives available to people who might build and place apartments on the market do not change, for example, the profitability of supplying office space. Holding constant these and other variables affecting cost, the number of apartments that landlords plan to supply depends upon the monthly rent that they expect to receive.

Quantity supplied– The quantity of a good that producers will plan to sell at each possible price, holding constant other factors that affect supply.

Supply curve– A curve (line) showing the quantity supplied of a good for each possible price, holding constant other factors that affect supply.

Supply price– The price at which sellers will just put a specific quantity of a good or service on the market. It is the minimum price that a seller will accept in return for selling one more unit of a good or service.

The *supply schedule* gives the number of apartments per month that landlords plan to supply at each alternative rental price. Like the demand schedule, the supply schedule exists for the given levels of other variables—here, *construction technology, resource and materials prices*, and *profitability of other alternatives available to landlords and potential landlords*. (Change in any relevant variable other than the rental price of apartments would create a new supply schedule.) The supply schedule in Table 2.4 shows that landlords plan to supply 400,000 apartments if the rental price is $300 per month and to supply 475,000 apartments if the price is $350. If the expected price increases from $300 to $350 per month, the **quantity supplied** increases from 400,000 to 475,000.

The **supply curve** is constructed and interpreted in the same way as the demand curve. (Use the supply schedule in Table 2.4 to draw a supply curve, which you can compare with Figure 2.2.) Suppose the market price is $450. The supply schedule or curve shows that the quantity supplied is 625,000. If the market price is $450, landlords would supply any quantity up to 625,000. They will not voluntarily supply more than 625,000.

The **supply price** aids in understanding why landlords are willing to supply less than 625,000 apartments, but not more than that quantity. The supply price—$450—is exactly sufficient to persuade landlords to supply a specified quantity. If the actual price is less than the supply price, say, $449, landlords will not supply the 625,000th apartment because $449 does not both cover the cost of production and provide an acceptable surplus (rate of return). The supply price, $450, is just sufficient to get the last unit to the market. It exactly covers the opportunity cost (which includes an acceptable surplus or rate of return) of producing the last unit. The opportunity cost, in turn, is the value of what the resources—land, labor, construction materials, the owners' contribution, and so on—could have produced

TABLE 2.4 SUPPLY SCHEDULE OF APARTMENTS IN GOTHAM CITY

	PRICE (MONTHLY RENT PER APARTMENT)	QUANTITY (APARTMENTS PER MONTH)
A	$500	700,000
B	450	625,000
C	400	550,000
D	350	475,000
E	300	400,000
F	250	325,000
G	200	250,000

The supply schedule gives the number of apartments per month that landlords would supply at each alternative price. It exists for given values of other variables: construction technology, resources and materials prices, and profitability of alternatives. If the price is $300 per month, the quantity of apartments supplied per month is 400,000. If the price is $350 per month, the quantity supplied is 475,000.

in their next best use. So the supply price is the minimum price that any producer would accept for supplying the last unit. The producer, of course, would be happy to receive a price higher than the supply price for the last unit.

Inspection of the supply curve in Figure 2.2 shows that the supply price increases as quantity increases. This positive relationship shows that the greater the quantity supplied, the greater the opportunity cost of the last unit supplied. An example clarifies why this happens. Suppose that more apartments are built and rented in Gotham City. To do so, workers and materials in Gotham City (and perhaps in other cities) would be diverted from the production of other goods and services. The opportunity cost of these new workers and materials is the value of what they currently produce. Workers and materials would be diverted first from the least valuable of their current uses. Perhaps they are attracted from building yet another amusement park that would just barely be profitable. Both the opportunity cost and wages necessary to attract the new workers might not be much higher than those of the workers currently producing apartments. But as apartment construction increases, workers and materials might be attracted from the construction of new health care facilities that are in greater demand than the amusement parks. Opportunity costs would be higher and the wage necessary to attract the workers would also be higher. The opportunity cost of producing additional apartments increases because the additional workers must be diverted from uses with increasingly higher values. It is this relationship that leads to the **law of supply**—namely, holding other variables constant, the quantity supplied of a product is positively related to its price.

Law of supply– As the price of some good changes with other factors constant, the quantity supplied for that good changes in the same direction.

Figure 2.2 Supply Curve for Apartments in Gotham City

The supply curve shows the quantity of apartments supplied per month at each alternative price. It is plotted from the supply schedule in Table 2.4. At point E, price is $300 per apartment per month and quantity supplied is 400,000 apartments per month. The diagram can also illustrate the supply price. The supply price is the price that must be paid to put a certain quantity of apartments on the market. If 400,000 apartments are on the market, the lowest price that any supplier would accept for the 400,000th apartment is $300. If the price were $299, the 400,000th apartment would not be supplied. The supply price therefore is $300.

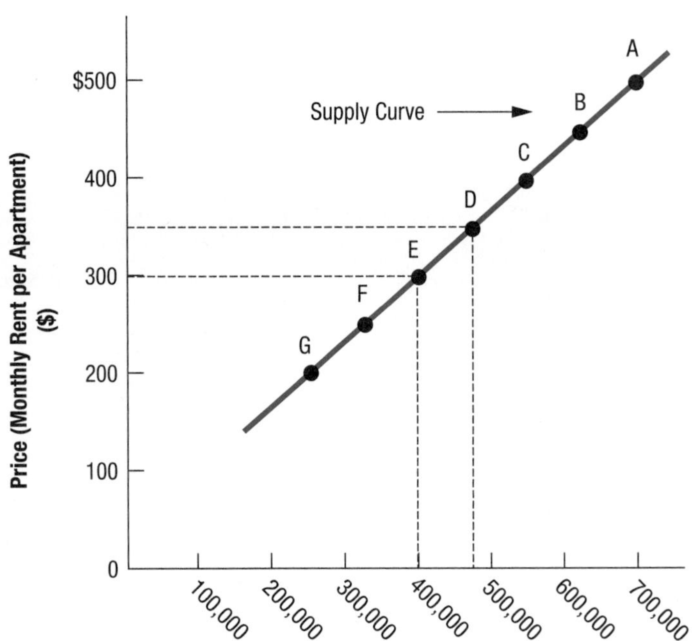

Now we put our understanding of the supply side of the market—the supply schedule, the supply curve, the supply price, and the law of supply—together with our understanding of the demand side. The two parts of a market interact to coordinate the plans of consumers and producers.

Putting the Pieces Together: Demand and Supply

In a market economic system, government does not tell producers how much to produce or what price they will receive for their product. Neither does it tell consumers what they can buy nor what they must pay for products. The decisions about what to buy and sell are coordinated through the laws of supply and demand with no central direction. An astounding fact about market economies, therefore, is that year in and year out producers and consumers simultaneously adjust their production and consumption until they are equal. It is unusual to have excessive stockpiles of fruit or automobiles at the end of a typical year; likewise, almost everyone who is willing to pay for a product can buy it. Exceptions occur, however, when producers slip up in planning. For example, during the holiday season, a toy or gadget occasionally becomes unexpectedly popular or else unpopular and either not enough or too much is produced; unexpected shortfalls or stockpiles result. In a market economy these are exceptions! History shows, however, that in command economies such coordination failures are the rule!

Suppose a supercomputer were programmed to ensure that the vast majority of the 15 million people of the New York metropolitan area would find places they choose to rent and provide the appropriate quantities of other goods (food, clothing, and so on), and that this could be done with little overcrowding of apartments or few vacant ones. We would be amazed and rightly so. Yet a market economy does this every day. How?

Table 2.5 puts the demand and supply schedules from Tables 2.3 and 2.4 together. These schedules show the quantity demanded and supplied of apartments at alternative prices. Individuals in the Gotham City apartment market do not affect the market price.

TABLE 2.5 DEMAND AND SUPPLY SCHEDULES FOR APARTMENTS IN GOTHAM CITY

PRICE(MONTHLY RENT PER APARTMENT)	QUANTITY DEMANDED (APARTMENTS PER MONTH)	QUANTITY SUPPLIED (APARTMENTS PER MONTH)
$500	400,000	700,000
450	475,000	625,000
400	550,000	550,000
350	625,000	475,000
300	700,000	400,000
250	775,000	325,000
200	850,000	250,000

The demand and supply schedules for apartments help us see how the plans of consumers and producers are coordinated in a market economy. Each individual consumer or producer assumes that the market price is outside his or her control, so these consumers and producers adjust their quantity demanded or quantity supplied to the market price. Suppose the market price is $250. Consumers wish to rent 775,000 apartments per month. But landlords will not place that many on the market. They are willing to supply only 325,000. Excess demand of 450,000 will push price up. As price increases, quantity demanded falls and quantity supplied increases. The originally inconsistent plans of consumers and producers come together as price adjusts. At a price of $400, the plans are exactly coordinated. Quantity demanded equals quantity supplied. The equilibrium quantity exchanged is 550,000 apartments.

They are like the potato farmer who can produce from fence row to fence row or withhold all of her potatoes from the market without changing the price of potatoes. They are also like the shopper who can spend all or none of his money on potatoes, again without affecting the price of potatoes. They are price takers.

Excess demand (shortage)– A situation in which quantity demanded exceeds quantity supplied at a given price.

If the market price is $300 a month, the number of apartments demanded is 700,000 a month and the quantity supplied is 400,000. At $300 the quantity demanded by consumers is greater than the quantity supplied by producers; this is an example of **excess demand**. People want more apartments than are available; landlords notice that they have unsatisfied customers. Someone will ask or offer a higher price (rent). Landlords will find that they are still able to lease their apartments at the higher price. As the price increases, the quantity demanded decreases—the law of demand. In addition, as the price increases, landlords will figure out ways to supply more apartments. The quantity supplied increases, illustrating the law of supply. As price goes up, the quantity that people plan to buy decreases and the quantity that other people plan to sell increases. Initially, the plans of consumers and producers are not coordinated. But as the price increases, the plans converge. At $400 per month, the quantity of apartments demanded and the quantity supplied are equal—550,000. (Work out on paper what happens if the market price is $450 a month.) The excess demand that exists at the lower price is automatically eliminated if the price of apartments is flexible. The price system *coordinates* the plans of consumers and producers.

Figure 2.3 puts the demand and supply curves of Figures 2.1 and 2.2 together. Suppose the market price is $500 a month. The figure shows that the quantity demanded is

Figure 2.3 Demand and Supply Curves for Apartments in Gotham City
Suppose the price is $500 per apartment per month. The figure shows that the quantity supplied at that price is 700,000 apartments per month and that the quantity demanded is 400,000. The difference is an excess supply of 300,000 apartments. This excess supply can be measured by the distance from A to B—AB.

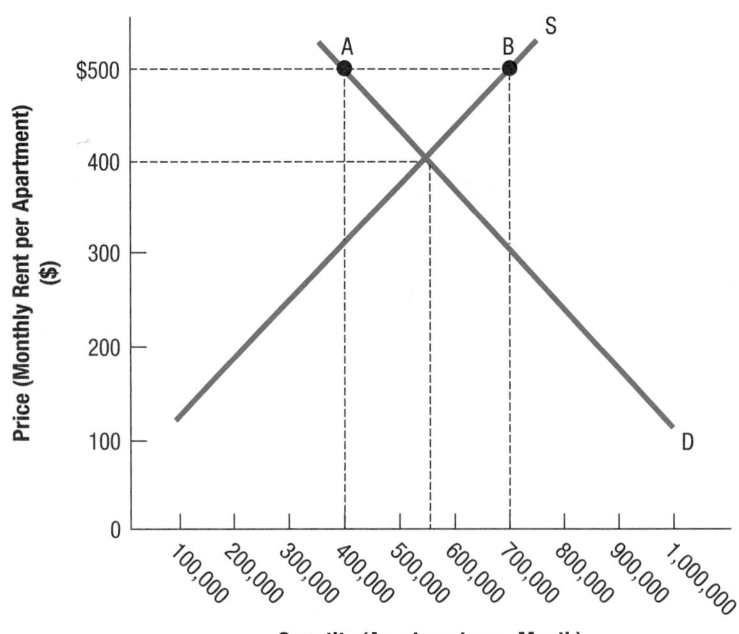

Excess supply (surplus)– A situation in which quantity supplied exceeds quantity demanded at a given price.

400,000 apartments per month and that the quantity supplied is 700,000 per month. The situation is one of **excess supply** because quantity supplied exceeds quantity demanded. The excess is 300,000 apartments: 700,000 minus 400,000. In the figure it is measured by the distance from A to B—AB. Many landlords have vacant apartments. Although the apartments are vacant, the landlords must pay taxes and perhaps make mortgage payments. They will try to entice consumers into the apartments by offering a lower price. The quantity demanded will increase. Some young people, for example, might decide to establish independent households because of the lower price. As the price falls, some landlords might decide to use their buildings for something other than apartments. The quantity supplied decreases.

Suppose the existing price is $300. As an exercise, use Figure 2.3 to explain to yourself why the price will increase. This exercise and the example in the previous paragraph show that *if the market price results in excess demand, the price will increase, and if it results in excess supply, the price will decrease.* The market price adjusts until the quantity demanded equals the quantity supplied—until the market is in **equilibrium**. Equilibrium is a situation that will continue indefinitely unless some outside force changes it. It occurs in competitive markets when quantity demanded equals quantity supplied. The price, $400, which equates the quantity demanded and the quantity supplied, is the *equilibrium price.* The quantity demanded and supplied (550,000) at that price is the *equilibrium quantity exchanged.*

Equilibrium– A state of rest for the economy or market. Market equilibrium occurs at the price at which quantity demanded equals quantity supplied—the equilibrium quantity exchanged.

This emergence of equilibrium is the essence of market coordination. It is how a market system determines how much of each good to produce and how to produce it. Moreover, the market system accomplishes these tasks without a central plan. The essence of a command economy—a planned economy—is that government orders individuals to produce certain goods and services. These orders are laws. In other words, in a command economy people are under legal obligation to obey a central plan. In a market economy, on the other hand, government establishes rules of behavior. Given these rules of behavior, individuals are free to decide what goods to produce and how to produce them.

COMPARATIVE SYSTEMS: AN INTRODUCTORY SKETCH

This section discusses coordination through the price system in a market economy and compares it with coordination in a command economy. We will then discuss the transition of former planned economies to market economies.

The Price System

Comparing a market economy to a command economy—capitalism versus centrally planned socialism—is not a matter of comparing no planning with planning. Planning occurs in any economy. The difference is *who plans* the coordination of economic activity and *how plans are enforced.* In a command economy, government plans what and how to produce. The plan is enforced by law. In a market economy, individuals plan and laws protect their transactions. As students, you plan your education: courses, major, and graduate school. In a command economy, your choices would not be allowed if they were inconsistent with the plan. Similarly, as consumers, you plan what to buy based on prices, your income, and your preferences. In a command economy, your choices might be frustrated if they were inconsistent with the plan. In the former Soviet Union, you could have afforded and wanted to buy a car, but you might have had to wait 10 years to buy one because the plan did not call for enough new cars to fulfill the demands of people who were willing and able to buy them at the price charged. In a market economy, the purchase could be immediate. In the United States, a producer plans how and how much to produce based on expected profitability. In a command economy, the manager of a state-owned enterprise produces according to the central plan and uses techniques determined by the central planners.

We assume that in a market economy consumers attempt to maximize their total satisfaction, and producers attempt to maximize their total profits. A competitive market has many consumers and producers. No single consumer or small group of consumers has any noticeable effect on the market price. Consequently, a single consumer does not worry that the price of, say, housing will go up if he buys more housing. In competitive markets, consumers are *price takers*, implying that they accept market prices as given. Given their circumstances, their economic choice is how much to consume.

Competitive producers, attempting to maximize their profits, also are price takers. No single housing producer or small group of housing producers has any noticeable effect on market price. Consequently, a competitive producer does not worry that the price of housing may fall if she attempts to sell more. Their economic choice is simply how much to produce.

There are two exceptions. First, suppose a product has only a single producer, such as the Windows operating system. Microsoft realizes that, holding everything else constant, to increase the planned sales of a new version of Windows, its must reduce the planned price. Consequently, a single producer affects the price when deciding how much to sell.

Second, what applies to a single competitive producer does not apply to all producers. In a competitive market, one housing producer does not noticeably affect the price of houses, even by increasing production by 10 percent. If, however, each of 10,000 producers put just 1 percent more on the market, the price would have to fall before all those houses will sell. An individual's decision to produce more or less will have no effect on others' production decisions because no one expects a single producer to affect market price. Likewise, because decisions about what to produce rely on market price, producers do not respond to what another producer does. For instance, suppose that Edward decides to produce 20 percent more houses. His decision does not affect how many houses Venus or other housing producers plan to produce because it does not affect the price. Consequently, the individual competitive producer is a price taker even though all producers acting together affect market price.

In a competitive market, all participants are price takers. They take market prices as given. Given their circumstances, their economic choices are simply how much to produce and consume.

Keywords: *price and demand and supply*

Access InfoTrac at http://infotrac.cengage.com

Information, Rationing, and Motivation in a Market Economy

In a market economy, prices play three roles: They inform, they ration, and they motivate. These roles are crucial in the coordination of consumer and producer plans. The price system informs producers and consumers about underlying changes in the economy. For instance, an increase in price signals to consumers and producers that a good has become more valuable. The price system also provides incentives that motivate consumers and producers to adjust to those changes. These incentives provide the motivation for change: conservation and increased production.

Informing. Suppose the apartment market in Gotham City is in equilibrium. In Figure 2.4, the equilibrium price and quantity are P_0 and Q_0. Now suppose the demand curve changes unexpectedly from D_0 to D_1. Perhaps population increases. Notice that we

Figure 2.4 **Effects of Change in Demand in the Apartment Market**
With the demand and supply curves D_0 and S_0, the equilibrium price and quantity in the apartment market are P_0 and Q_0. An increase in demand to D_1 disturbs the original equilibrium. The immediate effect may be no change in quantity and an increase in price to P_1. The increased price rations the original quantity of apartments to consumers who are willing to pay the most for them. P_0, however, is the supply price (opportunity cost) of an additional apartment. With the market price, P_1, above the supply price (opportunity cost), producers can profit by expanding output. Ultimately, the price increase motivates producers to expand output.

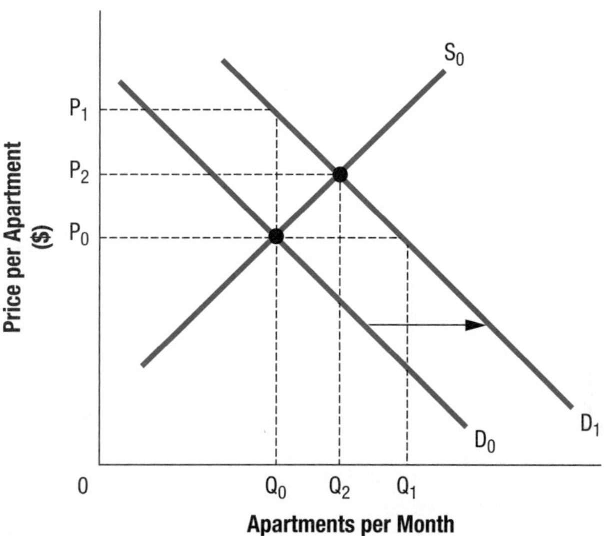

assume that one of the "other" variables has changed, which has caused a change in demand.[4] This demand increase means that at the same price consumers plan to rent more apartments. In contrast, an increase in the quantity demanded of apartments occurs if price falls and none of the "other" variables change. Because none of the other variables change, demand and the demand curve stay unchanged. For instance, consider the demand curve D_1 in Figure 2.4. The quantity demanded at the price P_1 is Q_0. If consumers in the city face a price of P_2, rather than P_1, their quantity demanded increases from Q_0 to Q_2.

The increase in demand that occurs when population increases might not be immediately obvious to the landlords or tenants. In any city, some people are moving out while others are moving in. An increase in population can occur either when fewer people leave or more people arrive. The immediate effect of the increased demand for apartments may be simply that apartments are leased more quickly and vacancy rates fall. Landlords will find that they can raise prices and tenants will find that they can get an apartment faster if they offer a higher price. The price increase will spread through the market, providing a signal to all participants that apartments are currently more valuable. This information, available to everyone, will generate numerous changes.

Rationing of Existing Apartments. The increase in demand raises the demand price for the quantity Q_0 from P_0 to P_1. Excess demand would exist if the price remained at P_0, but landlords discover that some applicants are willing to pay more than the going rate, P_0, for an apartment. Potential excess demand for apartments is eliminated as tenants bid up the price to the demand price, P_1. Even if the quantity of apartments

[4]We will examine changes in demand and supply in more detail in Chapter 3.

supplied does not increase, the excess demand disappears. This price increase *informs* people that apartments have become scarcer. If they expect the price increase to be permanent, the original residents of the town will reduce the quantity they demand of housing. Similarly, the new residents will demand a lower quantity at the higher price than at the lower price. In short, consumers automatically respond to more expensive apartments by reducing the quantity demanded. They conserve because it is to their advantage to do so.

People will choose to live in more crowded conditions, but this does not mean that excess demand exists—it means that increased *scarcity* has caused the equilibrium price to go up. The distinction between excess demand and increased scarcity is important. **Scarcity** is the economic condition common to all societies. It simply means that, in the aggregate, our wants exceed our abilities to meet them. Consequently, we must choose which wants to satisfy. Excess demand, on the other hand, persists only if price cannot adjust.

Scarcity– The common situation for all economies: Aggregate wants exceed the ability to meet them.

As we see, the price system automatically **rations**, or allocates, an available supply to consumers. This automatic rationing of a good that has become scarcer is a controversial feature of a market system. It results in the allocation of apartments on the basis of their willingness (ability) to pay. It makes no allowance for individual circumstances, and a higher price, therefore, changes consumption plans regardless of circumstances. Those people who are willing to pay the most for the good obtain it. But the rationing of apartments on the basis of willingness (and ability) to pay might result in people living in what others perceive as inadequate housing. (We discuss this question of rationing by price again in Chapter 3 in the Additional Insight entitled "Price Gouging and the Twin Hurricanes.")

Ration– To allocate a limited supply of goods and services to people.

Profit as a Motivation for Increased Apartment Production. At a price of P_1 (Figure 2.4) and quantity of Q_0, provision of an additional apartment—an increase in quantity supplied—generates **economic profit** because the price is greater than the minimum price necessary to rent the last apartment. The supply price, P_0, covers the opportunity cost of putting the last apartment on the market. It is important to remember that a minimum acceptable return is part of the opportunity cost. If price equals opportunity cost, the seller can sell at this price and earn the return necessary to stay in the business. If the market price is above the supply price, some landlord will find it profitable to put another apartment on the market. With the new demand curve D_1, the new demand price, P_1, clears the market if no more apartments are supplied. Because the market price rises above the supply price, it will be profitable to build new apartments. The higher price *informs* producers of the increased scarcity of apartments. Some landlords will think that the increased scarcity is temporary, but others will think that the price change is a signal that demand has increased. If market research confirms the demand increase, the possibility of earning profits *motivates* the adventuresome landlord to produce more apartments. Because the demand price is above the supply price, producing more apartments yields a higher return than producing other goods. Quantity supplied increases as existing or new producers put more apartments on the market.

Economic profit– A return to a producer in excess of the minimum necessary to induce the producer to continue to produce the product.

So long as the market price is greater than the supply price, producing more generates more profits. As producers place more apartments on the market, competition increases and the price falls. The increase in quantity supplied moves the market to a new equilibrium with price P_2 and quantity Q_2. The producers compete for the potential profits by producing more apartments. As they do so, price falls; beyond the quantity Q_2, profits cannot be earned by producing more. It is ironic that the pursuit of profits under competitive conditions eventually eliminates the opportunity for additional profits. The first landlord to get additional apartments on the market will make economic profits. The last one will cover costs and get the minimum acceptable return.

The increased demand in the apartment market automatically causes increased demand in input markets. Increases in construction wages, for instance, *signal* greater job opportunities, motivating people to become construction workers. If input prices change, the cost of production of other goods changes. So the effect of the increased demand for and therefore increased scarcity of apartments ripples into other markets. In each market, as price changes, individuals adapt their plans to new conditions. Price changes are the signals for individuals to consider changing their plans; profits are the motivation.

Information, Rationing, and Motivation in a Command Economy

In a command economy, even if the central planners want to respond to consumers, adjustment to changes in demand and supply is lower and subject to larger error than in a market economy. This is because the planners do not allow the price system to play its three roles of informing, rationing, and motivating.

Informing. If the demand for apartments in a particular area increases, the central planners could respond, as the market does, by allowing rent to increase. In a situation where the government rather than an impersonal market sets prices, governments are often unwilling to raise price. A price increase would meet political resistance. Furthermore, it is not just in one market that demand and supply changes cause equilibrium price to change. If planners adjusted prices in all markets where the equilibrium changed, it would be incredibly costly—both in terms of planning costs and politically. To avoid these complications, planners tend to keep prices constant, making it impossible for price changes to signal and inform individuals of changing demands and supplys. The information about the changing scarcities does not get generated or transmitted.

Rationing of Existing Apartments. In the former Soviet Union, the state committee on prices set about 500,000 prices. Prices of some products could not be changed without changing other prices. Because it is extremely expensive to set 500,000 prices, prices did not change often. Many prices changed no more than once every 10 years. If prices are not flexible, however, the price system cannot ration available supply. Excess demand and excess supply did not disappear in the Soviet Union, because prices did not adjust. For instance, excess demand for apartments persisted for years. Young couples, even those who could afford separate housing, had to live with their parents and perhaps others in small apartments. Exceptions included Communist Party and government officials. People with political influence got apartments. It was who you knew that counted, not what you would pay, unless you were willing to pay bribes. Similar situations arise in Berkeley and Manhattan that are just examples of the many cities in the United States and throughout the world where laws prevent apartment rents from being raised to market levels.

The market price system, by contrast, is anonymous. An increase in demand causes price to rise automatically and leads the economy to a new equilibrium. Because price increases spring from the adjustments of many individual planners, no single entity can be blamed for the price increase. In a command economy, on the other hand, a price increase must be approved by the central planners who, therefore, are blamed for it.

Motivation for Increased Apartment Production. Problems persist in a command economy even if the planners allow prices to rise. Setting new prices takes a long time. The higher prices result in economic profits. But in a command economy producers rarely share in these profits, undermining their motivation to increase production. One reform often tried in command economies is to let producers share in profits so they will be motivated to follow price and profit signals.

Alternatively, the central planners could order the production of more apartments. They first must be sure, however, that the demand increase is permanent. If not, they could make a serious error. In a market economy, if an individual (one of the many planners in the market system) expands production, that person bears the consequences. If the decision is a good one, the person profits. If not, the person bears the loss. Normally, the effects on the market would be inconsequential because one producer has little effect on the entire market. When central planners make a decision, however, they necessarily affect the entire market. If the decision is a good one, the planners receive little credit. (The politicians take the credit.) If they build too many apartments, the error can be easily traced to their planning decision, making it easy to penalize them. As a result, central planners often decide that the risks associated with inaction are less than the risks of significant changes. In other words, for the market producer, it is heads, I win; tails, I lose. For the central planner, it is heads, other people win; tails, I lose.

A command economy has limited ability to adjust to economic changes. Political factors limit the price or output adjustments that can be made, and economic changes require enormous amounts of information about the market in question and about related markets. Because planners or production managers rarely profit legally, motivation for change is often political rather than economic. On the other hand, a market economy with decentralized planning based on a price system does not require the large bureaucracy of central planning. It needs no centralized information about individual markets. And it has a built-in incentive system.

ADDITIONAL INSIGHT

Wal-Mart and FEMA

In the late summer of 2005, hurricanes battered the U.S. Gulf Coast. Even if the disastrous flooding of New Orleans had been avoided, the areas devastated by the hurricane would have experienced drastic shocks, affecting peoples' health, life, and ability to deal with routine daily affairs. Preparing for a response to an unexpected disaster—such as an earthquake or terrorist attack that occurs without immediate warning, or to an impending natural disaster, such as a hurricane that is three days away and heading in your direction— is difficult for an individual or for an organization. At least four categories of agents prepare for and respond to a disaster. First, each individual (household or family) prepares and responds. Given human nature, the preparation is often inadequate and we respond by making last-minute adaptations and reacting after the disaster occurs. If we have a warning to evacuate, we probably have not developed an evacuation plan and we will probably have to fill our car with gasoline. If we are going to board up our homes and businesses and be assured of having food, water, and medicine, many of us are going to have to purchase plywood and other necessary items either just before the disaster strikes or make do with what we can purchase or obtain afterward. Very often the individual will be the first and most important responder, but it is important that local inventories of necessary goods be available.

Another two categories, private business—such as Wal-Mart, Home Depot, Federal Express, and many smaller local businesses—and private charitable organizations such as the Salvation Army, the Red Cross, local charities, and local faith-based organizations—often provide these necessary goods. Businesses and charitable organizations of a regional or national scope, some of which are mentioned above, may be large and nimble enough to predict what people will want to buy or will need and have it in stock or be able to deliver it quickly. The business firms have the distinct advantage that they will profit by being right in their decisions. After the Florida hurricanes of 2004, some businesses reevaluated procedures that didn't work and developed new procedures. For instance, some businesses realized that satellite phones were desirable because cellular networks didn't stand up well to hurricanes. If businesses make mistakes, their bottom lines are affected, either directly or because of reputation effects. The large charitable organizations rely heavily on the public perception of their efforts because of their current and future dependence on fund raising. They too will have tried to prepare for the emergency.

It is also important to remember all of the small businesses, charities, and individuals, who see a local situation that requires action and take that action without requiring an okay from a higher level. Some managers of Wal-Mart stores made necessities available to people in distress, but we can be sure that many owners of small businesses did the same thing. The Red Cross and the Salvation Army provided food to the hungry, but we can be sure that local charities did as well. The citizens of the areas in distress have a tremendous advantage over the outsiders because they have much local knowledge about who might need help and about who can provide help. In some ways, the advantages of these private and nongovernmental agents are similar to the advantages of individuals in a market economy with a price system. People have incentives to help and they have the knowledge of local conditions that individuals have when they are making their normal economic decisions about buying and selling. It should not be surprising that this decentralized approach has advantages over the command economy approach that government agencies such as the U.S. Army, FEMA (the Federal Emergency Management Agency), or a state homeland security agency.

Government provides the fourth category of agents—government agencies and planners. Coping with a disaster may require that special legal rules, such as curfews, traffic rules for evacuations, and the establishment of shelters, be imposed and certainly requires special attention to law enforcement. These actions are similar to those that government undertakes to establish and enforce a system of private property and exchange; government has a comparative advantage in these activities. These agencies also may have to deal with public health matters and other public safety matters. The restoration of order, the evacuation of New Orleans after it got underway, and the medical evaluations at the airport showed government agencies effectively undertaking large-scale projects. Releasing of petroleum from the strategic petroleum reserve provides another example of effective governmental action.

Our analysis of the market system, however, suggests where the command-economy nature of government action creates problems. When responding, government agents must follow rules that constrain their actions. Just like central planners, government agents do not have the same individual discretion as private individuals because they must consider the political implications of their actions. They are limited in their freedom to respond to unique situations. Government responses work well when one size fits all, but when the action is best tailored to an individual situation, government responses work less well.

Source: Suggested by Mary L. G. Theroux, "Public and Private Responses to Katrina: What Can We Learn?" The Independent Institute, October 20, 2005, at http://www.independent.org/newsroom/article.asp?id=1589.

Systems and Coordination

This discussion of the provision of apartments in different economic systems shows that a market system provides goods to people based on their willingness (including ability) to pay. Command economies are much less successful in coordinating demand and supply. They run into problems of excess demand (shortages) and inequitable allocation based on personal characteristics rather than willingness to pay.

Market systems successfully coordinate economic activity. Price falls in response to excess supply and rises in response to excess demand so as to equate the quantity demanded and supplied of a good. A market system coordinates the interdependent actions of specialized producers and does so without a legally imposed central plan. It fosters the division of labor that is responsible for increasing the "wealth of nations." Because of competition producers have incentive to provide customers with products of the type and quality that they desire and treat them reasonably and honestly. If ABC Corporation attempts to pull a sharp one on its customers, it must be concerned that XYZ Corporation will take them away.

Historical experience shows that command economies have great difficulty in coordinating economic activity. They lack a market economy's ability to automatically and inexpensively collect information about consumer wants and production capabilities. Neither do they share the capability to automatically and inexpensively provide incentives and motivation for people to make wealth-promoting decisions. As a result, command economies, like the Soviet Union that emphasized industrial growth and military might, often experience excess demand or shortages of consumer goods. For instance, apartment rents or automobile prices did not change in response to excess demand. With continuing excess demand, the producer, the government monopoly, did not have to worry about quality. It can sell everything it produced even if the apartments and cars were low quality. Better a roof that leaks than no roof at all. USSR Automotive Company did not have to worry about competition from other producers—there were none. The next section briefly discusses experiences of some former Communist countries in their struggle to transform their command economies to market economies.

TRANSITIONS TO A MARKET ECONOMY: SOME EXPERIENCES

Transition economies, if they are to become successful market economies, must bring together the five pieces of a market economic system. Unfortunately, these are not five easy pieces, and all of them must fall in place at about the same time. As shown in Table 2.1 (in a different order), to work well, a market economy or price system must have the following:

- Reasonably stable prices and a well-functioning monetary system that facilitates voluntary exchange.
- A system of private property and property rights defined, established, and protected by law.
- Market incentives that are generated by a price system whose rewards and penalties motivate decision makers.
- Flexible prices that fluctuate in response to individuals' voluntary decisions and exchanges (market exchange).
- A legal system that is broadly obeyed and a culture that generates a climate of trust and respect for the legal and political systems.

We will discuss the progress of several transition economies in terms of these five pieces. Although the collapse and breakup of the Soviet Union—including its satellite states and the former Yugoslavia—happened almost two decades ago, some of these countries have made little progress toward establishing well-functioning market systems. Change continues, and the situation that we describe in fall 2008 may change by the time you read this. Several countries in Central Europe, including Hungary and Slovenia, have in effect created market economies. Others, such as Ukraine, have a long way to go. Russia, the largest and most powerful of the transition states, has serious problems. These countries' different rates of transition depend upon history, politics, tradition, and the economic situation when the transition began. Our discussion of transition experiences begins with a comparison of the performance of these countries' economies: Hungary and Slovenia began serious efforts to create market systems well before Russia and Ukraine. Almost every country that has switched from a command economy to a market economy has experienced tremendous instability in terms of inflation, high unemployment, and large reductions in total production. A convenient way to measure their performance is to compare total production in recent year, say 2007, with that country's total production in 1989. The end of the Cold War and the collapse of the Soviet system can be dated by the fall of the Berlin Wall in November 1989. Hungary and Slovenia had a total production in 2007 from 35 to 49 percent greater than their production in 1989. Russia just surpased its 1989 production level. Ukraineis producting about 30 percent less output than in 1989.

Keyword: *transition economy*

Access InfoTrac at http://infotrac.cengage.com

Stable Prices and the Monetary System

Many countries that abandoned Communism did so in part because economic growth had stagnated. Moreover, inflexible prices led to excess demand for many products—apartments, cars, and so on. Excess demand for many consumer products removed much of the incentive for business firms to produce high-quality products. They had no competition. The government had a monopoly on everything produced. Moreover, international trade restrictions eliminated foreign competition. Inflation and unemployment, however, were generally low under central planning. Inflation was low because prices were held down by law, by plan, and by inertia. Prices did not reflect the scarcity of goods and services. Unemployment was low because many people had make-work jobs where the value of what they produced was less than the cost of production.

As prices were freed, the suppressed inflation exploded, hidden unemployment became open, unemployment grew, and production fell drastically. These countries faced extremely difficult and painful economic problems. Initially, they had the pain of the transition without the rewards of a market economy. Our comparisons of these countries' performance skip past the early transition period and examine the period from 1997–2007. The performance measure is the country's total production in 2007 compared to its total production in 1989. For all of these countries total production dropped as they started to restructure their economies and at some point began to recover.

In Figure 2.5 the countries are listed according to the ratio of their 2007 GDP to their 1989 GDP times 100. If a country had a GDP of $2 billion in 1989 and $3 billion in 2007, its index number would be ($3 billion/$2 billion) times 100 or 150. Its GDP would have grown by (150 − 100/100): 50 percent. So Slovenia's index number, presented immediately after its name in each table, of 149 means that its GDP (adjusted for inflation) was 49 percent greater in 2007 than in 1989. Similarly, Ukraine's with its index number of 68 means that it had an 32 percent ((68 − 100)/100) lower GDP in 2007 than in 1989.

Figure 2.5 shows that Slovenia and Hungary, countries that have been among the more successful in the transition, have been more successful in stabilizing their inflation rates. Both Russia and Ukraine experienced inflation rates above 20 percent for particular years between 1997 and 2007; Slovenia and Hungary did not. Erratic and rapid inflation in many transition countries including Russia and Ukraine has hampered the ability of the price system to provide reliable and efficient information to decision makers. Inflation also tends to cause decision makers to focus on short-term results and investments with quick payoffs.

The lower and more stable inflation rates for Hungary and Slovenia, on the other hand, have been important in their more rapid recovery from the production declines that accompanied the collapse of the central planning systems. Their more stable

Figure 2.5 The Transition: Selected Countries

The three panels provide data on inflation, output growth, and unemployment for four transition countries—Hungary, Russia, Slovenia, and Ukraine. Hungary and Slovenia have been successful in transition. Since 1997 inflation and unemployment have been relatively low and stable. Output has grown steadily. Russia and Ukraine have not done as well in transition. Their problems in transition are particularly apparent in the negative output growth and rapid high inflation in the first part of this period. Ukraine's low unemployment is misleading because it reflects delayed economic reform.

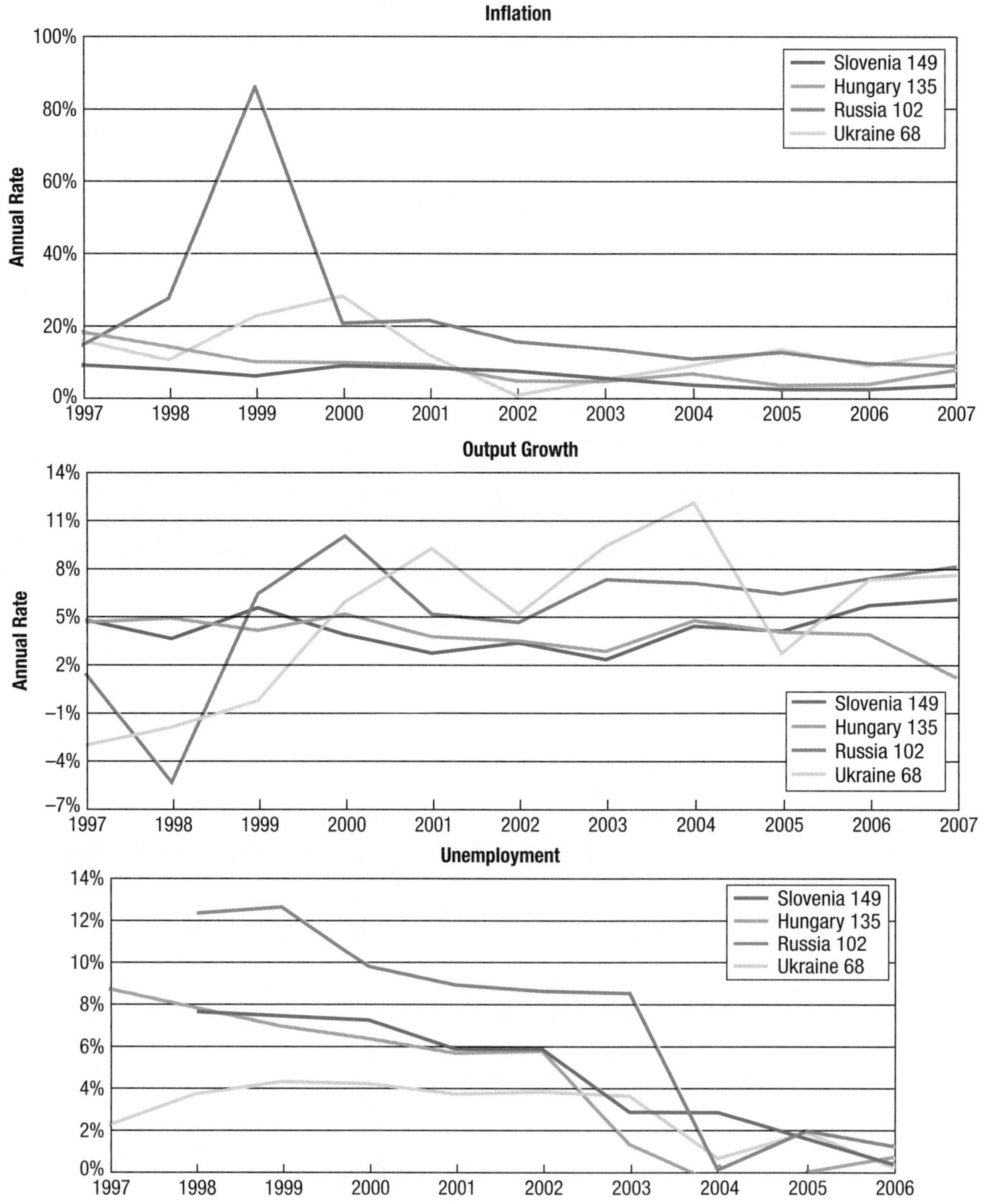

Source: European Bank for Reconstruction and Development (EBRD) Transition Reports.

inflation rates have been accompanied by steady output growth. In the later years, Russia and Ukraine have grown faster than the other two countries, perhaps because of how far they had fallen at the beginning of transition and their later start on market reforms.

Along with the more modest inflation and steady output growth, Hungary and Slovenia have had relatively low and steadily decreasing unemployment rates. Russia's unemployment was high in the early part of the period, and while falling remained well above that of the other countries.

Other Economic Reforms

The remainder of this section refers to four charts that rank countries on various aspects of the economic reforms necessary to develop a market economy. The European Bank for Reconstruction and Development (EBRD)[5] has rated a country's success in transition from 1 to 4.3 for many categories, with 1 indicating no progress and 4.3 indicating that the country has achieved norms for the category typical of that of "advanced industrial countries. The countries are arranged according to their index numbers in each figure. Most economists would agree that the top two countries in the figures (Slovenia and Hungary) have progressed farther in transition than the bottom two (Russia and Ukraine). After considering each of these figures, you will see that all of the countries have made substantial progress in establishing the basics of a market economy—flexible prices, private property, an appropriate system of laws, and market incentives—but the more successful ones have made more progress in establishing economic and political institutions and a culture conducive to market processes. Specifically, you will see that the more successful countries have made the most progress in both the first stages of transition—flexible prices and small—scale private firms, for instance—and the second stages—for instance, establishing a rule of law and sophisticated financial institutions.

Flexible Prices. Most of the countries of Central and Eastern Europe have allowed the prices of most goods to adjust to demand and supply conditions. Some have freed prices all at once, and others have done it gradually, but almost all have done so. Nevertheless, the ones that liberalized first, the success stories, have had a more successful transition than the remainder. Liberalization here is defined as the year in which a country first had a price liberalization score of 3 and a trade score of 4. A price score of 3 indicates substantial price flexibility, with only prices of "essentials" held down. The trade score indicates substantial trade liberalization with the only restrictions on international transactions being tariffs. As the bottom bar for each country in Figure 2.6 shows, the success stories liberalized prices and trade well before Russia and Ukraine.

As the top bars show, all four countries have by now liberalized prices. (Recall that 4.3 is the maximum possible score; the countries have all achieved a score of at least 4.) Moreover, only Russia and Ukraine have failed to remove most restrictions on international trade. In terms of flexible domestic prices, Hungary is slightly ahead of the other countries which have been slow in freeing prices of such items as electricity, energy, and public transportation. These prices have been held down for humanitarian and political reasons. Allowing these prices to increase to market-clearing levels would cause distress and could cause political unrest. Nevertheless, these price controls limit market coordination and impede economic restructuring.

---

[5]*European Bank for Reconstruction and Development (EBRD) Transition Report 2007.* We have converted the years of liberalization in Figure 2.6 to the EBRD scale of 1 to 4.3, taking Hungary as 4.3. In Figure 2.7, we took Hungary's private share of GDP as 4.3 and standardized those of other countries to this index. Finally, the EBRD indices for legal matters (Figure 2.7) were also converted to this scale.

Figure 2.6 Flexible Prices and Markets: Selected Countries
This figure shows that the success stories—Slovenia and Hungary—begin liberalizing earlier than the adversity stories—Russia and Ukraine. They also are somewhat farther along in liberalization. The numbers after the country name are index numbers that show the country's GDP in 2007 as compared to its 1989 GDP, which is indexed at 100.

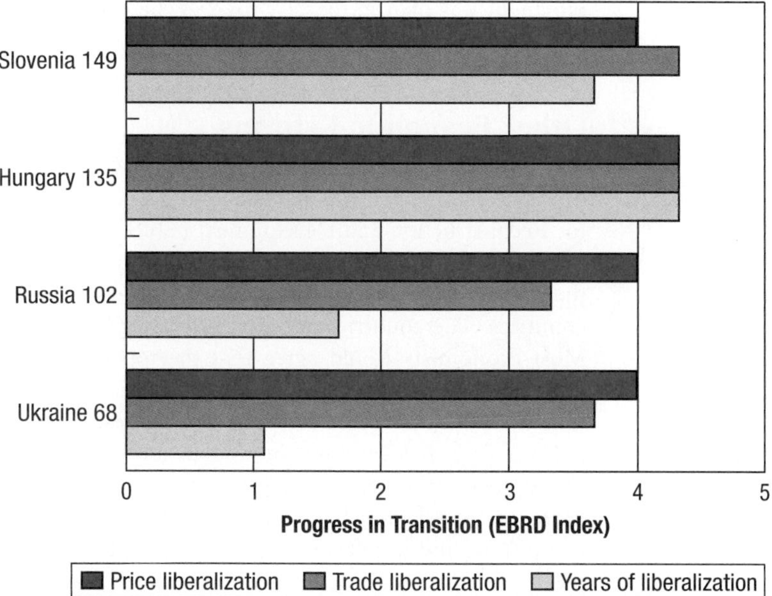

Source: European Bank for Reconstruction and Development (EBRD) Transition Reports

Another element that holds some of the price scores down is the fact some the transition countries continue to subsidize their state-owned enterprises (SOEs). One purpose of the subsidies is to prevent unemployment from increasing beyond its already high rates. Another purpose is to ensure that the SOEs continue to provide social services, such as health and education, to their employees, as they did under the previous system. Nevertheless, some SOEs are completely wasteful; the value of what some of them produced under central planning was actually less than the value of the resources that they used. This is probably still true in some transition countries. The transition economies use subsidies to keep inefficient and wasteful state-owned enterprises operating, impeding the economic restructuring necessary to privatize physical capital assets, both directly and indirectly. In a market economy, an enterprise that does not cover its full costs must reduce costs, increase revenues, or shut down. If it is shut down, its resources—land, labor, and capital—are released for use by other enterprises. Although the subsidization of SOEs has interfered with privatization, it has not prevented the creation of a large private sector in these economies or the establishment of property rights.

The Establishment of Private Property and Property Rights. The creation of private property requires creating private property rights and enticing entrepreneurs to start new business, and transferring SOE to private ownership. As seen in Figure 2.7 all four countries have large shares of their GDP produced in the private sector. Hungary is given a score of 4.3, reflecting 80 percent of its GDP produced in the private sector. The other three countries are close to this. With high shares of GDP produced in the private sector, all four countries have successfully privatized their economies. This is reflected in the high scores that they achieve with small-scale privatization. Entrepreneurs

Figure 2.7 **Private Property and Property Rights: Selected Countries**
The four countries have large private sectors and have promoted small-scale privatization. Hungary is somewhat ahead of the other countries overall and in large-scale privatization. Slovenia and Hungary are somewhat ahead of Russia and Ukraine in the extent and operation of their legal systems.

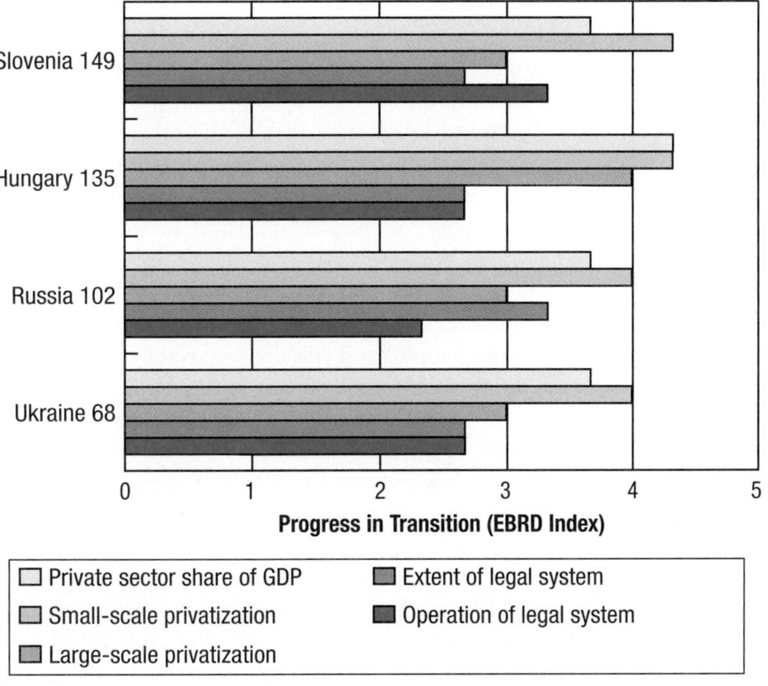

Source: European Bank for Reconstruction and Development (EBRD) Transition Reports.

have created new restaurants, repair shops, small manufacturing operations, and other small businesses that account for significant parts of these economies' private sectors. Similarly, many small SOEs have been transferred to private ownership. The legal system has enabled many private individuals to start new business and to purchase small SOEs and manage them effectively. Figure 2.7 suggests that these countries have reached advanced industrial status in terms of privatizing small business and that the other countries are not far behind.

The second aspect of privatization is the much more difficult task of privatizing large SOEs. Imagine a society in which most people are completely unfamiliar with the idea of owning stock in a company like Google. Imagine also that the people who currently manage Google were stripped of their authority and that ownership responsibilities were sold to people with absolutely no management or ownership experience. The problems would be enormous. Where would people find the resources to buy stock? How could they choose new managers? How could they know whether their managers were doing a good job? Establishing a corporate culture in these countries is difficult. In addition, many of these large SOEs provided their employees with health care, education, and recreation. Governments are reluctant to privatize such enterprises because the social services would be discontinued and many workers laid off. As Figure 2.7 indicates, large-scale privatization has been slower than small scale. Again Hungary has made the most progress with Russia second and Slovenia and Ukraine tied for third. The last three countries have 25 to 50 percent of the original state assets in private hands or moving to private hands. Countries, with substantial production still taking place in SOEs, have much to do to establish market incentives.

Keyword: *Russian economy*

Access InfoTrac at http://infotrac.cengage.com

The four countries have made substantial progress in setting up a legal framework for a market economy. As we will see, this process is not complete, but the extent of the legal system, the actual laws in place, is usually ahead of the operation of the legal system. The operation of the system relates to actual enforcement, its fairness, and its timeliness. In Figure 2.7 the extent of the system is measured by legal experts' evaluation of bankruptcy law. The figure shows that Russia has made the most progress in establishing bankruptcy law, but it and the other countries still have not passed appropriate legislation for bankruptcy. Perhaps, more importantly, the operation of the Russian bankruptcy law is ranked lower than that of the other three countries. Slovenia's law, on the other hand, has the most effective implementation. By and large, for the transition countries, the extent of the legal system tends to more highly rated than its operation.

Incentives. For market incentives to work well, prices must reflect cost and individuals must bear the costs and receive the benefits of their decisions. The interest rate that is charged for loans is an important price because it rations investment funds among competing uses. Suppose you wanted to build a house and planned to borrow the money from a bank to do so. Typically, you want plan to repay the bank on a monthly basis at a rate which would pay off the mortgage in 30 years. Suppose you could borrow the money at a zero interest rate. You then decide what house to build and contract for the resources—land, labor, and capital—to do so. Alternatively, suppose that you have to pay 10 percent interest. In this case, you certainly would build a less expensive house, because the total payment for the original one will include repaying what you borrowed plus interest. You will use fewer resources in building your house. In a command economy interest rates do not reflect cost and investment decisions are made without concern for cost of borrowing money. Without market interest rates to ration investment funds, the command economy had to so in some other way. The government had to decide what investments to make. Until the transition economies have market determined interest rates and well developed financial institutions, it will be difficult for interest rates to provide the appropriate information to investors. As Figure 2.8 shows, only Hungary has made substantial progress toward interest rate liberalization. Russia and Ukraine, in particular, still prevent free adjustment of interest rates and have substantial government involvement in the allocation of investment funds among investors.

Capital markets—both stock and bond markets—are important sources of finance for business. Allocating financial assets to enterprises in the appropriate way is necessary for economies to prosper. Many types of financial institutions other than banks are necessary. They include insurance companies, brokerages, and equity markets, like the New York Stock Exchange. The failures to more completely privatize large SOEs and the failure to enact and particularly to implement bankruptcy and other relevant laws suggest that some of the transition economies, at least, have not been able to fully implement market incentives. As Figure 2.8 shows, Hungary is ahead of the other countries in establishing effective security markets. Russia and Slovenia are at about the same, and Ukraine comes in last.

The figure also shows that Russian and Ukraine, reflecting the difficulties that they have had in large-scale privatization, are well behind the other countries in restructuring enterprises. To see how this relates to incentives, it is necessary to look at one of the major problems of command economies, namely motivating the managers of SOEs to make sound economic decisions. A central plan might provide a target of a certain number of suits of clothes. The enterprise would be allocated workers and cloth. Without profit as an incentive, managers would have incentive only to make the most suits possible, and so they would make them in one size only—small. Although it might seem unbelievable, such things happen under central planning. Consequently, in transition, it is important to provide the managers of these enterprises with appropriate incentives. This is also why it

Figure 2.8 Incentives: Selected Countries
Establishing effective market incentives requires prices that reflect opportunity costs and establishing ownership institutions that link rewards to actions. For interest rates to provide signals of opportunity cost necessary for making sound investment decisions, financial markets must be liberalized. Russia and Ukraine have made little progress in this area, and consequently cannot rely on interest rates as measures of opportunity costs. Similarly, they are behind Slovenia and Hungary in terms of developing institutions of corporate ownership, as reflected in the restructured enterprises score.

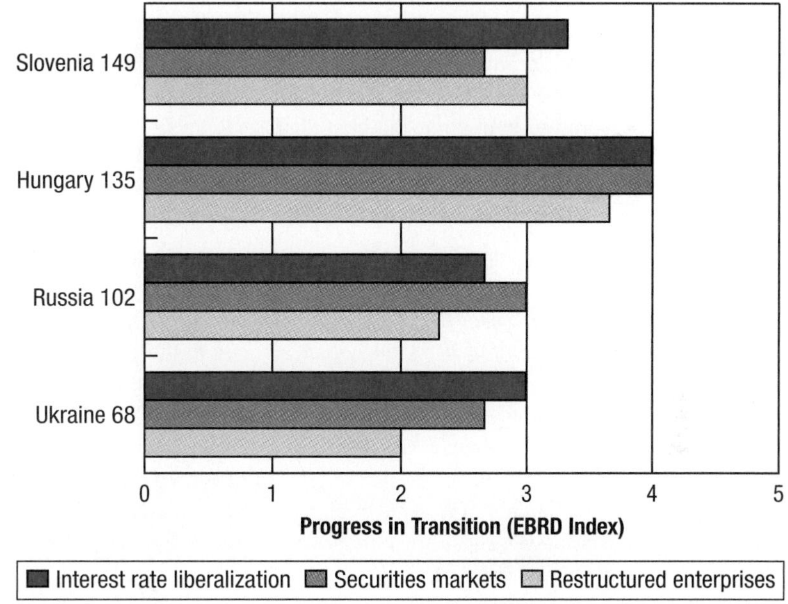

Source: European Bank for Reconstruction and Development (EBRD) Transition Reports.

is so important for the transition economies to privatize their SOEs. If the enterprises are privatized, the owners presumably will be interested in profits.

Different countries have used different schemes to achieve privatization. Managers and workers have been given partial ownership of their enterprises. Citizens have been given ownership shares in enterprises. Enterprises have been sold to foreign investors. In all such situations, the owners want profits. Contrary to what happens in a command economy, firms in market economies earn profits by finding cost-effective ways to produce what consumers want. If managers share in the profits through ownership, performance contracts, or in other ways, they will have an incentive to respond to consumer wants. They will also have incentive to use appropriate production techniques, to monitor workers, and to try to figure out better ways of doing things.

The information in Figure 2.8 indicates that Russia and Ukraine have done little to establish effective institutions that induce large firms and corporations to make decisions profitable for the firm and the economy. In particular, they subsidize big business and inhibit bankruptcy. Recall that bankruptcy is important in a market economy, so that firms that make uneconomic decisions lose control of resources, which, in turn, can be transferred to better decision makers. Slovenia and Hungary, on the other hand, are much less likely to subsidize big business and have developed sound bankruptcy procedures.

Culture That Respects the Legal and Political Systems. Each country must develop and enforce a system of contract, criminal, property, and tort law to carry out its economic transformation. Many of these countries have established much of the legal

INTERNATIONAL PERSPECTIVE

Cowboy Capitalism in Russia?

Criminal activity in Russia reminds some people of lawlessness in the Old West. After all, rustling, land grabbing, bank robbing, and other criminal activities are part of the Western saga, just like the cowboy. Perhaps a new capitalist economy breeds criminal and gang activity. Certainly Russia has a significant crime problem. Russians might be reassured to know that the chaotic criminal conditions that exist today are just a stage of capitalism; they could then expect crime to fall as the economy developed.

Numerous gangs operate in Russia. They deal in illegal goods, they smuggle, they bribe government officials, and they force legitimate businesses to pay for protection. They divert resources, such as oil, which they buy at below-world-market prices, from legitimate uses and sell them on the world market. Blackmail, threats, and murder are used to prevent competition or to learn business secrets.

It is an insult to the early settlers, however, to compare contemporary Russian lawlessness to conditions in the Old West. Because law enforcement did not spread west as fast as the settlers, criminal activity probably exceeded the norm in more established parts of the United States. Despite respect for the rule of law derived from a long history of established property law, vigilante groups, consisting of community leaders, operated outside the law. Superficially, this appears like gang activity. Unlike the Russian gangs, however, vigilante groups attempted to enforce the law, not victimize honest citizens.

In the early stages of capitalism in the United States, most prices were unregulated and few regulations prevented people from doing what they wanted, so long as other people were not harmed involuntarily. Unlike the situation in a command economy or in a society with price controls, unexploited gains from voluntary exchange did not exist and thus could not generate profits for gangs. Government officials lacked the power to prevent profitable activities; consequently, no reason existed to bribe them.

Russian history is different. Bribery of government officials was routine in the Soviet Union, and it was not considered wrong. It was a way to get things done. Evading price controls also was a way of life. As a result, life in the Soviet Union did not generate the respect for and trust of the legal system necessary for capitalism to work well.

In fact, the situation in Russia is more like developments in the United States during Prohibition. Prohibition made gang activity extremely profitable in the 1920s. Criminals profited from selling alcohol, some otherwise honest citizens enjoyed its consumption, and government officials profited by turning a blind eye to the situation.

No, gang activity in Russia does not result from an early state of capitalism; it is not cowboy capitalism. Furthermore, it will not automatically go away. The gangs who prospered during Prohibition in the United States outlasted Prohibition by decades. They moved into illegal gambling and drug sales, and they corrupted some labor unions. Furthermore, gang activity can harm an economy as well as the individual victims. As the wealth and power of gangs increase, they are more likely to infiltrate legitimate businesses and labor unions. Investors in industries where gangs are less prevalent will be reluctant to invest in gang-ridden ones. Evidence suggests that areas of southern Italy with the highest growth rates have the lowest crime rates, and vice versa. Although this is not conclusive, it is hard to disagree with the scholar who said that gangs "can therefore have serious consequences for the economic growth of the legitimate economy ... [They] may create monopolies in local enterprises, control entry ... [and collect] protection payments. New investment may be discouraged and old investment driven out."

Source: Suggested by Annelise Anderson, "The Red Mafia: A Legacy of Communism," Chap. 10 in *Economic Transition in Eastern Europe and Russia* (Stanford: Hoover Institution Press, 1995), 343.

structure important for their transition. As Figure 2.7 shows, the legal transition is not complete, but the countries receive similar ratings. Indeed, the rankings in the figure are closer than in the other figures. The culture necessary for a market economy differs substantially among these countries, as seen in Figure 2.9. This figure presents one

Figure 2.9 Cultures that Respect the Legal and Political Systems: Selected Countries
Although the countries are fairly close in terms of the legal transition (see Figure 2.9), Russia and Ukraine rate much lower than Slovenia and Hungary on measures of the rule-of-law, corruption, and political stability…

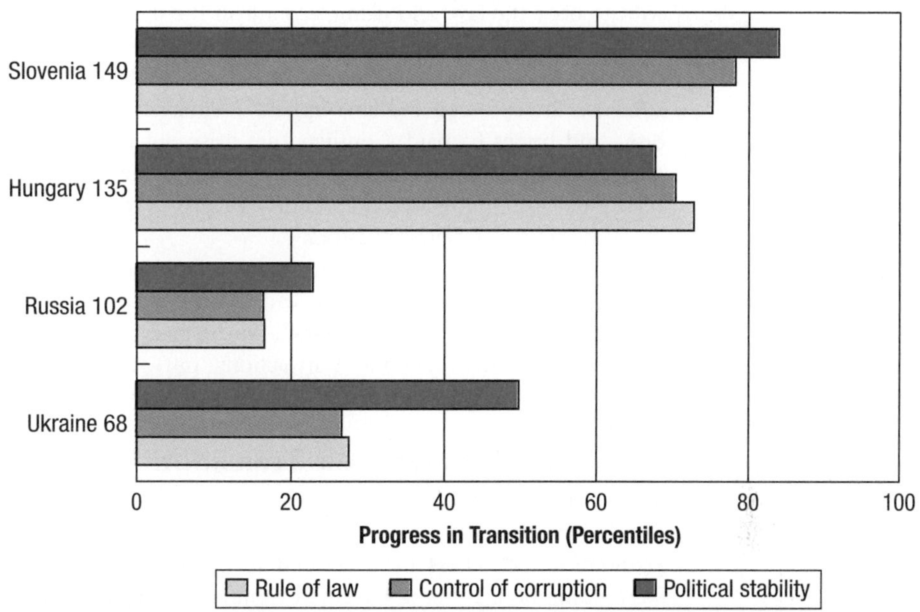

Source: World Bank Governance Data 1996–2007; http://info.worldbank.org/governance/wgi/sc_chart.asp. (See also endnote 6 in this chapter.)

ranking of respect for and enforcement of the laws. The rule-of-law is a measure based on crime rates, judicial effectiveness and predictability, and contract enforcement. The rankings along the horizontal axis in this figure are percentiles rankings. Thus, for Hungry, about 30 percent of all countries in the world rank higher and 70 percent rank lower, when considering the rule of law. For Russia, on the hand, the numbers are just about reversed: about 80 percent rank higher and 20 percent rank lower. It is not coincidental that Slovenia has progressed so much farther in transition than Ukraine.

Another part of a culture of honesty and trust relates to the use of government for private gain. It measures the frequency of bribes, business corruption, the illegal transfer of state-owned assets to private hands, and so on. As one study put it, "The presence of corruption is often a manifestation of a lack of respect of both the corrupter (typically a private citizen or firm) and the corrupted (typically a government official) for the rules which govern their interactions …"[6] Again, in terms of control of corruption, the success stories rank much higher than the adversity stories.

For a third measure of the effectiveness governance, we consider political stability. This is an attempt to measure the possibility of political violence that could lead to a

[6]D. Kaufmann, A. Kraay, and P. Zoido-Lobaton, "Governance Matters," World Bank Working Paper #2196, 1999. The World Bank states that the rule-of-law, control of corruption, and other governance indicators "reflect the statistical compilation of perceptions of the quality of governance of a large number of survey respondents in industrial and developing countries, as well as nongovernmental organizations, commercial risk rating agencies, and think-tanks. They in no way reflect the official position of the World Bank, its Executive Directors, or the countries they represent" (www.worldbank.org).

change in government. Again, the success stories have a reputation of much greater political stability than the adversity stories.

These measures of the honesty and trust in the "culture" indicate that individuals or firms doing business in low-rated countries cannot count on the people whom they deal with to obey the law, and cannot count on the judicial system to enforce it in an equitable manner. The cost of doing business is increased because of the necessity of making contracts as clear and comprehensive as possible. Resources must be used to ensure that contracts are enforced and laws upheld. Moreover, corruption may require that favors be done and bribes be paid. Conflicts that arise out of breach of contract often are settled only after costly renegotiations. Usually the business ends up with a less valuable contract. Such actions reduce the security of property rights and inhibit economic activity by domestic and foreign investors.

Moreover, political stability in some of these countries is hampered by violence and the threat of violence that might lead to an overthrow of the government. Uncertainty about the government and its future and the possibility of violence threatening one's person, property, or economic transactions only raises the risks and further inhibits investment.

Additional Thoughts on Transition Economies

Transition economies face diverse experiences on their different paths to market economic systems. They have different starting points. Some have had well-performing economies and others have decided to change their systems because their economies were doing poorly. Some have had significant private sector and recent experience with a market economy; others have had neither. Some have had a functioning government; others have had to establish national sovereignty and also a new economic system. In all cases, the transition has caused severe economic problems. Some countries have attempted a quick transition to a market economy, while others have taken a more gradual approach. Although they all have had extremely high unemployment and rapid inflation, some, such as Hungary, have stabilized their economies and created conditions conducive to sustained growth. Others, such as Russia, have a long way to go. Similarly, almost all of the transition economies have freed most prices, but they are reluctant to free the prices of necessities, such as food and shelter. Hungary, for instance has one of the freest price systems in the world.

Similarly, the transition economies recognize the need to improve incentives, particularly for the remaining state-owned enterprises, but they differ in their willingness to adopt market incentives. They have been slow to establish institutional and legal systems, such as bankruptcy law and procedures, to undergird their embryonic market systems. As new economic, legal, and political institutions evolve in the transition countries, they have marvelous opportunities to reap the benefits of market systems, while perhaps avoiding some problems of established market economies. Mounting evidence suggests that the economies that have reformed the fastest have had the most economic growth since 1989.[7]

Summary

Market economic systems must have a legal and institutional framework that supports private property and the validity of contracts. These systems work by allowing individuals to make voluntary exchanges; a price system evolves. For voluntary exchanges and a price system to work well in organizing an economy,

[7]Oleh Havrylyshyn and Thomas Wolf, "Determinants of Growth in Transition Countries," *Finance and Development* 36, no. 2 (June 1999). This issue has several articles on transition countries.[7]

prices must be free of government control and inflation must be avoided. A market system replaces centralized control with dispersed individual decision making as the method for approaching economic questions. It relies on incentives based on prices to encourage and to motivate people to respond to other peoples' abilities and desires when they choose what to produce and consume.

Division of labor and comparative advantage result in specialization that creates a need to coordinate the interdependent actions of the people in an economy. A market economy accomplishes this coordination with a decentralized price system. Understanding basic demand and supply analysis is crucial to understanding this coordination. Prices coordinate by informing producers and consumers about alternatives, by rationing existing supplies, and by motivating people to respond to market incentives. In a command economy, prices are often unable to perform these functions.

Transition economies are making uneven progress in the transformation of their economic systems. Some countries have stabilized their economies, freed prices, established private property rights, developed market incentives, and have created the beginnings of legal and institutional systems necessary for a market economic system. Most other countries have freed prices (to one degree or another), but they show great differences in the extent to which they have transformed other elements of their systems. In particular, the more successful transition countries have gone the farthest in establishing the five elements of a market system. Market systems are more efficient than planned systems because their use of the price system provides information in a timely way necessary to coordinate specialized activities. They also allow the price system to generate market incentives so that economic performance is automatically evaluated. Decisions consistent with consumer demands generate profits. The less successful transition economies have gone a long way toward privatization, but they have not been as successful in establishing a comprehensive legal system that is widely respected and obeyed. These economies have not performed as well because they have not been as successful in establishing the legal and political situation in which can expect long-term stability. Just as the Chinese farmers (discussed in the first part of this chapter) are reluctant to make long-term, potentially productive investments because they cannot be sure of the ownership of their land, economic agents in countries with fragile legal and political systems are reluctant to make long-term growth enhancing investments.

Key Terms

Relative price
Absolute advantage
Comparative advantage
Quantity demanded
Demand curve
Demand price
Law of demand
Quantity supplied
Supply curve
Supply price
Law of supply
Excess demand
Excess supply
Equilibrium
Scarcity
Ration
Economic profit

Review Questions

1. What are five characteristics of a successful market economy? Explain.
2. Why is average price stability important in a market system?
3. What are five questions that an economic system must answer?
4. Why is the division of labor important? Why does an increased division of labor make the coordination problem more difficult?
5. Define comparative advantage. Suppose Hugh can produce either four short stories per week or eight gallons of orange juice and Liz can produce either four short stories per week or four gallons of orange juice. At this time Hugh is producing four gallons of orange juice and two short stories per week and Liz is producing two short stories and two gallons of orange juice.
   a. Who has an absolute advantage in producing short stories? In orange juice?
   b. Who has a comparative advantage in producing short stories? In orange juice?
   c. Is there a basis for specialization and trade between Hugh and Liz? Explain in detail why or why not.
6. State the law of demand and illustrate it with a diagram. Show an example of a demand price on

your diagram and explain why it falls when quantity increases.

7. The supply price of corn increases as more corn is produced. Illustrate this fact with a diagram and explain why it happens.
8. The operation of the laws of demand and supply ensures that the market for apartments will be in equilibrium.
   a. Define equilibrium.
   b. Draw a diagram with demand and supply curves. Illustrate the equilibrium price and the equilibrium quantity exchanged.
   c. Suppose the market price is above the equilibrium price. Show the quantity demanded and the quantity supplied on your diagram.
   d. What will happen to cause this market to return to equilibrium?
9. Use a diagram or diagrams to (a) explain how price acts as a signal for consumers and producers and (b) explain how it acts as a motivator.
10. Why is coordination difficult to achieve in a command economy?
11. Draw a demand curve D_0 and a supply curve S_0 for apartments. Show the equilibrium. Now draw a new demand curve D_1 to the right of D_0; the new demand curve is caused by an increase in population. Explain how the price system will operate to signal and motivate producers and consumers to react to this new situation. What is the role of profits?
12. What have transition economies had to do in their attempts to create market economic systems?
13. Compare and contrast the effectiveness of the transition in Hungary with that of Ukraine.
14. According to the box titled "Cowboy Capitalism in Russia?" is the gang activity in Russia typical of the early stage of capitalism? Discuss.
15. In the comparison between FEMA and WalMart, it is suggested that WalMart (the private sector) does many things better than FEMA (the public sector) in disaster relief. Do you agree that the private sector has better knowledge about what needs to be done in disaster relief because of its profit motive. If so, why not turn all elements of disaster relief over to the private sector? If not, why not?
16. Economic News Online, http://www.swcollege.com/bef/econ_news.html. Go to this site, choose the Comparative Economic Systems category under World Economy, and choose an EconNews story that interests you. Read the full summary and answer the questions posed.

Web Sites

- Adam Smith Institute.
  As you might expect, a market-oriented Web site with information about Adam Smith and suggested readings for the "New Generation"—**http://www.adamsmith.org.uk/**
- Center on Budget and Policy Priorities.
  This research and policy institute examines government policies designed to assist low- and moderate-income people—**http://www.cbpp.org/**
- World Bank.
  The World Bank has data and papers on the transition economies. This URL takes you to the *Beyond Transition Newsletter*, which provides current information—**http://econ.worldbank.org/external/default/main?menuPK=51515855&pagePK=64256479&piPK=64165424&q=Beyond%20Transition%20Newsletter&theSitePK=469372.html**
- Brookings Institution.
  The Foreign Policy Studies research area at Brookings contains information about Russia, China, and other relevant countries—**http://www.brook.edu**
- European Bank for Reconstruction and Development.
  The EBRD provides financing for projects in transition economies and monitors the progress in transition—**http://www.ebrd.com**
- Center for Economic Reform and Transformation.
  CERT focuses on academic research that assists in understanding the transition to a market economy—**http://www.som.hw.ac.uk/cert**

CHAPTER 3

Competitive Markets and Government Policy: Agriculture

The U.S. agricultural sector generated over $282 billion in sales while using only 1 percent of the population. The industry's production feeds almost the entire nation with enough left over to account for approximately 8 percent of U.S. exports. Congress provides annual subsidies of $25 billion to support the industry. Why does agriculture need subsidies? What are the effects of these policies on the industry and the US economy?

Eliminating farm poverty is the intended goal of farm subsidies. Table 3.1 compares farm household income to U.S. household income. In 2006, the median income to farm operator households was $54,835, about 14 percent higher than the national median ($48,201) for all households. Average farm household income exceeds U.S. average household income by nearly 17 percent. Average farm household income has exceeded average U.S. household income every year since 1996.[1] In addition, farming is not a peculiarly risky business: a nonfarm business is six times more likely to fail.[2]

There are three basic classifications for farms. Table 3.2 lists these types, indicates what portion of the industry they represent, and their respective value of crop and livstock production. About 82 percent of all farms are classified as small family farms with sales less than $100,000 per year. These farms produce about 12 percent of the value of agricultural production. Family farms with sales between $100,000 and $249,999 are considered high sales small family farms. These farms produce about 9 percent of the value of agricultural production while they are only about 6 percent of the farming population. Commercial family farms generate gross sales equalling or exceeding $250,00 and represent 7.5 percent of all farms. Commercial family farms produce 58 percent of the value of production. Nonfamily farms, agribusinesses, generate sales equaling or exceeding $250,000. While nonfamily farms represent only 4.5 percent of U.S. farms, they produce 19 percent of the value of production. So who gets the subsidies?

Commercial and nonfamily farmers receive the largest share of farm subsidies. Their average income is nearly $200,000 and average net worth approaches $2 million.[3] Table 3.3 shows the average government payment to aid farmers by sales class. Clearly, the large farms receive a much greater payment than do small farmers. Consider also the 1,500 or so recipients in Stuttgart, Arkansas (ZIP code 72160), received $1.05 billion from 1995 to 2006—$87.5 million a year. The 20 largest payment recipients in Stuttgart totaled more than $912 million or 86 percent of all payments received in the ZIP code.[4] Annual

[1]U.S. Department of Agriculture, *Agricultural Income and Finance Outlook: Report of the Economic Research Service*, AIS-85 (December 2007), p. 50 (http://usda.mannlib.cornell.edu/usda/ers/AIS//2000s/2007/AIS-12-13-2007.pdf).

[2,3]Brian M. Riedl, "How Farm Subsidies Harm Taxpayers, Consumers, and Farmers, Too" *Heritage Foundation Backgrounder* 2043 (June 20, 2007).

[4]The Environmental Working Group presents details on subsidies received by individuals by ZIP code, county, and state on its Web site, http://www.ewg.org/farming

TABLE 3.1 INCOME TO FARM AND U.S. HOUSEHOLDS, 2002–2007

	2002	2003	2004	2005	2006
Median farm household	46,491	47,692	53,651	53,684	54,835
Median U.S. household	42,409	43,318	44,334	46,326	48,201
Average farm household	65,761	68,597	81,596	81,599	77,654
Average U.S. household	57,852	59,067	60,466	63,344	66,570

Source: USDA, ERS, "Agricultural Income and Finance Outlook" at (http://usda.mannlib.cornell.edu/usda/ers/AIS//2000s/2007/AIS-12-13-2007.pdf).

TABLE 3.2 U.S. FARM TYPES WITH VALUE OF AGRICULTURAL PRODUCTION (VOP), 2007

FARM TYPE	% OF FARM POPULATION 2006	CROP VOP	LIVESTOCK VOP
Small Family Farms	88.0	22.7	19.9
Low sales	*82.1*	*11.7*	*12.5*
High Sales	*5.9*	*11.0*	*7.4*
Commercial Family	7.5	58.2	61.7
Family Farms	95.5	80.9	81.6
Nonfamily	4.5	19.1	18.4
Total	**100.0**	**100.0**	**100.0**

Source: USDA, ERS, "Agricultural Income and Finance Outlook" at (http://usda.mannlib.cornell.edu/usda/ers/AIS//2000s/2007/AIS-12-13-2007.pdf).

TABLE 3.3 SHARES OF NET VALUE ADDED AND AVERAGE SUBSIDY/SUPPORT PAYMENT RECEIVED

SALES CLASS	% OF FARM POPULATION 2006	NET VALUE ADDED	AVERAGE GOVERNMENT PAYMENT
$1 million and above	1.7	47.8	$80,386
$500,000–$999,999	2.2	13.0	55,579
$250,000–$499,999	4.3	13.6	32,183
$100,000–$249,999	7.9	11.2	16,267
Below $100,000	82.9	14.4	4,898

Source: USDA, ERS, "Agricultural Income and Finance Outlook" at (http://usda.mannlib.cornell.edu/usda/ers/AIS//2000s/2007/AIS-12-13-2007.pdf).

subsidies create numerous adverse unintended consequences for farmers, taxpayers, and the public. Small farmers receive little or no subsidies. Subsidies contribute to overproduction which lowers overall prices to farmers. Subsidies increase farm land values, and support the buyout of small family farms. Congress pays farmers to keep 40 million acres of cropland from production. Government subsidies distort agricultural markets and prevent them from reaching allocative and technical efficiency.

INTERNATIONAL PERSPECTIVE

OECD Farm Policy: New Zealand Breaks the Mold

Farm policy in the United States is not unique. In fact, the U.S. support to farm producers, although large, amounted to 18 percent of gross farm receipts in 2004 compared to 33 percent support provided to producers by the European Union. The average for OECD (Organization for Economic Co-operation and Development) countries was 30 percent, but countries such as Iceland, Japan, and Korea supported farm receipts at 69, 56, and 63 percent respectively. Throughout the industrialized world, farmers have obtained substantial support and protection from their governments. This protection consists of barriers to free trade that permit domestic agricultural prices to rise above world market prices, price supports, deficiency payments, and various other subsidies. This near universal support might suggest that something in the nature of farming requires significant government help. The case of New Zealand, however, refutes that suggestion; its support for farmers is only 3 percent.

One argument that farmers "need" to be supported is fallacious. It relies on a fundamental fallacy—the all-or-nothing fallacy—that supposedly provides a national security argument for protecting farmers and agriculture. The argument is simple and persuasive. Food is necessary to survive. Farmers produce food. If domestic farmers go out of business, we may lose our independence, because we must rely on foreign countries for life's necessities. This argument, along with the relative and absolute decline in the number of farms and farmers in most developed countries, leads nonfarmers in some countries to want to protect agriculture. The fallacy is to conclude that if some farms or farmers are going out of business, all farmers are in danger of doing so.

Economic situations are rarely so cut and dried. In the United States the number of farms and farmers has declined for most of the twentieth century. Does this mean that the United States is in danger of becoming reliant on other, perhaps unfriendly, countries for its food supply? No! U.S. farms are producing more than ever. Only the high-cost farms and the high-cost farmers are leaving agriculture, and as they do, the supply price of U.S. farm products falls. The lower-cost farms and farmers would be able to supply the U.S. market at lower cost. So one example of the all-or-nothing fallacy is to think that if one farmer leaves agriculture, all farmers will leave agriculture. They don't. And as the high-cost producers leave, the remaining producers in the industry are the lower-cost ones.

New Zealand no longer accepts this fallacy, having eliminated almost all direct producer subsidies. Most of its government expenditures for agriculture are spent on research, disease control, and pest control. Government payments to farmers based on production have essentially been eliminated. New Zealand has also moved away from providing relief payments to farmers because of climatic disasters, encouraging farmers to undertake risk management. New Zealand permits marketing boards to attempt to influence market price, but overall its farmers, as we have seen, receive far less per farmer than do farmers in most other OECD countries, and New Zealanders pay far less to support agriculture.

New Zealand has demonstrated that a country can eliminate most agricultural protection without causing a crisis in its agricultural economy.

Source: OECD data from Organization for Economic Co-operation and Development, *Agricultural Policies in OECD Countries: Monitoring and Evaluation—Highlights* (Paris: OECD, 2005), 62 (http://www.oecd.org/dataoecd/33/27/35016763.pdf).

From 2005 to 2007, direct payments to U.S. farmers from U.S. taxpayers averaged over $17 billion per year. As we just saw, most of these payments go to rich and wealthy farmers. But these direct payments are only part of the support that government gives farmers. As the OECD shows, total support to farm producers averages three times this amount. This additional support comes from tariffs, price controls, and other government interference with the farm economy. Government farm programs interfere with farmers' production decisions, increase food costs, provide large subsidies to the wealthy, and do little to help poor farmers. The support that agriculture receives from the average citizen is an example of a program that redistributes income from the average citizen to a privileged group, a program that our political system has been unable to reform. To understand the difficulties of reform, we resume our discussion of demand and supply and bring in some political considerations.

DEMAND AND SUPPLY ANALYSIS

Demand and supply analysis shows how the market determines what to produce. The law of demand states that, at a lower price, consumers would plan to purchase more of a good—say, milk—during a week.[5] It also states the reverse. At a higher price, consumers would plan to purchase less milk per week. Conversely, the law of supply states that producers of milk would plan to sell less milk per week at a lower price. It also states that, at a higher price, they would plan to sell more. (Our statements about the laws of demand and supply assume that all factors other than price of the good stay constant.)

In a market economy, the laws of demand and supply lead to *equilibrium*. By definition, equilibrium exists when a situation has no cause to change. Market equilibrium exists when the quantity that people plan to buy at the market price is the same as the quantity that producers plan to sell at that price; no one wants to change behavior. To review the analysis from Chapter 2, suppose that, at the going price, consumers plan to buy more of a good—say, milk—than producers plan to sell. Consumers find their plans frustrated. They cannot buy the amount of milk they want, even though they are willing to pay the price. Producers find that they cannot satisfy their customers. Some consumer is likely to offer a higher price or some producer is likely to ask for one. Either way the offer will be accepted and the price will increase. According to the law of demand, at the higher price consumers will plan to purchase less. According to the law of supply, producers will plan to produce and sell more. Buyers buy less; sellers sell more. As the plans of consumers and producers converge, the market moves to equilibrium.

If this economic coordination (also discussed in Chapter 2) were accomplished once and for all, the price system's ability to coordinate might not be particularly important. Change, however, characterizes modern economies. New goods and services emerge. Consumers learn about new goods and learn more about existing goods. National population grows. Population grows in some parts of a country and declines in others. These and other changes that affect demand require an economic system to solve the coordination problem again and again.

Similarly, changes in factors affecting supply require the economy to adjust to new equilibriums. Supply is affected by changes in technology, in the prices of resources such as labor, and in the relative profitability of various activities. New production techniques, new goods, and new opportunities will be trademarks of the twenty-first century, just as they were of the twentieth. To understand why agriculture is so heavily subsidized, we must understand competitive markets—the first step is to understand demand and supply.

---

[5]In discussing demand and supply, we must include a time dimension. It would be meaningless to say that Nadia has a greater demand for milk than Ivan because she plans to purchase 20 gallons of milk and Ivan plans to purchase 2 gallons. For instance, Ivan may plan to purchase 2 gallons a day, and Nadia may plan to purchase 20 gallons a month. Ivan would have the greater demand.

TABLE 3.4 CHANGES IN DEMAND FOR MILK WHEN OTHER FACTORS CHANGE

ORIGINAL DEMAND		DEMAND WITH NEW CHEESE PRICE		DEMAND WITH NEW INCOME	
PRICE PER GALLON (1)	GALLONS PER WEEK (2)	PRICE PER GALLON (3)	GALLONS PER WEEK (4)	PRICE PER GALLON (5)	GALLONS PER WEEK (6)
$3.50	0	$3.50	0	$3.50	1
3.25	0	3.25	0	3.25	2
3.00	1	3.00	0	3.00	3
2.75	2	2.75	0	2.75	4
2.50	3	2.50	1	2.50	5
2.25	4	2.25	2	2.25	6
2.00	5	2.00	3	2.00	7
1.75	6	1.75	4	1.75	8
1.50	7	1.50	5	1.50	9
1.25	8	1.25	6	1.25	10
1.00	9	1.00	7	1.00	11

The original demand schedule for milk changes to a new demand schedule as other factors affecting demand change. The demand for milk decreases if the price of cheese decreases. The demand for milk increases if consumers' income increases.

Other Demand Factors

The maximum amount that consumers are willing to pay for an additional gallon of milk, the demand price, depends on how much they like milk (their preferences) and their income, among other factors. It also depends on the amount of other goods, such as cheese, that they consume, which, in turn, depends upon the prices of other goods. Consequently, the demand for any good—say, milk—depends on its price and other factors: for instance, consumers' preferences, consumers' income, and the prices of other goods.[6] A complete statement of the law of demand is that as the price of some good changes, keeping the other factors unchanged, the quantity demanded of the good changes in the opposite direction.

In Table 3.4, columns 1 and 2 present a market demand schedule for milk. Suppose that this demand results when the price of a pound of cheddar cheese is $5, the price of a gourmet chocolate chip cookie is $1.25, and consumers earn $900 per week.

Decrease in demand – A situation in which, at each price, consumers plan to purchase less of a good; it is depicted by a leftward shift of the demand curve. It may also be interpreted as a reduction in the value of an additional unit of the good, which emphasizes the downward shift of the curve.

Related Goods. Now suppose that the price of some related good changes. Say that the price of a pound of cheddar cheese drops to $3. As a result, consumers purchase more cheese. If they eat more cheese, then milk is less important. Consequently, for any given quantity of milk, consumers will not be willing to pay as much for an additional unit. Its demand price falls. For the sixth gallon of milk it decreases from $1.75 to $1.25. In Table 3.4, the demand schedule changes from that in columns 1 and 2 to that in columns 3 and 4. This is an example of a **decrease in demand** for milk because of a decrease in the price of a related good, cheese. For any given quantity of milk, consumers place a lower value on an additional unit—that is, the demand price decreases. Another way to see the decrease in demand is to note that for each possible price,

[6]To read about some of the other factors that affect demand, such as expected future prices, see Chapter 19 in James D. Gwartney, Richard L. Stroup, Russell Sobel, and David Macpherson, *Economics: Private and Public Choice* (Cincinnati: South-Western, 2003).

consumers plan to purchase less milk. For instance, at the price of $1.25, the planned purchase decreases from 8 to 6 gallons.

The demand curve changes from D_0, the original demand curve, to D_1, as shown in Figure 3.1, which plots information from Table 3.4. The downward movement in the entire demand curve reflects the decline in demand prices. Its leftward movement shows that for each price consumers' planned purchases have decreased.

Suppose the price of cookies increases. The law of demand implies that you now would buy fewer cookies. Assume that consuming cookies enhances your enjoyment of milk. Because you are consuming fewer cookies, milk is less important—the value that you put on an additional gallon of milk declines. Demand decreases, as in Figure 3.1.

Substitute – A good used in place of another good. An increase in the price of one good results in an increase in demand for the substitute good.

Complement – A good used with another good. An increase in the price of one good results in a decrease in demand for its complement.

So the demand for milk reacts the same way to a decrease in the price of cheese and an increase in that of cookies. Two goods are **substitutes** if a decrease in the price of one, say cheese, causes a decrease in the demand for the other, say milk. The price change for one good and the demand change for the other good move in the same direction. In the example in Table 3.4, cheese and milk are substitutes because a decrease in the price of cheese leads to a decrease in the demand for milk. In effect, the cheese substitutes for the milk in consumers' diets.

In contrast, cheese is a **complement** with hamburger because an increase in the price of cheese results in a decrease in the demand for hamburger. This might occur among people who really like cheeseburgers, but don't particularly like burgers or cheese alone. The price change for one good and the demand change for the other good are in opposite directions. Cookies and milk are complements in Figure 3.1 because an increase in the price of cookies leads to a decrease in the demand for milk.

Income. Now suppose that each consumer's income doubles. With this increase in income, each consumer might place a higher value on milk. In Table 3.4, the demand schedule resulting from the increased income is shown in columns 5 and 6. Demand has changed. Originally, the fourth gallon of milk was worth $2.25. Now it is worth $2.75.

Figure 3.1 A Decrease in Demand

The change in demand from D_0 to D_1 is a decrease in demand. At a price of $1.75, the quantity purchased decreases from 6 to 4 gallons per week. Quantity demanded decreases at every price. Alternatively, the demand price for the sixth gallon falls from $1.75 to $1.25. The demand price falls for every quantity.

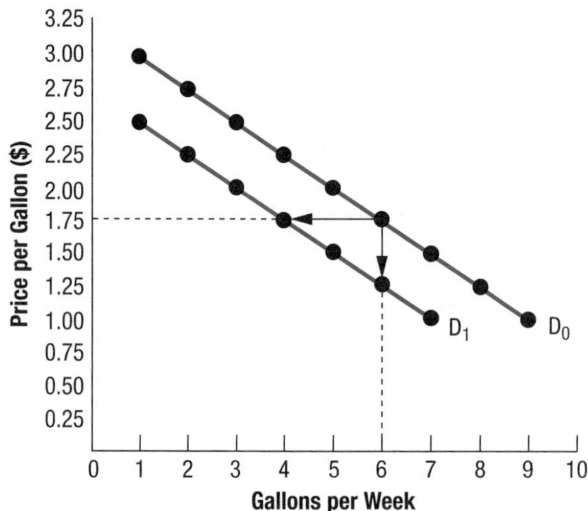

Increase in demand – A situation in which, at each price, consumers plan to purchase more of a good, depicted by a rightward shift of the demand curve. It may also be interpreted as an increase in the demand price, which emphasizes the upward shift of the curve.

This **increase in demand** means that consumers plan to purchase more at each price. For instance, at the price of $2.25, the quantity demanded is now 6 gallons; originally, it was 4 gallons.

Figure 3.2 shows the demand change from D_0, the original demand curve, to D_1, the new demand curve. The movement upward in the demand curve shows that, for each quantity, demand price increases. Alternatively, the move to the right shows that, for each price, consumers plan to purchase more.

In this example, the demand for milk increased when income increased. A good for which this happens is a **normal good**, one that consumers purchase more of when their incomes go up. Some goods—perhaps ramen noodles—are **inferior goods**. Nothing is inherently inferior about these noodles; it's just that as consumers' incomes go up, they place a lower value on them. For instance, if your income goes up, you may decide to eat more sushi. If you eat more high-end Asian food, you will have less room in your diet for ramen noodles. Thus, the demand for the noodles decreases, implying that it is an inferior good. Imagine an impoverished family that can't afford ramen noodles. If the family's income increases, it might place a higher value on them—ramen noodles would be a normal good for this family. If its income increases even more, the family may now decide to purchase fresh fruits and vegetables, reducing the value of ramen noodles. Ramen noodles now have become an inferior good for the family.

Keywords: *price cuts and demand*

Access InfoTrac at http://infotrac.cengage.com

Normal good – A good that consumers purchase more of when their income rises.

Inferior good – A good that consumers purchase less of when their income rises.

Other factors obviously affect demand. One is consumers' preferences. Consumers may change their minds about the benefit received from consuming certain goods. If so, the demand for the goods will change. Demand in a particular market also will change if the number of consumers in the market changes. This is so because market demand is just the sum of the demands of individual consumers. In short, the demand for a good depends upon the price of the good, consumers' income, the prices of related goods, consumer preferences, and the number of consumers.

Figure 3.2 An Increase in Demand

The change in demand from D_0 to D_1 is an increase in demand. At a price of $2.25, the quantity purchased would increase from 4 to 6 gallons per week, quantity demanded increases at every price. Alternatively, at a quantity of 4 gallons per week, the demand price increases from $2.25 to $2.75. The demand price increases for every quantity.

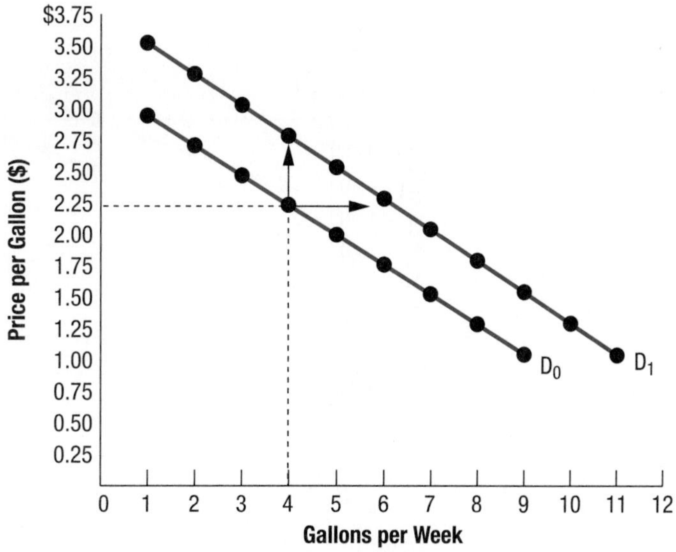

Other Supply Factors

Just as with demand, factors other than its price affect the quantity of, say, wheat that producers plan to supply; these other factors are those that affect production cost. These include the technology of wheat production, the prices of inputs, (say, fertilizer and labor) and the prices of goods (say, corn) that could be produced instead of wheat. A full statement of the law of supply, therefore, is that a change in the price of a good, keeping these other factors unchanged, results in a change in quantity supplied in the same direction as the price change.

Figure 3.3 shows the market supply curve, S_0, that exists when, for example, the price of fertilizer is \$0.25 a pound, the price of labor is \$10 an hour, the price of corn is \$4 a bushel, and a given technology exists. To find the quantity supplied for each price, choose a price on the vertical axis in Figure 3.3, say, \$2.20. The corresponding point on the horizontal axis gives the quantity supplied, 5 bushels. The supply price for 5 bushels, \$2.20, is just sufficient to cover the cost of the fifth bushel.

Increase in supply– A situation in which, at each price, producers plan to sell more of a good; it is depicted by a rightward shift of the supply curve. It may also be interpreted as a reduction in supply price for each quantity of the good, which emphasizes the downward shift of the curve.

What happens to the supply curve when other factors change? Suppose technology advances. Perhaps a new strain of wheat is developed that thrives with less fertilizer. Assuming the price of the wheat seed is unchanged, the cost of wheat production falls. The fifth bushel of wheat produced in the market might now cost only \$1.90 rather than \$2.20. In other words, the supply price of the fifth bushel falls from \$2.20 to \$1.90. Because of the cost reduction, a new supply curve, S_1, exists in Figure 3.3. Suppose the price had been \$2.20. Before the advance in technology, the quantity supplied was 5 bushels. But now a profit is earned on the fifth bushel because \$2.20 is greater than the new supply price. With the new supply curve, producers supply 8 bushels at \$2.20. In fact, with the new supply curve, more will be supplied at each price. The cost reduction leads to a movement of the supply curve to the right. This is an example of an **increase in supply**, where for each price producers plan to sell more.

Figure 3.3 An Increase in Supply

The shift in the supply curve from S_0 to S_1 is an increase in supply. At any price, the quantity supplied increases. For instance, at a price of \$2.20 the quantity supplied increases from 5 to 8 bushels per year. Alternatively, at any quantity the supply price decreases. For the fifth bushel, the supply price falls from \$2.20 to \$1.90.

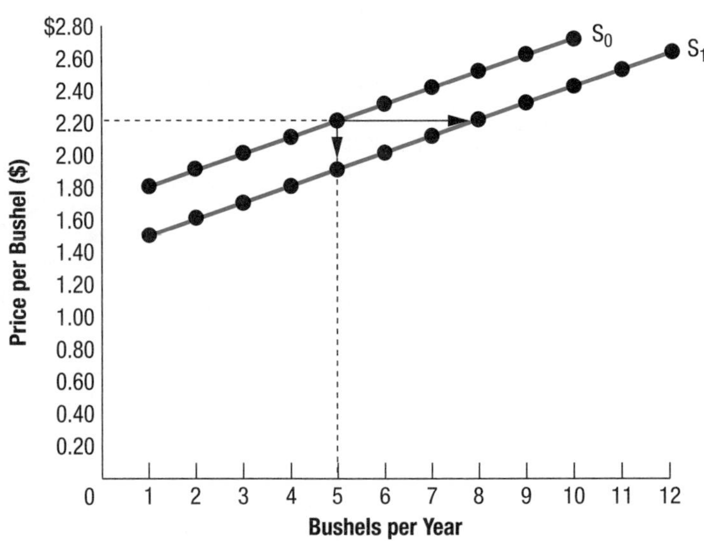

Figure 3.4 A Decrease in Supply
The shift in the supply curve from S_0 to S_1 is a decrease in supply. At any price, the quantity supplied decreases. For instance, at a price of $2.20, the quantity supplied decreases from 5 to 2 bushels per year. Alternatively, at any quantity, the supply price increases. For the fifth bushel, the supply price increases from $2.20 to $2.50.

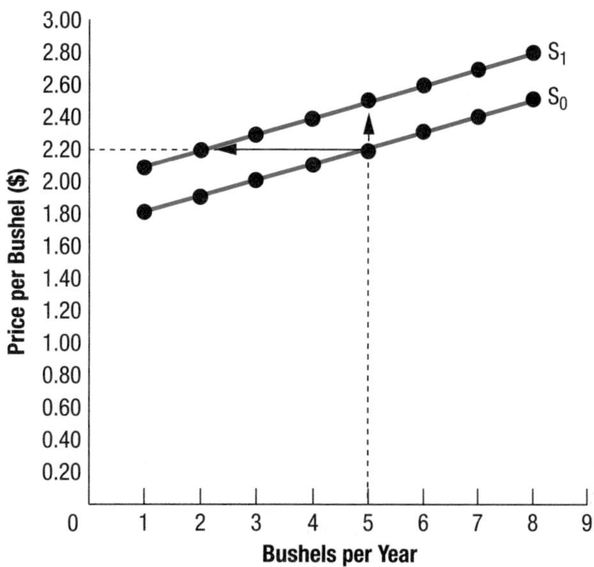

Keywords: *price increases and cost*

Access InfoTrac at http://infotrac.cengage.com

Decrease in supply– A situation in which, at each price, producers plan to sell less of a good; it is depicted by a leftward shift of the supply curve. It may also be interpreted as an increase in the supply price for each quantity of the good, which emphasizes the upward shift of the curve.

Now suppose the price of labor rises from $10 to $15 an hour. The cost of wheat production increases. The cost of the fifth bushel of wheat, the supply price, might go from $2.20 to $2.50 (Figure 3.4). With the increase in cost, the supply curve moves up, from S_0 to S_1. With S_0, if the price had been $2.20, the quantity supplied would have been 5. But with S_1, a price of $2.20 is less than the new supply price of the fifth bushel: producers will supply only 2 bushels. In fact, the quantity supplied will be less at any given price. The cost increase leads to a movement of the supply curve to the left. This is an example of a **decrease in supply**, where for each price producers plan to sell less.

Any farm, or any agricultural area, can produce different crops. To decide about wheat production, one must consider the profitability of these related crops. For instance, suppose the price of corn goes up. According to the law of supply, the quantity of corn supplied will increase. Farmers find it profitable to increase corn production, which requires transferring some land previously used in wheat to corn. Because corn has become more profitable, the opportunity cost of growing wheat has increased. Because the cost of wheat production is up, the supply price increases; in other words, the supply of wheat decreases, as in Figure 3.4.

In short, the supply of a good depends upon the price of the good, technology, the prices of inputs, and the prices of other goods that could be produced. The law of supply is that the quantity supplied changes in the same direction as the change in the price of the good, assuming that the other supply factors do not change. With our knowledge of what causes demand and supply to change, we now turn to how demand and supply changes affect the equilibrium.

HOW CHANGES IN DEMAND AND SUPPLY AFFECT EQUILIBRIUM PRICE AND QUANTITY

In Chapter 2, we studied price determination in competitive markets. Competitive markets have many well-informed buyers and sellers. No single buyer or seller has a noticeable effect on market price; buyers and sellers are price takers. Furthermore, people can participate in competitive markets solely in response to their evaluation of the advantage of doing so. Potential buyers need only consider whether the expected value of a purchase is worth its opportunity cost. Similarly, people can become producers simply because they expect to profit. Government laws and regulations do not prevent voluntary exchanges. How do competitive markets handle changes in demand and supply?

Changes in Demand

Figure 3.5 illustrates the market for cheese. The initial demand and supply curves are D_0 and S_0. As explained in Chapter 2, the equilibrium price and quantity exchanged are P_0 and Q_0. At P_0, consumers plan to purchase Q_0, and producers plan to produce and sell Q_0; equilibrium requires that quantity demanded equals quantity supplied. Suppose now that new medical studies, as they so often do, find evidence of much greater health dangers in eating dietary fat. Cheese is high in dietary fat, so consumers will place a lower value on cheese. Demand, as illustrated in Figure 3.5, decreases from D_0 to D_1. The reduction in demand for cheese causes a price decrease, which in turn causes a reduction in quantity supplied. The old equilibrium was at P_0 and Q_0; the new one is at P_1 and Q_1.

The simplicity of this change conceals the complexity of what is happening. Consumers have decided that cheese is less valuable. They want less at the initial price, P_0: an excess supply develops. Sellers have more cheese than they can sell. With the excess

Figure 3.5 The Effects of a Change in Demand
The decrease in demand from D_0 to D_1 creates an excess supply at the original equilibrium price, P_0. This excess supply creates pressure for the price to fall. As the price falls, the quantity supplied decreases. Equilibrium is restored at P_1 and Q_1. Both price and quantity exchanged decrease.

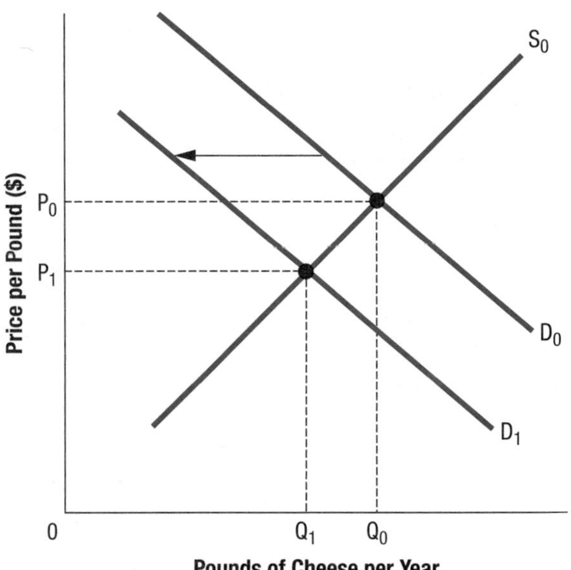

building up, some seller decides to cut price and possibly take customers away from other sellers. Or, some sharp consumer sees the excess building up and offers a lower price to take the cheese off the sellers' hands. Even though no central planner or government orders it to happen, the price falls. As it falls, the quantity supplied falls. As the quantity supplied falls, some inputs are released from cheese production. Some labor resources (people) are forced to find jobs in other industries. Because milk is used in cheese production, dairy farmers start producing less milk. Land that had been used for dairy farming is converted to other agricultural uses. Thus, the change in consumer preferences causes resources to be reallocated to products on which consumers now place a greater value relative to cheese. Although the market accomplishes this reallocation automatically, history shows that central planning, such as existed in the former Soviet Union, is often unable to do so.

Notice that the supply curve for cheese has *not* changed. The quantity supplied has decreased, but no change has occurred in technology, the prices of inputs, or the prices of other goods that might be produced. We sometimes read that a reduction in demand causes a reduction in supply, but that's false. The correct interpretation is that a decrease in demand (a leftward shift in the demand curve) results in a decrease in price, which causes the quantity supplied to decrease (a movement along the existing supply curve).

Cheese producers and dairy producers may have other responses. They may advertise that cheese is a healthful food, just as beef producers now advertise that beef is a healthful food. They might support research to develop a lower-fat cheese, as pork producers have developed lower-fat pork over the years. These efforts to protect their profits through advertising and research would lead to an improved situation for consumers and producers. In the face of falling prices, however, producers might use a political approach rather than attempting to satisfy consumers' changed demand. They might use political advertising, campaign contributions, and so on to entice the government to keep the price of cheese at its original level.

Changes in Supply

The impact of an increase in the supply of cheese is also easy to determine. Suppose that workers in the cheese industry receive lower wages. This lowers the cost of producing cheese and its supply price: supply increases from S_0 to S_1 (see Figure 3.6). The increase in the supply of cheese causes price to fall, resulting in an increase in quantity demanded. The old equilibrium was at P_0 and Q_0; the new equilibrium is at P_1 and Q_1.

Again, much is happening behind the scene. Producers have learned that it is cheaper to produce cheese. Fewer sacrifices are made to produce a pound of cheese, and because its opportunity cost is less, producers are willing to supply more at the going price. Producers try to sell more at P_0, but they fail. Excess supply develops. Again price falls, without a government planner giving any orders. As price falls, quantity demanded increases. As quantity demanded increases, consumers substitute the now cheaper cheese for other foods in their diets. The change in cost conditions leads to people consuming more cheese and less of other foods.

The demand curve for cheese, however, has not changed. The quantity demanded has increased, but no change has occurred in consumer preferences, income, the prices of related goods, or the number of consumers in the market.

Changes in Demand and Supply

The process is somewhat more complicated if both demand and supply change at the same time. Suppose that demand decreases and supply increases. A demand decrease means that consumers wish to buy less at the going price; a supply increase means that producers wish to sell more at the going price. As you might expect, whether the amount

Figure 3.6 The Effects of a Change in Supply
The increase in supply from S_0 to S_1 creates an excess supply at the original equilibrium price, P_0. The price falls in response to the excess supply, causing quantity demanded to increase. The new equilibrium is at a lower price, P_1, and a higher quantity, Q_1.

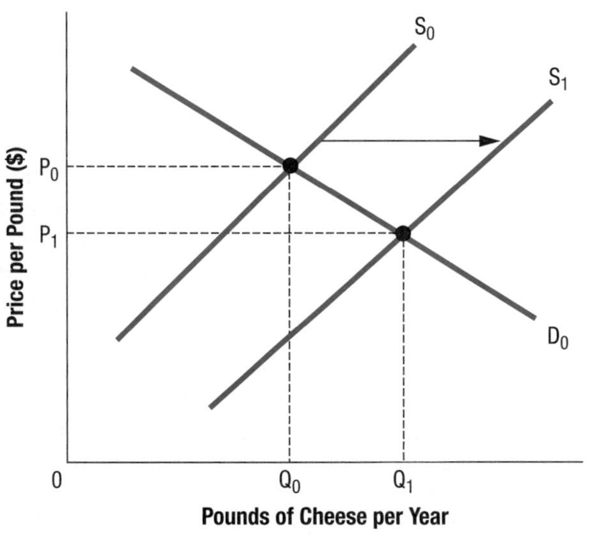

actually exchanged increases or decreases depends upon the relative size of the two changes. But for any quantity, consumers now place a lower value on cheese, and producers are willing to accept a lower price for it. Consequently, the price will fall.

Keywords: *law of supply and demand*

Access InfoTrac at http://infotrac.cengage.com

In Figure 3.7, the decrease in demand from D_0 to D_1 is a larger change than the increase in supply from S_0 to S_1. Consequently, quantity exchanged decreases from Q_0 to Q_1, but the quantity exchanged would have increased if the supply increase were large enough. Price falls, as it must, from P_0 to P_1.

Price changes for agricultural products occur frequently because of changes in demand and supply. Over time, the prices of many agricultural products, adjusted for inflation, have fallen. This long-term fall in agricultural prices is partially responsible for federal government intervention in agricultural markets.

U.S. FARM POLICY

Political support for U.S. farm policy derives from two sources. One is based on economic and historical characteristics of the industry. The other is based on the political influence of the recipients of farm subsidies. We first discuss the economic and historical characteristics of agriculture that have shaped farm policy. Then we consider the political aspects.

Economic and Historical Characteristics

As the Industrial Revolution progressed, household income in the small but growing industrial and urban parts of the U.S. economy surged ahead of household income in the farm sector. In 1840, slightly more than two-thirds of employed workers—3.7 million—were in agriculture. Although the number of workers in agriculture grew until the 1920s, the percentage has fallen since 1800. In 1920, more than one-fourth of U.S. workers—11.1 million—were still in agriculture, but since then the percentage of agricultural workers has dropped to about 2 percent, and the number has dropped to less than

Figure 3.7 The Effects of Changes in Demand and Supply
The decrease in demand from D_0 to D_1 and the increase in supply from S_0 to S_1 cause an excess supply at the original equilibrium price, P_0. The excess supply causes price to fall. Other factors equal, the increase in supply would also cause quantity to increase. But other factors are not equal. Demand has decreased. By itself a decrease in demand would cause quantity to decrease. Consequently, quantity might increase or decrease depending on the size of the supply increase compared to the demand decrease. In this example, the demand decrease is larger, so quantity falls.

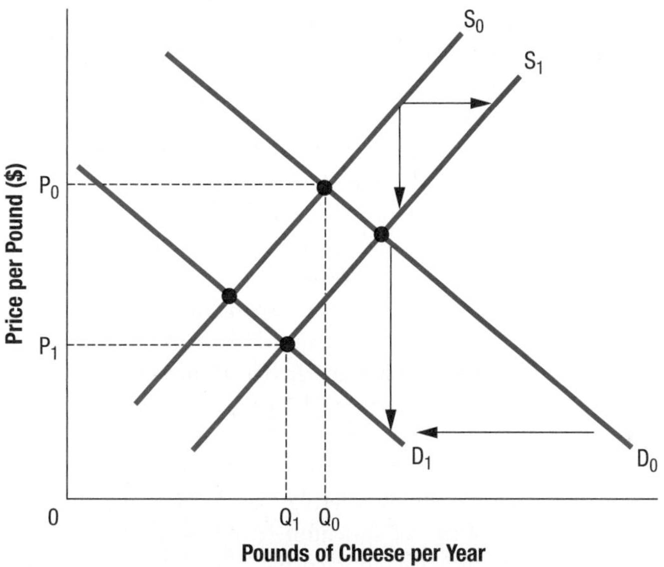

in 1840—about 2 million. This massive downsizing of agricultural employment was accompanied by large reductions in the number of farms. Price and income instability in agriculture caused by economic fluctuations in the economy and erratic weather at times forced thousands off the farm in a short time.

A substantial exodus from agriculture has accompanied economic development in most countries. Innovations in agriculture and industry, combined with education and research provided through the land-grant university system, have resulted in tremendous technical progress in U.S. agriculture. The supply of agricultural products has increased substantially. The demand for agricultural products—food, in large part—increases with income and with world population, but these increases have not been large enough to offset the large supply increases. First, increases in income do not cause proportionate increases in demand. For instance, if your income doubles, you probably would not double food consumption or the amount spent on food. You probably would not increase your food consumption at all, but you might spend more on food—not by eating more, but by eating better. Second, population has not grown nearly fast enough to counteract the huge increases in supply caused by technical progress. (To test your understanding, draw a diagram for the food market that illustrates these demand and supply changes.)

Suppose output per farmer doubles in 14 years, which is within the historical experience. If the number of farmers remains the same, this productivity growth will double farm output. The demand for food must double for farm prices to remain the same. Population and income simply grow too slowly to increase demand that much. If productivity grows rapidly, farm prices must fall, as they have over the past 100 years—about 0.5 percent per year. This price trend, based on farmers' greater ability to produce, is part of U.S. agriculture's success story. The falling prices indicate a greater availability (reduced scarcity) of food. But because the quantity demanded is not very responsive to price changes, prices would nosedive if agricultural employment remained the same as productivity increased.

Farmers have responded to this price trend by leaving agriculture. Consider the demand for and the supply of labor in agriculture. Because output per worker has increased, fewer workers can produce the same amount of agricultural products. Furthermore, because the price of agricultural products has decreased, the demand price for a given amount of labor has decreased. Both the productivity increase and the price reduction for farm output cause a decrease in the demand for farm labor. Economic development in the nonagricultural sector affects the supply of farm labor. Growth in manufacturing, services, and other sectors of the economy improves opportunities outside agriculture, increasing the opportunity cost of remaining in agriculture. Thus, the supply of labor to agriculture decreases. As Figure 3.8 shows, the result is necessarily a reduction of labor in agriculture. Because of the tremendous growth of opportunities outside agriculture, the supply decrease is larger than the demand decrease. Thus, wages in agriculture increase.

Farmers have also responded to the falling prices in agriculture by taking high-cost farms and farmland out of agriculture. Farms may be high cost because they have infertile land or adverse weather. In many parts of the country, forests stand on land like this, land that was farmed 75 years ago. Today, farming this land requires too much labor, fertilizer, and other inputs. In other places, shopping malls stand on land that was used for farming just a few years ago. This land also left agriculture because it is high cost even though it is fertile, easy to farm, and located close to markets; land has high opportunity cost in agriculture if it has valuable alternative uses. Farming even the most fertile agricultural land is costly, if the land is also a prime site for a shopping center.

Figure 3.8 The Demand for and Supply of Labor in Agriculture

The initial wage is W_0 and the initial amount of farm labor is L_0. Technical change and falling output price cause a decrease in the demand for agriculture labor. At the same time, economic development in the nonagricultural sector raises the opportunity cost of being in agriculture, causing the supply of labor to agriculture to decrease. The wage for workers in agriculture goes up, although the amount of labor goes down.

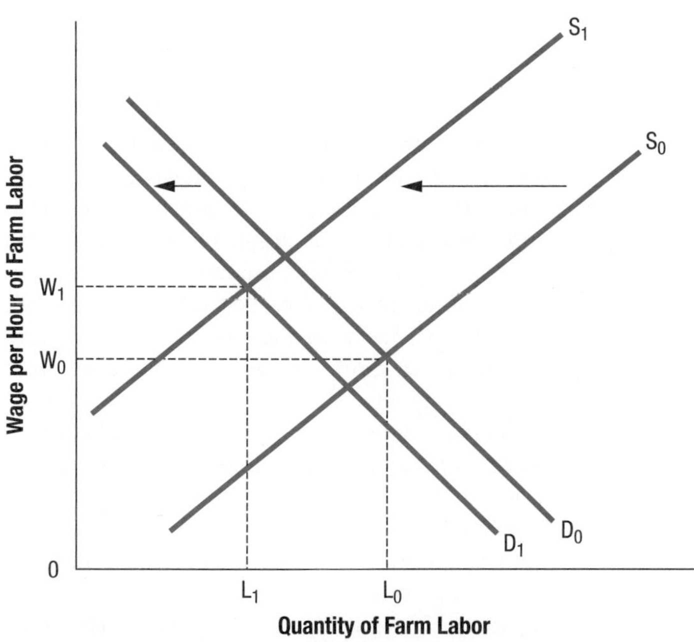

The tremendous productivity increases in agriculture have been accompanied by an enormous reallocation of labor resources (people) and land away from agriculture. This reallocation occurred in response to market forces, and in spite of government farm-support programs. Moreover, the reallocation has left the remaining farm population better off—relatively and absolutely. The median family income among people who call themselves farmers is above the median family income among nonfarmers, and the poverty rate is lower among farmers. Furthermore, the labor and land resources transferred from agriculture are now in more productive uses, increasing the total output of the economy.

The reforestation that has accompanied the land reallocations is a boon to the environment and the availability of relatively inexpensive farmland for suburban development has resulted in improved housing conditions in urban areas.

INFOTRAC College Edition

Keywords: *family farm and economic future*

Access InfoTrac at http://infotrac.cengage.com

Although productive, these reallocations can cause pain. Some family farms no longer are viable. Agricultural families see their children migrate to urban areas, breaking the family farming tradition. Some people promote subsidies to agriculture as a way of saving the rural agricultural environment. In terms of the population, however, it is too late to save the agricultural environment. The farmers have gone. Large family farms will continue to be profitable, even if government protection were completely eliminated. Their demand for resources and goods and services in rural areas, along with the many other advantages of rural life, would be sufficient to preserve many small towns.

Competitive Markets and Economic Profits

Two elements of agricultural markets are especially important for farmers. First, agriculture is risky; second, agricultural markets are competitive. Long-term changes in demand and supply of agricultural products create steady pressure to leave the farm; short-term events may create crisis conditions.

Risk. Most types of agriculture are risky; income for individual farmers from a single type of agriculture can fluctuate dramatically from year to year. At the beginning of a growing season, farmers make decisions about the use of their land, equipment, and labor in light of expected prices and profit. Often they borrow large amounts to buy land and to plant crops or build an inventory of livestock. The long lag between planting and harvesting crops or buying and selling livestock makes it hard for farmers to be sure they will have output to sell. Disease, pestilence, and localized bad weather (such as hailstorms) can wipe out a farmer's crop or herd. A run of bad luck can cause a farming operation tremendous financial and emotional stress.

INFOTRAC College Edition

Keywords: *crop insurance and income protection*

Access InfoTrac at http://infotrac.cengage.com

Besides this individual risk, farmers also face market risk. Unexpected price decreases because of a reduction in demand or increase in supply occur frequently in agriculture. The supply of farm products responds little to price changes in a particular year—after the potato crop is planted, the farmer has little opportunity to change quantity in response to a price increase or decrease. Nor does the demand for farm products—particularly broad categories of food such as meat, fruit, and vegetables—respond much to price changes. So in Figure 3.9 the original demand and supply curves, D_0 and S_0, for vegetables are quite steep. An increase in supply to S_1, perhaps caused by good weather, causes price to fall from P_0 to P_1. Price falls substantially because quantity demanded responds little to price change; thus, quantity exchanged increases only from Q_0 to Q_1. What happens to vegetable farmers' total revenue? Total revenue (price times quantity sold) in the original situation in Figure 3.9 is $0P_0$ times $0Q_0$. It is represented by the area of the rectangle $0P_0R_0Q_0$. In the new situation the relevant rectangle is $0P_1R_1Q_1$. By inspection, the area of $0P_1R_1Q_1$ is less than that of $0P_0R_0Q_0$. The new rectangle increases in area by $Q_0T_0R_1Q_1$ because more is sold, but the increase is more than offset by the reduction in

Figure 3.9 The Effect of an Increase in Supply

This figure shows a demand curve for which quantity demanded responds little to changes in price. Because of this unresponsiveness, an increase in supply (perhaps caused, ironically, by good weather) pushes price down by relatively more than it pushes quantity exchanged up. In this situation the total revenue for vegetable producers falls because of the supply increase. Before the supply increase, total revenue is measured by the area of the rectangle $0P_0R_0Q_0$; after, it is measured by the area of $0P_1R_1Q_1$.

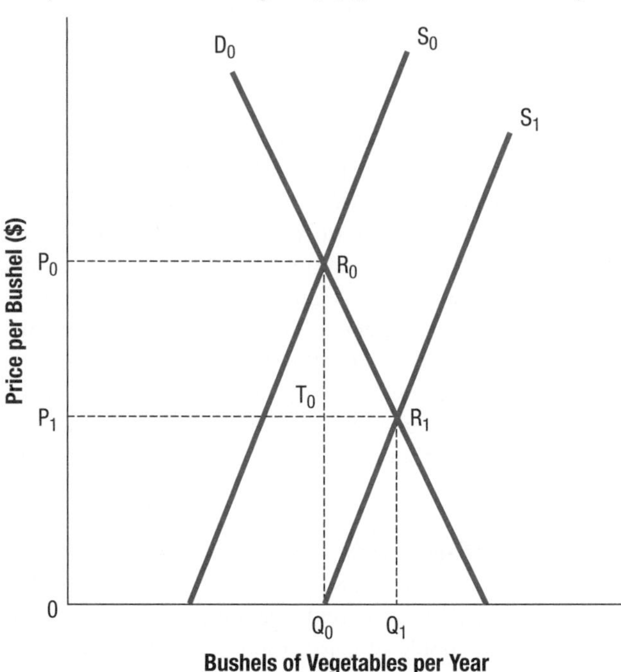

Competitive market – The two most important conditions (for this issues-oriented analysis) are that a market is competitive if the market has (1) many buyers and sellers so that both buyers and sellers are price takers and (2) easy entry of new producers so that new firms enter in response to economic profit and compete that profit away. More theory-oriented approaches add two conditions, namely that (1) firms in the industry produce the same or very similar products; and (2) both buyers and sellers have good information about market conditions.

area ($P_0R_0T_0P_1$) due to the lower price. Although farmers sell more, they receive less revenue than originally expected because the good weather leads to a large price decrease. Such an unexpected reduction in price can cause a large reduction in income, making it difficult if not impossible to repay loans and continue operation.

An analysis of an unexpected reduction in demand would show similar results. Because quantity supplied is relatively unresponsive to a price change, a reduction in demand causes a sharp drop in farm prices and farm income. Farmers experienced this during the Great Depression, when agricultural prices fell more than other prices in response to reduced demand. They also experienced it in the late 1990s when the Asian economic crisis reduced the demand for U.S. agricultural products. Moreover, farm products are subject to variation in demand because of foreign trade. Suppose Argentina has a bumper wheat crop. Argentine wheat may displace U.S. wheat in other countries, reducing the demand for U.S. wheat. Farmers face substantial market risk because weather is unpredictable and because quantity demanded and quantity supplied respond little to price changes. The fact that most agricultural markets are competitive magnifies the risk.

COMPETITION. Many agriculture industries—corn, wheat, beef, and poultry—are examples of competitive industries operating in **competitive markets**. In our issues-oriented approach we emphasize two characteristics of a competitive market:

- a large number of buyers and producers (sellers)
- free entry of new producers in response to profitable conditions

Pure economic theory also specifies that a competitive market or industry is one in which different producers produce identical (very similar) products and both buyers and sellers have good information about market conditions. The large number of buyers and sellers means that no one individual or small group of individuals can affect market price. The free entry condition means that profitable industries attract new producers that produce more of the product, until the profits are competed away. Let's use an agricultural example to explain.

Consider the kiwi fruit. This fruit, from China via New Zealand, has exploded in popularity in the United States. But the first California farmers to grow and sell kiwis took a big chance. Such innovative farm products as the Belgian endive and the ugli fruit have floundered in the U.S. market. The early kiwi farmers were successful; the price received for their product more than covered the marginal cost of production. Figure 3.10 describes the situation. As an approximation, assume that the supply curve for a particular year is vertical—VSR – S_0. Such a supply curve is sometimes called a very-short-run supply curve because it does not allow for adjustments in planned production. We assume that after the production decision is made for a particular year, farmers can do nothing to adjust the amount they sell. (Weather can affect the supply curve by moving it to the left or the right.) With demand curve D_0, the equilibrium price and quantity exchanged are P_0 and Q_0. The price these farmers receive is above their marginal cost of production, C_0, which includes a normal rate of earnings on the investment made by the farmers. (The marginal cost—supply price—is C_0 by assumption.) Therefore, the market price P_0 is above the supply price. This price gives existing farmers **economic profit**, which is a rate of earning greater than necessary to attract resources into the industry. If these farmers are operating at capacity, this situation is stable—they will continue to earn economic profits—until other farmers start growing kiwis.

Economic profit – A rate of earning in excess of the minimum necessary to attract economic resources into a particular use.

Figure 3.10 The Expansion of U.S. Kiwi Production

This figure shows that competitive farmers have incentive to supply food in response to consumer demand. At quantity Q_0, the demand price, P_0, is greater than the cost of producing an additional unit, C_0. Because a producer will receive a price greater than the cost of production for one more unit, some producer will increase profit by doing so. So long as the demand price is greater than the supply price, the very-short-run supply curve will march to the right, causing market price to fall and quantity exchanged to increase.

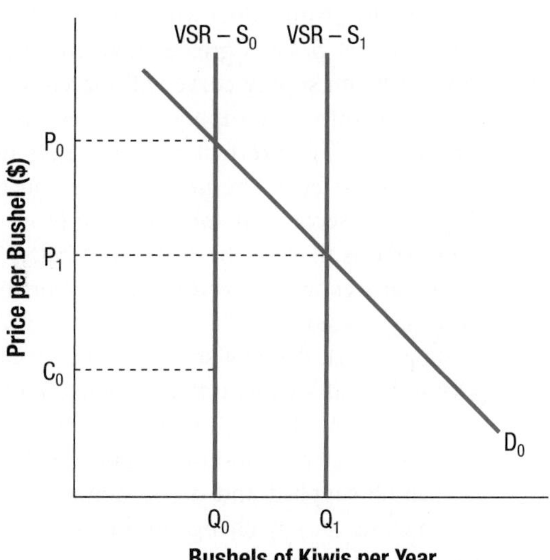

ADDITIONAL INSIGHT

What Does it Mean for a Farmer to Break Even?

According to the U.S. Department of Agriculture (USDA), the average wheat farmer in the Northern Great Plains had 527 acres of with costs of about $160 an acre. Can this farm prosper if it just breaks even? Operating costs—seed, fertilizer, and so on—were about $52 an acre. The average farm family provided most of the labor; the cost of labor per acre is therefore an implicit cost. The farmer does not directly pay this implicit cost to a third party. It is, however, an important opportunity cost. According to the USDA this opportunity cost was $11.60 per acre. This opportunity cost is then about $6,000 per year. If the farm business breaks even, the farmer at least has the $6,000. Moreover, suppose the farmer owns the land. In this region the opportunity cost of land is about $36 an acre; so with 527 acres the farmer also earns about $19,000. The farmer's income would also include an opportunity cost for the investment in machinery and equipment and for the investment in operating inputs—seeds and fertilizer must be purchased and used months before the crop is harvested and sold. Although the USDA does not have the average value of these investments in this report, for farms in the Intermediate Class the investment might be around $150,000. If the necessary return to keep resources in agriculture is 8 percent, this adds another $12,000. So the wheat farmer in the Northern Great Plains who breaks even still generates income: $37,000. Moreover, many of these farmers have off-farm employment, so their family income is much greater.

Suppose we consider the large family farms. If the farmer owns the business assets, the farm family average investment might be about $1.5 million. If the necessary return is 8 percent, then when this average large farm breaks even, the family earns $120,000 plus the opportunity cost of the labor provided by the family. Farm income is not actually this high because the farmers have borrowed to finance their investment. So a farmer who financed half of the investment with an 8 percent loan would have interest cost of $60,000 and a return on the owned part of the investment of $60,000. Since operating a large farm leaves little time for off farm employment, the opportunity cost of the labor would be well above that for the wheat farmer discussed above. Because many commercial farmers own a large proportion of their assets, when they break even, their income is indeed very high.

Other farmers will soon see their kiwi-growing neighbors driving BMWs; or perhaps the county extension agent will tell them about kiwis' profitability. As they become aware of the profits, they will invest in kiwi production, which increases supply. So long as the market price is greater than the supply price (marginal cost of production), the very-short-run supply curve will march to the right, as more and more farmers learn of the opportunity. As supply increases, the market price will fall. As more farms are converted to kiwi production, the supply price (marginal cost) will increase for at least three reasons. First, the new farmers and the new land may not be well suited to kiwi production. Second, as more orange groves are converted to kiwi production, the land transferred is likely to be better and better suited to orange production. Third, as more orange groves are converted, the opportunity cost of kiwis (the value of the oranges given up) increases.

Suppose that the very-short-run supply curve advances to VSR – S_1, pushing the market price to P_1 and the quantity exchanged to Q_1. Assume also that the supply price (marginal cost) rises to P_1. Because the market price equals the supply price, farmers no longer find it desirable to enter the industry. Supply will stop increasing. With quantity demanded equal to quantity supplied and no economic profits or losses the market is in equilibrium. No reason exists for any change in this market unless changes occur in other factors affecting demand and supply.

As new farmers began kiwi production the original ones saw steady erosion of their economic profits. Depending upon how long it takes to establish kiwi production, these profits may exist for a year or two or perhaps as long as five years. Farmers, who take the risks in producing new crops or have the good luck of being among the first producers, earn their rewards during this period. The economic profits eventually will be competed away; latecomers receive only a normal rate of earnings. Economic profits alert people that rewards are available to those who risk putting their resources into producing the product. Besides their information role, these profits motivate people to take action that benefits other members of society.

Farmers operate in an inherently risky, competitive industry. Competitive markets ensure that economic profit will be competed away. If farming is inherently more risky than other industries, the normal rate of earnings in farming will be greater than the normal rate of earnings in other industries, which compensates farmers for taking greater risks. In addition to the greater compensation, farmers have ways of reducing the risk that they face.[7]

- First, they can buy crop insurance to protect against natural disasters.
- Second, they can diversify. At one time the wisdom of diversification was explained with an agricultural example: "Don't put all of your eggs in one basket." In the nineteenth century, Ireland depended heavily on one crop—one variety of potatoes—and suffered famine when it failed. South American farmers, who rely on potatoes for subsistence, have diversified for centuries. They developed different varieties of potatoes for (1) different altitudes in the Andes, (2) different weather patterns, and (3) immunities to different diseases. If one failed, another would likely succeed.
- Third, U.S. farmers can use commodity market techniques to reduce their risk.[8]
- Fourth, market participants who are more willing to bear risk may voluntarily assume other participants' risks—for a price, of course. Poultry farmers, for instance, have shifted much of their market risk to large processors such as Tyson. Poultry farmers previously suffered unstable incomes because of the variability of input costs and output price. Most poultry farmers now contract with the processors, with most of the payment dependent upon how efficiently farmers convert feed into pounds of bird. The price variability still exists, but the processors, who bear the risk, are more efficient in handling it.

Keywords: *farming, competition, income, and successful farming*

Access InfoTrac at http://infotrac.cengage.com

Risk is not unique to agriculture; moreover, people who take on risk get rewarded for it. Producers who can produce in more or less risky industries will only stay in the more risky industry, if their earnings are greater. This implies that producers in risky industries have a higher normal rate of earnings. They require a bigger return to stay in the industry. The fact that farmers face risk does not distinguish them from other business people who face risk without the government providing them with price supports.

Keywords: *opportunity cost and farm*

Access InfoTrac at http://infotrac.cengage.com

PRICE CONTROLS

The most visible and costly farm programs have been those designed to increase the price that farmers receive for such commodities as corn, cotton, milk, peanuts, rice, corn,

[7]These arguments are beyond the scope of this book. For a discussion, see Bruce L. Gardner, *The Governing of Agriculture* (Lawrence, KS: Regents Press of Kansas, 1981).

[8]Chapter 6 in Gardner provides an accessible analysis of this topic.

tobacco, and wheat. Although the methods may differ from crop to crop and over time, the basic idea is that the government guarantees a minimum price for the product. The government might:

1. establish a minimum price—a price floor—and take appropriate action to maintain that price
2. use regulation to control supply and thus support the price
3. pay the farmer a deficiency payment, which is the difference between the market price and some guaranteed price

Price floor– A minimum price set by government, below which the market price is not allowed to go.

Price Floor. **Price floors** have been used extensively for crops, such as corn, rice, and wheat. The program is sometimes presented as a way to keep prices up in good years by allowing the government to buy and store some of the bountiful harvest, which in turn would be sold in lean years, increasing availability and reducing price. Although biblical in concept, the program has not worked in this way.

Suppose the government establishes a price floor for corn at P_1 as in Figure 3.11. The equilibrium price is P_0 and the equilibrium quantity is Q_0. The quantity demanded of corn falls from Q_0 to Q_1, but farmers plan to supply Q_2, which is more than consumers plan to buy. An excess supply of corn, as measured by the distance from Q_1 to Q_2, $Q_2 - Q_1$, emerges. To hold the price at P_1 someone has to buy the excess supply. The government, in effect, does so. Rather than buying the corn, in the typical program the government takes the corn as collateral in a loan to the farmer. The government lends an amount equal to the value of the corn put up as collateral, where the price floor is the value per bushel. If the market price stays below the price floor, the farmer defaults on the loan, sticking the government with the corn. The loan is called a *nonrecourse loan*, meaning that the government must accept the corn as full payment for the loan. The farmer is in a win-win situation. If the market price goes above the floor, she reclaims the corn

Figure 3.11 Price Floor for Corn
In equilibrium, the price of corn per bushel is P_0 and the quantity exchanged is Q_0. Now suppose the government sets a support price at P_1. Excess supply exists because quantity supplied is Q_2 and quantity demanded is Q_1. The excess supply, $Q_2 - Q_1$, will cause price to return to equilibrium unless something is done. In a price support program, the government buys the excess supply and stores it.

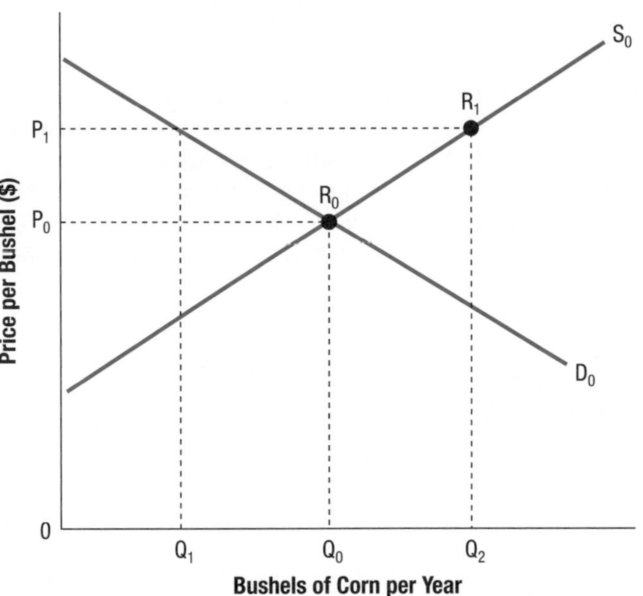

and sells it at the higher price. If the price stays below the floor, the government takes the corn and the farmer takes the money.

At the equilibrium price and quantity, total expenditures by consumers and total revenues of farmers are measured by the area $0P_0R_0Q_0$. With the price support, the total revenues increase to the area $0P_1R_1Q_2$. To purchase the quantity Q_1, consumers must pay a price higher than the equilibrium price. To buy the excess supply, consumers as taxpayers must pay the support price times the quantity $Q_2 - Q_1$.

Corn farmers earn increased revenue because they sell more at a higher price. Consumers—as direct buyers and taxpayers—spend more but receive less. Part of the cost of the program to consumers is the higher price they pay. Another part is the value of the consumption they give up. A price support program, if effective, eventually results in the government accumulating surpluses, which it must store. If it dumps the surplus on the domestic market during lean years, farmers become unhappy. If it tries to sell it on the world market, it has to subsidize the sale, violating free trade arrangements and upsetting friendly countries. Storing the excess supply is costly, and giving it away is difficult. Some might be sold, at subsidized prices, to developing countries, which otherwise would not buy it, and some might be given away in school lunch and commodity distribution programs.

Output Constraints. Eventually, the problems of storing the surplus corn created by the price floor above the equilibrium price create serious political problems. Two avenues of escape appear attractive. One is to reduce the storage and disposal problem by requiring or inducing farmers to limit their production. Suppose the government sets a price support of P_1 in Figure 3.12. To participate, farmers must take land out of production, which shifts supply to S_1 and eliminates the excess supply.

Farmers would have higher total revenue because quantity demanded responds little to a change in price. Thus, farmers lose the revenue measured by the area of the rectangle labeled A because of the smaller quantity exchanged. But they gain the revenue

Figure 3.12 Output Constraints for Corn
In equilibrium the price of corn per bushel is P_0 and the quantity exchanged is Q_0. Now suppose the government wants the price of corn to be P_1. The government can require farmers to take 15 percent of their land out of production in an effort to reduce output by 15 percent. If successful, the supply curve will decrease from S_0 to S_1, which will push the price up to P_1. The government will have established a higher price without causing excess supply. The government need not buy corn or make deficiency payments. Farmers, however, have strong incentives to evade the output constraints in various ways.

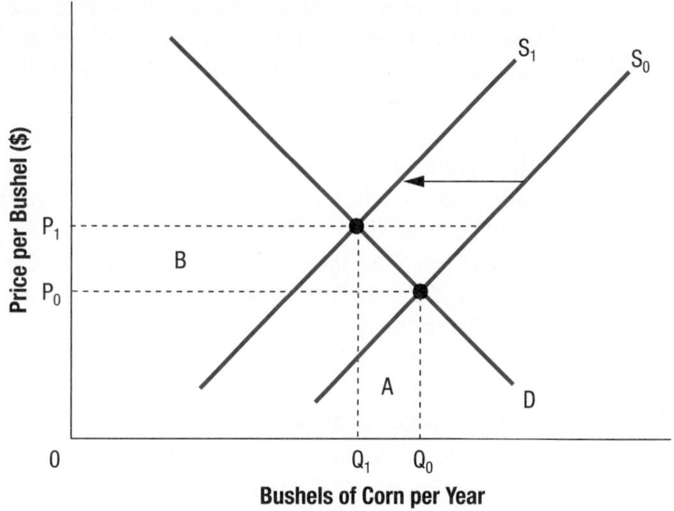

indicated by the rectangle labeled B. Because their output would be less, their total cost would be less. Therefore, their net profit would increase. In addition, farmers may be paid for taking their land out of production.

Output constraints appeal to politicians because they shift part of the burden of supporting farmers from taxpayers to consumers without causing excess supply. The costs of the programs are hidden because consumers pay higher prices for many different products rather than taxes for a few large items in the federal budget. Government programs are more popular if their costs are hidden.

Output constraints rarely work as advertised. Suppose the goal of the program is to reduce corn production by 10 percent. At first glance, taking 10 percent of the corn land out of production would seem to be the answer. But this won't work. First, farmers will take their less fertile land out of production. Second, they will farm the remaining 90 percent of their corn land more intensively by using more fertilizers, labor, and other inputs. Presumably, the farmers were farming at the lowest possible cost before any land was taken out of production. Now when they use more inputs per acre of land to produce corn, the opportunity cost of the corn is higher. Thus, the amount of corn produced will not fall by 10 percent, and the attempt to eliminate excess supply or deficiency payments will not succeed. Farmers also resent the bureaucratic controls needed to ensure that they keep the agreement and keep land idle. Idling good farmland is clearly wasteful. It was not uncommon in the 1960s and 1970s for 50 million acres of farmland per year to be idle because of farm programs. Paying people not to use their land is politically embarrassing as well as wasteful. A second avenue of escape from political embarrassment is to establish target prices and make deficiency payments.

Target price– A guaranteed price for a product. The product is sold at the market price and the government pays the producer the difference between it and the guaranteed price.

Target Prices and Deficiency Payments. Given the problems of storage and disposal, the government may tell farmers that they will be guaranteed a certain price for their crop, say, corn. This guaranteed price is the **target price**. But the government does not support this price; it does not buy the excess supply produced at the target price.

Farmers decide how much corn to produce on the basis of the target price. In Figure 3.13 with a target price of P_1, farmers plan to produce Q_2 bushels of corn per year. When this amount of corn reaches the market, the market price falls to P_2, the demand price for that quantity. There is no excess supply, but the price falls below the guarantee. So now the government must make good its promised target price to farmers. It makes a deficiency payment, which is the difference between the target price and the market price multiplied by the number of bushels of corn that the farmer sells.

The target price system seems to have several advantages over the price support system. First, no excess supply. Second, no direct export subsidies. Third, consumers avoid paying an elevated price for their corn flakes and other corn products.

But the target price system differs little from the price support system. Figure 3.13 shows a potential excess supply of $Q_2 - Q_1$, just as if a price support were set at P_1. The output of corn and the amount of money received by farmers are the same under both systems. The excess supply disappears because the price falls to P_2. For the last bushel produced, the supply price is P_1 and the demand price is P_2. Just as with the price support program, the cost of producing the last unit is greater than its value. Resources that could be used to produce something else are wasted. The government is, in fact, subsidizing buyers to take the potential excess supply off its hands. Thus, the target price system deals with excess supply by implicitly subsidizing domestic and foreign buyers.

The subsidy to foreign buyers arises both with price floors and target prices. With price floors, the subsidy only occurs if the domestic price is greater than the world. With sugar

Figure 3.13 Target Price for Corn

In equilibrium, the price of corn per bushel is P_0 and the quantity exchanged is Q_0. Now suppose the government sets a target price for corn at P_1. Farmers will produce the quantity Q_2 because the government has guaranteed the target price. But consumers will buy only the quantity Q_1 at that price. Therefore the target price will not be realized in the market. For consumers to buy the quantity Q_2, price must fall to P_2. To give the farmers the guaranteed price, the government must give farmers $P_1 - P_2$ per bushel as a deficiency payment.

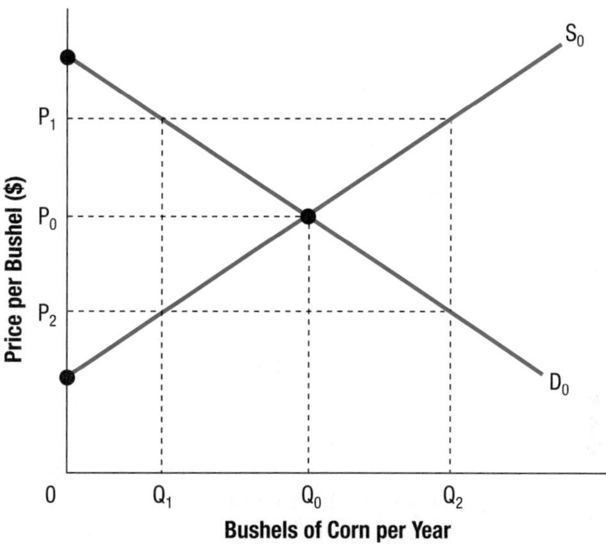

the U.S. price is higher than the world price, so rather than subsidizing foreign buyers, it is necessary to use tariffs or import quotas to keep foreign producers out of the U.S. market. Such policies, of course, fly in the face of the stated U.S. policy of free trade. With other products the U.S. price can create an excess supply, which the U.S. government may sell on world markets by providing subsidies to foreign purchases. This, too, is in contradiction to a free-trade policy and might violate certain international agreements. For these products a target-price system is a way to subsidize foreign buyers without seeming to do so. U.S. agricultural programs and government programs sometimes can be best understood by realizing that the politicians try to hide their consequences.

Keywords: *price support and United States price*

Access InfoTrac at http://infotrac.cengage.com

A price-floor system extracts subsidies from consumers for farmers in two ways. First, consumers pay higher prices for farm products. Second, consumers pay taxes so the government can buy the excess supply. A target price system results in a market price below the equilibrium price. It taxes consumers to pay farmers. With the target price system, all of the extra money for farmers comes directly from taxpayers, creating two political problems. One, the size of the subsidy is apparent to taxpayers. Two, farmers are clearly receiving of government transfer payments—welfare payments.

Political rent seeking– Attempt by certain individuals or groups to encourage government activity that will result in an economic advantage for them.

RENT SEEKING

Agricultural policies impose large costs on consumers and create difficulties for politicians and the government. You might wonder why we continue to have such agricultural programs. The answer may be **political rent seeking**. Political rent seeking occurs when people seek economic advantage through government action. It is in contrast to

Economic rent seeking– Attempt by people to gain an economic advantage through production of new or better products or through production of products at a lower cost.

economic rent seeking, which occurs when people seek economic advantage by producing new or better products or by producing products at a lower cost and selling for a lower price.

The size of the government giveaway programs to farmers shows that farmers are successful political rent seekers. Their success may seem strange because the farm population is less than 2 percent of the total population. How do farmers have enough political influence to warrant such preferential treatment?

The answer may be that farmers of a particular type, such as sugar farmers, are a small group of producers with a strong interest in getting a higher price for sugar. A small increase in the price of sugar can generate big profits for sugar farmers. So they are willing to put a lot of time, effort, and money into convincing members of Congress to raise the price of sugar. For instance, in 2004 political action committees associated with the growing of sugar cane and sugar beets contributed over $2 million to federal political campaigns.

Legislators weigh the gratitude that sugar farmers will have for a price increase against the reactions of numerous consumers to higher sugar prices. Although consumers far outnumber sugar farmers, no single consumer or small group of consumers has a big stake in the price of sugar. The increase in the cost of sugar results in only a small increase in any single family's cost of living. Even if they are aware of the program and its impact, most families probably won't even be angry enough to write a letter about it to a member of Congress. Few people would make political contributions to defeat legislators simply because they voted to increase the price of sugar.

A small group of committed people with a big stake in a desired political decision, like a higher price for sugar, has a good chance of obtaining that action. This is so because the cost of the action will be spread over a larger group of people. No single person will bear a large enough cost to attempt to defeat the proposed action. Consumer lobby groups, such as Ralph Nader's various enterprises, do exist, but these groups rarely have the power or resources of an industry lobby group.

The sugar industry is important in just a few states, but sugar PACs and presumably individuals in the industry made donations in 2004 to almost every Senate race. Not surprisingly, it obtains favorable legislation. The sugar industry is one of many in which the benefits are concentrated in a small group, and the costs are spread over a larger group. Similarly, the 130,000 farmers who receive the bulk of the corn and wheat subsidies are sufficiently concentrated to be a potent political force in several Midwestern states.

But how do a few thousand farmers in a couple of states exert sufficient political influence to obtain the government favors? The answer is *logrolling*, which might be defined as members of Congress trading votes to pass legislation of interest to each other. Thus, legislators from sugar-producing states vote to support wheat farmers, and, in return, members of Congress from wheat-growing states vote to support sugar farmers.

So, even if the peanut and rice farmers lack sufficient clout to enact their desired legislation, they can leverage their political influence through logrolling. Will the members of Congress from a state where corn growers have political influence vote for a sugar subsidy in return for votes for a corn subsidy? The ability of extremely small agricultural groups to obtain favorable government treatment suggests that they will—that such logrolling occurs.

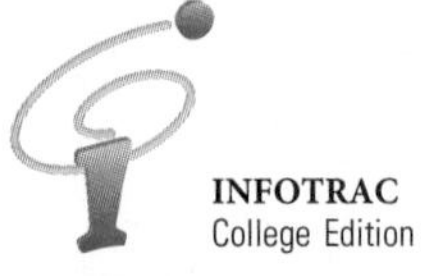

Keyword: *Farm bill*

Access InfoTrac at http://infotrac.cengage.com

The logrolling agreements need not be explicit—a wink and a nod will do—because of the way Congress handles farm legislation. Every five years or so, Congress considers farm legislation in a single omnibus farm bill. If you want your part of the farm program to pass, you must vote for the whole package.

ADDITIONAL INSIGHT

Price Gouging and the Twin Hurricanes

Governments sometimes impose price ceilings rather than price floors in markets where consumers can generate political power. Perhaps the most prevalent example of price ceilings, the maximum price that a seller can legally collect, is in the housing market. Rent controls exist in many cities throughout the world with the associated excess demands (shortages), personal discrimination, and illegal evasions of the price control. These behaviors are exactly the ones discussed in Chapter 2's analysis of command economies. People, who generally accept this analysis of price ceilings in the general case, often think they are appropriate as a response to a natural disaster. This opinion is so strong that about 30 states have explicit laws against price gouging if the president or the state's governor has declared an emergency. Florida, for instance, prohibits unconscionable prices for essentials in a declared emergency. Other states limit the permissible price increases to 10 percent, unless the seller can demonstrate a compelling rationale. Georgia prohibits any price increase at all.

As our analysis in Chapter 2 discusses, imposing an effective price ceiling will prevent the rationing of the available product to users who are willing to pay. An excess demand is created, and the price system is not permitted to play its information and motivation roles. Charging someone the maximum that he or she is willing to pay for a necessity in an emergency, when there is no alternative, is often considered exploitation. An example might be charging $10,000 for taking a seriously injured person five miles to an emergency room. The exchange that takes place is not the voluntary exchange discussed in Chapter 2. Many people would think it unfair, unconscionable, and, if not illegal, should be. The price gouging of people in dire straits in an emergency presents ethical as well as legal and economic challenges. The untold number of instances of both friends and strangers helping others during the hurricane tragedies demonstrates that many people meet this ethical challenge in conscionable ways.

We are more concerned, however, with the frequent complaints about price gouging that arise after a disaster because of supply disruption of, say, gasoline or because of a general demand increase for, say, lumber. As we have studied in this chapter either of these two events will cause a price increase. If quantity demanded of gasoline or of lumber is not very responsive to price and if the same is true of the quantity supplied, price will increase substantially. As you may remember, complaints about gasoline price increases could be found throughout the country after the twin hurricanes, Katrina and Rita. The price of gasoline jumped 20 or 30 percent to over $3 a gallon after Hurricane Katrina, even in areas of the country not hit by the hurricanes. Is it unconscionable to allow a 30 percent increase in price of gasoline that is already in stock in a state not directly hit by the hurricane, say Georgia or Oklahoma?

Because the hurricanes had such extensive effects on refineries, pipelines, oil production, shipping into New Orleans, and ground transportation, it's hard to come to grips with how markets responded to them. Let's consider a simpler situation in the gasoline market. In August 2003, gasoline prices in Phoenix rose from about $1.50 a gallon to $2.10 and then late in September fell back to $1.80, price changes similar to those that occurred in late summer 2005 in response to hurricanes. The price changes in Phoenix occurred because of a break in a pipeline, a pipeline that supplied 30 percent of Phoenix's gasoline. To cut consumption by 30 percent, the Federal Trade Commission estimated that price would have had to increase to $3.75 per gallon. In fact, the price only went to $2.10. Therefore, the price increase must have increased the quantity supplied to Phoenix, other things equal. How did this happen? Phoenix stations bought gasoline from the West Coast, which was delivered through the Los Angeles to Phoenix pipeline. To attract gasoline from Los Angeles (where it was more expensive anyway), Phoenix stations had to bid up the price. They were so successful that they attracted gasoline from refineries as far away as Northern California, Oregon, and Washington. We know this because the break in the Tucson to Phoenix pipeline caused prices to increase by diminishing amounts all the way up the West Coast. The higher price in Los Angeles attracted gasoline from and pushed price up in Northern California and so on up the coast. So the Washington state refineries were, in effect, providing gasoline to Phoenix and Washington state customers were sharing in the pain of the broken pipeline. The Phoenix stations also trucked in gasoline from Tucson, a more expensive way to transport gasoline. So prices went up in Tucson, as well, with the effects following the pipeline east to El Paso. With more trucks transporting gasoline to Phoenix, congestion occurred at the Tucson storage depots. The diversion of the trucks from serving areas surrounding Tucson spread the price increases throughout the area.

Just as with the twin hurricanes, the price increases spread throughout the West, even though the supply disruption was effectively contained to Phoenix. The price increase that followed the supply disruption served three purposes. It *informed* refiners, pipeline operators, and trucking operators that gasoline had become more valuable in Phoenix. The prices increase spread in waves from the east and west. Had this supply disruption in Phoenix been permanent, it would have *motivated* refineries in the west to increase production and those in the east—because they could no longer serve Tucson—to reduce production. The prices increases provided incentives (motivation) to consumers to reduce quantity demanded, with consumers in the West and Tucson, giving up some of the gasoline that they used for lower-value uses—maybe college students rode the bus rather than driving their cars. The price increases throughout the West *rationed* the available supplies to consumers.

Suppose the price of gasoline had risen to $3.75 a gallon in Phoenix and had remained at say $1.80 a gallon in Los Angeles. A consumer in Phoenix might have valued an additional gallon at $3.50 so that she could visit a sick friend. A consumer in Los Angeles may have been using the last gallon, valued at $1.80, to find a closer parking space. The Phoenix consumer would be willing to pay the Los Angeles consumer $3.50 for the gallon of gasoline. The LA consumer would accept any price above $1.80. If they trade in this range, both parties are better off and the increase in value is $1.70. Now suppose the price of gasoline goes to $2.10 in LA and Tucson. Consumers outside of Phoenix, the area directly hit by the supply disruption, now give up gasoline that has uses valued at less than $2.10; the gasoline they sacrifice is diverted to Phoenix. Consequently, Phoenix users would no longer have to give up the use of gasoline valued at amounts up to $3.75 a gallon. The gasoline station that raises its price to $2.10 in LA might make 30 cents profit and the LA consumer saves 1.80 because he doesn't buy that gallon of gasoline. So far, we have a profit for the station. It's selling the same gasoline that it would have sold for $1.80 for $2.10. But the Phoenix consumer is getting something worth $3.50 for only $2.10. She is better off by $1.40. Allowing prices to go up in LA and other places where costs had not increased led to this valuable trade; two parties in the transaction are better off, the third party is no worse off. The information and motivation to make this trade would be incredibly costly to gather in any way other than through the price system.

These are the types of trades made possible by the big gasoline price increases after the hurricanes. Yes, the producers and distributors of the gasoline made profits; but consumers benefited because the price increases were spread throughout the country so that people who placed higher value on the marginal units of gasoline were able to get them. Consumers who would not have been affected otherwise by the hurricane experienced losses. But the gains to consumers from being able to purchase gasoline for higher-valued uses outweighed the losses to consumers who sacrificed lower-valued uses of gasoline. It's hard to imagine how the government, which brought us the FEMA disaster relief after Katrina, could have figured out how to cope with the closed refineries, shutdown pipelines, and disrupted transportation. Individuals responding to market signals and making voluntary changes based on profitability were able to almost completely overcome any expected chaos in the gasoline market. Yes, there were a few cases of "unconscionable" price gouging and there were some spot shortages, but by and large people could get the gasoline they were willing and able to pay for. The people stranded in New Orleans, however, were not able to get the transportation they were willing and able to pay for because for whatever reason government prevented these trades from being made. In one example, some hotels had arranged for buses to transport people out of the French Quarter, at a price, but the government would not permit the buses to go to the hotels. Ironically, only one bus made it out of the Quarter; it was a renegade bus operated by an individual who charged unconscionably high price. Nevertheless, we suspect that the people who escaped on this bus were grateful for the possibly criminal actions of the bus operator.

In the previous chapter, we discussed how private-sector firms, such as Wal-Mart, had a response superior to FEMA's in terms of delivering market goods and services. There we suggested that the profit motive and local information improved the decentralized response. To that conclusion, we now add the ability of the price system to convey information, to ration, and to motivate, without relying on costly information, as another reason for the superior response.

Summary

In this chapter, we first discussed how the laws of demand and supply interact to determine market equilibrium. The equilibrium price and quantity are the price and quantity that coordinate consumers' and producers' plans. The price adjusts until the quantity that consumers plan to buy matches the quantity that producers plan to sell—until quantity demanded equals quantity supplied.

Changes in demand and supply cause the equilibrium price and quantity to change. For instance, an increase in demand means that consumers place a higher value on a particular product. This causes an increase in the equilibrium price and quantity. As price increases, quantity supplied increases.

An increase in supply means that producers can produce at a lower marginal cost. This causes a decrease in the equilibrium price and an increase in the equilibrium quantity. As price decreases, quantity demanded increases.

An increase in demand and an increase in supply both cause equilibrium quantity to increase. But the demand increase causes price to increase, and the supply increase causes price to decrease. When both changes happen together, we cannot predict what will happen to equilibrium price.

Federal farm programs supposedly are designed to attack farm poverty, preserve the family farm, and stabilize farm prices and income. Although these programs provide large benefits to wealthy farmers, they do not particularly help poor farmers or small family farmers.

Price-support programs and target-price programs give the biggest benefits to farmers who produce the most and thus surely have the most wealth. These programs are expensive for consumers. The price support programs lead to a large excess supply of farm products. Significant storage costs and waste result. Price-support programs and target-price programs both cause significant problems in international relations.

Farm-support programs appear to exist because small groups of farmers can organize into effective political groups. They use their political influence to seek political rents, and they do so quite successfully.

Key Terms

Decrease in demand
Substitute
Complement
Increase in demand
Normal good
Inferior good
Increase in supply
Decrease in supply
Competitive markets
Economic profit
Price floor
Target price
Political rent seeking
Economic rent seeking

Review Questions

1. What factors will lead to a change in demand? If the good in question is a normal good, briefly explain how each factor will affect demand.
2. Use your knowledge of demand to answer each of the following questions:
   a. How would a freeze in Florida affect the demand for oranges?
   b. The price of coffee falls. How is the demand for coffee affected?
   c. Income falls. How will this affect the demand for beans, an inferior good?
   d. How will a fall in the price of peanut butter affect the demand for jelly?
   e. The media report that red apples are sprayed with a substance that allegedly causes cancer. What would be the likely effect of this news on the demand for apples?
   f. How would an East Coast hurricane affect the demand and supply of lumber in the affected area?
3. Briefly describe the difference between a change in quantity supplied and a change in supply. What will cause each of these changes to occur?
4. Use a graph of supply and demand to illustrate each of the following:
   a. equilibrium price and quantity
   b. an increase in demand and its effect on the equilibrium values
   c. a decrease in supply and its effect on the equilibrium values

d. a relatively small decrease in demand and a relatively large increase in supply and their effect on the equilibrium values

5. Explain in words and use graphs of demand and supply to illustrate what happens to the price and quantity exchanged of each of the following:
   a. new cars in the United States, if the price of steel increases
   b. iPods, if the teenage population increases
   c. bread, if wheat-fertilizer prices increase
   d. fur coats, if conservation laws restrict the number of fur-bearing animals that can be harvested
   e. hamburgers, if the fight against "mad cow" disease raised the cost of growing cattle and consumers become more worried about getting the disease
   f. public transit in Washington, D.C. if a hurricane shut down refineries on the Gulf Coast that supply the East Coast with gasoline
6. Cite and briefly describe some specific examples of the U.S. government farm policy. Explain differences between the effects of price supports and target prices.
7. Suppose the government announced that it was going to treat the agricultural industry the same way that it treats the retail industry. That is, it will eliminate all price support programs and all deficiency payment programs. What would be the effect on farm poverty? On the number of farmers? On food production? On food prices?
8. Explain the risks involved with farming. Explain why government programs are not necessary for farmers to deal with these risks.
9. Some people argue that no reason exists today for government to be so heavily involved with agriculture. These people believe that agricultural programs exist to satisfy political constituencies. Given that only 2 percent of the U.S. population is in agriculture, how does agriculture gather so much political support?
10. Use InfoTrac or some other means to research a particular government program that benefits a specific agricultural crop, such as sugar, peanuts, or rice. Explain how the analysis in this chapter helps you to understand this program.
11. Based on the box titled "OECD Farm Policy," compare New Zealand's farm programs with those of the United States.
12. Explain the all-or-nothing fallacy (see the box on OECD farm policy). Can you think of other examples?
13. Using the information in the Additional Insight regarding price gouging and hurricanes, use a demand and supply diagram to illustrate what happened in Phoenix in August 2003. What would have happened if the governor of Arizona had immediately declared and emergency and frozen the market price at $1.50 per gallon? Use the diagram in your answer.
14. Economic News Online, http://www.swcollege.com/bef/econ_news.html Go to this site and choose the Equilibrium category under Fundamentals and choose an EconNews story that interests you. Read the full summary and answer the questions posed.

Web Sites

- Economic Research Service, United States Department of Agriculture.
  This site provides official statistics regarding U.S. agriculture and much more. A good source for information about the new farm bill—**http://www.ers.usda.gov**
- The Environmental Working Group.
  This site provides detailed data on U.S. government payments to farmers by state, ZIP code, and by individual recipient—**http://www.ewg.org/farming**
- The Agriculture and Food Policy Center at Texas A&M University.
  Land grant colleges and universities provide much research into and about agriculture. Their sites are designed to some extent to help farmers. They also provide much information about agriculture markets and government programs—**http://www.afpc.tamu.edu**
- Cato Institute.
  The Cato Institute is a market-oriented advocacy and research organization. A "farm bill" search returns numerous sources that are critical of government policies—**http://www.cato.org**
- The Heritage Foundation
  The Heritage Foundation is a market-oriented advocacy and research organization. An "agriculture subsidy" search returns multiple sources that are critical of government agricultural policy—**http://www.heritage.org**

APPENDIX TO CHAPTER 3

The Price Elasticity of Demand

OUTLINE

The price elasticity of demand and other elasticity measures are important tools of the applied economist. This appendix presents a brief discussion of demand elasticity. Its purpose is to explain the elasticity coefficient, to discuss the relationship between price elasticity and total revenue, and to discuss the determinants of price elasticity.

THE ELASTICITY COEFFICIENT

Coefficient of the price elasticity of demand– The percentage change in quantity demanded divided by the percentage change in price; it is a measure of the responsiveness of consumers to price changes.

The **coefficient of the price elasticity of demand** is the percentage change in quantity demanded divided by the percentage change in price. It shows the responsiveness of quantity demanded by consumers to a price change. It is in percentage terms to make comparisons among different products more meaningful.

The actual calculation of the elasticity coefficient requires a specific formula. In the demand schedule in Table 3A.1, a decrease in price from $2.75 to $2.50 causes quantity demanded to increase from 2,000 gallons per week to 4,000 gallons per week. The percentage increase in quantity demanded is 100 percent. The percentage change in price is about −9.1 percent. Dividing 100 percent by −9.1 percent gives an elasticity coefficient of about −11. The negative sign is usually dropped for convenience.

If the price increases from $2.50 to $2.75, however, quantity demanded falls from 4,000 to 2,000 gallons per week. The percentage decrease in quantity demanded is 50 percent; the percentage increase in price is 10 percent. Dividing 50 percent by 10 percent gives an elasticity of 5. Thus, the elasticity coefficient for the same prices on the demand schedule differs, depending on whether there is a price increase or a price decrease.

To overcome the problem of obtaining different elasticities between the same prices on the same demand schedule, numerous formulas have been developed. A convenient formula is always to use the lowest price and the lowest quantity as the base of the percentage changes in calculating the elasticity coefficient. Between the prices of $2.75 and $2.50, this formula gives the percentage change in quantity demanded as 100 percent and the percentage change in price as 10 percent. The elasticity coefficient is 10, which is between the two coefficients calculated previously.

TABLE 3A.1 A DEMAND SCHEDULE FOR MILK

PRICE PER GALLON	QUANTITY PER WEEK	TOTAL REVENUE PER WEEK
$3.00	1,000	$3,000
2.75	2,000	5,000
2.50	4,000	10,000
2.25	6,000	13,500
2.00	8,000	16,000
1.75	10,000	17,500
1.50	12,000	18,000
1.25	14,000	17,500
1.00	16,000	16,000
0.75	18,000	13,500

The demand schedule for milk is used to explain the elasticity of demand.

Price elastic– Demand is price elastic if the elasticity coefficient is greater than 1.0.

Price inelastic– Demand is price inelastic if the elasticity coefficient is less than 1.0.

Unit elastic– Demand is unit elastic if the elasticity coefficient equals 1.0.

The elasticity coefficient for the prices of $1.00 and $0.75 is the percentage change in quantity (2,000/16,000 times 100) divided by the percentage change in price ($0.25/$0.75 times 100). The coefficient is 0.375. So we have calculated elasticity coefficients greater than 1.0 and less than 1.0. Elasticity coefficients can also exactly equal 1.0. Demand is **price elastic** if the coefficient is greater than one. This means that the percentage change in quantity is greater than the percentage change in price. It is **price inelastic** if the coefficient is less than one. This means that the percentage change in quantity is less than the percentage change in price. If the percentage change in quantity just equals the percentage change in price, demand is said to be **unit elastic**.

THE RELATIONSHIP BETWEEN PRICE ELASTICITY AND TOTAL REVENUE

Total revenue is price times quantity. There is a simple relationship among total revenue, price change, and price elasticity. When price changes from $2.75 to $2.50 in Table 3A.1, total revenue increases from $5,000 to $10,000. As we have seen, the percentage increase in quantity is greater than the percentage decrease in price; thus, with the price decrease, total revenue increases. Conversely, when price falls from $1.00 to $0.75, total revenue decreases from $16,000 to $13,500. This happens because the percentage increase in quantity is less than the percentage decrease in price. This example illustrates a general rule. If demand is price elastic and price falls, total revenue will increase. Conversely, if demand is price inelastic and price falls, total revenue will decrease.

Similarly, if demand is price inelastic and price increases, total revenue will increase. Conversely, if demand is price elastic and price increases, total revenue will decrease.

Finally, in the special case of unit elasticity, changes in price will have no effect on total revenue. These relationships among elasticity, price changes, and changes in total revenue are evident in different parts of this book.

THE DETERMINANTS OF PRICE ELASTICITY OF DEMAND

The price elasticity of demand is a measure of the responsiveness of quantity demanded to price change. Consumers will be very responsive to price changes under three conditions. One condition is when several substitutes exist for the good whose price has changed. For example, if the price of chicken goes up, other prices unchanged, consumers will find it easy to substitute other meats for chicken. Conversely, if the good is meat and its price goes up, consumers will find it difficult to adjust their meat purchases to the extent that they could adjust their chicken purchases. Demand will be less elastic for meat than for chicken.

Another condition depends upon the importance of the good in consumer's budgets. Demand will be more elastic the larger the amount that consumers spend on the good. The demand for paper clips is probably price inelastic because consumers spend such a small part of their income on paper clips. Other things equal, the demand for restaurant meals will tend to be more elastic than the demand for paper clips because people tend to spend more per year on restaurant meals.

The third condition depends on how long consumers have to adjust. Demand will be more elastic the longer the time that consumers have to adjust to a price change. The sharp increase in the price of fuel oil used for home heating in the mid-1970s did not have much of an immediate impact on quantity demanded. Given time to adjust, however, people found many ways to reduce the quantity they demanded of fuel oil. They insulated their homes, bought sweaters, found substitute fuels such as wood, and in general conserved energy.

This experience tells us that any future sharp energy price increases will result in a reduction in quantity demanded of energy, and, importantly, the reduction will be larger if consumers expect the price to last for an extended period. Given flexibility and time, energy consumers—both firms and households—will find ways to conserve energy if its price indicates that it is scarcer.

Summary

Price elasticity of demand is an important concept. To calculate the elasticity coefficient, it is important to use a formula that gives the same result for a given price change: increase or decrease. The price elasticity of demand can be elastic, unit elastic, or inelastic. If it is elastic, a price decrease will increase total revenue. If it is inelastic, a price decrease will decrease total revenue. The opposite holds for a price increase. At least three factors affect the elasticity of demand. Demand is more elastic (1) the more substitutes there are for the product; (2) the smaller the amount spent on the product by consumers in a given period; and (3) the longer consumers have to adjust to a price change.

Key Terms

Coefficient of the price elasticity of demand
Price elastic
Price inelastic
Unit elastic

CHAPTER 4

Efficiency in Resource Allocation: How Much Do We Have? How Much Do We Want?

OUTLINE

INTRODUCTION

A lot of economics is concerned with determining how well the economy performs relative to specific goals and, where it falls short, with devising policies or plans that will get it on the right track. There is no universally accepted set of economic goals, but economists normally agree that the economy should achieve: (1) full employment of labor, (2) nonaccelerating rates of inflation, (3) economic growth, (4) equity in the distribution of income, and (5) efficiency in the allocation of resources. This chapter concerns the last of these goals—efficiency in the allocation of resources. Full employment is the subject of Chapter 13, inflation is addressed in Chapter 14, economic growth is examined in Chapter 2, and equity in the distribution of income is related to the discussion of poverty in Chapter 11.

This chapter has three principal themes. The first theme is that efficiency in resource allocation is a desirable goal, but that it is difficult to achieve, as evidenced by many instances of inefficiency in both the private and public sectors of the economy. The second theme is that, although efficiency in resource allocation is a desirable goal, other economic goals are also desirable, and there are instances when policies to achieve efficiency may exact a cost in terms of the achievement of other desirable goals. The third theme is that, although there are often conflicts between goals, there are also instances when policies to achieve efficiency may help to achieve other desirable goals.

THE MEANING OF EFFICIENCY IN RESOURCE ALLOCATION

Efficiency in resource allocation (allocative efficiency)– An allocation of resources that satisfies wants as fully as possible.

The fundamental premise of economics is that resources are scarce—that the amount available is not large enough to satisfy all human wants. Economists recognize that scarcity cannot be eliminated, but they also believe that its effects can be minimized. This can be accomplished by allocating resources so that wants are satisfied as fully as possible. An economy that does this has achieved **efficiency in resource allocation**, or, more simply, **allocative efficiency**. An economy that achieves allocative efficiency is producing the right things (those that individuals value most highly) in the right amounts.

The resource allocation problem has two parts: the allocation of resources in the short run (for example, a year) and the allocation of resources over the long run (for example, across several years). An economy that allocates resources efficiently in the short run

Static allocative efficiency– An efficient allocation of resources in the short run.

Dynamic allocative efficiency– An efficient allocation of resources in the long run.

achieves **static allocative efficiency**. An economy that allocates resources efficiently in the long run achieves **dynamic allocative efficiency**. Only a small percentage of the economy's resources, however—primarily nonrenewable resources such as minerals, fossil fuels, and timber—pose a long-run allocation problem. Accordingly, we will concentrate on the problem of achieving static allocative efficiency. When we refer throughout this chapter to the simpler term "allocative efficiency" please remember that static allocative efficiency is what we have in mind.

You will discover from reading this chapter that the U.S. economy exhibits many instances of *in*efficiency in resource allocation, or allocative *in*efficiency. You will also learn that allocative inefficiency is a problem that pervades both the private or market sector of the economy, and the public or government sector.

REQUIREMENTS FOR ACHIEVING EFFICIENCY IN RESOURCE ALLOCATION

The objective of economic activity is to satisfy wants, but economists have no direct measure of the "want-satisfying power" of goods and services. They are forced to work instead with proxy measures of the "benefits" that individuals derive from goods and services. Assuming that benefits can be measured (much more on this below), there is a two-part requirement for achieving an efficient allocation of resources to a specific good or service. The first requirement is that the benefits provided by a good or service must be equal to or greater than the costs of providing the good or service. The second requirement is that the *difference* between the benefits and costs must be as large as possible, or maximized. Properly measured, costs represent the largest possible benefits that would have been produced from other goods and services that must be given up to provide a specific good or service. Given this interpretation, *the rule for efficiency in resource allocation is nothing more than the commonsense notion that you're not doing the best you can until you maximize the difference between what you get and what you give up to get it.* It takes something more than common sense, however, to determine benefits and costs.

The easiest cases are those of goods and services that are produced and sold in markets where the demand curve provides the information needed to determine benefits, and the supply curve provides the information needed to determine costs. We begin our application of the requirements for allocative efficiency with two such cases.

THE COMPETITIVE MARKET: AN EXAMPLE OF EFFICIENCY IN RESOURCE ALLOCATION

The first case is one in which the amount produced and sold is determined solely by demand and supply. Figure 4.1 illustrates such a market in terms of the demand (D) for and supply (S) of apartments for rent in Kansas City. We have added additional labels, however, to the demand and supply curves to facilitate measures of benefits and costs.

The *height* of the demand curve for each apartment indicates the maximum monthly rent that buyers are willing to pay for that apartment. For example, Figure 4.1 indicates that there is a buyer who is willing to pay $800 for the 100,000th apartment, that there is a buyer who is willing to pay slightly less for the next apartment, one who is willing to pay $700 for the 200,000th apartment, and so on. Economists use the maximum amount that buyers are willing to pay for a unit of something as a measure of the benefit they perceive

Figure 4.1 A Competitive Market for Apartments
This figure illustrates a competitive market for apartments in Kansas City. Market equilibrium occurs at 450,000 units, where S = D or MB = MC. This is also the number of apartments at which total net benefit is maximized; thus, this market automatically achieves allocative efficiency.

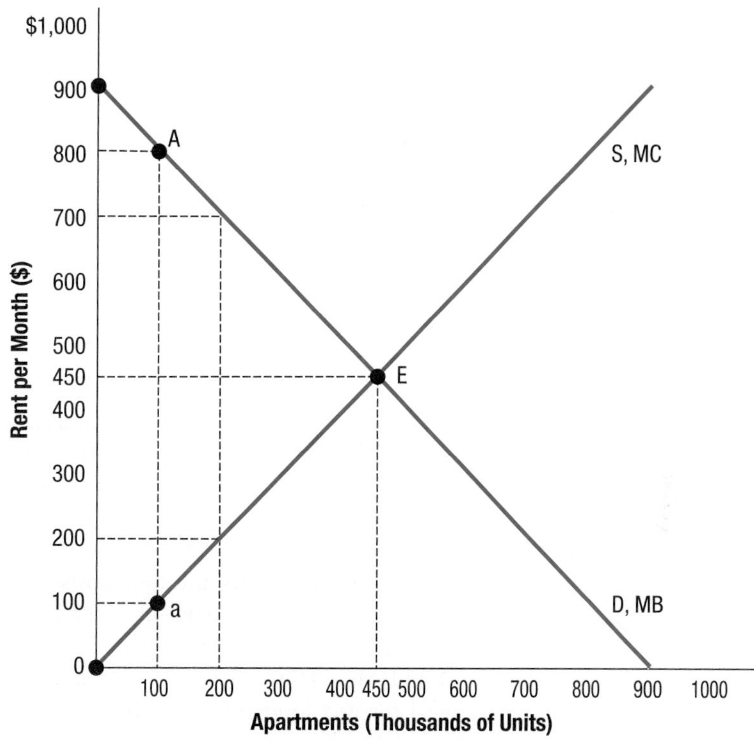

Marginal benefit curve (demand curve)– A curve that depicts the benefits from each additional, or marginal, unit.

Marginal cost curve (supply curve)– A curve that depicts the costs of providing each additional, or marginal, unit.

Total benefit– The sum of marginal benefits; also the area under the marginal benefit or demand curve.

from buying that unit. Thus, the demand curve for apartments is also a **marginal benefit curve**; it indicates the benefits buyers perceive from each additional, or marginal, unit.

The *height* of the supply curve for apartments indicates the minimum monthly rent that suppliers (owners) must receive for each apartment. For example, Figure 4.1 indicates that the supplier of the 100,000th apartment must receive at least $100 for that apartment, that the supplier of the next one requires a slightly larger amount, that the 200,000th apartment must fetch at least $200, and so on. Economists use the minimum amount that suppliers must receive as a measure of what must be given up, or the cost, to provide each apartment. Thus, the supply curve for apartments is also a **marginal cost curve**; it indicates the costs suppliers must pay to provide each additional, or marginal, unit.

The *area under* the demand curve (that is, the area between the demand curve and the horizontal axis) is a measure of the **total benefit** to buyers. This follows from the fact that the area under the curve between two quantities is the *sum* of all the marginal benefits between the two quantities. Thus, the total benefit from the first 100,000 units is $85,000,000—calculated as the sum of two areas under the demand curve: the rectangle bounded by the points $800, A, 100,000 units, and 0, and the triangle bounded by the points $900, A, and $800. The total benefit of all 900,000 units, or the area under the entire demand curve, is $405,000,000—the area of the triangle bounded by the points $900, 900,000 units, and 0.

Total cost– The sum of marginal costs; also the area under the marginal cost or supply curve.

The *area* under the supply curve (that is, the area between the supply curve and the horizontal axis) measures **total cost**, or the sum of marginal costs. Thus, in Figure 4.1, the total cost of the first 100,000 apartments is $5,000,000 (the triangle bounded by the points, 0, 100,000 units, and a). And the total cost of the first 500,000 units is $125,000,000—the value of a triangle with a height of $500 and base of 500,000 units.

Total benefits are greater than total costs all the way up to the last, or 900,000th apartment. (The reader should verify this by calculating the areas under the MB and MC curves.) But efficiency requires provision of the number of apartments where the *difference* between total benefit and total cost is *maximized*. This occurs at 450,000 units. This can be confirmed by noting that MB > MC for all apartments up to 450,000 units and that MB < MC for all apartment units beyond 450,000. Thus, each apartment rented up to 450,000 units *adds to* the difference between benefits and costs. Beyond 450,000 units, however, each apartment yields benefits less than costs, so each additional apartment *reduces* the total difference between benefits and costs. It follows that the total difference between benefits and costs must be the largest at 450,000 units.

Total net benefit– Total benefit minus total cost; also the area between the demand and supply curves.

An alternative way to approach this proof is to realize that the *difference* between total benefits and total costs is equal to the area *between* the MB and MC curves. This area, also known as the **total net benefit**, is maximized at 450,000 units, with a value of $202,500,000. This area can be calculated as the value of the triangle bounded by the points 0, $900, and E. Alternatively, it can be calculated that buyers are willing to pay $303,750,000 for 450,000 units (the area under the MB curve—remember?) and that sellers must receive $101,250,000 (the area under the MC curve), so the difference determined by comparing total benefits and total costs is also $202,500,000.

Markets that are highly competitive—in which neither buyers nor sellers can influence market price by their individual actions—will automatically clear at the intersection of D and S or MB and MC. Thus, they will automatically achieve allocative efficiency and there is no need for any kind of policy to ensure that such markets achieve allocative efficiency.

MARKET FAILURE: INEFFICIENCY IN THE PRIVATE SECTOR

Market failure– A situation in which a market fails to achieve allocative efficiency.

There are markets in the economy, however, that do not achieve allocative efficiency. When they do not, they are said to exhibit **market failure**. Here we examine several such cases, beginning with monopoly.

Monopoly

If some market participants have market power in the form of the ability to affect price by their own actions, the market will exhibit allocative inefficiency. A good example is that of a monopoly, a market in which only one seller exists. To illustrate this case, suppose that one firm owns all the apartment units in the Kansas City market.

As explained in Chapter 5, a monopolist will set a price for its product at the level where its profits are maximized. A profit-maximizing price is normally higher than a price that would result if determined by the forces of demand and supply. This makes a monopoly allocatively inefficient in the sense that *too little* is produced and *too few resources are allocated* to a monopolized market. Alternatively, a monopolist denies consumers the opportunity to buy additional units from which they would reap benefits greater than costs.

Profit–
Total revenue minus total cost.

Total revenue–
The price per unit times the quantity sold (the rectangle under the demand curve, where the height of the rectangle is the price per unit and the base of the rectangle is the quantity sold).

Profit is total revenue minus total cost. In determining profit, total cost is the sum of total variable and total fixed costs. In this illustration, we assume that total fixed costs are zero. **Total revenue** is the price per unit times the number of units sold. In Figure 4.2, total revenue is a *rectangle* under the demand curve. For example, total revenue from renting 100,000 apartments is $80,000,000—the product of a price of $800 and 100,000 units. This differs from the total benefit of $85,000,000 for these units—the total area under the demand curve, which equals the value of the total revenue rectangle plus the value of the triangle on top of it formed by the points, $900, $800, and 100 units.

Continuing with the calculations, the total cost of the first 100,000 units is $5,000,000 (the area under the supply curve—remember?). Thus, the profit realized by renting the first 100,000 apartments is $75,000,000. Although this is a lucrative option for the monopolist, it can do much better than that. Total profit from renting the first 200,000 units is $120,000,000 (total revenue of $140,000,000 minus total cost of $20,000,000), but it is even higher from renting 300,000 units; namely, $135,000,000 (total revenue of $180,000,000 minus total cost of $45,000,000). In fact, profit is *maximized* by renting 300,000 units at $600 per apartment. If a monopolist were to rent 450,000 units at $450 each, for example, profit would be only $101,250,000 (total revenue of $202,500,000 minus total cost of $101,250,000).

If the monopolist sets the apartment rent at $600 per unit—and it will, because this is the price that maximizes its profits—the number of apartments rented (300,000) will be less than the efficient number (450,000—where marginal benefit is equal to marginal cost). If only 300,000 units are rented, the difference between total *benefit* and total cost

Figure 4.2 A Monopolized Market for Apartments
This diagram illustrates the market for apartments in Kansas City, given the assumption that one firm owns all of them. Market equilibrium occurs where profits are maximized, at 300,000 units. There are deadweight losses equal to are MEm.

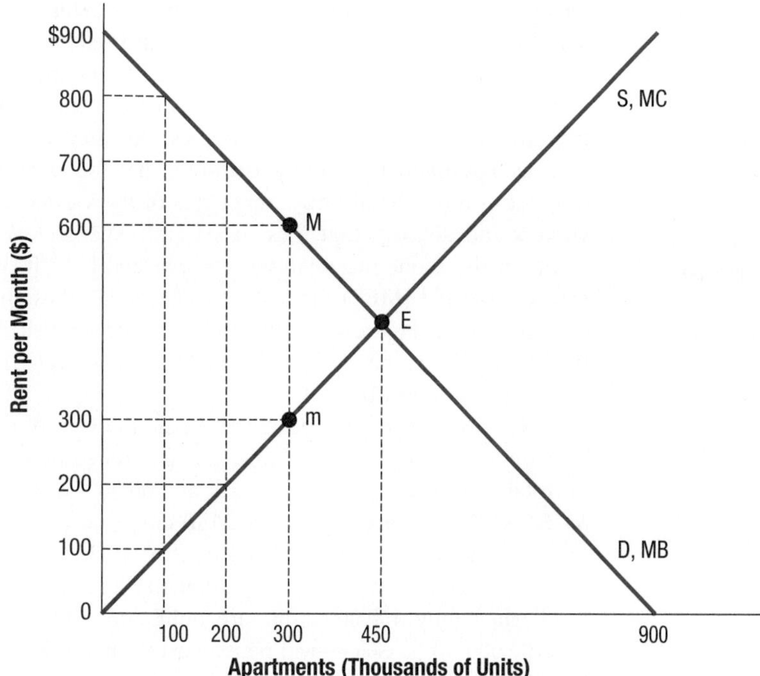

is *not* maximized. At 300,000 units, total benefit (the *area* under the demand curve) is $225,000,000 and total cost is $45,000,000, so the difference (or total net benefit) is $180,000,000. But this is smaller than the difference (total net benefit) of $202,500,000 between total benefits ($303,750,000) and total costs ($101,250,000) at 450,000 units. The difference of $22,500,000 ($202,500,000 minus $180,000,000) between the two total net benefit figures is a measure of the **allocative efficiency loss** due to the exercise of monopoly power. The reader should also recognize that this loss in total net benefits can be calculated directly as the value of the triangle bounded by the points M, E, and m. Economists often call this loss in allocative efficiency the **deadweight loss** from monopoly pricing.

Allocative efficiency loss (deadweight loss)– Maximum total net benefit minus actual total net benefit.

There are not many pure monopolies, but in some markets a few firms are so dominant that they have market power as a group. Inefficiency occurs in such markets, although to a lesser degree than in the pure monopoly case. The pure monopolies in the United States are firms to which government has given an exclusive franchise to supply a product. The most familiar of these are the public utilities that supply electricity and natural gas. Economists estimate that the efficiency losses from monopoly pricing in the U.S. economy amount to between 0.5 percent and 2 percent of total output, or between $60 billion and $240 billion for a $12 trillion economy. Many of the problems involved in attempting to reduce these losses by government intervention are discussed in Chapter 5.

Keyword: *deadweight loss, welfare loss*

Access InfoTrac at http://infotrac.cengage.com

External Benefits

In the competitive model for apartments in Kansas City, we assumed that the demand or marginal benefit curve provides an accurate measure of all the benefits realized from the rental units. That may not be the case, however. Suppose, for example, that the apartment buildings are particularly attractive; in fact, they are so attractive that they draw visitors from around the country just to view them. In this case, each visitor realizes benefits from the apartments that are in addition to the benefits realized by the renters of the apartments. Economists call these benefits **external benefits**. External benefits are external to the transaction between buyers and sellers, or benefits created by a market that are realized by individuals other than the buyers and sellers.

External benefit– A benefit created by a market that is realized by individuals other than the buyers and sellers.

It is not easy to determine the value of external benefits in real-world cases because they are not included in demand curves. But they are not impossible to estimate. In this case, we approximate them by assuming that the external benefits are at least as great as the cost of the time and travel expenses of the viewers. Suppose that we take a survey of viewers and discover that these costs and expenses average $100 per month per apartment. In the economist's jargon, the external benefit of each apartment—the **marginal external benefit** (MEB)—is $100. In Figure 4.3, these benefits are added to the demand or MB curve of Figure 4.1. The result is a curve labeled MSB, for **marginal social benefit**, where MSB is the vertical sum of MB and MEB (MEB is the vertical distance of $100 between MSB and MB).

Marginal external benefit– External benefit on the additional, or marginal, unit.

Marginal social benefit– The sum of the marginal benefit and the marginal external benefit.

With this change, total benefits become the sum of the marginal social benefits, or the area under the MSB curve. Now, the difference between total benefits and total costs, or total net benefit, is maximized at 500,000 units. At this level, total benefits are $375,000,000 (the area under the MSB curve) and total costs are $125,000,000 (the area under the MC curve), so total net benefit is $250,000,000 (the area bounded by $1,000, B, and 0). This is more than the total net benefits of $202,500,000 that would be realized when only 450,000 units are built and rented. Most of the extra $47,500,000—$45,000,000, to be exact—will be realized if only 450,000 units are rented. The remaining $2,500,000 (the area bound by e, B, and E) could be realized if renters received a subsidy

Figure 4.3 A Market for Apartments—With External Benefits
This figure illustrates the market for apartments in Kansas City with the assumed presence of external benefits. The market equilibrium is 450,000 units, where MB = MC. This is less than the efficient quantity of 500,000, where MSB = MC. Total net benefit is \$2.5 million larger at 500,000 units than at 450,000 units.

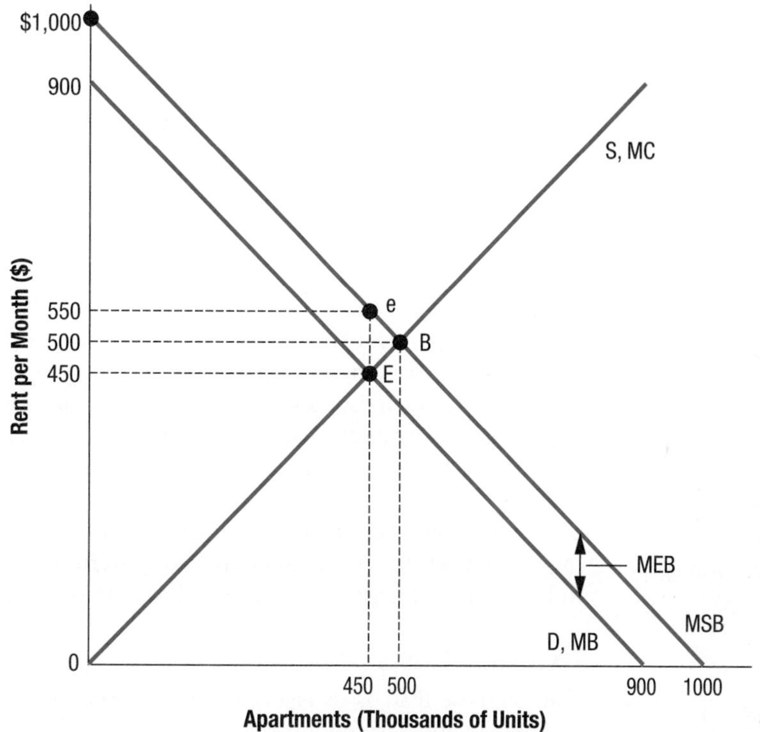

of \$100 a month for each unit rented. The subsidy would increase their willingness to pay for apartments by \$100 a unit, inducing them to rent an additional 50,000 units. Now this may strike you as a bad deal—an extra \$2,500,000 in net benefits for a subsidy of \$50,000,000 (\$100 times 500,000 units). It isn't, however, from an allocative efficiency perspective. The government could take the \$50,000,000 from taxpayers and transfer it to the renters. The losses of the taxpayers would just be offset by gains to the renters, so the net effect of the tax and transfer, alone, is zero. An additional 50,000 units would be rented, however, on which there would be a net gain of \$2,500,000. That is, when all gains and losses are added up, there is a net gain for society; that is, for taxpayers, renters, and viewers considered together.

This may be a fanciful illustration, but it underscores an important point: Whenever buyers cannot appropriate benefits, the market tends to allocate too few resources to the provision of the good or service. This point applies to less fanciful examples like primary and secondary education and public health. Primary and secondary education enhance the earning power of the persons educated, but turn them into better citizens as well, to the benefit of others (an external benefit). Public health measures, such as immunization, provide protection to the party immunized, but also some protection to people not immunized (an external benefit).

Public Goods

Goods and services differ in terms of the relative importance of external benefits. External benefits are most important in the case where, if a good is provided to one individual, all other individuals benefit from its provision. Economists call such goods public goods.

Public good– A good that provides benefits from which no one can be excluded.

National defense is the classic example of a **public good**. It is "public" in the sense that if it is provided to all, it bestows benefits on the public in general. That is, no one can be excluded from the benefits of national security. In such a case, it is likely that many individuals will not reveal their true willingness to pay, hoping for a "free ride" after other people pay for it. If many people reason this way, of course, we will not allocate enough resources to national defense even though the aggregate benefits from doing so may be large. In such a case, there is a need for government to levy taxes and use the proceeds to provide what the market cannot provide; that is, for the government to act on behalf of individuals.

Another important example of a public good is basic research. Private firms will undertake basic research provided that they can exclude others from using the knowledge they produce long enough to make an adequate return on their investment. Unlike national defense, it is possible, although difficult, to exclude others from using such knowledge. For example, patent protection can be secured for new discoveries. However, basic research produces fundamental knowledge—knowledge with potential for creating widespread external benefits—and precluding access to this knowledge through patent protection would cut off some of the external benefits derived from diffusing and utilizing that knowledge. Thus, some form of government support for basic research appears to be required to ensure an efficient allocation of resources to this activity.

Keyword: *public good*

Access InfoTrac at http://infotrac.cengage.com

External Costs

Now suppose that, as in Figure 4.1, no external benefits are associated with apartments in Kansas City. Assume instead that each apartment renter burns coal to produce heat, and that harmful byproducts—pollutants—of coal combustion escape from the apartments and drift across the city. People who are particularly sensitive to these pollutants suffer physically. Some become ill and miss work. Many see their doctor more frequently. Some curtail their outdoor activities. Some buy filtration systems for their homes. The income they forgo, the money they spend at the doctor, the value to them of the activities they give up, and their outlays for filtration systems are all examples of **external costs** imposed by apartment dwellers.

External cost– A cost created by a market that is paid by individuals other than the buyers and sellers.

Suppose that we have studied the problem and determined that there is an external cost of \$100 per apartment per month, or a **marginal external cost** (MEC) of \$100 per unit due to the air pollution created by renters. We examine the effects of this cost on efficiency by adding this \$100 to the MC curve in Figure 4.4. The result is a curve lying above the MC curve, labeled MSC for **marginal social cost**—the sum of MC and MEC. MEC is the distance between the MC and MSC curves.

Marginal external cost– The external cost on the additional, or marginal, unit.

Marginal social cost– The sum of the marginal cost and the marginal external cost.

Total costs are now measured as the area under the MSC curve, instead of the MC curve. Given this change, the difference between total benefits (the area under the demand or MB curve) and total costs, or total net benefit, is maximized at 400,000 units. Total net benefit at this level is \$160,000,000 (the area bounded by \$900, C, and \$100). If 450,000 units are rented, as in a competitive market, total net benefits will decrease by \$2,500,000 (the triangle CED) to \$157,500,000. Thus, the competitive market solution is marked by allocative inefficiency, or an allocation of too many resources to apartments in Kansas City.

Figure 4.4 A Market for Apartments—With External Costs
This figure illustrates the market for apartments in Kansas City with the assumed presence of marginal external costs. The market equilibrium is 450,000 units, where MB = MC. This is greater than the efficient quantity of 400,000 units, where MB = MSC.

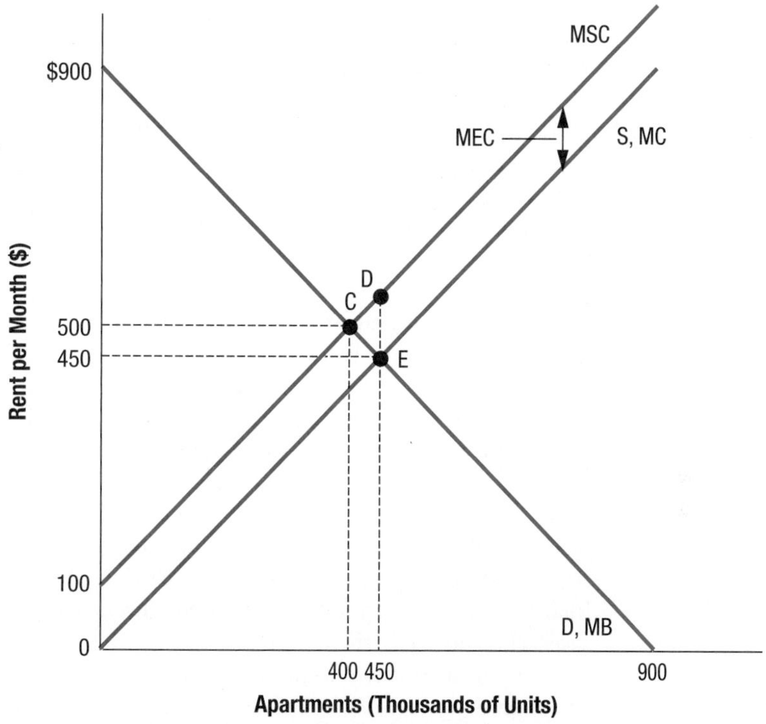

Keyword:
externalities, pollution

Access InfoTrac at http://infotrac.cengage.com

In cases such as this, the government may have to take action to reduce the number of apartments rented. The government could, for example, levy a tax equal to MEC per unit. If it did, there would be a net gain to society, or an increase in net benefits, of $2,500,000.

This is a contrived example, of course, but it underscores an important point: Whenever suppliers can escape paying for some of the costs of their actions, the market tends to allocate too many resources to the provision of the good or service. This point applies, moreover, to important real-world cases. For example, an EPA study found that air pollution regulations averted nearly $1.1 trillion in costs to individuals and the environment each year from 1970 to 1990.[1] Given that air pollution regulations did not eliminate air pollution, this is an underestimate of the external costs imposed by air pollution.

Imperfect Insurance Markets

Life is full of risks—poor health, death, accidents, fire, inflation, disability, natural disasters, unemployment, and poverty. The market system responds to these risks whenever it can by offering insurance. The very nature of insurance, however, makes it difficult to achieve efficiency in resource allocation in this sector of the economy.

Insuring against the risks of any event over which individuals have some control may make them less careful about avoiding the event. For example, having health insurance

[1] U.S. Environmental Protection Agency, *The Benefits and Costs of the Clean Air Act, 1970 to 1990.*

Moral hazard– The risk that insurance for an event will increase the probability of the event occurring.

Adverse selection– Self-selection that results in a pool of insured individuals dominated by high-risk, high-cost individuals.

may induce people to be less careful about maintaining their own health. Economics refers to the problem of insurance increasing the probability that claims will be made, or that the claims made will be more expensive, as **moral hazard**.

Moral hazard will flourish only if individual policyholders can shift the increased costs associated with their acts to others who are insured. If individual policyholders assume, however, that they can shift the costs of their actions to others, and act accordingly, the cost of insurance rises for the whole group. This discourages some individuals from buying insurance, especially individuals least in need of insurance—for example, those who are healthier. The market suffers from **adverse selection**—a situation in which self-selection results in an insurance pool of predominantly high-risk, and high-cost, individuals.

Ultimately, moral hazard and adverse selection result in too few people being covered by health insurance, or, what is the same thing, in an inefficiently small allocation of resources to health insurance. The problem is not confined to health insurance, however. Moral hazard and adverse selection make it difficult for the market system to provide the right amount of insurance against virtually any risk, including unemployment and poverty.

Adverse selection can also create allocative inefficiency in other types of markets. One example is the market for college student loans. College students, as a group, are an attractive pool of borrowers. They will realize high lifetime incomes and experience low rates of unemployment. What is true about the group, however, is not necessarily true about individual members of the group. The superior earning power of college students is no guarantee against the risk that *individual* students will not repay a loan in a timely manner, or the risk that the pool of borrowers will come to be dominated by individuals least likely to repay their loans.

This problem arises with borrowers in general, of course. Therefore, lenders protect themselves against risk of default by requiring collateral for a loan; for example, they retain the titles to cars and houses until auto and home loans are repaid. This protection is unavailable for student loans, however; that is, students cannot serve as collateral. This makes a loan to a specific individual relatively risky and requires the lender to charge a relatively high rate of interest to cover this risk.

A conflict arises, then, between individual and group risk of default in the market for college student loans—group risk of default is small, but individual risk of default is high. In the absence of a government guarantee against default, the rate of interest charged for student loans would reflect the relatively high individual risk of default. This rate would be higher than the one that reflects the group, or social, risk of default. If students had to pay the individual risk-of-default rate, there would be an inefficiently small allocation of resources to the market for college student loans. In this instance, a government guarantee against default would provide the necessary collateral, and the government would assume the relatively low risk associated with lending to college students as a group. Defaults would occur, but they could not be eliminated under any conceivable financing arrangement.

GOVERNMENT FAILURE: INEFFICIENCY IN THE PUBLIC SECTOR

The correction of market failures is often cited as a basis for government actions that affect the allocation of resources, such as government expenditures, subsidies, regulations, laws, and policies. Substituting government actions for private choices, however,

Government failure–Allocative inefficiency resulting from government activities.

is no guarantee of an improvement in the allocation of resources. In fact, there are many instances of **government failure**.

Rent Controls

Several local governments in the United States have adopted rent controls, placing an upper limit on rents that landlords can charge. These limits commonly keep rents *below* the market-clearing, or equilibrium, level. When this happens, landlords supply fewer units than the equilibrium quantity—too few for an efficient allocation of resources—resulting in less than maximum net benefits.

These points are illustrated in Figure 4.5, which represents the market for rental units in a city with rent controls. The equilibrium price (rent) and quantity are P_e and Q_e, respectively. The equilibrium quantity is also the allocatively efficient quantity. If landlords can charge no more than P_c because of the rent control, they will provide only Q_c units. At Q_c, MB exceeds MC, and net benefits are short of the maximum possible net benefits by the area bounded by C, M, and E.

Agricultural Price Supports

As explained in Chapter 3, the U.S. government has a series of programs designed to keep the prices of various agricultural commodities *above* the market-clearing, or equilibrium, level. Such prices induce farmers to produce more than market-clearing quantities—too much, in fact, from the perspective of allocative efficiency.

Figure 4.5 **A Market for Apartments—With Rent Controls**
This figure illustrates a market for apartments with rent controls. The market equilibrium without such controls is Q_e units, where S = D or MB = MC. This is also the efficient quantity. When the rent is limited to P_c, only Q_c units are supplied, and there is an efficiency loss equal to the area MEC.

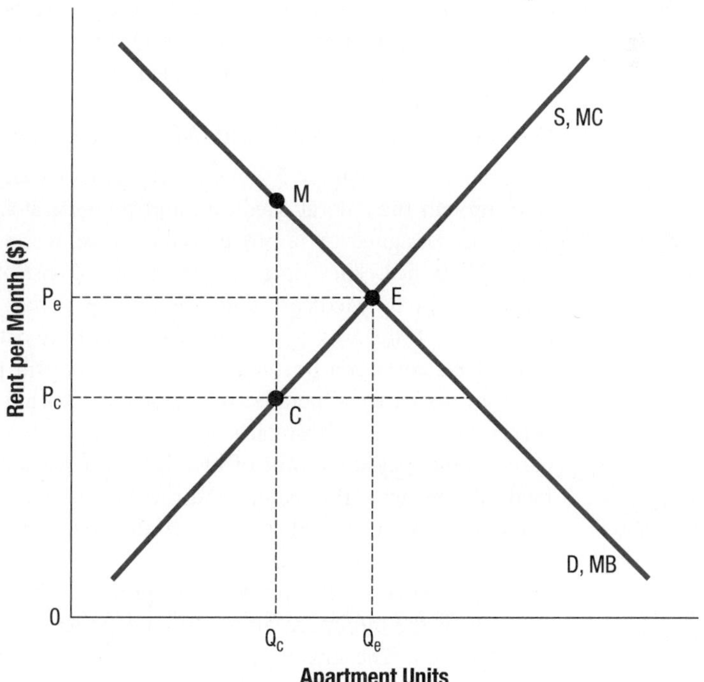

Figure 4.6 A Market for Wheat—With a Government-Supported Price
This figure illustrates a market for wheat with a government-supported price. The market equilibrium without government intervention is Q_e, the efficient quantity. When the government assures a price of P_s, the quantity is Q_s and there is an efficiency loss equal to the area ESM.

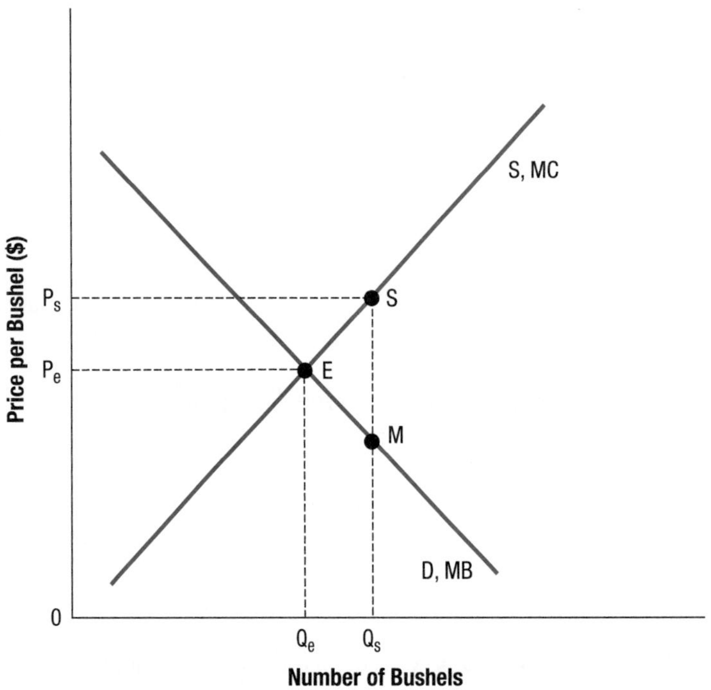

These points are illustrated in Figure 4.6, which depicts the market for wheat. The equilibrium price and quantity are P_e and Q_e, respectively. If the government supports the price at P_s, farmers will produce Q_s bushels, a quantity resulting in allocative efficiency losses equal to the area bounded by E, S, and M.

Keyword: *farm programs, price supports*

Access InfoTrac at http://infotrac.cengage.com

Government-Subsidized Medical Care

As discussed in Chapter 7, government provides large subsidies to consumers of health care through the federal Medicare and the federal-state Medicaid programs. These programs are designed to improve medical care access for the elderly (Medicare) and the poor (Medicaid). They do so by lowering the cost of each unit of medical care received or consumed by Medicare and Medicaid patients. For example, Medicare pays about 85 percent of the costs of a hospital stay, and the patient pays only 15 percent. Medicaid pays all the costs of a hospital stay, and the patient pays nothing.

From the patients' perspective, these cost-sharing arrangements drastically reduce the perceived price of a hospital stay. They make the perceived price (what the individual patient must pay for a unit of medical care) significantly less than the marginal cost of medical care (what the patient and the government together must pay to ensure the production of a unit of medical care). Acting solely on the basis of the price that they pay, patients buy too much medical care.

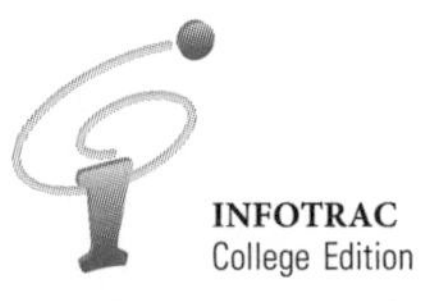

Keyword: *welfare loss*

Access InfoTrac at http://infotrac.cengage.com

These points are illustrated in Figure 4.7, which represents the market for medical care. MC is the minimum amount that suppliers must receive to pay the costs of providing each unit. The line P_c represents the amount that patients pay for each unit. The difference between MC and P_c per unit is the share of costs paid by the government.

Figure 4.7 A Market for Medical Care—With Government Cost-Sharing
This figure illustrates a market for medical care in which government shares part of the cost. The market equilibrium without government cost-sharing is Q_e, the efficient quantity. When the government shares part of the cost, consumers perceive a lower price, P_c. With cost-sharing, consumers buy Q_c units and there is an efficiency loss of the area ESM.

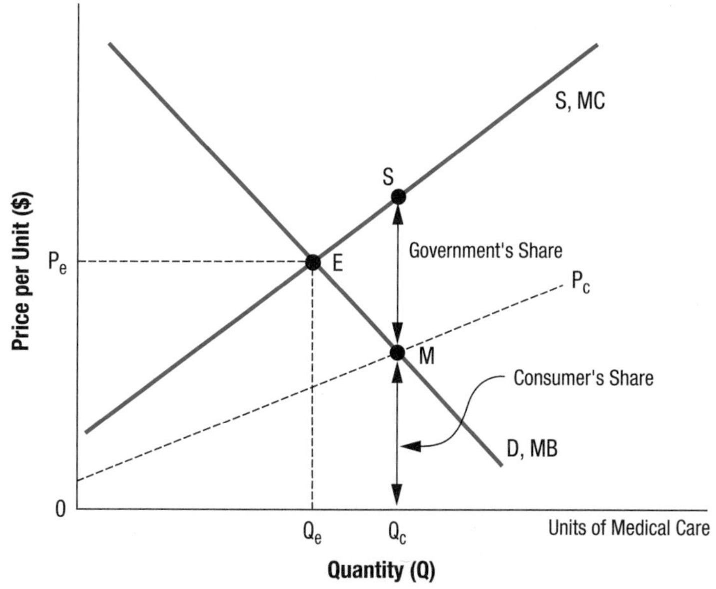

Consumers will want to buy all units for which the perceived benefit per unit—the marginal benefit—is greater than or equal to P_c. Thus, consumers will choose to buy Q_c, resulting in allocative efficiency losses equal to area bounded by E, S, and M.

Minimum Wage

The United States has a federal law requiring employers to pay workers in most occupations a minimum wage of $5.15 an hour. The intent of the law is to increase the income of low-wage workers. Whatever its merits in this regard (see the discussion in Chapter 13, which indicates that the minimum wage is not a very effective strategy for achieving this purpose), it is a source of allocative inefficiency.

This point is illustrated in Figure 4.8, which depicts the market for unskilled labor (the market most likely to be affected by the minimum wage). The demand or marginal benefit curve in this market reflects the benefits that employers get from hiring additional workers. The supply curve in this market reflects the amount that workers must receive in order to come to work, or the marginal cost—to them—of working. Net benefits are maximized where MB = MC, or at N_e workers hired. If the lowest wage that employers can legally pay, W_m, exceeds the market-clearing wage, W_e, as in this example, there will be less than the allocatively efficient quantity of labor hired (N_m rather than N_e) and efficiency losses equal to the area bounded by M, E, and m.

Keyword: *minimum wage*

Access InfoTrac at http://infotrac.cengage.com

Taxes

The ways in which governments finance their activities are also sources of allocative inefficiency. This is especially true of taxes.

The effect of taxes on allocative efficiency can be illustrated with the case of the general sales tax levied on retail purchases of goods and services. This tax is imposed by

Figure 4.8 A Market for Labor—With a Minimum Wage
This figure illustrates a labor market in which a legislated minimum wage, W_m, exceeds the equilibrium wage, W_e. Only N_m workers will be hired. This is less than the efficient quantity, N_e, and there are efficiency losses equal to area ME_m.

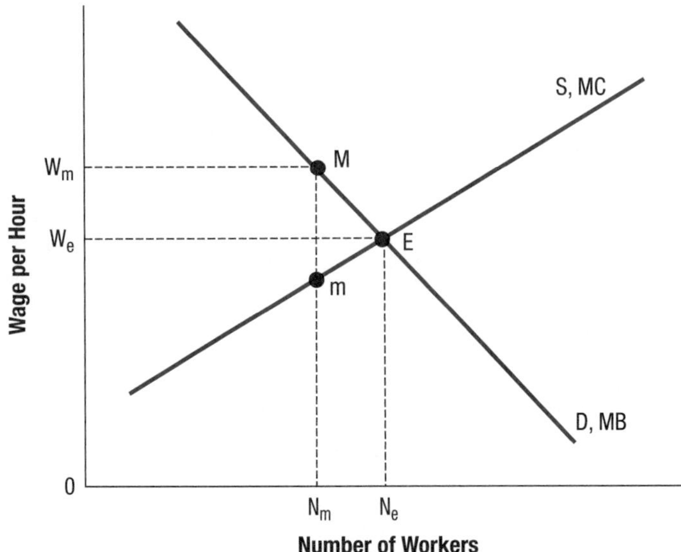

45 state governments at rates ranging from 4 to 7 percent. This tax is also imposed by local governments in 33 states, with additional local tax rates ranging from 1 percent to 7 percent. Maximum combined state and local tax rates range from 4 percent in Hawaii to 11.5 percent in Arkansas.

The general sales tax is commonly levied on sellers; that is, governments require sellers to send taxes to the tax authorities based on the sales they make. The tax itself is a percentage of the price at which a good or service is sold. Although sellers are liable for taxes on sales, they attempt to shift the tax to consumers in the form of higher prices. That is, their supply price (the price they require in order to supply a good or service) increases by the amount of the tax.

The effect of the tax is illustrated in Figure 4.9. The supply curve before the tax is S. After the tax is imposed, the supply curve rotates upward to S + T. The vertical distance between S and S + T is the tax. As illustrated, the tax is a constant percentage of the supply price before the tax is imposed. The pretax equilibrium is at P, the intersection of the demand curve and the supply curve before the tax is imposed. The pretax price and quantity are P_p and Q_p, respectively.

The tax raises the price to the buyer to P_b and lowers the price to the seller to P_s. The difference between the two prices ($P_b - P_s$ or B − S) is the tax per unit. Total tax revenue is equal to the rectangle bounded by P_b, P_s, S, and B.

The tax also lowers the quantity sold from Q_p (the pretax quantity) to Q_a (the after-tax quantity). Assuming that the supply curve before taxes is a marginal cost curve and the demand curve is a marginal benefit curve, the tax results in an inefficiently small quantity of goods and services sold. The allocative efficiency loss attributable to the tax is equal to the net benefits not realized because of the tax, or the area bounded by B, P, and S. Economists often refer to this area as the **excess burden** of the tax to distinguish it from the burden of the tax, where the latter is equal to revenues collected. The excess burden is also called the **deadweight loss** from taxation.

Excess burden of taxation (deadweight loss from taxation)– Net benefit not realized because of taxation.

Figure 4.9 A Market With a General Sales Tax
This figure illustrates a market with a general sales tax levied on sellers. The equilibrium after the tax is Q_a. This is less than the pretax equilibrium and efficient quantity, Q_p. There is an excess burden attributable to the tax of area BPS. Tax collections (the tax burden) equal area P_bBSP_s.

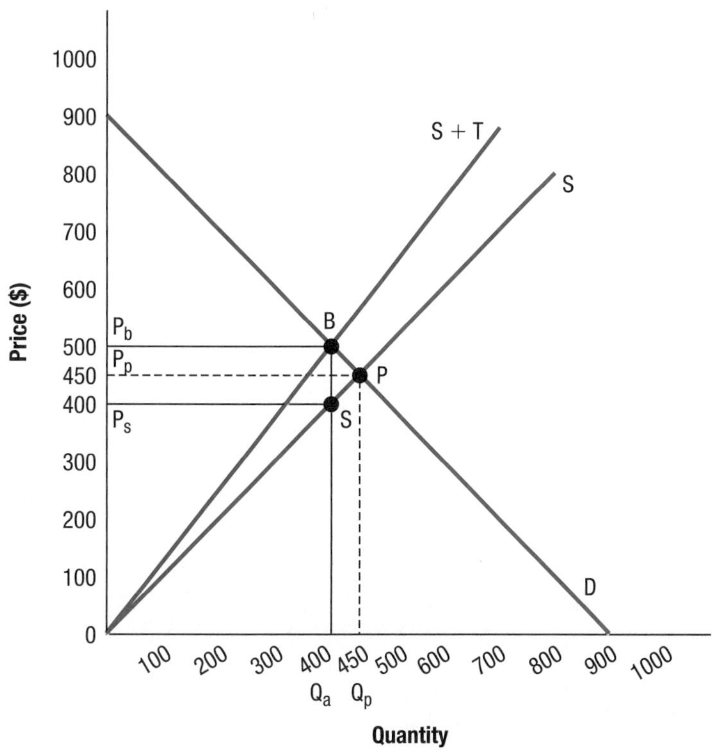

Keyword: *welfare loss (from taxation), deadweight loss (of taxation)*

Access InfoTrac at http://infotrac.cengage.com

The general sales tax is not alone in generating excess burdens or deadweight losses; all real-world taxes do this. In fact, the extra costs of raising tax revenue attributable to excess burdens appear to be substantial. For example, a widely cited study by Jorgenson and Yun estimates excess burdens of at least 30 cents for each dollar of taxes collected.[2] Given these and other similar estimates, the Office of Management and Budget requires federal agencies to increase tax costs by 25 percent for excess burdens when conducting benefit-cost analyses of government programs.[3]

Allocative efficiency can also be affected by the way in which the tax base is determined. The tax base for the individual income tax is equal to income *minus* various deductions, exclusions (also called exemptions), and deferrals. The final tax bill is also reduced by various tax credits. The effect of items such as these on allocative efficiency can be illustrated best by focusing on a particular case, the deductibility of mortgage interest on owner-occupied homes. This deduction reduced federal individual income tax collections by nearly $70 billion in 2005.

Consider Figure 4.10, which depicts housing decision variables for Bob and Mary. There is the usual downward-sloping demand curve, designated by D and MB. The marginal cost (MC) curve reflects all the costs of home ownership, including the interest

---

[2]Dale W. Jorgenson and Kun-Young Yun, "The Excess Burden of Taxation in the United States," *Journal of Accounting, Auditing, and Finance* 6, no. 4 (Fall 1991): 487–508.

[3]Office of Management and Budget, *Guidelines and Discount Rates for Benefit-Cost Analysis of Federal Programs*, Circular No. A-94, Revised, October 29, 1992.

Figure 4.10 The Effect of Tax Subsidies for Home Ownership
This figure illustrates the effect of federal subsidies for home ownership provided through the tax code. The subsidies reduce the cost of home ownership from MC to MC_t. They increase the quantity of housing purchased from the efficient level, H_e, to the inefficiently larger level, H_t, and create an efficiency loss equal to the area EST.

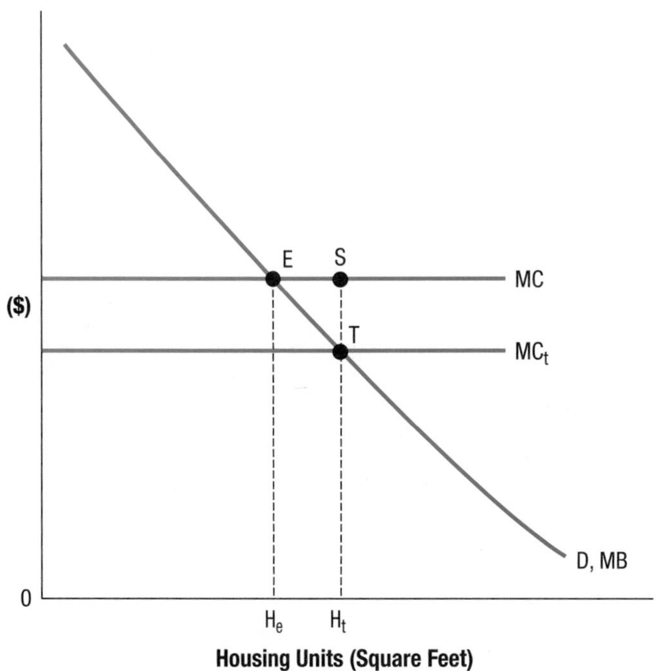

costs of money borrowed to finance a home mortgage. If interest costs are not deductible, the couple will buy H_e square feet and net benefits will be maximized. The deductibility of mortgage interest lowers the cost of home ownership, shifting the marginal cost curve down to MC_t. For example, if mortgage interest is $10,000 a year and Bill and Mary's annual income is $75,000, the deductibility feature lowers the tax bill—or cost of home ownership—by $2,500, the value of the deduction times the marginal income tax rate of 25 percent that this couple faces under the federal income tax code.

In the face of the lower cost of home ownership, the amount purchased will increase from H_e to H_t. Bill and Mary will have been induced by this feature of the tax code to buy too much housing and there will be losses in allocative efficiency equal to the area bounded by the points E, T, and S (the amount by which maximum net benefits are decreased).

Other tax breaks also induce taxpayers to do too much from an allocative efficiency perspective. For example, the exclusion of employer contributions for medical insurance (the largest tax break in 2005—$113 billion) will induce taxpayers to buy too much medical insurance. Roger Feldman and Brian Dowd[4] estimated efficiency losses from excess health insurance at 0.9 to 2.9 percent of national output, or $108 billion to $348 billion for a $12 trillion economy. A substantial part of this loss may be attributable to the exclusion of employer contributions for medical insurance. The deferral and preferential

[4] "A New Estimate of the Welfare Loss of Excess Health Insurance," *American Economic Review* 81 (March 1991): 297–301.

Capital gain– The market price of an asset minus the purchase price of that asset.

treatment of a **capital gain** (the difference between the market value of an asset and the purchase price of that asset) will induce taxpayers to earn too much of their income in this form. The accelerated depreciation of machinery and equipment will lower the cost of those items, inducing purchasers to buy too much of them. And the deductibility of property taxes on houses and the exclusion of capital gains from home sales will lower the cost of home ownership, just like the exclusion of mortgage interest, and induce taxpayers to buy too much housing. In fact, estimates by Poterba indicate that all the features of the tax code that favor expenditures on housing create allocative efficiency losses of about $600 per year for someone who owns a $100,000 home.[5]

Sales Taxes A similar tale can be told for the general sales taxes levied at the state level. As illustrated above, the rates associated with those taxes induce taxpayers to spend too little, creating allocative efficiency losses. There are many exclusions from the general sales tax base, however, especially for services, and these exclusions lower the cost of the exempted items relative to the cost of items subject to taxation. This produces a pattern of too much consumption of some items and too little of others. The net result is a system of sales taxation that is characterized by many instances of allocative inefficiency.

The Individual Income Tax and Personal Saving The decisions to consume and invest are not the only decisions affected by taxes. The overall division of disposable income into consumption and saving may also be affected. Individuals have the choice of spending all their income during the period in which it is received or saving it for future consumption. The amount that they defer to later periods will be influenced, in part, by the interest income that they earn on the portion that they save. The individual income tax applies to interest income, so it distorts the choice between present and future consumption, or, what is the same thing, current consumption and saving. This distortion is a source of additional efficiency losses from taxation.

HOW MUCH EFFICIENCY DO WE WANT?

We think that it follows from the above analysis that allocative inefficiency in the U.S. economy is an important problem. It does not necessarily follow, however, that eliminating it is always an appropriate strategy. One reason is that efforts to do so may make the distribution of resources or income more inequitable, and equity is also a desirable economic goal. Another reason is that attempts to achieve allocative efficiency may stifle innovation, and innovation can be an important means of satisfying wants more fully.

Efficiency Versus Equity: Tax Trade-Offs

We have so far ignored the possibility of desirable economic goals other than efficiency. Many people are concerned, however, about *who* reaps the benefits from and *who* pays the costs of alternative allocations of resources, or about *who* pays the tax bill. They want an allocation of resources or a distribution of the tax burden that treats particular individuals or groups equitably or fairly.

Since the tax system is such an important source of inefficiency, there is understandably considerable interest in redesigning it to reduce the excess burden of taxation. This could be done, for example, by reducing marginal income tax rates or by eliminating some of the exclusions, deductions, and credits pertaining to this tax. The largest

[5]James M. Poterba, "Taxation and Housing: Old Questions, New Answers," *American Economic Review* 82, no. 2 (May 1992): 237–242.

increase in efficiency via rate reductions could be achieved by reducing the highest marginal tax rate. This would tend to shift a greater portion of the tax burden, however, to lower-income taxpayers, and many people would consider this to be a less equitable distribution of the tax burden. Alternatively, the excess burden of taxation could be enhanced by taxing income that is currently excluded from the tax base. This could be done, for example, by eliminating the child-care tax credit, but many people would object to this on the grounds that the costs of this change would fall primarily on lower-income households. Many trade-offs between efficiency and equity such as these would be involved in any attempts to reduce the excess burden of taxation.

Isn't there a way to determine how far to go in reducing allocative inefficiency? The simple answer is "yes—at least in theory." The solution is to assign weights to the individuals who will benefit from and pay for the changes that will be made. If this could be done, the objective would be to make the change only if the *weighted* sum of the benefits from doing so were equal to or greater than the *weighted* sum of the costs. Ideally, we would go one step further and design the change so that we maximized the *difference* between the weighted sum of benefits and the weighted sum of costs.

The weights to which we refer tell us how much satisfaction one individual gets from the marginal dollar relative to other individuals. For example, if, as some believe, a dollar to a poor person is worth more than a dollar to a rich person, a dollar received by or given up by the former would be weighted more heavily than a dollar received by or given up by the latter.

INFOTRAC
College Edition

Keyword: *trade-off, leaky bucket*

Access InfoTrac at http://infotrac.cengage.com

Suppose that some evidence convinces us that a dollar to a poor person has twice the value of a dollar to a rich person. We could assign any weights to the two groups as long as the value for the poor person was twice as large as the value for the rich person. A weight of 1 for the poor person and 1/2 for the rich person would work, but so would 2 and 1, 10 and 5, and so on. The actual numbers are irrelevant; it's the ratio of the two that matters. These weights could then be applied to changes in the tax burden experienced by the two individuals. The difficulty, of course, lies in discovering the appropriate weights. Unfortunately, this has not been done, and the perceived equity costs of increases in allocative efficiency can be a powerful brake on changes that focus primarily on efficiency.

Efficiency Versus Innovation

There are trade-offs, as well, between achieving greater efficiency and more innovation in the economy. This is illustrated in the following case.

As we have seen, allocative efficiency calls for industries in which firms have little market power, and a case can be made for government regulation of firms with market power. The objective of such regulation is to keep firms with market power from charging prices that exceed marginal cost.

Chapter 5 develops examples of markets, however, in which prices greater than marginal cost are required to elicit the development of new products. This is especially true of industries that are highly dependent on knowledge and the creation of new knowledge as the basis for growth, such as the computer hardware and software industries, and the pharmaceutical industry. The leading firms in these industries must incur large and highly uncertain start-up costs for research and development and production. Prices greater than operating, or marginal, cost must be charged in order to finance the start-up costs required to compete in these industries. There is a clear trade-off in such cases between allocative efficiency and innovation. Both are desirable goals, however, and government regulation that opts for efficiency only may exact too high a price in terms of new product development.

INTERNATIONAL PERSPECTIVE

Does More Government Mean Less Growth?

Many economists are concerned that there may be a trade-off between the size of the government sector and the rate of economic growth. More specifically, they fear that more government may mean slower growth. A larger government sector requires higher taxes, and higher taxes may reduce work effort, savings, and investment. A larger government sector may also mean more regulation, and more regulation may require business firms to substitute investment in regulatory compliance for investment in goods-producing plant and equipment. More government need not mean slower growth, however, if it provides more education, research, social infrastructure, and political stability. Theory alone, then, will not help us determine whether more government means slower growth.

Considerable variation occurs across countries in terms of both size of government and rate of economic growth. Accordingly, several researchers have attempted to detect a relationship between government and growth by making cross-country comparisons. In the studies done to date, government's influence on the economy has been represented by either government expenditures or taxes. The research questions whether slower rates of growth have been associated with higher ratios of government spending or taxes to output.

Keith Marsden, using a sample of 20 countries for the period 1970–1979, found a statistically significant negative relationship between growth rates and tax shares: on average, a 1 percent increase in the ratio of taxes to output was associated with a 0.36 percent decrease in the rate of economic growth.[a] Charles Wolf and Randy Ross estimated that a 10 percent increase in the ratio of government spending to output was associated with a 1 percent decrease in the rate of growth, using a sample of 27 countries for 1972–1982.[b] Daniel Landau's study of the relationship between government expenditures and per capita economic growth shows results similar to those of Marsden and Wolf and Ross.[c] Alternatively, Mancur Olson found no reliable connection between the size of government and economic growth in his study of long-term secular growth,[d] and Frederic Pryor reached a similar conclusion based on his study of a broad range of market-based and command economies over the period 1950–1980.[e] Based on these studies, the evidence of a relationship between the size of government and the rate of economic growth is somewhat ambiguous. This issue is such an important one in making the choice between markets and government, however, that certainly we have not heard the last word from the research community.

---

[a] Keith Marsden, "Links between Taxes and Economic Growth: Some Empirical Evidence," World Bank Staff Working Paper 605 (Washington, D.C., 1983).

[b] Charles Wolf, Jr., Markets or Governments, 2nd ed. (MIT Press Cambridge, MA, 1994), 145–51.

[c] Daniel, "Government Expenditure and Economic Growth: A Cross-Country Study," Southern Economic Journal 49, no. 3 (January 1983): 783–92.

[d] Mancur Olson, The Rise and Decline of Nations (Yale University Press New Haven, CT, 1982).

[e] Frederic L. Pryor, "Growth and Fluctuations of Production in OECD and East European Countries," *World Politics* 37, no. 2 (January 1985): 204–237.

Efficiency and Equity

Efforts to achieve greater allocative efficiency do not always create conflicts of the type noted above. There are cases where we could increase efficiency and equity at the same time—or at least be unlikely to reduce equity significantly as efficiency increases.

Agricultural Price Supports Although federal farm programs supposedly are designed to attack farm poverty, we argue in Chapter 3 that the evidence clearly indicates that price-support and target-price programs give the biggest benefits to farmers who produce the most and surely have the most wealth. Given this result, it seems possible to reduce some of the allocative inefficiency created by these programs without seriously violating notions of equity.

Minimum Wage A similar verdict seems in order for the federal minimum wage. A recent study of this subject finds evidence that the minimum wage largely redistributes income among low-income families.[6] Thus, it seems possible to reduce the application of this measure, thereby reducing the allocative efficiency loss, without imposing significant additional costs on low-income families as a group. That is, most of the gainers and losers from such a measure would be in the same income category.

Medicare and Medicaid As noted above, government-subsidized medical care is an important source of allocative inefficiency. However, poor families and individuals benefit significantly from these subsidies through both of these programs. One potential solution to the problem of reducing allocative inefficiency without great harm to the welfare of these groups is to provide them with vouchers that they could use to pay for medical care directly. The vouchers could be issued in a smaller amount than the current subsidy because the existence of too much medical care is evidence that the care is worth less to consumers than the cost of providing it. The vouchers themselves would provide consumers of medical care with the incentive and the means to be more careful shoppers.

Efficiency Offsets to Inefficiency

Finally, there are cases in which one source of inefficiency is offset to some degree by other sources of inefficiency. Some tax examples illustrate this point clearly.

Excise taxes on cigarettes are a case in point. Cigarette smoking is a source of external costs in the form of secondhand smoke. Without excise taxes on cigarettes, there would be too many cigarettes consumed from an allocative efficiency perspective—just like the case explained earlier of the coal-burning apartments in Kansas City. Application of the excise tax reduces cigarette consumption, creating allocative efficiency losses from taxation but reducing efficiency losses from secondhand smoke. The two effects may or may not offset each other, but the excise tax works in this instance as a corrective measure. In a similar fashion, the allocative efficiency losses from gasoline taxes may be offset somewhat by *reduced* efficiency losses from the air pollution associated with oil refining or automobile travel, and the efficiency losses from excise taxes on alcohol may be offset somewhat by reduced efficiency losses from the external costs of alcoholism.

Keyword: *green taxes*

Access InfoTrac at http://infotrac.cengage.com

Summary

Efficiency in resource allocation is an important economic goal. To achieve allocative efficiency, resources must be allocated so that benefits are equal to or greater than costs, *and* marginal benefits must equal marginal costs. Competitive markets automatically fulfill these conditions, but there are many instances of allocative inefficiency in the U.S. economy—some in the market sector (cases of market failure), and some in the public sector (cases of government failure).

Several cases of market failure were examined. We found that:

- Monopoly pricing causes too few resources to be allocated to monopolized industries, creating allocative efficiency losses or deadweight losses from monopoly.
- The presence of external benefits from an activity causes too few resources to be allocated to that activity, resulting in allocative efficiency losses.
- Public goods are an extreme version of the external benefits case.
- External costs created by an activity cause *too many* resources to be allocated to that activity.
- Markets for some insurance products and credit are inherently inefficient because of moral hazard, adverse selection, and differences between individual and social risk.

[6] David Neumark and William Wascher, "Do Minimum Wages Fight Poverty?" *Economic Inquiry* 40, no. 3 (July 2002): 315–333.

Several cases of government failure were also examined. We found that:

- Rent controls cause too few resources to be allocated to markets for rental housing.
- Agricultural price supports cause too many resources to be allocated to agricultural markets.
- Government subsidies for medical care also cause too many resources to be allocated to medical care.
- The minimum wage causes too few workers to be employed.
- The tax system is a source of excess burdens or deadweight losses, resulting from high marginal tax rates and exceptions to the tax base.

When the various sources of inefficiency are viewed together, they indicate that allocative inefficiency may be a serious problem for the U.S. economy. It does not follow, however, that eliminating allocative inefficiency is a desirable thing to do. There are trade-offs between efficiency and equity and between efficiency and innovation. These trade-offs indicate that some inefficiency is desirable, but they also make it difficult to determine exactly how much this might be.

There are some instances in which the trade-off between efficiency and equity is not severe. Agricultural price supports and the minimum wage are cases in point. There may be instances in which policy can be designed to reduce efficiency losses without seriously compromising equity; the case of vouchers for medical care is an example. Finally, there are instances where government intervention that creates efficiency losses of one type reduces efficiency losses of another type, as exemplified by the so-called "sin taxes" (taxes on cigarettes and alcohol) and gasoline taxes.

Key Terms

Efficiency in resource allocation (allocative efficiency)
Static allocative efficiency
Dynamic allocative efficiency
Marginal benefit curve (demand curve)
Marginal cost curve (supply curve)
Total benefit
Total cost
Total net benefit
Market failure
Profit
Total revenue
Allocative efficiency loss (deadweight loss)
External benefits
Marginal external benefit
Marginal social benefit
Public good
External cost
Marginal external cost
Marginal social cost
Moral hazard
Adverse selection
Government failure
Excess burden of taxation (deadweight loss)
Capital gain

Review Questions

1. What do we mean by market failure? By government failure?
2. What conditions must be fulfilled to achieve efficiency in resource allocation?
3. Explain how a competitive market achieves allocative efficiency automatically.
4. Describe two cases in which the market produces an inefficiently small allocation of resources. Explain why.
5. Describe and explain two cases in which markets produce an inefficiently large allocation of resources.
6. Describe and explain two cases in which government policies cause too many resources to be allocated to an activity.
7. Draw a diagram in which you indicate the effect of a general sales tax levied on the seller. Identify the burden of the tax and the excess burden of the tax. What does your diagram imply about the common claim that the general sales tax is paid by the buyer?
8. A study has been done of a government program that provides the following benefits to, and imposes the following costs on, two groups of individuals:

	Group A	Group B
Benefits	$100 million	$50 million
Costs	$50 million	$75 million

   a. From the perspective of efficiency alone, should the program be undertaken? Why or why not?
   b. Suppose that group A consists of rich people and that group B consists of poor people, and that it has been determined that a dollar to a

poor person is worth three times as much as a dollar to a rich person. Should the program be undertaken? Why or why not?

c. What trade-off is illustrated by part b of this question? Explain.

9. Many communities in the United States experience droughts each year.

a. Use a supply-demand diagram to illustrate the effects of a drought on the equilibrium price and quantity of water in such a community.

b. Suppose the city authorities do not allow the price of water to change as indicated in your diagram. Use your diagram to illustrate the effect of such a pricing policy on allocative efficiency.

10. Suppose that the market for apartments for rent in your community is described by the following data:

Rent per Month	Apartments Demanded	Apartments Supplied
$2,000	0	20,000
$1,800	2,000	18,000
$1,600	4,000	16,000
$1,400	6,000	14,000
$1,200	8,000	12,000
$1,000	10,000	10,000
$800	12,000	8,000
$600	14,000	6,000
$400	16,000	4,000
$200	18,000	2,000
$0	20,000	0

Determine the following

a. The equilibrium quantity of apartments

b. Total benefit at equilibrium

c. Total cost at equilibrium

d. Total net benefit at equilibrium

e. Total revenue at equilibrium

f. Suppose that Bill Gateway buys all the apartments in your community and engages in monopoly pricing. As a result, the number of units rented falls to 7,000 (you might want to prove this as an advanced exercise) and the price rises to $1,400. How large is the efficiency loss from monopoly pricing?

11. Use the diagram you have constructed for your answer to question 11 (without Bill Gateway) to *illustrate and quantify* the efficiency losses from air pollution, assuming that each apartment produces smoke that impairs health in the community by an average of $400 per apartment per month.

Web Sites

- Want to learn more about taxes and expenditures of U.S. governments? Start by browsing the U.S. Department of Commerce, Bureau of Economic Analysis Web site—**http://www.bea.gov**
- What are your beliefs about taxation? What kind of tax policy would you design? Take the brief survey at *Tax Policy* to *Build Your Own Tax Policy in Just 10 Minutes!*—**http://www.taxpolicy.com/build.htm**
- Review some alternative tax systems as found on the Web sites for *Tax Policy & Reform Groups*—**http://www.taxsites.com/policy.html**. Which system is most interesting to you? How does it differ from the current tax system? Will it increase or decrease efficiency losses from taxation? Will it distribute the tax burden equitably?

CHAPTER 5

Market Power: Does It Help or Hurt the Economy?

OUTLINE

Monopoly Analysis
Market Power and Economic Efficiency
OPEC: A Few Sellers Acting Like a Monopoly
Market Power and Technical Progress
Government and Market Power

A government or society that promotes economic efficiency and technical progress runs into contradictions regarding the appropriate policy toward market power. Economic efficiency requires that market power be minimal; technical progress may require a more permissive view of market power. This tension between efficiency and progress unfolds in U.S. government policy. On the one hand, the United States has laws against firms agreeing to fix prices and laws that prohibit the purchase of one firm by another (the merger of two firms) if the purchase would create significant market power. So does the European Union and other industrialized countries. These same governments also grant monopolies—give market power—to firms that invent new products and processes. The purpose of such grants is to provide incentives for research and development and other forms of economic rent seeking. Government discourages the creation of market power through price fixing and mergers of independent firms, but its policies promoting technical progress—greater cost effectiveness and more innovations—may increase market power.

Furthermore, government sometimes helps firms attain market power for reasons other than promoting progress. It does so by helping firms fix prices above the competitive level, restricting new competition, and inhibiting foreign competition. Price floors and import tariffs for agricultural products can also be interpreted as government helping firms gain market power.

Firms can earn profits in various ways. Microsoft and Wal-Mart have established themselves in computer software and in mass retailing, respectively. They have done this even though many other firms (including Apple, IBM, Sears, and K-Mart) have fought to prevent it. Microsoft and Wal-Mart have attracted consumers with a preferable product-price combination. Much of their success comes from successful **economic rent seeking** (entrepreneurial behavior). The entrepreneurial behavior of Bill Gates and Sam Walton and others such as Mary Kay and Oprah Winfrey is responsible for much economic growth and creates large economic profits. As with Microsoft, successful economic activity sometimes results in market power.

Economic rent seeking– Actions taken by entrepreneurs to increase profits.

Market power exists when firms earn economic profit for long periods without attracting new competitors and without improving their products or reducing their production costs. It permits a firm or a few firms to set a price higher than the competitive equilibrium price. Market power requires: (1) a few firms in control of the product and (2) limitations on the entry of new firms. For instance, in the U.S. tobacco products industries—that is, the cigarette industry—four firms, on average, produce over 90 percent of total U.S. production. These tobacco firms are in a different market situation than the many firms in the furniture industries—in these industries, on average, the four largest firms account for only about 30 percent of U.S. production. As a result, firms in the tobacco products industries realize that their output affects market price, whereas a firm in the furniture industries would not normally expect its output decisions to do so.

Market power– A situation in which a firm or a few firms can affect the price received for their product, and new firms do not enter the industry in response to economic profit.

Monopoly–
An industry with a single producer of a good that has no close substitutes.

Oligopoly–
An industry with only a few producers or sellers of a good.

Cartel–
An organized group of producers who manage their output and pricing as if they were a monopoly.

This chapter discusses market power and some of its effects on the U.S. economy. A **monopoly**, a single seller of a product with no close substitutes, is the extreme in market power; it chooses its product's price and might be able earn profits without attracting competitors. The chapter explains how monopolies determine price and discusses the source of market power in the U.S. economy. Most U.S. industries with market power are **oligopolies**. An oligopoly consists of a few firms selling the same or similar products. To what extent do oligopolies have market power? To answer this question, the chapter examines **cartels**. A cartel is an organized group of producers who attempt to manage their output and pricing as if they were a monopoly. The chapter first examines market power in terms of efficiency, and then it examines market power in terms of technical progress, by which we mean both technological improvements that lead to economic growth and efficiency improvements that lead to more cost-effective outcomes.

MONOPOLY ANALYSIS

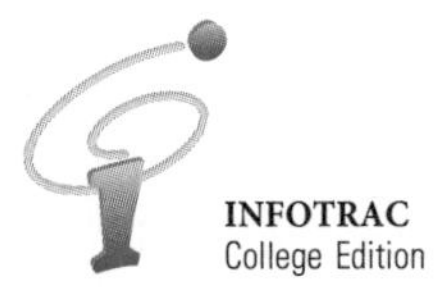

Keyword: *monopolies*

Access InfoTrac at http://infotrac.cengage.com

A monopolist is the sole producer of a good or service that has no close substitutes. One example is the distribution of electricity and natural gas. The monopoly arises because it is rarely cost-effective to build two or more pipelines or sets of transmission lines to serve the same local market. Currently, in most parts of the country, consumers of gas and electricity have only one supplier, and state government regulates it.[1] Other monopoly examples are found in small cities and towns. Throughout the country many such communities have only one provider of first-run movies and cable television. A quick Internet search indicates that Frostburg, Maryland; Lexington, Virginia; Davidson, North Carolina; Clemson, South Carolina; and Stillwater, Oklahoma, each have only one first-run theater. College students—and other residents—in these towns apparently have convenient access to only one theater. The theater monopolist's demand curve for attending first-run movies in these towns is the town's market demand curve. For example, in Figure 5.1, the output chosen by the monopolist determines the price that it can receive. If the monopolist chooses to attract a quantity of two moviegoers per week, the demand price, the maximum price at which that quantity can be attracted, is $8. For a larger quantity, three, the demand price is only $7. Clearly, the more people the monopolist wishes to attract, the lower the maximum price that it can charge. This conclusion is simply a restatement of the law of demand.

Contrast this with the situation facing the competitive firm. A competitive firm can sell as much or as little output as it produces without affecting its price; it is a *price taker*. Conversely, the quantity the monopolist chooses to sell affects price. The monopolist searches for the price that will maximize profit; it is a *price searcher*. Because the monopolist faces the market demand curve, its decision about how much to produce is more complicated than the competitive firm's decision. When it chooses an output, it also chooses a price. In contrast, the competitive firm chooses an output, but the market determines the price.

Marginal Revenue

Suppose the monopolist faces the demand situation posed by the first two columns in Table 5.1. At a price of $9, it can attract one moviegoer per week; at $8, it can attract two customers per week. At $9, its total revenue per week is $9 (column 3). At $8, its

[1]In some places the sale of electricity and natural gas is being deregulated and competition is being introduced. To create effective competition, the government must ensure that the owners of the distribution systems provide access to other firms that wish to sell electricity and gas.

Figure 5.1 The Monopolist Faces the Law of Demand

The monopolist is the only seller of the product. It can sell six units at $4. Alternatively, it can sell a larger quantity (seven units) if it accepts a lower price ($3). Suppose the price is $9. One unit is sold, and the total revenue is $9, which is the sum of the areas of the rectangles A and B. At $8, two units are sold, so total revenue is $16, the sum of the areas of A and C. At the lower price, the monopolist adds the area of C to total revenue for the first price, but must subtract the area of B. Thus, marginal revenue, the change in total revenue with a unit change in output, is the gain C minus the loss B. Because of the loss, marginal revenue is less than the new price.

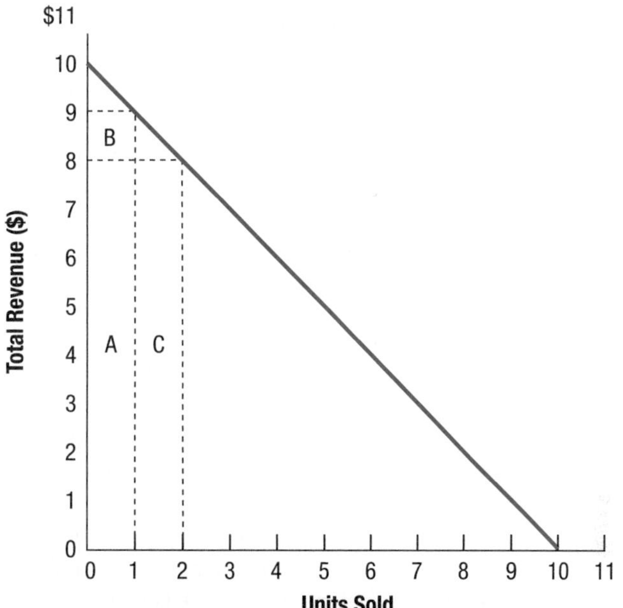

TABLE 5.1 DATA FOR THE MONOPOLY ANALYSIS

Q (1)	P (2)	TR (3)	MR (4)	MC (5)	TC (6)	PROFIT (7)
0	$10	$0	$—	$—	$0	$0
1	9	9	9	3	3	6
2	8	16	7	3	6	10
3	7	21	5	3	9	12
4	6	24	3	3	12	12
5	5	25	1	3	15	10
6	4	24	−1	3	18	6
7	3	21	−3	3	21	0
8	2	16	−5	3	24	−8
9	1	9	−7	3	27	−18

This table is based on the monopoly's demand schedule and marginal cost schedule. Given price and quantity, total revenue is price times quantity. Marginal revenue is then the change in total revenue with a unit change in output. Given marginal cost, total cost is the sum of successive marginal costs. Profit is total revenue minus total cost.

Q = Quantity per unit of time
P = Price per unit
TR = Total revenue = P × Q
MR = Marginal revenue = $TR_1 - TR_0$
MC = Marginal cost = $TC_1 - TC_0$
TC = Total cost = The sum of successive marginal costs
Profit = TR − TC

Marginal revenue– The change in total revenue associated with a one-unit change in the output sold by a producer.

total revenue is $16. By increasing its output from one to two tickets per week, it increases its total revenue by $7 per week. This change in total revenue with a unit change in output is **marginal revenue**. Marginal revenue is the private benefit to the monopolist of selling one more ticket.

It is easy to see why marginal revenue is less than price for the monopolist. When it plans to sell one ticket, it can charge $9. When it plans to sell two tickets, it must charge a lower price ($8) for the second ticket *and* the first one. Therefore, with a price of $8 rather than $9, the monopolist's increase in revenue is $8 from the second unit sold minus the $1 less that it earns on the first ticket now priced at $8; marginal revenue is $7. In comparison, the marginal revenue for a competitive firm is the same as price; the producer's marginal benefit for selling one more unit equals the marginal benefit to the buyer. Suppose the price of wheat is $5 per bushel. A wheat farmer might sell 1,000 bushels per year and receive $5,000 per year. If the wheat farmer instead had sold 1,001 bushels, she would receive $5,005 per year. With a unit increase in the number of bushels sold, the change in total revenue is $5—the price of a bushel of wheat. Marginal revenue equals price for the price taker because the price taker does not have to accept a lower price to sell an additional unit.

In Table 5.1, total revenue is in column 3 and marginal revenue is in column 4. Total revenue is price multiplied by quantity. Marginal revenue is the total revenue associated with a given quantity minus the total revenue associated with the preceding quantity. The total revenue associated with three tickets is the price ($7) times the quantity (three units), or $21. The total revenue associated with four tickets is $24. Thus, the marginal revenue associated with four tickets is $3, obtained as $24 – $21. If the monopolist decided to sell six tickets rather than five tickets (at $5 per ticket), it would have to lower its price to $4. As a result, total revenue would be $24 rather than $25. The marginal revenue would be negative; it loses $1 in revenue. It can take in more revenue by selling five tickets than by selling six tickets. As the example shows, marginal revenue decreases as output increases.

The Marginal Principle

To determine the output (tickets sold) that provides the greatest profit to the monopolist, we must include cost. For simplicity, Table 5.1 uses a special cost-output relationship. Marginal cost, the change in total cost with a one-unit increase in output, is constant at $3 per unit. We assume that for each ticket sold the monopolist must pay $3 to the movie producer and that the monopolist has no other costs. The first ticket sold requires the theater owner to pay the movie producer $3, and each succeeding ticket sold requires the same payment: $3. Therefore, the marginal cost of, say, the fourth ticket is $3. The total cost of producing four units is $12—$3 each for the first, second, third, and fourth units.

Marginal principle– To maximize profits, the producer should choose the output that equates marginal revenue and marginal cost.

The monopolist follows the **marginal principle** in choosing the output that maximizes profit. The marginal principle states that profit will be maximized if marginal revenue equals marginal cost. If marginal revenue is greater than marginal cost, the marginal principle implies that the monopolist should increase output because the addition to revenue is greater than the addition to cost. Profit must go up. Marginal revenue decreases as output increases and marginal cost is constant; therefore, they get closer as output increases, eventually reaching equality.

Table 5.1 shows that using the marginal principle leads the monopolist to an output where marginal revenue equals marginal cost. For instance, at an output of two units, marginal revenue ($7) is greater than marginal cost ($3). So, increasing output from one to two units increases the theater owner's total revenue by $7 and his total cost by $3. Profit increases by $4. At two units, profit is $10, compared to $6 at one unit.

Figure 5.2 **The Monopolist and Economic Efficiency**
Following the marginal principle, the monopolist chooses the output Q_2 that equates marginal revenue and marginal cost. It charges the highest price, P_2, consistent with selling that quantity. The marginal cost of the monopolist—under certain conditions—would be the supply curve for the competitive industry. If this industry were to become competitive, the equilibrium price and output would be P_1 and Q_4. So the monopolist restricts output below the competitive output and charges a price above the competitive price. It makes a profit given by the area P_1P_2MN.

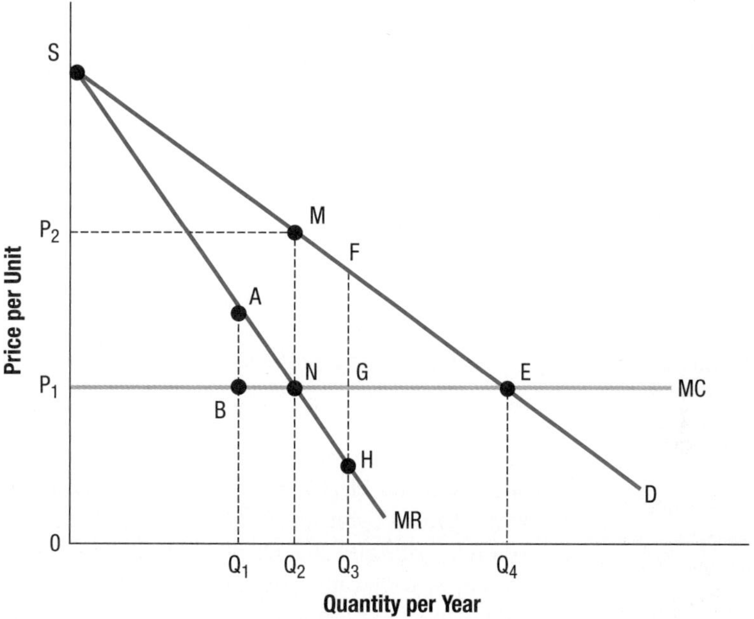

At five units, marginal revenue ($1) is less than marginal cost ($3). Decreasing output from five to four units increases profit by $2.

The profit-maximizing equilibrium may be easier to understand in a graphical analysis. Figure 5.2 shows a demand curve, a marginal revenue curve, and a marginal cost curve.[2] The marginal revenue curve lies below the demand curve. At output Q_1, marginal revenue is Q_1A and marginal cost is Q_1B. Increasing output slightly will increase profit by the distance AB. As long as marginal revenue is above marginal cost, increasing output will increase profit. Conversely, if output is greater than Q_2 (say, Q_3), decreasing output will increase profit. In summary, if output is less than Q_2, increasing it will increase profit; if output is greater than Q_2, decreasing it will increase profit. Therefore, the output that maximizes profit is Q_2.

The monopolist will sell its chosen output, Q_2, at the highest price possible, the demand price. This price P_2 is at the point where a vertical line from Q_2 intersects the demand curve. Given these demand and cost conditions, the monopolist will not want to charge a price higher than P_2. A monopolist cannot always increase its profit by increasing price. If the monopolist increases price, it reduces the quantity sold. Beyond a certain price, further increases do not pay.

[2]Here is a useful hint for drawing this diagram. For a straight-line demand curve, the marginal revenue curve is also a straight line. Furthermore, the marginal revenue curve lies halfway between the linear demand curve and the vertical axis. The marginal cost curve is a horizontal line, which is the assumption made in Table 5.1. We use the straight lines for convenience. All the results discussed would be the same for a curved demand curve and for a curved, upward-sloping marginal cost curve.

Monopoly and Competition Compared

Competitive market– For this issues-oriented analysis, the two most important conditions are that a market is competitive if the market has (1) many buyers and sellers so that both buyers and sellers are price takers and (2) easy entry of new producers so that new firms enter in response to economic profit and compete that profit away. More theory-oriented approaches add two conditions, namely that (1) firms in the industry produce the same or very similar products, and (2) both buyers and sellers have good information about market conditions.

Political rent seeking– The attempt to gain economic advantage through government action.

Efficient output– The output where marginal social benefit equals marginal social cost.

In Chapter 2 we discussed some of the characteristics of a market economy, and in Chapters 3 and 4 we discussed some of the characteristics of a **competitive market**. An industry operates in a competitive market if it has (1) many buyers and sellers so that both buyers and sellers are price takers; and (2) easy entry of new producers so that new firms enter in response to economic profit and compete that profit away. More theory-oriented approaches add two conditions, namely that (1) firms in the industry produce the same or very similar products, and (2) both buyers and sellers have good information about market conditions. A market economy composed mostly of competitive industries has several notable properties;

- First, decisions are impersonal; among the many decision makers, no single one has a decisive influence.
- Second, individuals can choose to buy products from or sell their labor to many different sellers and buyers. This freedom to choose limits the power of firms over customers and employees and vice versa.
- Third, the more firms in an industry, the less political power each is likely to have. All else being equal, the smaller the number of firms, the more easily they can organize for **political rent seeking**.

The existence of significant market power alters many of these properties:

- First, it makes markets personal. If the price of refrigerators increases, consumers blame General Electric or one of the other producers. In contrast, if the price of wheat goes up, consumers do not blame Farmer Jones.
- Second, significant market power limits the freedom to choose. Henry Ford supposedly said that his customers could have any color Model T that they wanted, so long as they wanted black. Only a producer with market power would dare be so unresponsive to consumers' tastes.
- Third, significant market power increases firms' effectiveness in political rent seeking.

Although impersonal markets, free choice, and political factors are important, economists often focus on the purely economic effects of market power. Suppose that the monopoly shown in Figure 5.2 becomes a competitive industry with no change in the marginal cost curve.[3] The minimum price that some producer would accept for the first unit of output is its marginal cost, P_1. The minimum price would be the same for any additional unit. This minimum price defines the marginal cost curve. Thus, the monopolist's marginal cost curve is the supply curve for the competitive industry. The demand curve also would remain unchanged. Therefore, under competition, price would be P_1, quantity would be Q_4, and economic profit would be zero.

Figure 5.2 suggests that a monopoly causes economic inefficiency because it restricts output to Q_2, compared to the output of the competitive industry, Q_4. As a result, the monopolist charges more—P_2 rather than P_1. By restricting output and increasing price, the monopolist drives a wedge between the demand price (marginal benefit to consumers) and the supply price (marginal opportunity cost of production) of the good. The value of one more unit of the good, the demand price, is greater than the value of the units of other goods given up to produce it—the opportunity cost or supply price. A potential gain from trade exists, but the trade is not made. So, output is less than the **efficient output**.

[3]Later in the chapter, we will discuss a situation in which changing a monopolistic industry into one with several firms will change the cost curve.

In contrast, under competition marginal revenue equals price. Both the consumer and the producer equate marginal revenue to price, resulting in the value of one more unit just equal to the opportunity cost of producing it. Consumers and producers make all trades that have a potential for gain because, in equilibrium, price measures both the value of one more unit and the cost of producing it—that is, demand price equals supply price. Under competition, the marginal private benefit received by the seller is the same as the marginal private benefit paid by the buyer. So if the marginal private benefit is greater than marginal opportunity cost, the item is produced and sold.

Under monopoly, the marginal private benefit to the seller is marginal revenue, and the marginal private benefit to the buyer is the price. The monopolist will choose to sell if her marginal private benefit (marginal revenue) is equal to or greater than marginal opportunity cost, but she will not produce and sell simply because the buyer's marginal private benefit, the maximum price that he is willing to pay, is greater than marginal opportunity cost. Marginal revenue must also be greater than marginal opportunity cost.

Some people object to monopoly because of monopoly profit. (Monopoly profit is a type of economic profit because it provides a return greater than the minimum return necessary to keep resources in the industry.) Unlike a competitive firm, a monopolist might earn monopoly profit in equilibrium. Monopoly profit, however, is not a loss to the economy; it is a transfer of income from consumers to the monopolist. People who dislike monopolies because of the profit they earn may be objecting to who earns the profit, not its existence. In fact, a monopolist has no guarantee of a profit. (A monopoly on slide rules probably would not be profitable.)

Perhaps the most fervent complaints about monopoly arise when the good monopolized is extremely important for its users, and its producer makes large profits—"blood money," according to an article in *Scientific American.*[4] An obvious example is the monopoly production and sale of breakthrough drugs: for instance, Lipitor, the widely used and highly profitable cholesterol-lowering drug, and Cialis. The possibility exists, of course, that expectation of such profits motivates pharmaceutical companies to undertake the research necessary to discover such drugs. In the next section, we explore the extent and sources of market power in the U.S. economy.

MARKET POWER AND ECONOMIC EFFICIENCY

Market power exists when a single seller or few sellers can adjust price or output in pursuit of greater profit and when profit fails to attract new firms into the industry. In the United States economy, many industries—such as the aluminum, automobile, beer, and cereal industries; computer operating systems; and the local telephone service—are dominated by a few firms. We raise three questions about this domination. One, has market power increased in the U.S. economy over the past 60 years? Two, to the extent that market power exists, why is it not eliminated by new competition? Three, does industry domination by a few firms allow them to exercise market power by raising market price?

The Trend in Market Power

Much evidence suggests that market power decreased in the U.S. economy until about 1980. It did increase in some industries such as the beer industry as Anheuser-Busch

---

[4]Tim Beardsley, "Blood Money? Critics Question High Pharmaceutical Profits," *Scientific American* 269 (August 1993): 115–117.

(Budweiser) and Miller became more prominent. In contrast, it decreased in the computing industry with the disappearance of IBM's dominance in computer hardware production. William Shepherd's comprehensive study concludes that market power in the U.S. economy fell from 1939 to 1958 and fell again from 1958 to 1980.[5] Competition increased, according to Shepherd, for three reasons:

1. The first is increased foreign competition, particularly in the manufacturing sector. As the European and East Asian economies recovered from the devastation of World War II and transportation costs declined, foreign competition became more intense. Government encouraged this greater competition by reducing barriers to foreign trade. As a result, U.S. producers of automobiles, televisions, other electronic equipments, and other products became less able to raise prices without attracting competition. The intensity of global competition has probably increased since 1980, the ending date for Shepherd's study.
2. Shepherd's second reason is government deregulation. The transportation sector is much more competitive than it was because government has eliminated some of its regulations. Interstate trucking, for instance, became more competitive after the late 1970s because no special permission or license beyond safety regulation and such is necessary to begin a freight transport business. Air transportation provides another example. Southwest Airlines, a small local carrier before deregulation, provides significant competition for other domestic airlines. Growing out of the Southwest, it has penetrated California and the Mid-Atlantic states, and it is now challenging in the New England states. Airfares are usually lower at airports serviced by Southwest. This new competition would not have been permitted before deregulation.
3. Third, Shepherd cites the federal government policies that made mergers and price fixing more difficult.

A fourth general reason, emerging after Shepherd's study, is the information revolution, which has increased competition in many industries. With easy access to information about prices and markets throughout the country and with lower transportation costs, the power of many local monopolies has diminished. Furthermore, business-to-business and business-to-consumer transactions are made with much more information because of the World Wide Web. As part of the information revolution, fiber optics and deregulation have increased competition in long-distance communications. Another communications revolution relates to new products and technologies that provide recorded recreation. Superstations, specialized networks, cable, and satellite dishes have created greater choices among programs, networks, and signal providers. And finally, new manufacturing technologies have allowed firms in some industries to operate at low cost, even at a small output rate.

In a later study, Frederic L. Pryor suggests that industrial concentration, which can be a basis for market power, began to increase in the 1980s.[6] Although data availability prevented his study from going beyond 1992, he contends that industrial concentration is likely to continue to increase. Although Pryor accepts Shepherd's analysis and finds it likely that changes in technology have reduced the relative advantage of large size, he believes that since 1980, the federal government has become more tolerant of mergers between firms in the same industry. Certainly, the evidence shows that the rate of such mergers has increased since 1980.

[5]William G. Shepherd, "Causes of Increased Competition in the U.S. Economy, 1939–1980," *Review of Economics and Statistics* 64, no. 4 (1982): 613–626.

[6]Frederic L. Pryor, "New Trends in Industrial Concentration," *Review of Industrial Organization* 18, no. 3 (2001): 301–326.

Barriers to Entry

Barrier to entry– Any condition that prevents new firms from entering an industry with the same cost conditions as existing firms.

Natural monopolies– Monopolies that exist if demand and cost conditions are such that only one firm can survive in an industry.

Keyword: *barriers to entry*

Access InfoTrac at http://infotrac.cengage.com.

To the extent that market power persists, it may do so because of **barriers to entry** that prevent firms from entering an industry with the same costs as existing firms. These have four major sources. First, technical conditions of production might be such that a technologically efficient factory operating at full capacity supplies most of the market. For instance, the output of a technologically efficient turbo generator factory would supply about 25 percent of U.S. production. Consequently, just a few firms produce turbo generators. The technical conditions of production create a barrier to entry. Indeed, some industries are **natural monopolies** because, in a free market, only one firm would survive. Such a monopoly cannot be broken into several firms without causing significant, unnecessary duplication. Imagine breaking a small-town electricity distribution system into five systems. Surely, cost would increase. In this situation, the monopoly with its lower cost may be more efficient than an industry with several firms. Because some natural monopolies produce goods and services of great importance to consumers, government often regulates them and sometimes even owns them. Natural monopolies, however, account for market power in only a few industries.

Second, an existing firm, or small group of existing firms, might control an essential input and thus have an absolute cost advantage over potential new firms. Firms in the aluminum industry have long had an advantage over potential rivals because they control most of the high-quality, accessible bauxite.

Third, existing firms in some industries—including the automobile, beer, and cereal industries—develop and maintain market power through product differentiation. A firm whose product is subject to competition from other firms with closely related products has at least one route to market power. If it can convince consumers that its product is superior to the related products, it can raise its price without sacrificing its sales completely. The product may actually be superior, or the firm may merely be convincing. Suppose an existing firm, say, Anheuser-Busch raises "brand" consciousness sufficiently to develop market power. Existing or potential rival firms may be unwilling or unable to invest in sufficient product development or marketing to recapture part of the Anheuser-Busch market.

Often a barrier to entry for new firms comes from the fourth source of monopoly, the government. The U.S. Postal Service is an example of a government-granted monopoly.

Nothing in the technology of first-class mail delivery, however, requires that it be one. The government also grants patents to people who invent new products or new ways of producing products, giving them the sole right to produce the product.

Furthermore, government grants protection from new firms in various other ways. For instance, taxes on goods imported from other countries—tariffs—protect domestic producers from foreign competition. Similarly, restrictions on the quantity of goods that can be imported—quotas—protect domestic producers. An example was a restriction on the number of cars that Japan could export to the United States. These restrictions allowed U.S. producers to charge U.S. consumers jacked-up prices. Governments also require that taxicab companies, physicians, and many other firms and professionals have licenses to operate. Whatever its purpose, licensing has the effect of excluding unlicensed people from the industry or occupation; it is a barrier to entry.

Some firms, however, achieve a dominant position in their industry because they provide their customers with a product that has a price-quality combination that other firms cannot match. One example might be Wal-Mart, which provides a type of retail service at a price that other firms apparently cannot match. Southwest Airlines may be another example. Wal-Mart's (and Southwest's) advantage appears to be due to cost advantages relative to other firms that have resulted from superior decision making by management

INTERNATIONAL PERSPECTIVE

The Battle Between American and Japanese Automobile Firms

The Big Three of the U.S. automobile industry emerged from World War II with more than 90 percent of U.S. car sales. This dominance continued into the 1970s. By 2004, however, the share had dropped to less than 60 percent. What happened?

Perhaps Sir John Hicks, a Nobel Prize–winning English economist, had the answer when he declared, "The best of all monopoly profits is a quiet life." Or, as a Chrysler executive said, "The real problem is that the U.S. car industry went to sleep for 20 years."[a]

History suggests that the postwar automobile industry exercised market power. It restricted output, and price increased; costs rose, and quality control faded. The industry was so lucrative that management could enjoy the quiet life. It was easier to share "monopoly" profits with the United Automobile Workers, the industry's trade union and its members, than to worry about costs. In addition, management allowed production methods to become obsolete and ignored quality problems. Consumers paid high prices for cars of mediocre quality. Autoworkers and management did well, and stockholders did all right but could have done better.

The energy crisis of the 1970s caught U.S. car producers off guard and increased the demand for smaller cars that got better gasoline mileage. Car imports, particularly from Japan, surged. The U.S. firms complained that Toyota and other Japanese firms had a protected home market and were subsidized by the Japanese government.

The Japanese cars, however, had more going for them than gasoline efficiency and perhaps government support. They were of higher quality and were cheaper to produce. Although Japanese wages were lower, the great shock was that the Japanese produced cheaper, higher-quality cars mostly because Japanese management was more effective. Rather than attempting to compete with Detroit's mass production techniques, Toyota's managers developed new techniques of car production. They made assembly line workers responsible for quality, whereas Detroit's mass production took responsibility away from workers. To Detroit's amazement, a Japanese worker could stop the assembly line if some production problem arose. Stopping the assembly line to prevent the production of defective cars was unheard of in Detroit. U.S. firms expected so many newly produced cars to be defective that they had repair shops at the end of the assembly lines. Nevertheless, the assembly line workers were not allowed or expected to do anything about it. In short, the Japanese adopted policies for quality control, inventory, and human relations that led to much greater productivity than U.S. firms could achieve. These improved management techniques are just as much an innovation, and perhaps just as important for growth and progress, as the many new products that have been introduced in the past 50 years.

In the 1990s, however, Chrysler, Ford, and GM improved quality and did well, particularly with light trucks (vans, SUVs, and pickups). Their share of car sales did not change much, but they had 73 percent of the car plus light trucks market. By 2004, as mentioned previously, this share was less than 60 percent.

[a]See John E. Kwoka, Jr., "Automobiles: Overtaking an Oligopoly," in Larry L. Duetsch (ed.), *Industry Studies*, 2nd ed. (New York: Sharp, 1998), 10. This study provides the basis for much of this discussion.

and a superior management system. They do not keep their management approach secret, but other firms cannot seem to match it. This type of cost advantage prevents them from competing effectively. Nevertheless, it is not an indication of the market power that leads to the economic inefficiency discussed in Chapter 4. Instead, it is the kind of success that results from economic rent seeking and leads to technical progress.

Most U.S. industries with market power are oligopolies—consisting of a few firms—rather than monopolies. Can a few market-dominating firms cooperate in choosing output and price? In the United States, such explicit cooperation is illegal. For instance, it is illegal for the owners of gasoline stations in a small town to agree to set a certain price for gasoline. Sometimes, however, the owners can achieve the same result without an explicit agreement. Perhaps they play golf together and simply come to understand that price cutting is not good manners. We examine this possibility in detail in the next section by studying the Organization of Petroleum Exporting Countries (OPEC) cartel. Since the early 1970s OPEC has been a powerful force affecting us every day through its direct effect on the price of gasoline and other products derived from crude petroleum.

OPEC: A FEW SELLERS ACTING LIKE A MONOPOLY

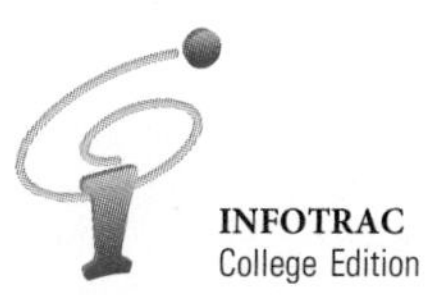

Keyword: *Organization of Petroleum Exporting Countries*

Access InfoTrac at http://infotrac.cengage.com.

Will industry domination by a few sellers allow them to exercise market power by raising price? In the United States it is illegal for firms to form a cartel and to agree to cut output or raise prices. But suppose it were legal. How effective would such an agreement be? OPEC, an organization of 11 petroleum-exporting countries, provides an excellent case study. (Although OPEC members are countries, not business firms, and may have objectives other than profits, OPEC provides an important example of a cartel.) In the early 1970s, these countries sold more than 90 percent of all petroleum exported to other countries. Petroleum production in these countries—for instance, Saudi Arabia, Iran, Venezuela, and Kuwait—had been increasing at the same time that production in the largest petroleum producers and consumers—the Soviet Union and the United States—had begun to decline. In 1970, the average U.S. price per barrel of oil at the well was $3.18. This average price started a roller coaster ride in 1974 when it rose to $7.67 and reached almost $40 in the summer of 1980. Some respected analysts expected $100-per-barrel prices by 1990, but the roller coaster headed down, with the price falling to $28.52 in 1982, $26.19 in 1983, and $24.09 in 1985 before it fell below $12 for a short time in 1986. The roller coaster headed up again starting in 2002. The price per barrel of West Texas crude oil reached $134 in 2008. Much of the price increase was generated by speculation in the oil commodities market by large hedge funds and sovereign funds. The ride down was swifter than anyone could imagine. Oil plummeted to $35 in January 2009. The current global recession and reduced driving habits have significantly reduced the demand for petroleum products.

Figure 5.3 shows the price of West Texas Intermediate Crude per barrel from June 1984 to December 2008. The figure shows that from 1987 through 1997 the price tended to remain between $18 and $22 per barrel, except for the period of the Gulf War, when it spiked to $36. In 1998 it fell to about $11 before it again climbed to about $35. From the beginning of 2002 until late 2005, it more than tripled, at times reaching $70 a barrel. The largest absolute price change in oil occurred during the period July 2007 to July 2008 when oil rose from $74 to $133 in one year.

In the mid-1980s, annual petroleum production in the Soviet Union and in the United States had increased compared to the mid-1970s. On the other hand, OPEC's Saudi Arabia—where petroleum is sometimes cheaper to pump than water in the United States—produced almost 50 percent less in the mid-1980s than it had in the mid-1970s. Other countries with reduced annual production were Kuwait, the United Arab Emirates, and Venezuela, all members of OPEC. Countries with sharply increased annual production were Mexico, the United Kingdom, and Norway, none of which are OPEC members.[7]

From 1991 to 1997, non–OPEC and OPEC production increased annually. In 1996 OPEC's production accelerated and received a boost in 1997 when Iraq's production increased, substantially. As mentioned above, prices began to fall in mid-1997 and reached

[7]Data can be found in various years' issues of the American Petroleum Institute's *Basic Petroleum Data Book*.

Figure 5.3 Monthly Petroleum Prices
This figure shows the price of West Texas Intermediate Crude per barrel from June 1984 to December 2008. The figure shows that from 1987 through 1997 the price tended to remain between $18 and $22 per barrel, except for the period of the Gulf War, when it spiked to $36. In 1998 it fell to about $11 before it again climbed to about $35. From the beginning of 2002 until late 2005, it more than tripled, at times reaching $70 a barrel. The largest absolute price change in oil occurred during the period July 2007 to July 2008 when oil rose from $74 to $133 in one year.

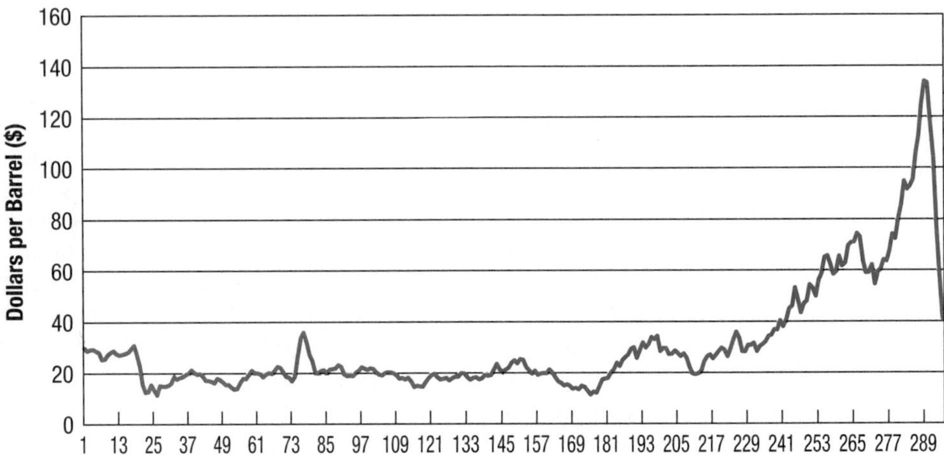

a low of about $12 in mid-1998. The falling prices were followed by almost a zero growth in non–OPEC countries' production, as Figure 5.4 shows. Since 2000, non–OPEC production has been increasing, but OPEC production has fallen and then increased. How are these price and production trends related to the OPEC cartel?

Figure 5.4 Petroleum Production (million barrels per day)
This figure gives annual oil production for OPEC and non–OPEC countries in terms of barrels per day. The up-and-down OPEC production since the mid-1990s contrasts with the steady upward trend of non–OPEC production.

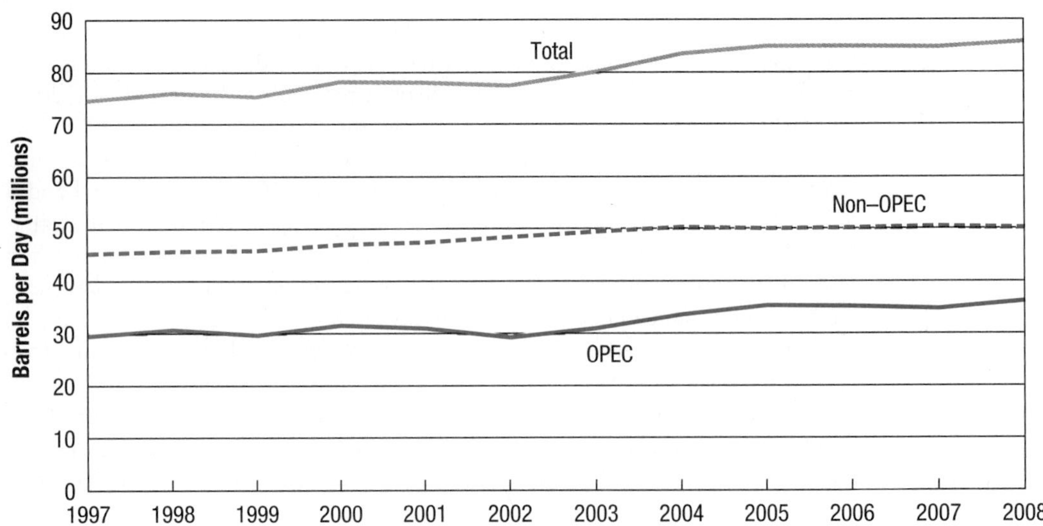

Source: U.S. Department of Energy, Energy Information Administration, *International Petroleum*, http://www.eia.doe.gov/.

Cartel Formation

Several of these changes in petroleum prices and production are consistent with OPEC acting as a cartel. For instance, the run-up in prices from 1973 to early 1980s probably resulted from OPEC output reductions. The sharp declines in the mid-1980s and the late 1990s were related to failures of cartel discipline and attempts by Saudi Arabia to stabilize oil prices. The rapid run-up since 2002, however, does not seem to be in response to OPEC actions. To see why the earlier price changes were likely related to OPEC actions and the later ones were not, we must discuss cartels in more detail.

To succeed, a cartel must restrict output and prevent entry of new firms. A successful cartel requires an ACE in the hole: agreement, cooperation, and enforcement. A cartel agreement requires that all important producers *agree* on both total output and the division of that output among cartel members. Its purpose is to restrict output and raise price above the competitive price. The agreement outlines a procedure for solving problems as they arise; it cannot, however, anticipate and solve all possible problems.

In a cartel, the members must continually *cooperate* and come to new agreements as conditions change. If they are successful, price will be above the marginal cost of production for each member of the cartel. For instance, the price of petroleum in early summer 2008 was above $133 a barrel in the United States. Some OPEC members can produce and deliver a barrel of petroleum to world markets for less than $5.

Every barrel a member country sells beyond its quota increases its profit by $128. Cheating is very profitable, as it is in any cartel. As long as a cartel member thinks it can cheat—produce more than its quota—without greatly affecting cartel price, it will be tempted to increase its profit by doing so. Therefore, a cartel must be able to *enforce* its agreement.

The Determinants of Cartel Success

All members of a cartel suffer from a split personality. On the one hand, they realize that the maximization of cartel profit is probably in the best interests of each member of the cartel. Thus, they agree to a common policy and cooperate in following and adapting that policy. On the other hand, if other members keep the agreement, each member realizes that it can increase its profit by cheating. Enforcement becomes necessary.

The fewer and more similar the firms, the easier it is to form and operate a cartel. In an industry consisting of two identical firms, the agreement that maximizes cartel profit requires that cartel output be divided evenly between the two firms. For instance, a national market might be split in two. Each firm could keep the profit it earns, and each would earn the same profit.

Furthermore, with only two members, it is easy to determine if the other firm cheats on an agreement. Suppose the market price falls below the expected cartel price. Either demand has decreased or the other member of the cartel is cheating by producing more than the agreed amount.

If cheating occurs, the noncheating firm probably will retaliate by also expanding output. The agreement will break down. Profit will decrease. Neither member wants this to happen. Because each firm can identify the cheater, the agreement may be self-enforcing. With just two identical firms in the industry, no explicit agreement is necessary to reach a cartel-type solution. This is why many economists think that some highly concentrated industries act as if they were monopolies, even in the absence of explicit cartel agreements.

It becomes progressively more difficult to agree on, cooperate with, and enforce a cartel policy (1) as the number of firms in the industry increases and (2) as the firms become less and less similar. With more firms it becomes more difficult for the agreement to include all or at least most of the major firms in the industry. One problem is the holdout. When Rockefeller Center was being developed in New York City, owners of a small piece of land in its midst refused to sell. Perhaps the owners had some sentimental attachment to the business that they operated on the land. Or perhaps they hoped to obtain a much higher price by holding out until the last minute.

A potential member of a cartel might behave in the same way, letting the other firms restrict their output so the holdout will benefit from the higher price without restricting its output. With such a bargaining position, the holdout firm might capture a larger share of the cartel profit. Rockefeller Center was built around the holdout, but continuing cartel success requires that almost all major players participate.

A second problem is that, with more firms, it becomes more difficult to detect cheating. If there are ten firms in the cartel and the cartel price starts to fall, then either there is a decrease in demand or at least one of the nine other cartel members is cheating. But which? Thus, each firm might think that it could cheat without being detected. As the detection of cheating becomes more difficult, the temptation to cheat becomes overwhelming.

If the firms are dissimilar, agreement also is harder to reach. Suppose there are only two firms, but one is a higher-cost firm. As you might think, to produce a given output at least cost, the lower-cost firm must produce a larger share of total output than the higher-cost firm. In the extreme case, the lower-cost firm would produce all of the cartel output. But now the initial bargaining becomes extremely difficult. The higher-cost firm will insist on a larger profit share than output share in return for accepting the lower output quota. The lower-cost firm will counter that profit shares and output shares should be the same. If the lower-cost firm has a large cost advantage, it may be able to force the other firm to accept and keep an agreement. It may do so by threatening to flood the market with output unless the higher-cost firm cooperates.

Problems of the OPEC Cartel

The OPEC cartel has had serious problems for at least three reasons.

1. First, there are 11 member and 6 to 10 nonmember countries that are important petroleum producers. It currently accounts for less than one-half of world production.
2. Second, the demand and supply for petroleum are different when consumers and producers have time to adjust completely to a price change.
3. Third, the member countries of OPEC have different and conflicting goals.

OPEC's initial success in the 1970s, measured by the increase in price from about \$3 a barrel to more than \$30 a barrel in less than a decade, was due to a number of factors. Political upheaval in the Middle East played an important role. OPEC also accounted for more than 90 percent of the world's exports. But OPEC did not have significant barriers to entry for new producers. As a result of major petroleum discoveries in Alaska, the North Sea, and Mexico and of numerous successful attempts to squeeze more petroleum out of existing fields, non–OPEC production grew substantially.

The petroleum pessimists in the 1970s thought that the supply of petroleum could be represented by a supply curve such as S_0 in Figure 5.5. On S_0, an increase in price from P_0 to P_1 does not cause an increase in quantity supplied. But the pessimists underestimated both the greed and the ingenuity of business owners. The incredible profit potential of \$30-a-barrel petroleum attracted a tremendous amount of resources into the industry. Given sufficient time for adjustment—five to ten years—the supply curve for petroleum looks more like S_1 in Figure 5.5. The increase in price engineered by OPEC

Figure 5.5 The Supply of Petroleum
If the supply of petroleum is similar to S_0, raising price does not induce an increase in quantity supplied. Many people believed that OPEC would be successful because they thought S_0 was a good representation of the supply curve for petroleum. It turns out, however, that the supply curve for petroleum is more like S_1 because the price increases engineered by OPEC resulted in big increases in quantity supplied by non–OPEC producers.

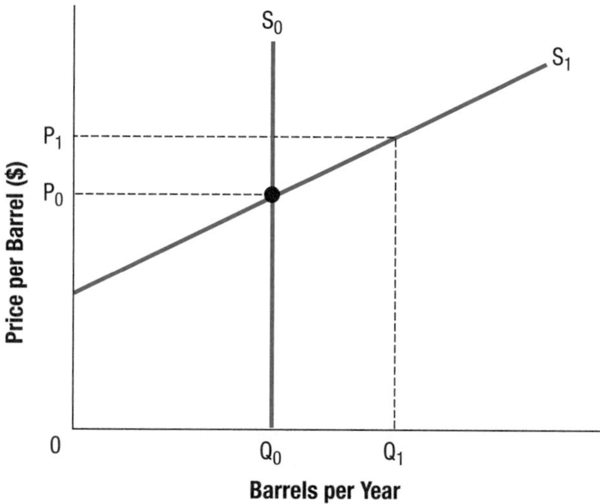

carried the seeds of its own destruction in the supply response of non–OPEC countries. At price P_1 quantity supplied ultimately increases from Q_0 to Q_1.

Just as the petroleum pessimists underestimated supply responsiveness, they also underestimated demand responsiveness to a price change. The pessimists thought that demand responsiveness was almost nil. It is only a slight exaggeration to say that they thought that the demand for petroleum products was vertical. When price increased suddenly and substantially in the 1970s, consumers were not able to adjust their purchases very much—at first. The demand for petroleum could be cut only so much by reducing (1) pleasure driving, (2) home heating in the winter, and (3) home cooling in the summer. But given time to adjust, people replaced their cars, furnaces, air conditioners, and houses with more energy-efficient ones.

Similarly, firms adopted more energy-efficient methods of production. The amount of energy used per dollar of national output has fallen every year since 1975. Thus, the demand curve for petroleum products—given several years for adjustment—is better represented by D_1 than D_0 in Figure 5.6. Here, an increase in price from P_0 to P_1 ultimately causes quantity demanded to fall from Q_0 to Q_1.

Finally, the OPEC countries differ substantially in terms of their petroleum reserves, their populations relative to their reserves, and in many other ways. They are not similar. Just as in any cartel, each country's self-interest conflicts with the objective of maximizing cartel profit. Countries with large reserves relative to their populations, such as Saudi Arabia, want to stretch their sales of petroleum and their profits over a long period of time. They fear that a low-output/high-price strategy will hasten the demise of petroleum as a major source of energy, preventing them from enjoying petroleum profits in the future.

Countries with large populations and small reserves want to get their profit now with a low-output/high-price strategy. They wish to use their profit to finance economic development and to reduce political tension. They do not care that such a strategy might result in an early replacement of petroleum as a prime source of energy because they

Figure 5.6 The Demand for Petroleum
If the demand for petroleum is similar to D_0, raising price does not induce a decrease in quantity demanded. Many people believed that OPEC would be successful because they thought D_0 was a good representation of the demand curve for petroleum. It turns out, however, that the demand curve for petroleum is more like D_1 because the price increases engineered by OPEC resulted in large decreases in quantity demanded after consumers had time to adjust.

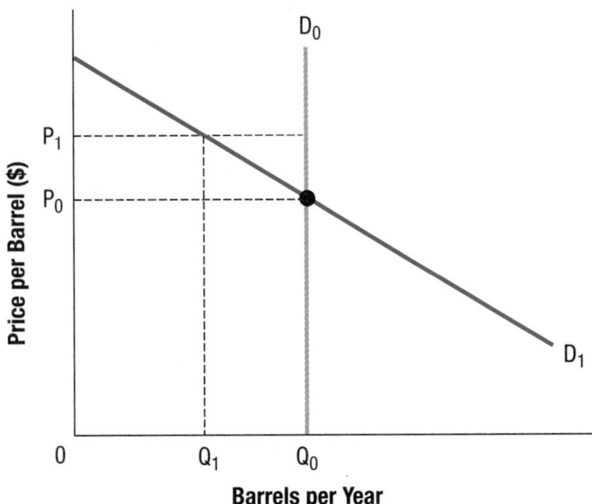

will not have any petroleum to sell in the future. The different objectives enhance the always-present incentive to cheat; thus, OPEC is "a confederacy of cheats."[8] Several important producers regularly violate OPEC agreements.

The largest producer in OPEC, Saudi Arabia, holds the cartel together. It is a very low-cost producer with a probable objective of establishing a cartel price that will stretch its profit over a long time. It is such a large and low-cost producer that it can cause wide swings in the price of petroleum. In the early 1980s, it supported the cartel price by substantially reducing its output. As a result, other countries could cheat with impunity.

In the mid-1980s, Saudi Arabia became an enforcer. It substantially increased its output, driving the price of petroleum temporarily below $10 a barrel. Other cartel members and perhaps nonmembers got the message: cooperate or the price will stay extremely low. New agreements were reached at a lower price level and a higher output level than existed in the early 1980s. A recent chapter in the OPEC saga started in 1998, when oil prices had fallen to around $12 a barrel, with Mexico receiving just $7 a barrel for a few shipments. OPEC countries had steadily increased their production, with their share of world production increasing from 30 percent in 1985 to 47 percent in 1998. Late in 1998, Luis K. Tellez, Mexico's energy minister, persuaded the OPEC countries and Norway to cut production. The cartel played its ace. OPEC production fell by more than 4 percent, and non–OPEC production barely changed relative to 1998. Mexico's and Norway's cuts in close cooperation with OPEC offset increases in other non–OPEC countries. By the end of 1998 petroleum prices were rising, and they approached $35 a barrel by the beginning of 2000. Large production increases by OPEC and the triumvirate of Mexico, Norway, and Russia in 2000 started prices on a downward slide to about $20 a barrel at the end of 2001. In 2001 OPEC again cut production, but Russia continued to increase

[8] "A Confederacy of Cheats," *The Economist*, June 10, 1989.

Figure 5.7 **Changes in Petroleum Production, 1998–2008**
This figure shows year-on-year changes in production starting in 1998. The assistance and encouragement that Mexico and the North Sea producing countries gave to OPEC from 1998 to 2002 contrast with the production increases for Russia beginning in 1999. In 2003 and 2004 OPEC—followed by Mexico and the North Sea producing countries in 2004—began increasing production, but the increases in 2004 were bigger than those in 2005.

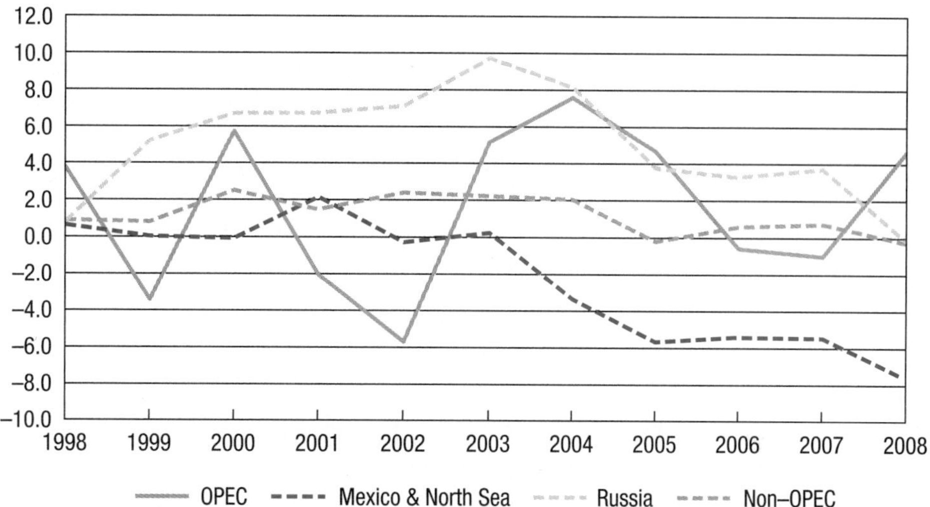

its production. OPEC's efforts to keep prices in the $25 to $30 range met resistance from countries not in the cartel.

We have now seen $100 plus for a barrel of oil. Is OPEC responsible for its resulting bonanza, and is it likely to persist? As Figure 5.7 shows, OPEC and its Mexican and North Sea producing allies cut output in 2001 and 2002, continuing the upward pressure on price. From 2003 to 2006, both OPEC and non-OPEC countries increased production at a decreasing rate. With prices going up so fast in these four years, the OPEC response was to expand output. Rather than causing the price increases with its output policy, OPEC moderated them. Part of the moderate response was in response to short-term profit taking and possibly cheating on output quotas, but another part presumably is Saudi Arabia's political and economic response to high oil prices. In the first half of 2005, Saudi Arabia may have been producing at more than a 25 percent faster rate than in 2002, which was well above its quota. (Note that these production figures vary by source and are subject to revision.)

Although the OPEC cartel's output policy probably has had little to do with the rapid price increases beginning in 2003, their past capacity decisions may have been important. If we assume that Saudi Arabia would prefer lower, sustainable oil prices than the levels of fall 2005 and summer 2008, then the reason that it and its allies within OPEC are unable to push prices down is their lack of capacity. Perhaps OPEC, and the world, are about to reach their peak of oil production. More likely, however, the Saudi investment decisions over the last decade underestimated the effects of political instability and demand growth. Consequently, prices have increased beyond the level desired by the enforcer.

The Energy Information Administration of the U.S. Department of Energy is projecting oil (West Texas Intermediate) prices to average above $60 through 2009. After 2006, the forecast for world oil prices adjusted for inflation is for the price to increase to

[9]"The Emperor's New Clothes," *Global Markets* 32, no. 25 (July 1, 2002): 1.

[10]"Analysts See Steady Oil Price for 2002," *The Oil Daily* 52 (June 24, 2002).

$78 a barrel by 2010 and remain between $78 and $95 through 2012. The demand and supply analysis of Figures 5.5 and 5.6 shows how such a scenario could play out. At $60 a barrel and current costs, producing an additional barrel of oil is incredibly profitable. Both OPEC and non–OPEC sources can be expected to respond to these prices. Similarly, the energy prices—particularly for transportation fuel and heating fuel—implicit in $60-a-barrel oil will result in increasing reactions by consumers.

The high prices for crude and accompanying profit opportunities are accompanied by:

- Huge investments in petroleum production and alternative technologies.
- Expanding supply in countries such as Russia, Angola, China, Algeria, Britain, India, Canada, and Azerbaijan.
- Projects in South Korea, China, Singapore, and the United States to expand production of drilling rigs.
- Refinery expansion in the United States by Chevron, ConocoPhillips, and Valero.
- Increased use of mass transit, increased sales of hybrid cars, and expansion of wind power.
- Increased investment and technological advancements in renewable and other alternative energy sources.

Do a Few Firms That Dominate a Market Have Market Power?

It is not easy to determine if a few firms that dominate a market have market power. The internal tensions caused by the entry of new producers, by the substitution of other products for the cartel's products, and by dissension and cheating in the cartel itself are not unique to OPEC. Any formal or informal agreement to restrict output and increase price is subject to similar tensions. In the absence of barriers to entry and government enforcement of agreements, formal and informal cartels are likely to be unstable. If government actively discourages cartels, it is even more difficult for them to function. In short, the market power of oligopolies is weaker: (1) the greater the number of firms; (2) the more dissimilar the firms; (3) when there is no powerful firm to enforce an agreement; and (4) over time, because of the responses of consumers and other producers to high prices and large profits.

MARKET POWER AND TECHNICAL PROGRESS

As we have seen, economic efficiency and a dispersion of economic and political power require industries in which firms do not have much market power. Technical progress, as we saw in Chapter 1, depends upon the development of new products and methods of production and on using existing technologies more effectively. Using existing knowledge better and creating new knowledge are ways in which entrepreneurs adapt to external changes and generate economic growth. Firms that are successful in adapting to new situations and in creating new knowledge can be expected to grow and might develop significant market power.

Some types of knowledge-based firms have several characteristics that may lead them to a monopoly or near monopoly. For instance, the development of a new medicinal drug or a new operating system for computers has huge start-up costs, and the product developed is essentially knowledge. After the knowledge of how to produce a new drug, operating system, or chip is developed, huge investments in plant and equipment might be required to produce the product. These large up-front costs are a much bigger part of the total cost of developing a drug or a chip than are the direct labor and material costs of producing one. Therefore the firm's marginal cost of production, after the knowledge

Figure 5.8 **Retail Gasoline Prices, 1999–2009**
This figure shows the sharp increase in gasoline prices beginning in 2002 and the dramatic decline in gasoline prices starting in August 2008.

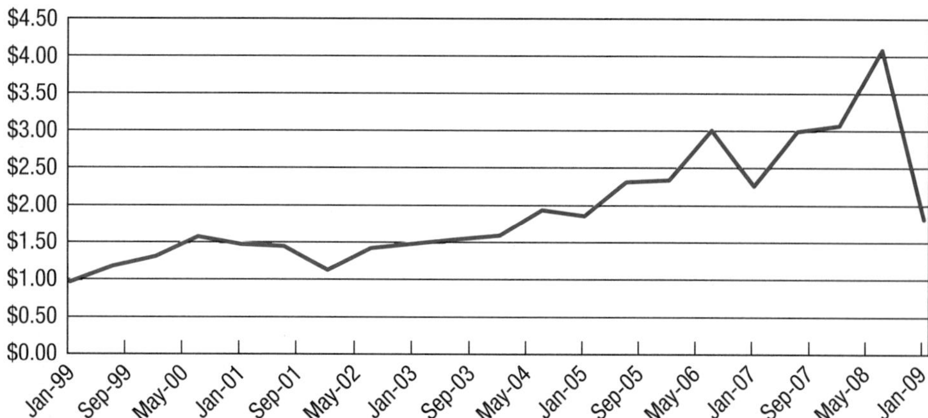

Source: U.S. Department of Energy, Energy Information Administration, *Retail Gasoline Prices*, http://www.eia.doe.gov/.

is developed and the investments in plant and equipment are made, is very low. For such firms to anticipate and actually make profits, they must be able to price well above marginal cost.[11] In short, a requirement for success is the ability to earn monopoly profits in production to cover the up-front development costs.

It is not just in the modern high-tech industries, however, that entrepreneurs and other firms' decision makers must develop new knowledge or learn to use existing knowledge in creative ways in a search for profits. The changing environment in which petroleum firms operate and have operated requires that they respond in new ways. Examples of the dynamic environment in the industry are numerous. Over the last 30 years, the price of oil, as we have seen, has fluctuated enormously. The sources of crude oil to refineries in the United States have been changing, along with its chemical composition. Environmental regulations have become increasingly strict.

In this section, we will discuss the petroleum refining industry's reaction to these changes. One of the industry's products, gasoline, is one whose recent price behavior is familiar. As Figure 5.8 shows, from 2004 to 2009 retail gasoline prices ranged from about $1.57 to $4.06 per gallon.

Gasoline prices, of course, are affected by the price of crude oil, but from August 2004 to August 2005 gasoline prices rose more than would be expected from the oil price increases. As the article "Gas Profit Guzzlers" in the September 25, 2005, edition of the *Washington Post* points out, this implies that it is not only the crude producers who are profiting. Refiners, both those integrated with crude producers, such as ExxonMobil, and independent refiners that purchase crude to refine, such as Valero Energy Corp., also profit. According to this article, Senator Dorgan of North Dakota wants to tax some of these profits away. As quoted in the Post article, he said, "They obviously are experiencing windfall or excess profits … They … are profiting in an extraordinary way at the expense of the American consumer."

We previously discussed why crude prices have increased and why crude production is profitable. In summary, it is because of unexpected demand increases in the face of

[11] W. Brian Arthur, "Increasing Returns and the New World of Business," *Harvard Business Review* 74 (July–August 1996): 100–109. The quotation is from 103.

Figure 5.9 Petroleum Refining Capacity
This figure shows the mircochange in refining capacity for the United States, East Coast states, and West Coast States.

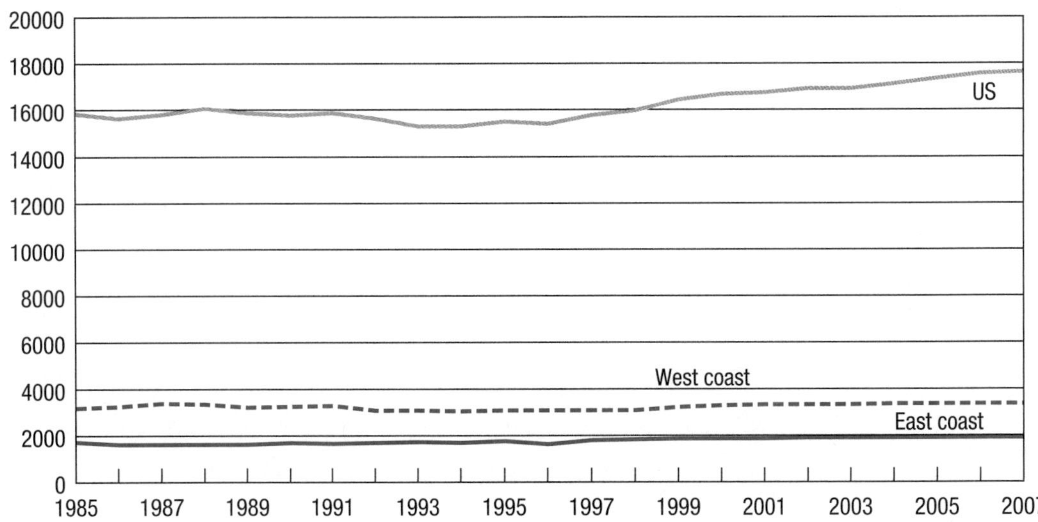

Source: U.S. Department of Energy, Energy Information Administration, *Retail Gasoline Prices*, http://www.eia.doe.gov/.

a slowly growing OPEC and world capacity. The slowly growing OPEC capacity, in particular, may be caused by cartel behavior or by the possibility that oil production is peaking. The increased refinery profits are caused by slowly growing refinery capacity. Could this slow growth in refinery capacity also be a result of cartel behavior?

Refinery capacity and the number of refineries have fallen in the United States over the last two decades. by more than one-half, and not a single new refinery has been built in the United States since the 1970s. Since 1990 over 2,600 mergers have occurred in the petroleum industry. As Figure 5.9 shows, U.S. refinery capacity has grown only 11 percent during the past 22 years. East and West coast refining capability remained nearly unchanged. This growth occurred because refineries have invested to increase the capacity of a given physical structure. The economics of refinery construction and its risks are such that this so-called "capacity creep" is a more cost-effective way to add capacity than construction of a totally new refinery. Increased imports of gasoline have also, in effect, provided capacity. These imports have more than doubled since the mid-1990s. Importing refined products is a way of overcoming slow growth in refinery capacity. It is not unusual to import rather than build domestic capacity. Look at automobiles and steel.

The concentration ratio—the percentage of refinery capacity in the United States owned by the four largest firms—increased from about 25 to 45 percent from 1981 to 2000. For the Upper Midwest (Illinois, Indiana, Kentucky, Michigan, and Ohio) it increased from about 55 to 75 percent. These are large increases in concentration ratios, and the concentration of production among a few firms may be sufficient to permit cartel behavior. In fact, the United States General Accountability Office believes that the mergers that occurred resulted in increased market power and increased prices. On average, however, it found that the mergers increased prices on the order of two cents a gallon. One reason that the mergers had such a small effect on price is that they resulted in more cost-effective operation. These cost savings moderated the increase in price.

Refineries are making substantial profits, but the evidence developed by the National Petroleum Council, an advisory group to the U.S. Department of Energy, suggests that from 1981 to 2002 the profit rates in the petroleum industry were slightly lower than

ADDITIONAL INSIGHT

Rita, Katrina, and Refineries: Economic or Political Rent Seeking

Utilization of refining capacity in the United States is intense. Consequently, any disruption of refinery operations has a large effect on the prices of gasoline and other refined petroleum products. If refiners and distributors were to maintain larger inventories, this price effect might be moderated. But sustained demand increases and modern inventory policies have resulted in smaller inventories. Because people cannot quickly adjust to higher gasoline prices, the effect of the disruptions is for them to spend more for essential transportation. Nevertheless, the inventory policy must lead to lower-cost operations overall, or the firms would not find it profitable to follow the policy.

We suggest in the text that refinery capacity grows in response to profits through capacity creep, and that imports are a more cost-effective source of refined products than would be the use of marginal U.S. capacity. Nevertheless, some politicians have attempted to provide a "solution" to the capacity "problem." In early October 2005, President Bush and the Republican Congress pushed a bill through the House of Representatives that would (1) provide federal land for new refineries and financial aid to build a refinery for the military; (2) compensate oil companies for regulatory delays; and (3) relax regulations that inhibit refinery expansion and gasoline supply.

Subsidizing the building of a new refinery could, of course, lead to a capacity increase. But if the market won't support it, this new subsidized capacity would displace already existing capacity. If the market would support it, it would be more profitable for firms to expand capacity through capacity creep. The market also suggests that imports may be another effective source of incremental supply. The case for subsidizing capacity expansion and particularly new refinery construction is weak.

Compensating refineries for regulatory delays and relaxing regulations may or may not be desirable. If the environmental, health, and safety regulations are well conceived and well executed, then meeting these regulations is part of the cost of gasoline production. It is appropriate that they be reflected in the price. If they are not well conceived and well executed, reform is in order. In other words, the regulations should be considered on their merits and are irrelevant for capacity expansion.

In another twist, politicians and policy makers in Oklahoma have noted the heavy concentration of U.S. refinery capacity in Louisiana and Texas. One newspaper source said that Oklahoma experts believe that capacity "should be focused more in the central states, such as Oklahoma [so that] natural disasters like Hurricane(s) Rita and Katrina" do not disrupt U.S. energy markets. Another expert noted the decline in refinery capacity in Oklahoma since 1981.

Admittedly, it seems odd to have so much refining capacity in the path of hurricanes (although moving it to Tornado Alley may not be the best response), but firms are expanding capacity in the Gulf Coast and on the West Coast. Does this not tell us that the firms believe that these locations are the most profitable? They don't think that locating refineries on these coasts is a mistake. If they did, they would have closed refineries there and expanded them in the central states. The people with the most pertinent knowledge about refineries and energy markets—and with the most incentive to use that knowledge profitably—are the people in the industry making these decisions. As they engage in economic rent seeking, they will, as we have seen, be making decisions that benefit their customers as well. The politicians are unlikely to be as knowledgeable about the industry, and their incentives are not so much focused on making profitable decisions as on decisions that have political benefits.[a]

[a]Sources for this discussion included David Ivanovich, "House Passes Bill to Aid Refineries," *Houston Chronicle*, October 8, 2005; and Janie Halencak and James Gutzmer, "Refineries Hot Topic at REDI Meeting," *Cushing Daily Citizen*, October 9, 2005.

those earned by other large American firms and that they were even lower in the refinery sector. Nevertheless, refiners have adjusted to new sources of crude, new technologies, environmental regulations, and inventory policies in ways that have resulted in a more efficient industry. They have expanded capacity even as they shut down refineries. They have also made the technical changes necessary to refine different types of petroleum profitably. The business firms in the refinery sector have also responded to various environmental, health, and safety regulations. They have developed new technologies and applied old technologies in innovative ways. The sustained profits generated over the last two years can be expected to provide incentive for the continued expansions of capacity, which are likely to continue to be capacity creep and imports, and for developing new ways of squeezing gasoline out of crude. The alternative to allowing profits and profit seeking to guide the investments would be some type of government industrial policy focused on refinery capacity. Senator Dorgan's legislation to tax the profits away would be a movement in this direction, and in the direction of the technical and business decisions being made by politicians and bureaucrats.

GOVERNMENT AND MARKET POWER

Economists have not reached consensus on government's role in dealing with market power, as they have, for instance, concerning farm policy. The conflicting implications of economic efficiency and economic growth create this lack of consensus. Promoting static economic efficiency requires limiting market power; promoting dynamic economic efficiency—technical progress—may require more permissive policies dealing with market power. Three general principles can guide policy toward market power in a way that reconciles the sometimes conflicting goals of efficiency and growth. First, government can limit mergers of firms that produce the same or similar products and prohibit price fixing. Second, government can encourage economic rent seeking by granting patents and copyrights and by supporting basic research. Finally, it must discourage political rent seeking so that government itself does not become a source of market power.

U.S. antitrust laws dealing with mergers and price fixing probably satisfy the first principle. They make it even harder for oligopolies to reach formal or informal agreements to exercise market power. These laws, particularly the Clayton and Sherman Acts, prohibit explicit conspiracies to fix prices, divide markets, restrict entry, and engage in other cartel behavior. They also help to maintain the number of firms in an industry by preventing mergers that would increase market power without providing offsetting benefits. As Shepherd argues, these laws enhance the tendencies for industries to remain or become competitive. Recall, however, that Pryor contends that antimerger enforcement became much less stringent in the last two decades of the twentieth century. Given the federal antitrust laws and the existing structure of industries in the United States, many economists believe that market power is not a major problem in the U.S. economy. They recognize that it exists, but they do not advocate government action—beyond the current antitrust laws—to reduce it. From this perspective, the merger wave in petroleum, particularly in the refining sector, apparently resulted in more efficient firms and perhaps some additional market power.

According to the second principle, government policy should not impede and perhaps should promote economic rent seeking. The tremendous growth in industrial economies in the past two centuries depended largely upon the entrepreneur seeking profit. To sustain progress, we must allow prices and price changes to relay information about scarcity and changing scarcity to entrepreneurs, and entrepreneurs must be allowed to reap profit from their innovations. Instead of breaking up or regulating firms that achieve market power and profits through economic rent seeking, government can play a positive role by increasing the incentive for innovation. As the experiences of General Motors and IBM show, the market power that is created is often temporary. Market power in a market economy is like the mythical gunslinger in the Old West: it lasts only until someone faster comes along.

The third principle implies that government must take care not to make political rent seeking more lucrative than economic rent seeking. Granting patents to innovators must not lead to granting market power to existing firms and interest groups. Political rent seeking—the attempt to gain economic advantage through government action—supports much market power. License systems support the market power of accountants, some cab companies, doctors, real estate dealers, and others. In almost every instance, the license system is requested by the industry or occupation. Moreover, the standards for obtaining and keeping a license are almost always set by the industry or occupation. Rarely does such activity lead to economic progress.

Summary

A competitive economy is efficient because the value of one more unit of any good (marginal benefit) is just equal to the opportunity cost of producing one more unit (marginal cost). If marginal benefit were greater than marginal cost, unrealized gains from trade would exist. This is because the value of the additional unit of a good would be greater than the value of the goods given up to produce it. The monopolist restricts output and raises price above marginal cost. Marginal benefit under monopoly is greater than marginal cost. Thus, the monopoly output is inefficient.

Yet the monopolist cannot raise price without limit. When price goes up, output goes down. Charging more and selling less is not always a good strategy. To maximize profit, the monopolist equates marginal revenue with marginal cost.

The U.S. economy is reasonably competitive. Efficiency loss due to monopoly appears limited. Moreover, profit attracts new firms into an industry. In addition, economic rent seeking—innovation—is important in many parts of the economy, in particular the knowledge-based industries.

Monopoly occurs for four reasons: (1) technology sometimes requires that a firm be so large that it can supply the entire market; (2) a firm might control essential inputs or have other absolute cost advantages; (3) a firm might use advertising and product development to gain a dominant position; and (4) government sometimes encourages monopoly.

The OPEC cartel shows how several firms in an industry might act like a monopoly. Although numerous countries produce petroleum, OPEC has succeeded in restricting petroleum output and raising price. Cooperation, however, is not perfect. Some countries cheat on the cartel agreement by producing more than their share. Enforcement activity by Saudi Arabia has increased OPEC cartel stability.

Analyses of cartels and of OPEC in particular show that agreement among firms—even if it is not an explicit agreement—might lead to monopoly. But cheating—which increases as the number of firms in the industry increases—and the entry of new firms destabilize such agreements. Government can promote competition through antitrust laws, but it must avoid impeding economic rent seeking.

Economic growth, as well as economic efficiency, is related to monopoly and competition. As they develop new products and processes, knowledge-based firms may achieve significant market power. Doing this on the merits of their products rather than through price fixing and mergers may promote economic growth. Even though such firms capture a large market share, government policy, in such circumstances, must recognize that reining in their profit-seeking behavior may reduce the incentive to innovate and thus impede economic growth.

Key Terms

Economic rent seeking
Market power
Monopoly
Oligopoly
Cartel
Marginal revenue
Marginal principle
Competitive market
Political rent seeking
Efficient output
Barrier to entry
Natural monopolies

Review Questions

1. List and briefly discuss the major sources of monopoly in the United States.
2. If a firm is a pure competitor, marginal revenue and price will be equal. If the firm is a monopoly, marginal revenue will be less than price. Justify these statements.
3. Suppose you are given the information about a monopoly that appears in the following table.

Quantity	Price	Marginal Cost
1	$50	$20
2	45	20
3	40	20
4	35	20
5	30	20
6	25	20
7	20	20
8	15	20
9	10	20
10	5	20

   a. What is the firm's total revenue for each quantity?
   b. What is the firm's marginal revenue for each quantity?
   c. What quantity and price should the firm choose to maximize its profits?
   d. Suppose the monopolist is currently producing five units of the good. What actions should it undertake, and why?
   e. Use the information above to plot the demand curve faced by the monopolist, the monopolist's marginal revenue and marginal cost curves, the profit-maximizing level of output, and the profits earned by the firm.
4. "A monopolist can charge whatever price it desires for its output." Is this statement true or false? Defend your answer.
5. State and defend the general principle to be followed in maximizing profits.
6. Use graphical analysis to compare and contrast the economic outcome of monopoly with the economic outcome of pure competition.
7. "Because a monopolist can extract a higher price than a firm that is a pure competitor, the monopolist will always earn a profit." Is this statement true or false? Defend your answer.
8. Why does the efficient output occur where marginal benefit equals marginal cost? Analyze in detail.
9. What is a cartel? What factors help to maintain a cartel? What factors encourage its dissolution?
10. Evaluate Senator Dorgan's quote that "They obviously are experiencing windfall or excess profits ... They ... are profiting in an extraordinary way at the expense of the American consumer," and its implications.
11. Evaluate the following statement: "Because monopoly results in economic inefficiency and in large profits for a few powerful corporations, we should enforce regulations to break up these firms or eliminate their profits."
12. According to the box titled "The Battle between American and Japanese Automobile Firms," why were the Japanese firms successful in the battle?
13. What are the advantages and disadvantages of allowing profits and profit-seeking behavior to determine refinery capacity investment in the United States?
14. Upon initial consideration, concentrating so much of the U.S. refining capacity on the Gulf Coast, an area prone to devastating hurricanes, seems like a mistake. Do you think it is a mistake? Justify your answer.
15. Go to http://www.swcollege.com/bef/econ_news.html and click on monopoly under the microeconomics section. Choose an article of interest, read the full summary and answer the questions. (Some of these questions may go beyond the materials in this course. If you run into such questions you may want to try to answer anyway, go to a different article, or just answer the ones that seem appropriate.)

Web Sites

- *Federal Trade Commission.*
  Visit the FTC to obtain even more information about competition, monopoly, and the federal government—**http://www.ftc.gov/ftc/economic.htm**
- *Energy Information Administration.*
  The Energy Information Administration provides a tremendous amount of information about the energy sector. This site is the source of much of the information for this chapter, and its reports have added a great deal to our analysis—**http://www.eia.doe.gov/**
- *International Energy Agency.*
  International Energy Agency is an organization that provides energy information and advice for its 26 member countries—**http://www.iea.org/**
- *Organization of Petroleum Exporting Countries.*
  OPEC's Web site is a great source of information about OPEC and its policies—**http://www.opec.org/home/**

CHAPTER **6**

Air Pollution: Balancing Benefits and Costs

OUTLINE

Keyword: *smog*

Access InfoTrac at http://infotrac.cengage.com

We live on a small planet with a thin, life-sustaining mantle of air, the quality of which is constantly threatened by economic activities. Millions of urban dwellers endure smog created by factories, power plants, and motor vehicles. Lakes and forests in the eastern United States and Canada suffer from acid rain produced by electric generating plants in the Midwest. Many scientists fear that the Earth will get warmer if we do not control our consumption of fossil fuels. Others contend that the Earth is losing its ozone shield, exposing the planet to greater concentrations of harmful ultraviolet rays.

To counter threats such as these, federal and state governments have adopted an imposing array of laws and regulations. Our focus in this chapter is the federal Clean Air Act. We examine some of the ways in which it has shaped environmental regulation and assess whether it has resulted in improved air quality. We also analyze the costs and benefits of air quality regulation and evaluate ways to reduce the costs of achieving cleaner air.

THE PRINCIPAL AIR POLLUTION PROBLEMS

The air pollution problem has several dimensions. The most important of these are: (1) poor-quality air in urban areas, (2) acid rain, (3) global warming, (4) ozone depletion, and (5) hazardous air pollutants.

Urban Air Quality

Urban air quality is measured in terms of atmospheric (ambient) concentrations of six common air pollutants: total suspended particulates, sulfur dioxide, carbon monoxide, nitrogen dioxide, ozone, and lead. Suspended particulates consist primarily of chemically stable substances such as dust, soot, ash, and smoke.

Sulfur dioxide is a pungent, toxic gas with beneficial uses: as sulfuric acid, as a bleaching agent, as a compound in preservatives, and as a refrigerant. It can be harmful to humans, plants, and structures, however, when airborne concentrations exceed critical levels—a problem created primarily by electricity generating plants that burn fossil fuels.

Carbon monoxide is a colorless, odorless, toxic gas produced by incomplete combustion of fossil fuels. It can be a silent killer when an automobile exhaust system is not ventilated properly and a chronic—but less lethal—problem when motor vehicles vent their exhaust gases into urban air sheds.

Nitrogen dioxide emissions are also caused by the incomplete combustion of fossil fuels, primarily by electric utilities and motor vehicles. Urbanites are victimized by nitrogen dioxide when it combines with other elements, such as ozone, to form smog.

Ozone is a form of oxygen with a pungent odor, created naturally in the upper levels of the atmosphere (the stratosphere) by a photochemical reaction with ultraviolet radiation from the sun. In fact, stratospheric ozone shields the Earth from the sun's harmful rays. Ozone is produced commercially and used in disinfectants, deodorizers, oxidizers, and bleaches. It is also produced when volatile organic compounds (chemically unstable hydrocarbons) are emitted from sources such as oil refineries and motor vehicles. As noted, ground-level ozone is a primary ingredient in smog.

Lead is a mineral with many beneficial uses, but it is toxic when inhaled or ingested, even in tiny doses. Lead in the atmosphere used to come primarily from motor vehicles; today it is largely a by-product of nonferrous smelters and battery plants.

The concern about urban air quality is based largely on its adverse effects on human health, property, safety, and visibility. Research shows that poor air quality contributes to bronchitis, asthma, lung cancer, and emphysema. Air pollutants can cause extensive damage to property, such as autos, houses, commercial buildings, and historic structures. Sulfur dioxide and ozone corrode and weaken many materials. Particulates and smog reduce visibility and the amenities associated with a clear vista. High levels of some pollutants, such as carbon monoxide, impair judgment and motor skills, increasing the risk of accident and injury.

Acid Rain

Acid rain–
A solution of sulfuric acid and precipitation.

Acid rain occurs when airborne sulfur dioxide is chemically transformed into a weak sulfuric acid solution that falls to the Earth as part of natural precipitation. Sulfur dioxide emissions come largely from Midwestern power plants. These emissions are transported long distances by the wind currents that flow from west to east in the Northern Hemisphere. Thus, acid rain falls primarily in the eastern United States and Canada.

Some lakes and streams in these regions have become highly acidified, impairing their ability to sustain life, and eastern forests have suffered retarded growth and increased mortality. Acid rain also corrodes materials, erodes and discolors paint, and deteriorates structures.

Keyword: *acid rain*

Access InfoTrac at http://infotrac.cengage.com

Global Warming

As fossil fuels burn, carbon dioxide is released into the atmosphere. The clearing of land (especially heavily forested land) reduces the Earth's capacity to absorb released carbon dioxide. The cumulative effect of burning and clearing has increased the level of atmospheric carbon dioxide.

Carbon dioxide is the principal **greenhouse gas**—a gas that helps the Earth retain heat from the sun. Rays from the sun that reach the Earth are partly absorbed and partly reflected into space. Some of the reflected energy is redirected toward the Earth by greenhouse gases, further warming the planet. Without these gases, the Earth would be too cold for human habitation. If greenhouse gases continue to accumulate, however, the warming they will cause could have serious consequences.

Keyword: *global warming*

Access InfoTrac at http://infotrac.cengage.com

Greenhouse gas–
A gas that helps the Earth retain heat from the sun.

Slight warming of the Northern Hemisphere has occurred during the past century. If the industrial nations continue to emit greenhouse gases at current rates, and today's Third World countries industrialize, the atmosphere may get even warmer. Scientists do not currently agree, however, on the likely rate or extent of global warming. Some predict only a slight warming trend, with little impact on the world's climate. Others predict warming sufficient to raise ocean levels, flood coastal population centers, and change the locations of the world's croplands and forests.

Stratospheric Ozone Depletion

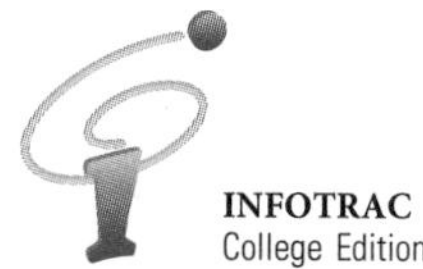

Keyword: *ozone depletion*

Access InfoTrac at http://infotrac.cengage.com

As indicated above, ozone is both a beneficial and a harmful gas. It is harmful when present in high concentrations in the lower atmosphere, but it is beneficial when present in the Earth's stratosphere. Ozone in the stratosphere prevents harmful solar ultraviolet radiation from reaching the Earth's surface. A reduction in the protection it provides would increase the incidence of skin cancer and possibly trigger genetic mutations.

When chlorofluorocarbons enter the stratosphere, they trigger a chemical reaction that destroys ozone. Chlorofluorocarbons are used primarily as aerosol propellants, refrigerants, foam-blowing agents, and cleaning solvents. Other gases, principally carbon dioxide and methane, increase the atmospheric concentration of ozone. Scientists are not certain about the effects of these conflicting forces on ozone levels. Measurements taken to date, however, indicate that significant decreases have occurred periodically in the ozone layer over Antarctica. Some computer models indicate a significant decrease in stratospheric ozone with continued growth in the use of chlorofluorocarbons.

Hazardous Air Pollutants

Keyword: *hazardous air pollutants*

Access InfoTrac at http://infotrac.cengage.com

The air also serves as a medium for transporting thousands of chemicals, many of which may be hazardous to humans, animals, and plants if inhaled or ingested. The Environmental Protection Agency (EPA) targeted 189 of these chemicals for regulation in the Clean Air Act of 1990. The primary impetus for these regulations is evidence that these chemicals impair human health, especially in the form of central nervous system damage and cancer.

THE ECONOMIC PERSPECTIVE

As noted above, pollution imposes costs—on humans, on the ecosystem, and on structures. Some would argue for drastic reductions in pollution in order to reduce these costs. Pollution is largely a by-product, however, of economic activities that produce beneficial goods and services. Economists recognize both the costs of pollution and the benefits of the economic activities that produce it. Accordingly, they argue for reducing pollution only if the costs avoided exceed the benefits given up. Alternatively, they find pollution acceptable only if the benefits from the activities that produce it exceed the costs attributable to the pollution.

The economic perspective can be illustrated with the use of a supply and demand diagram, such as Figure 6.1. The market represented is refined oil products, such as gasoline, kerosene, diesel fuel, and lubricating oils. Producers in this market face an ordinary, downward-sloping demand curve for their products; that is, additional quantities can be sold only at lower prices. There is an ordinary, upward-sloping supply curve; that is, additional quantities can be provided only at higher prices. The demand curve is also a marginal benefit (MB) curve—the height of the demand curve at each quantity (or marginal unit) is a measure of the benefit provided by that quantity (or marginal benefit). The supply curve is also a marginal cost (MC) curve—the height of the supply curve at each quantity (or marginal unit) is a measure of the cost of providing that quantity (or marginal cost).

External costs– Costs created by producers or consumers, but paid by others.

It is critical to recognize that the costs reflected in the supply or MC curve are only those paid by the producers of refined oil products. If oil refining emits pollutants as a by-product, and it does, the costs imposed by those pollutants, such as impaired health and ecosystem damage, are *not* reflected in the MC curve. Economists refer to the costs attributable to pollution as **external costs**—to convey the idea that they are external to (do not influence) market transactions between buyers and sellers. Pollution costs

Figure 6.1 Market for Refined Oil Products, with External Costs
In the presence of pollution, the efficient level of production is 400 million barrels and the efficient level of pollution is that associated with 400 million barrels. The market will clear, however, at 450 million barrels, resulting in too much production and too much pollution and efficiency losses equal to the area CDE.

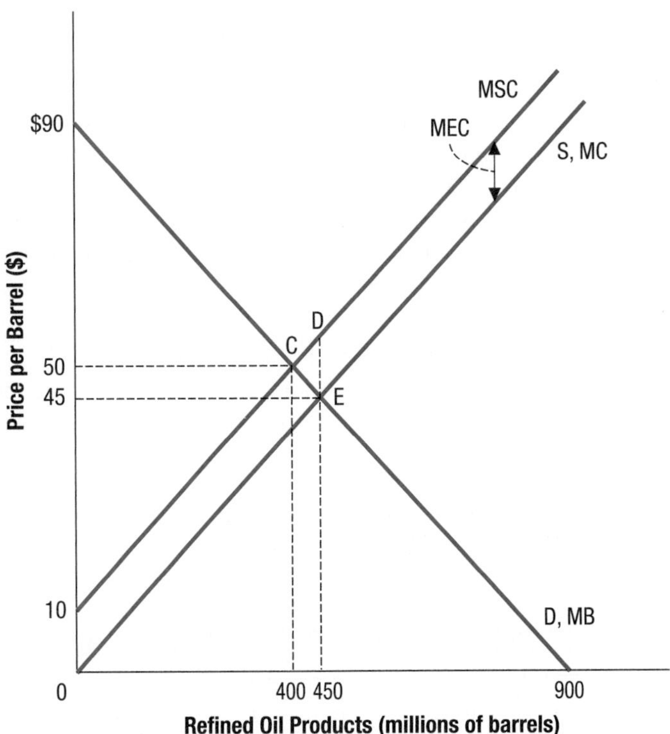

Marginal external costs (MEC)– External costs attributable to each additional unit of production.

Marginal social costs (MSC)– The sum of marginal costs and marginal external costs.

Efficiency loss from pollution– Marginal social cost (MSC) minus marginal benefit (MB), summed over all units produced for which MSC > MB.

attributable to each unit of output are called **marginal external costs**. The costs attributable to pollutants should be added to those paid by refiners to portray a complete picture of the costs of oil refining. We have done this in Figure 6.1 by adding marginal external costs to MC. When MC and MEC are added together, all of the costs to society from oil refining are accounted for; hence, the curve labeled MSC—for **marginal social costs**.

Figure 6.1 illustrates constant MEC, or MECs that are the same at each quantity of refined products. We assume this in order to simplify the example. In reality, the MEC of oil refining probably increases as the quantity refined increases.

The quantity of refined oil products will be determined, as usual, by the intersection of the supply and demand or MC and MB curves. Thus, 450 million barrels of refined products will be produced and sold at $45.00 a barrel. This level of production creates external costs of $4.5 billion—450,000,000 barrels times MEC of $10 per barrel—or the area marked by the end points: O, $10, D, and E. The MECs from the first 400 million barrels are entirely offset by buyers' willingness to pay for *both* the costs of refining and the MECs associated with refining. This is indicated by the fact that the demand or MB curve exceeds the MSC curve (remember, this curve includes all costs) for all units up to 400 million barrels. For each barrel beyond 400 million, however, MSC exceeds MB, or the social cost per barrel exceeds the benefits per barrel. This means that the market will produce too many barrels of refined oil products—50 million barrels to be exact. Society will lose an amount equal to the area CDE, or $250 million, on these units. Economists call this amount the **efficiency loss from pollution**. To eliminate these losses, the market would have to clear at 400 million barrels, but it won't do so because it is in the interest of both producers and buyers to ignore the costs of the pollutants emitted from oil refineries (they are external to market transactions—remember).

It is important to recognize that when both the benefits from economic activity and the costs of pollution are considered, the efficient level of pollution is *not* zero. The level of pollutants associated with 450 million barrels of refined products is too much, but reducing it below the level associated with 400 million barrels would be too little because the social costs saved by doing so would be less than the benefits sacrificed. Social costs saved on each barrel are indicated by the MSC curve and benefits sacrificed are indicated by the MB curve. Clearly, for units less than 400 million, the amount sacrificed (MB) exceeds the costs saved (MSC).

Pollution is not only inevitable in a market economy, but some pollution is acceptable, as in the case just reviewed. Some pollutants could be so harmful, of course, that the beneficial effects of economic activity are not sufficiently large to warrant producing any of them. This may be the case, for example, with lead used in motor fuels.

MARKET FAILURE: IS GOVERNMENT ACTION NECESSARY?

Property right–
A legally defined and enforceable right to use property for specific purposes.

Common property resource–
A resource that is the property of all.

Keywords: *Ronald Coase, Coase's theorem*

Access InfoTrac at http://infotrac.cengage.com

Coase's theorem–
The thesis that the assignment and enforcement of property rights can lead to the efficient level of pollution.

The case just examined is an example of market failure—a situation in which private decisions coordinated through the market produce allocative inefficiency. Many economists believe that government action, such as regulation, is necessary to correct market failures. Other economists question, however, whether government regulation is necessary to achieve a cleaner environment. They argue that government need only establish and enforce property rights to the natural environment.

Proponents of the latter view argue that the atmosphere is used excessively for waste disposal because polluters avoid paying a price to use it for this purpose. Normally, market prices for a particular use of a resource can be established only with clear **property rights**—legally defined and enforceable rights to use property in specific ways. A market for alternative uses of the atmosphere has never developed as have markets for other natural resources because the atmosphere is a **common property resource**—a resource that is the property of all. In the absence of the right to use property exclusively, no markets for particular uses of the resource are possible.

Ronald Coase, a winner of the Nobel Prize for Economics, recognized this aspect of the pollution problem and argued that a market in uses of the atmosphere would be established if the right to exclusive use, including the right to transfer that privilege to others, was given to some private party. He demonstrated that such a policy would yield the efficient level of pollution regardless of whether the use right was assigned to a polluter or to an environmentalist.[1]

We can illustrate **Coase's theorem**, using the information in Figure 6.1. If producers have the right to use the natural environment for waste disposal, they will choose (as above) to produce at 450 million barrels, where S = D or MC = MB. Would they be willing to produce less? Yes, provided that the amount that victims of pollution would be willing to pay them to reduce production is at least as large as the amount that they would be willing to accept.

The maximum amount that victims of pollution would be willing to pay oil refiners for reducing pollution is equal to the damages they suffer from pollution, or MEC. How much compensation would producers require in order to reduce pollution? In order to reduce

[1]Ronald Coase, "The Problem of Social Cost," *Journal of Law and Economics* 3, no. 2 (1960): 1–44.

INTERNATIONAL PERSPECTIVE

The Total Social Cost of the Automobile: Pollution and Much More

It is widely acknowledged that the privately owned, gasoline-powered automobile is a major source of air pollution throughout the world. Air pollution costs, however, are just one of several types of external costs attributed to the auto. Others include congestion, noise, accidents, increased vulnerability to recession, and oil-related national security expenditures.

All of the world's major oil-consuming nations experience the costs of congestion, noise, accidents, and pollution. All of the major oil-importing countries—such as the United States, Japan, Germany, Italy, France, and the United Kingdom—are susceptible to the costs associated with increased vulnerability to recession. These countries and others devote part of their national security expenditures to ensuring the continued flow of oil from unstable sources of supply.

Anyone who drives in a major urban area of the United States experiences firsthand the congestion that normally occurs during morning and evening rush hours. It has been estimated that these urban drivers annually waste between one and two billion hours stuck in traffic, and that the delayed delivery of goods and lost employee time amounts to a cost of $100 billion per year. But such costs are not confined to the United States. In Thailand, Bangkok's workforce loses an average of 44 days in traffic each year, costing the country several percentage points in potential gross domestic product (GDP). It has also been estimated that each driver in central London during peak traffic hours costs all other drivers on the highway about 80 cents per mile in wasted time.[a]

Consider also the economic costs to the oil-importing nations when they suffer an unanticipated oil cutoff. Oil prices suddenly increase, causing recessions. In fact, the largest decline in U.S. real GDP during the post–World War II era, 4.1 percent from 1974 to 1975, was initiated by a reduction in oil exports from the Middle East. The impact of this action reverberated far beyond the United States as total world GDP dipped about 6 percent below its trend value. Such outcomes can be blamed only in part on the world's love affair with the automobile—imported oil is used for many purposes other than transport—however, the world's appetite for gasoline heightens its vulnerability to oil supply disruptions.

And the world is vulnerable to oil supply disruptions. The politically volatile countries of the Persian Gulf produce about one-fourth of the world's oil and sit atop two-thirds of the world's known oil reserves. The first U.S.—Iraq war and its aftermath provided vivid evidence of the need for the United States and its allies to spend money to protect their interests in secure oil supplies from this region. The bill for this war—paid partly by the United States and partly by its allies—came to more than $50 billion, and it appears that maintaining readiness for future action will cost billions more each year.

The difficulty with these costs is that, because they are external costs, consumers of gasoline and other oil products ignore them. The challenge to policy makers, then, is to find ways to impose these costs on consumers. Economists have suggested a variety of ways to do this. Here we look briefly at three of them: (1) congestion pricing, (2) parking cash-outs, and (3) higher gasoline taxes.

Congestion pricing involves imposing a fee on vehicles that use urban roadways. Singapore has used a congestion pricing scheme since 1975, and officials are either planning or considering such schemes in Chile, France, Norway, the United Kingdom, the United States, and several other countries.[b]

Solo commuters are a principal cause of the pronounced congestion in central cities. Solo commuting is greatly facilitated when employers provide free parking for their employees. U.S. employers offer free parking because the Internal Revenue Code allows them to deduct any costs of employer-provided parking as a business expense and lets workers deduct the benefits from their taxable income, up to $155 per month. As a result, 95 percent of automobile commuters receive free or subsidized parking. *Parking cash-outs* require employers who provide free parking to offer a travel allowance worth the value of the parking space as an alternative. Employees who choose the less expensive options of car-pooling or public transit can pocket most of the allotted amount. Los Angeles County substituted travel allowances for free parking in 1990 and experienced a 40 percent decrease in the demand for parking.[c] The Internal Revenue Code could be modified to require all employers who currently provide free or subsidized employee parking to offer such a substitution.

Gasoline taxes in the United States average about 40 cents per gallon. They average $1.68 per gallon in Japan, $2.35 in the United Kingdom, $2.66 in Germany, $2.86 in France, and an astounding (to Americans) $3.64 per gallon in Italy. Although American travelers to these countries are puzzled by this practice, its purpose is clear: Officials in these countries have acted aggressively to reduce dependence on imported oil by levying higher gasoline taxes. As a by-product, they have also reduced the air pollution attributable to automobiles. So they have, in effect, charged automobile users more fully for the social costs of the automobile by shifting the costs from those who are not responsible to those who are.

[a] The data in this paragraph come from Marcia D. Lowe, "Reinventing Transport," in Lester D. Brown et al., *State of the World* (New York: Norton, 1994), 80–98.
[b] Kenneth A. Small, "Urban Traffic Congestion: A New Approach to the Gordian Knot," *The Brookings Review*, Spring 1993.
[c] Lowe, "Reinventing Transport," 96.

pollution, they would have to reduce production of refined oil products. If they reduced production below 450 million barrels, they would save costs equal to the MC of each barrel, but they would also sacrifice revenues equal to the amount they could charge for each unit. The amount they could charge is the same as the amount buyers are willing to pay, or the MB on each unit. Thus, they would be willing to reduce pollution only if they received the difference between what they could charge, MB, and what they would save, MC.

Starting at 450 million barrels, the victims of pollution are willing to pay more per barrel to have production reduced (MEC, or the distance between MSC and MC) than the minimum amount required as compensation by producers (the distance between MB and MC). This is the case for all barrels between 450 million and 400 million. Below 400 million barrels, however, the minimum compensation required for reducing production (MB − MC) exceeds the maximum victims will pay (MSC − MC). In theory, then, if victims could bargain freely with producers, they could pay producers enough to reduce production to the efficient level and no further.

We can also use Figure 6.1 to illustrate the case in which property rights have been bestowed on the victims of pollution. Here we start with a clean environment or zero pollution. Zero pollution means zero production of refined oil products. Now the relevant questions are: How much are producers willing to pay victims for the right to produce (and pollute) and how much compensation will victims require from producers? The maximum amount that producers would be willing to pay victims for the right to produce a unit of refined oil products is the difference between MB and MC—the difference between the maximum price they could charge buyers if they increased production by an additional unit and the cost of producing each unit. The minimum amount that victims would accept is MEC—the value of the damages they would suffer from each unit produced. The maximum amount that producers would be willing to pay (MB − MC) exceeds the minimum amount that victims would accept (MSC − MC) for all units up to 400 million. Thus, if producers could bargain freely with victims, they could pay them enough to secure the right to increase production to the efficient level.

If the world worked like this, the government would not need to intervene to eliminate excess pollutants (they would have to award property rights and enforce them, of course). Alas, it probably works this way only if the number of producers and victims is relatively small; smallness in numbers is required for the bargaining necessary for the affected parties to negotiate a mutually satisfactory payment arrangement. Real-world cases of air pollution most often involve too many affected parties for Coase's solution to work. Thus, some kind of government regulatory activity appears necessary as a means of achieving a cleaner environment.

AIR POLLUTION REGULATION: THE CLEAN AIR ACT

Keyword: *clean air act*

Access InfoTrac at http://infotrac.cengage.com

The Environmental Protection Agency (EPA) is the principal regulator of air pollution in the United States. Its basic authority comes from the Clean Air Act of 1963, as amended in 1965, 1970, 1977, and 1990. It is impossible to summarize neatly all the important features of the Clean Air Act; it is too long and too complicated and has been greatly expanded by administrative directives. We will focus instead on the principal regulatory tools or concepts upon which the EPA relies to carry out its regulatory responsibilities.

National Ambient Air Quality Standards (NAAQS)

Ambient concentrations– Concentrations of pollutants in the atmosphere.

The NAAQS are the upper limits permitted for concentrations in the atmosphere (**ambient concentrations**) of the six common air pollutants described earlier: particulates, sulfur dioxide, carbon monoxide, nitrogen dioxide, ozone, and lead. The limits have both a physical and a time dimension. For example, the standard for ozone is violated when the average hourly concentration is 0.12 part per million or more for more than one day per year.

The EPA believes that concentrations exceeding the NAAQS pose a significant health risk. The law requires that the NAAQS be set and achieved without consideration of costs. The law also requires that they be applied uniformly across the country.

Emissions Limits

The NAAQS govern concentrations in the atmosphere *after* pollutants have been released or emitted. The law also fixes limits on the amounts of certain pollutants that may be *emitted from* various sources. Limits have been placed on emissions of carbon monoxide, nitrogen dioxide, and hydrocarbons from automobiles; on emissions of toxic chemicals from industrial and commercial sources; and on emissions of sulfur dioxide and nitrogen oxides from electric generating plants.

Restricted Technology

The Clean Air Act requires not only that certain standards be attained or limits observed; it also places restrictions on the technologies that may be used to achieve them. For example, it requires automobile manufacturers to install catalytic converters with a minimum life of 100,000 miles. Vapor recycling equipment must be installed on new cars, and gasoline stations in areas where NAAQS for ozone are exceeded must install vapor-recovery devices on fuel-dispensing hoses. Stationary sources of pollution are subject to a variety of restrictions on the technologies they may use for pollution control. The resulting patchwork of permissible technologies is a source of great uncertainty to manufacturers, a major administrative burden for the EPA, and a source of excessive costs of air pollution regulation.

New Source Performance Standards

New commercial and industrial facilities—those established *after* a law is enacted—are often subject to more stringent technology restrictions than old facilities—those established *before* a law is enacted. The more exacting new source performance standards are a powerful incentive to keep older and more costly plants in operation longer.

Prescribed Fuels

The Clean Air Act also prescribes certain fuel requirements for motor vehicles. Gasoline stations in areas where ambient concentrations of carbon monoxide exceed EPA standards must sell oxygenated gasoline. Officials in areas that fail too often to meet ozone standards must develop and implement plans for increasing the percentage of motor vehicles powered by alternative fuels, such as methanol, compressed natural gas, liquid petroleum gas, and electricity.

Offset Requirements

Areas that fail to meet the ozone and carbon monoxide standards can accommodate new sources of pollution, such as new factories, but only if the pollution from new sources is offset by reductions in pollution from existing sources. In fact, the offset must exceed the addition. The ratio of offsets to additions ranges from 1.1 in areas that barely violate the standards to 1.5 in areas with serious air quality problems, like Los Angeles.

Emissions Trading

Emissions reduction credit– A credit for reducing emissions more than required by regulations.

The offset policy has stimulated development of markets in **emissions reduction credits**. Emissions reduction credits are earned by reducing emissions below the legally required level. For example, suppose that an oil refinery is required to reduce its emissions of sulfur dioxide by 100 tons per year and that it can reduce its emissions by 200 tons at reasonable cost. If it does so, it would receive emissions reduction credits for 100 tons of sulfur dioxide. These credits can be sold to firms seeking offsets for new sources of emissions.

Prevention of Significant Deterioration

To prevent air quality from deteriorating, the Clean Air Act also establishes limits on increases in pollution in areas that did not violate the NAAQS when they were established. In fact, the limits on additional pollution are stricter for areas that started with better air quality.

Monitoring and Compliance

The nature and significance of the air pollution problem varies greatly from place to place. Assuming that state and local authorities have greater knowledge of local conditions than federal officials, Congress has given state pollution control agencies the responsibility for issuing pollution permits, for monitoring sources of pollution, and for ensuring compliance with the standards.

EFFECTS OF THE CLEAN AIR ACT ON AIR QUALITY

The 1990 Clean Air Act Amendments require the EPA to conduct periodic, scientifically reviewed studies to assess the benefits and costs of the Clean Air Act (CAA). Two such studies have been published so far: *The Benefits and Costs of the Clean Air Act, 1970 to 1990* and *The Benefits and Costs of the Clean Air Act, 1990–2010*. In the first of these studies, the EPA estimated changes in emissions and air quality attributable to the CAA prior to 1990; that is, they isolated the effect of the CAA from other factors that could have produced changes in emissions or air quality. In the second of these studies, the EPA forecasted the additional changes in emissions and air quality that were likely to occur as a result of the CAA Amendments of 1990—again abstracting from the effects of other factors that might change emissions or air quality.

Table 6.1 summarizes the EPA's estimated and projected percentage reductions in emissions achieved by the end-dates of the two time periods.

Emissions of primary particulates were reduced 75 percent in the first two decades, due to vigorous efforts to reduce visible emissions from smokestacks. The projections for 1990–2010 indicate that most of the easy reductions of particulates have been

TABLE 6.1 ESTIMATED AND PROJECTED REDUCTIONS IN EMISSIONS OF CRITERIA POLLUTANTS ATTRIBUTABLE TO THE PROVISIONS OF THE CLEAN AIR ACT (IN PERCENT)

TIME PERIOD	PARTICULATES	SULFUR DIOXIDE	NITROGEN OXIDE	VOLATILE COMPOUNDS	CARBON MONOXIDE	LEAD
1970–1990	75	40	30	45	50	99
1990–2010	4	31	39	35	23	

Source: U.S. Environmental Protection Agency, *The Benefits and Costs of the Clean Air Act, 1970 to 1990;* and *The Benefits and Costs of the Clean Air Act, 1990–2010.*

achieved. Sulfur dioxide emissions are significantly lower in both periods, primarily due to electric generating plants installing stack scrubbers or switching to lower sulfur fuels (low-sulfur coal and natural gas). Nitrogen oxide emissions were reduced during the first time period mostly because of the installation of catalytic converters and other technologies on motor vehicles. Caps on nitrogen oxide emissions from electric generating plants account for most of the reduction expected in this pollutant in 1990–2010. The reduction in volatile organic compound (VOC) emissions, 1970–1990, was due primarily to the application of motor vehicle emissions control technologies. This is still the primary source of VOC reductions in 1990–2010, although there is significant assistance in the future from commercial sources. Most of the reductions in carbon monoxide emissions over the 40-year period are also attributable to motor vehicle emissions control technologies. Lead emissions reductions were due largely to the phase-out of leaded gasoline.

THE ECONOMICS OF THE CLEAN AIR ACT: HAVE WE GONE TOO FAR?

This is an impressive record and an encouraging forecast, but the EPA's own data hardly indicate complete control over emissions of the common pollutants, other than lead. Moreover, despite improvements in air quality since 1970, nearly 40 percent of the total population still lives in counties with air that fails to meet all of the NAAQS, acid rain still poses a problem in some areas of the United States and Canada, and the stratospheric ozone problem is far from solved. Given this view, some would argue that we have not done enough to reduce emissions. Emissions reduction is not a costless endeavor, however; for example, substantial outlays are required for emissions control technologies. Given this view of the issue, some would argue that we have gone too far; that the costs of achieving emissions reductions have been too large.

Economists attempt to resolve the issue by conducting benefit-cost analyses. The two EPA studies by the EPA referred to in the previous section reflect the kind of work that needs to be done.

Benefits and Costs of the Clean Air Act, 1970–1990

Benefits The lower emissions of pollutants attributable to the CAA from 1970 to 1990 translate into lower ambient concentrations of sulfur dioxide, nitrogen oxides, particulate matter, carbon monoxide, ozone, and lead. These lower concentrations yield a variety of benefits derived from improvements in human health, increased visibility, reduced soiling of items and structures, increased worker productivity, increased agricultural output, and ecological improvements.

TABLE 6.2 TOTAL ESTIMATED BENEFITS FROM THE CLEAN AIR ACT, 1970–1990

SOURCE OF BENEFIT	PRESENT VALUE (BILLIONS OF DOLLARS)
Fewer premature deaths	$17,971
Fewer cases of chronic bronchitis and other respiratory problems, and decreased productivity	$3,495
Reduced losses in IQ points	$399
Fewer cases of hypertension	$98
Fewer hospital admissions	$57
Reduced soiling damage	$74
Increased visibility	$54
Increased agricultural production	$23

Source: U.S. Environmental Protection Agency, *The Benefits and Costs of the Clean Air Act, 1970 to 1990,* ES-7.

Improvements in human health are the most important source by far of the benefits estimated by the EPA. Lower concentrations of pollutants mean fewer: (1) cases of premature death, chronic bronchitis, and other respiratory illnesses and symptoms, hypertension, strokes, heart disease, and impaired IQs; and (2) fewer hospital admissions. Increased visibility, reduced soiling, increased worker productivity, and increased agricultural output are much less important sources, but the EPA was also able to estimate the benefits from these sources. They did not estimate the benefits of ecological improvements, although this is a potentially significant source of benefits.

The benefits from all of these factors are subject to uncertainty, so the EPA produced a range of estimates. Table 6.2 presents the EPA's mean or central estimates of the benefits produced from 1970 to 1990. All estimates were corrected for inflation and for differences in time of occurrence (by discounting benefits—see Chapter 9 for a fuller explanation of this procedure).

Costs Consumers, business firms, and governments all incurred higher costs to comply with the Clean Air Act. The costs of providing goods and services (and their prices) were higher due to requirements to install, operate, and maintain pollution control equipment, to report on regulatory compliance, and to invest in research and development of new control technologies. Governments incurred costs of designing and implementing regulations and monitoring regulatory compliance. The EPA estimated total compliance costs for the 20-year period—adjusted for inflation and time of occurrence—at approximately $523 billion.

This is not the end of the cost story, however. Some of the expenditures on environmental compliance displaced productive investments. These decreases in investment reduced the nation's capital stock and labor productivity and eventually reduced the rate at which the economy grew. Thus, compliance costs should be supplemented with an estimate of the value of GDP foregone because of the lower rate of growth attributable to environmental compliance.

The EPA did not produce estimates of GDP foregone in its study of the 1970–1990 period, but a widely cited study by Jorgenson and Wilcoxen concludes that the growth *rate* of real GDP was reduced by about 0.2 percentage points annually from 1974 to 1985

TABLE 6.3 BENEFITS AND COSTS OF THE 1990 AMENDMENTS TO THE CLEAN AIR ACT, 1990–2010

PROGRAM	TOTAL BENEFITS	COMPLIANCE COSTS	REAL GDP FORGONE	TOTAL COSTS
Criteria pollutants reduction	$680 B	$170 B	$106 B	$276 B
Stratospheric ozone reduction	$500 B	$27 B	$17 B	$44 B
	$1,180 B	$197 B	$123 B	$320 B

Source: All figures except real GDP forgone are calculations based on data provided in U.S. Environmental Protection Agency, *The Benefits and Costs of the Clean Air Act, 1990–2010.* Real GDP forgone estimates are based on the authors' assumption that the ratio of real GDP forgone to compliance costs is the same in 1990–2010 as in 1970–1990.

as a result of the costs of all environmental rules.[2] This appears to be a small effect—and it is. Our calculations indicate that if real GDP had grown at a rate that was 0.2 percentage point higher than the actual rate each year between 1970 and 1990, the nation would have produced only an additional $327 billion of goods and services (corrected for time of occurrence) over the entire time period.

When environmental regulation increases compliance costs it also increases the costs and prices of goods and services produced by affected firms. This increase in prices lowers the buying power of workers' wages, or what is the same thing, the reward from working. They will react by decreasing hours worked, imposing an additional cost on society that the EPA has not accounted for. Although there is some evidence that this cost, by itself, is substantial, currently available empirical estimates of this cost are inconclusive.

INFOTRAC College Edition

Keyword: *cost benefit analysis and environmental regulation*

Access InfoTrac at http://infotrac.cengage.com

Given Jorgenson's and Wilcoxen's estimate, however, total costs of the CAA for the 1970–1990 time period are $523 billion, plus *some* portion of the $327 billion they estimate (remember, Jorgenson's and Wilcoxen's results pertain to more than air pollutants alone). This is certainly a large number, but it is dwarfed by the $22.2 trillion in total benefits (the sum of the benefits in Table 6.2). The EPA would appear to have a solid basis for arguing that, as of 1990, the regulations imposed by the Clean Air Act had a net beneficial impact on the economy.

Benefits and Costs of the Clean Air Act, 1990–2010

The second issue that the EPA addresses in its benefit-cost analyses is whether the 1990 amendments to the CAA are likely to yield benefits greater than costs over the period, 1990 to 2010. Since the amendments are *additional* regulations, they would be expected to have a smaller impact on both benefits and costs than the regulations cumulated up to 1990. This expectation is confirmed by the estimates reported in Table 6.3.

Table 6.3 reflects the EPA's separation of the 1990 amendments into two types: (1) changes in the regulations aimed at reducing criteria pollutants; and (2) changes in the regulations designed to reduce stratospheric ozone. The **criteria pollutants** affected by the 1990 amendments are particulates, sulfur dioxide, nitrogen oxide, carbon monoxide, and ozone in urban air sheds. The 1990 amendments aim to reduce stratospheric ozone by restricting chlorofluorocarbons and other volatile organic compounds.

Criteria pollutants–Pollutants that are subject to the National Ambient Air Quality Standards (NAAQS).

Although the gap between benefits and costs is not nearly as large as it is for the 1970–1990 period, projected benefits still exceed projected costs by nearly 4 to 1, even

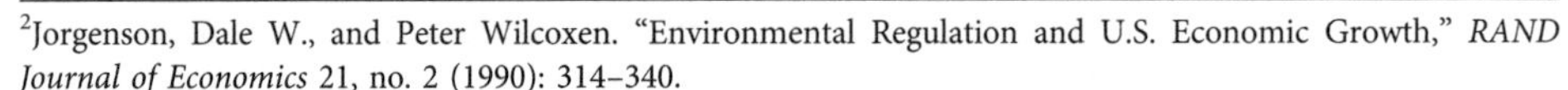

[2]Jorgenson, Dale W., and Peter Wilcoxen. "Environmental Regulation and U.S. Economic Growth," *RAND Journal of Economics* 21, no. 2 (1990): 314–340.

after adding an estimate for GDP forgone from productive investment displaced by compliance costs.

So, conventional economics shows that environmental regulation does not cause the widespread negative economic effects that are feared by some critics. These results do *not* necessarily mean, however, that we have an efficient level of environmental regulation.

We have efficiency in environmental regulation when *total benefits from regulation exceed total costs* and when the *marginal benefits from regulation equal the marginal costs.* The EPA's estimates clearly indicate that the total benefits from regulation exceed the total costs, but, by themselves, they cannot tell us if we have too little or too much regulation. The fact that benefits exceed costs in the aggregate also does not rule out the possibility that there may be ways to reduce the costs of environmental regulation. Annual costs of the CAA are probably in the neighborhood of $60 billion a year—certainly a worthy target for cost-reduction.

COST-REDUCING MEASURES

Economists have identified several ways to reduce the costs of environmental regulation without reducing environmental quality. The two that have received the most attention are (1) emissions taxes and (2) marketable emissions permits.

Emissions Taxes

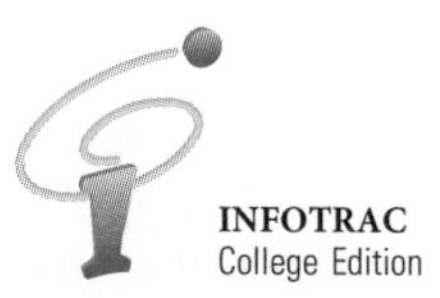

Keywords: *Pigovian taxes, pollution taxes*

Access InfoTrac at http://infotrac.cengage.com

One of economists' favorite solutions to pollution is an excise tax on emissions of pollutants, commonly called a *Pigovian tax* after its originator, the British economist A. C. Pigou (1877–1959). An **emissions tax** regulates the level of pollution by establishing a price that emitters must pay per unit of emissions.

A numerical example will show how an emissions tax works and how it can lower the costs of achieving a cleaner environment. Suppose that four coal-fired electric generating plants, each owned by a different firm, are initially unregulated. Each plant emits 4 tons of sulfur dioxide per day. Each of the plants could eliminate its sulfur dioxide emissions, but at widely varying costs per ton, as indicated in Table 6.4. The variation in cost per ton reflects factors such as differences in age of plant and access to low-sulfur coal.

Emissions tax– A tax charged polluters for each unit of pollutants emitted.

Marginal abatement cost– The cost of abating or eliminating an additional unit of pollutants.

Suppose now that the regulators have determined that if total emissions are greater than 8 tons there will be unacceptable harm to humans, plants, structure, animals, etc. To achieve this goal, they simply limit each plant to 2 tons and monitor emissions to make sure that they do not exceed two tons. In order to comply with the limit each plant is forced to reduce pollutants by 2 tons. The cost to them of doing this is indicated in Table 6.4 in the columns labeled MAC. MAC stands for **marginal abatement cost**. In the language of environmental economists, a ton that is abated is not emitted. Thus, MAC is the cost of *not* emitting, or eliminating, each successive ton of pollutants. With the 2-ton limit enforced, each plant abates 2 tons. This costs plant A $300, Plant B $600, Plant C $900, and Plant D $1,200, as indicated in row 6 of Table 6.4. Total abatement cost (TAC) is the sum of these costs, or $3,000 per day.

At this point the EPA's chief economist comes forward and suggests a way to reduce TAC. She argues that the government can achieve the same level of abatement (8 tons); but at lower TAC, if it lets the plants emit what they want—at the cost of a tax of $500 per ton for each ton that they emit. Each plant will now abate a ton only if the MAC of doing so is less than the tax. If the MAC exceeds the tax they will not abate, but emit and pay the tax. Applying this decision rule to the data in Table 6.4, we find that the responsibility for abatement shifts to the plants with the lowest MAC; Plant A abates 2 more tons and Plants C and D abate 1 fewer ton each. TAC falls from $3,000

TABLE 6.4 EFFECTS OF IMPOSITION OF A POLLUTION TAX OF $500 PER TON OF POLLUTANTS

	MAC PLANT A	MAC PLANT B	MAC PLANT C	MAC PLANT D	TAC
First ton abated (MAC_1)	$100	$200	$300	$400	
Second ton abated (MAC_2)	$200	$400	$600	$800	
Third ton abated (MAC_3)	$300	$800	$900	$1,200	
Fourth ton abated (MAC_4)	$400	$1,200	$1,200	$1,600	
Tons abated with uniform emissions limit of 2 tons	2	2	2	2	
Total cost of abatement with uniform emissions limit of 2 tons	$300	$600	$900	$1,200	$3,000
Tons abated with tax of $500 per ton emitted	4	2	1	1	
Total cost of abatement with tax of $500 per ton emitted	$1,000	$600	$300	$400	$2,300

per day to $2,300 per day as a consequence. The owners of Plants B and C are happy; they experience a reduction in costs, including both abatement costs and taxes ($100 for Plant C after taxes and $300 for Plant B after taxes). Government officials are happy, as well; they achieve their emissions objective and collect tax revenues of $1,000 that they can use for other government programs or to reduce other taxes. The owners of Plant A are likely to be unhappy; they experience an increase in abatement costs.

Marketable Pollution Permits

Suppose that the owners of Plant A have a lot of political influence and that they are successful in stifling passage of legislation that authorizes the $500 pollution tax. Another economist steps forward with another policy that she claims will accomplish the same things as the pollution tax, but at no cost to any of the plants. She suggests that each plant simply be issued two permits, each of which allows a plant to emit 1 ton of pollutants, but that the owners of the permits be allowed to sell them to others. She suggests, that is, the use of **marketable pollution permits**. Now the permit owners have to decide whether to hold or sell. If they hold a permit they save on abatement costs. If they sell a permit, they assume additional abatement costs. What will they do? Their choices are outlined in Table 6.5.

Marketable pollution permit–
A permit that can be bought and sold that allows a polluter to emit a specified quantity of a pollutant or pollutants.

When the permits are issued, and before any exchange of permits takes place, each plant emits 2 tons of pollutants and abates 2 tons. TAC at this point is the same as it was in the pollution tax case; namely, $3,000 per day (line 6). With the possibility of exchange, or permit transferability, the owners of each plant must decide how much they are willing to pay for a permit, if they contemplate buying, and how much they are willing to accept for a permit, if they contemplate selling. There will be an exchange or transfer of permits if someone is willing to pay more than someone else is willing to accept.

Let's work through the possibilities one permit at a time. Given the starting point of two tons abated, the maximum amount that all plants would be willing to pay for another permit (the first one traded) is what it would cost them to abate the ton themselves. That is, they would pay no more to emit the ton (buy a permit) than the MAC of that ton—that is, the MAC of the second ton abated. The minimum amount that they would accept is the MAC to them of the third ton; this is what it would cost them for abatement if they sold a

TABLE 6.5 EFFECTS OF MARKETABLE POLLUTION PERMITS

	MAC FIRM A	MAC FIRM B	MAC FIRM C	MAC FIRM D	TAC
First ton abated (MAC_1)	$100	$200	$300	$400	
Second ton abated (MAC_2)	$200	$400	$600	$800	
Third ton abated (MAC_3)	$300	$800	$900	$1,200	
Fourth ton abated (MAC_4)	$400	$1,200	$1,200	$1,600	
Tons abated with 2 non-transferable permits	2	2	2	2	
Total cost of abatement with 2 nontransferable permits	$300	$600	$900	$1,200	$3,000
Maximum amount would pay for 1st permit	$200	$400	$600	**$800**	
	(MAC_2)	(MAC_2)	(MAC_2)	(MAC_2)	
Minimum amount would accept for 1st permit (MAC_3)	**$300**	$800	$900	$1,200	
	(MAC_3)	(MAC_3)	(MAC_3)	(MAC_3)	
Maximum amount would pay for next permit	$300	$400	**$600**	$400	
	(MAC_3)	(MAC_2)	(MAC_2)	(MAC_1)	
Minimum amount would accept for next permit	**$400**	$800	$900	$800	
	(MAC_4)	(MAC_3)	(MAC_3)	(MAC_2)	
Permits sold	2	0	0	0	
Permits bought	0	0	1	1	
Tons abated with transferable permits	4	2	1	1	
Total cost of abatement with transferable permits	$1,000	$600	$300	$400	$2,300

permit. Under these conditions, Plant A will sell a permit to Plant D at some price between $300 and $800. Whatever they may agree to in this range will make both parties better off if the exchange is made. Once the exchange has been made, Plants A and D have to make a new calculation. Plant A is now abating 3 tons and Plant D is now abating 1 ton. Plant A is now willing to pay no more for another permit than the MAC, to them, of the third ton. Plant D is now willing to pay no more than the MAC, to them, of the first ton. Plants B and C are still willing to pay the MAC, to them, of the second ton. Plant A is willing to accept no less for a permit than the MAC of the fourth ton, Plants B and C are still willing to accept no less than the MAC of the third ton, and Plant D is willing to accept no less than the MAC of the second ton. Under these conditions, Plant A will sell another permit, this time to Plant C.

The possibilities for exchange have now been exhausted. Plant A ends up abating 4 tons; Plant B, 2 tons; Plant C, 1 ton; and Plant D, 1 ton. This is the same outcome as would be achieved with a pollution tax of $500 per ton, and the TAC is also the same as in that case. All parties, except the government, are as well off, or better off, than they were when no exchange of permits took place.

In spite of their apparently equivalent ability to reduce TAC, regulators in this country have opted for transferable permits over pollution taxes. In a fashion similar to our example, the EPA has issued emissions permits for sulfur dioxide to electric generating plants in two phases of a program to reduce acid rain. These permits allow electric generating plants in the aggregate to emit only one-half of the sulfur dioxide that they were emitting before the program was initiated. The EPA estimates that the exchange of sulfur dioxide permits for money will save $1 billion in costs (out of $5 billion) of complying with the acid rain provisions of the Clean Air Act. Economists have hinted, also, at large potential savings from using transferable permits for emissions of carbon dioxide and toxic chemicals.

Transactions costs– The costs of finding willing buyers and sellers and negotiating a mutually acceptable price.

The transferable permit is an effective regulatory tool, but it is not perfect. Its Achilles' heel is **transactions costs**—the costs of finding willing buyers and sellers and negotiating mutually acceptable prices for emissions permits. Both buyers and sellers face transactions costs, and they can be large enough to wipe out the margin between what buyers are willing to pay and sellers are willing to accept. Another problem with transferable permits is the government's practice of allocating them free of charge. This practice not only gives the recipients a valuable piece of property for nothing, but the government foregoes the opportunity to raise revenues—revenues that could be used to reduce other taxes.

Alas, pollution taxes are not defect-free, either. The primary difficulty they pose is the determination of the correct tax; that is, the tax that just induces producers to emit pollutants at the level desired by regulatory authorities. In case you didn't notice it, we were able to specify a tax in the above example that was just right, but we had all of the information that we needed to do this—a luxury that the real world rarely permits. Taxes do provide government with money that can be used to reduce other taxes, but it has no advantage over transferable permits in this regard if the permits are auctioned off instead of awarded free of charge.

Limiting Global Warming: Emissions Permits in an International Context

Increasing concerns about the prospects for global warming, and its possible consequences, led to a United Nations conference on the problem in Kyoto, Japan, in late 1997. Delegates from the industrialized countries agreed to reduce carbon dioxide emissions in their countries, although the United States has yet to sign the agreement. Given expected growth in the use of fossil fuels, the Kyoto Accord would require a 15 to 25 percent reduction in projected 2010 emissions. More than 130 of the world's less-developed countries—including Brazil, China, India, and Mexico—were exempted from the agreement, largely on the grounds that they could not afford to reduce carbon dioxide emissions.

The Kyoto protocol would be expensive for the United States. In fact, some estimates indicate that GDP in 2010 could be as much as 5 percent lower as a result of the changes

TABLE 6.6 COSTS PER TON OF ELIMINATING CARBON DIOXIDE EMISSIONS

	COST PER TON OF ELIMINATING EMISSIONS	
TONS PER DAY	DEVELOPING COUNTRY	DEVELOPED COUNTRY
First	$100	$300
Second	200	600
Third	300	900
Fourth	400	1,200
Fifth	—	1,500
Sixth	—	1,800

The developed and developing countries differ in terms of their costs of eliminating carbon dioxide. This provides an opportunity for the developed countries to purchase emissions permits from the developing countries.

INFOTRAC
College Edition

Keywords: *tradeable emissions permits, emissions permits*

Access InfoTrac at http://infotrac.cengage.com

required in the economy to achieve the Kyoto target. As should be clear from the above analysis, however, U.S. costs can be minimized by using emissions permits to allocate the responsibility for emissions reductions across U.S. emitters. The cost of the protocol can be further reduced by using emissions permits to allocate the responsibility for emissions reductions across countries.

Table 6.6 illustrates the value of trading permits between countries. Currently, eliminating carbon dioxide emissions probably costs more in developed countries than it does in developing countries because the developed countries must sacrifice higher-valued goods and services to achieve lower emissions than will the developing countries. The data in Table 6.6 reflect this assumption.

ADDITIONAL INSIGHT

Carbon Taxes

As noted in the text, the Kyoto protocol is designed to reduce carbon dioxide emissions. One way to accomplish this is to levy a carbon tax—a tax on different fuels based on the amount of carbon they contain.

A carbon tax is advocated as a cost-effective means of dealing with the problem of global warming. Such a tax would directly raise the price of fossil fuels—especially oil, natural gas, and coal—and the products derived directly from them, such as gasoline and electricity. This increase would encourage energy conservation and the use of relatively cleaner energy sources, such as solar and wind energy. The net result would be less carbon dioxide emitted to the atmosphere.

Economists have estimated the carbon taxes required to reduce carbon dioxide emissions to various target levels. Generally, they fall in the $100 to $400 per ton range. Manne and Richels estimate, for example, that a $250 tax per ton of carbon will be required to reduce long-run U.S. carbon emissions by 20 percent.[a]

The Congressional Budget Office calculates that a tax of $100 per ton of carbon amounts to $60 per ton of coal, $1.63 per thousand cubic feet of natural gas, $13 per barrel of oil, and 30 cents per gallon of gasoline.[b] Compared to projected year-2000 prices, a $100 carbon tax would be 256 percent of the price of coal, 53 percent of the price of natural gas, and 40 percent of the price of oil.

Carbon taxes in the $100 to $400 range would raise enormous amounts of revenue. A tax of $100 per ton, for example, would raise about $130 billion per year in the United States—about 2 percent of gross domestic product. Governments could choose to levy a carbon tax but offset the revenues raised by lowering other taxes, such as personal or corporate income taxes.

Although this would appear to simply offset the effects of one tax with effects from another, it is possible that a revenue-neutral carbon tax would have net beneficial effects. Not only would the carbon tax reduce the distortion created by people's failure to consider the external costs associated with fossil fuel use, but reducing income taxes would reduce the adverse effects these taxes have on incentives to work and invest. Unfortunately, imposition of the carbon tax, itself, would also distort the work decision, so the net effect of these tax-interactions is uncertain.

Carbon taxes also appeal to government officials who want to reduce the nation's trade deficit. As the carbon tax raises the price of oil, American consumers and producers would reduce the quantity they buy from foreign producers.

In spite of uncertainty regarding tax interactions, there is a lot of support for a carbon tax. The lineup of forces favoring a carbon tax, however, would not necessarily ensure passage of authorizing legislation. Forces opposing the tax are bound to be powerful, as it would have an adverse impact on the coal, oil, gas, and automobile industries. Higher energy prices could also trigger falling GDP and rising unemployment. Consumer groups could join the opposition because at least part of the tax would be passed on to them in the form of higher prices. We probably will witness a spirited and protracted debate if the carbon tax rises to the top of the policy agenda.

[a] Alan S. Manne and Richard G. Richels, "CO_2 Emissions Limits: An Economic Cost Analysis for the USA," *Energy Journal* 11, no. 2 (1990): 51–74.

[b] Congressional Budget Office, *Carbon Charges as a Response to Global Warming: The Effects of Taxing Fossil Fuels* (Washington, DC: Congressional Budget Office, 1990), iv.

In the absence of an international agreement, suppose that the levels of economic activity were such that 9 tons of emissions were produced—6 by the developed country and 3 by the developing country. Next, suppose that an international agreement is crafted with an emissions target of 6 tons. A Kyoto-like protocol would require the developed country to reduce emissions from 6 tons to 3 tons and leave emissions at 3 tons in the developing country. The cost of this protocol is the cost in the developed country of reducing emissions by 3 tons, or $1,800 ($300 for the first ton, $600 for the second, and $900 for the third).

Suppose, instead, that the international agreement allowed six marketable pollution permits for 1 ton each, with three permits going to the developed country and three permits going to the developing country. In this instance, the developed country would have an incentive to buy permits from the developing country, and the developing country would have an incentive to sell. The developed country would be willing to pay up to $900 for the first marketable permit because it would have to pay this cost anyway to abate pollution without the permit. The developing country would be willing to sell a permit for no less than $100 because it would have to pay this cost to reduce emissions by 1 ton if it sold a permit. The price paid would be somewhere between $100 and $900. A similar argument can be made for the developed country purchasing a second permit from the developing country, with a sales price somewhere between $200 and $600. They would not trade a third permit because the maximum price the buyer is willing to pay ($300) equals the minimum price the seller is willing to accept ($300). After the two permits change hands, however, the cost of reducing emissions falls from $1,800 to $600. The sale of the permits also transfers money from the developed countries to the developing countries, with the amount transferred depending on the sales prices that are established for the two permits.

Summary

The five most important air pollution problems are (1) poor air quality in urban areas, (2) acid rain, (3) global warming, (4) ozone depletion, and (5) hazardous air pollutants.

Air pollution is a source of concern primarily because of its harmful effects on human health. It also damages plants, animals, and property, and it impairs visibility.

Air pollution is an inevitable by-product of economic activity; it can be eliminated entirely only at great cost in terms of goods and services forgone. It should be reduced, from an economic perspective, but only so long as the reduction in marginal external costs is greater than or equal to the reduction in marginal benefits. Alternatively, pollution is acceptable as long as the marginal benefit from an activity that produces pollution is greater than or equal to the marginal social cost—which includes the cost attributable to pollution—of that activity.

Private-sector decision makers expand economic activities to the point where marginal social cost exceeds marginal benefit because they ignore the marginal external cost of pollution. This behavior produces excess pollution.

The presence of excess pollution is evidence of market failure. Market failure suggests the need for government regulation of economic activity. Coase's theorem raises the possibility that government regulation is unnecessary; that is, that government should confine itself to establishing and enforcing property rights to the environment. The conditions under which this prescription would suffice do not prevail in the real world, however.

Government has played an active role in establishing and enforcing regulations that constrain economic activities and choices that affect air quality, principally through the authority established by the Clean Air Act. The Clean Air Act establishes ambient air quality standards, emissions limits, restrictions on pollution abatement technology, constraints on motor fuel sales in certain areas, procedures for the trading of emissions credits and pollution permits, and an extensive federal-state partnership for implementing the act.

There is evidence that the Clean Air Act improved air quality prior to 1990 and that it will produce further improvements in air quality from 1990 to 2020. There is also evidence that the improvements achieved prior to 1990 produced benefits greatly in excess of costs and that the 1990 amendments to the CAA will produce benefits greater than costs, although by a much smaller margin. This evidence does not prove, however, that we have the right amount of environmental regulation.

Economists have suggested two principal approaches to reducing the costs of environmental regulation: (1) emissions taxes and (2) marketable pollution permits. If information were free, both approaches would reduce the costs of pollution abatement by the same amount.

Key Terms

Acid rain
Greenhouse gas
External costs
Marginal External Costs (MEC)
Marginal Social Costs (MSC)
Efficiency loss from pollution
Property rights
Common property resource
Coase's theorem
Ambient concentrations
Emissions reduction credits
Criteria pollutants
Emissions tax
Marginal abatement cost
Marketable pollution permits
Transactions costs

Review Questions

1. According to this chapter, what are the five most important air pollution problems? Briefly discuss them.
2. Explain and distinguish between the following concepts. Use specific examples, if needed.
   a. Marginal cost
   b. Marginal external cost
   c. Marginal social cost
3. "Generally, we would not expect the efficient level of pollution to be zero." Using graphical analysis, explain why this statement is true.
4. Suppose that a market for refined oil products is described by the following data:

Price	Quantity Demanded (Gallons)	Quantity Supplied (Gallons)
$2.00	0	20,000
$1.80	2,000	18,000
$1.60	4,000	16,000
$1.40	6,000	14,000
$1.20	8,000	12,000
$1.00	10,000	10,000
$0.80	12,000	8,000
$0.60	14,000	6,000
$0.40	16,000	4,000
$0.20	18,000	2,000
$0.00	20,000	0

   Suppose also that there are external costs of $1 per gallon associated with each gallon produced. Illustrate and determine the following:
   a. The equilibrium quantity of refined oil products
   b. The efficient quantity of refined oil products
   c. Total costs of pollution
   d. Efficiency losses from pollution
5. Using the diagram you have created for your answer to Question 4, identify the following:
   a. The quantity that would be produced if oil refiners (producers) were given property rights to the environment.
   b. The quantity that would be produced if victims of pollution (victims) were given property rights to the environment.
   c. The maximum amount that victims would pay producers to reduce production (and pollution) and the minimum amount that producers would accept.
   d. The maximum amount that producers would pay victims to increase production and the minimum amount that victims would accept.
6. What are the principal features of the Clean Air Act?
7. Has the Clean Air Act improved air quality? Explain.
8. Has the United States gone "too far" in reducing air pollution? Explain, citing relevant evidence.
9. Briefly explain why an emissions (Pigovian) tax reduces the cost of achieving cleaner air, using the example of the four plants developed in the chapter.
10. Briefly explain why marketable emissions permits reduce the cost of achieving cleaner air, using the example of the four plants developed in the chapter.

Web Sites

- *Council on Environmental Quality.*
  The CEQ produces annual reports that provide informative discussions of the nation's pollution problems and efforts to achieve a cleaner environment—**http://www.whitehouse.gov/ceq/**
- *Environmental Protection Agency.*
  The EPA Web site provides access to a wealth of information on environmental regulations and to the results of research related to these regulations—**http://www.epa.gov/**
- *Resources for the Future.*
  This private think tank provides summaries of state-of-the-art studies of research on natural resources and the environment—**http://www.rff.org/**

CHAPTER 7

Health Care: How Much? For Whom?

OUTLINE

The Rising Share of GDP Devoted to Health Care

The Growing Ranks of the Uninsured

Getting Our Money's Worth

Limiting Health Care Expenditure Growth

Keyword: *national health expenditures*

Access InfoTrac at http://infotrac.cengage.com

This chapter addresses the principal problems of the U.S. health care system and issues related to reforming that system. The principal problems are: (1) the rising share of GDP devoted to health care, (2) the growing ranks of the uninsured, and (3) wasteful spending. We do not assess the many proposals for health care reform, in general, a matter beyond the scope of this chapter. Instead, we consider what we believe to be some of the principal issues that must be resolved in any effort to reform the system.

THE RISING SHARE OF GDP DEVOTED TO HEALTH CARE

The dominant concern about the U.S. health care system is that it has been commanding a growing share of the nation's resources and that it threatens to continue to do so. As illustrated in Figure 7.1, national health expenditures (NHE) as a share of gross domestic product (GDP) grew from 5.9 percent in 1965 to 16.3 percent in 2007.

Figure 7.1 National Health Expenditures as a Percent of GDP

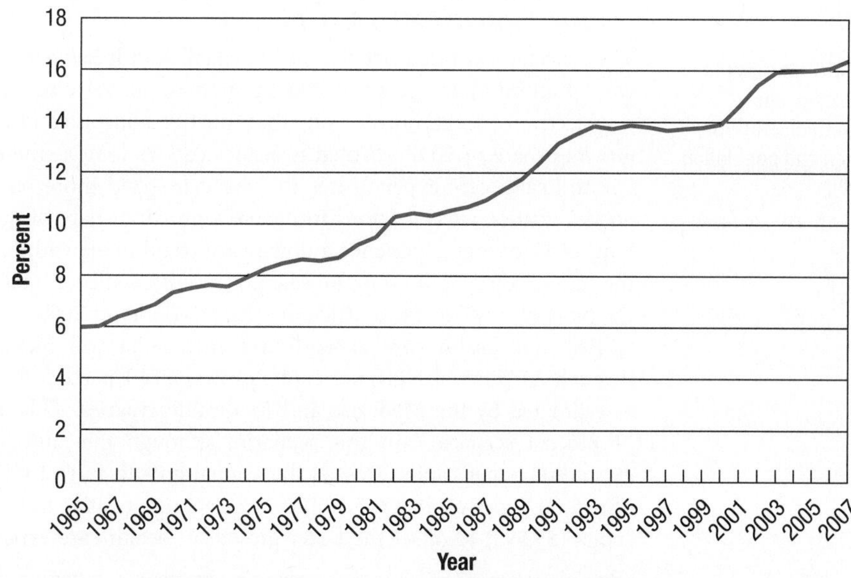

Source: *National Health Expenditures, Amounts by Type of Expenditure and Source of Funds, Calendar Year 1965–2017*, Centers for Medicare and Medicaid Services, Office of the Actuary.

Figure 7.2 Real NHE per Capita as a Percent of Real GDP per Capita

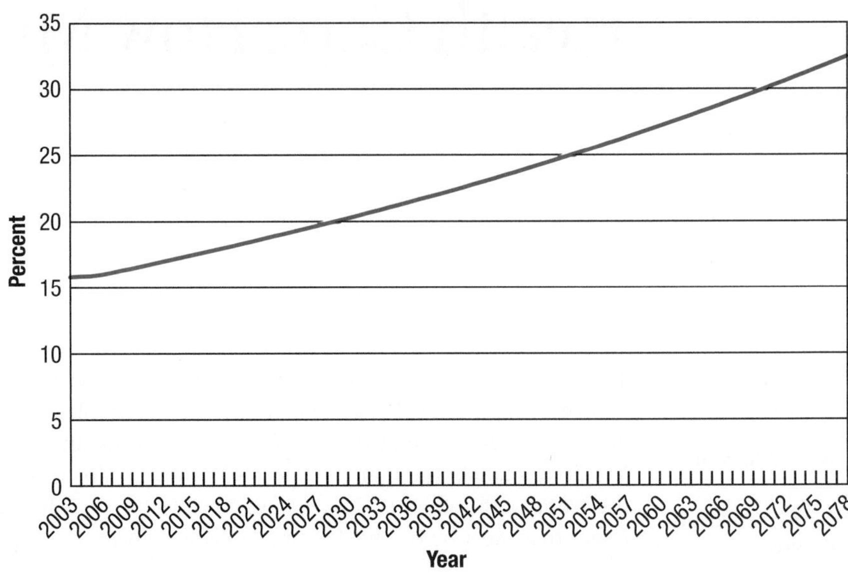

Source: For 2003–2014, *National Health Expenditures, Amounts by Type of Expenditure and Source of Funds, Calendar Year 1965–2017*, Centers for Medicare and Medicaid Services; for 2018–2078, authors' projections.

Real national health care expenditures per capita– National health care expenditures adjusted for inflation and population growth.

Real GDP per capita– Gross domestic product adjusted for inflation and population growth.

Actuaries in the Centers for Medicare and Medicaid Services expect **real NHE per capita** to grow 1 percent faster each year than **real GDP per capita**. If this does happen, the health expenditure share of GDP will reach 17.3 percent by 2014. If this trend continues beyond 2014, real NHE per capita will consume 32.4 percent of real GDP per capita by 2078, as shown in Figure 7.2.

How Much Can We Afford? Health Care versus Non-Health Care

The trajectory just described is not inevitable, but it has heightened concern about whether we can afford to devote an increasing share of our resources to health care. Affordability is a subjective concept, but it is one that must be addressed. One view is that we can afford a growing share of GDP devoted to health care as long as the economy grows enough relative to health care expenditures that we can spend more on health care *and* on all other goods. That is, we can afford to devote a growing share of our resources to health care as long as we do not experience a downward trend in expenditures on all other goods. This is the test of affordability employed by a recent Medicare Technical Review panel and it is the basis of a widely read article in *Health Affairs* in 2003.[1]

Real non-health care expenditures per capita will increase continuously from 2003 through 2078 if real NHE per capita grows only 1 percent faster than real GDP per capita, as estimated by the Medicare and Medicaid actuaries. This is shown in Figure 7.3 as the "1 percent scenario." In this scenario, although the annual growth in real health care expenditures per capita exceeds the annual growth in real GDP per capita, the initial level of real GDP per capita ($35,387) is large enough relative to the initial level of real NHE per capita ($5,593) to offset the faster growth in health care expenditures.

[1]Michael E. Chernow, Richard A. Hirth, and David M. Cutler, "Increased Spending on Health Care: How Much Can the United States Afford?" *Health Affairs* 22, no. 4 (2003): 15–25.

Figure 7.3 Projected Non-Health Care Expenditures per Capita

Source: Authors' projections.

Historically, however, the gap in growth rates has been close to 2 percent. If history repeats itself, real non-health care expenditures per capita will eventually decline in the 75-year projection period, as illustrated by the 2 percent scenario in Figure 7.3. Real non-health care expenditures per capita reach a peak of $41,175 in 2050 and decline thereafter.

If the actuaries are right, the 1 percent growth scenario would appear to be affordable. However, the share of the *annual* growth in real GDP per capita spent on health care would start at 17 percent and increase continuously throughout the projection period, reaching 59 percent in 2078.[2]

Keyword: *health care affordability*

Access InfoTrac at http://infotrac.cengage.com

There is a margin for additional increases in the ratio of health care expenditures to GDP for the next two or three decades in the 2 percent scenario although additional health care spending eventually becomes not affordable according to the proposed test of affordability. The nation would probably become unwilling to sustain the 2 percent gap between the growth rates of real health care spending per capita and real GDP per capita, however, well before it would become unwilling to sustain the 1 percent gap.

How Much Can We Afford? The Government Budget Constraint

Medicare– Federal health insurance program for people 65 and over.

Medicaid– Federal and state program that provides health care for low-income and disabled persons.

One likely source of the nation's unwillingness to sustain a rising share of GDP devoted to health care is the choices it would force upon the federal government. As shown in Figure 7.4, the Office of Management and Budget (OMB) projects that federal expenditures for **Medicare** and **Medicaid** will require a growing share of revenues projected under current law. Medicare and Medicaid expenditures are currently 25 percent of revenues; in 2060 they will be 46.5 percent of projected revenues.

This scenario provides Congress with difficult choices. It could finance the increase in Medicare and Medicaid expenditures by increasing the budget deficit. This option would reduce the rate of growth in potential real GDP, increase the trade deficit, and increase the risk of sustained inflation (for reasons spelled out in detail in Chapter 15). It could

[2]Ibid.

Figure 7.4 Projected Federal Expenditures for Medicare and Medicaid as a Percent of Projected Revenues

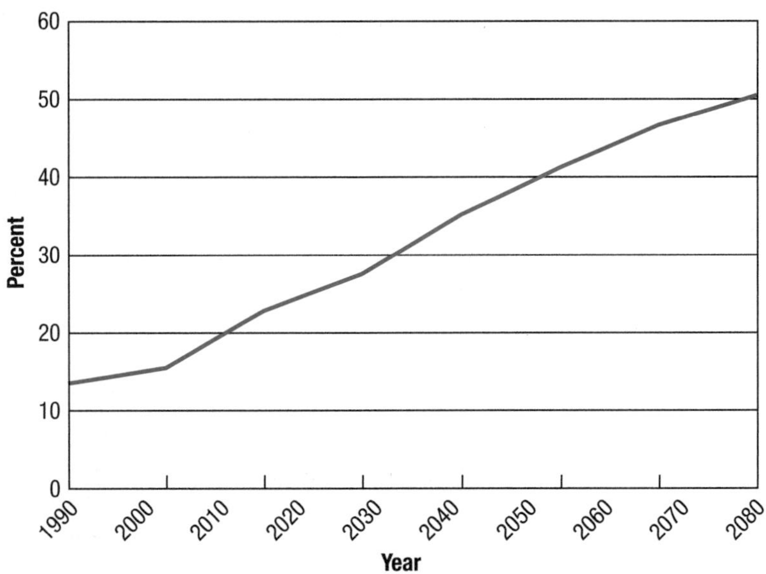

Source: Office of the President, *Budget of the United States Government, Fiscal 2009, Analytical Perspectives*, p. 188.

increase taxes, but the increase required (somewhere between 7 and 10 percent of GDP or a tax increase of 35–45 percent) would also wreak havoc on the economy. It could transfer resources from discretionary government programs, but it could not acquire all of the resources required to fund the increases in Medicare and Medicaid even if it wiped out all federal discretionary programs. Under these circumstances, it is easy to imagine that the federal government would lead the charge to bring rising health care expenditures under control. It would probably be aided in this effort by state governments, who also see Medicaid expenditures growing as a share of their budgets.

How Much Can We Afford? The Rising Household Burden

Ultimately, the burden of sustaining the relative growth in real NHE per capita falls on individuals. They pay health insurance premiums, either out of their own pockets or as reductions in take-home pay to cover the cost of employer-provided health insurance. They pay directly for expenditures not covered by insurance. They pay the taxes required to finance Medicare and Medicaid and other government health programs.

As you might suspect, an increasing share of GDP devoted to health care will be perceived by individuals or households as a growing share of the household budget spent either directly or indirectly on health care. Robert Hall, an economist at Stanford University, has estimated the burden that a typical household can look forward to as the health care share of GDP rises.[3] According to Jones's reporting of Hall's work, people now in their mid-60s have devoted about 16 percent of their preretirement income to health care. People now in their mid-20s will spend 35 percent of their preretirement

[3]"The Unbearable Forward Burden: Health, Education, and Retirement," Mimeo, Stanford University, February 18, 2003, as summarized by Charles Jones in *The Fiscal Problem of the Century*, Federal Reserve Bank of San Francisco News Letter No. 2003-27, September 19, 2003.

resources on health care, and people born in 2003 can expect to devote 56 percent of their preretirement resources to health care. Given these consequences, it seems likely that many individuals, acting in their roles as consumers, workers, or taxpayers, will feel the pinch and join efforts to slow down health care expenditure growth.

THE GROWING RANKS OF THE UNINSURED

Keyword: *uninsured*

Access InfoTrac at http://infotrac.cengage.com

Even if the rise in health care costs may be affordable in terms of the trade-off between health care and non-health care, it will not be affordable to all individuals. In fact, in spite of the world's highest expenditures for medical care, nearly 46 million Americans—more than 15 percent of the population—are without health insurance. Many who are insured are at risk of losing insurance coverage if they change jobs, or at risk of higher insurance costs if they contract an expensive disease.

This is not a new problem. The data illustrated in Figure 7.5 indicate that the number of Americans without health insurance has been rising at about a quarter million individuals per year since 1987, the first year for which data are available. Not only has the number of uninsured been rising but the increases in the uninsured have exceeded the increases in the population, resulting in a growing share of Americans without health insurances. As Figure 7.6 indicates, the percent of the population without health insurance has also generally trended upward for nearly the past two decades.

Health care insurance in the United States is closely linked to the workplace, with employers providing over 80 percent of the total. It is common, but inaccurate, to attribute lack of insurance to weak or no attachment to the workforce. More than 80 percent of the 46 million uninsured have some connection to the workforce, either as workers or as dependents of workers. The key to lack of workforce coverage is the size of a firm's labor force. The likelihood that a worker will not be covered is inversely related to the

Figure 7.5 Number of Individuals without Health Insurance

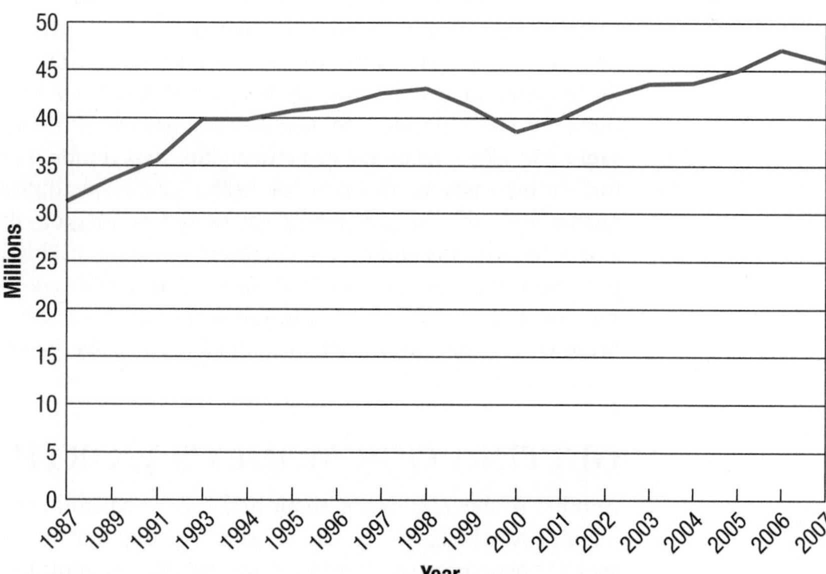

Source: U.S. Census Bureau, *Income, Poverty, and Health Insurance Coverage in the United States, 2007*, page 61, August 2008.

Figure 7.6 Percent of Population without Health Insurance

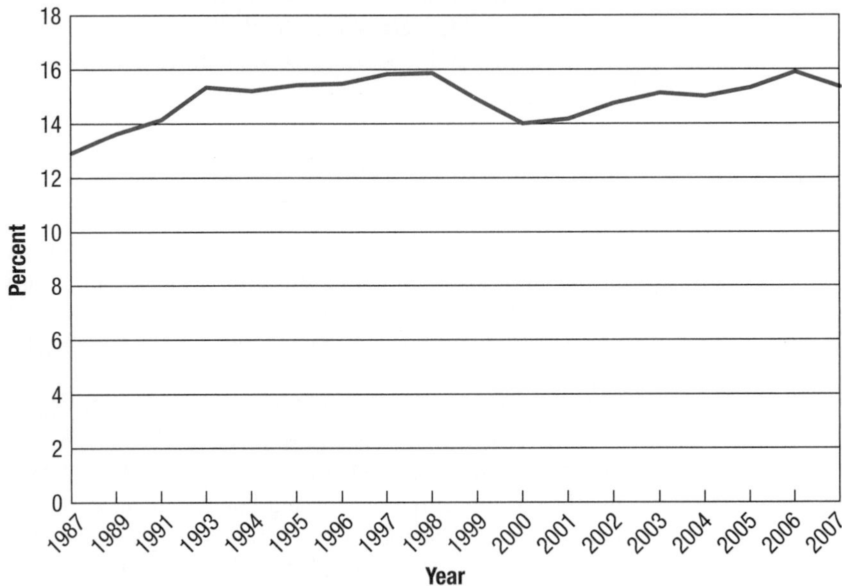

Source: Authors' Calculations, based on U.S. Census Bureau, *Income, Poverty, and Health Insurance Coverage in the United States, 2007,* page 61, August 2008.

size of the firm, measured by number of workers (that is, the fewer the number of workers, the greater the probability of no insurance). The problem is not necessarily lack of availability of health insurance to small firms, but the fact that health insurance cost per employee is much higher for small firms than for large firms. The higher costs stem from significantly higher insurance administration costs per employee and the higher risk of loss associated with smaller pools of employees.

The reader will probably note that the trend in the number of individuals who are uninsured is similar to the trend in the share of GDP devoted to health care. That is, the number of people who are uninsured has been rising at the same time that the share of GDP devoted to health care has been rising. There is not necessarily a cause-and-effect relationship between the two trends, but many observers believe that further increases in the ratio of health care expenditures to GDP will contribute to further increases in the percentage of the population that is uninsured. In a system that is heavily dependent on employer-provided health insurance, business firms will perceive the rising share of GDP devoted to health care as ever-growing upward pressure on the cost of health insurance. In order to stay in business, more and more firms will simply drop health insurance as a fringe benefit.

GETTING OUR MONEY'S WORTH

Another source of concern about health care expenditures is that we are not getting our money's worth. To an economist, we are getting our money's worth if two conditions are met: (1) benefits exceed costs for any specific expenditure; and (2) benefits per dollar of cost are equal across all expenditures. If the first condition is not met, we would be better off if the expenditure were eliminated, or cut back, if benefits and costs vary with the scale of expenditure. If the second condition is not met, we could gain by shifting expenditures from uses with relatively low benefits per dollar of cost to uses with relatively high benefits per dollar of cost. In both cases, the economists would say that we are not achieving efficiency in resource allocation, or allocative efficiency. (See Chapter 4 for a thorough analysis of this concept.)

A full review of this issue would require a book in itself. Here we concentrate on what we believe are four of the principal sources of allocative inefficiency in the health care sector: (1) the increasing share of third-party payments, (2) physician-induced demand, (3) defensive medicine, and (4) the federal tax subsidy of employer-provided health insurance.

Third-Party Payments

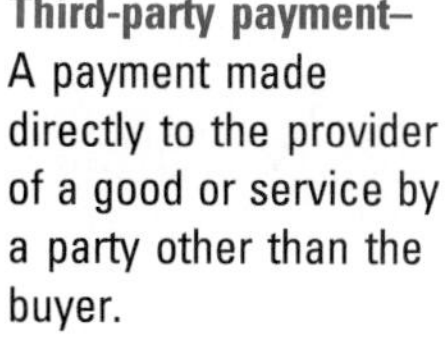

Health care is somewhat unusual in that patients are responsible for paying only a fraction of the cost of care directly. The share paid directly is called the out-of-pocket payment. The remaining share is paid by third parties—insurance companies, self-insured businesses, and government. This share is referred to as a **third-party payment**—a payment made to the provider of a good or service by a party other than the consumer.

Figure 7.7 illustrates the growth in third-party payments for health care since 1965. In 2003, third parties paid for 87.0 percent of all health care, up from 57.1 percent in 1965.

When third-party payments are involved, consumers pay directly for only part of health care costs. They pay out-of-pocket costs equal to the difference between the full cost of the health care received and the third-party payments for that care. The conventional view in economics is that this induces the production and consumption of too much health care; namely, health care for which benefits are less than costs. This situation is illustrated in Figure 7.8.

Figure 7.7 Third-Party Payments for Health Care as a Percent of National Health Expenditures

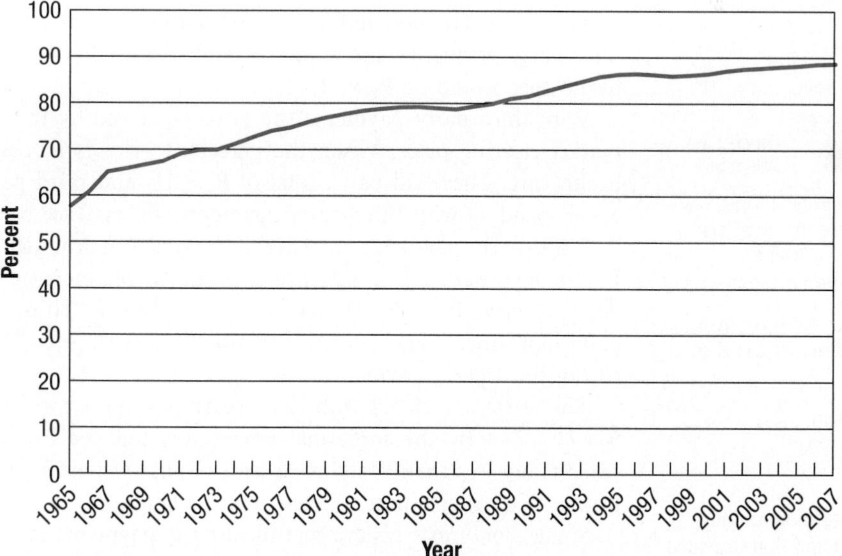

Source: *National Health Expenditures, Amounts by Type of Expenditure and Source of Funds, Calendar Year 1965–2017*, Centers for Medicare and Medicaid Services, Office of the Actuary.

Figure 7.8 The Effect of Third-Party Payments on Hospital Care
Consumers pay an out-of-pocket price of P_s, at which they demand H_2. In the absence of third-party payments they would purchase H_1 at price P_s—the market-clearing quantity and price. Third-party payments induce them to spend an additional A + B + C + D + E on health care. Of this amount, area C represents the welfare cost of third-party payments.

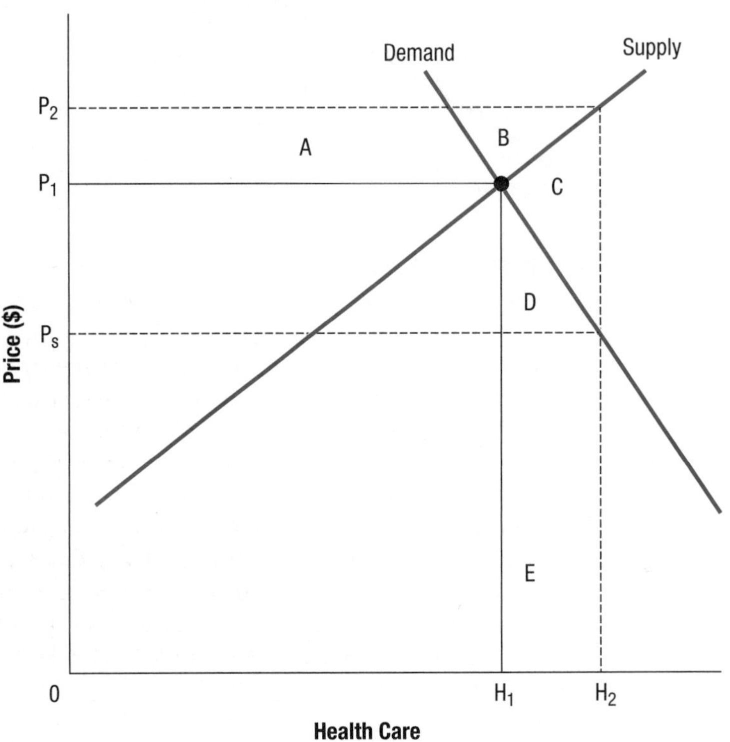

Figure 7.8 depicts the market for health care. The supply curve for health care is upward sloping. The demand curve for health care is downward sloping. In the absence of third-party payments, the market would clear at P_1, H_1 and the total amount spent on health care would be $P_1 \times H_1$.

With third-party payments the price perceived by the consumer, P_s, is less than the market-clearing price. When the perceived price is P_s consumers will buy H_2 units of health care. They will pay a total of $P_s \times H_2$ and third parties will pay $(P_2 - P_s) \times H_2$. Total spending with third-party payments will increase by the area A + B + C + D + E.

Third-party payments increase costs by the area under the supply curve from H_1 to H_2, or the area C + D + E. Third-party payments increase benefits by the area under the demand curve from H_1 to H_2, or the area D + E. Thus, third-party payments increase costs more than they increase benefits by area C. Area C is also known as the *welfare cost* of third-party payments.

The waste associated with third-party payments can be expressed either as area A + B + C + D + E—the additional expenditure induced by third-party payments for which benefits are less than costs, or as area C—the welfare cost of third-party payments. The former is obviously much larger than the latter.

Some economists believe that third-party payments are the principal cause of **wasteful spending** in the United States, but there is no apparent agreement about the amount of money represented by the area A + B + C + D + E.

Keywords: *third-party payments, welfare cost of health insurance*

Access InfoTrac at http://infotrac.cengage.com

Wasteful spending– Spending that provides benefits that are less than costs.

Physician-Induced Demand

The excess demand created by third-party payments is a good example of how consumer behavior can be affected by monetary incentives. Consumers are merely responding rationally to the incentive of a reduced price, and the wasted hospital care is a reflection of consumer choice. The outcome may not be socially desirable, but the consumer is still sovereign.

In the real world of health care, however, the doctor often has considerable influence on the care "demanded" by the patient. Because the doctor normally recommends a course of action, and the patient is presumably free to approve or disapprove, the consumer is ultimately sovereign in the sense that he has the final authority over health care expenditures. Most patients have little knowledge of medicine, however, so they often simply accept a physician's recommendation. This gives doctors considerable freedom to exercise their own preferences. At the very least, it affords them the opportunity to use their superior knowledge to persuade patients that particular services are necessary. If they use this opportunity to enhance their own income by prescribing health care that is ineffective or unnecessary, the doctor-patient relationship is a source of health care expenditure waste. We call health care prescribed by physicians to increase their own wealth **physician-induced demand**.

Physician-induced demand– Ineffective health care prescribed by physicians to increase their own wealth.

INTERNATIONAL PERSPECTIVE

Another Hidden Cost of Third-Party Payments

We have noted in the main text and in Figure 7.8 that third-party payments induce health care consumers to demand an inefficiently large amount of care, resulting in expenditures that yield benefits less than costs. This happens with third-party payments because only a small part of the health care cost is imposed on consumers; the remainder is paid by third parties. Just the opposite effect can occur, however. Third-party payments can impose costs on consumers that are not shared by third parties—this seems to be the case in Canada.

In Canada, most health care is paid for entirely by national health insurance. Thus, if the government were willing to pay for it, consumers would continue to consume health care until the benefit perceived on the last unit was zero (in Figure 7.8, this is where the demand curve would cut the horizontal axis). However, Canadian governments are not willing to pay for this much health care, and they place an overall limit on the amount that can be spent.

The result of the government expenditure limit is that the quantity of health care demanded often exceeds the quantity of health care supplied. In the face of such excess demand, patients often find that they have to wait for hospital and physician services.

Steven Globerman studied the problem of waiting for health care in British Columbia. He found that all patients together waited a total of 868,408 weeks for 10 types of hospital admissions in 1989, and that many of them experienced significant difficulty either at work or at home because of their untreated conditions. To put a cost on waiting, Globerman estimated the value of productive time lost. He did this by first multiplying the total time lost waiting by the percentage of patients experiencing difficulty while waiting, giving him an estimate of the amount of productive time lost. He then multiplied this number by average weekly industrial earnings in British Columbia in 1989. The resulting number—his estimate of the value of the productive time lost due to waiting—turned out to be about 0.2 percent of British Columbia's gross provincial product.

Undoubtedly, some cost is associated with waiting for hospital services in the United States, although we know of no estimates. The cost of waiting is probably concentrated on the uninsured. There appears to be little waiting among insured patients.

Source: Steven Globerman, "A Policy Analysis of Hospital Waiting Lists," *Journal of Policy Analysis and Management* 10 (Spring 1991): 247–62.

At least three conditions are necessary for the exercise of physician-induced demand. We have already touched upon two of these: (1) asymmetric information (physicians have information that is superior to patients' information) regarding the efficacy of health care alternatives; and (2) the desire of physicians to increase their own wealth. In addition, physicians' income must depend directly on the amount of health care that they prescribe. The first two conditions are surely present in the United States, although physicians as a group are undoubtedly motivated by more than money. The third condition is present where physicians practice fee-for-service medicine; that is, where a fee is charged for each service provided.

INFOTRAC College Edition

Keyword: *physician-induced medical care*

Access InfoTrac at http://infotrac.cengage.com

Recognition of these conditions has prompted a search for evidence of physician-induced demand. When experts evaluated medical records to determine if certain procedures are prescribed more often than warranted by risk-benefit considerations, they found indications that as much as one-third of certain common procedures (coronary bypass surgery, coronary angiograms, pacemaker insertions, carotid artery surgery, and upper gastrointestinal endoscopy) are inappropriate or of equivocal value.[4] Enormous variation also appears in care across different areas of the country and across countries. Phelps attributes most of the observed variation to differences in physician practices.[5]

Physician-induced demand does *not necessarily* cause variations in physician practices or the use of inappropriate procedures. This could be attributable, instead, to the inherent uncertainty of diagnostic medicine and variations in training and skills of physicians. Medicine, after all, is not an exact science, and honest differences of opinion arise within the medical community about the effectiveness of various procedures.

Economists have also identified several potential limits to the pure exercise of physician preferences, including:

1. *Potential competition.* Between 1965 and 1990, the number of physicians grew by nearly 110 percent while the U.S. population grew by only 28 percent. Observed patterns of physician location indicate clearly that doctors have been unable to hold on to their market share in the face of this increase in supply. (This is Phelps's conclusion in *Health Economics*, 186–92). This factor may moderate the exercise of physician-induced demand, just as the appearance of new foreign competitors reduces the market power of U.S. automobile manufacturers.
2. *Information monitoring by patients.* Many patients have some knowledge of the conditions for which they seek medical care and advice, and this knowledge is becoming easier to obtain over the Internet. If physicians suggest care that deviates significantly from what patients expect, they may not consent to the suggested care. Such patient self-monitoring constrains physicians in their pursuit of wealth.
3. *Second opinions.* Third-party payers may require second opinions before they agree to pay for expensive medical care. The threat of alternative diagnoses may make physicians more conservative in the care that they prescribe.
4. *Satisfaction maximization.* Maximizing satisfaction may be more important to doctors than maximizing wealth. If so, the amount of work—and income—that physicians create is probably less than the amount that they could create.
5. *Physician ethics.* Some physicians may simply consider it unethical to prescribe care that has questionable beneficial effects.

[4]David M. Cutler, "A Guide to Health Care Reform," *Journal of Economic Perspectives*, 8, no. 3 (1994): 14–15.

[5]Charles E. Phelps, Chapter 3, in *Health Economics* (New York: HarperCollins, 1992).

Cromwell and Mitchell estimate that each 1 percent growth in the number of surgeons has resulted in only one-tenth of a percent growth in surgeons' services.[6]

Rossiter and Wilensky found a similar effect for all physician types.[7] These results suggest that physician-induced demand is hardly even a minor source of increased spending for health care, perhaps for the reasons just noted.

Defensive Medicine

Defensive medicine– Medical procedures or diagnostic tests performed to reduce the risk of a lawsuit.

The U.S. legal system provides compensation to patients who can prove that they have been victims of medical malpractice. Doctors buy malpractice insurance as protection against the financial consequences of medical malpractice suits. The cost of malpractice insurance may have increased the rate at which doctors practice **defensive medicine**—medical care given to reduce the risk of a malpractice suit. The problem with defensive medicine is that this may be care with little value to the patient. The likelihood of this practice is increased if a third-party is making payments. This is because physicians are less reluctant to prescribe treatment of questionable value when they know their patients are not paying full cost.

Keyword: *malpractice insurance*

Access InfoTrac at http://infotrac.cengage.com

Defensive medicine need not be wasteful, however. It may result in higher quality care or a reduction in the number of high-risk procedures. Each of these outcomes provides value to patients.

According to some physicians, defensive medicine is a major factor in the growth of their medical costs. The most widely cited estimate, however, indicates that it explains less than 1 percent of all medical expenditures. Thus, it must be a miniscule source of wasteful expenditures.[8]

Federal Tax Exemption for Health Insurance

Keyword: *federal tax exemption for health insurance*

Access InfoTrac at http://infotrac.cengage.com

Employers pay for a significant fraction—more than 80 percent—of the health insurance premiums of workers in the United States. Good evidence indicates, however, that they shift the cost to employees in the form of lower wages (Phelps, *Health Economics*, 297). If this is the case, why don't employees just purchase their own insurance? They don't because their cost is lower if their employers pay for it. This happens because the federal income tax code exempts employee compensation received in the form of health insurance from the federal individual income tax.

The size of the exemption depends on the size of the insurance premium paid and the employee's marginal federal income tax rate. The marginal tax rate is the tax rate levied on the last dollar of taxable income. Currently, there are six marginal, or bracket, rates: 10, 15, 25, 28, 33, and 35 percent.

Suppose an individual in the 28 percent tax bracket has an insurance policy for which her employer pays a premium of $1,800 a year. If the worker were to buy the insurance herself, she would have to earn enough income before taxes to pay for both the insurance premium and her taxes on that income. In this example, she would have to earn $2,500 to realize the $1,800 after taxes to pay the premium [$1,800 = $2,500 – (0.28 × $2,500)]. A worker in the 35 percent bracket would have to earn $2,769 to buy the $1,800 policy. This means that the employee-provided $1,800 policy would cost the 28 percent taxpayer $2,500 and the 36 percent taxpayer $2,769 in the absence of the tax

[6]Jerry Cromwell and Janet B. Mitchell, "Physician-Induced Demand for Surgery," *Journal of Health Economics* 5, no. 4 (1986): 293–313.

[7]Louis F. Rossiter and Gail R. Wilensky, "Identification of Physician-Induced Demand," *Journal of Human Resources* 19, no. 2 (1984): 231–244.

[8]Roger Reynolds, John A. Rizzo, and Martin L. Gonzalez, "The Cost of Medical Professional Liability," *Journal of the American Medical Association* 257 (1987): 2776–2781.

exemption. Alternatively, both taxpayers enjoy exemptions from taxes worth $700 and $969, respectively. Thus, the tax exemption lowers the cost to them of health insurance by 28 and 35 percent, respectively.

The tax exemption reduces the price of health insurance, just as third-party payments reduce the out-of-pocket cost of hospital care. Given a downward-sloping demand curve for health insurance, the income tax exemption will increase the quantity of health insurance purchased (Phelps, *Health Economics*, 300–302). An increase in the quantity of health insurance will increase the quantity of health care demanded. In fact, Phelps estimates that the tax exemption for health insurance increases the demand for health care by 10 to 20 percent among the under-age-65 population (Phelps, *Health Economics*, 302). We are not certain, however, how much of this constitutes wasteful spending.

LIMITING HEALTH CARE EXPENDITURE GROWTH

As noted, we may be able, at least by some tests, to afford more health expenditures. There are, however, growing pressures to limit health care expenditure growth. Continued growth in the share of GDP devoted to health care will place a growing burden on both federal and state governments, on households, and on U.S. business firms. The growing pressure on business firms will increase the ranks of the uninsured. Increasing recognition of the scope of wasteful expenditures will temper the demand for more.

Limits on health care expenditures are not just the wave of the future, however. They are already here. In fact, they have been here for some time, primarily in the form of a fee schedule for Medicare and the growth of managed care organizations.

Managed Care

As health care costs became a larger part of the cost of doing business in this country, business firms began pressuring insurers to find a way that they could save money on health care costs. The solution chosen was **managed care**. Managed care is a general term for a variety of cost control practices used in managed care organizations. Health maintenance organizations, or HMOs, are the best-known of the managed care organizations, but they are only one of several types. There are also preferred provider organizations (PPOs), point of service plans (POSs), independent practice associations (IPAs), and others.

Managed care– Health care that is reviewed by someone other than the patient or provider to determine whether the right services are being provided and whether the cost of provision is minimized.

Traditionally, health care insurers in the United States reimbursed health care providers on the basis of services performed or on the basis of costs of provision. These methods of reimbursement created incentives for health care providers to increase fees, to increase services provided, and to adopt cost-increasing procedures and technologies.

In managed care settings, insurers pay less to medical care providers than did traditional insurers. One way they do this is through lower rates negotiated with providers. Traditional insurers did not negotiate lower rates because they believed that doctors would be less willing to see patients at lower rates. Managed care insurers do not strive for universal access to providers; they pick and choose with whom they want to contract. In return for lower prices, insurers provide patients. Lowering physician payments is an attractive way to save money because there is little that doctors will do about it. Doctors are trained primarily to practice medicine. If, in order to see patients, physicians must accept a reduction in income, most will do so and continue to practice. Some doctors retire early and others move into administrative jobs to avoid pay cuts, but the vast majority of doctors don't have that option.

Keywords: *managed care and cost savings, managed care and outcomes*

Access InfoTrac at http://infotrac.cengage.com

Utilization review– A process used to determine if the medical care prescribed by a physician is appropriate.

Managed care also saves money through restrictions on what services are provided, coupled with financial incentives for physicians to provide fewer services. Restrictions on services are accomplished by a process called **utilization review**. Managed care insurers use this process most aggressively to reduce hospital utilization and costs. They require second opinions before nonemergency admissions and withhold payment if they are not received. They monitor length of stay to see where extra days might be trimmed—and they trim them. Utilization review is also practiced at the physician level. Routine tests are scrutinized for need, as are referrals to specialists.

Financial incentives have reinforced these restrictions. In addition to lowering fees, managed care creates financial incentives for providers to provide fewer services. Some primary care physicians (general practitioners, internists, pediatricians) receive a fixed payment per patient. They must cover the costs of all medical services provided out of that amount. Thus, they lose money when more care is provided. Similar systems are in place at some hospitals.

Because different insurers use different payment schemes, reimbursement for services is a tangled web for providers. Physicians might be paid a fixed rate for some patients, a discounted fee for others, and a target payment for specific services for some or all of their patients. Many doctors probably have only a vague idea of how much they earn for each patient they treat.

Doctors are still paid more for doing more, but significantly less than under the traditional fee-for-service system. Managed care, however, is in some ways more generous to *patients* than what came before it. In exchange for tighter restrictions on utilization, managed care offers lower out-of-pocket payments. Most managed care plans charge very low fees—$5 or $10—per physician visit, substantially below what people paid in traditional policies. This is done in the hope that it will increase preventive care, thereby reducing the incidence of higher-cost health episodes. The goal of managed care is to limit use of the system when patients access it, not to keep them away from it.

Managed care has virtually taken over that part of the medical system financed by private insurance; nearly 95 percent of privately insured people are in managed care plans. Traditional insurance is largely confined to Medicare patients, although managed care is even making inroads among this population in some states (and must be used by Medicare patients in a handful of states).

The growth of managed care has had a major impact on the health care system. Its effect on health care expenditures can be seen clearly in Figure 7.1. After decades of increases in health care expenditures that exceeded GDP growth, national health expenditures grew only as fast as GDP from 1993 to 2000, an accomplishment that economists normally attribute to the growth of managed care. Unfortunately, it now appears that the savings from the adoption of managed care may be largely one-time savings (as many health care economists predicted); national health expenditures have been rising since 2000 at a faster rate than GDP is growing, and many health care economists predict that this will continue to be the case.

Monetary savings are not the only concern, of course. If managed care saves money but adversely affects health outcomes, the cost savings might not be worth it. Managed care has changed the type and intensity of treatment provided in some settings, but not, apparently, at the expense of effective outcomes. The worst fears that people have about managed care seem to be overblown, but patients still do not like what they perceive to be managed care's intrusions on their freedom of choice.

Less high-tech care is provided under managed care, but there is more routine and chronic disease care. On balance, these two incentives roughly cancel each other. People are neither better nor worse off in managed care. But the change is not ideal. Over the longer term, the incentives in managed care could be quite damaging. The lower rate of use of intensive care in areas with greater managed care enrollment raises the significant issue of whether managed care will have an adverse effect on new innovations. As noted below, these innovations have produced enormous benefits, and it would be bad policy to discourage further innovation.

Limiting Expenditure Growth Rationally

Although managed care has been somewhat successful in slowing the rate of expenditure growth, that's not all that we necessarily want from health care reform. Economists argue that we should limit expenditures rationally. The American public also appears to have a strong preference for insuring the uninsured. As we will argue next, doing so may be the rational thing to do.

We can limit expenditures rationally while limiting expenditure growth by first eliminating expenditures that yield benefits less than costs. If there is not enough money for all remaining expenditures, then we should eliminate expenditures according to benefits per dollar of cost, trimming those that yield the smallest benefits per dollar of cost. If benefits cannot be measured, we should eliminate expenditures according to effectiveness per dollar of cost, trimming those that yield the smallest effectiveness per dollar of cost, or, what is the same thing, trimming expenditures with the highest cost per unit of effectiveness.

Benefit-Cost Analysis. If benefits can be measured, expenditure decisions can be made using benefit-cost analysis. Here we consider an important example of the potential usefulness of this tool.

There are two primary sources of benefits from medical advances: reduced mortality or increased life expectancy, and reduced morbidity or enhanced quality of life. Up to now, economists have been more successful in valuing increases in life expectancy than in valuing enhancements in the quality of life.

David M. Cutler and Srikanth Kadiyala have analyzed life expectancy in the United States and found that it improved fairly steadily throughout the last century.[9] Life expectancy at birth in 1900 was less than 50 years, while today it is 77. Gains prior to 1950 can be explained largely by reductions in infant mortality and infectious diseases. The former are due to improved diet, sanitation, housing, and education. Reductions in infectious diseases are largely due to the development and diffusion of effective pharmaceutical weapons. Since then, the gains in life expectancy are closely associated with declining mortality among the elderly, chiefly from advances made in treating heart disease and strokes. In fact, death rates from cardiovascular diseases, both among the middle-aged and the elderly, have fallen to half of what they were in the mid-1960s.

To a large extent, then, the value of improved health care technology is linked to the increase in life expectancy due to medical advances in treating cardiovascular illness. The economist's task is to estimate the value of the extra years of life produced by these advances.

Value of a life–The value people put on their own lives, inferred from what they must be paid to incur small but predictable increases in the risk of dying.

The starting point is to estimate the **value of a life**. The dominant approach to this in economics is to infer the value people put on their own lives from what they must be paid to incur small but predictable increases in the risk of dying. As an example of how this works, suppose that moving from a job in retail sales to housing construction increases a worker's chance of a fatal accident by one in 5,000 each year. In other words, if 5,000 workers made the move, expected on-the-job fatalities would increase by one per year. Suppose further that employers would have to pay each worker an extra $1,000 annually to accept the higher-risk employment. The group would gain $5 million, then, as compensation for the death that will occur. The value that they place on a life, therefore, is $5 million. Formally: The value of a life = the increase in earnings required to assume additional risk divided by the increase in risk. In this case, the value of a life equals $1000 divided by 0.002, or $5,000,000.

[9] *The Economics of Better Health: The Case of Cardiovascular Disease*, from Cutler's Web site.

TABLE 7.1 DETERMINATION OF THE PRESENT VALUE OF ADDITIONAL LIFE YEARS FROM MEDICAL ADVANCES IN TREATING CARDIOVASCULAR DISEASE

FVLY	YEARS VALUE DELAYED	DISCOUNT FACTOR	PVLY
\$100,000	31	$(1.03)^{76-45} = (1.03)^{31} = 2.500$	\$100,000/2.500 = \$40,000
\$100,000	32	$(1.03)^{77-45} = (1.03)^{32} = 2.575$	\$100,000/2.575 = \$38,835
\$100,000	33	$(1.03)^{78-45} = (1.03)^{33} = 2.652$	\$100,000/2.652 = \$37,707
\$300,000			\$116,542

Once this value is established, it is necessary to determine what it means in terms of the average value of an additional *year* of life. A typical adult thinking about how much risk they would be willing to accept in return for more money might have about 40 years left to live. If so, that adult is implicitly valuing her life at about \$125,000 per year. A large number of studies have used a methodology like this to assess the value of years of life. A rough consensus is that a year of life is worth about \$75,000 to \$150,000. As a rough approximation, one could use a value of \$100,000 for an additional year of life.

According to the study by Cutler and Kadiyala, the average American aged 45 can expect to live 4.5 additional years today over 1950 solely because cardiovascular disease mortality has declined. Suppose that three years of this is a result of medical advances, with the rest being due to behavioral changes. If each additional year of life is worth \$100,000 per year to the person affected, the benefit from medical advances totals \$300,000. The additional years of life are tacked on to the end of life, however, so they won't be realized until around 30–35 years later. These are *future* values. To determine what they are worth to the 45-year-old, we must determine their *present* value—that is, value to the individual at age 45.

This is done by discounting each future value as follows:

$$PVLY_{45} = FVLY_t/(1 + i)^{t-45}, \qquad (7.1)$$

where PVLY is the present value of a life year at age 45, FVLY is the future value of a life year in year t, $(1 + i)^{t-45}$ is the discount factor, and i is the discount rate.

Table 7.1 shows how this equation is applied in the case where the additional life years are delayed until ages 76, 77, and 78, or for 31, 32, and 33 years. We use $i = 0.03$ or 3 percent, the real rate of return on long-term U.S. government bonds realized historically. The net result of discounting is to reduce the value of the additional life years from \$300,000 to \$159,186.

These benefits must be compared to the increased costs due to medical advances. The typical 45-year-old can expect to consume about \$40,000 in present value of resources devoted to cardiovascular disease over their remaining life. Virtually all of this is for medication, surgeries, and other long-term therapies that were not available in 1950.

Clearly, the present value of the benefits from these medical advances is greater than the costs. For every \$1 spent, there is a return of nearly \$3. Advances in cardiovascular disease treatment appear to have been worth it for the 45-year-old in this example.

Kevin Murphy and Robert Topel of the University of Chicago have applied methods similar to these to the entire population for the period 1970–1990.[10] They estimated that the additional life years attributable to reduced mortality from cardiovascular disease over this period are worth over \$31 *trillion* in present value for the population as a

[10]"The Economic Value of Medical Knowledge," September 2001, Authors' Web sites.

INFOTRAC College Edition

Keywords: *medical research and returns, economic benefits of medical research*

Access InfoTrac at http://infotrac.cengage.com

whole. They estimated, further, that the additional life years attributable to reduced mortality from all sources over this time period are worth nearly $57 trillion. Although not all these benefits can be attributed to medical advances, they are so large that it is hard to escape the conclusion that many medical advances have been well worth the investment. Besides, these are lower-bound estimates, which include nothing for any improvements that have occurred in morbidity or quality of life.

Moreover, Murphy and Topel estimate that potential future gains are also very large; they estimate that the benefits of reduced mortality from *eliminating* cancer would be worth roughly $47 trillion and the benefits of reduced mortality from *eliminating* heart disease would be worth about $48 trillion. They figure that even modest progress in reducing mortality from these diseases would have great value. For example, a 10 percent reduction in cancer deaths would be worth over $4 trillion. In fact, even a $200 billion research program on cancer would be worthwhile if it reduced cancer deaths by only as little as 1 percent.

INFOTRAC College Edition

Keywords: *costs of uninsured, costs of insuring uninsured*

Access InfoTrac at http://infotrac.cengage.com

Insuring the Uninsured. Another use of resources that is likely to be rational is insuring the uninsured, even though doing so would increase health care expenditures in the absence of offsetting reductions.

Uninsured individuals suffer adverse health outcomes from lack of access to the health care system that insurance would provide. They are less likely to get access to preventive and screening services and they are more likely to have serious diseases detected when the diseases are in their later stages. As a result, they are less likely to be diagnosed and treated in a timely fashion. As a result, they often have higher mortality rates and greater impairment of quality of life.

Miller, Vigdor, and Manning have reviewed the literature on the consequences of uninsurance and the costs of those consequences.[11] Based on this review, they estimate the value of health foregone each year because of lack of insurance at $65 to $130 billion. According to the authors this is a lower-bound estimate of the annual benefits that would be realized by providing insurance to the uninsured.

Halley and Holahan estimate that it would cost about $34 billion a year to insure the uninsured if provided with full Medicaid-like coverage, or $69 billion if provided with full private insurance coverage.[12] Although additional work on both sides of the benefit-cost ledger remains to be done, the results of these studies suggest that the benefits of insuring the uninsured are likely to exceed the costs by enough to make it an attractive policy option. They also suggest that spending more money on health care can be the rational thing to do—in spite of the growing share of expenditures relative to GDP—as long as there is a net gain to society from doing so.

Eliminating the Federal Tax Exemption for Health Insurance. We have already explained how the federal tax exemption for employer-provided health insurance increases the demand for health insurance. Although we don't know for certain the extent of the waste created by this inducement, it may be rational to eliminate it as a means of constraining expenditure growth.

Elimination of this exemption has been proposed to Congress many times, most recently as part of President Clinton's health care reform package, but Congress has refused to eliminate it.

The exemption was granted initially to encourage employer-provided insurance as a means of helping workers secure the lower premiums that come with group purchases of insurance. Many in Congress may believe that the elimination of the exemption would undo this advantage. The exemption tends to benefit primarily workers in larger firms,

---

[11]Wilhelmina Miller, Elizabeth Richardson Vigdor, and Willard G. Manning, "Covering the Uninsured: What is it Worth?" *Health Affairs Web Exclusive*, March 31, 2004, W4-157–W4-167.

[12]J. Halley and J. Holahan, "Covering the Uninsured: How Much Would it Cost?" *Health Affairs Web Exclusive*, June 4, 2003, W3-250–W3-265.

and they can secure favorable premiums anyway, because of their numbers. In fact, the exemption may not have had anything to do with the development of the employer-provided insurance market; that can be attributed largely to the competition among insurers for clients that look more profitable based on their experience rating. Take the exemption away, and they would still be the most profitable risk pools.

Thus, two problems actually arise with the exemption: (1) It leads to excessive health care spending (as already alleged); and (2) it is unnecessary as a means of increasing the availability of low-cost insurance. But that's not all. Because its value to workers rises with the marginal tax rate, the exemption provides a greater subsidy to higher-income workers than to lower-income workers. This pattern violates most notions of equity. In addition, the subsidy contributes to the federal deficit by the same amount as equivalent direct federal expenditure. This is not a trivial effect; the exemption amounted to more than $100 billion in 2004.

This is a formidable array of problems. Why, then, does the exemption persist? Probably because it provides a subsidy to the purchase of health care from which thousands of insurance companies, thousands of hospitals, hundreds of thousands of doctors, millions of businesses, and scores of millions of workers benefit. Together they form an almost irresistible force against significant political change. Given the rapidly rising concern about the level of health care spending, we may be closer than ever to the time when economics will triumph over politics on this issue, but we would not bet on it.

Voucher– A coupon that can be used to pay for something, such as health care or health insurance.

HEALTH CARE VOUCHERS. One rational way to reduce overspending for health care would be to replace the current system of reimbursement with a system of vouchers. Their use has been suggested most often for Medicare and Medicaid patients. **Vouchers** are coupons that can be used to pay for something, in this case health care at hospitals or doctors' offices chosen by the recipient. Alternatively, the individual could be required to use the voucher to purchase a conventional health insurance policy or to participate in a lower-cost managed care system. In fact, the voucher program could be tailored to encourage recipients to choose managed care by providing a slightly larger voucher for those who do.

INFOTRAC College Edition

Keywords: *medical vouchers, Medicare vouchers, Medicaid vouchers*

Access InfoTrac at http://infotrac.cengage.com

The government could save costs by issuing vouchers for a smaller amount than it currently spends. Economists argue that this could be done without materially reducing beneficial health care to the recipients, because they would be faced with a greater share of the costs of their own care and make better health care choices. Proponents of vouchers also stress that their use would enhance price (and cost) competition by health care providers for Medicare and Medicaid patients.

Critics of vouchers stress that they may not work as intended because recipients may make poor choices of health insurers or providers. Some proponents answer that, if this was a problem, the government could provide accurate information about the merits of alternative insurance policies and providers. A similar role for government, however, was rejected as part of the ill-fated Clinton health care reform proposal.

Summary

The focus of this chapter is on the rising cost of health care in the United States. Except for a seven-year period in the 1990's, national health expenditures (NHE) have increased steadily relative to GDP. Official projections indicate, moreover, that NHE will grow from just under 16 percent in 2003 to nearly 19 percent of GDP by 2003, and if real national health expenditures per capita grow only one percent per year faster than real GDP per capita projected trends indicate that NHE will be one-third of GDP by 2078.

These trends raise the question: Can we afford to spend more on health care? One view is that what is relevant is the trade-off between health care and non-health care. According to this view we can afford more health care as long as non-health care expenditures do not decline. This is projected to be the outcome over the next 75 years if real health care expenditures per capita grow only 1 percent per year faster than real GDP per capita. If the growth rate differential is 2 percent per year non-health care expenditures eventually decline.

Another view is that it is the perceived burden of health care expenditures that counts. If so, then the growing burdens of health care spending on governments, households, and business firms indicate that we will reach the point where we can't afford more health care spending sooner than indicated by the trade-off between health care and non-health care expenditures. The growing number of individuals without health insurance will also add to the pressure to limit health care spending.

The trend toward limits on health care spending is reinforced by the perception that much health care spending is wasteful; that it yields benefits less than costs. The most important case is that of third-party payments, which produce both wasteful spending and welfare costs. Probably next in line as a source of wasteful spending is the federal tax exemption of employer-provided health insurance. Physician-induced demand and defensive medicine appear to cause very little wasteful spending.

Some suspect that physicians have induced patients to over-consume health care. Several checks on physician-induced demand, however, keep it from becoming an important source of excess health care spending. Existing evidence of ineffective and inappropriate care cannot necessarily be attributed to independent, self-serving practices of physicians.

Physicians purportedly prescribe unnecessary procedures as a defensive measure against possible malpractice lawsuits. The costs associated with this practice, however, probably do not exceed 1 percent of health care costs.

Employer-provided health insurance enjoys a substantial subsidy in the form of a federal tax exemption of health insurance premiums. This exemption stimulates the purchase of more insurance and indirectly induces consumers to buy health care of questionable value.

There is already considerable effort in the United States to limit the growth of health care expenditures. The prime example is managed care, an approach that did slow expenditure growth from 1993 to 2000. Managed care no longer appears to be limiting expenditure growth, however.

Ideally, limits on expenditure growth would be achieved in a rational manner. This means that expenditure choices by the payers of health care costs would be made by comparing benefits and costs or by inducing individual consumers of health care to consider the full costs of health care when purchasing health care or health insurance.

The ideal tool for making such choices on the part of payers is benefit-cost analysis. Use of this tool indicates that the payoff from medical advances has been enormous, considering increases in life expectancy, alone. This is especially true of medical advances in treating cardiovascular disease. Economists estimate, moreover, that the payoff from further small reductions in heart disease and cancer are so large that even very expensive research programs that produced such outcomes would be worth it. The application of benefit-cost analysis also indicates that it would be rational to insure the uninsured.

Other rational approaches to limiting health care expenditure growth are the elimination of the federal tax exemption of employer-provided health insurance and vouchers. The federal tax exemption for employer-provided health insurance induces excessive health care spending and provides a larger subsidy to higher-income employees. Nevertheless, it enjoys considerable political support. Vouchers harness the cost-cutting power of consumer choice and may be an effective means of reducing health care expenditures.

Key Terms

Real NHE per capita
Real GDP per capita
Medicare
Medicaid
Third-party payment
Wasteful spending
Physician-induced demand
Defensive medicine
Managed care
Utilization review
Value of a life
Vouchers

Review Questions

1. Briefly describe the relationship between national health expenditures (NHE) and GDP over the period 1965–2078. What is the basic assumption that accounts for NHE rising relative to GDP from 2014 through 2078?
2. One way to decide whether we can afford more health care spending is by reference to the trade-off between health care spending and non-health care spending. Explain this test of affordability and explain the results of applying it, referring to the 1 percent and 2 percent scenarios.
3. Describe the likely impact of health care spending on the federal budget.

4. Describe the likely impact of health care spending on household budgets.
5. How many Americans are uninsured? Why is this number likely to grow?
6. What do we mean by "too much" health care? Illustrate and explain briefly how third-party payments cause too much health care to be produced and consumed.
7. Suppose that the risk of dying in an automobile accident is reduced by 1 in 10,000 through the use of front seat air bags and that 10,000 auto buyers choose to purchase these air bags as an option at a price of $250. What is the implicit value of a life to these buyers? Explain how you got your answer.
8. Suppose that a year of life is worth $150,000 and that a new treatment for diabetes increases life expectancy for a 40-year-old woman by 2 years. Suppose, further, that the treatment will cost $50,000 in present value per woman. If the discount rate is 3 percent ($i = 0.03$) determine if this treatment is worth the cost.
9. Carefully define physician-induced demand. Can it explain the large amount of ineffective and inappropriate care? Why or why not?
10. "Defensive medicine is one of the primary causes of excessive health care spending." Is this statement true or false? Justify your answer.
11. How can the federal tax exemption for health insurance make the net cost of an insurance policy negative?
12. What are the key elements of managed care? Evaluate managed care in terms of its effect on the rate of increase in health care expenditures.
13. In theory, vouchers should reduce excess health care spending. Explain why.

Web Sites

- *Health Affairs: The Policy Journal of the Health Sphere.*
  The most cited health policy journal. Contains original, peer-reviewed research articles, many of which are understandable by a lay audience—http://www.healthaffairs.org
- *Kaiser Commission on Medicaid and the Uninsured.*
  An arm of the Kaiser Family Foundation. Provides links to information on the uninsured, Medicaid, health care reform, and related topics—http://www.kff.org/about/kcmu.cfm
- *Center for Medicare and Medicaid Services.*
  Provides links to health care data, including national health expenditures—http://www.cms.hhs.gov

CHAPTER 8

Crime and Drugs: A Modern Dilemma

OUTLINE

In his *Wealth of Nations*, Adam Smith contended that government in a market economy has three major responsibilities: to provide national defense, to establish an exact system of justice, and to ensure the availability of certain public works and institutions. These responsibilities cannot be adequately or efficiently met by the market economy. Because they are essential, government must act. Although national defense is self-explanatory, Smith's conception of an exact system of justice and of public works requires explanation. For him, an exact system of justice requires "protecting, as far as possible, every member of the society from the injustice or oppression of every other member of it ..." Public works and institutions consist of (1) laws and infrastructure, such as roads and canals, that facilitate commerce; (2) institutions for the education of the young; and (3) institutions for the instruction of people of all ages. The educational institutions contribute to the wealth of nations through their effect on commerce. Smith argued, however, that users of the public works and institutions should be expected to pay at least some of the expenses based on the amount used.

The framers of the U.S. Constitution intended to perfect the union that had been established by the Articles of Confederation so as to "secure the blessings of liberty to ourselves and our posterity." The Preamble says that federal government responsibilities are to "establish justice, insure domestic tranquility, provide for the common defense, [and] promote the general welfare." The Preamble is consistent with Smith's ideas of the proper responsibilities of government: national defense, internal order, and undertaking public works that promote commerce. It should not be surprising that a view of government similar to Smith's bubbled up in eighteenth-century America. Jefferson, Madison, and others were directly influenced by Smith, and indirectly because they were steeped in the same philosophers.

In a similar vein, Paul Johnson, a British historian, once told Margaret Thatcher that governments "might quite properly do all kinds of things, such as run schools and build roads, but there were only three things they were compelled to do. The more of the optional things they did, the more likely it was that they would neglect the three essentials. So what were the three? They were external defence, internal order, and the maintenance of an honest currency. These things must be done by government because nobody else could do them."[1] Johnson went on to say that governments often failed to provide "an honest currency"; in other words, Johnson argued that governments often cause inflation, a topic that we discuss in Chapter 14. Although the British government currently provides an "honest currency," Johnson believed that it was doing a bad job with the second duty, maintaining internal order.

[1]Paul Johnson, "The Real Job of Government: External Defence, Internal Order and an Honest Currency," *Spectator*, October 9, 1999, 27.

Figure 8.1 Selected Crime Facts
Rapidly growing expenditures on crime control had little effect on the public's perception that too little is spent on crime control until the mid-1990s. Nevertheless, the expenditure growth may have influenced the reduction in property crime rates that occurred throughout the period and the reduction in violent crime rates that began in the mid-1990s.

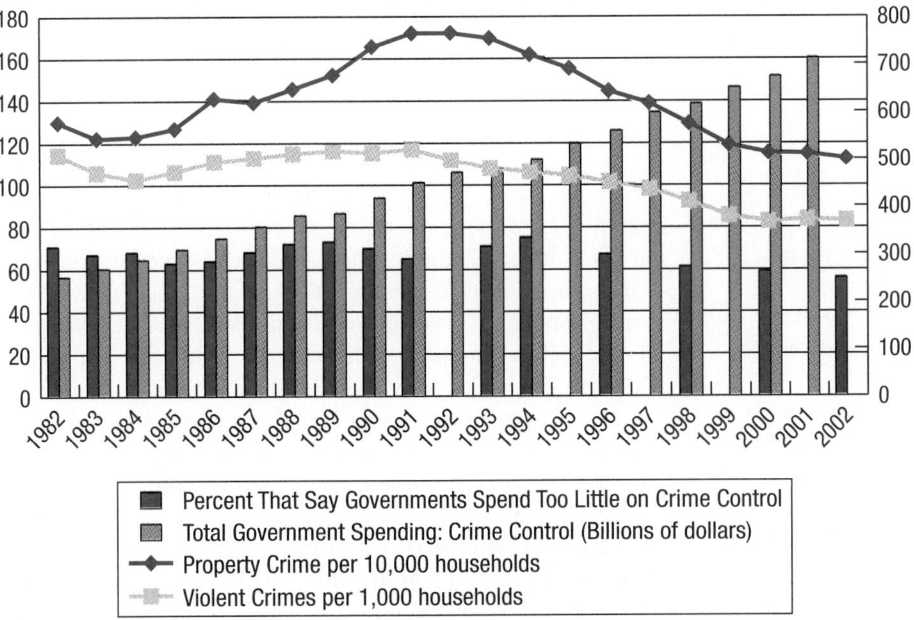

Source: Kathleen Maguire and Ann L. Pastore, eds. *Sourcebook of Criminal Justice Statistics* [online] (Washington, D.C.: U.S. Department of Justice, Bureau of Justice Statistics), various years.

A majority of U.S. citizens, according to opinion polls, also believe that federal, state, and local governments are not doing a good job in fighting crime, which is one aspect of "maintaining internal order." Surveys (2002) show that 56 percent of the population believes that governments should spend more on crime control. This percentage has varied between 56 and 75 percent since 1983 (see Figure 8.1). The highest figure, 75 percent, was in 1994. The reason for the concern about crime is evident in other polls, which find that over one-third of the population fears walking at night in some areas within a mile of their home. This percentage increased from 40 percent in 1989 to 47 percent in 1994 and dropped 30 percent in 2001. By 2005 it had risen back to 38 percent. Similarly, since 9/11 the percentage of the population that thinks the crime rate has increased over the previous year has increased from 41 percent, its lowest value in recent history, to 67 percent.[2]

The bars in Figure 8.1 (measured against the left axis) show the high percentage of the population that believes that governments spend too little on crime control. It also shows the rapidly increasing expenditures (in inflation-adjusted dollars) from 1983 to the present, which failed to reduce people's concerns about the amount spent on crime control until the mid-1990s. One of the lines in Figure 8.1 (measured against the right axis) shows

[2]The data used in the introduction are from Kathleen Maguire and Ann L. Pastore, eds. (various years) *Sourcebook of Criminal Justice Statistics* [online] (Washington, D.C.: U.S. Department of Justice, Bureau of Justice Statistics). Current version is available at http://www.albany.edu/sourcebook. See the Gallup Poll for October 2005 at http://www.pollingreport.com/crime.htm for the most recent results.

that the property crime rate (theft, burglary, and motor vehicle theft) has fallen steadily since about 1990, with little apparent effect, at first, on people's desire to spend more on crime control. The figure also shows that violent crime rates (murder, rape, robbery, and aggravated and simple assault) increased from the mid-1980s to the mid-1990s. Since the mid-1990s the violent crime rate has fallen, corresponding to the fall in the percentage of the population that thinks the government spends too little on crime control. People's perceptions of crime or fears about crime, not surprisingly, are associated with the incidence of violent crimes.[3]

Crime rates are so high in the United States, at least in part, because of the illegal markets for various drugs. These illegal markets cause much property crime and personal violence. Although the casual use of illegal drugs—as well as alcohol and nicotine—has declined from its peak in the 1970s, frequent users of marijuana, cocaine, heroin, and increasingly methamphetamine continue to create profitable, but illegal, markets. Violence is endemic on the supply side of these markets. On the demand side, heavy users of illegal drugs often support their habits by committing property crimes, often accompanied by violence.

Keywords: *crime, drugs, and government*

Access InfoTrac at http://infotrac.cengage.com

This chapter explores government's role in crime control. It focuses on Adam Smith's exact system of justice and the Constitution's goal of establishing justice and ensuring domestic tranquility. First, it discusses crimes in which one person uses force to violate another person's rights. Second, it discusses the so-called victimless crimes created by criminalizing voluntary transactions between two people, for example, the purchase and sale of marijuana. In both cases, the rationale for government action is discussed. The chapter then discusses drug policy. In subsequent chapters we discuss the government's role in secondary and college education, which relates to another of the Smithian roles of government and perhaps to the general welfare clause of the Constitution's Preamble.

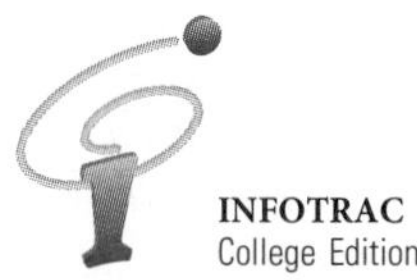

Keyword: *victimless crimes*

Access InfoTrac at http://infotrac.cengage.com

PUBLIC GOODS

Understanding the concept of a *public good* is important for understanding the role of government in crime and drug control. Public goods theory provides a rationale for government's role in the market economy. A **public good** has two characteristics. One characteristic is that a public good is a **nonexcludable good**; preventing or excluding people from consuming it is difficult. For instance, if a strong police effort makes streets safe, it is difficult to restrict the feeling of security to people who voluntarily pay for the police effort. In contrast, it is easy to restrict the use of a private good, such as a candy bar, to people who pay for it. So a public good is nonexcludable and a private good is excludable.

Public good– A good that is nonexcludable and nonrival.

Nonexcludable good– A good that is impossible or extremely difficult to exclude nonpayers from consuming.

The other characteristic is that a public good is a **nonrival good**; an individual can consume a public good without reducing the amount available to other people. For example, one person can enjoy the sunshine without diminishing his neighbors' enjoyment. Or, to continue the safe-streets example, one person enjoying the safety does not reduce the feeling of security available to anyone else. Again, in contrast, if one person eats a candy bar, a private good, other people cannot consume it. So a public good is nonrival and a private good is rival. Thus, a public good is nonexcludable and nonrival; a private good is excludable and rival.

Nonrival good– A good that one person can consume without reducing the amount available for others to consume, such as a feeling of security in a safe city.

[3]These crime rates are computed from victimization surveys, which ask people if they have been victims of crimes; victimization rates probably provide the best evidence about crime rates over time because they are more accurate than crimes reported to the police.

The government may be able to provide a public good more effectively than the private sector for at least three reasons. First, it is costly to exclude people from the benefits of a public good. In the secure-streets example, a private supplier would have to identify when people are enjoying the secure streets and bill them for the security, in much the same way that an electric utility sends a monthly utility bill. Monitoring people's street use would be more costly, however, than monitoring their electricity use. Government provision of secure streets, on the other hand, requires that citizens pay taxes, but this payment does not vary with use, which frees the government from the cost of measuring use.

Second, in addition to the opportunity costs of the resources used for measuring street use, monitoring the use of some public goods may incur privacy costs. People do not want a private firm or government recording where they go or whom they visit.

Third, private provision of a public good, like security or national defense, may be economically inefficient. The opportunity cost of providing security for one more person is zero; the good is nonrival. Nevertheless, a private firm would charge an additional user a price greater than its zero marginal cost. The market price would be greater than its zero supply price. Therefore, too little of the good would be used. If the government finances the public good through taxation, the price to an additional person of consuming security is zero. No one is excluded from the public good by its price. Because the marginal cost of providing the good is also zero, the zero price leads to efficient use of the public good. People consume it up to the point where marginal benefit equals the zero marginal cost.

Government Enforcement of Property Rights

As discussed in Chapter 2, a decentralized market economy requires a government to establish and enforce property rights. An individual with property rights in a good has an exclusive right to use or sell the good within certain constraints. Property rights allow the voluntary transactions of a market system to work well. Dave is more likely to buy a car from Joanna if he feels fairly sure that it will not be stolen or that the government will not take it. Imagine an economy in which the government does not establish and protect property rights. Individuals would have to provide for their own protection. With no government protection of property, more theft would occur. To counter the theft, individuals would use more resources to protect their property.

In this imaginary economy, if Hugh is skilled in protecting his property, he makes it easier for other people to protect theirs. To see how this might happen, suppose people in a neighborhood earn a reputation for protecting their property well. Some people in the neighborhood could take advantage of that reputation. For instance, imagine that Hugh and a few other people organize a Neighborhood Watch. Missy, who lives in the neighborhood, could receive some benefit from the watch without participating in the program. If she acts in this way, she is a *free rider*. A **free rider** uses goods or services provided by others without paying for them. Hugh and his colleagues may not be able to collect any fees or volunteer work from some of the people whose property rights they are defending just by establishing the watch. Some people might be free riders because they expect the Neighborhood Watch to exist and provide protection whether they contribute or not, so why contribute?

Free rider–
An individual who uses goods or services provided by others without paying for them.

Hugh and his colleagues will try to prevent free riding by concentrating on protecting their own property. For instance, they will put security locks on their doors but not on the free riders' doors. They may have security patrols only on their own property. But security patrols in the neighborhood will, by their presence, provide some protection to the free riders' property as well, even though the level of protection will be less than the efficient level. The marginal social benefit of the protection equals the marginal private benefit to Hugh (and his colleagues) plus the marginal benefit to the free riders. Hugh and his colleagues, who pay all of the cost, will expand protection to the point where their marginal private benefit equals marginal cost. But marginal social benefit is greater than their marginal private benefit. Therefore, Hugh will not expand protection to the efficient level (marginal social benefit equal to marginal cost). If the free riders were willing to share the cost, Hugh would be willing to supply more protection.

It is cheaper to have a single agency provide security for a town instead of having several types of neighborhood watch groups. Rather than having security patrols concentrate on particular pieces of property, it is probably cheaper and more effective to provide security for the entire town. In other words, monopoly provision of property rights protection may be cheaper than the alternative of individuals providing their own protection, because it is a natural monopoly. Notice, however, that gated communities provide one way that people can get more security privately than is provided by the government and avoid the free-rider problem. A developer perceives that people will pay more for housing if they believe the area is more secure. He then develops the gated community as a way of providing private security.

Another point is that property rights protection requires use of force: *coercion*. Rather than allowing individuals to decide what type of force to use to protect their rights, many people believe that coercive powers should be reserved for representative government.

Finally, because providing property rights protection to one more person does not increase cost, charging for it is inefficient. One more person can consume property rights without reducing their availability to everyone else. In other words, the establishment and enforcement of property rights is a public good because exclusion is difficult and it is nonrival.

CRIME AND CRIME CONTROL

Gary Becker, the Nobel Prize–winning economist and sociologist, was one of the first economists, and perhaps the most influential, to analyze crime and its control using the basic tools of economic analysis.[4] Becker and many other economists assume that criminals, just like law-abiding citizens, are systematic evaluators of the feasible choices before them. These economists also assume that people are willing to substitute among goods. The implication is that, given a large enough compensation, many people will take actions that they ordinarily would not choose to take. For instance, a person who says, "You cannot pay me enough to live in New York City," or "You cannot pay me enough to live in Stillwater, Oklahoma," almost always means that the market wage in the city is not high enough to induce her to live in that city. Offered a large enough compensation, these people would be willing to live in the other city. In other words, many people are willing substitute more material goods (greater monetary compensation) for the amenities that they give up by moving to a less desired city.

These systematic evaluators compare the cost and benefit of undertaking a particular action, and they act if the marginal benefit is greater than the marginal cost. Under given conditions, some people find that the marginal benefit of a criminal act is greater than the marginal cost; they commit the crime. Other people choose not to be criminals because they anticipate that the marginal benefit will be less than the marginal cost, including psychological costs and the expected punishment costs. Because people are willing to substitute, an increase in the expected benefit of a crime or a reduction in the expected

---

[4]Gary S. Becker, "Crime and Punishment: An Economic Approach," *Journal of Political Economy* 76, no. 2 (1968): 169–217.

Keyword: *economic aspects of crime*

Access InfoTrac at http://infotrac.cengage.com

cost will lead more people to crime. Conversely, if the benefit decreases or the cost increases, some criminals will decide to drop their criminal careers.

Economists also think of individuals as creative and resourceful.[5] For instance, when tax rates go up, many people become creative in finding legal ways to avoid the tax. In general, when laws are changed to restrict behavior, people respond by figuring out ways around the restriction. Jensen and Meckling discuss people's response to the 55-miles-per-hour highway speed limit imposed by the federal government in the 1970s.[6] CB radios and radar detectors became more popular. To avoid the penalties associated with speeding, people searched for better devices to reduce the costs of their traffic violations. The demand for such devices fell when the speed limit was raised to 65 miles per hour and more in some states. In this section we explore the implications of the economic approach to crime and crime policy.

An Economic Approach to Crime and Crime Control

Keyword: *causes of crime*

Access InfoTrac at http://infotrac.cengage.com

An individual commits a crime, according to the economic approach, when the expected marginal benefit of the crime is greater than the expected marginal cost. The marginal benefit is the material or psychological reward coming from the crime. The marginal cost is the material or psychological cost of the decision. This general analysis is applicable to any situation. It is more suitable, however, for some issues than for others. The economic approach is particularly useful in analyzing property crime and the illegal behavior of consenting adults in undertaking illegal voluntary actions—prostitution, use of illegal drugs, and illegal gambling. Crimes of violence associated with these crimes also suit this analytical approach. The economic approach may be less useful, however, in analyzing murder, rape, and other acts of violence from which the perpetrator receives only psychological benefit.

An economic approach to crime control implies that government can control crime, particularly property crime, because it can create conditions in which crime does not pay. According to this approach, crime decreases if potential criminals believe their chances of getting away with, say, a bank robbery have decreased. They will hesitate if they think that, upon getting caught, they are more likely to receive a speedy trial and, upon conviction, a harsh punishment. Besides making crime less profitable, government can reduce crime by jailing criminals. First, imprisonment raises the cost of crime, making the choice less attractive. Second, it reduces the supply of crimes because some of the people most likely to commit crimes have been locked up. This works because:

1. Offenders tend to repeat their criminal activity.
2. An imprisoned criminal is not immediately replaced by a new offender.
3. Imprisonment does not increase after-prison criminal activity.

Because property rights protection is a public good, it can be more efficiently provided by government. Crime control is one part of property rights protection. Government, through the political process, is responsible for determining how much crime control to provide. Everyone benefits from crime control, but, because it is a public good, many people would not voluntarily pay full value for it. As free riders, people reason that they will get the crime control because other people will pay for it. But if everyone reasons this way, we will have too little crime control. To overcome this free-rider problem, people agree to let the government tax them and to use the resources gained from taxation to provide the crime control.

---

[5]Michael C. Jensen and William H. Meckling, Chapter 1, The Nature of Man, in Michael C. Jensen (ed.), *Foundations of Organizational Strategy* (Cambridge, MA: Harvard University Press, 1998).

[6]Ibid.

ADDITIONAL INSIGHT

Hurricanes and Crime

The disaster that hit New Orleans in the wake of Hurricane Katrina provides another example of the ability of the economic approach to crime to explain events. At least three types of crimes occurred. People stole items from vacant stores that were important in their day-to-day lives. Other people stole entertainment systems, major appliances, and many other valuables. Recall that the economic approach to crime suggests that people consider the costs and benefits of their choice and act accordingly. People who would not ordinarily steal because they are fundamentally honest—the psychological cost of theft is high—may have taken food and water because their value was high and also because the emergency situation reduced their scruples against theft.

Other people, perhaps less scrupulous, observed that the expected cost of arrest, conviction, and punishment was less because the police were otherwise occupied. With the expected cost very low, these people chose to take advantage of the situation. Although most of these people may have committed criminal acts in the past, some of them no doubt committed crime for the first time.

Finally, some other crimes—murder, rape, assault, and interfering with the rescue and recovery efforts—also occurred. Although the media clearly exaggerated the extent of these crimes, some people did commit them. The economic approach formally can explain this behavior, but it is pathological behavior that requires psychological and sociological explanations as well.

Some people argue that the economic approach to behavior cannot explain the instances of social cooperation that are evident after disasters, including the flooding of New Orleans. According to E. L. Quarantelli, a sociologist, looting and violence are rare after disasters. New Orleans provided some examples, as did the blackout in New York City in 1977, but even with some disorder, Quarantelli, who has studied many disasters, finds that "volunteerism will explode, violence will be rare ... and the vast majority of the rescues will be accomplished by the real first responders—the victims themselves."[a] Most economists would not find voluntary social cooperation after a disaster surprising. They could put it in a benefit-cost framework, but again they may also leave it for other disciplines to explain.

[a]See Jesse Walker, "Nightmare in New Orleans," *Reason, December* 2005.

If government can, in fact, control crime, the allowed amount of crime is a political decision. Why do we decide to allow so much? Figure 8.2 shows the marginal social benefit and cost of reducing the crime rate through crime control activities. As the amount of resources used for crime control increases, the number of crimes and, therefore, the probability of being a victim decrease. The marginal social benefit of reducing crime and the probability of being a victim decrease as the crime rate decreases. The feeling of security increases as the probability of being a crime victim decreases, say, from 63 percent to 62 percent for a particular time period. The feeling of security also increases as that probability decreases from 3 percent to 2 percent. Most people would not value the latter decrease as much as they value the former; in other words, people would be willing to pay more for the decrease from 63 to 62 percent than for the decrease from 3 to 2 percent. If the chances of being a victim are already low, a given reduction in the probability of being victimized would be worth less.

The marginal social cost of reducing the probability of being a victim increases as the amount of crime control increases, as shown in Figure 8.2. The marginal social cost increases for three reasons. First, to reduce crime, more resources must be devoted to crime control. As more resources are devoted to crime control, their opportunity cost increases.

Figure 8.2 The Efficient Level of Control: Crime or Terror
Equating the marginal social benefit and cost of crime control gives the efficient level. Because the marginal social benefit is positive at that level, the efficient level of crime control does not result in elimination of crime—additional benefit results from additional crime reduction. The additional benefit is less than the additional cost. Interpreting the analysis in terms of terrorism control, the terrorist crimes of September 11, 2001, could have had the effect of shifting MSB to MSB′. The efficient level of terrorist control then increased, causing marginal social cost to increase along MSC.

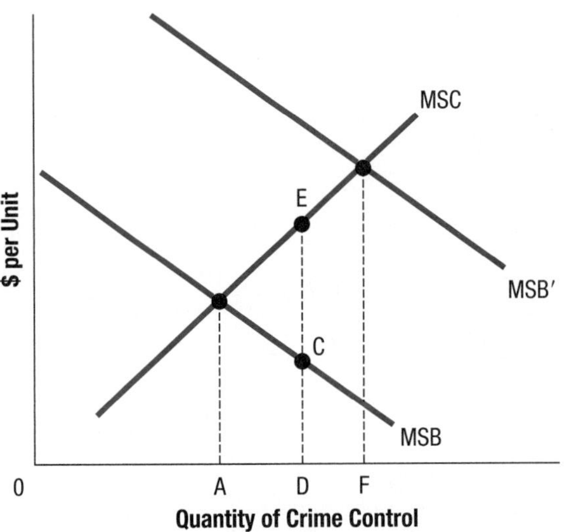

These resources must be pulled from other government programs, such as defense, AIDS research, and aid for the homeless—or from taxpayers' pockets.

Second, it takes more resources to reduce crime by a given amount if the crime rate is already low than to reduce it by the same amount if the crime rate is high. The first stage of crime reduction is easy—catch the incompetent criminals. As the crime rate decreases, however, only the most talented or the luckiest criminals will be in business. It will be more difficult to deter the more talented criminals.

Third, as the amount of crime falls, reducing it further eventually requires an assault on our freedom. By and large, U.S. citizens and their representatives prefer one type of mistake in our judicial system to another. Specifically, we believe punishing the innocent is a worse mistake than not punishing the guilty. Our unwillingness to accept confessions that police obtain by trickery or threat might be interpreted as a way of protecting the innocent. If we had less respect for civil rights, the conviction rate for crimes could increase. The crime rate might drop, but many people believe that the cost would be too high.

The intersection of the marginal social benefit (MSB) and marginal social cost curves in Figure 8.2 gives the efficient level of crime control and, implicitly, the efficient level of crime. An increase in crime control from A to D reduces everyone's chance of being a crime victim. At D the marginal social benefit is DC, which is the value that people would place on the increased security and reduced crime rates. The extra cost of an increase in crime control (of a lower crime rate) is DE. This marginal social cost includes the opportunity cost of using more resources for crime control, including the value of lost freedom, if any. Given the circumstances, the crime rate associated with D is too low. It costs more than is gained to increase crime control from A to D.

Just as it suggests that it is possible to spend too much on crime control, the analysis suggests that it is possible to spend too much on antiterrorist actions. Suppose we change the horizontal axis in Figure 8.2 to Quantity of Terrorism Control. Before the terrorist of attacks of September 11, 2001, the point A might measure the efficient quantity of terrorist control in the United States. The attacks and threats of further attacks changed the perceptions of the threat of terrorist activity and can be interpreted as increasing the marginal social benefit of control from MSB to MSB′. Now at A, the marginal social benefit is much greater than the marginal social cost. Small increases in expenditures on control now have a greater benefit than cost. More spending on control is desirable until the control level reaches F.

Several observations are relevant. First, the increase in the marginal social benefit of control occurs because people believe the world is a more dangerous place than they previously believed. Second, at the quantity F, marginal social benefit is greater than it was before the attacks. The fact that MSB is greater implies that people feel less secure than they did before the attacks, even with the increased expenditures on terrorism control. Given the available techniques of control, it is too costly or perhaps impossible to achieve the previous level of security. Third, although the marginal social cost curve hasn't changed, marginal social cost has increased along the existing marginal social cost curve. The increased resources going to antiterrorism activities have an opportunity cost that increases as the resources devoted to control increase. The extra government use of resources comes at the expense of other government programs or of private spending. In addition, a large nonmonetary cost is imposed on people. Every airline passenger pays a higher time cost for any given flight. Moreover, people are subjected to the indignities of searches of their belongings and their persons. In addition, some freedom has been sacrificed with the increased probability of being held on suspicion of terrorism, perhaps without the customary legal rights. Controversies about the Patriot Act and electronic eavesdropping on Americans reflect this movement along the MSC. Finally, as more resources are devoted to terrorism control, more effective ways to control terrorism might be developed. We can also expect technological change that will reduce the cost. This combination of learning by doing and development of new technology may shift the marginal social cost curve to the right, allowing us to feel more secure at a lower cost.

This analysis suggests that we have so much crime and so many terrorist acts because they are costly to control. Control may be costly because many people are willing to be criminals or terrorists. Or it may be costly because of the problems, such as poor economic prospects in some inner cities, rural areas, and other parts of the world.

A Comparison of Crime Trends in the United States and England

The economic approach provides a framework useful in understanding the causes of falling U.S. crime rates. A crime occurs when a person decides that the benefit from committing the crime outweighs the cost. Let's assume a crime of tax evasion that pays each taxpayer who commits it $50,000. Let's also assume 1,000 potential tax evaders. Suppose the only cost of the crime is the psychological cost to the criminal. Different people place a different value on being honest. Assume that 300 people choose to commit the crime. The other 700 people value their honesty at more than $50,000. One way to reduce the number of tax evaders is to convince some of the 300 people to place a greater value on honesty. This example implies that one way to reduce crime is to have "better" people; unfortunately, we don't know how to persuade people to place a greater value on honesty. An implication of this example, however, may be that somehow improving the economic and social environment for children is a long-term strategy for crime control.

A direct way to increase the cost of the crime is to use government resources to arrest the criminal, to convict the criminal, and to impose punishment, including incarceration. The objective would be to increase the expected cost of the crime. If a person were fined

$100,000 for the tax evasion and the chance of getting caught was 50 percent, most people might be deterred from the tax evasion. Increased enforcement and better opportunities in the legal sector of the economy also increase the costs of crime. Because the cost to the criminal (for instance, imprisonment or loss of a professional license) increases with the opportunities available, a well-educated person with good job skills faces a higher cost of crime than does a person with poor job skills. Again, the analysis implies that the economic and social environment helps determine if people become criminals. In particular, people in an economy with good employment opportunities face higher costs of crime.

A comparison of crime trends in the United States and England (including Wales) provides insights about criminal behavior. It may be surprising to learn that (with the exception of murder and rape) crime rates are lower in the United States than in England. More remarkably, English crime rates remained stable or increased from 1981 to the mid-1990s, when they begin to fall. Over the same period, almost all types of U.S. crime rates fell. The two panels of Figure 8.3 illustrate these trends for burglary and vehicle theft.

The following summarizes the data in these charts and for other types of crimes.[7]

1. The English burglary rate was just 40 percent of the U.S. rate in 1981 but it was about two-thirds greater than the U.S. rate in 1999.
2. The English rate of vehicle theft was 50 percent greater than the U.S. rate in 1981; by 1999 it was almost twice the U.S. rate.
3. The English assault rate was just above that of the United States in 1981 but more than doubled the U.S. rate in 1999.
4. The U.S. rape rate was 18 times that of England in 1981 and was two times the English rate in 1996.
5. The U.S. murder rate was nine times that of the England in 1981 and was four times the English rate in 1999.

Examining similar data, James Q. Wilson implies that reduced punishment in England and increased punishment in the United States is at least part of the explanation for the changing situation.[8] Certainly, the expected cost of crime is greater in the United States than in England. Days at risk combines the probability of being convicted of crime with the time served if convicted to develop an expected cost of crime based on the economic approach. As seen in Figure 8.4, the risk of days served for burglary and vehicle theft is greater in the United States than in England; moreover, the risk increased in the United States until the mid-1990s and fell in England over this same period.[9] Figure 8.4, when compared with Figure 8.3, suggests that increases in the costs of crime are associated with reductions in crime rates and that decreases in cost are associated with increases in crime. (A more thorough study would be required to demonstrate the conclusion. The example simply illustrates an approach that economists use to support their theoretical arguments.)

Not everyone shares the view that the increased cost of crime in the United States is an important cause of the falling crime rate. Indeed, some criminologists believe that fourfold increase in the number of American prisoners has had little effect on the crime

---

[7]See David P. Farrington, Patrick A. Langan, and Michael Tondry (eds.), *Cross-National Studies in Crime and Justice*, Bureau of Justice Statistics, U.S. Department of Justice (September 2004), NCJ 200988, http://www.ojp.usdoj.gov/bjs/ These results, except for murder and rape, are drawn from victimization surveys, which are more reliable than data drawn from police reports.

[8]James Q. Wilson, "Criminal Justice in England and America," *Public Interest* 126 (Winter 1997): 3–14.

[9]Ibid.

Figure 8.3a Trends in the Burglary Rate

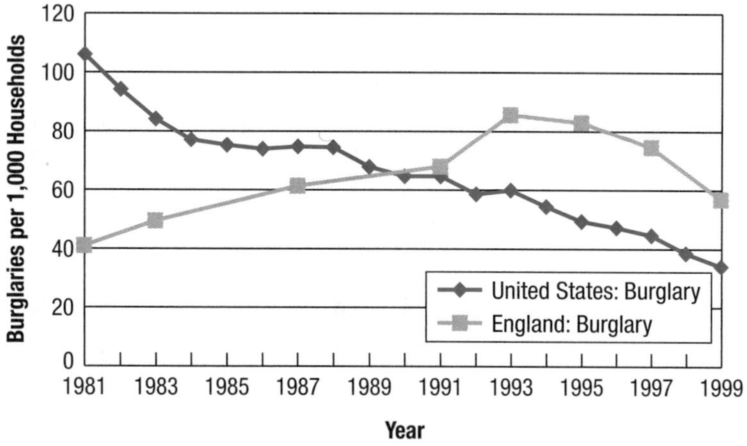

Burglaries per 1,000 Households

120
100
80
60
40
20
0

1981 1983 1985 1987 1989 1991 1993 1995 1997 1999

Year

United States: Burglary
England: Burglary

Figure 8.3b Trends in the Vehicle Theft Rate
Burglary and vehicle theft are now higher in England than in the United States. Burglary rates have dropped steadily in the United States, but they rose in England until the mid-1990s when they began to fall.

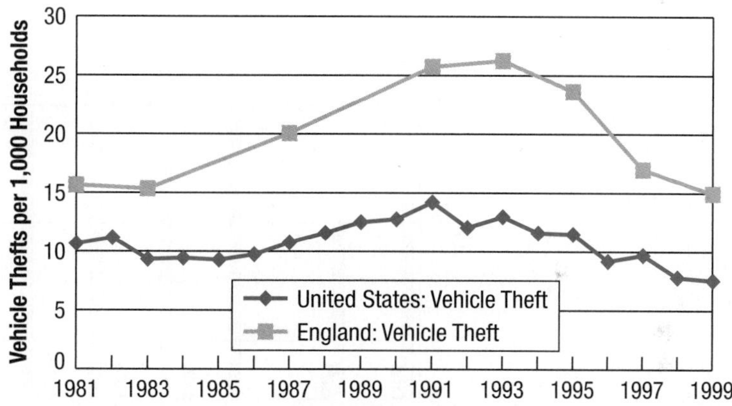

Source: David P. Farrington, Patrick A. Langan, and Michael Tondry (eds.), *Cross-National Studies in Crime and Justice*, Bureau of Justice Statistics, U.S. Department of Justice (September 2004), NCJ 200988.

rate. Rather than or in addition to the increased chance of punishment, some criminologists attribute falling crime rates to the following factors:

- Reduction in drug use or stabilization of drug makers.
- Demographic and population changes that reduce the number of people in crime-prone categories—(e.g., young males).
- A stronger economy and improvements in social and economic conditions.
- Greater police visibility through wider implementation of problem-oriented or community-oriented policy.
- Community- and youth-oriented programs that promote safer schools and neighborhoods.
- Gang abatement programs.
- A collective conscience shift toward greater civility and mediation.[10]

[10]Dale Steffensmeier and Miles D. Harer, "Making Sense of Recent U.S. Crime Trends, 1980 to 1996/98," *Journal of Research in Crime and Delinquency* 36, no. 3 (1999): 235–274.

Figure 8.4a Days at Risk for Burglary

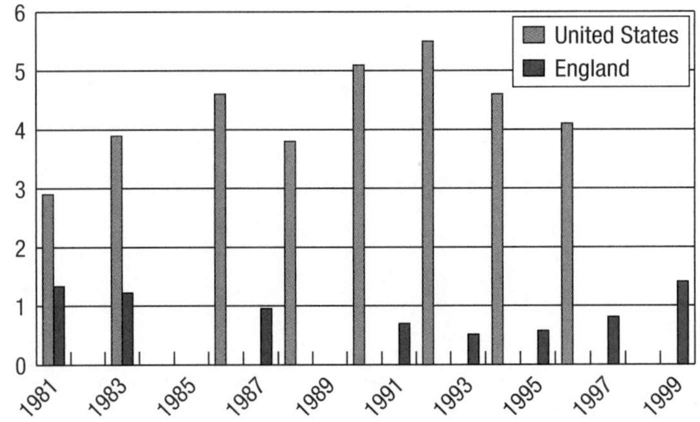

Figure 8.4b Days at Risk for Vehicle Theft

Days at risk of serving prison time for burglary and vehicle theft are greater in the United States than in England. The increasing risk of punishment for burglary in the United States mirrors the falling victimization rates until the mid-1990s. Similarly, the decreasing and then increasing risk of punishment for burglary in England mirrors the rise and fall of the burglary rates.

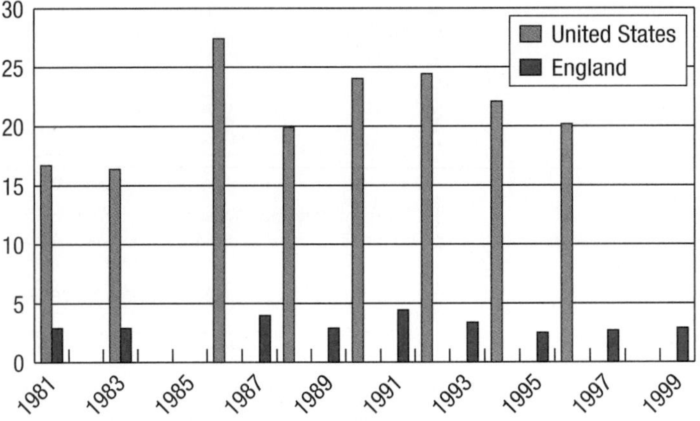

Source: David P. Farrington, Patrick A. Langan, and Michael Tondry (eds.), *Cross-National Studies in Crime and Justice*, U.S. Department of Justice (September 2004), NCJ 200988.

Steven Levitt, the coauthor of *Freakonomics*, rejects the suggestions that better police strategies, a stronger economy, and changing demographics have caused the dramatic drop in crime. He agrees that reduction in drug use, particularly changes in the crack cocaine market, is one important source of decline. Another important source is simply more police. He argues that the increased rate of imprisonment, both because it keeps criminals off the streets and because of its deterrent effect, is a third important causal factor. His fourth important cause of the reduced crime rate results from the Supreme Court's abortion decision, *Roe vs. Wade*. He argues that the legalization of and increased rates of abortion explain part of the drop in crime. The abortion hypothesis is simple. It is that unwanted children are more likely to become criminals and that many of the abortions that occur reduce the number of unwanted children.[11]

[11]See Steven D. Levitt, "Understanding Why Crime Fell in the 1990s: Four Factors that Explain the Decline and Six that Do Not," *Journal of Economic Perspectives* 18, no. 1 (2004): 163–190.

Regardless, part of the pattern of U.S. crime rates and punishment relates to illegal drugs. The peak of the cocaine epidemic occurred at about the same time as the peak in the murder rate. In the next section, we examine the interrelationships between drugs and crime.

DRUG LEGALIZATION: COMPETING VIEWS

In any year, more than 10 percent of all arrests reported to the FBI are for prostitution, drug abuse, gambling, and drunkenness (not including driving while intoxicated). These arrests are for voluntary transactions between buyer and seller that have little direct effect on anyone outside the transaction. Why do we make voluntary transactions crimes? In particular, why do we expend so much of our crime-fighting resources in combating the drug trade?

Liberty: An Argument for Legalization

Keyword: *decriminalization and drugs*

Access InfoTrac at http://infotrac.cengage.com

Some people argue that illegal drugs should be legalized. They argue that each responsible individual should have the freedom to engage in any voluntary transaction, as long as it does not impose substantial, involuntary harm on a third party. To John Stuart Mill, the nineteenth-century economist who made this argument, individual liberty was an extremely important value. Similarly, Milton Friedman, an advocate of drug legalization, writes, "I believe that adults—by this I mean people whom we regard as responsible, and as a practical matter this means people who are neither insane nor below a certain age—should be responsible for their own lives ... People's freedom to make their own decisions is my fundamental objective."[12]

The argument that people should be allowed to make their own decisions is subject to two qualifications. One qualification is that children should not have this freedom. If, say, cocaine was legal, the argument requires that children be forbidden to use it until they reach a certain age. Indeed, it may require strong policies to ensure that children do not use it.

The second qualification is that people should not be allowed to sell themselves into slavery. If you sell yourself into slavery, you relinquish your freedom to make your own decisions. The question then arises of whether dependence on drugs—alcohol, cocaine, or what have you—is equivalent to drug users selling themselves into slavery. The evidence shows that drug dependence is a powerful force that ruins many lives. Nevertheless, evidence also suggests that the ideas that most drug users become addicts, or even that all addicts remain addicts until they die, are wrong. An unqualified acceptance of the liberty argument implies the decriminalization of the use of such drugs as marijuana, cocaine, heroin, and methamphetamines.

Paternalism: An Argument against Legalization

John Kaplan rejects Mill's libertarian principle that would allow people to engage in self-destructive activity in the absence of involuntary harm to others. He argues that people, through government, can "morally attempt to keep others from likely harm even though they themselves are foolish enough to take the risk. After all, Mill's view that all adults must be assumed to know their own best interest is certainly contrary to fact, as most of

---

[12]Milton Friedman, "Stop Taxing Non-Addicts," *Reason*, October 1988, 24.

us see it."[13] Opinion polls support Kaplan's argument; only a small percentage of the U.S. population—usually less than 5 percent—strongly favors legalizing all drugs.

Public opinion is not completely consistent. The large majority in favor of prohibiting such dangerous drugs as cocaine and heroin opposes prohibiting alcohol and nicotine. We know that alcohol and nicotine are responsible for more deaths and illnesses, and that alcohol is related to more crime than all the prohibited drugs combined. Of course, if we legalized the prohibited drugs, they might generate more problems than alcohol and nicotine.

Morality: An Argument against Legalization

William J. Bennett, Irving Kristol, and James Q. Wilson, along with many other social scientists, argue that government has a responsibility for prohibiting the use of mind-altering drugs, regardless of (1) whether such drug users are fully responsible and (2) the absence of involuntary harm to others. Wilson flatly states this neoconservative position: "Drug use is wrong because it is immoral, and it is immoral because it enslaves the mind and destroys the soul."[14] In this view, the possibility that marijuana or any other drug may be of limited danger to health is irrelevant. The immorality of drug use is in its purpose, which, in this interpretation, is to withdraw from society and civilization.

For people who take this position, the immorality implicit in the use of mind-altering drugs resolves the seeming contradiction in the failure to prohibit nicotine. Although the use of tobacco is arguably as dangerous, medically, as the use of various controlled substances, it does not debase life; it only shortens it. Alcohol, of course, is another matter. According to Wilson, drug users lack such virtues as self-control, sobriety, and the ability to delay gratification. The immorality lies in the effects of drug use on the moral character and on the subsequent harmful effects on society.

The Final Analysis

The inconsistent treatment of alcohol (a mind-altering drug), nicotine, and cocaine suggests that our drug laws do not follow from Mill's or Friedman's libertarian argument, Kaplan's paternalism argument, or Wilson's neoconservative morality argument. Kaplan tempers his position by stating that the general argument that government should not interfere in basically private behavior is sound practical advice. He simply concludes that the cost of legalization is greater to society than the cost of prohibition. Similarly, Friedman makes his case more persuasive by arguing that drug prohibition causes more harm to innocent third parties than the harm that would be caused to third parties by legalization. In short, both Kaplan and Friedman take a pragmatic approach to drug policy, attempting to weigh the costs and benefits of various actions. Wilson's position, however, leaves little room for a pragmatic analysis.

A POSITIVE ANALYSIS OF DRUG POLICY

To analyze the effects of prohibiting a drug such as cocaine requires an alternative. For simplicity, suppose that cocaine is available on demand from government-owned stores. The price paid includes a substantial government tax. Thus, the alternative is similar to the legal situation for liquor in some states. Assume that the supply curve is flat, S_0 in

---

[13]John Kaplan, *The Hardest Drug: Heroin and Public Policy* (Chicago: University of Chicago Press, 1983), 104. This book includes an excellent discussion of these issues.

[14]As quoted by "Reclaiming the War on Drugs," *Empower America*, brochure, October 1996. See also James Q. Wilson, "Against the Legalization of Drugs," *Commentary*, February 1990, 23–28.

Figure 8.5 **The Effect of Drug Prohibition on Drug Use**
The supply and demand curves, S_0 and D_0, show the market for cocaine when cocaine is legal. Prohibition causes supply to decrease to S_1 and demand to decrease to D_1. Price goes from $20 to $100 per gram, and quantity exchanged falls from Q_0 to Q_1.

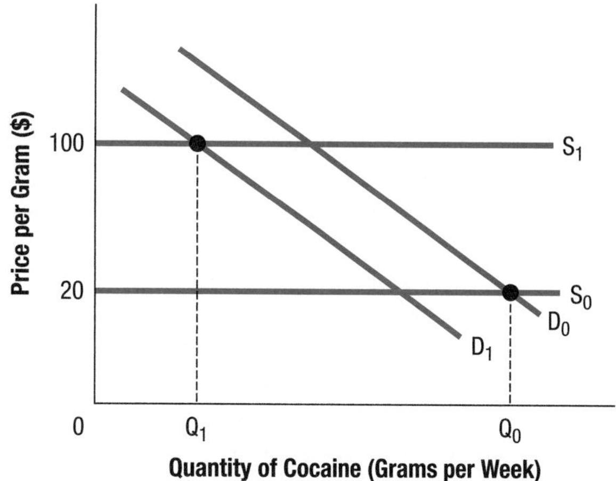

Figure 8.5. This supply curve is the market marginal cost of cocaine. Including a heavy rate of taxation, this marginal cost might be on the order of $20 per gram. Initial users might get 50 doses per gram. Therefore, the cost per dose could be as low as 40 cents.[15] In Figure 8.5 the demand curve, as usual, holds several factors constant: the price of other drugs, income, the method of distribution, laws, and consumer preferences.

Now suppose new laws make cocaine and other drugs—except alcohol and nicotine—illegal. Assume that possession and use of the illegal substances would be a felony. Furthermore, selling these substances would be an even more serious felony.

In the new situation, assume the method of distribution matches the one observed in the United States today. A cartel buys cocaine in other countries and exports it to the United States. Presumably, this cartel chooses an output that maximizes profit. After the cocaine arrives in the United States, the cartel distributes it to wholesalers throughout the country. These wholesalers distribute it to city wholesalers, who, in turn, may distribute it to another level of wholesalers, and so on until it reaches local retailers. The several layers of distribution protect the importers and large wholesalers from detection by the authorities. The large difference between the price they pay for their raw material—coca leaves—and the price they receive for their product—cocaine—is partly due to monopoly restriction of output. The price differential also partly reflects extra compensation that the sellers require to cover the cost, including the risk of punishment, of evading the drug laws.

Each level of distribution includes compensation for the risk of supplying an illegal product. Additional risks exist for distributors closer to the street. Retail distributors trying to claim a particular neighborhood market sometimes kill other distributors and bystanders.

As the transactions progress beyond the well-organized deals between large wholesalers, the system of property rights established by organized crime disintegrates. Organized crime imposes stiff penalties for stealing rather than buying a major shipment of drugs from a large wholesaler. The penalty—death—is more severe than the penalty imposed by law for, say, hijacking a truckload of whiskey. But the retailer and the

[15]See John Kaplan, "Taking Drugs Seriously," *Public Interest* 92 (Summer 1988): 41.

wholesalers close to the retailer cannot call on a large organization to enforce their property rights. Deals at this level are made through openings in bulletproof doors. Thus, two factors cause the large increase in cost and therefore large decrease in supply of cocaine in the United States. One factor includes the cartel system of smuggling cocaine into the United States. The other factor is the risk of punishment for distributing an illegal product and the risk associated with a lack of government-enforced property rights. As a result, if cocaine becomes illegal, the supply curve in Figure 8.5 shifts to S_1.

Demand also changes—from D_0 to D_1—when the product becomes illegal. First, it may decrease because many people avoid illegal activities. This effect may be offset, however, by other people who enjoy violating the law. Second, it will decrease because the deterioration of property rights under the illegal system raises the nonprice costs of buying the good. It is now more difficult to find a supplier of the good. To buy the good, you must deal with people who may murder you if you fail to pay. If you develop a reliable connection at the street level, your connection may be arrested and out of circulation at any time. Then you must go through the dangerous process of finding another supplier. Third, it will decrease because of the legal penalties associated with possession and use. Fourth, it will decrease because of the risk of buying a product in an irregular market. The customer has little recourse if the product purchased is not what it is supposed to be. (This point is comically illustrated by a widely reported arrest of a cocaine buyer. The buyer reported to the police that he had been sold fake cocaine. The police investigated and found that the substance contained only a small amount of cocaine. Nevertheless, the cheated buyer was arrested for possession.) It may be contaminated with toxic substances used to dilute it. According to the Drug Facts available online at the White House's Office of National Drug Control Policy, "adulterants include caffeine (in Miami), chalk, laundry detergent, and rat poison (in Memphis), meat tenderizer (in Boston), baby laxatives (in Baltimore and Memphis), and talcum or baby powder (in Billings, El Paso, and Washington, D.C." Overdoses, some deadly, occur from taking substances of inferior quality or unknown purity.

The effects of changes in supply and demand are easy to see in Figure 8.5. The price increases from $20 to $100 per gram, and the quantity exchanged decreases from Q_0 to Q_1.

The experience of people who have tried to reduce their use of cocaine supplements the economic analysis. People who have requested treatment for cocaine dependence either through hot lines or clinics have reported spending, on average, from $450 to $800 per week on cocaine. Extremely heavy users have spent as much as $2,000 to $3,000 per week. According to one survey, almost 50 percent of the people who called a cocaine hot line said they had sold cocaine to finance their habits. About 25 percent of them stole at work, and about 35 percent stole from families and friends. About 15 percent had lost their jobs because of cocaine, and about 30 percent had lost their spouses. The illegal use of cocaine clearly involves substantial cost to other people in the economy. In particular, cocaine abusers are similar to heroin abusers in how they finance their habits. If they are unable to support their habits legally, they often resort to crime to support them.[16]

It seems clear that drug prohibition reduces drug use and drug abuse. Usage is less when the drug is illegal and the price is higher. A major exception might arise if drug

---

[16]See Mark S. Gold, Andrew M. Washton, and Charles A. Dackis, "Cocaine Abuse: Neurochemistry, Phenomenology, and Treatment," 142–43, and Sidney H. Schnoll et al., "Characteristic of Cocaine Abusers Presenting for Treatment," 173–76 in *Cocaine Use in America: Epidemiologic and Clinical Perspectives*, eds. Nicholas J. Kozel and Edger H. Adams, National Institute on Drug Abuse, Research Monograph 61, U.S. Department of Health and Human Services (Washington, DC: U.S. Government Printing Office, 1985).

pushing is an important route to drug dependence. The drug pusher supposedly entices people—sometimes young people in the schoolyard—into drug abuse. This is similar to the approach that tobacco companies used when they distributed free cigarettes on college campuses: Hook a customer, and you may have one for life, albeit a shortened life. This may have been a good strategy for a tobacco company that expected to remain in business for a long time, but it seems less apt for drug dealers. Dependence on heroin or cocaine requires more than a couple of doses. Giving drugs away means less for the dealer-user, with no certainty of a future payoff. Furthermore, the target customer might be an undercover drug agent. Even if the pusher creates a dependent customer, either the pusher or the new user might be arrested before the pusher profits on the initial investment. Drug pushing seems to be an investment with little payoff because buyer-seller relationships are unstable.

In fact, heroin and cocaine use spread like an epidemic. Availability is the key. If people have access to and use heroin, they share their knowledge and their drugs with their friends. Heroin use begins much like a sexually transmitted disease: A friend infects a friend, and, with some promiscuity, the disease soon spreads through a social network.[17]

Keyword: *narcotics, control*

Access InfoTrac at http://infotrac.cengage.com

Cocaine use apparently is similar. One study, for example, found that almost 90 percent of the initial use of cocaine took place at a party or other informal social event. About 70 percent of new users obtained it from friends or relatives. Only 5 percent of the new users obtained it from dealers.[18] Kaplan concludes that the drug pusher is a myth. If this is correct, making drugs illegal results not in dealers pushing drugs on nonusers, but in reducing their general availability and young people's exposure to them.

Does Increased Enforcement Work?

Laws against selling and possessing certain drugs reduce their use by reducing (shifting) supply and demand curves. The relatively larger reduction in supply leads to a price increase. The law of demand, then, implies that the quantity of drugs purchased decreases further along the new demand curve. Some economists argue, however, that increased enforcement will not work. They say that the quantity demanded of illegal drugs responds little to price; therefore, an increase in price caused by increased enforcement leads to only a small decrease in quantity. Total expenditure for drugs could increase. Drug dealers would be better off—except, of course, for the ones caught.

The Effects of Policies to Reduce Supply If the drug is sold in a market with significant monopoly power, increased enforcement will reduce cartel profits. Because of the monopoly by the cartel, any increase in cost caused by greater enforcement will reduce the cartel profits.

Different customers, however, may have different responses to a price increase. Over any significant period of time, say, six months, almost every user will decrease cocaine consumption. Figure 8.6 shows the demand curve, D_c, for a casual user of cocaine. If price goes from P_0 to P_1, the quantity demanded falls from Q_0 to Q_C. The percentage reduction in quantity is greater than the percentage reduction in price; quantity demanded responds vigorously to the price change. As the figure shows, the casual user spends less; the shaded area labeled A measures the reduction in expenditure because quantity demanded is less. The increase in price leads to an offsetting increase in expenditure measured by the shaded area labeled B. Because the area of A is greater than the area of B, the net effect is for the casual user to spend less when price goes up. Given that the objective of the law is to reduce cocaine use, the increased enforcement works.

[17]See Kaplan, *The Hardest Drug.*

[18]Dale D. Chitwood, "Pattern and Consequences of Cocaine Use," in *Cocaine Use in America*, 114–115.

Figure 8.6 **Demand Curves for a Casual and a Dependent Cocaine User**
If the price of cocaine goes from P_0 to P_1, the casual cocaine user reduces quantity demanded from Q_0 to Q_C. The percentage reduction in quantity demanded is greater than the percentage increase in price. The casual user reduces expenditures on cocaine by the amount represented by shaded area A (due to lower quantity demanded), and increases expenditures by the shaded area B (due to higher price). By inspection, it is clear that the net effect is a reduction in expenditure. The dependent user, on the other hand, reduces quantity demanded from Q_0 only to Q_D and, by inspection, increases expenditure.

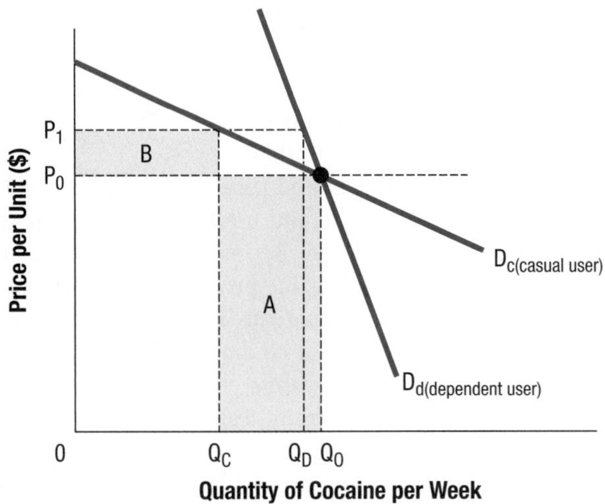

The user, of course, may substitute other substances for cocaine: alcohol, heroin, or methamphetamine, for instance.

Figure 8.6 also shows the demand curve, D_d, for a dependent user of cocaine. If price goes from P_0 to P_1, the quantity demanded falls from Q_0 to Q_D. But this user is dependent. The higher price reduces quantity demanded only slightly. Here, the percentage decrease in quantity is smaller than the percentage increase in price. The dependent user buys slightly less cocaine if price increases, but spends more. (Using the steeper demand curve, can you identify the areas that represent the expenditure reduction because of a reduced quantity and the expenditure increase because of an increased price?)

Many people would attack drug use and abuse in this country by going after the foreign sources. But cultivation of coca or opium poppies is possible and profitable over a large part of the world. Coca and opium poppies are traditional crops in many countries. It is unlikely that the U.S. government can convince or afford to bribe farmers in all parts of the world to grow other crops. The implicit position of these farmers is that if U.S. consumers do not want the product, they need not buy it. This, by the way, is the same position that the U.S. government and U.S. tobacco companies take with regard to U.S. exportation of cigarettes.

Similarly, production and distribution of illegal drugs are profitable and easy to conceal. Although increased enforcement can raise the cost of producing and distributing drugs, it is not clear that any acceptable policies can eliminate their supply. If an answer to drug use and abuse exists, it may lie on the demand side.

The Effects of Policies to Reduce Demand The second way that the laws work is by reducing demand. The effect of increased enforcement is to make the buyer-seller relationship less certain. Buyers and sellers both get arrested. New connections must be made. Particularly with increased enforcement, a new connection—buyer or seller—may be an undercover officer. Given the increased risk, some of the more reliable sellers leave the market. Also because of the increased risk, others may choose to deal in a more concentrated form of the drug. With greater enforcement, the product becomes more variable in purity and more subject to adulteration with toxic substances, leading to more overdoses, deaths, and serious illnesses. These effects will decrease the demand of users and potential users for the drug. But it is a harsh way to reduce demand. It brings to mind a quote from the Vietnam War: "We had to destroy the village to save it."

Many people argue that a better way to reduce demand is through education about the dangers of drug use and abuse. We certainly agree that young people need accurate information about all drugs—legal and illegal. If the opportunity cost of enforcement is a reduction in benefits from education about drugs, a careful study of alternatives would be important.

Social conditions may also be important determinants of drug use and abuse. Some drug use, no doubt, stems from the tendency of young people to take risks. Another part stems from the boredom and alienation experienced by suburban youth. The poverty, despair, and chaos of inner cities also contribute to drug use. A society without inner-city poverty, suburban alienation, and risk-taking youth probably would have a lower demand for drugs. But do we know how to change such social conditions enough to make a large and timely effect on drug use? The economic analysis of drug prohibition, on the other hand, suggests that it works. It reduces use, and increased enforcement of the laws reduces use even more.

Unintended but Inevitable Consequences of Drug Prohibition

Many people argue that drug laws and their increased enforcement have important undesirable and inevitable consequences. First, drug prohibition creates criminals where there were none before. Ten percent of the population above the age of 11—more than 20 million people per year—commits crimes simply by using illegal drugs. Almost one million people are arrested for drug use each year. The law, intended to protect potential users by keeping them away from drugs, makes criminals out of more than 10 percent of the adult population.

Furthermore, the drug user consumes products that are unsafe because they are exchanged in illegal markets and because our government at times sprays the raw material with toxic substances. Of course, the illegal drugs also are unsafe because of their chemical properties. It is an open question, however, whether the more common illegal drugs would be more dangerous, if legal, than alcohol or nicotine. A significant part of the health problems related to drug use is a result of the drug laws.

Another undesirable consequence is that some users commit numerous property crimes in order to buy drugs. In fact, as discussed earlier, increased enforcement—which causes a price increase—may lead to increased crime because dependent users spend more for illegal drugs at higher prices. Many drug users commit crimes. In 1997, 19 percent of all state prisoners and 16 percent of all federal prisoners reported that they committed their crimes to get money for illegal drugs. This was up from 16 and 10 percent in 1991. Similarly, in 2002 just over 16 percent of all jail inmates reported that they had committed their crimes so that they could buy drugs. We might assume that these people would not have committed their crimes if their drug of choice could be purchased legally.

It is sometimes argued that drug use causes crime in addition to the crimes committed to get money for drugs. Although they do not mention getting money to buy drugs, many other state and federal prisoners were using alcohol or other drugs at the time of their offenses. Does this mean that drug use causes crime? Would crime rates increase if more people were using drugs that are currently illegal? We cannot be sure, but it is not correct simply to assume that these people would not commit felonies if they were sober. Many drug-using criminals were criminals before they were drug users.

In addition, prohibition has created opportunities for many people to earn large incomes as drug dealers. For youth—especially those in the poor areas of large cities—the quickest way to a BMW is through dealing illegal drugs. This opportunity would decrease if drugs were legal. At the wholesale and import level, drug prohibition is a bonanza for organized crime. The profit from drug dealing is enormous—and almost all of it is available because of drug prohibition.

Large profits in illegal drugs also lead to corruption of public officials. Police officers realize that their salaries are low relative to the earnings of some drug dealers. Moreover, the police know that many citizens see nothing wrong with drug use. In such circumstances, bribes may entice some police officers, judges, prosecutors, prison guards, and other public officials into corruption. The drug war, as currently prosecuted, may lead to police corruption in other ways. The police have the right to confiscate any assets they think are linked to drug dealing. These assets can include your money, your house, and your car. Suppose you are stopped for a traffic violation. If they find the slightest evidence of an illegal substance in your car, the police can confiscate it. If your assets are confiscated, to retrieve them you must prove that they were not somehow obtained from or involved in illegal drug transactions. It is sometimes difficult to prove a negative. Moreover, in some instances, the police keep the assets or a portion of the assets for the use of the police department. This creates an obvious incentive for improper police behavior. Although the courts have not ruled such action unconstitutional, many people believe that it diminishes our constitutional liberties. Finally, if any of us condone illegal drug activity, respect for the law diminishes.

In short, drug prohibition causes a link between drug use and crime. If drugs were available legally, crimes committed to finance drug use would decline. Our experience with outlawing products and establishing price controls has taught us that such laws will be broken. Thus, the link between drug prohibition and crime is undesirable but arguably inevitable.

Unintended but Perhaps Avoidable Consequences of Drug Prohibition

Several unintended but perhaps avoidable consequences of the drug laws affect this country. One may be an increased use of cocaine at the expense of marijuana. Cocaine is an inherently more dangerous drug than marijuana. Periods of extensive cocaine use lead to depression, sexual problems, convulsions, unconsciousness, and death.[19] Babies with low birth weights, brain damage, and malformations are a tragic consequence of crack cocaine use by pregnant women.

Ironically, increased enforcement of drug laws may have increased the attraction of cocaine relative to marijuana. The price of cocaine per gram is much higher than the price of marijuana. It is much easier to smuggle a million dollars' worth of cocaine than to smuggle a million dollars' worth of marijuana. The greater weight and bulk of marijuana make it easier to detect in transit than cocaine. The penalties for smuggling or wholesaling cocaine were, at times, not much greater than for smuggling or wholesaling marijuana. Therefore, the laws and more aggressive enforcement of the laws have caused the supply of marijuana to decrease more than the supply of cocaine.

Changes in retail prices of cocaine, heroin, and marijuana support this analysis. According to Michael Grossman, from 1975 to 2003 the price of cocaine and heroin

[19]Ibid., 121–24.

fell about 90 percent. The real price of marijuana increased by about 10 percent. It first increased by about 70 percent as the War on Drugs heated up. Then from 1991 to 1996 it fell by about 40 percent and since then has risen about 10 percent.[20]

Another unintended and related consequence of increased enforcement of the drug laws may have been the development and widespread use of crack cocaine. The crack epidemic was related to the increased purity of street cocaine. One reason for this increased purity is that the penalty for dealing cocaine is similar whether the cocaine is 35 percent pure or 70 percent pure, making it relatively more profitable to deal in the purer or more concentrated product. Whatever the dangers of cocaine and whatever its addictive properties, it is clear that the more concentrated the product, the greater these dangers. Moreover, crack cocaine is smoked, which means that its effects are almost immediate compared to the slower effects of inhaled cocaine. The immediate reinforcement obtained from smoking crack is one of the reasons it may be more addictive.

Yet another unintended consequence of increased enforcement of drug laws is recruitment of teenagers and preteenagers into selling drugs. These children are lured by the fame and fortune of successful drug dealers. Drug dealers use these children for street activities with a high risk of arrest. This keeps the dealers out of jail, while the children arrested in these high-risk activities receive mild treatment from the courts. Thus, tragically, children become valuable gang members. It is ironic that current drug enforcement is leading young people into drug dealing, when everyone agrees that one goal of drug policy should be to keep young people away from drugs.

Another consequence of current drug policy is the siphoning of resources from fighting nondrug-related crime. Almost everyone would agree that a basic premise of crime control is to protect people from involuntary harm. Our drug control policies run counter to this premise. First, as we have seen, drug prohibition creates numerous crimes that result in involuntary harm to innocent bystanders. Second, using so many resources for drug control almost inevitably drains resources from crime control. Effective deterrence requires a high probability of being caught combined with a quick trial and sure punishment if convicted. Clogging the courts and prisons with drug offenders reduces the probability of being caught, swiftly convicted (if guilty), and surely punished for nondrug crimes. In short, the opportunity cost of drug prohibition may be high.

Evidence is accumulating that the War on Drugs is causing increases in other types of criminal activity. Recent studies have found that increased drug arrests are associated with higher property and violent crime. Contrary to conventional wisdom, increased arrests for producing, dealing, and possessing "hard drugs" (cocaine and heroin) are associated, other things being equal, with increases in both types of crime. Using enforcement to reduce drug use in hopes of reducing crime doesn't appear to work. Any reductions in crimes because enforcement leads to less drug-crazed behavior, fewer gang battles for markets, and fewer crimes committed to obtain drugs is offset by the increased crimes that occur because of the enforcement. Crime could and apparently does increase, perhaps because drug dealers now decide to switch to other types of criminal activity, because drug users have adverse psychological responses to withdrawal, and because crime control resources—police, legal system, and prison cells—are diverted to drug enforcement.[21]

---

[20]See *Drug and Crime Facts* at http://www.ojp.usdoj.gov/bjs/drugs.htm and *What America's Users Spend on Illegal Drugs: 1988–2000*, prepared for the Office of National Drug Control Policy (Cambridge, MA: Abt Associates, Inc., December 2001), available at http://www.whitehousedrugpolicy.gov; and Michael Grossman. "Individual Behaviors and Substance Use: The Role of Price," NBER Working Paper 10948 (Cambridge, MA: National Bureau of Economic Research, December 2004).

[21]See Edward M. Shepard and Paul R. Blackley, "Drug Enforcement and Crime: Recent Evidence from New York State," *Social Science Quarterly* 86, no. 2 (2005): 323–342.

INTERNATIONAL PERSPECTIVE

Dutch Drug Policy

Drug policy in the Netherlands differs from that of the United States in significant ways. The Dutch drug policy emphasizes risk reduction for individual drug users, their neighborhoods, and the general society. Possession, distribution, production, advertising, and international trade of all drugs, except for medicinal or scientific purposes, are illegal. So far, this sounds like U.S. drug policy, but the application is different. Dutch law explicitly distinguishes between soft drugs, such as marijuana, and hard drugs, such as cocaine and heroin.

Dutch law permits nonenforcement if to do so is in the public interest. Using this expediency principle, official Dutch policy is that the possession of small amounts of soft or hard drugs for personal use will not be prosecuted. Regulations permit the establishment of coffeehouses and other retail sites for the sale of marijuana for personal use. Coffeehouses are strictly regulated. Advertising, hard drugs, nuisances, sales to persons younger than 18 years of age, and large quantities sold per transaction are strictly prohibited.

The Dutch rationale for decriminalizing retail sale and use of marijuana is straightforward. The government argues that marijuana, unlike heroin and other hard drugs, does not create an unacceptable risk for users. Moreover, the government rejects the gateway hypothesis, by which the use of marijuana for physiological or psychological reasons leads to hard drug use. The Dutch position is that it is all but impossible to prevent people, including young people, from obtaining marijuana. Experience in the United States, which has had strong enforcement of its harsh drug laws, may confirm the Dutch position. Consequently, the Dutch argue, obtaining and using marijuana in a legal, controlled environment is better for young people than obtaining and using it in an illegal, uncontrolled environment where, Dutch authorities believe, young people are much more likely to be introduced to hard drugs. This argument implies that if marijuana is a gateway drug in the United States, the gateway is through illegal purchase rather than use.

The effect of Dutch policy on drug use and abuse is not easily determined. The best evidence suggests that as more coffeehouses opened, marijuana consumption among young people increased substantially, either because consumption became more accepted or because coffeehouse owners were able to increase the demand for their product. Nevertheless, young people's use of marijuana in the Netherlands is less than in the United States.

Furthermore, the incidence of hard-drug addiction in the Netherlands is no higher than in other European countries and in the United States. Dutch tolerance of marijuana does not obviously increase the demand for hard drugs. The Dutch also follow a harm-minimization policy in the treatment of hard-drug users. Needle exchanges are available, and methadone, a heroin substitute, is freely available to addicts on a maintenance basis. Although addicts are encouraged to reduce methadone use, it is not required. Moreover, methadone clients may use alcohol and other drugs in moderation. This program is designed to inhibit the addicts' health deterioration and perhaps to allow them to function in society. With this approach, only about 12 percent of the diagnosed Dutch AIDS patients were intravenous drug users, compared to about 24 percent in the United States and 38 percent in Europe in general. Again, little, if any, evidence exists that this nonpunitive approach has caused any substantial increase in addiction.

The Netherlands' more lenient drug policy is something for citizens and policy makers to consider. One pertinent question is whether soft and hard drug use is greater in the Netherlands than it would be under alternative policies. It apparently is no greater than in the United States. Other factors being equal, however, what might be the effect of changing U.S. drug policy? This is a question to be answered by positive analysis. Another pertinent question is, what should be the objective of U.S. drug policy? This normative issue turns on one's ideas about liberty, pragmatics, and morality.

Sources: *Drug Policy in the Netherlands: Continuity and Change*, Ministry of Health, Welfare, and Sport, Utrecht, The Netherlands, http://www.minvws.nl; and *Dutch Cannabis Policy*, Fact Sheet 1, Netherlands Institute for Alcohol and Drugs, Utrecht, The Netherlands, http://www.niad.nl.

Unintended Consequences of Drug Legalization

Many people argue that significant third-party effects of drug use exist. If prohibition reduced alcohol consumption, legalization of alcohol has had significant third-party effects. The legalization of cocaine and other illegal drugs presumably would have similar effects.

First, alcohol abuse by pregnant women has caused many children to suffer from fetal alcohol syndrome. Certainly, this effect of alcohol use is an unintended consequence. If the elimination of prohibition leads to increased use of drugs by pregnant women, an increased incidence of birth problems is an unintended consequence.

Second, drug (alcohol) abuse has led to the breakup of many families and to serious problems for many families that do not breakup. This is another unintended consequence of drug legalization. Some people might argue that these first two unintended consequences are confined to the family unit and thus are not third-party effects, but the effect on children must be of concern to the rest of society, and specifically to government.

Keyword: *decriminalization, medical marijuana*

Access InfoTrac at http://infotrac.cengage.com

Third, alcohol abuse has been responsible for the deaths of many innocent individuals in automobile accidents. Here is a clear third-party effect that requires government action. For instance, scarce police resources must be used to keep drunken drivers off the highways.

Fourth, alcohol abuse means that we have more automobile accidents and higher automobile insurance rates for everybody. We also have more illness and higher medical insurance rates for everybody. Presumably, the legalization of illegal drugs would have similar effects on automobile and health insurance.

EVALUATION: HAWKS, DOVES, AND OWLS

This analysis of the relationship between crime control and drug control could lead to a pessimistic conclusion. If we continue to follow the current policy, drug-related crime levels will remain high. Drug users, drug dealers, and some public officials will engage in criminal acts. On the other hand, if we legalize drugs, many more people—including young people—will become drug users and abusers. Can we find a middle ground?

Competing Views in Practice

Peter Reuter characterizes the debate between the advocates of strict prohibition, such as William Bennett, and those of legalization, such as Milton Friedman, as one between hawks and doves. According to him, hawks perceive the drug problem as one of values—users and sellers care nothing about right and wrong. Drug use, according to hawks, implies a concentration on short-term benefits and a lack of concern for others. Hawks consider drug use an evil that requires tough enforcement of prohibition as a means of restoring fundamental values. Reuter points out that, in addition to the crime and violence inherently associated with prohibition, hawkish policies may threaten constitutional guarantees. For instance, surveys show that a majority of adults agree that searches of a known drug dealer's house should not require court-approved search warrants.

Doves, according to Reuter, believe that the greatest drug problems are those associated with prohibition, not use. They are particularly concerned about the violence inflicted on third parties and about the threat to constitutional guarantees of freedom. Doves believe that if adults have appropriate information they will make informed choices about drugs and that government and society should not interfere. Reuter fears, however, that dovish policies risk a large increase in drug use and abuse.

According to Reuter, owls—Kaplan seems to fit—believe that the drug problem is one of drug abuse, addiction, and associated disease.[22] In their view, drug use and abuse result from bad social conditions. Although owls would retain prohibition, bold, demand-side intervention is the core of their policy. Rather than minimizing drug use or minimizing enforcement costs, owls want the lowest level of enforcement compatible with keeping initiation down and encouraging the dependent to seek treatment. Drug control is also not the only goal, and higher drug use may be accepted in return for better performance with respect to some other social goal, such as reduced spread of HIV infection.

Current Policy

Hawks, doves, and owls agree that an important goal is to keep young people away from drugs. The use of alcohol, nicotine, and various illegal drugs by young people peaked in the early 1980s. Figure 8.7 shows the trend beginning in 1988 and ending in 2007 of one measure of such drug use, the percentage of college students that used the substance in the previous year. Alcohol use fell throughout most of the 1990s and then stabilized. In 1990, 89 percent of college students reported they used alcohol while that percentage fell to 81 percent by 2007. Cigarette use started to increase at the beginning of the 1990s, peaked again at the end of the decade, and then began to fall. Use of the three illegal drugs increased in various years in the early 1990s. While the use of marijuana fell from 34 percent in 2000 to 31.8 percent in 2007, the use of cocaine increased from 4.8 percent to 5.4 percent and the use of amphetamines increased from 6.6 percent to 6.9 percent. The War on Drugs has not managed to prevent the rebound in the use of drugs by college students.

Data on admissions to specialty substance abuse treatment centers also suggest that the War on Drugs has not reduced the demand for treatment. Figure 8.8 shows since the mid-1990s, the number of people going for treatment for cocaine abuse has fallen slightly. For

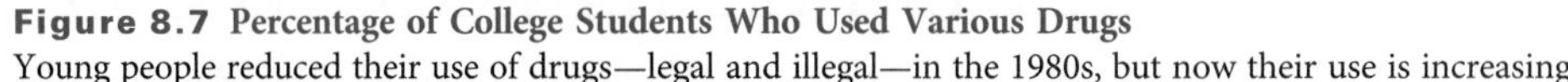

Figure 8.7 **Percentage of College Students Who Used Various Drugs**
Young people reduced their use of drugs—legal and illegal—in the 1980s, but now their use is increasing.

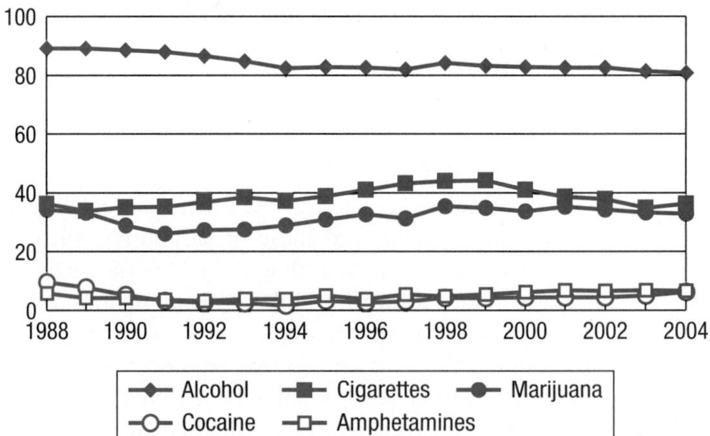

Source: L. D. Johnston, P. M. O'Malley, J. G. Bachman, and J. E. Schulenberg, Monitoring the Future Study: *National Survey Results On Drug Use, Vol. II, College Students and Adults Ages 19–45* (Bethesda, MD: National Institution of Drug Abuse, 2008), Table 9.2, page 259. http://monitoringthefuture.org/pubs/monographs/vol2_2007.pdf.

---

[22]Peter Reuter, "Hawks Ascendant," *Daedalus* 121, no. 3 (1992): 15–52. Reuter, a self-proclaimed owl, denies that the imagery is loaded. Based on his reading of Winnie-the-Pooh, Owl is "learned (he can misspell long words) but unrealistic and self-deluded," fn. 8, p. 48.

the other three drugs considered—heroin, marijuana, and meth—the number of admissions has been increasing: slowly for heroin and rapidly for marijuana and meth. The increase in admissions for marijuana and meth abuse is of concern for two reasons. One, the effect that prohibition has on increasing the potency of the prohibited product, in this case marijuana, may be part of the reason for its increased abuse. The other disturbing portent is the possible emergence of a meth epidemic. In California in 2004, meth accounted for one-third of all admissions for substance abuse treatment. It accounted for more admissions than any other single substance. Meth is a particularly vile substance, if abused. Moreover, it is easily prepared in a makeshift meth lab. Unlike homegrown marijuana, home-cooked meth generates serious negative external effects in terms of toxic substances.

Economists often analyze a program's effectiveness assuming that it has a fixed budget. Suppose that a drug program were given the approximate $13 billion that the federal government spent on drug control in 2006. Including state spending, total government spending in 2006 may be greater than $40 billion. Is this the efficient amount, the amount where marginal social benefit equals marginal social cost? We do not know; furthermore, it is extremely difficult to find out.

Consequently, the policy question often becomes whether the amount allocated is used most effectively. For instance, is the split between marijuana and cocaine control appropriate? The answer depends on whether the *equimarginal principle* is satisfied. The equimarginal principle requires that in the allocation of a fixed budget the last dollar spent on one activity should yield the same marginal benefit as the last dollar spent on any other activity. For instance, if the last dollar spent on marijuana enforcement yields a marginal benefit of $3 and the last dollar spent on cocaine enforcement yields a marginal benefit of $8, too much is being spent on the former. A dollar taken away from marijuana enforcement causes benefits to fall by $3. Switching this dollar to cocaine enforcement yields a benefit of $8 for a net gain of $5. As this switching continues, marginal benefit will fall for cocaine enforcement and rise for marijuana enforcement until the marginal benefits are equalized.

Some analysts have quantified some of these trade-offs. For instance, one estimate in 1997 was that an additional million dollars spent on treatment would reduce cocaine

Figure 8.8 **Admissions to Specialty Substance Abuse Treatment Centers by Substance**
The figure shows the rapid growth of admissions into substance abuse programs by abusers of marijuana and meth.

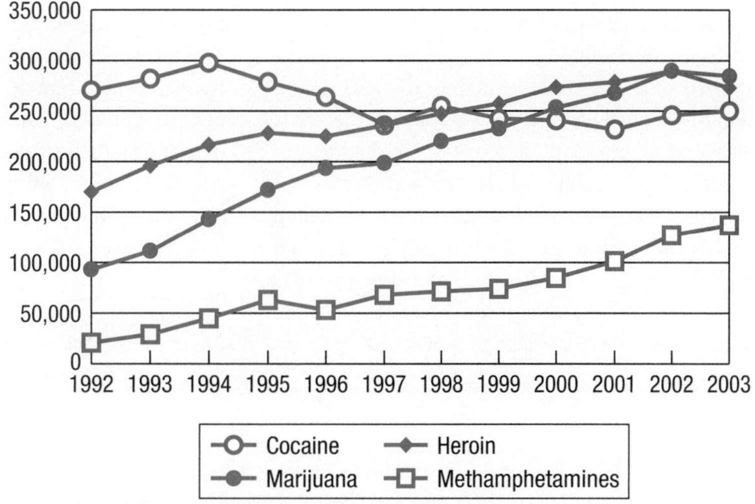

Source: Office of Applied Studies, Substance Abuse and Mental Health Services Administration, Treatment Episode, U.S. Department of Health & Human Services.

consumption about 108 kilograms, whereas the same amount spent on enforcement would reduce it by 75 kilograms. Clearly, if the objective is to reduce cocaine consumption, efficiency would be increased by switching dollars from enforcement to treatment. A more recent study found that resources allocated to treatment and education reduced drug abuse mortality rates, whereas resources spent on enforcement were associated with increases in such mortality rates. If the objective is to save lives, resources should be switched from enforcement to prevention and treatment.[23]

Owlish Criticism

Owls argue that enforcement still concentrates too much on marijuana. They believe that marijuana is less dangerous to the individual than cocaine. Hawks might respond that marijuana is as dangerous to social values as other illegal drugs, and that the danger to

ADDITIONAL INSIGHT

Why Attempts to Reduce Foreign Production of Coca Leaves and Opium Have Little Effect on U.S. Drug Use

Drug policy in the United States remains hawkish. According to the Department of Justice, in 2007 the federal government spent approximately $13.8 billion on drug control. State governments spent about the same amount. (According to the National Center on Addiction and Substance Abuse at Columbia University, states spent almost $80 billion dealing with substance abuse, both legal and illegal in 2002). The federal expenditures on control consisted (in round numbers) of $3 billion on treatment and research, $4 billion on domestic law enforcement, and $3 billion on efforts to reduce the imports of illegal drugs into the United States. The equimarginal principle requires that the last, say, $1 million spent on each of these categories should yield the same marginal benefit. Owls believe that this condition is clearly violated.

An analysis of prices shows that efforts to reduce the production of coca leaves and opium—the raw materials for cocaine and heroin—can have only a small effect on the street price in the United States. It's not hard to see why. The coca leaf necessary to produce just over 2 pounds of cocaine costs about $300, but the cocaine might then sell for about $150,000 on the street in $100 units. If the raw material price goes up by $1,000, the street price would only have to go to $100.67 to pass the full cost to the customer. In other words, tripling the price of the raw material would at most push the price up by only 0.67 percent. Similarly paying a pilot $500,000 to fly 500 pounds into the United States costs $1,000 per pound. If increased enforcement caused the pilot to require $1,000,000 for the flight, the cost goes up by only $1,000 a pound. Because the cost for 2 pounds goes up by $2,000, the necessary increase in the street price (based on the calculation above) would be 2 × 0.67–less than 2 percent. Because the increased efforts to reduce imports of coca leaf have had little effect on price or availability, reducing the effort to limit foreign imports would have little effect on cocaine use. In other words, the marginal benefit of an additional $1,000,000 spent to reduce imports is quite low. The marginal benefit of spending $1,000,000 on treatment, on the other hand, is much higher. Even if the objective is to reduce cocaine consumption, reallocating funds to treatment or demand reduction would appear to have more effect on consumption than the marginal funds spent on reducing imports. The equimarginal principle, discussed in the text, provides a useful way to think about drug control.

Source: Suggested by Peter Reuter, "The Limits of Supply Side Drug Control," *Milken Institute Review* 3, no. 1 (2001): 14–23.

[23]See Edward M. Shepard and Paul R. Blackley, "U.S. Drug Control Policies: Federal Spending on Law Enforcement Versus Treatment in Public Health Outcomes," *Journal of Drug Issues* 34, no. 4 (2004): 771–85; and Jonathan P. Caulkins, Peter Reuter, Martin Y. Iguchi, and James Chiesa, "How Goes the "War on Drugs?" An Assessment of U.S. Drug Problems and Policy. Occasional Paper, RAND Corporation, 2005.

the individual is less significant for social policy. Owls and hawks, therefore, because of different objectives, disagree about the allocation of the enforcement budget. Owls emphasize harm minimization to individuals, whereas hawks emphasize minimization of illegal drug use.

Reuter argues that the hawks are ascendant. First, he cites increased enforcement budgets, increased severity of laws, and increased punishment for drug possession and sale. As further evidence, he cites the unwillingness of the U.S. government to allow the therapeutic prescription of marijuana to people with AIDS, cancer, and glaucoma. Reuter suggests that the main reason for this prohibition, and the prohibition of heroin's use for pain relief for the terminally ill, is to signal that these drugs have no redeeming social value.

Keyword: *drug abuse, economic aspects, health aspects*

Access InfoTrac at http://infotrac.cengage.com

Similarly, HIV infection spreads partly because drug addicts share needles. To combat its spread, Canada and several European countries, including Britain, the Netherlands, and parts of Switzerland, have syringe-exchange programs. Syringe exchange is almost taboo in the United States, perhaps because it would imply that the HIV costs of needle sharing are greater than the costs of heroin use by addicts. Vancouver in Canada has gone farther. It has established a clinic where users can take their illegally purchased heroin and inject it under clinical conditions.

Owls might argue that the increased activity in the War on Drugs has not been decisive in changing U.S. drug use behavior. Except for a period in the early 1990s, resources expended in it have increased steadily. At first, it might seem that the reduction in illegal drug use in the 1980s was directly caused by the War on Drugs. Cigarette use, however, also declined, perhaps due to education programs. If illegal drug use and cigarette use had not grown in the 1990s, these explanations would appear plausible. But anti-drug education programs and the War on Drugs continued and increased in the 1990s, but drug use—legal and illegal—increased. Presumably, marijuana and other illicit drug use declined and then rebounded, in part, for the same reasons as alcohol and cigarette use. Figure 8.9 shows that during the 1980s young people increasingly disapproved of both heavy drinking and heavy marijuana use. This disapproval peaked in the early 1990s

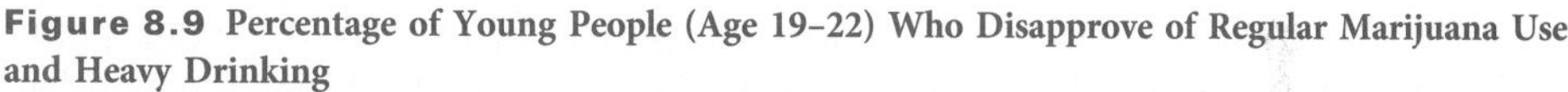

Figure 8.9 Percentage of Young People (Age 19–22) Who Disapprove of Regular Marijuana Use and Heavy Drinking

The percentage of young people (age 19–22) who disapprove of regular marijuana use and of heavy drinking increased until the early to mid-1990s and has since fallen. Not surprisingly, this is the mirror image of the percentage that uses various drugs.

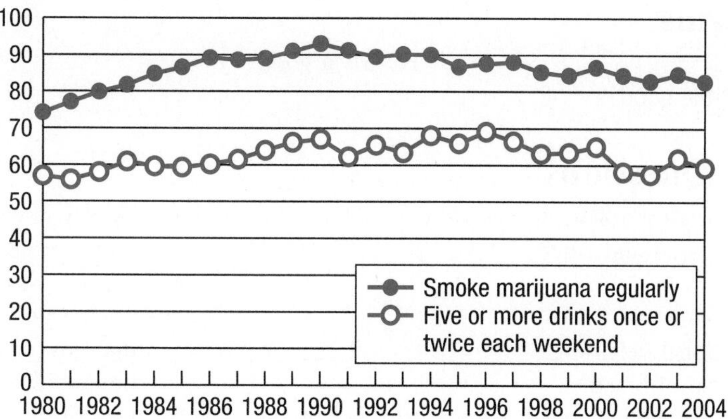

Source: L. D. Johnston, P. M. O'Malley, J. G. Bachman, and J. E. Schulenberg, *Monitoring the Future Study: National Survey Results On Drug Use, Vol. II, College Students and Adults Ages 19–45* (Bethesda, MD: National Institution of Drug Abuse, 2008), Table 6.2, page 195. http://monitoringthefuture.org/pubs/monographs/vol2_2007.pdf

and has fallen, although not to the levels of 1980. The resurgence of drug use by college students suggests that neither education nor a harsh war on drugs is sufficient to restrain it. Owls argue for other approaches.

Hawks, nevertheless argue for a continuation of current punitive drug policies. Without it, they believe that drug use would be even higher. Owls oppose legalization, but they would reduce the punitive nature of current policy and reorient it toward education and treatment. They also would make greater distinctions between types of drugs and enforcement measures. They believe that the current expenditures would yield greater benefits if they were reallocated. Neither hawks nor owls have convincing explanations for the recent upsurge in drug use.

Summary

Free riders can consume public goods without paying for them because it is difficult to prevent people from using public goods. Furthermore, it is inefficient to exclude people from using public goods because the marginal cost of one more user is zero. The existence of public goods provides a rationale for government action in the economy because it is often inefficient for the private market to supply public goods. Imagine the results if national defense were provided through a private market.

One type of crime, broadly defined, occurs if one person violates another person's property rights. The provision of a system of property rights is an important responsibility of government and is an example of a public good. The enforcement of property rights—crime control is an example—is also a public good. Therefore, crime control is an important responsibility of government. The efficient level of crime occurs when the marginal social benefit of crime control equals its marginal social cost.

Drug prohibition is a major cause of crime. A simple way to reduce drug-related crimes is to legalize drugs. Obviously, if drugs were legal, most direct drug crimes—possession and sale—would be eliminated. Furthermore, crimes committed to obtain money to buy illegal drugs would decrease because legal drugs could be cheaper than illegal drugs. Finally, the corruption of public officials that accompanies illegal drug markets would be eliminated.

With the huge profits eliminated from illegal drug markets, inner-city youth would have less incentive to become criminals. Gang activity and indiscriminate violence would decrease in the inner city.

On the other hand, drug legalization would increase the supply of such drugs as cocaine and heroin. Demand also would increase because of legalization, so drug use would increase. If it is true that cocaine use is more dangerous than marijuana use, a possible strategy would be to relax marijuana prohibition and strengthen cocaine prohibition. The debate over drug policy in the United States will continue.

Key Terms

Public good
Nonexcludable good
Nonrival good
Free rider

Review Questions

1. Which of the following would be classified as a public good and why?
   a. clean air
   b. universities
   c. national defense
   d. a loaf of bread
2. Why are public goods generally provided by the government rather than by private firms?
3. Have you ever had a free-rider problem in a group project? How did you resolve it?
4. Because of high crime rates, crime prevention is often a political issue. Do these high rates imply that government should increase crime prevention activities? Defend your answer.
5. Describe recent crime trends in the United States. Why have U.S. crime rates fallen?

6. Describe recent crime trends in England and the United States. Why have crime rates fallen more in the United States than in England?
7. Is the economic theory of crime as presented in the text useful for short-term crime control? For long-term control? Discuss.
8. Some people argue that marijuana and other illegal drugs should be legalized, because people should have the freedom to do as they please. They also argue that downloading and reproducing music should be illegal. Are they being inconsistent?
9. Government restrictions on drug use seem inconsistent with the way alcohol and nicotine (both drugs themselves) are treated. Why do you believe we see this inconsistency?
10. How might the legalization of cocaine affect its market price and quantity? Use graphical analysis to aid in your answer.
11. Why is the cost of drugs likely to increase and the demand for drugs likely to decrease in the face of prohibition?
12. "Making drugs illegal results in dealers pushing drugs on nonusers." Is this statement true or false? Defend your answer.
13. What are the pros and cons of drug laws and their increased enforcement?
14. People come to different conclusions about the desirability of Dutch drug policy. How can people look at the same situation and come to different conclusions?
15. The chapter argues that present drug laws ensure that drug-related crimes will continue. On the other hand, legalization would ensure increased drug use and abuse. Could any actions be undertaken to improve the situation?

Web Sites

- National Criminal Justice Reference Service. "NCJRS is a federally funded resource offering justice and substance abuse information to support research, policy, and program development worldwide." Extensive information on crime and justice—http://www.ncjrs.gov/
- The Media Awareness Project.
  This site is "A worldwide network dedicated to drug policy reform. We inform public opinion and promote balanced media coverage." This site contains massive amounts of information. It does not support the War on Drugs—http://www.mapinc.org/
- Kathleen Maguire, and Ann Pastore, eds. *Sourcebook of Criminal Justice*. Washington, D.C.: U.S. Department of Justice, various years. This source provides fascinating information about the U.S. criminal justice system—http://www.albany.edu/sourcebook
- *Monitoring the Future Study*. University of Michigan.
  This annual survey tracks drug use among young people—http://www.monitoringthefuture.org
- Office of National Drug Control Policy.
  This is a site that supports current drug policy. It too contains massive amounts of information—http://www.whitehousedrugpolicy.gov/
- The National Center on Addiction and Substance Abuse at Columbia University.
  This site is focused on substance abuse and its costs—http://www.casacolumbia.org/
- Common Sense Drug Policy.
  Another informative site oriented toward changing U.S. drug policy—http://www.csdp.org/

CHAPTER 9

College Education: Is It Worth the Cost?

OUTLINE

Americans have long viewed a college education as a ticket to a better life. It is—but it is an expensive ticket. A bachelor's degree from a public college or university in 2005 cost the typical student over $73,000. The largest part of this, over $54,000, was the money the student could have earned if she had not attended college. The remaining $19,000 was money spent on tuition, fees, books, and transportation. Receipts from tuition and fees, however, covered only part of the costs of producing that degree; an additional $33,000 came from other sources—primarily from state government appropriations. Accordingly, society invested over $106,000 in the typical bachelor's degree.

Given these costs, it is easy to understand why students, parents, taxpayers, and legislators wonder if a college degree is "worth it." We will show in this chapter that a college degree yields high rates of return—for both students and society. On the one hand, these findings suggest that it pays for students to invest in a college education. On the other hand, the high rate of return for students raises a question: If a college education is such a good investment for them, why should they get government support? The short answer (which we will explain in detail) is: (1) to ensure that society invests enough in college education; (2) to ensure that students borrow enough to finance their college education; and (3) to increase college enrollment by students from lower-income households.

HOW TO EVALUATE AN INVESTMENT

As noted, the typical college student (and/or the student's family) invests a lot of money in acquiring a college education. We are interested in determining whether this is a wise investment. The decision to invest in a college education, however, is relatively complex. Thus, we begin with a simplified example that illustrates how investment decisions, in general, are made.

Imagine that your friend, Tom, offers you the opportunity to invest in his new enterprise, Tom's Tops, a business that will make and sell customized T-shirts, sweatshirts, tank tops, and so on. Tom asks you to invest $1,000 today and another $1,000 one year from today. In return, he promises to pay you $700 two years from today, $950 three years from today, and $902 four years from today. You are certain that Tom will pay you these amounts on these dates, but you are uncertain whether this is a wise investment.

The investment decision you must make involves three steps:

1. Identify and estimate the costs (C) you expect to pay and the benefits (B) you expect to receive, and list them by date.
2. Adjust your estimates of C and B for date of occurrence.
3. Compare the adjusted Cs and Bs, using an investment decision rule.

TABLE 9.1 BENEFITS AND COSTS OF INVESTING IN TOM'S TOPS

(1) TIME (t)	(2) BENEFITS (B)	(3) COSTS (C)
0	\$0	\$1,000
1	\$0	\$1,000
2	\$700	\$0
3	\$950	\$0
4	\$902	\$0
Total	\$2,552	\$2,000

Determine Costs and Benefits

The elements of the first step are displayed in Table 9.1, which lists each of the expected costs and benefits according to the time (t) at which they will be made or realized. The present date, or "today," is designated by $t = 0$. One year from today is designated by $t = 1$, two years from today by $t = 2$, and so on. The investment decision itself is to be made at $t = 0$, or today. Given the elements in Table 9.1, a little addition quickly indicates that expected benefits (\$2,552) are greater than expected costs (\$2,000). Before you jump to conclude that you should invest in Tom's Tops, however, you must adjust each of the benefits and costs for time of occurrence.

Adjust for Date of Occurrence

To understand why the second step, adjustment for time of occurrence, is necessary, consider the following example. Suppose that you are offered the choice between receiving \$1,000 today or \$1,000 one year from today. Which would you choose? Unless you are quite unusual, you would choose \$1,000 today because you can invest the money today and end up with more than \$1,000 a year from now. How much more depends upon the return on your investment. If you invest the money in a U.S. government bond that pays an interest rate, i, of 3 percent, you will have \$1,030 a year from now. Thus, \$1,000 today has the same value to you as \$1,030 one year from today, or, put differently, \$1,030 one year from today is worth only \$1,000 to you today.

Future value (FV)– The value at a future date of a current amount of money.

Present value (PV)– The current value of a future amount of money.

Discount factor– The value of the divisor $(1 + i)^t$ used to discount a future value.

As the example points out, the **future value (FV)** of a sum of money is larger than the **present value (PV)** of that sum. Formally,

$$FV_t = PV_0(1 + i)^t, \tag{9.1}$$

where t may be any value equal to or greater than 0, and the 0 subscript denotes the present.

Alternatively, the present value of a sum of money is less than the future value of that sum, or

$$PV_0 = FV_t/(1 + i)^t. \tag{9.2}$$

Applied to the current example, $\$1,030 = \$1,000\ (1.03)^1$, and $\$1,000 = \$1,030/(1.03)^1$, where \$1,030 is the future value at $t = 1$, and \$1,000 is the present value at $t = 0$. Equation 9.2 indicates that the future value of an amount of money must be divided by a **discount factor**, $(1 + i)^t$, to determine what that future amount is worth to the investor today.

Table 9.2 shows the results of applying Equation 9.2 to the data in Table 9.1. Columns (1), (2), and (5) in Table 9.2 are the same as the three columns of Table 9.1. Column (3)

TABLE 9.2 BENEFITS AND COSTS OF INVESTING IN TOM'S TOPS, ADJUSTED FOR TIME OF OCCURRENCE

(1) TIME (t)	(2) BENEFITS (B)	(3) $(1-i)^t$	(4) PVB_t	(5) COSTS (C)	(6) PVC_t
0	$0	1.000	$0	$1,000	$1,000
1	$0	1.030	$0	$1,000	$971
2	$700	1.061	$660	$0	$0
3	$950	1.093	$869	$0	$0
4	$902	1.126	$801	$0	$0
Totals	$2,552		$2,330	$2,000	$1,971

in Table 9.2 depicts the value of the discount factor for each value of t from 0 to 4 when the value for i is 0.03. Column (4) contains the present values of the benefits (PVB) listed in column (2). For example, PVB_t when $t = 2$ is $\$700/(1.03)^2$ or \$700/1.061 (= \$660). Column (6) contains the present values of the costs (PVC) listed in column (5).

Present value decision rule– A rule used to determine if an investment is financially sound; an investment is financially sound according to this rule if the sum of the present value of benefits is equal to or greater than the sum of the present value of costs.

Apply an Investment Decision Rule

The first two steps in the investment evaluation are now complete. The third step is to decide if the investment is worthwhile. We can apply two investment decision rules for this purpose. The first is the **present value decision rule**. According to this rule, an investment is worthwhile if the *sum* of the present value of benefits (PVB) exceeds or equals the *sum* of the present value of costs (PVC). This is equivalent to the rule that the sum of the *present value of net benefits* (PVNB, where PVNB = PVB − PVC) must be greater than or equal to zero.

We apply this decision rule to the data in Table 9.2 by adding columns (4) and (6) and comparing them. The sum of the PVBs, \$2,330, clearly exceeds the sum of the PVCs, \$1,971. Alternatively, the PVNB is greater than zero, or \$359 (= \$2,330 − \$1,971). Thus, according to both versions of the present value decision rule, the investment in Tom's Tops is worthwhile.

Rate of return decision rule– A rule used to determine if an investment is financially sound; an investment is financially sound according to this rule if the rate of return on the investment is equal to or greater than the rate of return on the best alternative use of funds.

The second decision rule is the **rate of return decision rule**. According to this decision rule, an investment is worthwhile if the rate of return on the investment is greater than the rate of return on the best alternative use of your money. To apply the second decision rule, you must be able to calculate the rate of return. The **rate of return (ROR)** is the discount rate, r, which makes the *sum* of the PVCs *equal* to the *sum* of the PVBs, or which makes PVNB = 0. That is, you must substitute r for i in the discount factor and solve the following equation for the value of r:

$$[\$1{,}000/(1-r)^0]-[\$1{,}000/(1-r)^1]=[\$700/(1-r)^2]-[\$950/(1-r)^3]-[\$902/(1-r)^4]. \tag{9.3}$$

Rate of return (ROR)– The discount rate, r, at which the sum of the present value of costs is equal to the sum of the present value of benefits.

If several time periods are involved, as in this investment, the value of r can be determined fastest by using a financial calculator or a computer program that calculates rates of return. We have relieved you of this task and already determined that the solution value for r in Equation 9.3 is 0.10, or 10 percent. This solution is confirmed by the data in Table 9.3, where the sums of the PVBs and PVCs are determined using r = 0.10 in the discount factor in column (3). Note that at this discount rate, the sums of both the PVBs and the PVCs are \$1,909, so PVNB = 0. If 10 percent exceeds the rate you could

TABLE 9.3 CONFIRMATION OF A 10 PERCENT RATE OF RETURN FROM INVESTING IN TOM'S TOPS

(1)	(2)	(3)	(4)	(5)	(6)
TIME (t)	BENEFITS (B)	$(1 - i)^t$	PVB_t	COSTS (C)	PVC_t
0	$0	1.000	$0	$1,000	$1,000
1	$0	1.100	$0	$1,000	$952
2	$700	1.210	$635	$0	$0
3	$950	1.331	$820	$0	$0
4	$902	1.464	$742	$0	$0
Totals	$2,552		$1,909	$2,000	$1,909

earn on the best alternative use of the money you lend to Tom, this investment is worthwhile. In our example, you should make the investment in Tom's Tops if the U.S. government bond is your best alternative, because you would earn only 3 percent on that investment.

Monetary benefits and costs– Benefits and costs valued in dollars.

Nonmonetary benefits and costs– Benefits and costs not valued in dollars.

Social benefits– Benefits that accrue to all individuals; applied to college education, benefits to students and nonstudents.

Social costs– Costs paid by all individuals; applied to college education, costs to students and nonstudents.

Student benefits– Benefits of a college education to students.

Nonstudent benefits– Benefits of a college education to nonstudents.

Student costs– Costs of a college education paid by students.

Nonstudent costs– Costs of a college education paid by nonstudents.

INVESTING IN A COLLEGE EDUCATION: MONETARY BENEFITS AND COSTS

Now let's use this framework to determine the payoff for a typical student and for society from investing in a college education. The first step, identifying and estimating the benefits and costs by date, is more complicated that it was for the investment in Tom's Tops. Benefits and costs fall into two general classes: monetary and nonmonetary. **Monetary benefits and costs** are those that can be easily valued in dollars. **Nonmonetary benefits and costs** are those that are difficult or impossible to value in dollars. The procedures we have outlined above can be applied only to monetary benefits and costs.

The principal monetary benefits and costs of a college education are listed in Table 9.4. The broadest measures are of social benefits and social costs. **Social benefits** are benefits that accrue to both students and nonstudents. Similarly, **social costs** are costs that are paid by both students and nonstudents. The benefits that accrue only to students are called **student benefits**. We use the word "student" here to mean the primary unit that benefits or pays; this may be the student, alone, or the student and his or her family. The benefits that accrue to nonstudents are **nonstudent benefits** of a college education. **Student costs** are costs paid by students. **Nonstudent costs** are costs paid by nonstudents.

The principal monetary student benefit is the *increase* in lifetime earnings *after taxes* attributable to a college education. If the student is a recent high school graduate, this benefit is equal to lifetime earnings after taxes with a college degree *minus* lifetime earnings after taxes with a high school diploma. Taxes are deducted from earnings because students do not directly benefit from the taxes levied on their earnings. The taxes that should be deducted are those based on earnings. The most important of these are federal and state individual income taxes and the payroll tax for Social Security.

The increase in tax revenue from the lifetime earnings of college graduates is used to finance government expenditures that provide benefits—primarily to nonstudents. The benefits from these expenditures are the principal monetary nonstudent benefits from college education.

TABLE 9.4 MONETARY BENEFITS AND COSTS OF A COLLEGE EDUCATION

SOCIAL BENEFITS
Student Benefits
Increase in earnings, after taxes
Nonstudent Benefits
Benefits financed by increased tax revenue
Benefits financed by nonstudent private sources
SOCIAL COSTS
Student Costs
Net tuition, fees, books, and transportation
Earnings forgone, after taxes
Nonstudent Costs
Costs paid by government
Costs paid by nonstudent private sources

The principal monetary student costs are student outlays for net tuition (tuition minus the value of scholarships and fellowships received), fees, books, and transportation, and earnings forgone after taxes. Earnings forgone are equal to what students could earn after taxes if they were not attending college minus the earnings after taxes they receive from a job while in college. Since the typical college student works only part-time, earnings forgone are substantial.

The principal monetary nonstudent costs are outlays made by federal and state governments in the form of appropriations, grants and contracts, and scholarships. A small share of monetary external costs is paid by private sources, primarily in the form of gifts and income from endowments.

Student rate of return (ROR)– Rate of return realized by students from investing in a college education; the discount rate at which the sum of the present value of student benefits is equal to the sum of the present value of student costs.

Social rate of return (ROR)– Rate of return realized by students and nonstudents from investing in a college education; the discount rate at which the sum of the present value of social benefits is equal to the sum of the present value of social costs.

Estimates of these benefits and costs can be used to determine both the PVNB and the ROR from investing in a college education. Actually, we can make two types of estimates. The first type produces the PVNB and the ROR from the student's perspective—the *student PVNB* and the **student ROR**. These are determined using estimates of student benefits and student costs. The second type produces the PVNB and the ROR from a social perspective—the *social PVNB* and the **social ROR**. These are determined using estimates of social benefits and social costs.

The Student's Perspective

In this section, we illustrate how investment analysis can be used to determine the student PVNB and ROR. Our subject is the typical recent high school graduate who enrolled in a public college in the fall semester or quarter of 2000 with the goal of earning a bachelor's degree.

If the student has earned a degree (more on this later) it would have taken her 4.57 years to do so (not the 4 years that parents hope will be the case). During that time, she would have "paid" \$82,369; \$21,101 for net tuition, fees, books, and transportation related to her schooling, and \$61,269 in the form of after-tax earnings foregone (after allowing for \$5,200 of earnings per year from working part-time while in college). All of these are real costs; that is, they have been adjusted for inflation, using the Consumer Price Index.

The monetary prize for enrolling is the expected *increase* in real lifetime earnings after taxes that she will realize with her degree. This real earnings differential is illustrated in Figure 9.1 by the vertical distance between the two lifetime real earnings profiles in Figure 9.1.

Figure 9.1 **Real Lifetime Earnings after Taxes of a Typical Individual with either a High School Diploma or a College Degree**

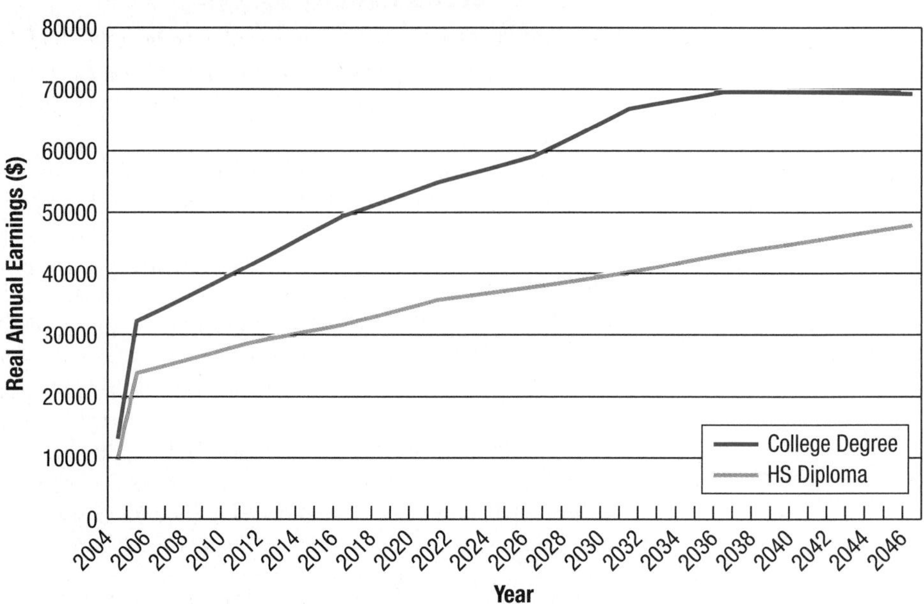

These profiles reflect estimates of the average before tax real wage (the actual wage less inflation) earned by high school and college graduates (with a bachelor's degree) of various ages working full-time in 1997–1999.[1] We created these profiles by assuming that the 1997–1999 age distributions of real earnings would remain unchanged, but that all real earnings would grow by 1.1 percent a year.

The total benefits from a bachelor's degree are equal to the differences in real earnings summed over the working lifetime of the typical college graduate. For the 42 years depicted in Figure 9.1 this amounts to $831,955, or an average of $19,808 per year.

The untutored reader may leap to the conclusion at this point that a college education is *really* worth it; after all, the costs of a bachelor's degree are only $82,369 and the expected benefits are $831,955. The informed reader knows, however, that the costs and benefits must be discounted. We will do this shortly.

Before we do this, however, we must allow for the fact that the student *will not necessarily pay the costs or receive the benefits indicated so far*. The typical college student is *at risk of dropping out* during the time normally spent working toward a degree. This changes the expected costs that would be paid. The typical student is also *at risk of not completing a degree* even if she or he doesn't drop out during the time normally spent working toward a degree. This reduces the expected benefits that would be realized.

Data from the National Center for Education Statistics indicate that the typical entering student drops out of college and never completes a degree at a rate of about 4 percent per year of those who enter.[2] That is, 4 percent drop out the first year, 8 percent have dropped out by the end of the second year, 12 percent by the end of the third year, and so on, up to six years. Very little completion occurs after six years. Application

---

[1]U.S. Census Bureau, *The Big Payoff: Educational Attainment and Synthetic Estimates of Work-Life Earnings*, Current Population Reports (July 2002), P23–210.

[2]U.S. Department of Education, National Center for Education Statistics, *Descriptive Summary of 1995–96 Beginning Postsecondary Students: Six Years Later*, Statistical Analysis Report NCES 2003–151.

Figure 9.2 Costs and Benefits of a College Degree

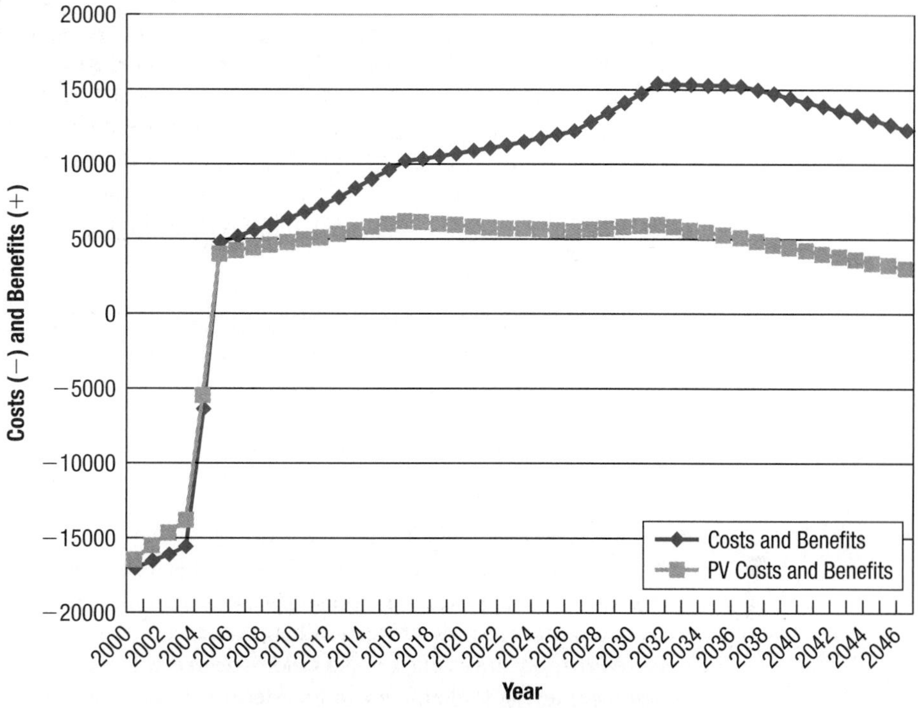

of these percentages to the years spent working toward a degree reduces the costs of tuition, fees, books, and transportation each year by 4 percent, 8 percent, 12 percent, etc. The probability of dropping out also reduces the estimate of earnings forgone. The expected cost of tuition, fees, books, and transportation falls from $21,101 to $18,727 and the expected cost of after-tax earnings forgone falls from $61,269 to $54,330 after these adjustments are made. Thus, the total costs fall from $82,369 to $73,057.

Data from the same source indicate that, even though 77 percent of students who start college persist in working on a degree for up to six years, only 58 percent of those who start ever complete the degree. This means that the typical college enrollee will realize only 58 percent of the $831,955 in additional lifetime after-tax earnings, or $482,534.

This is a big adjustment, but even after this is done, benefits still exceed costs by $409,476. Now, let's discount. The appropriate discount rate is the rate of return that the typical student could earn on a comparable investment. In this case, the comparable investment should be one that is long-term and relatively risk-free, such as long-term bonds of the federal government. The real rate of return realized on these assets over the last 50 years—3 percent—is the rate that we have used for discounting the costs and benefits of a college education.

The effect of discounting is illustrated in Figure 9.2. The "Costs and Benefits" profile is projected *un*discounted costs and benefits, after adjustments for the probabilities of dropping out (and never completing a degree) while working toward a degree and for not completing a degree within six years. The "PV Costs and Benefits" profile reflects the effect of discounting on both costs and benefits. Values below the horizontal axis indicate net costs and values above the horizontal axis indicate benefits.

Discounting costs and benefits at 3 percent and summing the annual discounted values yields an estimate of $67,411 for the present value of costs and an estimate of

TABLE 9.5 SUMMARY OF ESTIMATED COSTS, BENEFITS AND REAL RATE OF RETURN FROM INVESTING IN A COLLEGE DEGREE

ROW	MEASURE	AMOUNT
(1)	Costs [= (2) – (3)]	$82,369
(2)	Net tuition, fees, books, transportation	$21,101
(3)	After-tax real earnings foregone	$61,268
(4)	Benefits [= (5) + (6)]	$842,754
(5)	College graduate after-tax real earnings	$2,417,892
(6)	High school graduate after-tax real earnings	$1,575,138
(7)	Costs (1), adjusted for probabilities of dropping out and completion	$73,057
(8)	Benefits (4), adjusted for probabilities of dropping out and completion	$482,534
(9)	Present value of adjusted costs (7)	$67,411
(10)	Present value of adjusted benefits (8)	$215,787
(11)	Student real rate of return	9.51 Percent

$215,787 for the present value of benefits. Thus, investing in a bachelor's degree clearly is worthwhile according to the present value decision rule.

Given that the present value of benefits exceeds the present value of costs, the real rate of return from investing in a bachelor's degree will exceed the real rate of return on the assumed next best alternative (a long-term U.S. government bond). Our calculations indicate that the *real rate of return from investing in a bachelor's degree from the typical student's perspective is 9.51 percent.* This is greater than the 3 percent the student could expect to earn on a long-term U.S. government bond. Thus, the investment in a bachelor's degree is clearly worth it if the relevant alternative is the long-term bond.

The reader who has persevered to this point may have followed the general argument, but lost track of the specific estimates and how they are related to each other. Table 9.5 may provide a helpful guide. The cost estimates are summarized in order of increasing accuracy in rows (1), (7), and (9). The benefit estimates are summarized in order of increasing accuracy in rows (4), (8), and (10). Row (11) contains the estimated real student rate of return.

The so-called typical students may argue that the long-term bond is not the relevant alternative; that they could do better by investing in stocks. Stocks have earned a much higher real rate of return historically than bonds, about 7.5 percent versus 3 percent. The real rate of return for the typical student from investing in a bachelor's degree still exceeds the real rate of return on stocks, however. Moreover, the returns from stocks vary widely from year to year; thus, they are subject to considerable risk.

Merely arguing that stocks are subject to considerable risk, however, does not clinch the argument in favor of investing in a college education. The returns from a college education are also subject to risks that we have not considered. For one thing, there is a wide variation in earnings realized by college graduates. For example, the rate of return will not be as high as in our example for the graduates who end up in jobs after graduation that individuals with a high school diploma could fill. *Students who perform poorly while in college, who take little mathematics, or who study majors leading to low-paying jobs should also expect to earn a lower real rate of return.* (See the Additional Insight Box "Does Where You Go to School Matter?" for additional discussion.) Thus, there is more to the college investment decision than we have been able to analyze.

ADDITIONAL INSIGHT

Does Where You Go to School Matter?

The results of our rate of return analysis should encourage high school graduates who are trying to decide whether to invest their time and money in a college education. But prospective students must decide where, as well as whether, to go to college. Before they decide where to go, they may want to know whether a degree from an elite college is worth more than a degree from a less prestigious one.

The lack of attention to this question is surprising, given the voluminous literature on the rates of return from investing in a college education. Nevertheless, finding the necessary detailed individual and institutional information is difficult.

Fortunately, this situation is about to change as more data become available from the National Longitudinal Study of the High School Class of 1972. In fact, the results of a study based on these data provide interesting answers to the question of whether college reputation makes a difference in terms of post-college earnings. Estelle James and colleagues found that the choice of school can provide a slight advantage in later earnings, but only if one is fortunate enough to graduate from a selective private Eastern institution.[a] They found a much larger earnings advantage associated with a student's choices and achievements while in college, regardless of the institution. The choice of major is important, with higher earnings advantages to engineering majors and to business majors who function as managers after college, as opposed, for example, to education majors, especially if they function as teachers after college. A significant payoff follows from taking lots of math regardless of major. The biggest payoff of all, however, is for a high grade point average. Apparently, what matters most is not which college or university you attend but what you do while you are there.

[a] Estelle James, Nabeel Alsalam, Joseph C. Conaty, and Duc-Le To, "College Quality and Future Earnings: Where Should You Send Your Child to College?" *American Economic Review* 79, no. 2 (1989): 247–52.

The Social Perspective

As noted, the social rate of return is based on a comparison of *social* benefits and *social* costs. As illustrated in Table 9.4, the social costs easily valued in dollars are the student costs already examined, plus costs paid by nonstudents. Social benefits consist of (1) the student benefits already estimated, (2) the benefits produced by the government expenditures financed by the increase in income and Social Security taxes paid by college graduates, and (3) the benefits produced by funds provided by private nonstudent sources. Benefits from government expenditures vary in terms of the ease with which they can be valued in dollars, but they cannot, in general, be easily valued. Nor can the benefits produced by funds provided by private nonstudent sources. We resort, instead, to the assumption that the benefits from these two sources are equal to the revenues provided. This is probably an underestimate of the benefits from privately provided funds—Why would they be provided voluntarily unless the providers perceived benefits at least as great as costs? We do not know how good this assumption is as an estimate of the benefits from publicly provided funds.

Our typical college graduate will pay $718,155 in income and Social Security taxes (a rate of 22.9 percent applied to lifetime earnings before taxes of $3,136,047). Our typical high school graduate will pay income and Social Security taxes of $206,692 (a rate of 11.6 percent applied to lifetime earnings of $1,781,830). The difference in taxes—$511,463—is our estimate of the nonstudent benefits from publicly provided funds. Nonstudents will pay $3,320 for each college graduate from private funds. Thus, nonstudent benefits from both public and private sources will total $514,783.

ADDITIONAL INSIGHT

Education and Economic Growth

This chapter indicates that a college education is a major contributor to the income of individual graduates. Likewise, economists' estimates indicate that education has made major contributions to growth in national income. Studies based on "growth accounting" indicate that investment in education at all levels tends to explain directly about 15 to 20 percent of recorded growth in U.S. national income, and that higher education accounts for about one-fourth of this effect.[a] Another 20 to 40 percent of income growth generally is attributed to growth in knowledge and its application, and higher education is believed to contribute importantly to this process.

[a] The leading developer of the art of growth accounting was Edward F. Denison, who produced several estimates of the contribution of education to economic growth. For a good review of his work, see "Accounting for Slower Growth: An Update," in J. Kendrick (ed.), *International Comparisons of Productivity and Causes of Slowdowns* (Cambridge, MA: Ballinger, 1984).

On the cost side, public and private nonstudent sources will provide $33,504.

Given that the nonstudent benefits greatly exceed the nonstudent costs it would appear that a college education is worth a lot more from a social perspective than it is from a student perspective. The real social ROR is only 10.14 percent, however, or just 0.63 percentage points higher than the real student ROR. This is a consequence of differences in the timing of the nonstudent benefits and costs. The nonstudent costs must be paid up front while the nonstudent benefits are delayed. The wait involved for benefits greatly reduces their present value relative to the present value of costs.

Keywords: *college education and social rate of return*

Access InfoTrac at http://infotrac.cengage.com

INVESTING IN A COLLEGE EDUCATION: NONMONETARY BENEFITS AND COSTS

Up to now we have emphasized the benefits and costs that we can value in dollars, but additional benefits and costs may be attributed to a college education. We have excluded them from our present value and ROR calculations, but relevant examples exist in all four benefit and cost categories.

Nonmonetary Student Benefits

Robert Haveman and Barbara Wolfe have examined a number of education benefits commonly left out of present value and ROR calculations, some of which may be attributable to a college education.[3] According to them, education enhances the value of leisure.

Better-educated parents improve their children's intellectual development, occupational status, and future earnings. Education produces improved health. Education enables people to make better choices among consumer goods, locations, jobs, and prospective mates. Education also increases the returns people realize from savings, and the educational experience itself is a source of satisfaction to many students.

Their discussion suggests that these effects are important sources of benefits. In their 1984 study, they estimated that parents place a value of $300 to $1,800 on the

[3]Robert H. Haveman and Barbara L. Wolfe, "School and Economic Well-Being: The Role of Non-Market Effects," *Journal of Human Resources* 19, no. 3 (1984): 382; and "Accounting for the Social and Non-Market Benefits of Education," in John F. Helliwell (ed.), *The Contribution of Human and Social Capital to Sustained Economic Growth and Well-Being: International Symposium Report* (Organization for Economic Cooperation and Development, 2001), 221–250.

contribution that each additional year of the parents' college education makes to the intellectual development of each of their children. They also estimated that parents are willing to pay $360 annually per additional year of college for its effect on their attainment of desired family size and child spacing. They calculated that an additional year of college is worth $100 per year in terms of its effects on improved consumer decisions. They also estimated that the value of better health that an additional year of education produces is worth up to $3,000 per year. The lower rate of smoking among college graduates is an example of how college education contributes to better health.

Haveman and Wolfe do not claim that their estimates are definitive. They do suggest, however, that benefits not easily measured might be as valuable as benefits from increased earnings. Clearly, if estimates such as these were included in the present value and ROR calculations, both the student and social payoffs would be larger.

Nonmonetary Student Costs

Some other effects that are hard to measure in dollars are nonmonetary student costs. One important example is the cost that comes from overeducation. Overeducation occurs when college graduates end up working at jobs for which they believe they are overqualified. Tsang and Levin argue that overeducation may lead to job dissatisfaction, adverse workplace behavior, deteriorating health, and lower productivity.[4] If the dollar values of these effects were counted as part of the cost of college education, both the student and social RORs would fall.

Nonmonetary External Benefits

Keywords: *social benefits and education, nonmarket benefits and education*

Access InfoTrac at http://infotrac.cengage.com

Keyword: *overeducation*

Access InfoTrac at http://infotrac.cengage.com

We categorize three primary types of nonmonetary external benefits: *research spillovers, knowledge spillovers*, and *community benefit spillovers*. Essentially, each of these is a benefit of a college education not captured by the student and not easily valued.

The nation's colleges and universities are major producers of research, the benefits of which are often widely dispersed among the populace at large. Most of these benefits, however, are by-products of education for advanced degrees or separately contracted activity. Thus, the external benefits from research produced solely as a consequence of providing a bachelor's degree—the focus of this chapter—are likely to be small.

A college graduate with a bachelor's degree acquires a stock of knowledge that not only serves as the basis for personal earnings but may enhance earnings prospects of others. The specific knowledge a college graduate acquires may also spur better personal decisions by others and contribute to better community decisions, as well. Thus, the college graduate's general knowledge produces benefits that spill over into society at large.

We know of no estimates of the value of these effects. The general role of the stock of knowledge in the economic growth process appears important enough, however, that it has stimulated the development of a whole new branch of economic inquiry. As the results of this research accumulate, they will quite likely indicate that the social rate of return from college education is higher than we have come to expect on the basis of what we currently know.

Colleges and universities may also provide a variety of events or experiences for both students and nonstudents. Art shows, musical programs, plays, public addresses, and athletic contests provide benefits that spill over into the local or regional community. Although benefits from events such as these can be valued using information on admission fees, we know of no general estimates of their magnitude.

[4]Mun S. Tsang and Henry M. Levin, "The Economics of Over-education," *Economics of Education Review* 4, no. 2 (1985): 93–104.

INTERNATIONAL PERSPECTIVE

Rates of Return Around the World

Investment in education is almost universally accepted as worthwhile. In fact, the value of investing in education has been confirmed by studies of rates of return around the world. The following table summarizes the social rates of return estimated in many of these studies, arranged by region and level of education.

The table depicts rates of return on investment in primary, secondary, and tertiary education. Tertiary education is advanced (postsecondary) education, including college education. The estimates reported in this table indicate that investment in education is a productive use of society's resources throughout the world. It promises relatively higher rates of return, however, in lesser-developed countries and at lower levels of education. The higher rates in lesser-developed countries reflect the relatively greater shortage of educated people at all levels in these countries.

The rates in this table are probably high enough to justify investment in education at all levels throughout the world, but they do indicate that the less-developed countries should give a high priority to achieving universal primary and secondary education.

Average Social Rate of Return on Investment in Education by Geographical Region and Level of Education (Percentages)

	Level of Education		
Region	Primary	Secondary	Tertiary
Sub-Saharan Africa	24	18	11
Asia	20	13	12
Latin America	18	13	12
Developed countries	14	10	9

Source: George Psacharopoulos, "Returns to Investment in Education: A Global Update," *World Development* 22, no. 9 (1994): 1325–1343.

Nonmonetary External Costs

Some external costs of college education not valued in dollars include, for example, the extra demands a college or university may place on local schools, police and fire departments, and community social services, or extra local traffic congestion. Including these costs in present value and ROR calculations would lower both of them.

IS GOVERNMENT SUPPORT NECESSARY?

Our estimates for a typical college graduate suggest a social rate of return high enough (10.14 percent) to justify using society's resources to invest in college education. In fact, the high social rate of return suggests that we should allocate an even bigger share of national resources to college education. That is, national output would be higher if we diverted resources from other uses and devoted them to college education.

A high student rate of return (9.51 percent) indicates that a large share of high school graduates should be investing in bachelor's degrees. Some economists would argue, in fact, that investing in a college education is such an attractive option to students, per se, that government support for students and educational institutions is unnecessary. To determine whether this is the case, we examine three rationales often advanced for government support of college education:

1. To ensure that society invests enough in college education.
2. To ensure that student borrowing reflects the social risk of default.
3. To increase enrollment of lower-income students.

Figure 9.3 The Market for College Degrees

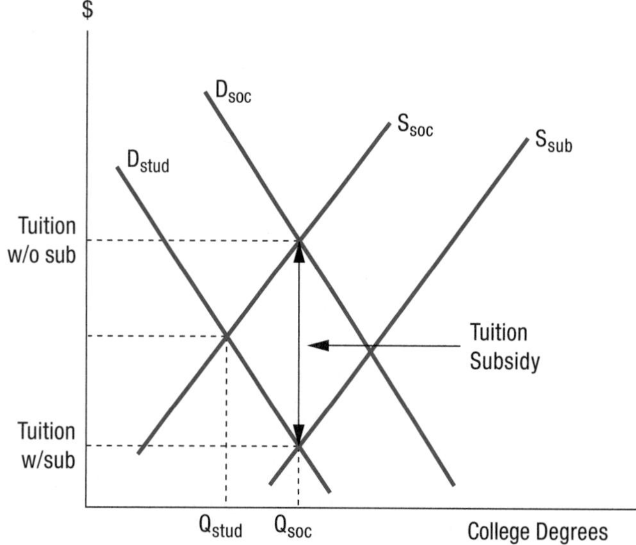

Ensuring that Society Invests Enough in College Education

As noted, the student ROR is almost as large as the social ROR. This implies that students would voluntarily invest in about as much college education as society desires because it is worth nearly as much to them as it is to society. This is not the case, however, when an adjustment is made in the real student ROR for the costs covered by government.

The student ROR is dependent upon the percentage of the total cost of a college education that students must pay. Currently, net tuition and fees cover only about a third of the total operating costs of public four-year institutions, and federal and state governments pick up about 58 percent of the tab. If government support were withdrawn, students would face the prospect of higher tuition and fees. At the same time, however, withdrawal of government support would permit a reduction in taxes, so students could expect lower taxes in exchange for higher tuition.

Student rate of return without government support– The student rate of return from investing in a college education when government pays none of the costs.

A reduction in taxes would increase the student ROR, while an increase in tuition and fees would reduce the student ROR. We expect the student ROR to *fall* when lower taxes are exchanged for higher tuition and fees because the student must pay the tuition and fee increase much sooner than the benefits from lower taxes will be realized. This is, in fact, what happens for our typical college graduate. The **student rate of return without government support** is *only 6.96 percent.* Under these circumstances, students would underinvest in college education and a government subsidy would be necessary to achieve the socially desired level of investment.

We have constructed Figure 9.3 to illustrate why students would underinvest and how a subsidy can be used to correct for this problem. This figure depicts the investment choice in terms of the demand for and supply of college degrees. The downward-sloping demand curves indicate that students want more degrees the lower the price. The upward-sloping supply curves indicate that more degrees will be provided the higher the price.

The locations of the two demand curves also depend on the expected rate of return from investing in a college degree. The expected rate of return for D_{stud} is 6.96 percent—the student rate of return without a government subsidy. The expected rate of return for

D_{soc} is 10.14 percent—the social rate of return. The supply curve labeled S_{soc} reflects the marginal cost to society of producing college degrees.

If students were required to pay all the costs now paid by government, the market would clear at the intersection of D_{stud} and S_{soc} and there would be Q_{stud} degrees produced. The socially efficient number of degrees, however is Q_{soc}, where D_{soc} and S_{soc} intersect. Thus, the market would produce too few degrees. To achieve Q_{soc}, the government could provide a subsidy to students equal to the difference between S_{soc} and S_{sub}, lowering the cost enough to induce students to buy Q_{soc} degrees.

Ensuring that Student Borrowing Reflects the Social Risk of Default

In 2002–2003, college students at all levels borrowed $57.3 billion to finance the costs of a college education, or over $4,400 per full-time equivalent student. More than 60 percent of bachelor's degree recipients graduated with some debt. In fact, the median debt owed at graduation was over $17,000, nearly as much as the typical college graduate spends on tuition, fees, books, and transportation.

The federal government provided 88 percent ($50 billion) of the money borrowed in 2002–2003. A little over $22 billion in federal funds were provided through two subsidized loan programs. Under the Federal Family Education Loan (FFEL) Program, private financial institutions lend money to students or parents and the federal government pays a portion of the interest on the loans and guarantees the loans against losses resulting from default, death, or disability. Under the William D. Ford Direct Loan (FDL) Program the federal government makes subsidized loans directly to students.

This figure illustrates that students would invest in too few college degrees if they had to pay the full costs of a college education. Under these circumstances, they would perceive D_{stud} and S_{soc} and invest in Q_{stud} degrees, or fewer than the efficient number of degrees, Q_{soc}. Government could ensure investment in Q_{soc} by providing a subsidy equal to $S_{soc} + S_{sub}$.

The student loan programs convey substantial financial benefits to borrowers in both cases, including interest rates below those on private loans and the deferment of debt service. Given that there is such a highly developed credit market in this country and that students can expect to earn a relatively high rate of return on their investment in a college education, many critics of the federal student loan program question whether such a government subsidy is justified.

College students, as a group, constitute an attractive pool of borrowers. They will realize higher lifetime incomes than non-graduates and also experience lower rates of unemployment. What is true about the group, however, is not necessarily true about individual members of the group. The superior earning power of college students is no guarantee against the risk that *individual* students will encounter financial difficulty and be unable to repay a loan in a timely manner.

The same problem arises, of course, for many individuals with whom lenders do business. Lenders normally protect themselves in those instances by requiring collateral for a loan, such as the title to a car or house until the loan on each is repaid. Student loans have no such protection for lenders; that is, students cannot serve as collateral. This makes a loan to a specific individual relatively risky and requires the lender to charge a higher rate of interest to cover this risk.

A conflict arises, then, between individual and group risk of default in the college student loan market; group risk of default is low, but individual risk of default is high. From a social perspective, the risk premium on student loans should reflect the lower group risk. The FFEL Program reduces the risk premium required by lenders, while the FDL Program

ADDITIONAL INSIGHT

The Demand for Education

The fact that a college education represents a sound investment for individuals does not necessarily mean that students decide to attend college solely, or even primarily, based on estimated rates of return. In fact, the evidence indicates that they are strongly influenced by the same factors—such as the price of the good or service itself, consumer income, and the prices of related goods and services—that determine their demand for other goods and services such as food, housing, and health care.

Higher education is subject to the law of demand; that is, a higher price, in terms of net tuition and fees (after a deduction for scholarships and fellowships) is associated with a smaller number of students enrolled. In fact, Leslie and Brinkman found this relationship confirmed in 25 studies of the demand for higher education.[a] According to their calculations, enrollment in U.S. higher education in 1982 could be expected to drop about 2.1 percent for each $100 increase in net tuition.

The demand for higher education is also affected by the income of students and their families. For example, in their seminal study of the demand for education in the United States, Campbell and Siegel found that the influence over time of tuition on enrollment was apparent only after controlling for changes in income.[b] Their findings have been confirmed repeatedly, most recently by economists studying the determinants of enrollment in public colleges in New York, New Jersey, and Pennsylvania who determined that a 1 percent increase in income in these states increases the demand for public higher education by 1.67 percent.[c] These economists also found a relationship between the demand for public education and the price of private higher education. A 10 percent increase in the price of private colleges increased the demand for public higher education by 2.8 percent in the three states.

Information such as this on the determinants of the demand for higher education should be of great interest to officials of both public and private colleges who are responsible for determining tuition and financial aid policy. Proper application of this kind of information would enable them to predict the effects of certain policy changes on enrollment and institutional revenues more accurately.

---

[a] Larry L. Leslie and Paul T. Brinkman, "Student Price Response in Higher Education," *Journal of Higher Education* 58, no. 2 (1987): 181–204.

[b] Robert Campbell and Barry Siegel, "The Demand for Higher Education in the United States 1919–1964," *American Economic Review* 57, no. 3 (1967), 482–494.

[c] Cindy Kelly and Suzanne Tregarthen, "Price Plays Key Role in College Selection," *The Margin* 7 (Fall 1991): 60.

directly assumes some of the risk. Given the difficulty in determining the magnitude of the difference between group and individual risk, there is an unsettled debate about whether these programs provide too much or too little risk reduction.

Increasing Enrollment of Lower-Income Students

One argument often invoked to justify government support for college students is that it increases the enrollment of lower-income students. This section examines the principal types of support, the federal Pell Grant and state government appropriations, to determine how well they have accomplished this objective.

Pell Grants. The Pell Grant program provides cash assistance directly to college students, based on their own and their parents' income and assets. It is the largest government program providing grants directly to students—over $16 billion appropriated in 2008–2009.

The Pell Grant is an income-tested transfer payment—one in which the payment falls as income rises. Pell Grants are not confined, however, to students from low-income families. First, students from families with middle-class incomes are eligible. Second, the grant award tends to be larger for students attending more expensive schools, and attendees at these institutions are more likely to come from higher-income families. Third, some students from higher-income families establish independent status so that they can qualify for a Pell Grant on the basis of their income instead of their parents' income. Nevertheless, the proportion of students receiving Pell Grants generally declines as family income rises.

The Pell Grant lowers the net cost, or price, of a college education. The law of demand (see the Additional Insight box "The Demand for Education") predicts that this will result in an increase in enrollment. The available evidence indicates that this has been the case, although the Pell Grant has failed to appreciably increase the number of lower-income enrollees. The primary reason why this is so appears to be that the grant covers only part of the total cost of a college education and that low-income families lack the means to finance the remainder or are reluctant to borrow enough to make up the difference.

State Appropriations. One of the largest sources of support to college students in public colleges and universities is money appropriated by state legislatures to these institutions. The institutions use these funds to cover a large share of their costs, allowing them to charge lower tuition and fees. Thus, state appropriations provide indirect tuition support. Indirect tuition support is so large, in fact, that it appears to reduce potential tuition by nearly 60 percent. If each 1 percent reduction in tuition increases enrollment by 0.3 percent (a number consistent with the studies cited in "The Demand for Education" box), the indirect tuition support provided by state appropriations increases enrollment by 18 percent.

There is some concern, however, about how this support is distributed across income classes. Most likely, a large part of the support goes to middle- and high-income students. This pattern follows from the structure of higher education. Public institutions of higher learning are arranged according to a three-tiered structure in many states: junior colleges, four-year colleges, and comprehensive universities. Educational costs increase more than tuition in moving from the junior colleges to the comprehensive universities; thus, the more comprehensive the institution, the greater the indirect tuition support. Students from lower-income families are overrepresented in less comprehensive institutions and underrepresented in more comprehensive institutions. Thus, indirect tuition support is related directly to family income. So, although indirect tuition support increases enrollment, the enrollment increase is likely to be concentrated more heavily on middle- and upper-income students.

Summary

A college education is a large investment from both the student and society perspectives. We determine the soundness of an investment by comparing the sum of the present value of benefits with the sum of the present value of costs. Social benefits and social costs are the broadest measures of benefits and costs. Social benefits are the sum of student benefits and nonstudent benefits. Social costs are the sum of student costs and nonstudent costs. Some benefits and costs are easy to value in dollars; some are not. The former are called monetary benefits and costs; the latter are referred to as nonmonetary benefits and costs.

The principal monetary student benefit to a college graduate is his or her increase in lifetime earnings after taxes. Monetary student costs are composed of outlays for net tuition, fees, books, and transportation, and after-tax earnings forgone while in college. The principal monetary nonstudent benefit is represented by the increase in taxes associated with increased lifetime earnings. The principal monetary nonstudent costs are the funds provided by state government appropriations and income from private nonstudent sources.

We illustrate how benefits and costs are measured and compared, using an example for a hypothetical public college student who earns a bachelor's degree in 4.57 years. Data for such an individual yield a real rate of return for the student of 9.51 percent, and a real rate of return for society of 10.14 percent.

Many nonmonetary benefits and costs accompany a college education. Examples are easy to come by, but currently available estimates of monetary value are not widely enough accepted to warrant their inclusion in rate-of-return calculations.

The estimates based on monetary benefits and costs alone indicate underinvestment in college education by both students and society. The high student rate of return, however, raises the issue of need for government support of higher education.

If government support for colleges and universities was withdrawn entirely, and if the money now spent by governments for this purpose was given back as a tax reduction, college students would face higher tuition but reap higher after-tax earnings. The effect on tuition outweighs the effect on after-tax earnings, however, and the net effect is a lowering of the student rate of return to 6.96 percent. Since this rate of return is well below the social rate of return, government support would be necessary to realize all socially justified investment in college education.

Governments provide several types of support to student borrowers. Government loans are necessary to correct for market failure resulting from a difference between private and social risk.

We examined the Pell Grant program to determine whether it is likely to increase access to higher education for lower-income students. The Pell Grant is structured to provide more aid to lower-income students, and it has increased college enrollment by this group, but not by much.

Indirect tuition support in the form of state appropriations was also evaluated. The typical pattern of indirect tuition support increases lower-income students' access to a college education, but it probably increases access even more for middle- and upper-income students.

Key Terms

Future value (FV)
Present value (PV)
Discount factor
Present value decision rule
Rate of return decision rule
Rate of return (ROR)
Monetary benefits and costs
Nonmonetary benefits and costs
Social benefits
Social costs
Student benefits
Nonstudent benefits
Student costs
Nonstudent costs
Student rate of return
Social rate of return
Student rate of return without government support

Review Questions

1. Using the following data and an interest rate of 3 percent (0.03), calculate the sums of the PVBs and the PVCs. Also determine the rate of return.

t	B	C
0	$0	$3,000
1	$1,100	$0
2	$1,210	$0
3	$1,331	$0

2. Explain why benefits and costs must be adjusted for time of occurrence.
3. Explain the nonmonetary student costs and student benefits of a college education. Do they appear to raise or lower the student rate of return from investing in a bachelor's degree? Explain.
4. What distinguishes calculations of the student rate of return from calculations of the social rate of return? Which is likely to be larger? Explain why.
5. Explain why, if governments withdrew their support for college education and, at the same time, reduced taxes levied to provide this support, too little money would be invested in college education.
6. Explain the difference between individual and social risk in the market for student loans. What are the implications of this difference for public policy?
7. "The provision of indirect tuition support has substantially increased lower-income students' access to higher education." Is this statement true or false? Defend your answer.

Web Sites

College Board

- Provides information on college costs—**http://www.collegeboard.com/**
- Provides pdf copies of the latest version of *Education Pays*—**http://professionals.collegeboard.com/data-reports-research/trends/education-pays-2006**

Grapevine

- A source for information on state tax support for higher education—**http://www.grapevine.ilstu.edu/**

U.S. Census Bureau

- Get a copy of *The Big Payoff*—**http://www.census.gov/prod/2002pubs/p23-210.pdf**

U.S. Department of Education, National Center for Educational Statistics

- The National Center for Educational Statistics provides a wealth of data on the demographic and financial aspects of college education, including enrollment, graduation rates, and financial aid. Also provides access to the six-year follow-up study of postsecondary students—**http://nces.ed.gov/programs/digest/**

CHAPTER 10
Educational Reform: The Role of Incentives and Choice

OUTLINE

Education is becoming increasingly important as the economy becomes increasingly dependent on knowledge and technology. The increased monetary return to a college education over the last quarter of the twentieth century reflects this increasing importance. The falling real wage of high school dropouts and high school graduates with no college is another indicator of education's importance in the modern economy. Perhaps in response to the increased return to education, state and federal governments have been pouring resources into K–12 (kindergarten through high school) education. Unfortunately, these increased resources have had little, if any, effect on the academic performance of high school seniors. Because of public education's familiarity and importance, we have strong but conflicting opinions about it. For instance, many people would say that the improvements in education depend upon obtaining more resources to raise teachers' salaries and to reduce class size. Still others would say that public schools are well provided with resources, but they must use them much more efficiently.

In this chapter, we consider some of the evidence that suggests that the U.S. public school system does not perform as well as those in comparable countries. We use simple quantitative analysis to examine the alleged failures of public schools and then use basic economics to analyze some of the problems of and proposals for public education.

THE NATURE OF THE PROBLEM

Evidence that U.S. public school performance is not the best in the world comes from international comparisons of the math and science achievement of high school seniors. According to the U.S. Department of Education, the Third International Mathematics and Science Study (TIMSS) "is a fair and accurate comparison of mathematics and science achievement in the participating nations. The students who participated in TIMSS were scientifically selected to accurately represent students in their respective nations." In particular, "Because the high enrollment rates for secondary education in the United States are typical of other TIMSS countries, our general population is not being compared to more select groups in other countries." The study concludes, "The performance of U.S. students in mathematics and science at the end of secondary school is among the lowest of those countries participating in TIMSS. This is true for all students as well as for students in advanced mathematics and physics."[1]

[1]The quotations are from the U.S. Department of Education's National Center for Education Statistics, *Pursuing Excellence: A Study of U.S. Twelfth-Grade Mathematics and Science Achievement in International Context*, NCES 98–049. Washington, D.C.: U.S. Government Printing Office, 1998. Available at the National Center for Education Statistics Web site: http://nces.ed.gov/fastfacts/ The countries are Australia, Austria, Canada, Cyprus, Czech Republic, Denmark, France, Germany, Hungary, Iceland, Italy, Lithuania, the Netherlands, New Zealand, Norway, Russian Federation, Slovenia, South Africa, Sweden, Switzerland, and the United States.

Figure 10.1 **Science and Math Scores for OECD Countries Compared with per-Pupil Spending** Countries are ranked by science achievement from left to right with scores measured on the right axis. The figure shows that U.S. Students perform less well in math and science than students in comparable countries. Expenditures, measured on the left axis, show no obvious relationship with scores.

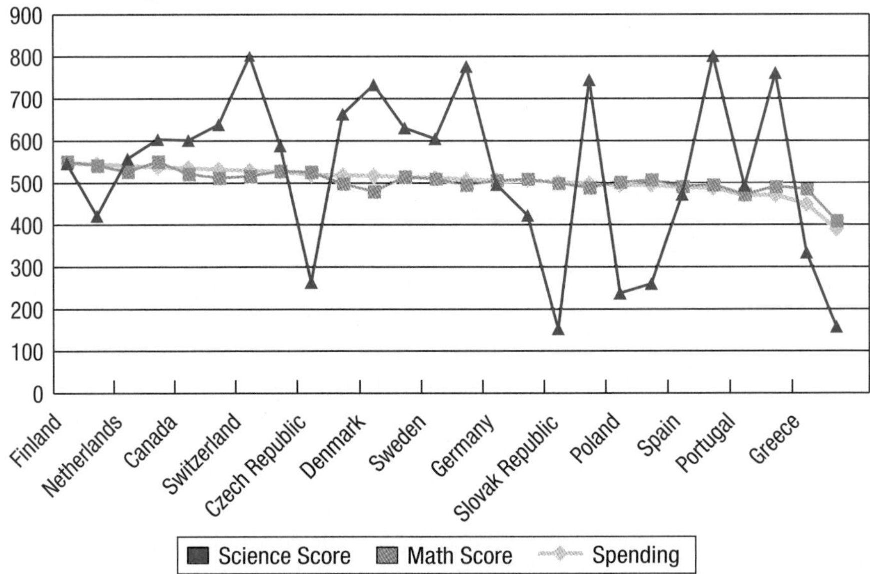

Source: OECD Program for International Student Assessment (PISA), http://www.pisa.oecd.org/

Another study of math and science achievement by the Organisation for Economic Co-operation and Development (OECD), an organization of higher-income countries, gives similar results.[2] Figure 10.1 ranks the United States and 20 other OECD countries by their science scores, with the highest-scoring country on the left. The scores are measured on the left axis. The first bar for each country is the science score; the second, math. The figure shows that the math and science performance of U.S. students was generally below those of other countries. Why do high school graduates in other countries outperform U.S. high school graduates? It is not because other countries spend more per pupil. Cumulative spending per pupil is measured on the right axis. The United States spends more per pupil than any other country in Figure 10.1 except Switzerland.

Figure 10.2 offers further evidence that the United States cannot fix public schools by throwing money at them. Since 1977, spending per pupil in United States adjusted for inflation has increased by more than two-thirds, but achievement scores, represented by math achievement in the figure, have been flat. The tentative conclusion is that we are spending more with no accompanying increase in student achievement.

Eric Hanushek and Steven Rivkin studied the growth in expenditures per pupil from 1970 to 1990. Over this period, rising real wages for teachers and falling pupil-teacher ratios pushed cost per pupil up. But more resources were also being used with each student. The reduction in the number of pupils per teacher alone was large enough to cause the real expenditure per pupil to grow at a 1.4 percent annual rate.

One reason that the decline in the pupil-teacher ratio has failed to produce increased achievement could be that more instructional resources were devoted to special education.

[2]See the OECD Program for International Student Assessment (PISA), http://www.pisa.oecd.org/index.htm for this international comparison of students across industrialized countries.

Figure 10.2 **Trends in per-Pupil Expenditures and Mathematics Achievement of 17-Year-Old Students**
We see in this figure that the increase in per-pupil spending shows no accompanying increase in math achievement.

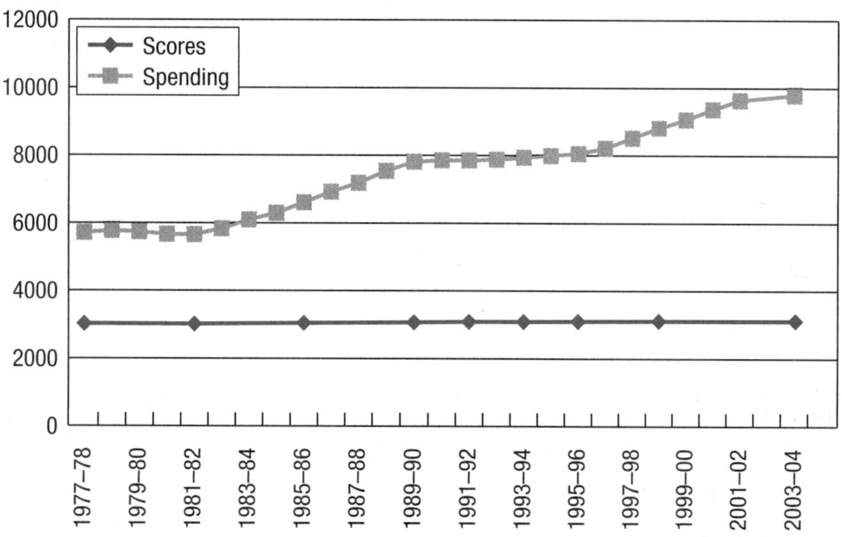

Source: National Center for Education Statistics, http://nces.ed.gov/

Keyword: *international aspects of education*

Access InfoTrac at http://infotrac.cengage.com

Even after adjusting for this factor, however, the pupil-teacher ratio fell, but as we see in the figure, achievement did not increase. The conclusion that fewer pupils per teacher is not associated with improved learning outcomes is consistent with the conclusion of many empirical studies, which find that smaller class size and fewer pupils per teacher have no consistent positive effect on achievement.[3]

The upward trend in per-pupil expenditures and the flat trend in achievement suggest inefficiency in resource use. The economist Eric Hanushek, a leading authority on K–12 education, summarizes our knowledge in this way: "Studies of class size and pupil-teacher ratios, of teacher education, and of teacher experience give little if any support to policies of expanding these resources … it is useful to clarify precisely what is and is not implied by the data. Perhaps the most important fact to underscore is that this finding does *not* [our emphasis] imply that all schools and teachers are the same. Quite the contrary. Substantial evidence suggests that there are large differences among teachers and schools. The simple fact remains that these differences are not related to teacher salaries or to other measured resources devoted to the program."[4]

Hanushek and other economists who have studied public education would probably agree with Thomas Jefferson that "The truth is that the want of common education with us is not from our poverty, but from the want of an orderly system. More money

[3]Eric A. Hanushek and Steven G. Rivkin, "Understanding the Twentieth-Century Growth in U.S. School Spending," *Journal of Human Resources* 32, no. 1 (1997): 35–69, provides the information discussed in the previous two paragraphs.

[4]Eric A. Hanushek, "Conclusions and Controversies about the Effectiveness of School Resources," *FRBNY Economic Policy Review* 4, no. 1 (1998): 17–28.

is now paid for the education of a part than would be paid for that of the whole if systematically arranged."[5]

We now consider government's role in K–12 education. After discussing the arguments for public support of education, we develop a model of student achievement. With this model we show that student achievement improves if its marginal benefit increases or its marginal cost decreases. From this perspective, achievement tests can be used to increase the benefits of achievement to students, and improved instruction may result in reduced costs to them.

ARGUMENTS FOR PUBLIC SUPPORT OF SCHOOLS

Thomas Jefferson, a pioneering education advocate, argued that universal primary education would provide external benefits to society and that such education should receive government support. For instance, in a letter to George Washington, Jefferson wrote: "It is an axiom in my mind that our liberty can never be safe but in the hands of the people themselves, and that, too, of the people with a certain degree of instruction. This is the business of the state to effect, and on a general plan."[6] Moreover, in another letter he wrote, "If the condition of man is to be progressively ameliorated, as we fondly hope and believe, education is to be the chief instrument in effecting it."[7]

We can all agree with Jefferson that K–12 education and college education generate external benefits, and at the same time some can argue that K–12 education does not require government support to achieve the efficient amount. With low high school graduation rates, say, 50 percent of the relevant population, the marginal social benefit may be greater than the demand price—marginal external benefit exists. A slight increase in the high school graduation rate then generates benefits to other people as well as for the graduating individual, whose benefit is measured by her demand price for education. But suppose a 90 percent graduation rate. The external benefit of a slight increase in the graduation rate might then be zero. In Figure 10.3, marginal social benefit is greater than marginal private benefit (demand) from 0 to F. At F and beyond marginal external benefit is zero, so MSB = MPB = D. Now suppose that supply is S_1. Given the demand situation, the equilibrium quantity of education—the quantity that would be purchased in a market economy—is E_1. But at E_1 MSB is greater than MPB that in turn equals MSC (supply). Therefore, marginal social benefit is greater than marginal social cost, so the people in the economy would be better off if more education were produced. The efficient level with this supply curve is, in fact, E_2. Unless education is somehow required or made more inexpensive, not enough education is produced.

Now, suppose the supply curve is S_2, the equilibrium quantity is E_3. It is also the efficient quantity. External benefits of education exist, but at the margin they are exhausted at F. If supply is S_2, private benefit—the demand price—is high enough to call forth the efficient level of education without government subsidies. The seeming contradiction

[5]Thomas Jefferson to Joseph C. Cabell, 1820. ME 15:291. Jefferson did not, however, think that state-controlled and state-provided education was the answer. "Education is here placed among the articles of public care, not that it would be proposed to take its ordinary branches out of the hands of private enterprise, which manages so much better all the concerns to which it is equal; but a public institution can alone supply those sciences which, though rarely called for, are yet necessary to complete the circle …" Thomas Jefferson, "6th Annual Message, 1806," in A. A. Lipscomb and A. E. Bergh (eds.), *The Writings of Thomas Jefferson, Memorial Edition*, vol. 3 (Washington, DC: Thomas Jefferson Memorial Association, 1903–4), 423. See http://etext.virginia.edu/jefferson/quotations/for this and other Jefferson quotations.

[6]Thomas Jefferson to George Washington, 1786. ME 19:24.

[7]Thomas Jefferson to M. A. Jullien, 1818. ME 15:172.

Figure 10.3 The Efficient Level of Education
In this figure, the marginal social benefit (MSB) is greater than the marginal private benefit (MPB) of education from 0 to F, implying that the marginal external benefit (MEB) of education is positive. The MEB gets smaller with increasing levels of education. For levels of education greater than F, MSB = MPB. Because MPB is the same as demand, the market equilibrium quantity of education, when supply is S_1, is E_1. The market equilibrium E_1 is not efficient because MSB > MSC (marginal social cost). One way to reach the efficient level of education in this case is for government to subsidize education. With supply S_2, market equilibrium is E_3, which is efficient because MSB = MSC. Because MEB declines to zero, the market equilibrium is efficient in some circumstances and not in others.

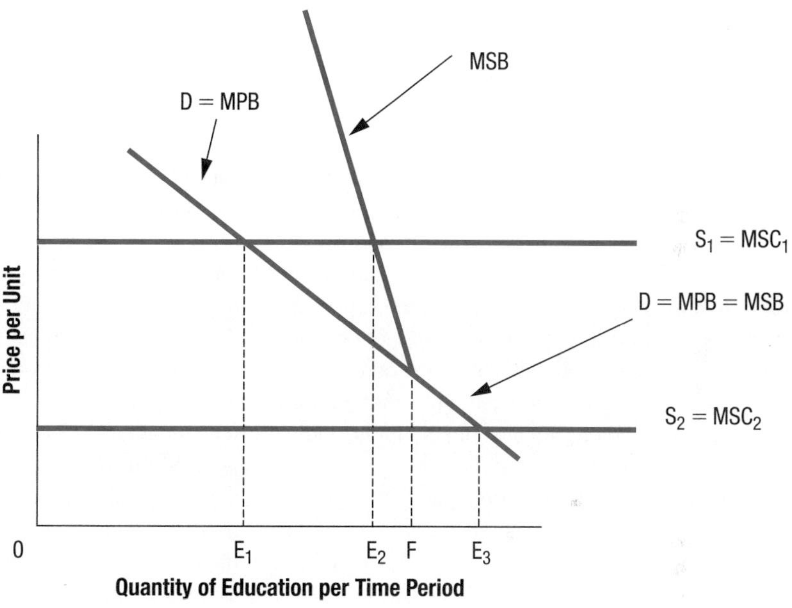

between the existence of external benefits and the market operating efficiently is resolved by noting that at the equilibrium quantity, E_3, marginal external benefit is zero; one more unit adds nothing to the total external benefit because the total external benefit is at a maximum.

Keywords: *economic aspects of federal aid to education, economic aspects of public schools*

Access InfoTrac at http://infotrac.cengage.com

In a modern economy that is moderately wealthy, the case for supporting higher education or even high school education on the basis of marginal external benefit may be weak. The private benefit of education may be sufficient to result in an educational level that exhausts marginal external benefit. Nevertheless, citizens support tuition subsidies for higher education and they provide universal K–12 education with no tuition charge. Why? Some economists would suggest that the amount of education that private, unsubsidized exchange would generate is not enough to exhaust the marginal external benefits due to economic growth. In other words, because of its effect on economic growth, education has external benefits no matter how high the level of education. Others suggest that equality, or the ideal of equal opportunity, may provide the answer, bringing up the issue of fairness or justice.

Some people argue that justice exists in a market economy because it is organized around voluntary exchange. Given the initial distribution of wealth and ability, people interact voluntarily, taking actions that they believe will increase their well-being. According to Henry Simons, late of the University of Chicago, "Such justice connotes exchange of equal values, as measured objectively by organized markets."[8]

[8]Henry Simons, *Economic Policy for a Free Society* (Chicago: University of Chicago Press, 1948), 4.

ADDITIONAL INSIGHT

Jefferson, Smith, and Public Schools: Standards and Local Control

Adam Smith and Thomas Jefferson were advocates of public education. Smith believed that government could facilitate or even require that everyone obtain "the most essential parts of education ... to read, write, and account ... [moreover government can establish] in every parish or district, a little school" where even the poorest family could send their children with the expense of the school shared between the family and the government.[a]

For almost half a century, Jefferson promoted his general plan for education in the State of Virginia. His original proposal was that county government would use tax revenue to finance a three-year education for all (free) children and would assist talented students from families too poor to pay for the child's education beyond the third year. Any other student could continue beyond three years, provided only that tuition was paid. Counties and divisions within counties would establish and control the schools.

Both Smith and Jefferson were reluctant to make even primary education compulsory because to do so would interfere with parents' freedom. They entertained the idea, however, that individuals without the abilities conferred by primary education should be deprived the full rights of citizenship. Even so, neither one consistently supported zero tuition for all students as a way to give everyone a chance to meet the citizenship criteria. Jefferson was willing to compromise on his government-financed, three-year education, if that was necessary to establish a version of universal education. He believed that the well-to-do opposed his plan for free tuition because they would be paying for the education of the poor. In one letter, he wrote: "The modification of the law, by authorizing the alderman to require the expense of tutorage from such parents as are able, would render trifling, if not wholly prevent, any call on the country for pecuniary aid."[b]

Jefferson and Smith apparently would have had no problem with a mixed system of K–12 education that included private schools, home schooling, and public schools dependent at least in part on tuition paid by the family. They did, however, have standards. To obtain "the honours of graduation," Smith said, "it is not necessary that a person bring a certificate of his having studied a certain number of years at a public school. If upon examination he appears to understand what is taught there, no questions are asked about the place where he learnt it."[c] In his 1779 proposal to the Virginia General Assembly for the "General Diffusion of Knowledge," Jefferson provided for county-appointed overseers responsible for ensuring that the local school met standards set by the College of William and Mary.

Jefferson advanced two arguments for universal education. One was that the experiment in self-government could work only if most people were literate and numerate. Jefferson's other objective was to ensure that the most talented students were educated beyond the primary level. He would provide public support for the most talented students from poor families, so that they could advance their education. Jefferson's purpose was to create an aristocracy based on merit and talent rather than inheritance. He did not want to waste the abilities of talented but poor students. As he put it, "By ... [selecting] the youths of genius from among the classes of the poor, we hope to avail the State of those talents which nature has sown as liberally among the poor as the rich, but which perish without use if not sought for and cultivated."[d]

Although Jefferson favored government support for education, he was convinced that what we would call K–12 education should *not* be subject to state control. "If it is believed that ... elementary schools will be better managed by the governor and council, the commissioners of the literary fund or any other general authority of the government than by the parents within each ward, it is a belief against all experience. Try the principle one step further, and ... commit to the governor and council the management of all our farms, our mills, and merchants' stores. No, my friend, the way to have good and safe government is not to trust it all to one, but to divide it among the many, distributing to every one exactly the functions he is competent to."[e]

---

[a] Adam Smith, *An Inquiry into the Nature and Causes of the Wealth of Nations*, bk. 2 (1776; 1979; reprint, Indianapolis: Liberty Press, 1981), 785.

[b] Thomas Jefferson to Joseph C. Cabell, 1816. ME 14:413.

[c] Smith, *Wealth of Nations*, bk. 2, 764–65.

[d] Thomas Jefferson: Notes on Virginia Q.XIV, 1782. ME 2:206.

[e] Thomas Jefferson to Joseph C. Cabell, 1816. ME 14:420.

Commutative justice– A norm for a market economy based on voluntary exchange. Voluntary exchange means exchange of equal market value.

Distributive justice– Equality among people, providing a norm of equal opportunity, with the hope that equal opportunity combined with commutative justice will move people toward equality.

Simons refers to justice emerging from voluntary exchange as **commutative justice**, and he believed it important both for economic efficiency and for fairness. Commutative justice by itself, however, is not complete for Simons; **distributive justice** or equality, for him, is another important goal of the good society. Simons concludes therefore that "Equality of opportunity is an ideal that free societies should constantly pursue, even at much cost in terms of other ends … Inequality … is overwhelmingly a problem of investment in human capacity, that is, in health, education, and skills. It can hardly be scratched by possible redistributions of wealth … Save as the bride of liberty, equality is pale and deadly dull, if not revolting. But the ultimate liberty is that of men of equal power."[9]

Taxpayers may support public education because of its perceived external effects, including its effects on economic growth, or they may do so to promote equal opportunity. Regardless, for any given level of education, obtaining it at the lowest opportunity cost is desirable, just as it is for achieving any level of environmental quality. Many analyses of the cost-effectiveness of public education, including our section, "The Nature of the Problem," are like Hamlet without the Prince of Denmark—they omit the students. In the next section we resolve this problem by considering students' incentives to excel.

THE ECONOMICS OF STUDENT ACHIEVEMENT

What explains the level of student achievement? Although economics can't provide all the answers, it does provide a way to think about it. The economic perspective is that students (or the parents of young children) make choices about academic achievement much as they make other choices. They assess the benefits and costs of academic achievement, and the chosen level of achievement reflects perceived benefits and costs. More specifically, it assumes that students compare the marginal benefit and cost of additional achievement, aim for higher achievement if the marginal benefit exceeds the cost, and aim for lower achievement if the marginal cost exceeds the marginal benefit.

For the typical student, additional achievement requires additional time spent on learning, which has an opportunity cost: the value of the next best alternative use of his time. Better jobs, better chances of receiving college scholarships, and better chances of being admitted to a desired college are among the perceived benefits from additional effort. Students will work harder on achievement as long as the benefit they expect from additional effort is greater than the cost of their best forgone opportunity.

The relevant costs and benefits are those perceived by individuals. Individual costs will differ because of differences in individual ability and alternative opportunities. Individual benefits will differ because of individual differences in aspirations, knowledge, and experiences. Given a relatively wide distribution of individual abilities and alternative opportunities, and the inherent difficulty in raising test scores at the margin, aggregate student achievement is subject to increasing marginal cost, as illustrated by the marginal cost of achievement (MCA_1) curve in Figure 10.4. Given a wide distribution of individual aspirations, knowledge, and experience, aggregate student rewards from additional effort are subject to decreasing marginal benefit, as illustrated by the marginal benefit of achievement (MBA_1) curve in the figure.

According to this model, at low levels of student achievement, marginal benefit is greater than marginal cost, and increases in student achievement will occur. At some point, however,

[9] Ibid., 6–9.

Figure 10.4 The Chosen Level of Achievement: The Student Perspective
From the perspective of the student or the student's family, the marginal benefit of achievement (MBA) for the student decreases with increases in achievement and the marginal cost of achievement (MCA) for the student increases with achievement. With the curves MBA_1 and MCA_1, the chosen achievement level will be A_1. Increases in marginal benefit and decreases in marginal cost will increase achievement.

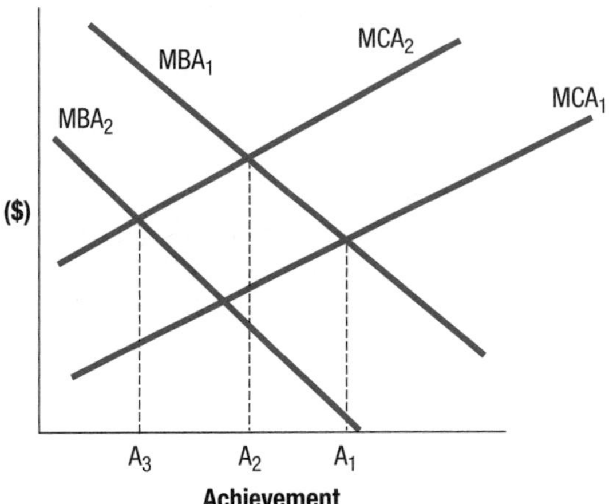

MCA begins to exceed MBA, and increases in student effort—and achievement—will cease. The equilibrium level of student achievement, A_1, occurs where $MCA_1 = MBA_1$.

Figure 10.4 also shows that this model can explain a downward drift in test scores. Suppose A_1 is the equilibrium level of achievement historically. An increase in perceived costs of academic achievement, shifting the MCA curve from MCA_1 to MCA_2 would reduce the equilibrium level to A_2. If the increased cost is accompanied by a decrease in perceived benefits that shifts the MBA curve from MBA_1 to MBA_2, the equilibrium decreases farther to A_3.

An increase in MCA can reflect either an increase in the opportunity cost of achievement or an increase in the difficulty of learning. The opportunity cost increases with increases in the value of the alternative uses of the time that would be required for studying. An example for older students is the increasing reward from part-time employment. Another is the lure of television. MCA also may increase because of school policies that make it more costly for students to learn. For instance, peer pressure to not succeed academically may increase in response to widespread adoption of grading practices that rank students against each other instead of against an absolute scale of achievement.

A decrease in MBA means that the perceived rewards from achievement have decreased. A decrease could occur if college admission becomes less selective and employers place a smaller value on in-school achievement. Or students may aspire to imitate individuals whose success appears to have little to do with academic achievement, such as entertainers, sports stars, or drug dealers. All of these factors can weaken the perceived link between achievement and the consequences of achievement, or what is the same thing, reduce the perceived MBA.

The model implies that achievement increases if the MBA curve increases (moves to the right) or the MCA curves decreases (moves to the right). To improve performance, ways must be found either to increase the marginal benefit of achievement relative to marginal cost or to decrease the marginal cost of achievement relative to marginal benefit. One way might be to reduce the number of hours teens can legally work. This would reduce the opportunity cost of achievement, shifting the MCA curve from MCA_2 to MCA_1 and increasing the level of achievement, say, from A_2 to A_1, as in Figure 10.4.

Another idea is to make driving privileges contingent upon a minimum level of academic achievement. This would increase the perceived benefits of achievement, shifting the MBA curve from MBA_2 to MBA_1, and increasing the level of achievement, say, from A_3 to A_2, as in Figure 10.4. A third option is to improve instruction for K–12 education, another way to shift MCA_2 to MCA_1. Parents themselves, in fact, are in a position to make such changes for K–12 students.

We next consider how high-stakes testing can increases the marginal benefit of achievement. Then we move to school organization to consider alternatives that might result in improved instruction and thus lower the marginal cost of achievement.

HIGH-STAKES TESTING

The skills developed in school are important keys to success, both on the job and in college. Many U.S. high school students, however, do not choose to achieve at high levels. The approximately one-half of students who do not attend college seldom perceive a connection between performance in school and immediate prospects for a job. For those who do attend college, high school performance has little effect on admission, except for those seeking to enter the most selective colleges. Perhaps as a result, half of those who attend college fail to graduate, in part because they enter college with insufficient knowledge and skills.

High-stakes testing– Focuses on achievement testing, with demonstration of achievement important for completing high school and for subsequent employment opportunities and college admission.

High-stakes testing is one way to strengthen the connection between school performance and prospects for employment and college. With high-stakes testing, students take achievement tests and their test scores affect grade promotion, high school graduation, employment, and college admission. Most students are currently tested in each course and do well enough to be promoted from grade to grade and to graduate. Course grades are averaged to obtain a grade point average (GPA), which determines class rank. Both GPA and class rank are often used as criteria for college admission. Some high school students also take the American College Test (ACT) or Scholastic Aptitude Test (SAT), and their scores also may affect college admission. Thus, we have a widespread system of testing in this country, and test scores may affect grade promotion, graduation, and college admission (although not often employment). This system differs considerably, however, from high-stakes testing.

High-stakes testing uses *achievement tests* designed to determine the degree to which a test taker has mastered a broad subject area, not specific course content. The tests are *universal tests*; that is, all students take them at a certain grade level. They use *absolute performance standards*, not relative performance standards such as "curves." A passing grade is established without reference to how others do on the test. The subject matter of the tests is similar to that used in achievement tests in other countries; thus, the tests are *internationally referenced.* Finally the tests are *analytically oriented*, rewarding analytical and problem-solving skills more than memorization.

Achievement tests are not standardized tests of general ability, such as the SAT exam. Instead, they concentrate on the core principles of a subject. Students prepare for them by taking specific courses and studying specific materials, but the courses and materials are carefully designed to teach these principles. Properly designed, these courses and materials provide students with a clear understanding of what they must know and do to succeed on the achievement tests.

High-stakes testing would establish high expectations for all students, regardless of family income and location, instead of the vastly different expectations and standards for different students that have long characterized the U.S. educational system. Proponents of achievement tests for everyone argue that the traditional practice of allowing

ADDITIONAL INSIGHT

The Effects of High-Stakes Testing on Achievement

In a series of studies summarized by Tom Loveless,[a] John Bishop has found that high-stakes testing results in improved performance. Many countries have high-stakes exit exams that are curriculum driven. Bishop finds that students from these countries do better on standardized international math and science exams. In Canada, some provinces have the exit exams; others don't. Bishop again finds that students in the provinces with the exit exams perform better on standardized tests.

Interestingly, Michigan offers scholarships to students who meet certain standards tests of core academic subjects. No penalties attach to failure. Nevertheless, the positive incentive of the scholarship is sufficient for improved overall achievement. The New York State Regents program also has had demonstrable positive effects on achievement.

Is the improved achievement a sufficient benefit to offset the increased cost? It is difficult, if not possible, to do a plausible benefit-cost study of high-stakes testing. A national consensus seems to exist for improved academic achievement. Perhaps one way to do this is through smaller class sizes, although the evidence for this is weak. Another way perhaps is with high-stakes testing. As Caroline Hoxby has said, that the cost per pupil of a well-designed high-stakes testing program is much lower than the cost per pupil of a meaningful reduction in class size.[b]

[a] See Tom Loveless, "Test-Based Accountability: The Promise and the Perils," *Brookings Papers on Education Policy* (2005), 137–56.
[b] See Sybil Eakin, "Technos Interview: Caroline M. Hoxby," *Technos: Quarterly for Education and Technology* 10, no. 2 (Summer 2001): 4.

students to choose watered-down courses (commercial math versus algebra, for example) effectively denies them equal opportunity to succeed in the workplace of the future or in higher education. High-stakes testing would severely limit this practice.

The absolute grading scale associated with high-stakes testing is an external standard; that is, a standard imposed by state or national authorities. Adoption of such a standard would strengthen the incentives of students and teachers to work together toward a common goal. Without an external standard, teachers might judge individual students relative to their classmates. Students perceive this and apply peer pressure to discourage classmates from "wrecking the curve." An external standard, by contrast, unites teachers and students in a common objective: to perform well.

The labor market for skilled workers is international, and U.S. students find themselves increasingly in competition with workers from other countries. Thus, the standards that prevail in U.S. high-stakes testing should equal those in the countries whose students have been outperforming U.S. students.

The labor market of the future will also require a larger share of the workforce to have more problem-solving ability. The proponents of high-stakes testing recognize this and argue for courses, texts, and tests that better prepare students to be problem solvers. Under high-stakes testing, students would develop the ability to put core principles to work in solving real-life problems.

The other part of high-stakes testing involves raising the stakes. Simply put, this requires that test scores have consequences: that they affect events of high value to students, such as promotion, graduation, college admission, and employment. Diplomas certifying different achievement levels and transcripts displaying course grades and achievement test results would make high school performance more meaningful. Such information would be useful for colleges and employers; with increased information about students' performance, colleges and employers would give it greater weight in admission and employment decisions.

U.S. educators and government officials have responded to the relatively poor performance of U.S. students primarily by requiring them to take more courses in "solid" subjects, such as math and science. Taking more courses is not sufficient to ensure that students will learn enough to match the performance of students in other countries. According to studies by Becker and Rosen, and Steinberg, increased student effort is essential, and significant increases in effort are unlikely without the prospect of greater rewards from studying than students now perceive. As they and many others put it, why study harder?

- It is highly unlikely that a student will have to repeat a course or a grade.
- Graduation from high school, by itself, is sufficient for admission to a large majority of colleges.
- Colleges and universities are willing to correct deficiencies through remedial courses.
- Employers do not use school performance as a criterion for hiring.[10]

If they are right, ways must be found to require underperforming students to repeat courses or grades, to implement performance-based college admission criteria, to put the colleges and universities out of the remedial education business, and to encourage use of student performance data as a criterion for employment.

One way to raise the stakes is to use achievement test scores rather than course grades to make grade promotion and graduation decisions. As noted previously, good grades do not necessarily mean mastery of a subject when grading relies on relative rather than absolute performance.

Many students who want a college education will exert more effort to achieve higher test scores if the scores determine college admission. Many public colleges and universities base admissions on ACT scores, high school grade point averages (GPA), and rank in high school graduating class, and they have raised the minimum required for each of these in recent years. The ACT exams require knowledge of subjects that students are expected to have regardless of where they went to high school. In that sense, they are achievement tests and they are useful substitutes until state exams emerge that reflect the standards the state wants to achieve.

Students who plan to enter the labor force directly from high school will also exert more effort to achieve higher test scores, if employers use them as a criterion for hiring. Employers currently do not make much use of measures of high school performance, apparently because a high school GPA is not an accurate indicator of the desired skills and abilities. Again, achievement tests could change employers' practices.

The Economics of Investing in High-Stakes Testing

High-stakes testing appears to be a "good thing," but it can be achieved only at additional cost to both students and society. Is it worth it? Like all such questions in economics, the answer depends on the additional costs and benefits associated with the activity.

The effect of high-stakes testing is illustrated in Figure 10.5. From the students' perspective, high-stakes testing increases the benefits of academic achievement. The higher the payoff in terms of promotion, graduation, employment, and college admission, the higher the benefit per unit of achievement. Thus, the adoption of more rigorous tests with high stakes—tests that measure achievement and are universal, internationally referenced, and analytically oriented—shifts the MBA curve from MBA_1 to MBA_2. As students and their

[10]William E. Becker and Sherwin Rosen, "The Learning Effect of Assessment and Evaluation in High School," *Economics of Education Review* 11, no. 2 (1992): 107–18; and Laurence Steinberg, "Standards Outside the Classroom," in Diane Ravitch (ed.), *Brookings Papers on Education Policy* (1998), 319–58.

Figure 10.5 The Effect of High-Stakes Testing on Student Achievement
High-stakes testing and its acceptance by colleges and employers shifts the marginal benefit of achievement to the right. At the original achievement level, marginal benefit is now greater than marginal cost. Because achievement is now perceived as more valuable, students find it worthwhile to incur higher opportunity cost and reach the new chosen achievement level, A_2.

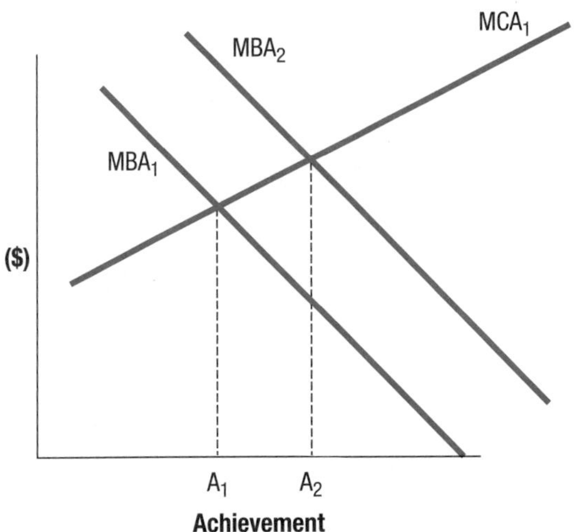

families recognize the increased benefits of achievement, students will incur the costs necessary to move to higher achievement levels: from A_1 to A_2.

The improved achievement, however, is gained at other costs. States and local districts must bear the costs of developing, implementing, and grading the achievement tests. To be high-stakes tests, they must be valid measures of the degree to which students have mastered the relevant material. It is crucial that the tests be well designed and focus on analytical ability rather than memorization or rote procedures. Only if the tests are validated will colleges and employers rely heavily on them. Implementation of high-stakes testing will have benefits and costs. The benefits are related to improved student achievement; the costs are the opportunity costs of the testing program. We have little evidence available to make the public policy benefit-cost calculation.

Keyword: *high-stakes testing*

Access InfoTrac at http://infotrac.cengage.com

By focusing on students' (and their families') decision making, we conclude that a sufficient element in increasing student achievement is to increase the payoff to achievement. We have suggested that state government can do this by requiring that students take high-stakes tests that are meaningful measures of core academic achievement. The results of these tests must be available to employers, colleges, and universities at the individual level.

Keywords: *educational tests* and *measurements* and *international aspects*

Access InfoTrac at http://infotrac.cengage.com

The Harvard Business School recently made its grading policy high stakes; the faculty changed a policy that prohibited the revelation of grades (except for those ranking in the top 20 percent of the class) to employers. The faculty decided to change the policy because many students found it easier to coast than to strive for the top 20 percent. For a class of, say, 100, employers didn't know whether a candidate was twenty-first or last in rank, so some students didn't try as hard because they thought it didn't matter. If Harvard Business School students, who pay high tuition and give up high-paying jobs to attend, require high stakes for motivation, certainly many high school students require them even more. Teachers, public schools, or state school boards could increase stakes, just as the Harvard Business School did. To understand why they have not done so, it is useful to examine the way public education is delivered.

Figure 10.6 The Effect of Teaching Effectiveness on Student Achievement
The original marginal benefit and marginal cost curves are the same as in Figure 10.5. Improved teacher effectiveness shifts the marginal cost of the achievement curve to MCA_2. Students choose to increase their achievement from A_1 to A_2 because the cost of doing so has declined. Figures 10.5 and 10.6 show two different ways of increasing achievement.

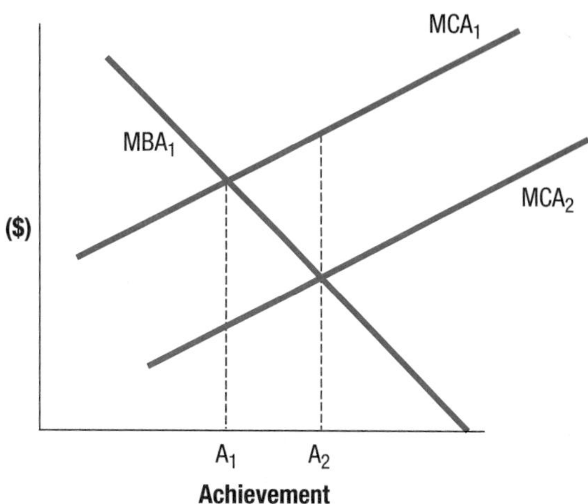

THE ECONOMIC ORGANIZATION OF PUBLIC EDUCATION

Hanushek and other economists conclude that the public schools waste a significant part of their resources. If so, we could attain the current achievement levels at lower cost, or we could attain higher levels for the same cost. In this section, we change the focus from the student to the teacher and the school. If we interpret an improved learning environment or improved teaching as reducing the student's opportunity cost of achievement, Figure 10.6 shows how we expect an improved economic organization of public education to increase achievement. It shifts the marginal cost of achievement, moving the equilibrium from A_1 to A_2.

Keyword: *economic aspects of public schools*

Access InfoTrac at http://infotrac.cengage.com

A discussion of other government enterprises that have wasted resources helps in understanding the current organization of U.S. public education and how it might be changed. The only enterprises that can survive significant inefficiency for long periods are government-protected monopolies that receive government subsidies—for instance, the large state-owned enterprises (SOEs) in China and in the former Soviet Union. To understand why SOEs perform poorly, we will first analyze why markets perform well in organizing a private economy. From this analysis we will derive three principles of economic organization and show that SOE organization is inconsistent with these principles.

Decision Making and Markets

To understand why SOEs perform so poorly compared to market organizations, we analyze entrepreneurial decision making in a market economy. Suppose Alfonso has inherited land with buildings in Vienna, Austria. Alfonso, a Californian, did not know that he had an Austrian relative and he speaks no German. Alfonso can easily locate certain information about the land—its area, its location, the sizes of any buildings, and the portion that is covered by a structure—but other information, such as the quality of the

General knowledge– Knowledge that is easy to transfer to another person, including people in another part of the organization or the economy.

Specific knowledge– Knowledge that is costly to transfer to another person and is particularly costly to transfer to someone in another part of the organization or the economy.

building; how to navigate Austrian laws, regulations, and bureaucrats; and the pros and cons of alternative uses of the property, is more difficult to transmit. The information that is easy to transmit we call **general knowledge** and the information that is hard to transmit we call **specific knowledge**. Profitable decisions about using the property require specific knowledge; consequently, if Alfonso is going to make a "good" decision, he must spend time in Vienna, learn German, and gain an understanding of the Viennese economy. If the bequest stipulates that Alfonso must retain ownership of the property and manage it himself, he can either make the best decision possible given the general knowledge or he can bear the cost of developing the specific knowledge and then decide. Neither alternative is as likely to lead to the best use of the property or to Alfonso gaining as much wealth as he would if he could get the specific knowledge without cost. Alfonso's situation resembles that of the head of a state department of education, the CEO of a large corporation, or an industry planner in Beijing: He does not have the specific knowledge necessary to make good decisions for the dispersed units of his organization.

If Alfonso has inherited the right to sell the land along with the right to use it, he has another alternative. He can sell it to someone who has the specific knowledge. Actually, he would sell the right to make decisions about the land and to obtain income from it. Selling the decision rights to the highest bidder reduces the chance of a bad decision being made, and it minimizes the cost of using specific knowledge by shifting (at low cost) the decision to someone who has the knowledge. An auction, for instance, could sell, or *assign*, the decision rights to the person who believes that she has the most useful specific knowledge. Potential buyers of the property will compete for it, with the person who thinks he has the best knowledge and most profitable ideas about using the property being the highest bidders. Let's say that Helga places the highest bid and acquires the decision rights. Thus, the market assigns decision rights to the person with the most valuable *specific* knowledge.

The market also automatically *evaluates* decisions. In private market transactions, each party to the transaction is trying to make the best possible decision. In market transactions between individuals and small firms, the objective is to increase profit or, more generally, to increase individual well-being. In earlier chapters, we learned that voluntary transactions benefit both parties and that they are efficient, increasing net social benefit. Alfonso's decision to sell the Viennese property to Helga will likely make Helga and him better off and result in the property being devoted to its most profitable use. Given Alfonso's lack of specific knowledge, selling is probably his most profitable decision. But how do we know that buying is right for Helga? We don't. The market, however, will provide an automatic evaluation. If she is successful, her venture will be profitable, and, if she is so inclined, she can leverage this investment into a bigger one. With successive investments, her wealth increases. Helga, like other entrepreneurs, might make mistakes. If her decision to buy Alfonso's property is not profitable, someone else might buy the decision rights over the property, perhaps at a bankruptcy sale. The crucial point is that the market will automatically evaluate the decisions and make appropriate adjustments.

Finally, Alfonso, Helga, and other participants in the Viennese property market have incentives to make good decisions. If their decisions increase wealth, they can command additional resources or they can use their wealth for various types of consumption. Conversely, if their decisions decrease wealth, they will command fewer resources and have reduced consumption choices. The market, therefore, automatically *rewards* wealth-maximizing decisions.

The market process that we have just described illustrates another way that the price system economizes on information. In Chapter 2, we discussed how the price system generates, summarizes and, and transfers information. Here we see that markets can make it unnecessary to transfer information because they transfer decision authority to people who have the most valuable specific information. In situations where specific information is important, markets exemplify three important organizing principles:

- Assign decision rights
- Evaluate the profitability of decisions
- Reward profitable decisions

Knowledge of various types can be costly to transmit—that is, be specific knowledge. *Tacit knowledge*, which might be learned on the job through trial and error, is one type that is costly to transmit. This is knowledge that is difficult to put into words. For instance, the knowledge about how to ride a bicycle is hard to transmit verbally. The development of the automatic bread machine provides another example of tacit knowledge. Matsushita, the Japanese electronics company, decided to produce an automatic bread maker. Given the idea, their engineers had an easy time creating the machine. The only problem was that the bread turned out poorly. To figure out how to make good bread, Matsushita apprenticed a couple of engineers to one of the best bakers in Tokyo. Although the engineers had studied the theory of making bread and had collected information from bakers, not until they became personally and directly involved in making bread did they understand how to design the bread machine.[11]

Although *local knowledge*, based on particular characteristics existing at a particular time, is not necessarily tacit, it may also be costly to transmit to the relevant decision maker. Let's suppose that an engineering firm designs a steel plant. It could send the blueprints to a construction manager, and she could build the plant following the blueprints. In contrast, some successful steel firms bring together the engineering firm, the construction firm, and the steel firm's customers and employees to plan and carry out the project. As one steel executive put it, he uses a design-engineering firm, but "At the same time, we have a lot of local knowledge about where things are, how things work, so we have an active role in projects."[12]

One steel firm puts the new plant's general manager in charge of the construction. Because the prospective general manager will be evaluated on the plant's performance, she has an incentive to adopt changes in the plant's construction that would improve future profits. Moreover, she has the authority—the decision right—to make changes in the construction project without consulting her boss. Steel firms that have decentralized decision rights in this way have built plants whose actual capacity exceeded the engineered capacity by 25 percent. For every four plants that it builds, this company, in effect, gets a fifth one free.

Other types of knowledge that are difficult to transmit are scientific knowledge and assembled knowledge. *Assembled knowledge* is knowledge developed in an organization, as its members interact. For instance, the workers at Monarch Marking Systems in Ohio had significant specific knowledge about their manufacturing process. By making workers responsible and rewarding them for cutting costs, Monarch Marking reduced floor space requirements by 70 percent, reduced past-due shipments by 90 percent, and doubled productivity.[13]

The crucial element in these examples is that people in one part of an organization have important knowledge that is costly to transmit to other decision makers. By

---

[11]Ikujiro Nonaka and Hirotaka Takeuchi, *The Knowledge-Creating Company: How Japanese Companies Create the Dynamics of Innovation* (New York: Oxford University Press, 1995).

[12]John Schriefer, "Completing Mill-Construction Projects Faster and Smarter," *New Steel*, July 1, 1996, 48.

[13]"Firm Shelves Empowerment as Workers Focus on Projects," *Wall Street Journal*, October 17, 1997.

realizing the importance of the specific knowledge, these business firms were able to tap into it.

As the discussion about property in Vienna illustrated, specific knowledge is important in the economy. The beauty of the market organization is that it results in an efficient use of information by assigning decision rights to people who have specific information. As a result, specific information does not have to be transferred. Because different bits of specific information are often widely distributed, their existence implies the importance of decentralized decision making, which requires that these decentralized decision makers, who must be able to act without getting permission, be evaluated and provided with incentives. A market organization provides this evaluation and motivation at low cost. Because specific knowledge is important in organizations, the three organizing principles exemplified in markets provide the framework for an **economic approach to organization**. To summarize these principles, we note that markets automatically:

Economic approach to organization– An approach that mimics the market in designing a profit or nonprofit organization. In particular, it assigns decision rights to people who have relevant specific knowledge, evaluates those decisions in relation to the organization's objective, and rewards decisions that advance the objective.

- *Assign* decision rights to individuals with the most useful specific knowledge, or, if cheaper or more profitable, they *transfer* the specific knowledge to people who already have the decision rights. In either case, people who have the relevant specific knowledge make decisions.
- *Evaluate* decisions, using profitability as the performance measure.
- *Reward* good decisions by providing good decision makers with more resources that can be used for consumption or investment.[14]

Decision Making and State-Owned Enterprises

In a centrally planned SOE, such as public education in California or a steel mill in China, decisions, by definition, are made at the center. These decisions can be well informed regarding general knowledge and specific knowledge available at the center, but they cannot be well informed about specific knowledge that is dispersed throughout the system. It is too costly to transfer all of the relevant specific knowledge to the center. In large organizations, both private and state-owned, centralized decision making is costly because it fails to use dispersed specific knowledge or because it expends resources attempting to transfer specific knowledge to the center. The alternative is to decentralize by assigning the decision rights to people in the field with the knowledge.

Any goal-oriented organization, SOE or private, must evaluate the success of its transactions. The transactions can be either internal ones affecting resource allocation, or external ones between people in the organization and outsiders. If large organizations decentralize decision rights, they must develop means to evaluate employees' decisions. Large private organizations presumably use the same evaluation measure that markets use: profit. But a large private organization usually lacks the market's *automatic* procedures for evaluating decision profitability. Consequently, if it decentralizes decision making, it must use scarce resources to develop and use an evaluation system. A large SOE has an additional disadvantage in evaluation: It typically rejects profit as an evaluation measure.

As with evaluation, if SOEs and large private organizations decentralize, they must develop procedures—rewards—that induce employees to make the appropriate decisions. The market rewards good decisions automatically with wealth and its accompanying

[14]Over the last three decades of the twentieth century, Michael C. Jensen of Harvard University and William H. Meckling, late of the University of Rochester, wrote several papers about specific knowledge and organizational design. These papers have been reprinted in Michael C. Jensen, *Foundations of Organizational Strategy* (Cambridge: Harvard University Press, 1998). See also James A. Brickley, Clifford W. Smith, Jr., and Jerold L. Zimmerman, *Managerial Economics and Organizational Architecture*, 2nd ed. (Chicago: Irwin, 2001).

opportunities, which appeals to the self-interest of creative people striving to advance their careers. In recent years, large private organizations in the United States that have decentralized have attempted to mimic market rewards, using various kinds of incentive pay. The central managers know that they have creative employees with profitable ideas throughout the large organization. The key is to give them decision-making responsibilities, evaluate their performance (decisions), and reward their creativity. SOEs also could use rewards to motivate desired behavior. In practice, however, SOE managers tend to compensate employees without regard to whether their actions advance the organization's goals.

In short, SOEs violate the three principles of an economic approach to organization. Many decisions made at the center are made without using the dispersed specific knowledge of many employees. They also are reluctant to use market-like evaluation systems or provide market-like rewards. State departments of education and school districts, particularly large ones, have organizational problems similar to those of SOEs.

Decision Making and Public Schools

A state department of education (SDE) is, in effect, the central planning office of a state-owned enterprise. It establishes ground rules for the curriculum, chooses textbooks, establishes detailed qualifications for teachers, provides substantial funding, sets standards, perhaps establishes high-stakes testing, and assesses the effectiveness of local schools or school districts. An SDE is apt to be politicized and to be responsive to special interest groups, as well as to schoolchildren and their parents. Special interest groups usually include the teachers' unions, environmental organizations, and other organizations promoting ideological and religious ends. The resulting conflicts are detrimental to learning and provide grounds for agreeing with Thomas Jefferson that "If it is believed that … elementary schools will be better managed by … any … general authority of the government than by the parents within each ward, it is a belief against all experience."[15]

Following SDE guidelines, a local school district (LSD) board hires the district superintendent and with him oversees the physical plant, plans new construction, oversees the hiring of principals and teachers, and participates in salary determination. LSD superintendents often serve at the pleasure of the school board, which in turn is elected. Superintendents naturally will be concerned with satisfying the LSD board and the SDE. Although school board members are typically not professional politicians, their objectives often will differ from what parents want for their children. Given the political influences on both the state and the school district, what satisfies the school board and the SDE may not be what the parents and students desire.

Assignment of Decision Rights. Politicians, state bureaucrats, and local administration place two burdens on effective decision making in public education. First, they have decision rights about curriculum, teacher qualifications, and textbook selection that restrict the choices of principals and teachers, the very individuals who have useful specific knowledge regarding these and other issues. For instance, regulations often prevent principals from employing staff they feel sure would do an excellent job in the classroom. SDEs and teachers' unions impose certification requirements that interfere with the judgment of local administrators; the result, if not the intent, is to discourage potential teachers and reduce the supply of teachers. If certification requirements contributed to better teaching, they would have benefits as well as costs. Unfortunately, no consistent evidence indicates that advanced degrees in education lead to better teaching. SDEs and

---

[15]See the box "Jefferson, Smith, and Public Schools: Standards and Local Control" for the quotation.

Keyword: *teacher evaluations*

Access InfoTrac at http://infotrac.cengage.com

colleges of education benefit, because these requirements increase the demand for their services. Teachers' unions promote the requirements for the same reasons that other unions impose certification requirements on their members: to convince customers that the certificate will ensure good service—whether it is relevant or not—and to prevent other people from competing with the union members. As a result, some people who might be excellent teachers never even apply for positions because the cost of certification is too great.

Similarly, centralized textbook selection creates an environment that politicizes textbook choice, creating two problems. First, a teacher, school, or school district cannot use a book not approved for purchase. Second, textbook writers focus on obtaining adoptions in key states. To do so, they focus on satisfying the majority of the textbook committee. An innovative textbook that only a small percentage of the teachers or schools want to use is unlikely to be chosen by a state textbook committee. Therefore, even the small market that might exist for an innovative textbook is foreclosed because public school teachers who want to use it would not be allowed to do so. The statewide textbook committee stifles the innovative book. Consequently, authors of textbooks for primary and secondary schools have little incentive to innovate. In contrast, authors of college textbooks do not have to get a statewide committee to adopt their books; they simply need to convince a sufficient number of college instructors.

The second burden on decision making is the large number of objectives that state politicians and bureaucrats and, to a degree, local bureaucrats impose on principals, teachers, and schools. Academic objectives may include equal opportunity for all students to achieve their potential, or focus on the most talented students, or focus on students with special needs. Nonacademic objectives might include promoting community service, providing sex education, developing a drug-free America, saving the environment, and winning athletic championships.

Evaluation. Just as superintendents and principals are responsible to elected and appointed politicians, teachers are responsible to their supervisors. Once a teacher achieves tenure, however, he or she receives only cursory evaluation from supervisors. Short of moral turpitude, it is unusual for a teacher to be dismissed or even to be reprimanded effectively. This is not because tenure makes it impossible to dismiss a teacher based on performance evaluation, although union protections and tenure do make it costly to do so. A big part of the reason is that, having earned tenure, most teachers are no longer subject to serious evaluation. Teachers' unions aim to ensure that all teachers are treated the same way. For instance, in the typical LSD all teachers with the same college degree, say MS, and the same years of experience receive the same salary. Their performance is irrelevant in their salary determination. Consequently, the supervisors have little incentive to conduct serious evaluations. Evaluation and performance critiques are difficult and can create personal tensions. If they have no effect on salary, it is simply easier to avoid serious evaluations. Without a history of evaluations, it is difficult to document poor performance.

Again this contrasts with some colleges and universities that have meaningful merit evaluation systems. Department heads and deans are willing to put time and effort into evaluation because the evaluations have consequences for salary decisions.

Reward System. In addition to making evaluations irrelevant, the reward system does not encourage excellence. As Adam Smith wrote: "It is in the interest of every man to live as much at his ease as he can; and if his emoluments are to be precisely the same, whether he does, or does not perform some very laborious duty, it is certainly in his interest, at least as interest is vulgarly understood, either to neglect it altogether, or if he is subject to some authority which will not suffer him to do this, to perform it in as careless and slovenly manner as that authority will permit."[16]

Given that teachers operate in a system where city hall and state government interfere with their professional judgment and impose numerous mandates that require them to spend time on activities of little academic merit, it is surprising how effective most teachers are in making achievement easier for students—that is, how well teachers teach. In fact, most teachers perform much better than the Adam Smith quotation implies that they would. The reason, of course, is that many teachers teach because they want to help students achieve, but they perform well *in spite of* the organizational structure rather than because of it. Moreover, some teachers are demoralized because their excellent performance is not rewarded in systematic ways.

INFOTRAC
College Edition

Keywords: *merit* and *pay* and *teachers*

Access InfoTrac at http://infotrac.cengage.com

Because public school teachers lack the right to make certain education decisions and because the organization's objectives go beyond student learning, they may with justification doubt that they should be evaluated and rewarded on the basis of their students' academic progress.

The organization of schools violates the three organizing principles: By not assigning the teachers appropriate decision rights, the organization is unable to use teachers' specific knowledge about learning. No simple way exists for parents and students to evaluate teachers. And because rewards are the same for all teachers regardless of their performance, spending resources on evaluation would be in vain.

GOVERNMENT POLICY

The federal government provides less than 10 percent of the public education budget. Its major effects on public education policy in the United States in the twentieth century were on school desegregation and education for the disabled. In both instances, states had failed to provide equal treatment for their citizens. The major failure today of state public school systems, from the perspective of equal opportunity, is the failure to uniformly provide decent education to children in poverty areas—the inner city, rural poverty areas, and on Native American reservations. At least three policy approaches are actively promoted. One approach is to spend more per pupil. The other approaches rely on improved efficiency to improve results, although they too could accommodate additional spending.

The spend-more approach, which might take "Stay the course" as its motto, does not appear promising. As the initial analysis in this chapter showed, increases in real spending per pupil over the last 35 years have been large, and the results in terms of achievement have been minimal.

No Child Left Behind is an accountability approach that might take as its motto "Improve or else." It assumes that central planners or policy makers can establish goals, require testing, and develop pedagogy for schools to achieve better results. It provides some additional resources for failing schools and ultimately presents them with the stark alternative of improvement or closure. It requires that parents be given the option and the resources to move their children to other schools. No Child Left Behind had bipartisan support when it was passed. It has since become politically charged, with the opposition asserting that the administration and Congress have not supplied the resources necessary to implement the act.

[16]Adam Smith, *An Inquiry into the Nature and Causes of the Wealth of Nations*, bk. 2 (1776; 1979; reprint, Indianapolis: Liberty Press, 1981), 760.

The bipartisan support for the act was generated when the choice elements in the original proposal were largely eliminated. Choice, however, is becoming an important part of the policy dialogue. Forty-one states have provided for school choice by creating charter schools. A charter school gets public funding on a per-pupil basis and is exempt from many of the regulations that public school administrators must deal with. With its emphasis on parental choice, the charter school approach is one that relies on market-like mechanisms to improve children's educational experience. About 750,000 students are in charter schools, with another 50,000, or slightly more, attending private schools with vouchers financed either from public education funds or private scholarship funds. In addition, about 1 million children are being home schooled. Choice is at least as significant a policy initiative as No Child Left Behind (NCLB). Its motto might be "Consumer choice."

"Improve or Else"

The Education Commission of the States (ECS) is an organization that provides support to state policymakers and to the public on education policy. It asserts that NCLB has established "improvement of public education" as one of the highest national priorities. In its report to the nation on NCLB, the commission describes the goals of the legislation: "To eliminate gaps in achievement between students who have traditionally performed well in school and those who have not, and ensure all students are proficient in reading and mathematics by the 2013–14 school year; to guarantee every classroom in the nation is staffed by a highly qualified teacher; and to make all schools safer and more productive learning environments."[17] The ECS is tracking the progress that states are making toward achieving these goals with over 2,000 indicators grouped into seven major categories: "standards and assessments, adequate yearly progress, school improvement, supplemental services, safe schools, report cards and teacher quality."[18]

According to ECS, in March 2004 all states were on track to meeting half of the 40 requirements of NCLB, and some states were much farther along. The ECS, however, saw several looming problems:

- Few states have made plans to implement high-quality professional development for all teachers.
- Only 10 states have well-designed plans to ensure that both new and veteran teachers are qualified to teach in their subject areas.
- Fewer than half the states have made progress in making sure that scientifically based technical assistance is provided to low-performing schools.
- Many states do not have in place the technology infrastructure needed to collect, disaggregate, and report data at the school, district, and state levels. NCLB doesn't require the development of statewide data systems but, without them, states will have difficulty meeting a number of the law's requirements.[19]

This is probably enough detail about NCLB to give you the idea that it is an essentially top-down, 10-year plan to improve public education. Its innovations are to require testing of all students, to set performance goals, and to narrow group disparities in academic achievement. By setting performance standards based on testing and holding schools and districts accountable for achieving the standards, NCLB has introduced high-stakes testing for schools and, to a much lesser extent, students. As previously

---

[17]Education Commission of the States, *State Implementation of the No Child Left Behind Act: Respecting Diversity Among States*, ECS Report to the Nation (July 2004): iv.

[18]Ibid.

[19]Ibid., v.

discussed, high-stakes testing that holds students accountable can be expected to induce students to achieve more, but focusing the stakes on teachers and schools is designed to induce teachers and schools to improve students' performance. It is an indirect approach that takes the current organization of public schools as a given and attempts to get better results.

Evidence is accumulating that states with high-stakes accountability systems for public school systems have achieved some improvement in results on standardized tests. Martin Carnoy and Susanna Loeb measured student and school accountability by state and used this measure in an analysis of the factors affecting improvement in standardized test scores for eighth-grade math. Taking into account expenditures per pupil, enrollment, and other variables, they found that increases in their accountability measure were associated with increases in math achievement. Margaret Raymond and Eric Hanushek measure only state accountability and use it in a study that compares fourth-grade standardized test scores in 1996 with eighth-grade scores in 2000. The idea is to see how the same group of students does after four years. They found that students in states with greater school accountability showed more improvement than in states with less. They also found that students in states that simply provided school report cards showed essentially the same improvement as those in states with strong accountability systems.[20]

NCLB narrows the objectives of public education to some extent by focusing educators' efforts on core academic achievement. Schools that are not meeting certain objectives must refocus, or eventually they will suffer serious consequences. As we discussed in our analysis of high-stakes testing for student accountability, it is important that these objectives be appropriately chosen and that tests meet certain criteria. Developing and grading such tests is costly. If the tests are not carefully designed and administered, however, problems can develop.

At this time, many states have multiple-choice achievement tests. Although such tests have the advantage of being easy to grade, they also are limited in their ability to measure students' analytical knowledge of a field. The tests are also subject to manipulation by the state and by teachers. The greater the stakes for the teacher or the school, the greater the "temptation to skew the reports … 'whether [in the words of the legislative report] by intentionally falsifying data, or simply stretching the rules to create more favorable data.'"[21] Numerous reports exist of teachers, sometimes prompted by school administrators, actually helping students cheat on standardized tests.[22]

Administrators in many school districts stretch the rules on universality, conveniently placing low-performing students in special education categories that exempt them from the test.[23]

In addition to cheating and fudging the data, administrators and teachers distort the curriculum in an attempt to increase the pass rate. In Texas, many schools use a couple of months before the achievement test to drill students on techniques to pass the test. Math and English classes, and sometimes other classes, ignore the normal curriculum and "teach to the test." If the test was less predictable and more analytical, normal teaching practices would "teach to the test" without distorting the curriculum.

---

[20]See Tom Loveless, "Test-Based Accountability: The Promise and the Perils," *Brookings Papers on Education Policy* (2005): 137–156; for a discussion of Martin Carnoy and Susanna Loeb, "Does External Accountability Affect Student Outcomes? A Cross-State Analysis," *Educational Evaluation and Policy Analysis* 24, no. 4 (2003): 305–311; and Eric Hanushek and Margaret Raymond, "High Stakes Research," *Education Next* 3, no. 3 (2003): 48–55.

[21]Peter Schrag, "Too Good to Be True," *American Prospect*, November 30, 2002, 48.

[22]Labi Nadya, "When Teachers Cheat," *Time*, December 20, 1999, 86.

[23]Schrag, "Too Good to Be True," 48.

Keywords: *No Child Left Behind and innovations; No Child Left Behind and testing; No Child Left Behind and progress*

Access InfoTrac at http://infotrac.cengage.com

No Child Left Behind is an experiment to determine whether increased control from Washington and from state departments of education can improve educational outcomes in the United States. Its emphasis on school accountability and increased focus on core academic achievement, both tied to extensive testing, are significant innovations. Its approach adopts and reinforces the current organization of public schools described in the section on Decision Making and Public Schools. One underlying, implicit hypothesis is that public education, in general, must narrow its focus; in effect, the federal government has seized the decision right to establish overall objectives of public education. Another implicit hypothesis is that schools and teachers are not performing well because they are unqualified, technically inept, or not trying. As seen in the ECS concern about looming problems, the NCLB solution is professional development of teachers and making sure that teachers are qualified to teach their subjects. This approach reinforces that top-down approach that SDEs have tried over the years. The NCLB uses punitive measures applied to low-performing schools to provide incentives to individuals for improvement. It does nothing to recognize the specific knowledge that teachers and principals have that could allow them to lower students' cost of achievement.

In an attempt to transfer this specific knowledge to central levels, state capitals, and the U.S. Department of Education, NCLB requires schools to provide detailed information to the states, and the states to Washington. The cost of doing so will be high. As the ECS says regarding looming problems, most states don't have the technology to accumulate and report the necessary information, and in the absence of sophisticated data systems, the states may be unable to meet the reporting requirements. As we discussed in Chapter 2, central planning has costly information requirements.

"Consumer Choice"

Competition among schools and choice for parents provide another approach to public school reform. As we have seen, choice is making inroads into the U.S. education system. Several states and cities, including Florida and Milwaukee, have instituted voucher programs targeted to low-income families. Private organizations are providing scholarships for low-income families to send their children to private schools. Charter schools are flourishing. Home schooling has grown tremendously. Before the charter school movement and home schooling, feasible choice existed only for families that had sufficient resources to make private school practical or to provide sufficient choice of housing location, so that the quality of neighborhood schools could influence residential location.

Evidence from surveys in 1993 and 1999 shows that the parents of most of the students in private schools were "very satisfied" with the schools and their academic standards. In contrast, the parents of less than half of the students who attended assigned public schools were "very satisfied." The surveys showed that parents who had choice among public schools or had chosen schools by their choice of residence were more satisfied than parents whose children attended assigned public schools.

Higher income obviously provides greater opportunity to attend private schools, but it also provides better choice among public schools because it provides greater choice among places to live. About one-half of the students from families with a $30,000 income or less attend assigned public schools based on where their parents reside, which in turn is not chosen based on the local school system. Only 30 percent of students from higher-income families attend assigned public schools.[24]

[24]Data from National Center for Education Statistics at http://NCES.ed.gov/index.html. See *Condition of Education* (various years), *Digest of Education Statistics* (various years), and "Trends in the Use of School Choice: 1993–1999" (2003).

ADDITIONAL INSIGHT

School Choice: A Review of Some Favorable Research

Herbert J. Walberg, in a recent review of the research on the effectiveness of school choice, made the following observations.[a]

- Most studies show that students whose families choose charter schools demonstrate improved performance on tests. Few if any studies find their performance getting worse. Parents are more satisfied with the charter schools. It is notable that the public cost of charter schools per pupil is less than for the regular public schools.
- Many studies show that choice improves performance of regular schools, as would be expected with competition.
- Parents use academic atmosphere as an important factor in choosing a school.
- Student performance is better at private schools, other things equal. A major difference between private schools and public schools is that the former tend to have stronger principals, more decentralized decision making, a greater focus on learning, closer parent-teacher interaction, and, in the former, parents who are dissatisfied move their possibly dissatisfied students to other schools.
- Limited evidence shows that choice serves students with disabilities well. In the choice schools, these students experience much less harassment and many fewer physical assaults.

[a] See Herbert J. Walberg, "Comment," *Brookings Papers on Education Policy* (2005), 156–62.

This information implies that children in higher-income families obtain the "presumably" better education their parents desire. Caroline Hoxby's empirical studies reinforce the point. She concludes, "Parents who have greater choice are more involved in their children's schooling. Parents' influence on school policy, which is greater when choice is greater, will reflect, on average, their stated preferences for tougher curricula and stricter school atmospheres."[25]

Why are parents and students more satisfied if they have choice among schools, such as private or charter schools? To succeed, the teachers in a private or charter school must offer a product parents demand. Because parents are more likely than politicians, education bureaucrats, and teachers to emphasize the well-being of their children, they would choose and evaluate schools that focus on their children's basic education and preparation for life after high school. For some children this would be a college preparatory curriculum; for others, it would be a curriculum focused on desirable vocational education. All graduates would have to meet certain state standards. Competition among schools would lead to a variety of educational programs well suited for their clientele, just as competition among colleges and universities does.

The introduction of competition and choice for K–12 education could be accomplished with a system of vouchers used at existing public schools and independent public schools—charter schools—or at the two types of public schools and at private schools. By allowing parents to spend vouchers and additional money at such schools, consumer evaluation of the schools would work like consumer evaluation of other goods and services. To succeed, schools would have to provide students the educational experience their parents demand. We believe that parents would choose schools on the basis of their reputation in motivating students to succeed academically and in motivating their own

[25] Caroline M. Hoxby, "What Do America's 'Traditional' Forms of School Choice Teach Us about School Choice Reforms?" *FRBNY Economic Policy Review* 4 (March 1998): 56.

INTERNATIONAL PERSPECTIVE

Choice and Sorting

In the United States, we have not had enough experience with empowered school choice to evaluate its likely effect on the sorting of students by family, class, or ability. The available evidence suggests that parents are more satisfied, students are generally safer, and they develop civic virtue, but information about sorting is limited and inconclusive.[a]

The United Kingdom and Sweden provide some information. The United Kingdom has had limited school choice since 1988. Its experience suggests that less sorting by socioeconomic status occurred after the choice had been expanded than before, when choice was restricted by residence. Just as in the United States, in the United Kingdom, the neighborhood school concept implies that upper-income families have choice, whereas lower-income families have less discretion.

In Sweden, families choose among regular (public) schools and independent (essentially charter) schools. Both types are tuition free, and the independent schools get reimbursed on a somewhat lower same scale than the regular schools. The independent schools must meet certain standards and have nondiscriminatory admission policies. The effect of the competition has been to improve achievement. Adverse side effects apparently have not occurred. In particular, low-income families are as likely to send their children to independent schools, as are high-income families. Thus, sorting does not increase. Moreover, the independent schools accept special needs students.[b]

[a] See Patrick J. Wolf, "Comment," *Brookings Papers on Education Policy* (2005), 162–68.

[b] See Herbert J. Walberg, "Comment," *Brookings Papers on Education Policy* (2005), 156–62.

children. Parents have specific knowledge about their children that is invaluable in matching them with appropriate educational programs. Along with the parents, teachers develop specific knowledge about themselves and about their students that allows them to develop effective pedagogic techniques.

With the schools competing for students, their principals would evaluate teachers on their success with students. We have good reason to believe that good teachers make learning easier for many students. Although quantitative measures such as experience and degrees are not particularly useful in identifying good teachers, principals and other teachers can identify them. If the principal is evaluated and rewarded by the ability of her teachers to motivate learning, that is, to teach well, the principal has the incentive to seriously evaluate teachers and use her specific information to identify and reward good teaching.

Some economists have long argued that competition among the providers of education will lead to existing public schools improving their performance.[26] Caroline Hoxby has studied the effects of existing competition (1) among suburban school districts, (2) within school districts, and (3) between private and public schools. She concludes that: "Public schools can and do react to competition by improving the schooling they offer and by reducing costs. They are not passive organizations that allow their students and budgets to be withdrawn without responding. Realistic increases in the competition they face produce significant improvements in students' test scores, educational attainment, and wages."[27]

The inefficiency of the U.S. public school system is, we argue, largely a result of its organization and lack of competition. Like other SOEs, it lacks clearly specified objectives

[26] Milton Friedman, Chapter 6, The Role of Government in Education, in *Capitalism and Freedom* (Chicago: University of Chicago Press, 1962).

[27] Hoxby, "What Do America's 'Traditional' Forms of School Choice Teach Us about School Choice Reforms?" 55.

and it is much too centralized. Because the system is a public system with multiple and sometimes conflicting objectives, it is difficult for the decision makers to know and take the appropriate action. People who have much specific knowledge about particular students and the operation of a particular school—parents, teachers, and principals—lack sufficient authority to make decisions that they are best able to make. The people with the greatest stake in the operation of the public school system—students and parents—rarely have a meaningful role in its evaluation. The teachers and principals who, along with students, make up the system can discern no clear relationship between their performance and their rewards. When administrators and teachers see a link between performance and rewards, they respond. Quoting Hoxby again, "[P]ublic schools' responses do not depend just on whether they lose students; the responses also depend on the fiscal rewards and penalties attached to gaining or losing students. When competition has little fiscal implication, a public school is less likely to react. When cost competition is weakened by a large price wedge (like that between public and private schools), public schools reduce costs less than they do when cost competition is on a more level playing field (like that between two similar public school districts)."[28]

"IMPROVE OR ELSE" AND "CONSUMER CHOICE"

Keywords: *education and innovations*

Access InfoTrac at http://infotrac.cengage.com

A narrow economic policy might be to provide all students with educational vouchers and let them spend these at the school of their choice. The vouchers, money that can be used only for education, could be varied in size by family income to narrow opportunity gaps. The schools could be private or public, and profit or nonprofit. The curriculum could be subject to certain state requirements and accountability through testing could be imposed.

Some economists believe that this approach would lead to efficiency and innovation in education and provide the United States with a superb primary and secondary education industry much like the superb U.S. college education industry. This approach, however, does not appear feasible at this time. Feasible policies appear to be accountability (NCLB) and expanded choice.

Keyword: *educational vouchers*

Access InfoTrac at http://infotrac.cengage.com

Although an economic approach to the organization of the educational system might call for privatization, in the absence of privatization this approach does not necessarily dictate either "Improve or else" or "Consumer choice." One can argue that the assignment of decision rights about basic education—and perhaps the study of national history and political institutions—is appropriate at the state or national level because of the external effects of education. The centralized decision maker(s) could use testing to evaluate whether schools are meeting these objectives. Finally, the national or state decision maker(s) could certify schools that meet the standards and prohibit uncertified schools from operating.

Keywords: *charter schools and testing*

Access InfoTrac at http://infotrac.cengage.com

Parents and students could then have extensive choice among available schools for their children. Market-like forces work to improve the performance of all schools as they attempt to attract students. It is important to remember that these market-like forces already provide many higher-income families with choice of schools for their children, either through private schools or residential choice. To narrow the equal opportunity gap, lower-income families could receive targeted vouchers that could be spent on education at the discretion of the family. Joseph P. Viteritti implies that commutative and distributive justice require no less: "It is what parents think that will matter. Children will attend a particular school because their parents believe it to be the one that best accommodates their particular wants

[28]Ibid.

and needs—be it a district, charter, independent, or religious school. These choices will not be limited to families that are well off. The next generation of schooling will promote both liberty and equality."[29]

Summary

Critics of public education in the United States complain that U.S. high school graduates perform less well than high school graduates in other countries with similar standards of living. The United States spends more per pupil on education than almost any other country, but even as expenditures have increased, performance on math and science achievement tests, if anything, has declined.

Thomas Jefferson was an early proponent of universal education. He believed that such education is necessary to preserve liberty and to improve living standards. Given the current level of education in the United States, it is possible that external benefits of K–12 education are zero, suggesting that government subsidization is unnecessary for economic efficiency. Equal opportunity, however, provides a firmer basis for government subsidy than does economic efficiency.

If the critics are justified in their concern about the relatively poor performance of U.S. high school graduates, the solution to the poor performance problem requires that we understand the determinants of student achievement. Imagine that students and their parents choose an achievement level based on the marginal benefit and marginal cost of achievement to them. This perspective suggests that achievement will increase if the perceived marginal benefit increases or the perceived marginal cost decreases. The widespread adoption of high-stakes testing could increase marginal benefit. High-stakes testing implies universal achievement tests that certify that an individual has a certain level of understanding about the subjects tested. To set high stakes, these tests must have consequences, such as opportunities for employment and for higher education.

In this context, schools and teachers facilitate learning by reducing the marginal cost of achievement. For an organization or an economy to perform well, decisions must be made by people with appropriate information. Appropriate information is often specific information, which means that it is costly to transmit. Consequently, to use specific information effectively, the people who develop it must use it. In a market, decision-making rights are assigned to people based on their willingness to pay for them. If a person has specific information that makes a certain decision right valuable, that person can purchase the right. Markets automatically evaluate these decisions, using profit as a criterion, and they automatically reward good decisions with the profit.

Like any other organization, managers of a school system must decide who makes decisions, how the decisions are evaluated, and how they are rewarded. State departments of education often control decision rights that may more appropriately be assigned to principals and teachers at local schools. By centralizing decision rights, the state ignores much specific information held by principals and teachers. As a political organization, the public education system responds to politicians and bureaucrats, and to that extent it is less responsive to students and parents. The centralization of decisions made at the state level and in large local school districts combined with teachers' unions makes it difficult to evaluate local decision makers—teachers and principals—and to reward their performance.

No Child Left Behind basically accepts this public school organization and attempts to work with it by making two types of changes. One, it narrows the focus of public education to emphasize goals established in Washington. The two goals that have received emphasis are to improve student achievement in core academic subjects and to narrow the learning gap between and among different ethnic groups. Two, it requires extensive testing with high stakes for schools.

Choice is another policy being adopted. Choice relies upon parents and at some point the students themselves to evaluate a school's performance, and it empowers the decision makers to select other schools. Some school districts' clientele—parents and students—currently have little opportunity or incentive to evaluate the district's performance because they are trapped in the district. Higher-income families have a greater incentive to evaluate the district's performance because they have greater flexibility about where they live, and for them

[29]Joseph P. Viteritti, "School Choice: How an Abstract Idea Became a Political Reality," *Brookings Papers on Education Policy* (2005), 137–156.

private schools are more practical. Consequently, suburban schools and private schools, which are subject to competition, do a better job of satisfying their clientele, the parents and students. This "consumer choice" relies upon parents and children contributing an important element to the evaluation of schools.

Key Terms

commutative justice
economic approach to organization
distributive justice
high-stakes testing
general knowledge
specific knowledge

Review Questions

1. What does the chapter identify as the problem or problems with U.S. public schools?
2. The chapter discusses two possible rationales for government support of education. What are they? Evaluate them.
3. The model of academic achievement presented in this chapter suggests that high school and college students choose a level of academic achievement that is a compromise between achievement and other goals. For what other goals have you sacrificed a small amount of academic achievement? What changes would lead you to place a higher value on academic achievement?
4. What are the four characteristics of high-stakes testing, and why is each characteristic important?
5. Suppose high-stakes testing results in greater achievement. If so, does that mean that it is the preferred education reform?
6. Some states require students to take additional mathematics and science courses. Will this lead to U.S. students performing at the same level as students in other countries? Why or why not?
7. Which of the following is specific knowledge and which is general knowledge and why?
   a. the distance to Washington, D.C.
   b. the ability to ride a bicycle
   c. the U.S. Bill of Rights
   d. the ability to read a map
   e. the way to win at poker
   f. the plot of *Romeo and Juliet*
8. This chapter suggests that giving parents more control over their children's education would be to the children's advantage. Do you agree? If not, why not? If so, does this imply that home schooling is a method of education superior to education in a school system? Explain.
9. Specific knowledge of profitable opportunities is scattered throughout the economy or throughout a business firm. How does a market economy make use of specific information? How does a business firm managed from the top down make use of specific information?
10. What are the three elements of an economic approach to organization?
11. Think of your introductory economics class as an organization. Suppose the professor's objective is to have the highest average score on a standardized test of any introductory economics class of about the same size and composed of similar students. Who has the relevant decision rights in the class? What are the roles of evaluation and rewards in attempting to achieve the objective?
12. Compare and contrast the approach to education reform implicit in No Child Left Behind and in charter schools.

Web Sites

- Education Week on the Web.
  Online newspaper covering hot topics in education in the U.S. and internationally. Pulls stories from top U.S. newspapers in the daily news section. Also has special reports on issues such as charter schools, school choice, and technology in the classroom—**http://www.edweek.org/**
- OECD Program for International Student Assessment (PISA).
  Web site for a new international test to compare students across industrialized countries—**http://www.pisa.oecd.org/**
- U.S. Department of Education—Research and Stats.

Source for U.S. government reports and evaluations of education in the U.S.—**http://nces.ed.gov/quicktables/**

- National Education Association.
A good source for ideas about improving education by providing more resources—"Stay the course"—**http://www.nea.org**
- Center for Education Reform and the Citizen's Guide to Education Reform: School Choices.
Sites that support reform—**http://www.edreform.com/** and **http://www.schoolchoices.org/**

CHAPTER **11**

Poverty: Old and New Approaches to a Persistent Problem

OUTLINE

The Scope of the Problem

Antipoverty Effectiveness of Government Transfers

Income-Tested Transfers and Income from Work

Making Work Pay

Making Fathers Pay

In 1962, Michael Harrington's book *The Other America* was published. The "other Americans" were the poor who lived in a land of plenty, primarily out of sight and out of mind. Harrington's work stirred the conscience of many Americans, including President John F. Kennedy, who directed his Council of Economic Advisers to study the problem. After Kennedy's assassination, President Lyndon Johnson embraced the issue and, in his State of the Union Address in 1964, declared "war" on poverty.

In the next decade, the federal government introduced new antipoverty programs and expanded old programs. According to the federal government's official measure, the U.S. poverty rate fell from 17.3 percent in 1965 to 11.1 percent in 1973, and government initiatives have been credited with much of this success. The successes of this decade were short-lived, however. The poverty rate started to grow in 1974 and has remained above the 1973 level ever since. It did fall steadily from 1992 to 2000, reaching 11.3 percent in 2000—just a little above the 1973 level—but it increased thereafter, reaching 12.7 percent by 2007.

Some interpret this as a sign that we are losing the war on poverty, although they do not necessarily agree on the causes of our failure. Some attribute it to cutbacks in government assistance to the poor. Others argue that this assistance is the wrong kind or is focused on the wrong people. Still others contend that government assistance actually increases the poverty rate by inducing recipients to work less. Finally, some claim that the official poverty data overstate the poverty problem, and that more accurate measures actually show that we have come closer to winning the war than is commonly acknowledged.

There is, in short, no universal agreement among economists about the extent or causes of poverty in the United States. Not surprisingly, they also disagree about what we should do to reduce poverty further. This accounts, perhaps, for the wide variety of approaches to solving the poverty problem in the United States. Some are old and time-tested, some are new and have yet to pass the test of time. This chapter is designed to provide you with a primer on what has been attempted, what is currently being done, and what might be done next.

THE SCOPE OF THE PROBLEM

Poor person– A person who lives in a family with money income below the poverty threshold.

Official poverty threshold– The annual cost of a nutritionally adequate diet multiplied by three.

Individuals are poor whenever their resources are insufficient to provide what society considers an acceptable minimum standard of living. We have, however, many possible definitions of resources and acceptable minimum standards of living. Thus, we have many possible measures of poverty. The most frequently cited measure is the official poverty measure. According to this measure, a **poor person** is one who lives in a family with money income below the official poverty threshold. The **official poverty threshold** is the annual cost of a nutritionally adequate diet multiplied by three. This multiplier is based on the idea that the poor should not have to spend more than one-third of their income for food—the proportion that they did spend for food when the official poverty measure was developed in the early 1960s.

The government adjusts the poverty threshold each year for changes in the Consumer Price Index. The poverty threshold also increases (though not uniformly) as family size increases. In 1959, the official poverty threshold for a family of four was $2,973. To compensate for price increases between 1959 and 2004, the government increased this threshold from $2,973 to $19,307. In 2007, the poverty threshold ranged from $10,590 for a single individual to $42,739 for a family of nine or more.

Money income– Measure of income used to determine the official poverty rate; includes earnings (before taxes), interest, dividends, and private and government cash transfers, such as alimony and child support payments, Social Security benefits, unemployment benefits, and payments from the Temporary Assistance to Needy Families program.

The other half of the official measure of poverty—resources available—is the gross (before tax) money income reported to the Census Bureau in its periodic surveys of income. **Money income** includes earnings before taxes, interest, dividends, and private and government cash transfers, such as alimony and child support payments, Social Security benefits, unemployment benefits, and payments from the Temporary Assistance to Needy Families (formerly Aid to Families with Dependent Children) program. If a family's money income is less than its relevant poverty threshold, all members of that family are counted as poor.

Figure 11.1 shows the number of people in poverty each year from 1959 through 2007, according to the official measure. Nearly 40 million people were poor in 1959. The number of poor people declined significantly from 1959 to 1969 to 24 million and remained around 25 million until 1978. From 1979 to 1993, the number of poor people trended generally upward, nearly reaching the 40 million mark again at the end of this period. After 1993 the poverty population plummeted, reaching a low of 31 million in 2000. Then the number of poor people rose again, reaching to over 37 million by 2007.

Poverty rate– The number of poor people divided by the U.S. population.

The number of poor people divided by the U.S. population yields the **poverty rate**. Figure 11.2 illustrates how the poverty rate has behaved from 1959 to 2004. The trend in the poverty rate is similar to the trend in the poverty population from 1959 to 1979. From 1980 through 1993, the poverty rate varied between 12.8 and 15.2 percent, averaging

Figure 11.1 Number of People In Poverty, 1959–2007

The number of people in poverty in the United States, according to the official measure of poverty, can be described as a series of trends: a rapid decline in the 1960s, followed by stability in the 1970s, a significant increase in the early 1980s, a small decline in the last half of the 1980s, a rapid increase in the early 1990s, a large decrease from 1993–2000, and a large increase since then.

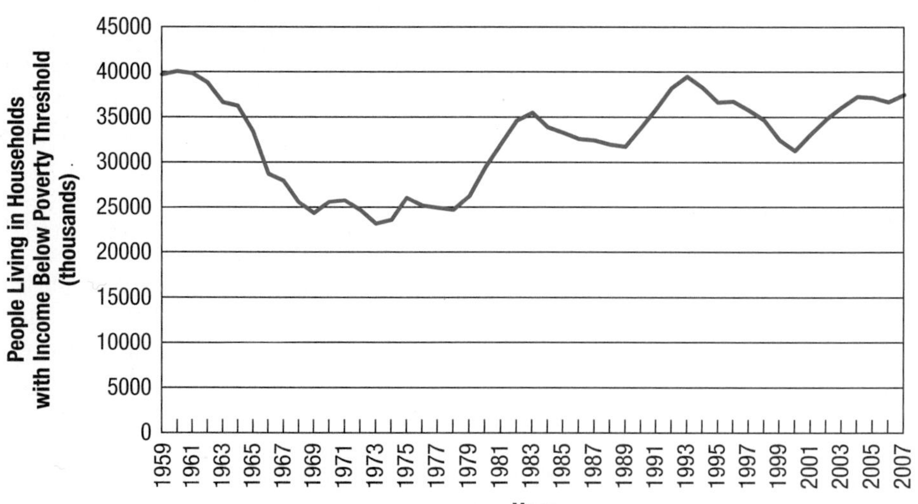

Figure 11.2 Official Poverty Rate, 1959–2007
The official poverty rate fell rapidly from 1959 to 1973. It has never been as low as it was in 1973, although it came close in 2000. It was at about the same level in 2004 as it was in 1989.

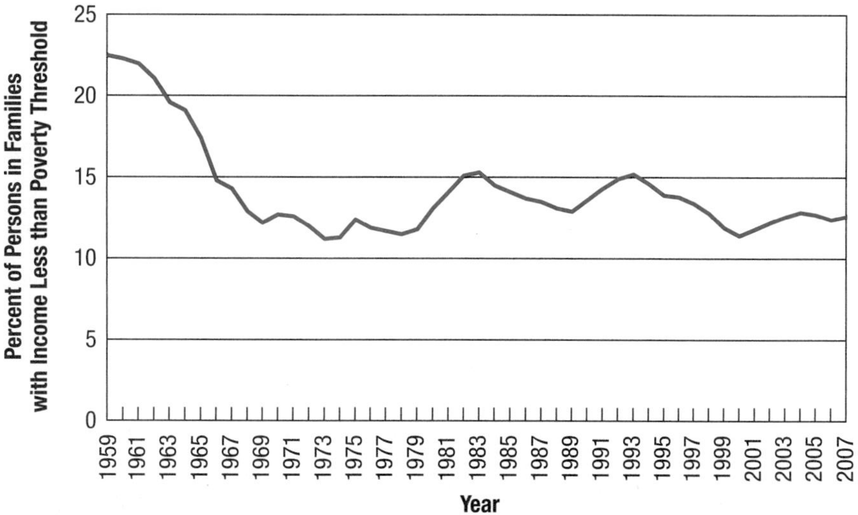

14.0 percent. It fell to 11.3 percent in 2000 and increased to 12.5 percent in 2007. The poverty rate is now slightly below where it was 15 years ago. Some would interpret this as lack of progress in solving the poverty problem. Others would cite the fact that the U.S. population has grown by over 120 million people since 1959 (from 178 million to 300 million) and argue that we have done a remarkable job in holding the line on poverty.

The biggest success story has been the reduction in the poverty rate for people age 65 and older, as illustrated in Figure 11.3. In 1967, the poverty rate for the aged was more

Figure 11.3 Poverty Rate, all Ages and 65 Years And Over, 1966–2007
Thirty-five years ago, the poverty rate for the elderly was more than twice as high as the poverty rate averaged over people of all ages (the official poverty rate). By 1982, the elderly poverty rate had fallen below the all-ages poverty rate, where it has remained ever since.

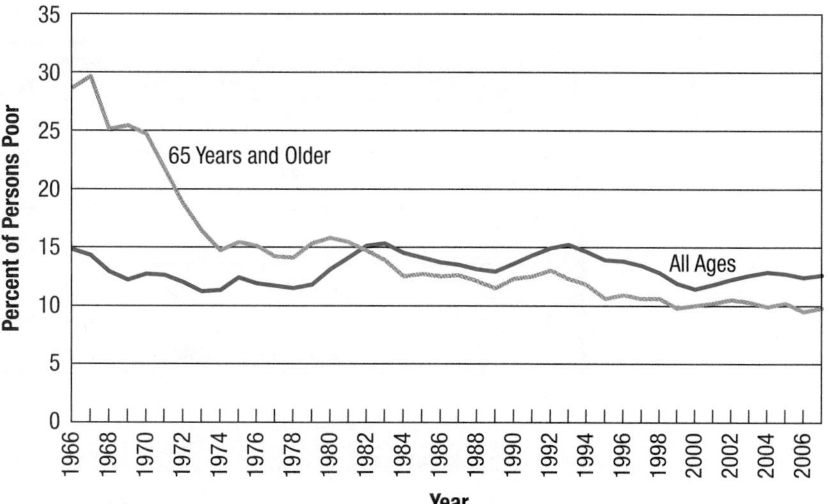

Figure 11.4 **Poverty Rate, Persons Living in Female-Headed Households, 1959–2007**
The poverty rate for people living in female-headed families fell from 50 percent in 1959 to less than 30 percent in 2001. It was slightly above the 30 percent mark again in 2004.

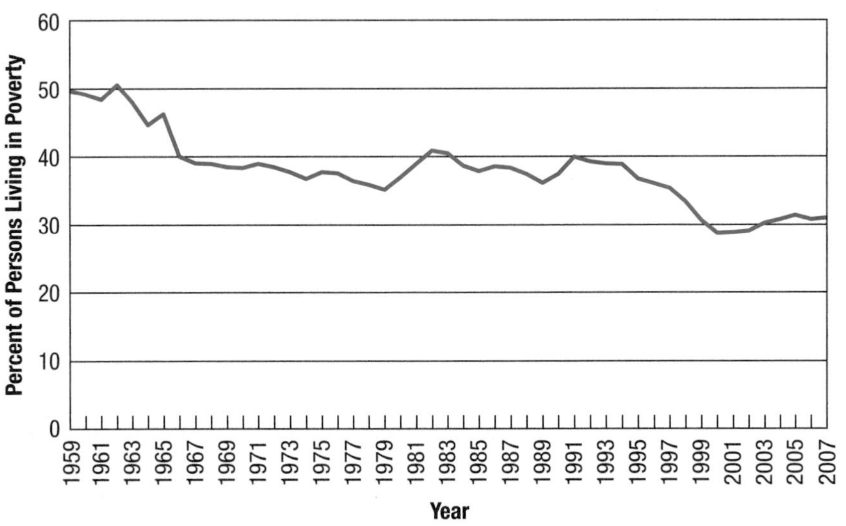

Keywords: *poverty in the United States, historical poverty data, poverty trends*

Access InfoTrac at http://infotrac.cengage.com

than twice that of the all-ages poverty rate (the same measure as the official poverty rate). By 1982, however, the poverty rate for the aged had fallen below the all-ages poverty rate, where it has remained ever since.

There has also been a significant reduction in the poverty rate for persons living in female-headed families, as illustrated in Figure 11.4. Progress here has been concentrated in two time periods: 1959–1979 and 1991–2001. Racial minorities have also fared relatively well in the last decade, as illustrated in Figure 11.5.

Figure 11.5 **Poverty Rates by Race, 1973–2007**
The poverty rates for people living in black and Hispanic households fell both absolutely and relative to the poverty rate in white, non-Hispanic families in the 1990s.

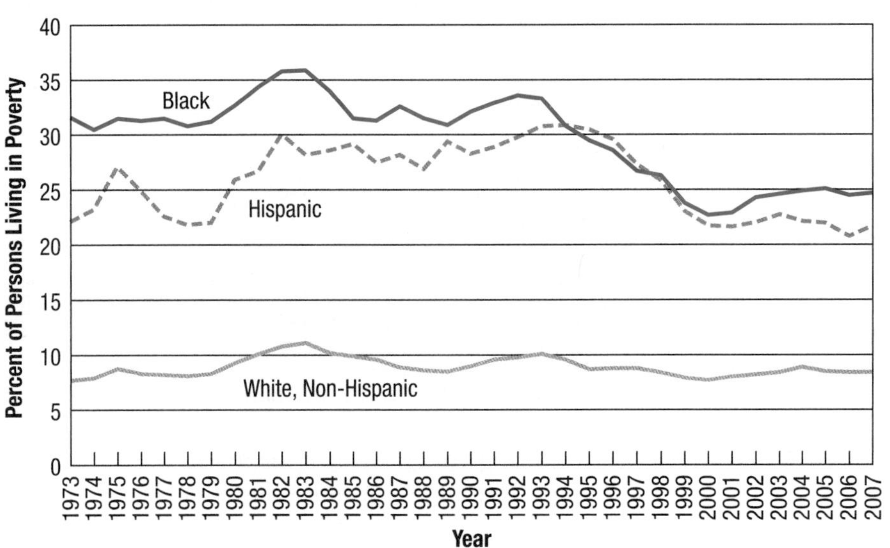

ANTIPOVERTY EFFECTIVENESS OF GOVERNMENT TRANSFERS

Transfer–
Cash, goods, or services paid for by taxpayers and provided to beneficiaries of government programs free of charge.

The official poverty rate reflects the number of people who are poor *after* they receive various government cash transfers. As we will see, government cash transfers significantly reduce the number of people who are poor according to the official measure of poverty. The actual poverty rate is even lower than the official rate, however, if the value of various government noncash transfers is added to the measure of income that is used to determine the official poverty rate.

Table 11.1 provides a list of the principal government income-tested expenditures or aid in 2002. These expenditures are also commonly referred to as **transfers**. An **income-tested**

TABLE 11.1 FEDERAL AND STATE AND LOCAL GOVERNMENT INCOME-TESTED BENEFIT PROGRAMS, FISCAL YEAR 2002 ($ MILLIONS)

Program	$ Millions
Medical Aid	**282,468**
Medicaid	258,216
Other Medical Aid	24,252
Cash Aid	**102,157**
Supplemental Security Income	38,522
Earned Income Tax Credit (EITC)	27,830
Temporary Assistance for Needy Families (TANF)	13,035
Other Cash Aid	22,770
Food Aid	**39,306**
Food Stamps	24,054
Other Food Aid	15,252
Housing Aid	**35,566**
Section 8 Low-Income Housing Assistance	18,499
Low-Rent Public Housing	8,213
Other Housing Aid	8,854
Education Aid	**30,484**
Federal Pell Grants	11,364
Head Start	8,172
Subsidized Stafford and Stafford/Ford Loans	7,523
Other Education Aid	3,425
Other Services	**22,215**
Child Care	10,911
TANF Services	6,147
Other	5,157
Jobs and Training Aid	**7,352**
TANF Work Activities	2,272
Job Corps	1,532
Other Jobs and Training Aid	3,548
Energy Aid	**2,152**
Total Federal, State and Local Government Aid	**521,700**
Total Cash Aid	102,157
Total Noncash Aid	419,543

Source: Appendix K-Spending for Income-Tested Benefits, Fiscal Years, 1968–2002, *Green Book: Background Material and Data on Programs Within the Jurisdiction of the House Committee on Ways and Means* (2004). Available at http://www.gpoaccess.gov/wmprints/green/

Figure 11.6 **Pre-Transfer and Official Poverty, 1979–2007**
This figure compares the official poverty rate with the pre-transfer poverty rate. It indicates that the poverty rate would be 6 to 7 percentage points higher in the absence of government cash transfers.

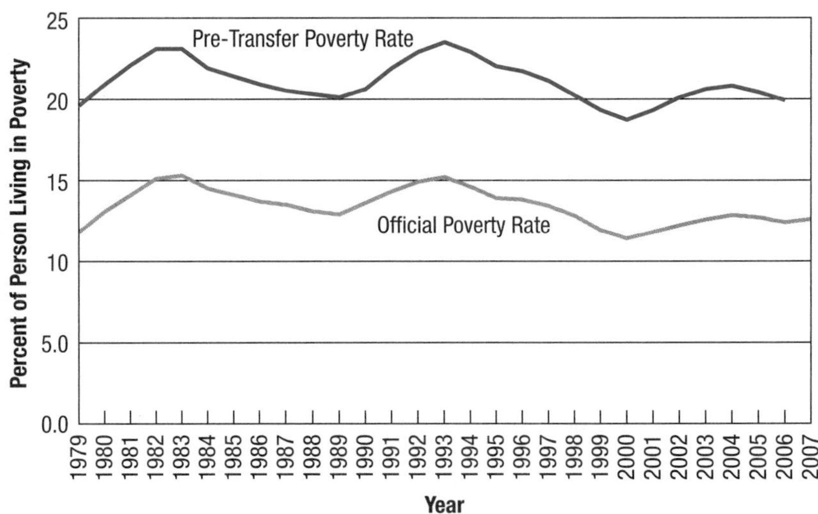

Income-tested transfer–
A transfer, the amount of which falls as a beneficiary's income increases (also called a means-tested transfer).

Cash transfer–
A transfer in the form of cash.

Noncash transfer–
A transfer in the form of goods or services.

Pre-transfer poverty rate–
An estimate of the poverty rate without the income provided by government cash transfers.

transfer (also called a means-tested transfer) is one that decreases as income increases. About a fifth of the 2002 income-tested aid was provided as cash **(cash transfer)**; the remainder was provided as **noncash transfers**. Together, the cash and noncash transfers were about 5 percent of GDP.

The antipoverty effectiveness of government cash transfers can be determined by comparing the pre-transfer poverty rate with the official poverty rate. The **pre-transfer poverty rate** is an estimate by the Census Bureau of what the poverty rate would be without the income provided by cash transfers. Figure 11.6 shows that government cash transfers have been a uniformly important factor in reducing poverty throughout the period 1979–2007 (the data on pre-transfer poverty begin in 1979). In the absence of income from government cash transfers the poverty rate would have averaged 20.5 percent; with the income from government cash transfers, the poverty rate averaged 13.3 percent. Government cash transfers reduced the average poverty rate by 7.2 percent, or nearly 35 percent of the pre-transfer level.

As Table 11.1 indicates, government also transferred a large amount of economic resources in the form of noncash transfers in 2002, especially for medical care, food, and housing. It has, in fact, been allocating significant amounts of money to these purposes for several decades. Government also levies taxes on income received by the poor—the Social Security payroll tax and state and local income taxes. The federal income tax bill for the poor is reduced, however, by the Earned Income Tax Credit (more on this below). That is, taxes, per se, increase the poverty rate, but the EITC reduces the poverty rate. Noncash transfers also reduce the poverty rate.

Figure 11.7 shows that the poverty-reducing effects of noncash transfers and the EITC greatly exceed the poverty-increasing effect of taxes. The net effect of the adjustment for taxes, the EITC, and noncash transfers has been to reduce the poverty rate below the official poverty rate throughout the period 1979–2006 by an average of 2.8 percent per year.

Table 11.2 shows the effects of taxes and transfers on the poverty *population* in 2003. It is clear from this table that government programs have had a significant effect on the poverty population, led by the poverty-reducing power of cash transfers. It is also clear from Table 11.2 that the EITC more than offset the effect of the payroll and income taxes in 2006.

Figure 11.7 Poverty Rate Before Cash Transfers, Official Poverty Rate, and Poverty Rate after Taxes and Cash and Noncash Transfers, 1979–2007

This figure shows that the poverty rate would be 6 to 7 percentage points higher in the absence of government cash transfers, but also that the poverty rate would be 2 to 3 percentage points lower than the official rate if noncash transfers and taxes were included in the measure of household resources.

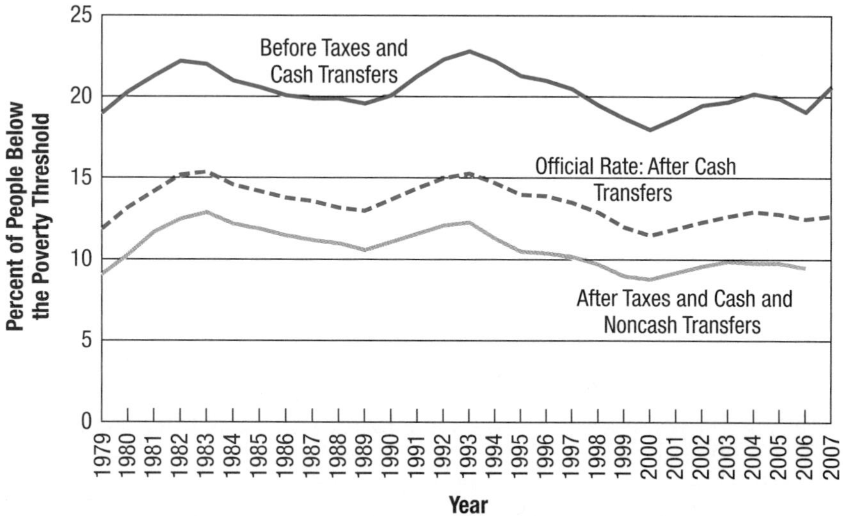

TABLE 11.2 EFFECT OF TAXES AND TRANSFERS ON POVERTY, 2006

	PERSONS POOR (THOUSANDS)	PERSONS REMOVED FROM POVERTY (THOUSANDS)
Before Taxes and Transfers	56,029	
After Cash Transfers	36,460	19,569
After Cash Transfers and Taxes (including EITC)	33,911	2,549
After Cash Transfers, Taxes, and Non-Cash Transfers	27,729	6,182
		28,300

Source: U.S. Census Bureau, *Current Population Survey, 2007 Annual Social and Economic Supplement.*

Some interpret the poverty rate after adjustments for all transfers and taxes as evidence that the poverty problem has been solved, or at least that it is not as bad as the official measure indicates. Others do not, citing the relatively high poverty rates that still prevail in female-headed, black, and Hispanic families. Still others argue that we have not solved the poverty problem as long as we have a fifth of the population living in pre-transfer poverty. They believe that we have failed to provide a meaningful solution to poverty to the degree that people live in families where the adults are unable to earn enough money to escape poverty without government transfers.

Keywords: *pre-transfer poverty, post-transfer poverty, government transfers and poverty*

Access InfoTrac at http://infotrac.cengage.com

INCOME-TESTED TRANSFERS AND INCOME FROM WORK

A thorough examination of why the pre-transfer poverty rate hovers near 20 percent of the population is well beyond the scope of this book. Some economists argue that part of the problem lies, however, with government transfers themselves. On the one hand, they provide the means to escape poverty. On the other hand, they provide incentives to the poor to do less to earn their own way out of poverty. This is especially true of the income-tested transfers, those in which the transfer falls as a recipient's income increases.

As illustrated by Table 11.1, a working poor adult is potentially eligible for a package of income-tested transfers, including TANF, Food Stamps, the EITC, Medicaid, and housing assistance. We will focus on the benefits from TANF, Food Stamps, and the EITC in this section because they are widely available as a package. Benefits from housing assistance also vary inversely with income, but only about 20 percent of poor families receive housing assistance. Benefits from Medicaid are extremely important to the poor, but they do not vary inversely with income.

Keywords: *Food Stamps, Food Stamp Program*

Access InfoTrac at http://infotrac.cengage.com

Food Stamps

The Food Stamp Program (FSP) helps people buy food. To be eligible, gross household income cannot exceed 130 percent of the relevant poverty line for the particular household. Most FSP beneficiaries are provided debit cards that they can use when they purchase food.

ADDITIONAL INSIGHT

The Tide Has Risen, but Most Boats Have Not

Real national output in the United States has grown dramatically since the Johnson administration launched the "war on poverty" in 1965, averaging nearly 2.8 percent per year. The nation's distribution of income has become significantly more unequal, however. For example, the share of total money income received by the richest quintile has increased from 43.8 percent to more than 49 percent, while the share going to every other quintile has fallen. To describe it metaphorically, the tide has risen, but most boats have not.

A flurry of research in recent years has focused on the subject of growing income inequality. Much of it concerns the nation's labor markets and the distribution of wages. According to this research, real earnings growth did indeed slow in the 1970s and 1980s relative to earlier decades, and earnings became less equally distributed.[a] One apparent factor in this trend is the economic shift from goods production to services production. Industries involved in producing services typically have paid lower wages and exhibited more variation in their wage structures than industries involved in producing goods. Increased wage inequality has also marked the goods-producing industries, however, so other explanations must be sought.

One of the more popular explanations focuses on the growing gap between the earnings of well-educated and poorly educated workers, presumably spurred by faster-growing demand for skilled workers. The nation's trade deficit also may have added to the problem because a greater proportion of unskilled labor produces this country's imports than its exports. Many of these imports could have been made by low-skilled workers in this country but were made abroad, reducing the demand for unskilled domestic workers.

The declining influence of unions on wage-setting practices also may have played a role. Less-skilled workers have typically received significant wage benefits from union membership. The maturing of the Baby Boom Generation (individuals born in large numbers between 1945 and 1965) probably had some effect, as it flooded the labor market with record numbers of younger entrants, driving down their wages relative to those of older workers.

Finally, some of the increased inequality in family income is undoubtedly caused by changes in family composition. Married-couple households—as a proportion of all households—have fallen dramatically in the last 30 years, to be replaced by single-parent family households and nonfamily households, groups that have traditionally exhibited greater inequality of income than married-couple households.

Economists are carefully examining these and many other possible explanations of the growing inequality in the distribution of income. What they find may matter a great deal in the design of future social and economic policy.

[a]Gary Burtless, "Has Widening Inequality Promoted or Retarded U.S. Growth?" unpublished manuscript, April 22, 2002. Available from The Brookings Institution Web site, http://www.brookings.edu

Gross income (GI)– Income that serves as the basis for determining the benefits from transfer programs; usually income from earnings and nonincome-tested cash transfers, such as Social Security benefits.

Deductible (D)– An allowance for essential needs that is disregarded in determining benefits from a transfer program (also called the *disregard*).

Basic benefit (BB)– Maximum benefit paid by an income-tested transfer program; normally when gross income of the beneficiary is less than or equal to the deductible.

Benefit (B)– Amount received by a beneficiary from an income-tested transfer program.

Benefit reduction rate (BRR)– Ratio of the change in the benefit to the change in gross income in an income-tested transfer program.

Break-even gross income (BEGI)– The gross income at which benefits become zero in an income-tested transfer program.

Target efficiency– The degree to which transfer program benefits are confined to the poor.

The amount of aid they receive depends on their **gross income (GI)**—income from before-tax earnings and non income-tested transfers (such as Social Security benefits)—and their **deductible (D)** expenditures for basic needs that the FSP disregards in determining the amount of Food Stamps that will be provided. If GI is less than or equal to D, the recipient gets the maximum or **basic benefit (BB)**. If GI is greater than D, the **benefit (B)** falls by $1 for each $3 increase in GI. This is a **benefit reduction rate (BRR)** of 0.3, or 30 percent.

When GI is equal to or greater than D, the relationship between these variables can be expressed as Equation 11.1:

$$\mathbf{B = BB - BRR\ (GI - D).} \qquad \mathbf{(11.1)}$$

Table 11.3 illustrates the determination of monthly benefits for a family of three in 2004. The value of the basic benefit that year was $371 a month. The minimum deduction that year was $134 a month. It would have been larger than this for many families, but we assume the minimum in this illustration. Thus, B is $371 for all GI equal to or less than $134.

The rows in the remainder of the table reflect the application of Equation 11.1. Each row is, in fact, set up just like Equation 11.1. For example, the second row of numbers fits the equation, 371 = 371 − .3 (134 − 134), the third row of numbers fits the equation, 341 = 371 − .3 (234 − 134), and so on. For these two rows, and throughout the table, B falls by $30 for every $100 increase in GI.

When gross income reaches $1371.0 benefits are zero. The level of gross income where benefits are equal to zero is called the **break-even gross income**. The break-even gross income (BEGI) can be determined by substituting BEGI for GI and solving Equation 11.1 when B = 0. That is, Equation 11.1 becomes: 0 = BB − BRR (BEGI − D). Solving this equation for BEGI yields:

$$\mathbf{BEGI = [BB + (BRR \times D)]/BRR.} \qquad \mathbf{(11.2)}$$

Using Equation 11.2, BEGI = [371 + (0.3 × 134)]/0.3 = 1371.

The break-even gross income is an indicator of the **target efficiency** of a transfer program—the degree to which program benefits are confined to the poor. In general, the lower the break-even gross income relative to the poverty threshold, the greater the target efficiency. In this case, the monthly break-even gross income of $1,371 is 109 percent

TABLE 11.3 DETERMINATION OF FOOD STAMP BENEFITS, FAMILY OF THREE IN 2004

B (1)	BB (2)	BRR (3)	GI (4)	D (5)
371	371		0	
371	371	0.3	134	134
341	371	0.3	234	134
311	371	0.3	334	134
281	371	0.3	434	134
251	371	0.3	534	134
101	371	0.3	1034	134
0	371	0.3	1371	134

Source: Background Material and Data on Programs Within the Jurisdiction of the House Committee on Ways and Means, Section 15, Other Programs, *Green Book: Background Material and Data on Programs Within the Jurisdiction of the House Committee on Ways and Means (2004)*. Available at http://www.gpoaccess.gov/wmprints/green/

of the 2004 monthly poverty threshold of $1,255 for a family of 3. Thus, some (but not very many) Food Stamps were provided to families that were not poor.

Food Stamps provide both food and income support. The income support aspect of the Food Stamp Program is reflected in its focus on monthly income, facilitating relatively quick changes in benefits when income changes. The food stamp benefit serves as a supplement to a family's other resources, usually Supplemental Security Income, TANF, and earnings. In at least 14 states, TANF families receive more each month in Food Stamps than in TANF cash.

INFOTRAC College Edition

Keywords: *Earned Income Tax Credit, Earned Income Credit*

Access InfoTrac at http://infotrac.cengage.com

Earned Income Tax Credit (EITC)

The federal tax code has provided an earned income tax credit (EITC) since 1975. As the label implies, this is a credit against income tax liability. To be eligible, the taxpayer must have dependents and a relatively low adjusted gross income (AGI—income from all sources less adjustments to income, such as excess employee business expenses and contributions to individual retirement accounts). The credit is refundable; taxpayers may receive a credit even if their tax liability is less than the credit. The refundable portion of the EITC is about 90 percent of the total. Several states have also adopted EITCs.

For a worker with two or more children in 2008, the federal credit was $4,824 for an AGI less than $38,646.

Although it is obvious from the relatively high break-even EITC that the program provides benefits to families that are not poor, about half of the EITC goes to families with incomes below the poverty line.

Temporary Assistance for Needy Families (TANF)

TANF is the nation's safety net program for low-income families. TANF is financed by the federal government through block grants to the states. The amount given to each state is based on how much the state received from the federal Aid to Families with Dependent Children (AFDC) program in the middle 1990s, just before TANF was established as a replacement for AFDC. Each state is allowed to design and implement its own TANF program, including benefit levels and criteria for eligibility.

TANF households are limited to five years of support in a lifetime, but states may impose shorter lifetime limits. TANF recipients are required to engage in work or "work activities," such as job training, looking for work, or schooling. States may refuse to provide additional benefits to families who have additional children while on TANF assistance.

The basic transfer varies widely, ranging from a low of $170 per month for a family of three in Mississippi in 2008 to a high of $923 per month in Alaska. States may disregard some of the income received from work in figuring monthly benefits. They may also treat certain expenses associated with the transition from welfare to work as disregarded income, such as childcare and transportation. The states vary greatly in the level and composition of disregards.

INFOTRAC College Edition

Keyword: *economic aspects of inflation*

Access InfoTrac at http://infotrac.cengage.com

It is difficult to generalize about TANF, given the existence of 51 different programs (the 50 states and the District of Columbia). The Urban Institute completed a study for 12 states, however, that examined how TANF affects household income and the benefit reduction rate as a family of three attempts to move from welfare to work.[1] The 12 states are Alabama, California, Colorado, Florida, Massachusetts, Michigan, Minnesota, Mississippi, New Jersey, New York, Texas, and Washington.

For these 12 states in 1998, the basic benefit (BB) averaged $459 a month, deductions or disregards (D) averaged $200 a month, and the benefit reduction rate (BRR) averaged

[1]Gregory Acs, Norma Coe, Keith Watson, and Robert Lerman, "Does Work Pay? An Analysis of the Work Incentives under TANF," Occasional Paper no. 9 (Urban Institute: July 1998).

TABLE 11.4 DETERMINATION OF TANF BENEFITS, FAMILY OF THREE IN 2002

B (1)	BB (2)	BRR (3)	GI (4)	D (5)
459	459		0	
459	459	0.6	200	200
399	459	0.6	300	200
339	459	0.6	400	200
279	459	0.6	500	200
0	459	0.6	965	200

Source: Authors' calculations based on information in Gregory Acs, Norma Coe, Keith Watson, and Robert Lerman, "Does Work Pay? An Analysis of the Work Incentives under TANF," Occasional Paper no. 9 (Urban Institute: July 1998).

0.60. Table 11.4 shows how TANF benefits fall as gross income rises for these basic parameters of the program. As noted in the bottom line, TANF benefits become zero at a gross income of $965 a month—about 82 percent of the poverty line for a family of three.

The underlying TANF benefit equation in 1998, for GI greater than or equal to D, was

$$\mathbf{B = \$459 - 0.60\,(GI - D).} \tag{11.3}$$

When B = $0 and D = $200, GI = $965.

TANF + Food Stamps + EITC

Given the low break-even gross income for TANF payments, they are not large enough, even in conjunction with earnings, to elevate the typical working welfare family above the poverty line. Working welfare families are also eligible, however, for Food Stamps and the EITC.

Table 11.5 (somewhat dated, but still instructive) shows effective marginal tax rates for a family of three, in which the family head earns progressively more income from work. Three sources of additional income from work are considered: moving from a state of "no work" to 20 hours of work per week at the minimum wage, from 20 hours of work at the minimum wage to 35 hours of work per week at the minimum wage, and from 35 hours per week at the minimum wage to 35 hours per week at $9.00. The effective marginal tax rate is the change in welfare payments and net tax liability resulting from a change in earnings. In this example, welfare payments consist of TANF payments and Food Stamps and net tax liability is taxes paid after the deduction of the EITC.

TABLE 11.5 EFFECTIVE MARGINAL TAX RATES FOR A FAMILY OF THREE RECEIVING TANF, FOOD STAMPS (FS), AND EITC IN MEDIAN STATE, 1997

WAGE-TRANSFER PACKAGE	FROM NO WORK TO 20 HRS @MINIMUM WAGE	FROM 20 HRS TO 35 HRS @MINIMUM WAGE	FROM 35 HRS @MINIMUM WAGE TO 35 HRS @$9 PER HR
TANF, FS, EITC	0.12	0.28	0.65

Source: Table 4 in Gregory Acs, Norma Coe, Keith Watson, and Robert Lerman, "Does Work Pay? An Analysis of the Work Incentives under TANF," Occasional Paper no. 9 (Urban Institute: July 1998).

ADDITIONAL INSIGHT

Welfare Reform: Then and Now

In 1996, President Clinton signed a Republican-sponsored bill, the Personal Responsibility and Work Opportunity Reconciliation Act, called "historic" welfare reform legislation by its proponents. Politics often makes strange bedfellows, but the nation's long record of failure to reduce its welfare rolls bred bipartisan support.

With the stroke of Clinton's pen, the federal government reduced its planned financial commitment to the poor and appeared to bow out of an active role in solving the nation's poverty problem. Planned federal expenditures for various poverty programs were reduced by $56 billion over the next six years. To ensure that this expenditure reduction target was met, the federal programs for Aid to Families with Dependent Children (AFDC) and Job Opportunities and Basic Skills (JOBS) were changed from entitlements to block grants to the states. The resulting program was renamed Temporary Assistance for Needy Families (TANF). Since its inception, each state has received a fixed sum of money each year from the federal government. The amount given to each state reflects what they received under the old AFDC program prior to passage of the 1996 law, and it has come with a lot of strings attached.

In order to continue to receive federal support, each family head on welfare must find work within 2 years or face the loss of benefits. A lifetime limit of 5 years was also imposed on all recipients of welfare benefits. Each state is also subject to new federal regulations as a condition of the federal block grant it receives. Within 5 years, at least 50 percent of a state's welfare recipients must be working at least 30 hours per week. To appreciate the magnitude of this task, consider that in 1995 only 3.7 percent of the women on AFDC worked full-time. In fact, to hit the federal target, the states had to find jobs for more than 2 million people.

By some estimates, up to one-quarter of the nation's welfare recipients are virtually unemployable. Reasons include unwillingness to work, difficulty in retaining jobs, chronic mental or physical problems, lack of basic skills, and serious language deficiencies. The average recipient has the reading and math skills of a typical eighth-grader and 30 percent have basic skills below the minimum of all women in the lowest-skill occupation (household workers).[a]

In spite of these difficulties, Wisconsin, which cut its welfare caseload by 44 percent between 1987 and 1996, showed that the targets can probably be met. But the Wisconsin approach was to spend more, not less, on the poor, investing millions in job training, health benefits, childcare, and other support. The Wisconsin experience indicates, moreover, that preparing a person to leave the dole for good usually takes about 18 months of support—only then do the savings begin. Robert Haveman claims, in fact, that no inexpensive way exists to do the task right. For those who might think otherwise, he asks them to consider all the support that unaided families give their children before they finish their education and embark on the path to a meaningful career.[b]

Not all states wanted to or could afford to take the Wisconsin route. The federal block grants were sufficient for the first 4 years of the program, judging by the fact that not all available federal money was spent. That was not the case in 2001 or 2002, in the wake of a recession and substantial budget difficulties at the state level. Problems in funding TANF appeared, especially in states with relatively high unemployment rates, few welfare recipients currently working, and large immigrant populations. The urge to simply deny welfare benefits may grow on the part of state officials in order to keep from cutting other state programs.

Howard Chernick and Andrew Reschovsky estimated that, over the course of several years, states would respond to the imposition of block grants for welfare by reducing benefit levels by about 20 percent.[c] They expected total welfare spending to decline by more than this as more stringent eligibility constraints and lower benefits reduced the number of beneficiaries. Fortunately, this "race to the bottom" did not occur. Apparently, as long as state economies are doing reasonably well, there is a willingness to provide funds to facilitate the transition from welfare to work. State support for TANF may be in harm's way in a recession, but it should not be assumed that reduced support suggests dissatisfaction with the aims of the 1996 welfare reform law.

---

[a]Robert Haveman, "From Welfare to Work: Problems and Pitfalls," *Focus* 18, no. 1, Special Issue (1996): 21–24.
[b]Ibid
[c]Howard Chernick and Andrew Reschovsky, "State Responses to Block Grants: Will the Social Safety Net Survive?" *Focus* 18, no. 1, Special Issue (1996): 25–29.

Keywords: *TANF and work incentives, EITC and work incentives*

Access InfoTrac at http://infotrac.cengage.com

Workers moving from no work to part-time work at the minimum wage experience a loss in TANF payments and Food Stamps and increased tax liabilities that exceeds the gain in the EITC by 12 cents per dollar of earnings. In the transition from part-time to full-time work at the minimum wage, the loss in TANF and Food Stamps and increased tax liabilities exceeds the gain in EITC by 28 cents per dollar of earnings. In the transition from full-time work at the minimum wage to full-time work at $9 an hour, the net effect is a loss of 65 cents for each additional dollar earned.

These results indicate that the package of benefits working welfare families receive is structured to penalize participants less for working part-time at low wages than for working full-time at higher pay.

This result is not surprising. Throughout the minimum wage earnings range, the BRRs for TANF and Food Stamps are largely offset by deductions for essential needs and the EITC. The increase in earnings from $5.15 an hour (the minimum wage) to $9 an hour places the worker in the range, however, where the EITC begins to decline, reducing its power to offset the BRRs for TANF and Food Stamps.

The bottom line is that the core antipoverty programs probably do not discourage heads of low-income households from working—at least, not at minimum wage jobs. They may, however, discourage them from seeking work at higher pay. Whether the net effect of these incentives increases or decreases poverty in the United States has not yet been determined by empirical studies.

MAKING WORK PAY

AFDC was transformed into TANF in an attempt to increase the degree to which the poor work their way out of poverty by gainful employment. TANF does this largely by requiring single mothers to find jobs and by establishing a lifetime limit on the duration of TANF benefits. This strategy has reduced the TANF rolls. It may, in fact, be a necessary condition for reducing poverty among TANF clients, but it is unlikely to be sufficient, for three important reasons. First, the economy must generate enough jobs for TANF clients; no welfare program can do this. Second, TANF clients appear to need help in order to successfully transition from welfare to work, especially with childcare and medical expenses. Third, the jobs that TANF clients get must pay an adequate wage.

Unemployment Policy

Since the passage of the legislation establishing TANF there has been more than a 25 percent increase in the percentage of single mothers who are working. Proponents of TANF claim this as an accomplishment of TANF. TANF was born, however, in the midst of the longest peacetime economic expansion in the last century so it is arguable whether the precipitating factor behind the rise in employment rates of single mothers was TANF or the economy.

Keywords: *poverty and unemployment*

Access InfoTrac at http://infotrac.cengage.com

One way to analyze the issue is to compare the pre-transfer poverty rate and the unemployment rate. As noted above, the pre-transfer poverty rate is a measure of what the poverty rate would be without government transfers or, alternatively, a measure of the ability of low-income households to escape poverty primarily by working. As indicated in Figure 11.8, the pre-transfer poverty rate has hovered between 19 and 23 percent for the last two decades. As Figure 11.8 also shows, however, the variations that have occurred in the pre-transfer rate virtually mimic the unemployment rate over the same period. This relationship strongly suggests that the ability of the economy to generate jobs is an important determinant of the poverty rate. The persistence of the pre-transfer rate also suggests that the market can solve only *part* of the poverty problem by generating jobs.

Figure 11.8 Pre-Transfer Poverty Rate and Unemployment Rate, 1979–2007
Variations in the pre-transfer poverty rate generally occur at about the same time, in the same direction, and in similar magnitude, as variations in the unemployment rate. This suggests, but does not prove, that the variations in the unemployment rate cause the variations in the pre-transfer poverty rate.

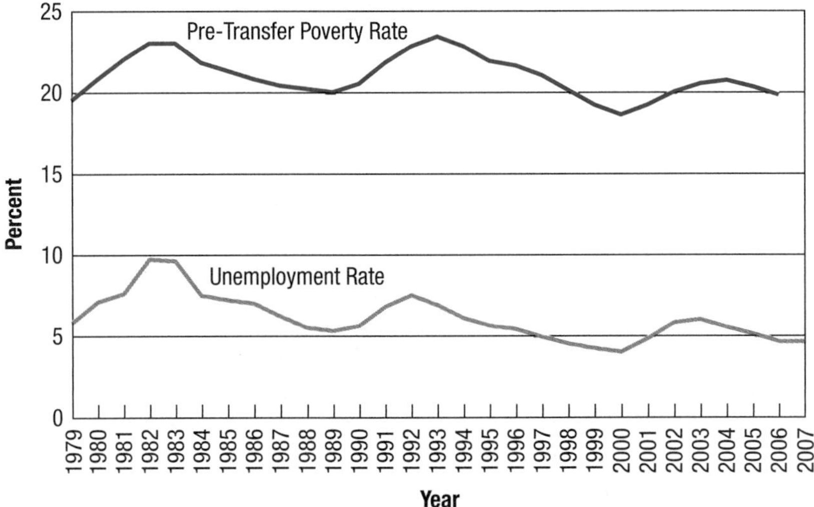

Figure 11.9 shows that variations in the unemployment rate and variations in the poverty rates for selected groups were similar from 1979 to 1993–1994, but that poverty rates for blacks, Hispanics, and female-headed households fell more rapidly than the unemployment rate after 1994. This suggests that something other than the robust performance of the economy was at work, such as the new work requirements imposed by TANF. The reduction in unemployment that occurred in the 1990s began, however,

Figure 11.9 The Unemployment Rate and Poverty Rates for Selected Groups, 1973–2007
Variations in the poverty rate for female-headed families, blacks, and Hispanics tended to mimic variations in the unemployment rate except during the 1990s. The relatively more rapid decline in the poverty rate in this decade for these groups may reflect a generally tighter labor market in that decade, rather than the switch from AFDC to TANF.

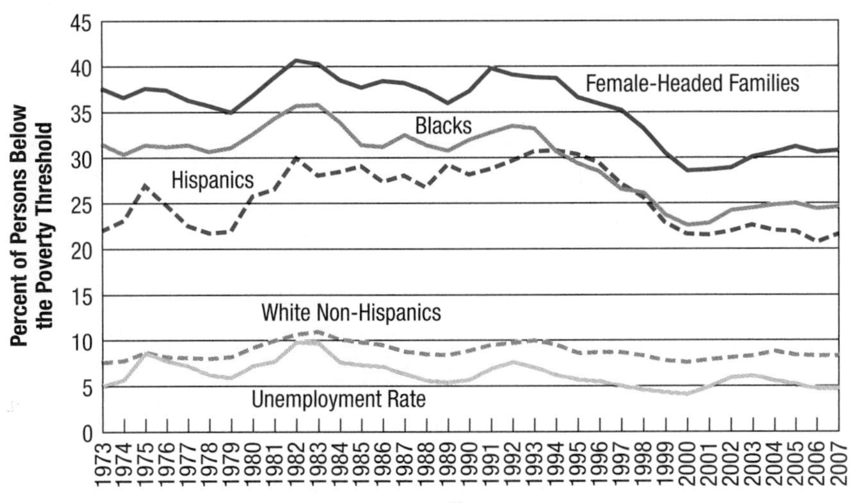

when the economy was already at a lower level of unemployment than it was at the beginning of the fall of the unemployment rate in the 1980s. The fact that labor markets were much tighter in the 1990s than in the 1980s may account for the relatively rapid gains for blacks, Hispanics, and female-headed households.

Researchers will eventually sort out the relative importance of the economic expansion and TANF in explaining the reduction in poverty recorded in the 1990s. In the meantime, it is hard to escape the conclusion that a robust economy is a precondition for the success of government efforts to reduce poverty by increasing income from earnings among low-income families. The macroeconomic policies designed to reduce unemployment that are discussed in Chapter 13 are rarely considered antipoverty tools. Yet they may be vital in any effort to make lasting progress against the poverty of the working poor.

Childcare Assistance

Over 20 percent of the mothers who leave the TANF rolls for work return to TANF within two years. Although they encounter a variety of obstacles while working, two of the more prominent are the costs of childcare and loss of Medicaid benefits.

The lack of affordable childcare can significantly hinder the labor market participation of adults in poor families. Childcare in organized facilities is expensive. In the absence of subsidies, a single mother moving from welfare to work will find that childcare costs eat up a substantial share of her income; thus, childcare costs can reduce her incentive to work.

Both the federal government and state governments have programs that provide some form of childcare assistance. The most prominent of these are the Dependent Care Tax Credit, the Child Care and Development Fund, the Dependent Care Assistance Program, and the Child Tax Credit.

Both the federal government and about half the state governments have a Dependent Care Tax Credit (DCTC) that provides a credit against income tax liability for childcare expenses for working taxpayers. In 2008 eligible expenses for the federal credit are limited to $3,000 for one qualifying child, or $6,000 for two or more qualifying children.

The Child Care and Development Fund (CCDF) is a federal government block grant that provides the states with money to help low-income working families pay for childcare. States use this money, and sometimes some of their own money, to provide subsidies for childcare. Like TANF benefit payments, the amount available and conditions of eligibility vary from state to state.

The Dependent Care Assistance Program (DCAP) is a federal program that allows an employer to provide up to $5,000 in assistance to employees to help them pay certain child and dependent care expenses, childcare included. This assistance is exempt from federal income and payroll taxes. An employer may provide this assistance as part of an employee's salary, or the employee may agree to receive the assistance in lieu of an equivalent amount of salary. Because the benefit of this program is taxes saved, the value of the exemption is greater for taxpayers at higher income levels who pay higher tax rates.

The federal tax code also provides a Child Tax Credit (CTC) of $1,000 per dependent child under age 17 for single taxpayers with income of $75,000 or less. It is phased out above the $75,000 threshold at a rate of 5 percent.

Although these programs reflect something of an awakening to the childcare problem, they have not significantly reduced the difficulty that the poor have in working and paying for childcare at the same time. The DCTC provides virtually no benefits to the poor; less than 1 percent of the total credit goes to families with adjusted gross incomes less than $10,000. It is doubtful that the working poor can afford childcare in the first place.

Moreover, in many poor two-parent families, only one parent works (probably because of high childcare expenses!), making the family ineligible for the credit. To top it off, the DCTC is not generally refundable. The CCDF is better targeted to the poor, but the amount available to a poor family depends on where it lives. DCA has been adopted by only a small percentage of employers and employees. The CTC is available to the working poor, but, by itself, will cover only 10 to 15 percent of the costs of childcare.

Proponents of these approaches to reducing poverty generally argue for an expansion of the amount of money provided the states by the CCDF. They also argue for making the DCTC wholly refundable and adjusting the maximum amount to cover a larger percentage of childcare expenses. Expanding the percentage of childcare expenses covered by the credit, as is often suggested, would largely help the nonpoor and significantly increase program costs. It would be more target-efficient to provide vouchers for childcare services directly to the poor.

Medical Protection

Policy makers have long feared that the potential loss of Medicaid benefits deters families from leaving welfare for work. Accordingly, Congress, under the Family Support Act of 1988, required states to expand Medicaid coverage for up to 12 months for families leaving TANF for work. Under waivers, some states have expanded coverage for up to 24 months.

The law that established TANF broke the direct link between eligibility for cash assistance and Medicaid. Families who leave TANF for work are still eligible, however, to receive 12 months of Transitional Medicaid Assistance (TMA). And once transitional Medicaid benefits are exhausted, Medicaid now provides coverage to all children younger than 6 living in families with incomes below 133 percent of the federal poverty level. If the parent in a family of three worked 35 hours a week and earned $9 per hour, the family's earnings would still fall below 133 percent of the poverty threshold, and any children ages 6 and younger would still be covered by Medicaid. Given this coverage, it is unlikely that Medicaid regulations should deter a parent from moving from no work to at least a part-time job.

Keywords: *childcare and poverty, childcare assistance*

Access InfoTrac at http://infotrac.cengage.com

The bigger problem is that the parent would need to find health insurance for herself before the end of the first year of employment, when TMA runs out. After a year of steady employment she might get employer-provided health insurance or be able to purchase reasonably priced individual coverage. But there are many instances in which these options are not available. There is a need, then, for the expansion of health insurance coverage to adults in low-income families.

Keywords: *TANF and Medicaid*

Access InfoTrac at http://infotrac.cengage.com

Minimum Wage

The working poor are poor partly because their wages are so low. Considerable interest exists, then, in policies that increase the rewards that workers realize from their efforts. The three most-discussed policies are (1) expanding the EITC, (2) raising the minimum wage, and (3) providing wage subsidies. The features of the EITC have been examined previously. Here we concentrate on the minimum wage and wage subsidies.

The federal minimum wage is currently $6.55 per hour. Even full-time work at this wage cannot eliminate poverty. Thus, even though Congress increased the minimum wage in 2008, political pressure for further increases cannot be ruled out.

Although few people—economists included—question the motive for raising the minimum wage, economists note that a higher minimum wage generates additional unemployment. Empirical studies show that the minimum wage increases unemployment primarily in low-wage industries and among teenagers. Apparently, no studies have discovered a significant effect on the full-time working poor. Nevertheless, their employment prospects may be adversely affected because the working poor are concentrated in low-wage industries.

A further difficulty with a higher minimum wage is its target inefficiency. A policy is target-inefficient when a large share of the benefits it provides is distributed to individuals other than those whom the policy is designed to assist. Of the 3.9 million workers who earned the minimum wage when it was $3.35 per hour, less than 10 percent were household heads of poor families. A further increase in the minimum wage would probably go largely to nonpoor individuals as well.

Wage Subsidies

Wage subsidy– Subsidy paid to an employer equal to a percentage of the difference between a designated maximum wage and a worker's wage.

In a program of wage subsidies, low-wage workers would receive a subsidy for each hour worked. The **wage subsidy** would equal some percentage of the difference between a designated maximum wage and the worker's wage. To illustrate, suppose that the designated maximum wage is $10 per hour and the subsidy percentage is 50 percent. Someone earning a wage of $6.55 per hour would receive a wage subsidy of $1.73 per hour [= 0.5($10 − $6.55)], thus increasing the effective wage to $8.28 per hour. If a person were earning $8 per hour, the wage subsidy would be $1, and the effective wage would be $9.

A wage subsidy can be more effectively targeted to the poor than can the minimum wage, provided it is restricted to principal family workers. Unlike the minimum wage, a wage subsidy probably would not reduce employment. It does not require employers to pay workers more than they are worth as employees, as does the minimum wage. The prospect of the government picking up part of the tab for labor costs, however, may provide employers with an incentive to reduce the wage they are willing to pay.

Paradoxically, a wage subsidy does not guarantee increased work effort, as one would expect a higher effective wage to do. This is because the higher wage increases the opportunity cost of leisure, inducing people to work more. On the other hand, a higher wage enables an individual to maintain a given standard of living by working less. The net effect is uncertain.

Keywords: *minimum wage and poverty, minimum wage and unemployment*

Access InfoTrac at http://infotrac.cengage.com

Labor Market Discrimination Policy

We have noted previously that poverty rates are higher in families headed by females, blacks, and Hispanics than in families headed by non-Hispanic whites. Such differences raise the specter of discrimination and suggest that poverty may be, at least to some extent, caused by discrimination.

The purpose of this section is to explore the relationship between poverty and discrimination. We begin by examining the extent of labor market discrimination. We then look more closely at possible links between labor market discrimination and poverty and briefly examine some of the implications of those linkages for public policy toward discrimination.

Keywords: *wage subsidy, wage subsidy and poverty*

Access InfoTrac at http://infotrac.cengage.com

The Extent of Labor Market Discrimination Table 11.6 contains data for full-time wage and salary workers in the fourth quarter of 2008, as compiled by the Bureau of Labor Statistics. The data are reported as earnings ratios—the ratios of the average earnings by individuals in selected groups to the average earnings of white males. They indicate, for example, that average white female earnings were 79 percent of those of the average white male, the average black male earned 75 percent of the average white male's pay, and so on.

Although these data represent only one recent year, the general pattern displayed here has persisted for as long as reliable data have been collected; that is, white males have always out-earned the other groups represented in Table 11.6. As a general rule, differences

TABLE 11.6 RATIO OF AVERAGE EARNINGS OF FULL-TIME WORKERS IN SELECTED GROUPS TO AVERAGE EARNINGS OF FULL-TIME MALE WORKERS, FOURTH QUARTER, 2008

GROUP	RATIO
White women	0.792727
Black men	0.751515
Black women	0.671515
Hispanic men	0.677576
Hispanic women	0.607273

Source: Calculated from data in U.S. Department of Labor, Bureau of Labor Statistics, *Median Usual Weekly Earnings of Wage and Salary Workers*, Fourth Quarter 2008.

in earnings reflect a host of factors that distinguish one worker, or group of workers, from another. Discrimination is one of these factors, but the list also includes education, training, work experience, occupation, location, hours worked, work effort, industry, marital status, verbal skills, intelligence, and others. The trick is to separate the effect of discrimination from the effects of all the other factors that could explain differences in earnings.

Many economists have attempted to do this, using various empirical or statistical techniques. No reliable measure exists, however, for discrimination. Thus, using these approaches economists can determine only the share of observed earnings differentials that can be attributed to factors other than discrimination. The portion not explained by factors other than discrimination could be a result of discrimination; it is not possible to know for certain.

According to the data in Table 11.6, black males appear to pay a 25 percent earnings penalty for being black. Empirical studies indicate, however, that as much as half of this penalty can be attributed to differences in experience, education, location, veteran and marital status, number of children, and hours worked.[2] Thus, the earnings differential between black males and white males produced by discrimination is probably no larger than around 13 percent of white male earnings—and possibly less (some of the differential may be due to other omitted factors).

According to the data in Table 11.6, white females appear to pay a 21 percent earnings penalty for being female. Time on the job is interrupted more often and for longer periods of time for women than for men, however, primarily for child rearing. This puts women at a disadvantage in the labor market in terms of work experience. In fact, the evidence suggests that perhaps half of the observed pay difference between white women and men can be explained by differences in experience.[3] Another 5 to 6 percent of the 22 percent differential can probably be attributed to occupational segregation.[4] Simply put, women are overrepresented in relatively lower-paying clerical and service occupations and underrepresented in relatively higher-paying precision production, crafts, and repair occupations, and also among operators, fabricators, and laborers. Several studies have shown that at least half of the occupational wage differential is eliminated when

[2]Francine Blau and Andrea Beller, "Black-White Earnings over the 1980s: Gender Differences in Trends," *Review of Economics and Statistics* 74, no. 2 (1992): 276–286.

[3]Mary Corcoran, "The Structure of Female Wages," *American Economic Association, Papers and Proceedings* 68, no. 2 (1978), 165–170.

[4]Erica Groshen, "The Structure of the Female/Male Wage Differential," *Journal of Human Resources* 26, no. 3 (1991): 457–472.

job characteristics are held constant; that is, higher pay by occupation in part reflects compensation for less attractive working conditions.[5]

As was the case for differences between black people's earnings and white people's earnings, we do not know for certain how much of the differential in male and female earnings reflects labor market discrimination. Differences in work experience and working conditions, however, appear to account for more than half the observed earnings differential. Some of the unexplained variation, moreover, can be attributed to pre–labor market discrimination—that is, to gender differences in socialization. Overall, it seems reasonable to infer that labor market discrimination produces no more, and possibly less, than a 10 percent difference in male and female earnings.

The data in Table 11.6 also suggest substantial earnings penalties for Hispanic males and females. The evidence indicates, however, that the wages of Hispanics living in the United States are only slightly below (5 percent at most) those of non-Hispanic whites after adjusting for differences in education, age, hours worked, marital status, region, fluency in English, and place of birth.[6] Lack of fluency in English has been an especially important factor keeping Hispanics out of higher-paying professional and managerial occupations.

This quick review of the evidence indicates that unexplained differences in pay do exist between apparently identical white and black workers, between male and female workers, and between Hispanic and non-Hispanic white workers. The unexplained pay differences appear no larger, however, than the 13 percent penalty paid by blacks, and they are probably less for both females and Hispanics. These differences should be viewed, moreover, as upper limits; they may represent the effects of discrimination, but they may also result from unmeasured differences in productivity.

These results are not surprising when viewed in the context of economic theory. Wage discrimination can arise from the unwillingness of employers to hire members of a certain race, ethnic group, or gender. Such choices, however, inevitably require employers to pass up more productive employees in favor of less productive employees. This will elevate costs of production above the level achievable in the absence of discrimination and eventually drive discriminating firms from the market. Thus, economic theory suggests that normal market forces will tend to moderate the extent of labor market discrimination.

How Much Does Labor Market Discrimination Contribute to Poverty?

Frankly, we doubt that discrimination has much to do with poverty, for several reasons. First, although poverty rates are higher among blacks, Hispanics, and female-headed families, 48 percent of the poor live in families headed by white males. Thus at the very least, nearly half the poor are not subjected to labor market discrimination.

Keywords: *poverty and discrimination*

Access InfoTrac at http://infotrac.cengage.com

Second, some evidence indicates that the earnings differential between white males and others is smaller for lower-paying occupations than it is for higher-paying occupations. For example, women's wages were 82 percent of men's wages in service occupations in the fourth quarter of 2008, while the percentage was 69 percent for management, business, and financial occupations according to the data in U.S. Bureau of Labor Statistics, *Usual Weekly Earnings of Wage and Salary Workers: Fourth Quarter of 2008*. This is a significant fact because the poor will be working, if at all, in the lower-paid occupations. In fact, evidence of discrimination against the so-called average worker is irrelevant in determining the contribution of discrimination to poverty in the United States.

---

[5]See, for example, David MacPherson and Barry Hirsch, "Wages and Gender Composition: Why Do Women's Jobs Pay Less?" *Journal of Labor Economics* 13, no. 3 (1995): 426–471.

[6]Leonard Carlson and Caroline Swartz, "The Earnings of Women and Ethnic Minorities, 1959–1979," *Industrial and Labor Relations Review* 41, no. 4 (1988): 530–546.

Third, evidence suggests that the earnings differential between white males and others is smaller among individuals with less education—that is, among individuals more likely to be poor. For example, in 1993, the black–white earnings ratio for full-time male workers with less than a high school education was 0.97.[7] Discrimination seems to be a bigger factor in creating wage differences among more-educated workers competing for higher-paying jobs than among less-educated workers competing for lower-paying jobs.

Fourth, poverty rates have persisted even though earnings differentials have narrowed over time. We have already presented evidence of the failure of the poverty rate to fall appreciably since 1975. During the same period, however, female/male earnings ratios (white female/white male, black female/black male, Hispanic female/Hispanic male) in the United States rose from 0.58 to 0.78 for whites, from 0.75 to 0.86 for blacks, and from 0.68 to 0.86 for Hispanics.[8]

Fifth, the earnings penalty imposed by discrimination would be too small in most cases to cause poverty—that is, to lower a family's income from above the poverty threshold to below the poverty threshold. In other words, if the income lost because of discrimination were somehow restored to the victims of discrimination, it would not be enough in most cases to raise their income above the poverty threshold.

Whether such a restoration would be sufficient to raise a family's income above the poverty threshold depends on (1) how close the family's income is to the poverty threshold; (2) how much of that income is derived from wages; and (3) how large the restoration would be (or the size of the discrimination penalty). It is impossible to apply a combination of all these factors to the poverty data short of a lengthy study, but we can suggest an upper limit by using some general characteristics of the poverty population.

The typical poverty family in the United States is a three-person household. The poverty threshold in 2008 for this family was $17,330. Assuming a discrimination penalty of 13 percent, the largest possible penalty would have been $2,253 (= 0.13 × $17,330). But this is the penalty for a worker whose entire income is from wages and whose hourly wage is at least $10 per hour. Most poor workers do not do nearly this well in the labor market. This computation is based, moreover, on a penalty percentage (13 percent) that our previous discussion suggests is too high for many victims of discrimination. Let us assume, however, that every female-headed, black, or Hispanic family with an income below the poverty threshold suffers from a discrimination penalty this large. If even this much income were given to each family in these three categories, only about 17 percent of the families would be elevated above the poverty threshold.

Policy Implications Much of the above discussion suggests that labor market discrimination is not a significant source of poverty in the United States. Thus, even if policies aimed at reducing labor market discrimination, such as affirmative action, were successful in reducing discrimination, they would have little effect on the poverty rate. A stronger link is probable between poverty and occupational segregation, and some hope that reducing the latter will also lower the poverty rate. So far, however, we have failed to accomplish this through public policy.

MAKING FATHERS PAY

The increase in female-headed families has focused attention on the poor record of absent fathers in supporting the children they leave behind. Nearly one of every two

[7]R. K. Filer, D. S. Hammermesh, and A. S. Rees, *The Economics of Work and Pay*, 6th ed. (New York: HarperCollins, 1996), 552.

[8]Ibid., 556–558.

children born today will become eligible for child support by an absent parent at some point before reaching age 18. Currently, however, courts award child support to only 58 percent of eligible parents. The process of setting the award is expensive and contentious. The size of the award as a percentage of the noncustodial parent's income varies greatly. Awards are extremely difficult to collect; fewer than 30 percent of awardees receive the full amount awarded on a regular basis.

Even if welfare parents were fully employed, many of them could earn no more than their annual welfare grant. It seems unreasonable in view of this fact to expect these parents to be totally self-supporting. One way to reduce poverty without creating total dependency is to supplement, rather than replace, the earnings of single parents who have custody of minor children. Some of this supplement must come from public assistance, but some can (and should) come from private child support.

Child Support Assistance

Child support is an important strategy in making work pay because it increases and stabilizes the income of low-income working adults. Combined with a mother's earnings, regular child support is a key income support that can help move families out of poverty. To the extent that fathers have the ability to pay, strengthened child support enforcement means that more low-income families will be able to leave welfare and sustain low-wage employment, and those who are already working will benefit from a higher standard of living.

To this end, the federal government has moved to develop new enforcement tools and to compel states to strengthen their individual child support programs. In addition, some states have introduced pass-through legislation, which allows for a portion of the noncustodial parent's payment to go directly to custodial parents who are recipients of cash assistance.

The first step in this direction at the federal level was the establishment of the Child Support Enforcement program, which created a bureaucracy to enforce private child-support obligations for all AFDC recipients and for others on request. Legislation passed in 1984 required the states to adopt expedited procedures for obtaining child-support orders from the courts, to establish child-support guidelines for the courts, and to initiate automatic paycheck withholding for child support beginning one month after failure to pay.

The Family Support Act of 1988 stiffened federal resolve on this issue. Starting in November 1990, states were required to provide for immediate wage withholding for all cases handled by the Office of Child Support Enforcement. Starting in 1994, withholding was required for all support orders.

The Personal Responsibility and Work Opportunity Reconciliation Act of 1996 (P.L.104-193) included strict child support enforcement and paternity-establishment policies. The law required state agencies operating the federal child support program to use a range of enforcement tools. States failing to comply with these requirements are penalized by deductions from their TANF block grants. The law also provides for the development of a National Directory of New Hires, which requires employers to report all new hires to child support enforcement authorities; the development of a Financial Institutions Data Match Program, which requires all states to enter into agreements with financial institutions to match the records of parents who are delinquent in their child support obligations; and the application of the Uniform Interstate Family Support Act, which seeks to consolidate and simplify the process of collecting child support across state lines.

States may apply penalties for failure to pay child support obligations. Penalties vary by state but they include revoking licenses, imposing work requirements on delinquent parents, denying Food Stamps to delinquent parents, withholding income tax refunds, and denying passports. The 1996 legislation also strengthened penalties for TANF recipients who failed to cooperate in child support collection activities and established new performance goals for paternity establishment.

Keywords: *child support assistance, child support insurance*

Access InfoTrac at http://infotrac.cengage.com

Child Support Assurance

Some believe that government should go beyond simply collecting money from absent fathers; that child support *assistance* should become child support *assurance*. In a child support assurance (CSA) system, a family would be guaranteed a certain amount of child support regularly and on time each month. To fund the guaranteed payment, the government would collect the child support owed by the noncustodial parent. If it were unable to collect, the government would still provide child support to the family at the guaranteed level and continue to pursue collection. If a low-income, noncustodial parent paid support but the amount was less than the guaranteed level, then the state would supplement that parent's payment up to the guaranteed level.

New York has run a CSA-like program for more than a decade. The New York Child Assistance Program (CAP) began as a demonstration project to test CSA as an alternative to welfare. The project was judged to be so successful that any county that wishes to do so can now offer CAP as an alternative to TANF. The success of CAP persuaded the California legislature to authorize a similar demonstration project beginning in 2003. Minnesota has received a grant from the U.S. Department of Health and Human Services (HHS) to design a CSA project in the context of TANF. HHS has solicited proposals from states for additional feasibility studies and demonstration projects.

Summary

This chapter begins by developing a historical perspective on the poverty problem. The primary focus is on the official measure of poverty and the official poverty rate. The official poverty rate declined significantly during the 1990s, nearly reaching an all-time low in 2000. Even then, 11.3 percent of the population lived in a family with income below the official poverty threshold. Since then, however, the poverty rate has returned just under its 1989 level of 12.8 percent.

The elderly have a poverty rate below the official rate, but people living in black, Hispanic, and female-headed households experience poverty at a much higher rate than the average.

In the absence of government transfers, around 20 percent of the population would normally live in poverty. Government cash transfers have provided enough income to the poor to reduce the poverty rate by 6 to 7 percentage points. Accounting for taxes increases the poverty rate, but taxes paid by the poor are more than offset by the Earned Income Tax Credit. Noncash transfers also reduce the poverty rate. The poverty rate after all transfers (cash and noncash) and taxes are accounted for has been two to three percentage points below the official poverty rate.

The three most common sources of support for poverty families, other than income from work, are Food Stamps, the EITC, and TANF payments. Each of these is an income-tested transfer. None is generous enough, by itself, to elevate very many families above the poverty threshold. Benefits from both the food stamp and TANF programs fall as income from work increases above a deduction for essential needs, raising the possibility that the loss of benefits discourages people from working. The net effect of the three programs together probably does not discourage the poor from working at low wages but may adversely affect the transition from low to higher wages.

The establishment of the TANF program is a clear signal that Congress wants to increase the percentage of income that the poor receive from work. Accordingly, this chapter reviews several programs or policies designed to achieve that objective.

An examination of the relationship between unemployment and poverty suggests that policies to reduce unemployment are an important part of any strategy to reduce poverty.

Data gathered to date on people who return to TANF after leaving TANF for work indicate that there is a need for more effective childcare assistance. It is believed that TANF clients are reluctant to leave TANF for work because of a fear that they will lose Medicaid benefits. This may be the case for adults, but not necessarily for children.

Increases in the minimum wage are often mentioned as a means of increasing the rewards from work. These suggestions are unlikely to come from economists, who emphasize the unemployment-creating effects of the minimum wage and its poor target efficiency.

Wage subsidies are also mentioned as a means of increasing the rewards from work. They find favor with economists because they may encourage work and can be made target efficient.

The relatively high incidence of poverty among blacks, Hispanics, and female-headed households raises the possibility that poverty may be reduced further by policies that discourage labor market discrimination. This prospect arises because of the higher wages received by non-Hispanic white males relative to non-Hispanic females, black males, black females, Hispanic males, and Hispanic females. We conclude, however, that labor market discrimination accounts for very little of actual wage differentials, and that dramatic reductions in labor market discrimination would have a small impact on poverty. Therefore, fighting poverty through policies to reduce labor market discrimination is not a promising route.

The final programs we consider are government efforts to assist single mothers with collecting child support payments from absent fathers. Efforts to date have resulted in significant increases in the amount of child support collected. Some believe, however, that the government should assure or guarantee child support payments while making further efforts to get fathers to pay.

Key Terms

Poor person
Official poverty threshold
Money income
Poverty rate
Transfers
Income-tested transfer
Cash transfer
Noncash transfers
Pre-transfer poverty rate
Gross income (GI)
Deductible (D)
Basic benefit (BB)
Benefit (B)
Benefit reduction rate (BRR)
Break-even gross income
Target efficiency
Wage subsidy

Review Questions

1. Currently, in-kind transfers are not included in the official measure of resources that individuals have available to meet their basic needs. Do you believe these transfers should be included? Defend your answer.
2. "Instead of enacting new transfer programs to eliminate poverty, we should concentrate on policies that would reduce unemployment." Do you agree or disagree with this statement? Defend your answer.
3. What government programs have been the most effective poverty reducers? Justify your answer.
4. The average female earned 78 percent as much as the average male in 2001. Explain why this comparison overstates the degree of labor market discrimination against females.
5. Evidence indicates that there is some labor market discrimination against blacks, Hispanics, and females, but such discrimination has little to do with poverty. Explain why.
6. Congressperson Smith argues that government transfers have worked to alleviate poverty. Congressperson Jones argues that these transfers have worked to increase poverty. Who is correct? Defend your answer.
7. Suppose that a person works 1,800 hours a year at the minimum wage. How large will this person's EITC be? Assume that total income from wages and AGI are equal. Show your calculations.
8. Congress is currently debating the pros and cons of the various methods of increasing the earnings of the poor: increasing the minimum wage, expanding the earned income tax credit, and granting wage subsidies. You are called before the House to testify. Briefly outline your views on these various programs.
9. The prospect of paying childcare expenses and the fear of losing Medicaid are both barriers to leaving TANF for work. Which of these two is really the bigger barrier? Explain.
10. What factors would you consider in designing a child support assurance program? Why?

Web Sites

- ***U.S. Census Bureau, Historical Poverty Tables***
These tables are a source of data on various measures of poverty in the United States—**http://www.census.gov/hhes/income/histinc/histpovtb.html**
- ***The Green Book***
This is an indispensable annual compilation of information and data on poverty and income redistribution programs. The latest (2004) version can be accessed at—**http://www.gpoaccess.gov/wmprints/green/**
- ***Income, Poverty, and Health Insurance Coverage in the United States: 2004***
This is the latest issue of the Census Bureau's annual survey of poverty in the United States—**http://www.census.gov/prod/2004pubs/_p60-226.pdf**

CHAPTER **12**

Tracking and Explaining the Macroeconomy

OUTLINE

This chapter introduces many of the concepts used to measure the economy's performance. As measures of the economy's performance, they provide helpful information to households, firms, and policy makers, which is why the news media bombard us with data based on these concepts.

Information on the economy's performance helps households, firms, and the government make better decisions. Suppose a person is considering quitting his job to search for a better one. Chances of success are better if the economy is performing well than if it is performing poorly. Similarly, a graduating college senior might postpone going for a master's degree if the economy is performing well and good jobs are relatively plentiful. However, she might decide to continue her education immediately if it is performing poorly, with good jobs hard to find. This information about continuing education and the job market, in turn, is important for university decision makers in responding to changes in the demand for advanced degrees.

In another situation, suppose you are an entrepreneur thinking about starting your own business. If the economy is expected to perform well, now might be a good time to get your plans underway. Similarly, now might be a good time to expand an existing business. Conversely if the economy is performing poorly or expected to decline, you might want to postpone such plans.

Finally, information about the economy's current and prospective performance is important to government policy makers, who compare the nation's economic performance with both its past performance and that of other countries. If the economy is performing poorly, policy makers can try to enact policies to improve its performance. If the economy is performing well, no policy action is necessary. Instead, policy makers can concentrate on taking credit, whether it is deserved or not.

The performance of the economy is always an important issue in election years, and it can be decisive in presidential elections. Many experts believe that the first President Bush lost his bid for reelection in 1992 primarily because of the economy's mediocre performance. They also believe that President Clinton's bid for reelection in 1996 was successful partly because of the economy's strength. A recession at the beginning of his first term, along with a slow growth of unemployment in the recovery, was partially responsible for the strong challenge to the reelection of the second President Bush. The improving economy as the election approached was a factor in his reelection. More recently it is clear that economic conditions played a significant role in the 2008 election. Oil prices and, consequently, gasoline prices reached an all time high even in real terms in the first half of the election year. The financial collapse in September and rising unemployment caused the National Bureau of Economic Research to declare that the economy was in a recession that begun in December 2008. As of this writing in February 2009, it is not known how long or deep the recession will be.

In addition to discussing various concepts used to measure the economy's performance, this chapter introduces aggregate demand–aggregate supply analysis. As we shall see, aggregate demand and aggregate supply determine the nation's output and price level. Because aggregate demand and supply change over time, output and the price level also change.

Because they determine output and the price level, aggregate demand and supply are important in determining the nation's unemployment and inflation rates. We consider unemployment in Chapter 13 and inflation in Chapter 14. Aggregate demand and supply also help to determine the nation's budget and balance of payments surpluses and deficits. We cover the federal government's budget in Chapter 15 and the nation's balance of payments in Chapter 18.

GROSS DOMESTIC PRODUCT (GDP)

Gross domestic product (GDP)– The market value of all final goods and services produced in the economy over the relevant time span, usually one year.

Final goods– Goods purchased (or available to be purchased) for final use.

Intermediate goods– Goods purchased for resale or for use in producing other goods.

In judging the nation's economic performance, the nation's output is clearly important. Various measures of output exist, but the most frequently used is gross domestic product. **Gross domestic product (GDP)** is the market value of all final goods and services produced in the economy over a year.

Only final goods and services are counted in GDP. **Final goods** are those purchased (or available to be purchased) for final use. By definition, final goods are not used to produce other goods. In contrast, **intermediate goods** are purchased for resale or for use in producing other goods. Automobiles and bread are final goods because they are typically purchased for final use. Steel and flour are intermediate goods because they are used in the production of other goods.

If all goods—intermediate and final—were counted as part of GDP, part of the nation's output would be counted twice. To illustrate, part of the steel industry's output is used in the production of automobiles. If the outputs of both the steel and automobile industries were included in GDP, the part of the steel industry's output that is used in the production of automobiles would be counted twice, first as part of the steel industry's output and second as part of the automobile industry's output. The same would happen if the outputs of both the flour and bread industries were included in GDP. To prevent multiple counting of the nation's output, only final goods and services are included in GDP.

GDP is an estimate of the market value of all final goods and services. It is the sum of the market value of each final good or service. The sum must be in value (dollar) terms because it is not meaningful to add the physical units of the various goods and services. In estimating the nation's output, it would, for example, make no sense to add together the numbers of automobiles and toothbrushes produced. If the automobiles produced sell for $15 billion and the toothbrushes for $1 billion, it does make sense to say that this amounts to $16 billion of production.

The GDP calculation is made using market prices or implicit market prices to value final goods and services. The market price of each good or service is used because, as we have seen, it measures the value of an additional unit of the product to consumers. Even with the use of market prices, accurate comparisons of the nation's output in different time periods are difficult.

Finally, GDP is a measure of production, not sales. All goods produced during the year are counted in GDP, regardless of whether they are sold or added to business inventories. Suppose firms produced $100 billion worth of automobiles in 2006, but they sold only $90 billion worth. The automobile industry's contribution to GDP in that year would be $100 billion, not $90 billion, with $90 billion sold and $10 billion added to business inventories.

As defined, GDP excludes many transactions. It excludes purchases of used or second-hand goods because these goods were counted when they were produced. It also excludes

Keyword: *consumption*

Access InfoTrac at http://infotrac.cengage.com

financial transactions such as the purchase of stocks or bonds because they involve an exchange of financial assets, not production.

GDP'S COMPONENTS

GDP has four parts: personal consumption expenditures, gross private domestic investment, government purchases of goods and services, and net exports of goods and services.

Consumption

Personal consumption expenditures– Household purchases of durable and nondurable goods and services.

Personal consumption expenditures (consumption) consist of household purchases of durable goods (such as automobiles, appliances, and furniture), nondurable goods (such as food, clothing, and cigarettes), and services (such as medical and dental care, legal advice, and hairstyling). Of these expenditures, most are for nondurable goods and services. The distinguishing characteristic of these goods and services is that they last only a short time. Durable goods, on the other hand, last much longer; even so, their contribution to GDP is recorded when they are produced rather than over their life span.

As shown in Table 12.1, personal consumption expenditures account for almost 70 percent of GDP. Thus, they make up the largest part of GDP by a wide margin. As a percentage of GDP, these expenditures vary little from year to year; they are a relatively stable component of GDP.

Gross Investment

Gross private domestic investment– Firms' purchases of new equipment, purchases of all newly produced structures, and changes in business inventories.

Gross private domestic investment (gross investment) is (1) the purchases of new equipment by firms; (2) the purchases of all newly produced structures; and (3) changes in business inventories. Thus, a firm's purchase of a new computer system or a new software package is treated as investment. The construction of a factory and the construction of residential housing, including apartment houses and homes, are also classified as investment.

TABLE 12.1 GROSS DOMESTIC PRODUCT AND ITS COMPONENTS, 2008, FOURTH QUARTER (BILLIONS OF CURRENT DOLLARS)

	$BILLIONS	PERCENT OF GDP
Gross domestic product	**14,264.6**	100
Personal consumption expenditures	**9,930.2**	70
Gross private domestic investment	**1,948.4**	14
Government purchases of goods and services	**2,914.9**	20
Net exports of goods and services	**−528.9**	−4
Exports of goods and services	1,758.5	12
Imports of goods and services	2,287.4	16

GDP has four components: personal consumption expenditures, gross private domestic investment, government purchases of goods and services, and net exports of goods and services. The largest component, by a wide margin, is personal consumption expenditures.

Source: U.S. Department of Commerce, Bureau of Economic Analysis, *National Income and Products Account, Gross Domestic Product*, January 30, 2009. (http://www.bea.gov/national/index.htm#gdp)

ADDITIONAL INSIGHT

Measured GDP and the Underground Economy

Over the years, many economists have become concerned that measured GDP may drastically underestimate the nation's level of economic activity because of the existence of an underground economy. The *underground economy* consists of economic activity that avoids official detection and measurement. The activities are either inherently illegal or not reported to avoid taxes, detection by the Immigration and Naturalization Service, or for other reasons. Examples of the former include illegal drug trafficking, bookmaking, and prostitution. Examples of the latter include the failure to report receipts by owners or managers of restaurants, bars, and various retail establishments, the failure to report income from tips and casual or part-time work, particularly by people who would lose such benefits as unemployment compensation, welfare payments, or, in the case of illegal migrants, residency. Although an underground economy has always existed, studies show that its share of GDP has increased substantially since 1960. Estimates for Germany, Sweden, and the United States put its share in 1960 at 2 percent, 3.5 percent, and 2 percent, respectively. Although by its nature, the exact size of underground economy is difficult to measure, the evidence is overwhelming that it increased after 1960. By 1995, comparable estimates of its size were 13.2 percent for Germany, 16 percent for Sweden, and for the United States, 9.5 percent. The underground economy is larger in Germany and Sweden than in the United States, possibly because these countries are more heavily taxed and regulated.[a] In general, higher payroll and other taxes and increased regulations of all types cause the underground economy to grow.

The incentives to avoid taxes and to evade costly regulations existed in 1960, just as they do today. Even if the incentives had not increased substantially, underground economic activity might have increased. The incentive to "cheat" the government is offset by the disincentive offered by potential punishment and, perhaps more important, by the disincentive created by a guilty conscience. If one can convince himself that everyone else is doing it, or herself that government regulates and taxes unfairly, then this disincentive is reduced. It is likely that the increased size of the underground economy is due both to increased taxes and regulations and to less concern about obeying the law.

The existence of a large underground economy implies that those not participating in the underground economy carry a disproportionate share of the tax burden. If those who participate in the underground economy paid taxes, tax rates could be reduced significantly without loss of tax revenue. In addition, the underground economy may be less efficient. The various activities must be carried out covertly, which often precludes the most efficient means of production and distribution. Also, most or all transactions must be conducted with cash, which is disadvantageous in many instances. These factors, however, are offset to some degree by the lack of government regulation and by the greater flexibility, including part-time and at-home work, in the underground economy.

Various suggestions have been made to reduce the size of the underground economy. These include reducing tax rates, making the tax system more equitable, devoting more resources to law enforcement, and increasing the penalties for participating in the underground economy. It must be recognized, however, that with existing tax rates (or even lower ones) a strong economic incentive exists for people to participate in the underground economy. Moreover, given its shadowy nature, one cannot be optimistic about reducing its size by devoting more resources to law enforcement. For these reasons, a large underground economy is likely to persist for the foreseeable future.

[a] Bruno Frey and Friedrich Schneider, "Informal and Underground Economy" in Orley Ashenfelter, *International Encyclopedia of Social and Behavioral Science*, bk. 12, Economics (Amsterdam: Elsevier Science Publishing Company, 2001).

Finally, because GDP is a measure of production, not sales, changes in business inventories are included in investment. To understand the reason, suppose that firms produced $100 billion worth of automobiles in 2006, but sold only $90 billion worth in that year. If the automobiles were sold to households, the $90 billion would be counted as consumption

Keyword: *underground economy*

Access InfoTrac at http://infotrac.cengage.com

Keyword: *investment*

Access InfoTrac at http://infotrac.cengage.com

Capital stock– The nation's accumulated stock of structures, producers' durable equipment, and business inventories.

and included in GDP. Because $10 billion worth of automobiles were not sold, business inventories increased by that amount. This $10 billion increase in inventories must be included in GDP to measure accurately the contribution of the automobile industry's production to GDP in 2006. Investment is the best classification for this increase in inventories.

So far, we have discussed gross private domestic investment, or gross investment. Part of gross investment merely replaces structures and equipment that have worn out or been destroyed during the period. To determine the part of gross investment that adds to the existing stock of structures and equipment, we subtract consumption of fixed capital from gross investment to obtain *net private domestic investment*, or net investment. *Consumption of fixed capital* consists of depreciation, an estimate of the deterioration of the nation's structures and equipment, and an allowance for accidental damage to them. To illustrate, gross investment was at an annual rate of $1,948.4 billion in the fourth quarter of 2008. Of this amount, $1,853.3 billion was used to replace structures and equipment that had deteriorated or been destroyed, yielding net investment of only $95.1 billion, obtained by subtracting consumption of fixed capital from gross investment.

Net investment is an important concept because it implies a change in the nation's capital stock. The nation's **capital stock** is its accumulated stock of structures, producers' durable equipment, and business inventories. Gross investment is the amount of newly produced structures and producers' durable equipment plus changes in business inventories. Because part of gross investment simply replaces structures and equipment that wear out or are destroyed during the period, only net investment adds to the nation's capital stock.

The capital stock is important because it is a major determinant of the nation's productive capacity. All other things being equal, an increase in the nation's capital stock (positive net investment) implies an increase in the nation's productive capacity. With the increase, the economy will be capable of producing more goods and services, discussed in Chapter 1.

In the fourth quarter of 2008, gross investment accounted for approximately 14 percent of GDP. In contrast, net investment was only about 0.7 percent. Gross investment in 2004 accounted for about the same percent of GDP, but net investment was about 4 percent of GDP. One reason net investment was such a smaller percent in fourth quarter of 2008 was due to the recession that had begun over a year earlier. In addition to constituting a smaller proportion of GDP than consumption, 17 percent rather than 70 percent, investment also exhibits greater instability from year to year.

Government Purchases

Government purchases of goods and services– The purchases of federal, state, and local governments.

Government purchases of goods and services are simply the purchases of federal, state, and local governments.[1] These purchases include procurement of military hardware; construction of dams, highways, and schools; and payment for the services of accountants, teachers, and other government employees. State and local governments account for most governmental purchases.

In 2008, government purchases accounted for approximately 20 percent of GDP—perhaps a surprisingly low percentage. The primary reason for the low percentage is that *government transfer payments* are excluded from GDP.

Government transfer payments include Social Security benefits, Medicare and Medicaid payments, and unemployment compensation. Like purchases of goods and services, transfer payments involve payments by government; unlike them, the government

[1]With regard to government purchases, the U.S. Department of Commerce now distinguishes between government consumption and investment. For convenience, however, we refer to government purchases rather than government consumption expenditures and gross investment.

receives no goods or services in return. Because transfer payments involve no production of goods and services, they are excluded from GDP. Although excluded, these payments are obviously important.

Net Exports

Net exports of goods and services– The amount by which foreign spending on domestically produced goods and services is greater (or less) than domestic spending on goods and services produced abroad.

Exports– Goods and services produced in this country and purchased by foreigners.

Imports– Goods and services produced abroad and bought by persons in this country.

Net exports of goods and services is the difference between exports of goods and services and imports of goods and services. **Exports** are produced in this country and purchased by foreigners. **Imports** are produced abroad and purchased by persons in this country. Because GDP is a measure of domestic production, exports are included in GDP. Consequently, exports are added to consumption, gross investment, and government purchases to arrive at GDP. Because imports are produced abroad, they are excluded from GDP. They are subtracted from consumption, gross investment, and government purchases because those components include the purchases of goods produced both here and abroad. Suppose a household purchases a new car made in Japan. The purchase is counted as consumption. Similarly, suppose a firm purchases machine tools made in Sweden. The purchase is included in gross investment. Because the various components of GDP include both domestic and foreign production, imports must be subtracted from those components to guarantee that only domestic production is included in GDP. If the subtraction were not made, the nation's output of goods and services would be greatly overstated.

Rather than treating exports and imports separately, we take the difference between them to arrive at net exports. This concept may be interpreted as the amount by which foreign spending on domestically produced goods and services is greater (or less) than domestic spending on goods and services produced abroad. This difference may be either positive or negative. In recent years, imports have exceeded exports. The difference, therefore, has been negative.

In 2008 (fourth quarter), exports of goods and services totaled $1,758.4 billion, approximately 12 percent of GDP. Imports of goods and services were $2,287.4 billion, about 16 percent of GDP. Net exports of goods and services equaled a minus $528.9 billion, obtained by subtracting $2,287.4 billion from $1,758.4 billion.

Keyword: *Net exports*

Access InfoTrac at http://infotrac.cengage.com

Keyword: *gross domestic product*

Access InfoTrac at http://infotrac.cengage.com

NOMINAL GDP, REAL GDP, AND THE GDP DEFLATOR

GDP is calculated by adding the market values of various goods and services. Unfortunately, quantities *and* prices change over time. Because GDP reflects changes in both quantities and prices, it is difficult to compare the output of goods and services in different years by comparing GDP in different years.

To illustrate the problem and its solution, consider the following example. We assume, for simplicity, only one good (good A) and two years (2007 and 2008). The relevant quantities and prices are shown in Table 12.2.

As indicated in the table, 6 million units of good A were produced in 2007. The price per unit was $1,000. With only one good, the nation's GDP in that year was $6 billion, obtained by multiplying 6 million (the number of units produced) by $1,000 (the price per unit). In contrast, 6.3 million units were produced in 2008 at a price per unit of $1,100. GDP in that year was therefore $6.93 billion, obtained by multiplying 6.3 million by $1,100.

A GDP of $6 billion in 2007 and $6.93 billion in 2008 seems to indicate that the nation's output of goods and services increased by about 15 percent. Thus, a person might conclude, incorrectly, that 15 percent more goods and services were available to members of society in 2008 than in 2007. Table 12.2 shows that the number of units produced

TABLE 12.2 QUANTITIES, PRICES, AND GDP: A SIMPLE EXAMPLE

YEAR	NUMBER OF UNITS PRODUCED	PRICE PER UNIT	GDP
2007	6 million	$1,000	$6 billion
2008	6.3 million	1,100	$6.93 billion

This table shows that output increased by 5 percent and price increased by 10 percent from 2006 to 2007. Consequently, GDP increased by about 15 percent.

increased from 6 million to 6.3 million, which is only a 5 percent increase in the quantity of good A available in 2008. Why does GDP overstate the increase in output? It does so because most of the increase in GDP in this example is due to the increase in good A's price. In 2007, the price was $1,000. In 2008, it was $1,100. This 10 percent increase in price plus the 5 percent increase in quantity gives the 15 percent increase in GDP.

This example illustrates the problem. To deal with it, we first construct a price index and then divide, or deflate, GDP by the appropriate price index number to compensate for the change in the price level.

Price index– A measure of the price level for a given period relative to the base period.

A **price index** measures the price level for a given period relative to the base period. By definition, it is the price for the period in question divided by the price in the base period multiplied by 100:

$$\textbf{Price index} = \frac{\textbf{Price for period in question}}{\textbf{Price in base period}} \times 100$$

To explain this index, we start by selecting a base period; let's select 2007. We first compute the price index for the base period. In this case, the price for the period in question, the numerator, is the same as the price in the base period, the denominator: $1,000. Thus, the price index for the base period (2007) is 100. We can now compare the price level in other periods with the base period by continuing to use the formula. Suppose the price of good A was $1,100 in 2008 and $1,000 in 2007 (the base period), so we have $1,100 divided by $1,000 equal to 1.1. Following the formula, multiply this by 100, making the 2008 price index number 110. Because the price index for the base period is standardized at 100, it is easy to see that the price level in 2008 is 10 percent higher than the price level in 2007 (the base period).

Table 12.3 shows the price index numbers for 2007 and 2008, along with the data from Table 12.2. Note that GDP from column 4 of Table 12.2 appears as nominal GDP in column 5 of Table 12.3. **Nominal GDP** is GDP measured on the basis of current, or nominal, prices. Nominal GDP in 2007 is calculated using 2007 prices, while nominal GDP in 2008 is calculated using 2008 prices.

Nominal GDP– GDP measured on the basis of current, or nominal, prices.

If prices change, nominal GDP gives a false impression of the nation's output of goods and services. To correct for price changes, divide, or deflate, nominal GDP by the price index. The result is real GDP. In equation form, the relationship is

$$\textbf{Real GDP} = \frac{\textbf{Nominal GDP}}{\textbf{Price index (in decimal form)}}.$$

Note that we divide nominal GDP by a price index written as a decimal rather than as a percentage. To convert from percentage to decimal form move the decimal point two places to the left, which is the same as dividing by 100.

TABLE 12.3 DEFLATING GDP

YEAR	NUMBER OF UNITS PRODUCED	PRICE PER UNIT	PRICE INDEX	NOMINAL GDP	REAL GDP
2007	6 million	$1,000	100	$6 billion	$6 billion
2008	6.3 million	1,100	110	$6.93 billion	$6.3 billion

By deflating, or dividing, nominal GDP by the price index, we obtain real GDP. Adjusting for the price change indicates that output increased by 5 percent from 2006 to 2007.

Real GDP– GDP measured on the basis of constant prices; reflects only changes in quantities.

Real GDP is GDP measured on the basis of constant prices. To calculate real GDP in 2007, divide nominal GDP in 2007 ($6 billion) by the price index number for that year in decimal form (1.00), giving

$$\textbf{Real GDP} = \frac{\textbf{\$6 billion}}{\textbf{1}} = \$6\,\textbf{billion}.$$

Real GDP in 2007 is $6 billion, the same as nominal GDP.

To calculate real GDP in 2008, repeat the procedure by dividing nominal GDP in 2008 ($6.93 billion) by the relevant price index number (in decimal form) 1.10, yielding

$$\textbf{Real GDP} = \frac{\textbf{\$6.93 billion}}{\textbf{1.1}} = \$6.3\,\textbf{billion}.$$

Real GDP in 2008 is $6.3 billion, which is less than nominal GDP in that year. This change occurs because we deflated nominal GDP in 2008 by the price index, eliminating the effect of higher prices on GDP. Recall that the price of good A increased from $1,000 in 2007 to $1,100 in 2008, a 10 percent increase. By dividing nominal GDP in 2008 by 1.10—the price index (in decimal form) in 2008—we have calculated GDP *as if* price had not changed.

By deflating nominal GDP, we obtain real GDP, a measure of the nation's output that reflects only changes in quantities. (Changes in nominal GDP reflect changes in both quantities and prices.) Because changes in real GDP measure only changes in quantities, real GDP is a better measure of the nation's output of goods and services than is nominal GDP.

In our example, we assumed only one good.[2] To deflate nominal GDP, a price index for *all* final goods and services must be used. This index is called the implicit price deflator for GDP, or the GDP deflator. The relationship between nominal GDP, real GDP, and the GDP deflator is

$$\textbf{Real GDP} = \frac{\textbf{Nominal GDP}}{\textbf{GDP deflator}}$$

GDP deflator– A weighted average of the prices of all final goods and services produced in the economy.

The **GDP deflator** is a weighted average of the prices of all final goods and services produced in the economy. It uses a weighted average because the various goods and services are not of equal importance. At present, the GDP deflator has 2000 as its base year. Nominal GDP, real GDP, and the GDP deflator for 1979–2008 are shown in Table 12.4.

[2]With many goods and services, it becomes more difficult to calculate real GDP and the GDP deflator. For a discussion of the U.S. Department of Commerce's procedures, see J. Steven Landefeld, Robert P. Parker, and Jack E. Triplett, "Preview of the Comprehensive Revision of the National Income and Product Accounts: BEA's New Featured Measures of Output and Prices," *Survey of Current Business* 75, no. 7 (1995): 31–38.

TABLE 12.4 NOMINAL GDP, REAL GDP, AND THE GDP DEFLATOR, 1979–2008

YEAR	NOMINAL GDP (BILLIONS OF CURRENT DOLLARS)	REAL GDP (BILLIONS OF 2000 DOLLARS)	GDP DEFLATOR
1979	2,563.3	5,173.4	49.6
1980	2,789.5	5,161.7	54.0
1981	3,128.4	5,291.7	59.1
1982	3,255.0	5,189.3	62.7
1983	3,536.7	5,423.8	65.2
1984	3,933.2	5,813.6	67.7
1985	4,220.3	6,053.7	69.7
1986	4,462.8	6,263.6	71.2
1987	4,739.5	6,475.1	73.2
1988	5,103.8	6,742.7	75.7
1989	5,484.4	6,981.4	78.6
1990	5,803.1	7,112.5	81.6
1991	5,995.9	7,100.5	84.4
1992	6,337.7	7,336.6	86.4
1993	6,657.4	7,532.7	88.4
1994	7,072.2	7,835.5	90.3
1995	7,397.7	8,031.7	92.1
1996	7,816.9	8,328.9	93.9
1997	8,304.3	8,703.5	95.4
1998	8,747.0	9,066.9	96.5
1999	9,268.4	9,470.3	97.9
2000	9,817.0	9,817.0	100.0
2001	10,128.0	9,890.7	102.4
2002	10,469.6	10,048.8	104.2
2003	10,971.2	10,320.6	106.3
2004	11,734.3	10,755.7	109.1
2005	12,421.9	10,989.5	112.8
2006	13,178.4	11,294.8	116.4
2007	13,807.5	11,523.9	119.7
2008	14,280.7	11,671.3	124.3

Nominal GDP and the GDP deflator increased annually from 1979 to 2004. Except for decreases in 1980, 1982, 1991, and 2001, real GDP also increased. Real GDP may be obtained by dividing nominal GDP by the GDP deflator.

Source: National Bureau of Economic Research, Gross Domestic Product, *National Income and Products Account,* January 30, 2009. (http://www.bea.gov/national/index.htm#gdp. Bureau of Labor Statistics, http://www.bls.gov/CPI/#tables)

Keyword: *United States economic conditions*

Access InfoTrac at http://infotrac.cengage.com

THE NATION'S ECONOMIC PERFORMANCE

Over the years, the U.S. economy has performed well. From 1929 to 2005, the nation's output of goods and services increased at an average annual rate of 3 percent. At first glance, a 3 percent growth rate appears modest, but it implies that output doubles every 24 years.

Business cycles– Recurring fluctuations in the general level of economic activity.

Expansion phase– The business cycle phase during which real GDP, employment, productive capacity use, and profits increase while unemployment falls.

Peak– The highest point in the business cycle, during which real GDP is at a maximum and employment, profits, and productive capacity use are high.

Contraction phase– The phase of the business cycle during which real GDP, employment, productive capacity use, and profits decrease while unemployment rises.

Despite its upward trend, output does not grow steadily; it sometimes declines. The 1930s saw dramatic changes in GDP. With the advent of the Great Depression, U.S. output decreased at a 7 percent rate from 1929 to 1933. As the nation recovered from the Depression, it increased at a 10 percent rate from 1933 to 1941. Since 1960, GDP has continued its long-run upward trend accompanied by sharp, short-run fluctuations. Figure 12.1 shows GDP on an annual basis from 1960, with GDP measured on the left axis. Although the upward-sloping line may give an impression of steady growth, this impression is misleading. The jagged line in the figure shows the annual growth rate, with the percentage given on the right axis. Examining the jagged line, it is easy to see that during some years, output grew relatively rapidly, while in others, it grew less rapidly or even declined. Calculations for some longer periods show that real GDP grew at an average annual rate of 1.8 percent rate from 1988 to 1991, but that it grew at a 5.0 percent rate from 1982 to 1988 and at a 4.3 percent rate from 1991 to 2000. Since 2000 until the beginning of the current recession (December 2008) the average annual growth rate has been 2.4 percent.

As measured by real GDP, the nation's level of economic activity has fluctuated throughout its history. The recurring fluctuations in the level of economic activity are **business cycles**. A business cycle has four phases: expansion, peak, contraction, and trough. (See Figure 12.2.) During the **expansion phase**, real GDP increases relatively rapidly. As it does, employment increases and the unemployment rate decreases. Also, a higher percentage of the nation's productive capacity is used and profits increase. As the unemployment rate falls and a higher percentage of productive capacity is used, however, wages and prices start increasing or increase more rapidly.

Eventually, a **peak** occurs. At the peak, real GDP is at a maximum. Employment, capacity use, and profits are high; unemployment is low. With unemployment low and capacity use high, wages and prices will increase more rapidly, and inflation may become a problem.

After the peak, the economy enters the **contraction phase**. During the contraction, real GDP decreases. With the decline, employment decreases and the unemployment rate rises. The percentage of the nation's productive capacity used falls. Profits also fall. With the increase in the unemployment rate and reduction in capacity use, wages and prices increase less rapidly or fall.

Figure 12.1 Real GDP: 1960–2008

Real GDP, as measured in 2000 prices, increased substantially from 1960–2008, as can be seen in the relatively smooth line, with its measure on the left vertical axis. It did not, however, increase steadily. As the jagged line, with its measure of the right vertical axis clearly shows, real GDP increased more rapidly in some years than in others. This jagged line also shows the growth rate of real GDP starting falling in 2005 and continued through 2008.

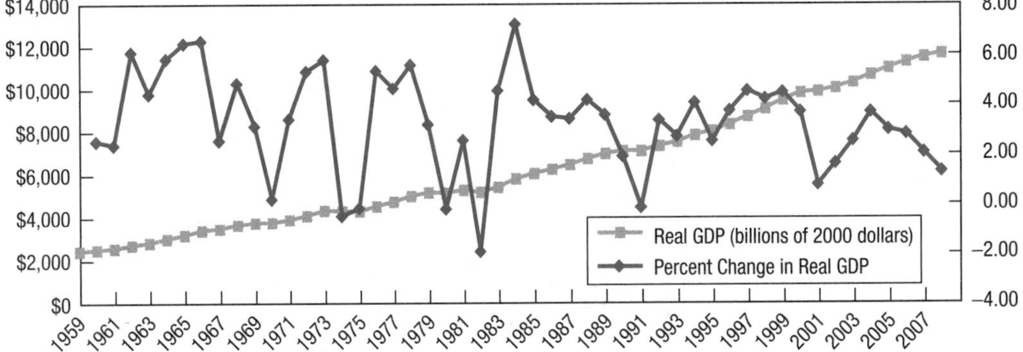

Source: U.S. Department of Commerce, Bureau of Economic Analysis, National Economic Accounts, February 2009.

Figure 12.2 **Phases of the Business Cycle**
Although real GDP increases over time, it does not increase steadily. Instead, it grows rapidly, reaches a peak, falls, reaches a trough, and repeats the cycle. This figure shows the four phases of the business cycle: expansion, peak, contraction, and trough.

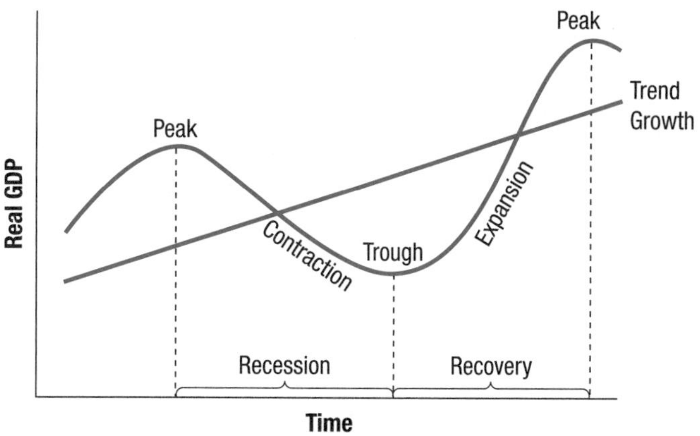

Trough–
The lowest point of the business cycle, during which real GDP is at a minimum and employment, profits, and productive capacity use are low.

Eventually, a **trough** will be reached. At the trough, GDP is at its low point. Employment, capacity use, and profits are low. The unemployment rate, however, is high. With high unemployment and low capacity use, there is little or no upward pressure on wages and prices. Indeed, wages and prices may fall.

The expansion phase is sometimes called a *recovery*. The contraction phase is often referred to as a *recession*. When a recession is particularly severe and prolonged, it is called a *depression*, for example, the Great Depression of the 1930s. Although we have had a number of recessions since the 1930s, none is in the same class as the Great Depression, when output decreased by about 30 percent from 1929 (peak) to 1933 (trough) and the unemployment rate increased from 3.2 percent to 24.9 percent.

Although each business cycle (as measured from peak to peak or trough to trough) has the same four phases, they *differ* in duration and intensity. Historically, contractions have averaged 18 months in length with the longest contraction lasted 65 months and the shortest lasted only 6 months. Expansions have averaged 35 months, with the longest lasting 120 months and the shortest, 10 months. The most recent contraction, or recession, began in March 2001 and lasted 8 months. The previous recession in 1990–1991 also lasted about 8 months. The last two recessions have been shorter than average and milder than most. In fact, in the last one output actually grew slightly.

The longest expansion in American economic history began in March 1991 and continued to March 2001. From 1991 through 2000, GDP grew at 3.6 percent per year, while unemployment fell to 4 percent and inflation remained low. The most recent exansion began November 2001 and ended December 2008, a duration of 73 months. The average annual growth of this exansion was about 2.6 percent.

Like the long-run trend, cyclical movements in real GDP have important implications for the economy. In addition to representing fluctuations in the nation's output, they are closely related to unemployment and inflation. As the economy enters the contraction phase, unemployment increases and becomes a major problem at or near the trough. As the economy recovers, unemployment may continue to increase for a while, but eventually it starts to fall. As the recovery continues, however, the price level may rise. Indeed, as the economy approaches the peak, inflation may become a major problem.

Both the long-run trend and cyclical movements of real GDP are determined by aggregate demand and aggregate supply. Because of their importance, we devote the rest of this chapter to a careful development of these concepts.

ADDITIONAL INSIGHT

Real GDP and Social Welfare—Hurricanes, Terror, and Other Considerations

Real GDP measures an economy or society's production of final goods and services in a year at market value. Is it also a measure of social welfare? Or to ask a related question, if GDP increases, can we conclude that a society is better off? With regard to the first question, the answer is no. GDP has nothing to say about many important elements of the good life—freedom, equality of opportunity, justice, and human development. With regard to the second question, the answer is a qualified yes. Most economists and perhaps most people would agree that an increase in goods and services available to a society's members will increase social welfare, assuming that no individual has an associated decrease in goods and services.

As recent natural disasters and terrorist acts have reminded us, not all measured production of final goods and services results in people having a greater availability of goods and services. According to early estimates by the Congressional Budget Office (CBO), the value of the capital stock destroyed by hurricanes Katrina and Rita amounted to somewhere between $70 and $130 billion. The CBO also estimated that between 300,000 and 500,000 jobs were lost. The CBO midpoint estimate for lost GDP in the second half of 2005 was $27 billion. The lost production was concentrated in energy production and reductions in consumption partly because of higher energy prices and partly because of the economic disruptions. This lost production was offset by additional production for replacement investment and government purchases. The CBO expects the losses in energy production, housing services, and consumption to continue throughout 2006 and into 2007. Nevertheless in 2006, the increased production because of replacement investment and government purchases will more than offset the losses. By 2006 increases in GDP due to the hurricanes will more than offset the decreases. No one would argue, of course, that the increase in GDP because of the hurricanes will result in more goods and services being available than would have been available if the hurricanes had not occurred.[a]

Similarly, it was estimated that terrorists destroyed over $16 billion of physical assets on September 11, 2001, in New York City. Their destruction did not affect measured GDP in 2001 and will never be a direct offset to GDP. (It enters the national accounts as consumption of fixed capital, affecting net domestic product.) The cost of business interruptions and dealing with the crisis—rescue, clean up and so on—amounted to at least $65 billion, which in turn was part of GDP for 2001and 2002. It has been estimated that the overall costs of Katrina and Rita will amount to even more—$140 billion.

One effect of the terrorist threat is to increase the demand for security. In response, the federal government has increased its spending on defense and security. This increased spending has drawn resources from other uses in the public and private sectors. Just as GDP makes no adjustment for hurricane cleanup, environmental pollution, or resource depletion, it makes no adjustment for reduced well being because of the perception of a greater risk of terrorist activity. Just as the economic activity associated with cleaning up the hurricanes contributes to GDP, so does the economic activity associated with enhanced security.[b]

Furthermore, GDP does not include a significant amount of production of final goods and services. The output produced by the family outside the scope of the market is not included in GDP. This includes all aspects of managing a household, childcare, do-it-yourself projects, gardening, and so on. In principle, this production could be included in GDP, but assembling accurate data would be very costly. Because these activities do not go through the market, market prices would have to be estimated. Because this production is not included it GDP, an increase in GDP can occur without any increase in production. If people went to restaurants for all of their meals, GDP would increase. If we assume, however, they purchase the exact meals they would have prepared at home, no increase in production occurs. Regardless, measured GDP increases. Over time, a larger and larger percentage of meals have been bought in restaurants, which lends an upward bias to measured GDP.

Real GDP has other defects as a social welfare measure. In particular, it provides no information as to the distribution of that output. Suppose GDP increased by 5 percent. We might conclude that society's welfare increased. Assume, however, that the increase in GDP was accompanied by a significant redistribution of income from the poor to the rich. In particular, suppose households with above-average incomes received large increases in income and those with below-average incomes experienced large decreases. Given the reduction in incomes for those at lower income levels, we might conclude that welfare decreased rather than increased.

GDP is a measure of the nation's output of goods and services, and social welfare depends, in part, on this output. Social welfare also depends on leisure. Over time, the length of the workweek has declined. In 1900, the average nonagricultural workweek was more than 50 hours. Today, it is about 40. In addition, we now have longer paid vacations and more holidays. The increase in leisure is widely regarded as having a positive effect on welfare. As before, suppose GDP increases by 5 percent. Suppose, however, that the increase in output is accomplished by significantly lengthening the workweek. Given the reduction in leisure, it is not clear that the increase in output is an improvement in social welfare.

GDP is a measure of the market value of goods and services produced in a year. Although an increase in GDP, other things equal, makes members of society better off, other things may not be equal. Consequently, GDP is an imprecise measure of social welfare. On its own terms, GDP provides a useful measure of market production in an economy. It is an element of social welfare, but it must be supplemented by many other factors.

[a]Douglas Holtz-Eakin, *Macroeconomic and Budgetary Effects of Hurricanes Katrina and Rita*, CBO Testimony, Committee on the Budget, U.S. House of Representatives, October 6, 2005.
[b]Economic Consequences of Terrorism, Ch. 4. *OECD Economic Outlook* 71 (June 2002).

Keywords: *terrorism and economic aspects, natural disasters and economic aspects, hurricanes and economic aspects*

Access InfoTrac at http://infotrac.cengage.com

Aggregate demand curve–
A curve showing the quantity of final goods and services (real GDP) that will be purchased at each price level (GDP deflator).

DETERMINING THE NATION'S OUTPUT AND PRICE LEVEL

Over time, the nation's output increases, but not steadily. It increases more rapidly in some years than in others. Similarly, the price level increases, but not steadily. As we shall see, aggregate demand and aggregate supply determine the nation's output and price level. By determining output and the price level, aggregate demand and supply also help to determine the nation's unemployment, inflation, and output growth rates. Finally, aggregate demand and supply help to determine the nation's budget and balance of payments surpluses or deficits.

Aggregate Demand

An **aggregate demand curve** shows the quantity of final goods and services (real GDP) that will be purchased at each price level (the GDP deflator). As discussed earlier, the quantity of final goods and services purchased can be divided into the amounts spent for consumption, investment, government purchases, and net exports.

Movements Along an Aggregate Demand Curve An aggregate demand curve, AD in Figure 12.3, like the demand curve for a single product, slopes downward and to the right. As the price level (as measured by the GDP deflator) decreases, the quantity of final goods and services purchased (as measured by real GDP) increases.

Both the demand curve for a single product and the aggregate demand curve are negatively sloped, but for different reasons. As you may recall from earlier chapters, nominal income and the prices of other goods and services are assumed constant in deriving the demand curve for a single product. As the price of the product falls, the product becomes less expensive relative to other goods and services. Consequently, individuals buy more of it.

This explanation is *not* appropriate for the derivation of the aggregate demand curve. When the price level falls, the prices of *all* final goods and services fall. Consequently, we

Figure 12.3 The Aggregate Demand Curve
An aggregate demand curve shows the quantity of final goods and services (real GDP) that will be purchased at each price level (the GDP deflator). The aggregate demand curve is negatively sloped.

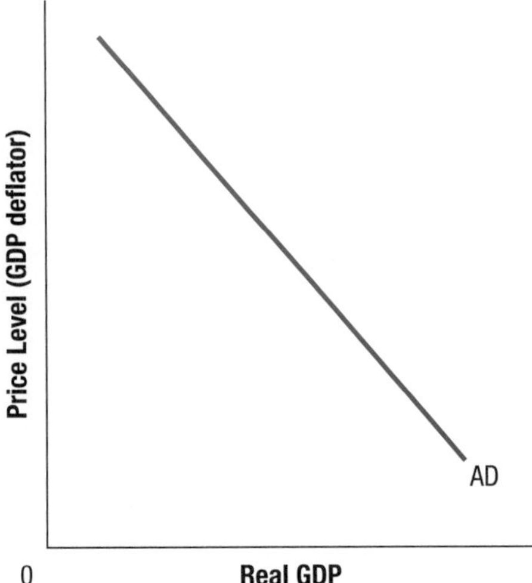

cannot argue that more will be purchased because one product is becoming less expensive relative to other goods and services.

The aggregate demand curve owes its negative slope to three effects:

- Price level on real balances and hence consumption
- Price level on interest rates and hence investment and consumption
- Price level on exports and imports

Real balance effect–The change in consumption caused by a change in the price level that changes the real value of financial assets that have fixed dollar values.

The first effect has to do with the impact of the price level on financial assets that have fixed dollar values. These assets include currency and checking account balances. As the price level rises, their purchasing power declines. As the real value of these assets erodes, households can be expected to reduce the real amount that they spend on consumption. Suppose you have a balance of $1,000 in currency and in your checking account. If the price level is 100, the real value of these money balances is $1,000. If the price level were to double (to 200) the real value would be only $500. If your real money balances decline in this way, you are likely to reduce the real amount that you spend on consumption. The effect of changes in the price level on real balances and then on consumption is the **real balance effect.**

Interest rate effect–The change in consumption and investment caused by a change in the price level that ultimately causes interest rates to change.

As we have just seen, an increase in the price level tends to reduce consumption—one component of aggregate demand—through its impact on real balances. The increase in the price level and decrease in real balances also have an impact on aggregate demand through the interest rate. When a reduction in real money balances occurs, households and firms may attempt to maintain their spending by borrowing more. As they borrow more, interest rates rise. The increase in interest rates increases the cost of borrowing. As a result of this **interest rate effect**, firms will invest less in new plants and equipment. Higher interest rates also discourage housing construction and purchases of new automobiles and other consumer durables. Thus, an increase in the price level tends to reduce investment and consumption—two components of aggregate demand—through its impact on interest rates.

The third and final effect of the price level on aggregate demand is through exports and imports. As discussed earlier, exports and imports are important to the U.S. economy.

Foreign trade effect– The change in net exports caused by a change in the price level that causes a change in the relative desirability of domestic and foreign goods and services.

The amounts that the United States exports and imports depend, in part, on the price level in the United States relative to the price level abroad. Suppose the price level in the United States rises and the price level abroad is constant. U.S. exports will be less competitive in world markets and will therefore decline. Similarly, as the price level rises in the United States relative to the price level abroad, households and firms will buy fewer goods produced in this country and more goods produced abroad because goods produced here are now relatively more expensive. Like the reduction in exports, this increase in imports reduces net exports and, therefore, aggregate demand. We can conclude that an increase in the U.S. price level results in the **foreign trade effect** that tends to reduce net exports, a component of aggregate demand, by increasing the price of U.S. products relative to foreign products.

Shifts in the Aggregate Demand Curve We have just explained why the aggregate demand curve is negatively sloped. We now consider the causes of shifts in the aggregate demand curve. One factor is changes in the degree of optimism (or pessimism) among households and firms. Suppose households were to become more optimistic about the future state of the economy. They may, as a result, spend more of their incomes on consumption. If they do, consumption will increase, and because consumption is a component of aggregate demand, aggregate demand will increase. This increase in aggregate demand is shown in Figure 12.4 as a shift in the aggregate demand curve from AD_0 to AD_1. With the shift, aggregate demand is now greater at each price level. A similar shift occurs if firms become more optimistic about the future state of the economy. The only difference is that if firms become more optimistic, investment increases.

Fiscal policy– Use of government purchases and taxes to achieve full employment and other economic goals.

The aggregate demand curve will shift for other reasons. For our purposes, we focus on changes caused by changes in the nation's fiscal and monetary policies. **Fiscal policy** is the use of government purchases and taxes to achieve full employment and other economic goals. Government purchases are one component of aggregate demand. If government purchases increase, the aggregate demand for goods and services increases and the aggregate demand curve, as shown in Figure 12.4, shifts to the right. If taxes are reduced,

Figure 12.4 A Shift in the Aggregate Demand Curve
An increase in aggregate demand is shown by a rightward shift in the aggregate demand curve. The aggregate demand curve may shift to the right because policy makers are pursuing an expansionary fiscal or monetary policy.

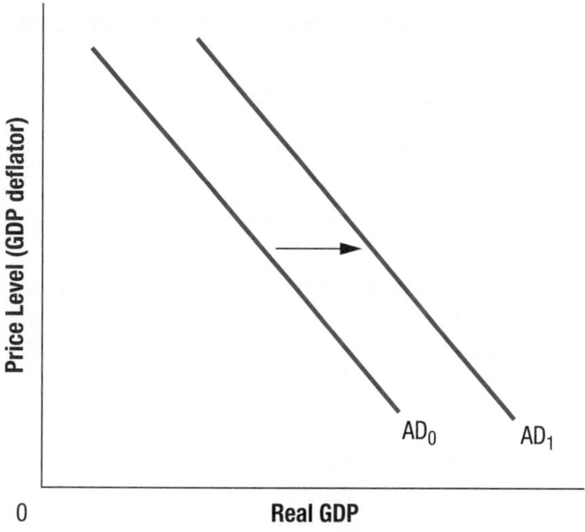

households find that their after-tax income, or disposable income, is higher. Because of the increase in their disposable income, households will increase their consumption. Because consumption is one component of aggregate demand, the aggregate demand for goods and services rises and the aggregate demand curve shifts to the right.

As demonstrated, both an increase in government purchases and a decrease in taxes cause aggregate demand to increase. Thus, we define an expansionary fiscal policy as an increase in aggregate demand brought about by an increase in government purchases, a decrease in taxes, or some combination of the two.

A decrease in government purchases or an increase in taxes has the opposite effect on aggregate demand. Both reduce aggregate demand, thereby causing the aggregate demand curve to shift to the left. Thus, we define contractionary fiscal policy as a decrease in aggregate demand brought about by a decrease in government purchases, an increase in taxes, or some combination.

Money supply– Currency (including coins), checkable deposits, and traveler's checks.

A change in the money supply also affects the aggregate demand for goods and services. For the purposes of this chapter, we define the nation's **money supply** as its currency (including coins), checkable deposits, and travelers' checks. These items are considered money because they are generally accepted as payment for goods and services.

If the nation's money supply increases, the aggregate demand for goods and services increases and the aggregate demand curve shifts to the right. The increase in aggregate demand occurs for at least two reasons. First, the increase in the money supply increases real balances. As a result, households increase their consumption. Second, the increase in the money supply reduces interest rates. Lower interest rates mean firms will invest more in new plant and equipment. Similarly, lower interest rates encourage housing construction and purchases of new automobiles and other consumer durables. The increase in real balances and the decrease in interest rates cause consumption and investment to increase. Because consumption and investment are components of aggregate demand, aggregate demand increases and the aggregate demand curve shifts to the right.

Monetary policy– Use of the money supply to achieve full employment and other economic goals.

The nation's money supply can be altered by the Federal Reserve, an independent agency of the federal government discussed at length in Chapter 14. The Federal Reserve conducts U.S. monetary policy. **Monetary policy** is the use of the money supply to achieve full employment and other economic goals.

Keywords: *fiscal policy, monetary policy*

Access InfoTrac at http://infotrac.cengage.com

As shown, an increase in the money supply causes aggregate demand to increase. Thus, we define expansionary monetary policy as an action by the Federal Reserve to increase the money supply. In contrast, we define contractionary monetary policy as an action by the Federal Reserve to decrease the money supply. A decrease in the money supply causes aggregate demand to decrease.

Aggregate Supply

Aggregate supply curve– A curve showing the quantity of final goods and services (real GDP) that will be produced at each price level (the GDP deflator).

An **aggregate supply curve** shows the quantity of final goods and services (real GDP) that will be produced at each price level (the GDP deflator). Aggregate supply curve AS is depicted in Figure 12.5.

Movements Along an Aggregate Supply Curve The aggregate supply curve in Figure 12.5 has two segments: a positively sloped segment up to price level P_1 and a vertical segment from P_1 up. The positively sloped segment of AS is like the supply curve for a single product. As the price level (as measured by the GDP deflator) increases, the quantity of goods and services (as measured by real GDP) supplied increases. In deriving the positively sloped segment of the aggregate supply curve, it is assumed that wage rates and other input prices (as well as the labor supply, capital stock, and technology) are constant. Consequently, when the price level rises from, say, P_0 in Figure 12.5 to P_1,

Figure 12.5 The Aggregate Supply Curve
An aggregate supply curve shows the quantity of final goods and services (real GDP) that will be produced at each price level (the GDP deflator). The aggregate supply curve is positively sloped until the full employment level of output, GDP_{FE}, is reached. It then becomes vertical.

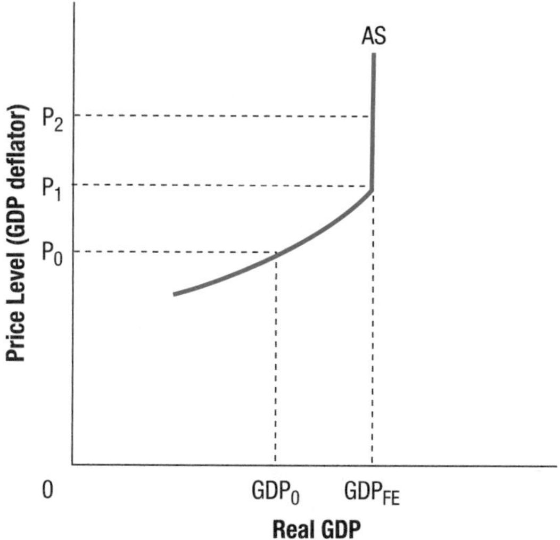

firms find it profitable to increase production and output increases from GDP_0 to GDP_{FE}. As firms expand production, they hire more workers. The rise in employment causes the unemployment rate to fall. In terms of the production possibilities curve, the economy is moving from a point inside the curve to the curve.

Once price level P_1 is reached, the aggregate supply curve becomes vertical at output GDP_{FE}, the full employment output level. At this point the economy has reached the production possibilities curve. Suppose the price level rises from P_1 to P_2. Wage rates and other input prices can no longer be assumed constant. With the economy at full employment, individual firms may increase output by offering higher wage rates to attract workers from other firms. These increases in output are offset by the decreases in output experienced by firms that lose workers. Thus, despite the increase in the price level and wage rates, total output is unchanged.

Shifts in the Aggregate Supply Curve We turn now to the causes of shifts in the aggregate supply curve. As discussed, the positively sloped segment of the aggregate supply curve is derived assuming that wage rates and other input prices are constant. For most firms, wages and salaries are the largest expense, typically accounting for 70 to 75 percent of all expenses. Consequently, wage and salary increases cause a major cost increase. This cost increase means firms must receive higher prices to continue producing the same amounts. Thus, a wage increase causes the aggregate supply curve to shift from AS_0 to AS_1 in Figure 12.6. An increase in the prices of other inputs will shift the aggregate supply curve in the same manner.

In deriving the aggregate supply curve, the nation's labor supply, capital stock, and technology are assumed constant. If the labor supply or the capital stock increases, the aggregate supply curve shifts to the right. Similarly, if technological progress occurs, the aggregate supply curve shifts to the right. One such shift is shown in Figure 12.7. Note that, with the shift, the full employment level of output increases from GDP_{FE} to GDP'_{FE}. This is because increases in the labor supply and capital stock and technological

Figure 12.6 The Impact of a Wage Rates Increase on the Aggregate Supply Curve
The positive slope of a portion of the aggregate supply curve is due to the assumption that wage rates and other input prices are constant. If wage rates rise, the relevant portion of the aggregate supply curve shifts to the left.

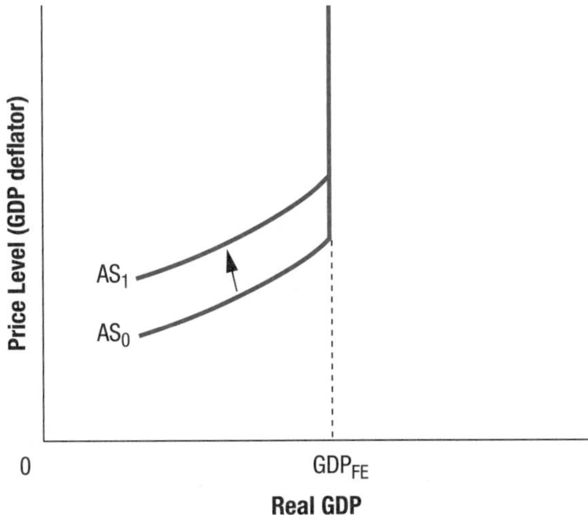

progress increase the nation's productive capacity. If wage rates or other input prices rise, however, the full employment level of output (see Figure 12.6) does not change, because the nation's productive capacity is unaltered.

Aggregate Demand and Supply Interaction

In Chapter 2, you saw that the demand for and supply of a particular good determine its equilibrium output and price. Similarly, aggregate demand and supply determine the equilibrium levels of real GDP and the GDP deflator. In Figure 12.8, the aggregate

Figure 12.7 The Impact of an Increase in the Capital Stock on the Aggregate Supply Curve
The aggregate supply curve is drawn on the assumption that the economy's labor supply, capital stock, and technology are constant. If the capital stock increases, the aggregate supply curve shifts to the right.

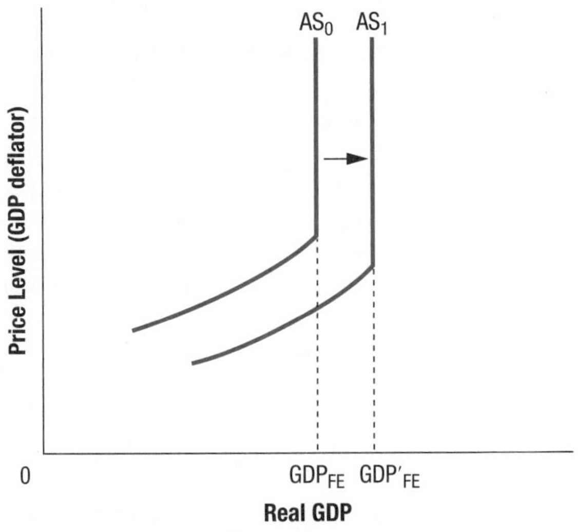

Figure 12.8 **Aggregate Demand and Supply**
The equilibrium combination of output (real GDP) and the price level (GDP deflator) is given by the intersection of the aggregate demand and supply curves. In this case, the equilibrium level of output is GDP_0 and the equilibrium price level is P_0.

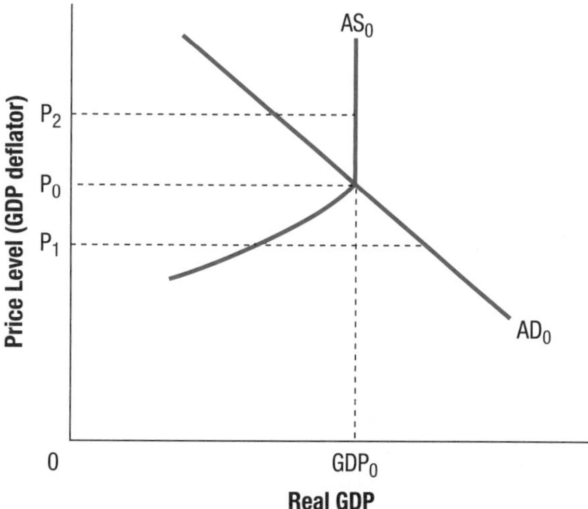

demand curve is AD_0 and the aggregate supply curve is AS_0. The equilibrium levels of real GDP and the GDP deflator are GDP_0 and P_0, respectively, given by the intersection of these aggregate demand and supply curves.

To show that GDP_0 and P_0 must be the equilibrium combination of real GDP and the GDP deflator, consider alternative price levels. Suppose that the price level is P_1, which is less than the equilibrium price level. At P_1, the aggregate quantity demanded exceeds the aggregate quantity supplied, implying that purchasers would like to buy more goods and services than firms are willing to produce. Firms find that they cannot maintain their desired levels of inventories because purchasers buy their products faster than they are produced. In addition to firms finding that they are not producing fast enough to maintain their sales, some customers are finding that they cannot buy all that they are willing to buy at the current prices. A general excess demand exists for goods and services. This excess demand puts upward pressure on prices, causing the price level to rise. As the price level rises, firms become willing to produce more and consumers cut back on their purchase plans. The price level will continue to rise until it reaches the equilibrium level, P_0. At P_0, purchasers buy the quantity of goods and services that firms produce. Consequently, neither purchasers nor firms have an incentive to alter their behavior.

Suppose that the price level is P_2, which is above the equilibrium price level. At P_2, the aggregate quantity supplied exceeds the aggregate quantity demanded, implying that purchasers are unwilling to buy as many goods and services as firms are willing to produce. This excess supply of goods and services places downward pressure on prices. As a result, the price level falls until the equilibrium price level, P_0, is reached.

In this example, P_0 is the equilibrium price level because it is the only price level at which purchasers are willing to buy the same quantity of goods and services that firms are willing to produce. At any other price level, either excess aggregate demand or excess aggregate supply exists, and the price level changes until the equilibrium price level is restored.

In Figure 12.8, the equilibrium level of real GDP is GDP_0, the full employment level of output. We know that GDP_0 is the full employment level of output because the

ADDITIONAL INSIGHT

The Long Boom

Since 1980, the United States has had three recessions and three expansions. Following the severe recession that began in July 1981 and lasted 16 months, the economy began a long expansion that lasted until June 1990. The mild recession that started in July 1990 and ended in March 1991 provided a brief pause for the U.S. economy, which then began its longest expansion ever—10 years. This expansion ended in March 2001, with this second mild recession ending before the end of 2001. The current expansion is now in its fifth year.

The severe recession that began in 1981 followed the Federal Reserve's contractionary monetary policy that subdued the rapid inflation of the late 1970s and 1980. The inflation rate did drop, but the nation's output and employment fell, and the unemployment rate increased. Real GDP fell by 2.2 percent in 1982, a large decrease by historical standards. The unemployment rate increased steadily, reaching a high of 10.8 percent in November 1982 (the trough).

The economic expansion that followed the November 1982 trough was the nation's third longest expansion, almost eight years. During the expansion, the unemployment rate fell steadily, reaching 5.3 percent in 1989. With the economy at or near full employment, prices started rising more rapidly. As a result, the Federal Reserve reduced the growth rate of the money supply. Although this policy succeeded in reducing the inflation rate, it was one of the factors causing the recession of 1990–1991. Other factors include (1) increases in debt—household, business, and government—which contributed to cutbacks in spending; (2) cuts in defense and in state and local spending, and (3) the impact of the savings and loan crisis on households and firms.

As previously stated, both the 1990–1991 and 2001 recessions were both short and mild. Real GDP increased in 1990 and fell by only 0.2 percent in 1991. Real GDP actually increased in 2001. Similarly, the unemployment rate in March 1991 (the trough) was only 6.8 percent, although it continued to increase, reaching a high of 7.8 percent in May 1992. Starting in the third quarter of that year, however, the economy began to grow more rapidly and the unemployment rate finally began to fall. Similarly, in 2001 the monthly unemployment rate rose to just 5.7 percent, but it continued to rise until June 2003, reaching a high of 6.3 percent.

This 1991–2001 recovery is the longest one in American history. It started slowly, but soon gained momentum with real GDP growing every year, including 2001 the year of the last recession. Remarkably, the unemployment rate continued to fall through 2000, reaching a low of 4 percent. The recovery that began at the end of 2001 was known as a jobless recovery because the unemployment rate continued to increase well after the trough. As the unemployment began to fall it returned to a relatively low 5.4 percent in December 2004 and 4.9 percent in December 2005.

This latest recovery has overcome three remarkable difficulties. It began just after the terrorist attacks of September 11 that many observers thought would cause the economy to remain in the recession and probably deepen the recession. The federal tax cuts at the beginning of 2001 probably helped the economy to emerge from the recession. The recovery has also had to cope with large increases in energy prices even before the hurricanes that disrupted petroleum markets. Such large energy price increases in the past have been associated with either a contraction or inflation and sometimes both. Finally, it has had to cope with disruptions to the economy because of the hurricanes. The ability of the economy to cope with these strong, negative shocks may be related to the reasons that we have had such a period of expansion with little inflation and only two short recessions. Professor John Taylor of Stanford University notes that the mild recessions of the early 1990s and in 2001 were just blips in what he calls the "Long Boom" that started in November 1982 and has continued through 2005. Figure 12.1 nicely illustrates this "Long Boom" and the decreased variability in growth rates that accompanied it.

What accounts for this remarkable period in American economic history? Professor Taylor, an Undersecretary of the Treasury for International Affairs in the second Bush administration, attributes it to sound monetary policy. Robert Rubin, Secretary of the Treasury during part of the Clinton administration, attributes much of the 1990s expansion to sound fiscal policy that balanced the federal budget and led to reductions in interest rates. The economic boom of the late 1990s resulted from a surge of investment that led to investment accounting for an unusually large part of GDP growth. Investment was spurred by new technologies and by monetary and fiscal policies that lowered the rate of interest.

Figure 12.9 Changes in Aggregate Demand and Their Impact on Real GDP and the Price Level The initial equilibrium combination of output and the price level is GDP_0, P_0. If aggregate demand decreases (to AD_1) with wage rates and other input prices constant, output and the price level fall. If aggregate demand increases (to AD_2), the price level rises. Output, however, remains constant because the economy is already at full employment.

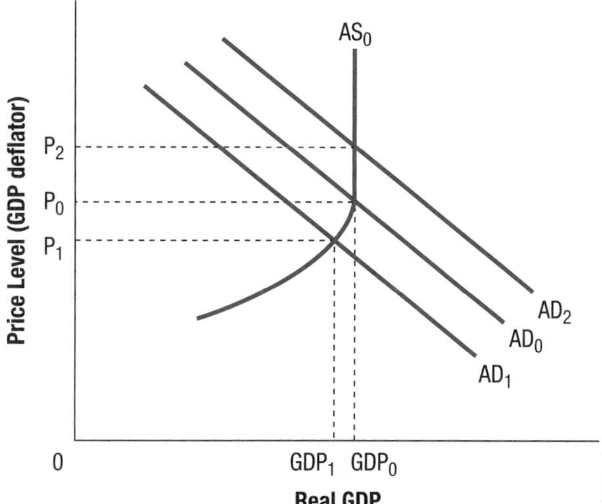

aggregate supply curve becomes vertical at that output level, indicating that the nation's productive capacity is fully utilized. There is no guarantee, however, that GDP will be at its full employment level. Suppose that, in Figure 12.9, aggregate demand falls from AD_0 to AD_1. With aggregate demand AD_0, real GDP was GDP_0—the full employment level of output. With the reduction in aggregate demand, purchasers now buy less at each price level. As a result, both real GDP and the GDP deflator fall. As real GDP decreases, firms reduce employment and the unemployment rate rises. With wage rates and other input prices constant (or slow to adjust), the unemployment rate may be above the full employment rate of unemployment for a substantial period of time.

Just as aggregate demand may fall from AD_0 to AD_1, it could increase from AD_0 to AD_2. When aggregate demand increases to AD_2, purchasers buy more at each price level. This increase in aggregate demand causes the price level to rise to P_2. It does not, however, alter real GDP. With the economy already producing at the full employment level of output, GDP_0, the increase in aggregate demand results in higher output and input prices, but not higher output.

Summary

Gross domestic product (GDP) is the market value of all final goods and services produced in the economy over the relevant time span, usually a year. GDP, the most frequently cited measure of the nation's output, is divided into four components: consumption, gross investment, government purchases, and net exports.

In compiling GDP, market prices are used. This makes it difficult to measure the nation's output because both quantities and prices change over time. To overcome this problem, we first construct a price index, a measure of the price level for a given period relative to the base period. Once this price index—the GDP deflator—is constructed, we divide, or deflate, nominal GDP by the GDP deflator to obtain real GDP. Thus, the relationship between real GDP, nominal GDP, and the GDP deflator is

$$\textbf{Real GDP} = \frac{\textbf{Nominal GDP}}{\textbf{Price deflator}}$$

Nominal GDP reflects both quantity and price changes. In contrast, real GDP reflects only quantity changes. Because real GDP reflects only quantity changes, it is a better measure of the nation's output.

The GDP deflator is a weighted average of the prices of all final goods and services produced in the economy. It is the most comprehensive measure of the nation's price level.

Historically, the economy has performed well. Since 1929, output has increased at an average annual rate of about 3 percent. It has not, however, increased steadily. Periods of rapidly increasing real GDP have been followed by periods of slowly rising or even falling real GDP. These fluctuations in the level of economic activity are called business cycles.

An aggregate demand curve shows the quantity of final goods and services that will be purchased at each price level. Similarly, an aggregate supply curve shows the quantity of final goods and services that will be produced at each price level.

The nation's equilibrium output and price level are given by intersection of the aggregate demand and supply curves. Because aggregate demand and supply change over time, output and the price level also change over time.

Fiscal policy is the use of government purchases and taxes to achieve full employment and other economic goals. Similarly, monetary policy is the use of the money supply to achieve those same goals. Through the use of fiscal and monetary policy, policy makers can alter aggregate demand and, hence, the nation's output and price level.

Key Terms

Gross domestic product (GDP)
Final goods
Intermediate goods
Personal consumption expenditures
Gross private domestic investment
Capital stock
Government purchases of goods and services
Net exports of goods and services
Exports
Imports
Price index
Nominal GDP
Real GDP
GDP deflator
Business cycles
Expansion phase
Peak
Contraction phase
Trough
Aggregate demand curve
Real balance effect
Interest rate effect
Foreign trade effect
Fiscal policy
Money supply
Monetary policy
Aggregate supply curve

Review Questions

1. Define GDP. Why are only final goods and services included? Why are changes in business inventories included?
2. List and briefly describe GDP's major components.
3. Describe the effects of each of the following on U.S. GDP:
   a. A hurricane that destroys a dam and floods a major city
   b. A ban on U.S. imports from Germany
   c. The legalization of marijuana
   d. U.S. involvement in a war in the Middle East.
4. What is the underground economy? Why do people participate in the underground economy? How might its size be reduced?
5. What is the difference between nominal and real GDP?
6. "An increase in nominal GDP means that more goods and services are available to society." Using a specific example, explain why this statement is true or false.
7. Fill in the blanks in the following table:

Year	Nominal GDP (billions of current dollars)	Real GDP (billions of 1992 dollars)	GDP Deflator
2005	–	4,800.0	120.0
2006	6,500.0	5,000.0	–
2007	9,000.0	–	150.0

8. Discuss the business cycle and its phases. What are the short- and long-run implications of the business cycle for growth of real GDP?
9. What is the aggregate demand curve? Why is it negatively sloped?
10. What factors may cause the aggregate demand curve to shift? Graphically, illustrate both an increase and a decrease in aggregate demand.
11. Carefully explain why the aggregate supply curve has two segments: a positively sloped segment and a vertical segment.
12. What factors will cause the aggregate supply curve to shift? How will these factors affect the two segments of the curve?
13. Using graphical analysis, explain why the equilibrium levels of GDP and the GDP deflator are determined by the intersection of the aggregate demand and supply curves.
14. Over the last three decades, there have been several episodes of increasing oil prices due to political events. The United States imports much of the oil that it uses. What effect does a large increase in oil prices this have on real GDP and the GDP deflator? Defend your answer.

Web Sites

- ***Economic Policy Institute***
  The Economic Policy Institute focuses on research and education and seeks to promote a prosperous and fair economy. Among its web features are "economic indicators" and "economic snapshots"—**http://www.epinet.org/**
- ***Economics Resource Center***
  This site by South-Western Cengage provides links to other sites through such features and Status of the Economy and Economic Data Online. It also presents "debates" on current economics topics—**http://www.swcollege.com/bef/economics.html**
- ***Economic Research***
  The St. Louis Federal Reserve Bank site for their economics research contains links to data and to the many publications of the bank, many of which are accessible to students—**http://www.research.stlouisfed.org/**
- ***Econ Data and Links.***
- A megasite—**http://www.csufresno.edu/Economics/econ_EDL.htm#UNITED%20STATES**

CHAPTER 13

Unemployment: The Legacy of Recession, Technological Change, and Free Choice

OUTLINE

One of the goals that Americans expect the economy to achieve is full employment of labor. Figure 13.1 indicates that the U.S. unemployment rate has fluctuated around the 6 percent level over the past 45 years, with the unemployment rate exceeding 6 percent in 16 years out of the last 45 years, or roughly one-third of the time. For reasons that we will explain, economists believe that the economy achieves full employment when no more than 6 percent of the labor force is unemployed. Thus, by this test, the unemployment rate has been unacceptably high quite often in recent U.S. history and the unemployment problem shows no signs of disappearing from the social problems agenda.

In this chapter, we explain why unemployment is a social problem, how the unemployment rate is determined, why a 6 percent unemployment rate is the full employment target,

Figure 13.1 Annual U.S. Unemployment Rate, 1960–2008

The U.S. unemployment rate has varied greatly over the past 45 years, exhibiting an irregular pattern of fluctuations above and below 6 percent.

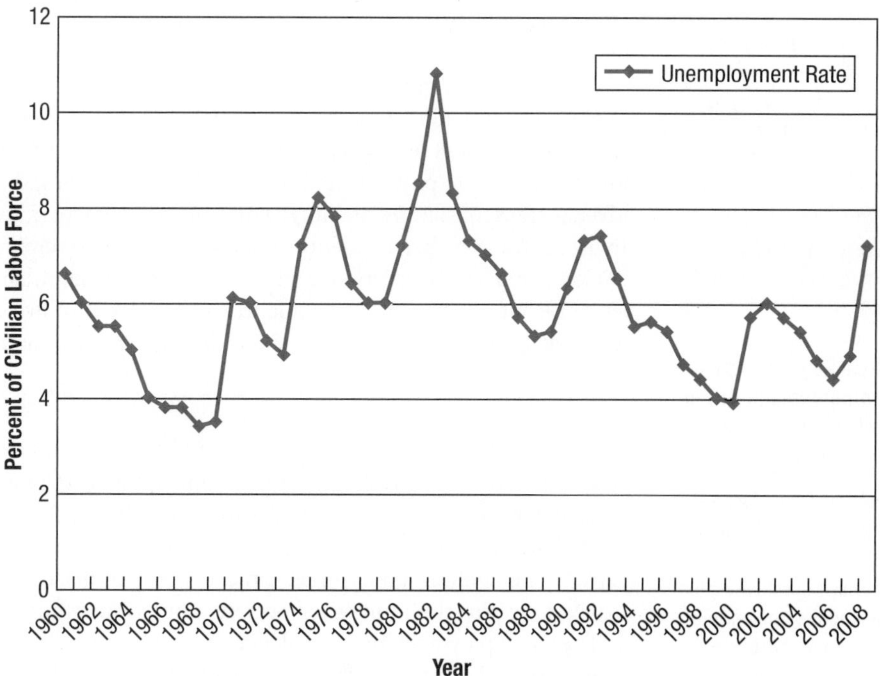

why the unemployment rate sometimes exceeds 6 percent, and what the government might do to reduce the unemployment rate. Although the chapter emphasizes unemployment in the United States, we also draw some lessons from unemployment in Europe.

COSTS OF UNEMPLOYMENT

Unemployment produces both economic and non-economic costs. These costs differ for the individual and for society.

Economic Costs

For the individual, the most obvious economic cost of unemployment is the loss of income that the person would have received if employed. This lost income may be partially offset by unemployment compensation, food stamps, or other government transfer payments. In general, however, these kinds of benefits are less than the income lost. As a result, the individual's economic position deteriorates.

So long as the period of unemployment is short, the impact on the individual is not severe. The individual and family may be able to maintain their standard of living by spending from savings. As time passes, however, the family may be forced to alter its lifestyle by spending less for food, clothing, and entertainment. More drastic changes might include moving to less expensive housing and selling assets. Ultimately, the individual and family may become impoverished.

For society, the cost of unemployment is the goods and services that could have been produced by the unemployed. To illustrate, the U.S. unemployment rate increased from 3.2 percent in 1929 to 24.9 percent in 1933. As a result, the nation's output of goods and services fell by about 30 percent, a decrease in output that has not occurred since then.

Non-Economic Costs

Keywords: *unemployment (economic aspects); unemployment (psychological aspects)*

Access InfoTrac at http://infotrac.cengage.com

In addition to economic costs, individuals experiencing prolonged unemployment are subject to other costs. Many unemployed persons experience anxiety, stress, loss of self-confidence and self-esteem, and depression. It is, after all, frustrating and depressing to apply unsuccessfully for job after job. It is also frustrating to be unable to buy what you and your family want and to not know when you will be able to do so.

High unemployment rates are associated with a higher incidence of alcoholism and drug abuse, as well as higher crime and suicide rates. Prolonged unemployment has an adverse effect on physical and mental health. Prolonged unemployment also has an adverse effect on family stability. High unemployment rates are associated with higher divorce rates, a higher incidence of child abuse, and increased infant mortality.

Compared to the economic costs of unemployment, these non-economic costs are very difficult or impossible to quantify. They are, however, no less real and should be acknowledged when considering the costs of unemployment.

Unemployment rate– The percentage of the civilian labor force that is unemployed.

Civilian labor force– The number of people 16 years of age or older who are employed plus the number of people not employed but looking for work.

THE UNEMPLOYMENT RATE

More attention is probably paid to the unemployment rate than to any other economic statistic. Given the costs associated with unemployment, this is not surprising.

The **unemployment rate** is the percentage of the civilian labor force that is unemployed. The **civilian labor force** is the number of persons 16 years of age or older who are working *plus* the number of persons not working but looking for work.

The unemployment rate is calculated monthly on the basis of household interviews. Interviewers visit nearly 60,000 households scattered throughout the United States each month and ask questions about each member of the household 16 years of age and older. The answers to the questions allow the government to classify each member of the household as employed, unemployed, or not in the civilian labor force.

People are defined as employed if they did any work at all as paid employees in the previous week or worked 15 hours or more as unpaid employees in a family business. People also are employed if they have jobs but do not work because of illness, bad weather, vacation, labor-management disputes, or personal reasons.

People are unemployed if they had no job, were available for work, and had actively looked for work during the past four weeks. Also counted as unemployed are persons waiting to start new jobs within 30 days or waiting to be recalled to jobs from which they had been laid off.

As noted, the civilian labor force consists of people 16 years of age or older who are either employed or unemployed. Persons 16 years of age and older who are neither employed nor unemployed are not in the civilian labor force. Persons not in the labor force include

- College students who do not have jobs (and are not looking for jobs).
- Homemakers and retired persons not looking for jobs.
- Persons without jobs who have become discouraged and stopped actively looking for jobs.

In calculating the unemployment rate, only people in the civilian labor force are included. Suppose that 7 million people are unemployed, 135 million are employed, and the civilian labor force is 142 million. Application of the following equation yields the unemployment rate (UR), where U refers to the number of people unemployed and LF is the number of people in the civilian labor force:

$$\mathbf{UR = (U/LF) \times 100}$$

In the equation, the ratio of the number of persons unemployed (U) to the civilian labor force (LF) is multiplied by 100 to express the unemployment rate as a percentage. With 7 million persons unemployed and a civilian labor force of 142 million, we have the following:

$$\mathbf{UR = (7\ million/142\ million) \times 100 = 4.9\ percent}$$

The unemployment rate summarizes the average experience of all cohorts in the labor force. There are significant differences from the average, however, for some labor force cohorts. Figure 13.2 illustrates the annual unemployment rates for four cohorts: teenagers (16 to 19 years old), African-Americans, Hispanics, and all workers. Generally, the rates for the four groups move together, but there are relatively persistent differentials between them.

These differences in unemployment rates have two important implications. First, they imply that an increase in the overall unemployment rate is not shared equally. Suppose the unemployment rate increases by 1 percentage point. Because the unemployment rate for African-Americans is about twice the unemployment rate for all workers and the teenage unemployment is about three times the unemployment for all workers, the African-American and teenage unemployment rates will rise about 2 and 3 percentage points, respectively. Second, the different unemployment rates among demographic groups may indicate the necessity of different policies to reduce the unemployment rates of the various groups. (See Additional Insight: Job Opportunities and Discrimination.)

Figure 13.2 Annual Unemployment Rates for Selected Labor Force Cohorts, 1973–2004
Annual unemployment rates for teenagers, African-Americans, and Hispanics exhibit fluctuations that are similar to fluctuations in the annual unemployment rate for all workers, but at higher rates of unemployment.

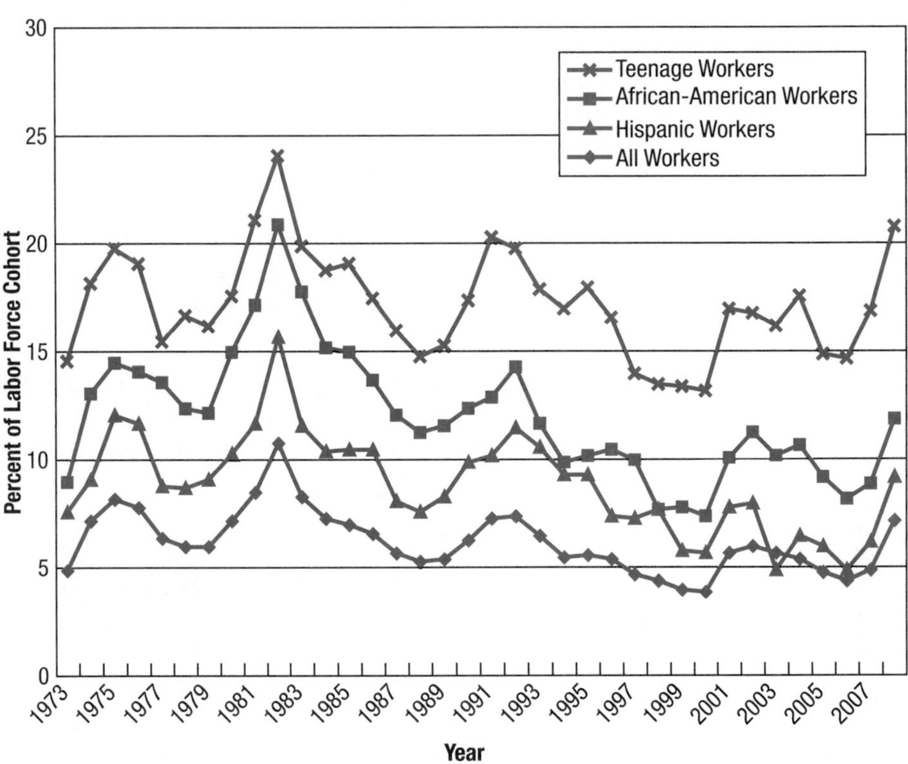

Keywords: *unemployed workers, employment discrimination*

Access InfoTrac at http://infotrac.cengage.com

PRINCIPAL TYPES OF UNEMPLOYMENT

Economists distinguish between three principal types of unemployment—frictional, structural, and cyclical. They do this because each type has different causes and different implications for public policy.

Frictional Unemployment

Frictional unemployment– Temporary unemployment arising from the normal job-search process.

Frictional unemployment is temporary unemployment arising from the normal job search process. It takes time for the labor market to match the job seeker with the available job. It includes persons entering the job market for the first time (or reentering after an absence). It also includes persons who have quit jobs to search for better ones. Finally, it includes some of the people who have been laid off or fired.

Structural Unemployment

Structural unemployment– Unemployment caused by structural changes in the economy that eliminate jobs.

Structural unemployment arises when jobs are eliminated by changes in the structure of the economy. These changes occur because of technological progress and shifts in the demand for goods and services. Technological progress creates new jobs and eliminates old ones. The production process in many industries, for example, is becoming increasingly computerized. As a result, some production line workers are losing their jobs. At the same time, new jobs—such as computer repair technician and software engineer—are

ADDITIONAL INSIGHT

Job Opportunities and Discrimination

The unemployment rate for African-Americans is about double that for whites and has been for years. Is this differential in unemployment rates due to discrimination? Before answering, we must analyze the situation.

Employers consider workers' productivity in their hiring decisions (see the Appendix to this chapter). At a given wage, hiring the most productive workers minimizes the firm's costs and maximizes its profits. Unfortunately, African-Americans typically receive less education and on-the-job training than whites. Moreover, the education that African-Americans do receive is often inferior to that of whites. With less education and on-the-job training, some African-Americans are less productive and are denied employment because of their low productivity. In fact, much—perhaps most—of the differential in unemployment rates is due not to job discrimination, but to differences in productivity, which, in turn, may be related to discrimination in the amount and quality of education that African-Americans receive.

Given that the unemployment rate for African-Americans is relatively high, the way to reduce it is to eliminate the cause. Their productivity would be enhanced by more and better—that is, more equal—education. Improving access to better schools and ensuring that persons from disadvantaged homes have the financial resources through student loan and other programs would go far to eliminate the differential in unemployment rates between African-Americans and whites.

Affirmative action programs to provide African-Americans with greater educational and job opportunities may be desirable. Quotas, however, are probably undesirable because they contribute to racial tensions and can result in reverse discrimination.

To the extent that African-Americans are the last to be hired and the first to be fired, stabilizing output and employment at their full employment levels is another way of reducing the differential in unemployment rates. With stability of employment, African-Americans will gain valuable experience and on-the-job training. Also, with full employment, employers are less able to discriminate because of the limited number of prospective employees. With less than full employment, employers are more able to discriminate on the basis of race because they can choose from a large number of unemployed workers of all races.

While some people find jobs almost immediately, others may search for several months. Consider a young man who has no job when he graduates from college. He must first identify available jobs and apply for them. Then he must wait for prospective employers to examine his credentials, check his references, interview candidates, and decide whom to hire. Even after he receives a job offer, the effective date of employment may be some time in the future. All in all, the job search process is time consuming, which is one reason why college students are urged to start interviewing early in their senior years.

Because it takes time to find a job, some frictional unemployment is inevitable. Although it may be unpleasant, it is temporary. Moreover, it is an aspect of an efficiently functioning economy because it results from people searching for the best (higher-paying?) jobs. As we indicate by the title of the chapter, frictional unemployment is a product of free choice. Those who are successful in finding higher-paying jobs will have also found higher-productivity jobs, and to this extent, the nation's output of goods and services increases. Because frictional unemployment is temporary and serves some useful social functions, it is not normally a matter concerning policy makers.

appearing. Even so, displaced production line workers may lack the skills necessary for these new jobs. Similarly, the demand for some goods and services declines over time, while the demand for others rises. Again, workers who lose their jobs in the declining industries may not have the skills needed in the expanding industries.

As with frictional unemployment, the problem is not caused by a lack of jobs. Jobs are available. Structural unemployment reflects a mismatch between the skills of prospective

INFOTRAC College Edition

Keywords: *structural unemployment, technological unemployment*

Access InfoTrac at http://infotrac.cengage.com

workers and the skills needed in the vacant jobs. Michigan may have unemployed automobile workers and unfilled computer science jobs. Similarly, Oklahoma may have a surplus of oil field workers and a shortage of airplane mechanics.

Although structural unemployment resembles frictional unemployment in that the problem is not a lack of jobs, it differs in two important, and related, respects. First, a person who is frictionally unemployed has marketable job skills. A person who is structurally unemployed does not and might benefit from substantial retraining or additional education to become employable. Second, a frictionally unemployed person can look forward to obtaining a job soon. A structurally unemployed person—without new training or additional education—faces a bleak future of long-term unemployment broken, perhaps, by sporadic employment spells. Because it is long-term, policymakers regard structural unemployment as a more serious problem than frictional unemployment.

INFOTRAC College Edition

Keywords: *unemployment, types of*

Access InfoTrac at http://infotrac.cengage.com

Cyclical Unemployment

Cyclical unemployment– Unemployment resulting from the business cycle.

Cyclical unemployment is the unemployment resulting from the business cycle. Cyclical unemployment increases in the contraction phase of the business cycle and falls in the expansion phase of the business cycle. Although both types of changes in the cyclical unemployment rate can be problematic (for reasons explained below), *increases* in cyclical unemployment appear to be of greater policy concern. Such increases occur as business firms reduce output and lay off or discharge workers in response to a contraction in the business cycle. Unlike frictional and structural unemployment, cyclical unemployment is characterized by a job shortage. The unemployment rate increases during the contraction phase of the business cycle and reaches a maximum at or near the trough. As the economy enters the expansion phase of the business cycle, firms increase output and employment, and the unemployment rate falls. The unemployment rate decreases during the expansion phase and reaches a minimum at or near the peak.

FULL EMPLOYMENT AND THE NATURAL RATE OF UNEMPLOYMENT

Full employment– The state of the economy where the rate of unemployment equals the natural rate of unemployment.

Natural rate of unemployment– The normal rate of unemployment around which the unemployment rate fluctuates.

Full employment is the state of the economy where the rate of unemployment equals the natural rate of unemployment. The **natural rate of unemployment** is the normal rate of unemployment around which the unemployment rate fluctuates. The normal rate of unemployment around which the unemployment rate has fluctuated since 1960 is about 6 percent. To illustrate this, we have reproduced Figure 13.1 (as Figure 13.3) and fitted a linear trend line to the data. The trend line is virtually constant at 6 percent.

The natural rate consists largely of frictional and structural unemployment. The year-to-year fluctuations around the natural rate reflect cyclical unemployment. Cyclical unemployment, in turn, reflects the contraction (when the unemployment rate is above the trend) and expansion (when the unemployment rate is below the trend) phases of the business cycle.

The economy achieved an unemployment rate of 6 percent in only 5 of the 45 years between 1960 and 2004: in 1961, 1971, 1978, 1979, and 2002. It was at or within 5 percent—an unemployment rate between 5.7 and 6.3 percent—of the target rate of 6 percent in 10 of the 45 years, or about one-fifth of the time. It was above 6.3 percent in 16 of the 45 years, or a little over a third of them. It was below 5.7 percent in 19 of the 45 years, or about 40 percent of the time.

Figure 13.3 **Annual Average Unemployment Rate and Linear Trend Line, 1960–2008**
A linear trend line fitted to the data on the unemployment rate indicates that 6 percent is the unemployment rate around which fluctuations occur.

Economists are concerned about deviations significantly above *and* below 6 percent. Deviations above the 6 percent rate produce the economic and non-economic costs of unemployment described above. Deviations significantly below the 6 percent rate pose the threat of accelerating inflation, a problem we will analyze in Chapter 14. Given that the economy can operate below the 6 percent rate, the full employment level of output (the level of output produced when 6 percent of the labor force is unemployed) is clearly less than the upper limit on output. The upper limit, or output ceiling, appears to be reached when the unemployment rate is between 3.5 and 4 percent.

THE MINIMUM WAGE: AN UNNATURAL CONTRIBUTOR TO THE NATURAL RATE

Keywords: *full employment*

Access InfoTrac at http://infotrac.cengage.com

As noted, both structural and frictional unemployment contribute to the natural rate of unemployment. Both of these factors are a consequence of the normal operation of the labor market; hence, they are natural contributors to the natural rate. The minimum wage also contributes to the natural rate of unemployment, but it is not a consequence of the normal operation of the labor market; hence, we call it an *unnatural contributor* to the natural rate.

A federal minimum wage—25 cents per hour—was first imposed in 1938. Over the years, the federal minimum wage has been increased and the number of covered workers expanded. In 2007, the minimum wage was increased to $5.85 from the previous level of

\$5.15 established in 1997. It was increased each year and is scheduled to increase to a level of \$7.25 in July 2009. More than 80 percent of the nonagricultural labor force works in jobs that must pay at least the federal minimum wage. Many states have also passed minimum wage legislation. At least 10 states will impose a minimum wage higher than the Federal rate in July 2009. Oregon and Washington are the highest at \$8.40 and \$8.55 per hour, respectively.

The expressed intent of the minimum wage is to help the working poor. It is possible for a family headed by a person working full time at the minimum wage to have an income below the poverty line. By imposing the minimum wage, it is argued, a worker's income will be increased and a family's standard of living improved. Increasing the minimum wage is a particularly attractive way to alleviate poverty to politicians because it does not require an increase in transfer payments or the taxes to pay for them.

Although advocates of a high minimum wage have the best of intentions, the outcome is likely to be different from what they expect. In Figure 13.4, we plot the demand for and supply of *low-skill* workers. We focus on low-skill workers because the equilibrium wage rate for high-skill workers is likely to be above the minimum wage. Consequently, the minimum wage will have no direct effect on them.

Suppose a minimum wage (W_m) higher than the equilibrium wage (W_e) is imposed, as in Figure 13.4. The increase in the wage causes the quantity of labor demanded to fall from H_e to H_m while the quantity of labor supplied increases to H_s. Because firms cannot pay less than the minimum wage, they will hire only H_m hours of work. As a result, workers seek H_s hours of work but are hired for only H_m hours. The difference between these two quantities ($H_s - H_m$) is a measure of the unemployment created by imposition of the minimum wage.

The imposition of the minimum wage causes firms to discharge or decline to hire workers with minimal skills and experience. Many teenagers fall into this category, so it is not surprising that they are among those most adversely affected by the minimum wage. The evidence indicates that a 10 percent increase in the minimum wage reduces

Figure 13.4 **Effects of a Minimum Wage on the Labor Market for Low-Skilled Workers**
Imposition of a minimum wage at W_m reduces the number of labor hours from H_e to H_m and increases the unemployment of labor hours from zero to $H_s - H_m$.

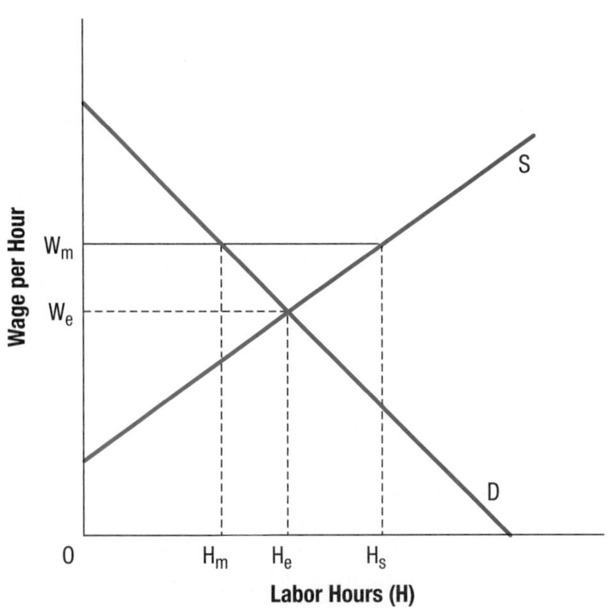

teenage employment by 1 to 3 percent. Young adults (ages 20 to 24), women, and African-Americans are also adversely affected, but to a lesser extent.[1]

The impact of the minimum wage on teenagers is unfortunate. Many of them lack work experience and have few skills. Consequently, they have difficulty getting jobs. But without jobs, they cannot get experience and upgrade their skills—a vicious circle. Because the minimum wage can make it prohibitively expensive for firms to hire teenagers, many economists believe that the minimum wage should not apply to them or that they should be subject to a lower minimum wage.

Structurally unemployed persons may also be adversely affected. A minimum wage may increase the cost of providing on-the-job training, making it more difficult for the structurally unemployed to find jobs. To ease this problem, some economists have recommended that the long-term unemployed either be exempt from minimum wage legislation or be paid a lower minimum wage.

Another problem with a minimum wage is that it may increase labor market discrimination. As noted, at the minimum wage, firms wish to hire only H_m hours of work, but workers are seeking H_s hours. The excess supply of hours provides employers with the opportunity to choose among job seekers on the basis of personal characteristics unrelated to ability to do the job. As a result, they are in a better position to discriminate—if they desire to do so—among prospective workers.

Those workers who remain employed after the imposition of a higher minimum wage have higher incomes. But does this mean that the lot of the working poor has improved? Unfortunately, increases in the minimum wage are less beneficial to the working poor than supposed. More than half of the low-wage workers in the United States are members of households with above-average family incomes. These workers include high school and college students with part-time jobs and spouses with low-wage jobs. Consequently, only part of the increase in incomes created by the minimum wage for those fortunate enough to find work accrues to the working poor.

If the goal is to help the working poor, the earned income tax credit approach is a better solution. As discussed in Chapter 11, working families with low incomes may deduct the credit from the taxes they owe. For families with very low incomes, the credit exceeds the tax liability. Consequently, they will receive a payment from the federal government. Because the earned income tax credit does not raise labor costs to firms, it does not reduce the quantity of labor demanded and, hence, employment.

CAUSES OF RECESSIONS

Recession– A decline in real GDP for two or more consecutive quarters.

High rates of unemployment are generally equated with recessions in the financial or popular press. This is not quite right. A **recession** is defined by the National Bureau of Economic Research as occurring when real GDP falls for two or more consecutive quarters. It is possible for a recession to occur without a high rate of unemployment, but the two generally occur at about the same time. We are being only a little imprecise, then, when we switch from explaining causes of high rates of unemployment to explaining causes of recessions.

Demand Shocks

Using the model of aggregate demand–aggregate supply developed in Chapter 12, we can distinguish between two basic causes of recessions. Recessions occur when there is a

[1]Charles Brown, Curtis Gilroy, and Andrew Kohen, "The Effect of the Minimum Wage on Employment and Unemployment," *Journal of Economic Literature* 20, no. 2 (1982): 487–528.

Figure 13.5 Effects of a Demand Shock on GDP and the Price Level
A demand shock shifts the AD curve leftward, creating lower GDP (from GDP_1 to GDP_2) and a higher unemployment rate (not shown).

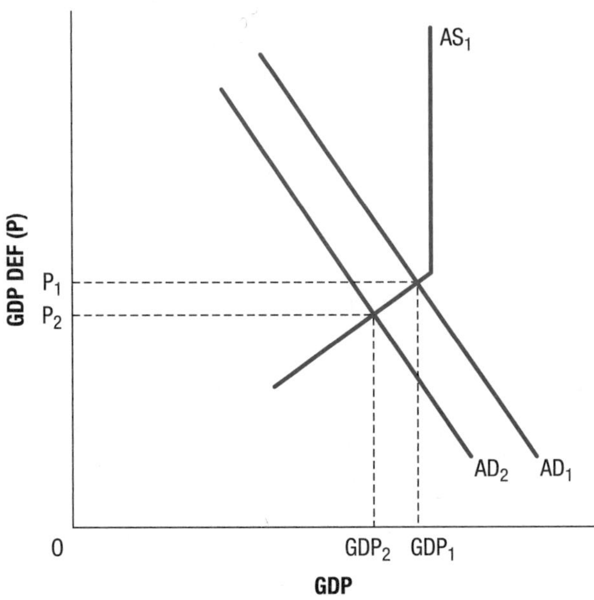

Demand shock– A contraction in aggregate demand large enough to cause a recession.

Supply shock– A contraction in aggregate supply large enough to cause a recession.

Maximum potential real GDP– The largest output the economy can produce; the vertical portion of the aggregate supply curve.

significant contraction in either aggregate demand (AD) or aggregate supply (AS). A contraction in aggregate demand *large enough to cause a recession* is called a **demand shock**. A contraction in aggregate supply *large enough to cause a recession* is called a **supply shock**. Thus, recessions occur primarily because of demand or supply shocks. Small leftward shifts in either AD or AS do *not* qualify as demand and supply *shocks*.

Figure 13.5 illustrates the effects of a demand shock on the economy. The economy is initially in equilibrium at full employment (at P_1, GDP_1); a little below the economy's **maximum potential real GDP**—the vertical portion of the aggregate supply curve. An adverse demand shock occurs, shifting the aggregate demand curve from AD_1 to AD_2. The level of real GDP falls from GDP_1 to GDP_2, moving the economy from full employment to less than full employment and a higher unemployment rate (not shown). The price level (GDP DEF) also falls. The adverse demand shock could be from any of a number of possible sources: for example, increased consumer pessimism that results in falling expenditures for consumption; increased producer pessimism that results in falling expenditures for investment; a reduction in the rate of growth of the money supply; or falling government expenditures for national defense, to name a few.

Supply Shocks

Figure 13.6 illustrates the effects of a supply shock on the economy. The economy is initially in equilibrium at full employment (P_1, GDP_1). A supply shock shifts the upward-sloping portion of the aggregate supply curve to the left resulting in a lower level of real GDP and a rising unemployment rate. A supply shock could occur from any of a number of possible causes, including rising oil prices (such as those that occurred in 1973 and 2008), and natural disasters that destroy part of the nation's private (factories, factory equipment) and public (roads, bridges, airport runways) capital stock. As explained in the Additional Insight box, Hurricanes Katrina and Rita created a supply shock that incorporated all of these events. Figure 13.6 shows that supply shocks not only reduce

Stagflation– Simultaneous stagnation (a reduction in real GDP) and inflation (an increase in the GDP deflator) created by a supply shock.

Active macroeconomic policy– The deliberate use of expansionary monetary or fiscal policy to reduce cyclical unemployment (also called **stabilization policy).**

Passive macroeconomic policy– The intentional reliance on market forces or automatic stabilizers to reduce cyclical unemployment.

Expansionary fiscal policy– Fiscal policy to reduce unemployment that increases the difference between government expenditures and tax collections.

Expansionary monetary policy– Monetary policy to reduce unemployment that normally involves an increase in the money supply.

Keywords: *expansionary fiscal policy, expansionary monetary policy*

Access InfoTrac at http://infotrac.cengage.com

Figure 13.6 Effects of a Supply Shock on GDP and the Price Level
A supply shock shifts the upward-sloping portion of the AS curve leftward, creating lower GDP (from GDP_1 to GDP_2) and a higher unemployment rate (not shown).

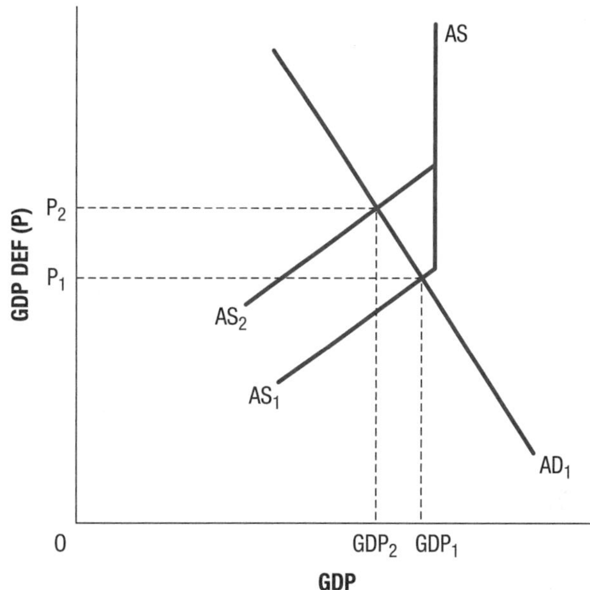

real GDP, but also increase the price level, creating stagnation (a reduction in real GDP) and inflation (an increase in the GDP deflator), or **stagflation**.

POLICIES TO REDUCE UNEMPLOYMENT

Cyclical Unemployment

There are two general approaches to reducing cyclical unemployment: **active macroeconomic policy** and **passive macroeconomic policy**. Active macroeconomic policy (also called **stabilization policy**) is the deliberate use of expansionary monetary or fiscal policy to reduce unemployment. Passive macroeconomic policy is the intentional reliance on market forces or automatic stabilizers to reduce the unemployment rate.

The effect of active macroeconomic policy is illustrated in Figure 13.7. There the economy is assumed to be in a recession, at GDP_1 and P_1. Active macroeconomic policy shifts the aggregate demand curve from AD_1 to AD_2, resulting in full employment real GDP (at GDP_2) and a lower unemployment rate (not shown). Active macroeconomic policy can involve either fiscal policy or monetary policy. Fiscal policy to reduce unemployment (also called **expansionary fiscal policy**) increases the difference between government expenditures and tax collections. Monetary policy to reduce unemployment (also called **expansionary monetary policy**) normally involves an increase in the money supply.

Each policy will shift the aggregate demand curve to the right by increasing one or more components of aggregate demand. Expansionary fiscal policy will normally consist of an increase in government expenditures or a reduction in taxes or some combination of the two. An increase in government expenditures directly increases the government

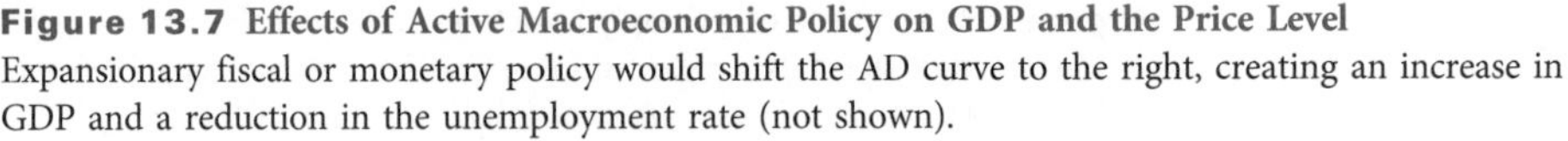

Figure 13.7 Effects of Active Macroeconomic Policy on GDP and the Price Level
Expansionary fiscal or monetary policy would shift the AD curve to the right, creating an increase in GDP and a reduction in the unemployment rate (not shown).

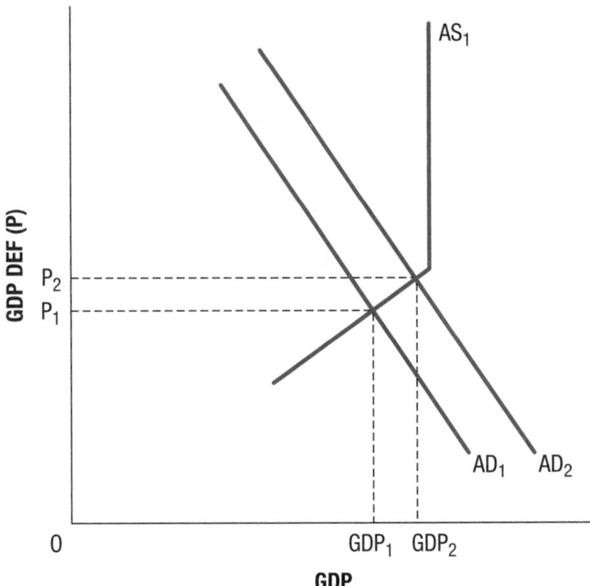

purchases (G) component of aggregate demand (remember? AD = C + I + G + NX). A reduction in taxes indirectly increases either the C or I components of AD; C, if consumption taxes or individual income taxes are reduced, I, if corporate taxes are reduced.

As explained in the appendix to Chapter 14, the money supply normally increases through the lending activities of the banking system. Thus, an increase in the money supply corresponds to an increase in lending to households for the purchase of consumer durables or houses, thereby increasing the C and I components of AD. An increase in the money supply also corresponds to an increase in lending to business firms for the purchase of plant and equipment, thereby also increasing the I component of AD.

In the real world of active macroeconomic policy, it is difficult to change fiscal or monetary policy just the right amount needed to achieve full employment. Policymakers are uncertain as to the magnitude of the changes in government purchases, taxes, and the money supply necessary to restore or maintain full employment. Even if policymakers accurately estimate the necessary increase, political and other considerations may prevent adoption of the appropriate policy. Members of Congress, for example, are often reluctant to reduce government spending or raise taxes in an election year.

Active macroeconomic policy must also be applied at the correct time; that is, it must be applied so that it reduces, rather than increases, fluctuations in the unemployment rate. Suppose that the unemployment rate rises. If policymakers act in a timely manner, the application of expansionary fiscal and monetary policies can reduce the unemployment rate. Suppose, however, that they are slow to act. By the time they agree on a new set of policies to reduce the unemployment rate and these policies have an impact, the economy may be at the peak of the business cycle. If it is, their actions could result in a higher price level than anticipated.

Most economists believe that active macroeconomic policy plays a valuable role in reducing the economy's instability. They concede that policymakers have made mistakes in the past but, on balance, are optimistic that policymakers can do better in the future.

Figure 13.8 Effects of Passive Macroeconomic Policy on GDP and the Price Level
If wages are flexible downward, the AS curve will eventually shift rightward, creating an increase in GDP, a reduction in the price level, and a decrease in the unemployment rate (not shown).

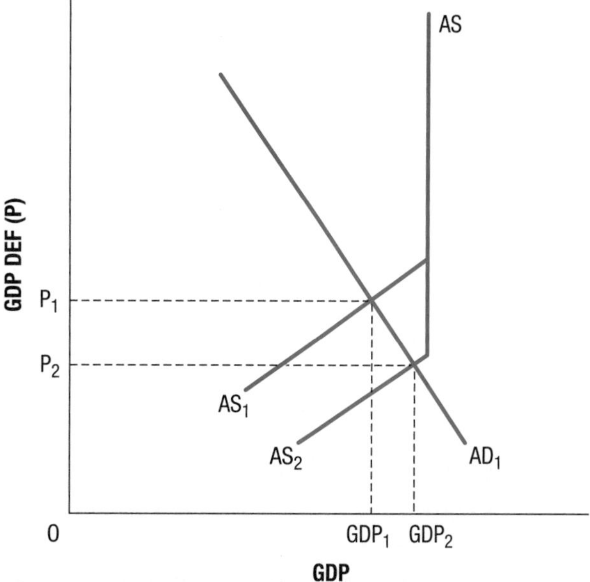

Some economists believe, however, that stabilization policy actually increases the economy's instability and that policymakers should abandon its use. They argue that we should take a passive approach to solving the unemployment problem.

The effect of passive policy that relies on the operation of market forces to reduce unemployment is illustrated in Figure 13.8. The economy is initially in equilibrium at less than full employment (P_1 and GDP_1). Whether this state of the economy persists depends on the flexibility of wage rates and other input prices. Given the relative importance of labor costs as a share of total costs (around 70 percent), however, the flexibility of wage rates is the critical factor. If wage rates fall in response to the increase in unemployment, aggregate supply increases from AS_1 to AS_2, thereby increasing GDP to the full employment level and reducing the unemployment rate (not shown). It should also be noted that the average price level falls as well. So even if nominal wages fall, falling prices of goods and services may result in no change to real wages.

Most economists believe, however, that wage rates are "sticky" in the short run. That is, they fall slowly (or in a growing economy, grow more slowly) in the face of high rates of unemployment (an excess of the supply of labor relative to the demand for labor). One reason they are sticky is that long-term contracts establish the wage rates of many workers. Most labor union contracts, for example, cover three years. Even in industries where wage rates are not set by contract, they usually are adjusted only once a year. Another reason they are sticky has to do with the minimum wage. Most workers receive wage rates well above the legal minimum wage. But some workers receive only the minimum wage, which cannot legally be reduced. For these and other reasons, wage rates are sticky in a downward direction. Because wage rates are slow to respond to an increase in unemployment, economists believe that unemployment caused by a reduction in aggregate demand may persist for too long—up to two or three years.

ADDITIONAL INSIGHT

Mother Nature Batters the Coast, But Not the Economy: The 2005 Hurricane Season from the Perspective of Basic Macroeconomics

In September 2005, Hurricane Katrina slammed into the Gulf Coast, killing more than a thousand people, forcing hundreds of thousands to flee inland, and destroying homes, businesses, roadways, and bridges. Recovery had barely begun when Hurricane Rita arrived, adding to the scope of the damage.

At the time this is written, it is too early for a full accounting of the costs imposed by these events, but what we do know already indicates that Katrina, alone, was the most costly natural disaster in recent U.S. history. Estimates reported by the Congressional Budget Office (CBO) to Congress indicate that the damage to the private and public capital stock could approach $140 billion.[a] The hurricanes also disrupted the nation's natural gas and oil supplies and shut down about 20 percent of the country's oil refining capacity, driving up gasoline prices and threatening to drive up the cost of heating with natural gas by 40 to 50 percent during the winter of 2005–2006. Katrina and Rita together were expected to result in (mostly) temporary job losses totaling 480,000. Prices in general, as measured by the Consumer Price Index, were expected to rise by 1 percentage point for the year following the hurricanes, primarily as a result of the direct and indirect effects of increases in energy prices.

Estimated Net Effect of Hurricane Katrina on Real Gross Domestic Product (billions of 2005 dollars at annual rates)

	2005	2006		2007	
	2ND HALF	1ST HALF	2ND HALF	1ST HALF	2ND HALF
Energy production	−18 to −28	−8 to −10	−5 to −7	−5 to −7	−5 to −7
Housing services	−1 to −2	−2 to −4	−1 to −3	0 to −2	0 to −2
Agricultural production	−1 to −2	0	0	0	0
Replacement investment	6 to 12	16 to 34	16 to 35	16 to 35	12 to 25
Government spending on goods and services	6 to 10	12 to 18	14 to 20	10 to 16	7 to 11
Effect of higher energy prices on non-energy consumption	−6 to −10	−5 to −7	−2 to −5	−1 to −3	0 to −2
Other consumption	−8 to −12	−2 to −4	−1 to −3	−1 to −3	0 to −2
Real GDP	**−22 to −32**	**11 to 27**	**21 to 37**	**19 to 36**	**14 to 23**

Source: Congressional Budget Office.

Although these impacts were expected to significantly disrupt the regional economy, the estimated effect on real GDP is quite small. The table on page 14 indicates that net losses are likely to be confined to the second half of 2005. Even then they would range from only $34 to $54 billion, a trivial sum in a $12 trillion economy. After 2005, the effects of increased expenditures for replacement investment and government purchases of goods and services are large enough to more than offset the lingering effects of the hurricanes.

To sum up, in terms of the aggregate supply-aggregate demand model of this chapter, we expect:

1. A very small leftward shift in the 2005 AD curve, followed by a very small rightward shift in the 2006 and 2007 AD curves.
2. A moderate leftward shift in the upward-sloping portion of the 2005 and 2006 AS curves, followed by a moderate downward shift in the upward-sloping portion of the 2007 AS curve.

3. A little stagflation (rising prices and rising unemployment) in 2005, but a reversal of this pattern by the end of 2007.

The small impact on real GDP is due partly to the fact that the Louisiana and Mississippi economies produce only a small share of national output, and the impacts are confined to only a part of those economies. The small impact on real GDP is also due to the offsetting effect of increased private expenditures for recovery and rebuilding (primarily the I component of GDP) and expansionary fiscal policy, that is, an increase in government purchases of goods and services (the G component of GDP). The reversal of the initial inflationary impulse is due to the automatic operation of market forces; principally, to eventually falling energy prices that will shove the AS curve rightward. Given the relatively small negative aggregate impacts that are likely, the 2005 hurricane season qualifies as neither a demand shock nor a supply shock.

[a] Douglas Holtz-Eakin, "Macroeconomic and Budgetary Effects of Hurricanes Katrina and Rita," Testimony before the House Budget Committee, October 6, 2005.

One advantage that passive policy of this variety has over active policy is that the price level does not rise. This is probably only a small advantage when the economy is in a recession; the benefits of reducing the unemployment rate via active policy may be well worth the costs associated with the modest price increases that are likely to occur. If the economy is at full employment, however, the verdict is different. At that stage in the business cycle, further increases in aggregate demand increase the risk of accelerating inflation.

Automatic stabilizers– Features of government taxes and expenditures that automatically increase aggregate demand in a recession.

The other type of passive macroeconomic policy is reliance on **automatic stabilizers** to reduce the unemployment rate. Automatic stabilizers are features of government taxes and expenditures that automatically increase aggregate demand in a recession. When the economy is in a recession, tax receipts from income and consumption (sales or excise) taxes automatically fall as income and expenditures fall. The reduction in taxes will increase, or offset the fall in, the C component of AD. Some government expenditures automatically increase in a recession, such as outlays for unemployment compensation, food stamps, housing assistance, health care, and income support. The increase in government expenditures will indirectly increase, or offset the fall in, the C component of AD, by providing households with more spendable income.

The only problem with automatic stabilizers is that they offset only part—about a third—of the decrease in AD that occurs in a recession.

Structural Unemployment

In the late 1950s and early 1960s, the U.S. unemployment rate increased. Most economists believed that the increase was due to inadequate aggregate demand. But some argued that rapid structural change was causing structural unemployment to rise.

With structural unemployment, the problem is not caused by a lack of jobs. As old jobs are destroyed, new ones are created. Instead, the problem is that the displaced workers fail to meet the skill and educational requirements of the new jobs. In this situation, expansionary fiscal and monetary policies are ineffective because the jobs created are like those already available.

In retrospect, it is clear that the increased unemployment of the late 1950s and early 1960s was cyclical rather than structural. Even so, there is little doubt that mismatches between the skill and educational levels of unemployed workers and those of existing job vacancies are a problem. To put it differently, even if no cyclical unemployment exists, the nation's unemployment rate will be 3 to 4 percent per year because of structural unemployment.

One possible solution to this problem is government programs that retrain displaced workers. With new job skills, these workers should be able to compete more successfully in the job market. Another possibility is to provide subsidies to firms that will employ these workers and train them on the job. Still another possibility is to help workers relocate to areas where jobs exist. Without assistance, prospective workers may be reluctant or unable to relocate. Alternatively, firms may be given favorable tax or other treatment to induce them to build or expand plants in areas with labor surpluses. Finally, prospective workers might be induced to continue or resume their educations. Without more education, many of them will have great difficulty in finding jobs—or at least good jobs—in a technologically advanced economy.

Starting in the 1960s, the federal government has sponsored various job training programs. Unfortunately, the results have been mixed. In some programs, enrollees have failed to complete their training. In others, enrollees were trained for jobs that were virtually nonexistent. In still others, enrollees were trained with obsolete equipment. Finally, the placement record of many of these programs is disappointing. Despite the mixed results to date, job training programs are probably necessary to reduce structural unemployment. Because we live in a dynamic society, some structural unemployment will always be present. Even so, many economists believe that we can reduce it and thus reduce the natural rate of unemployment.

Frictional Unemployment

For the most part, frictional unemployment exists because searching for a job is time consuming. Job seekers have imperfect information about vacancies, salaries, retirement and fringe benefits, and working conditions. Similarly, prospective employers have imperfect information about job seekers and their qualifications. With imperfect information, job seekers and prospective employers must search for the best matches of jobs and job seekers' qualifications.

To reduce frictional unemployment, job seekers and prospective employers require better information about job vacancies and job seekers' qualifications. In an attempt to reduce the cost of this information, the U.S. Department of Labor's Employment and Training Administration, in cooperation with the states, has established a system of One-Stop Career Centers that pull together all the employment, training, and education programs designed to help job seekers find jobs. These centers provide access to Internet information about jobs and job seekers, such as through the publicly supported America's Job Bank. Many other sites exist, providing information about jobs and applicants.

Keyword: *job search*

Access InfoTrac at http://infotrac.cengage.com

Although providing job seekers and prospective employers with more information is desirable, it may have the unintended effect of increasing worker turnover. If it is easier to find another job, workers are more likely to quit their present jobs. If it is easier for employers to find new workers, they are more likely to fire present employees. The increases in the number of people who quit jobs and in the number of firings result in a higher turnover rate. The effects of the higher turnover rate, in turn, tend to offset the effects of the faster placement of job seekers.

Keyword: *job training*

Access InfoTrac at http://infotrac.cengage.com

Another approach to reducing frictional unemployment is to implement apprenticeship programs similar to those in Austria and Germany. These programs ease the transition from high school to full-time employment and provide some on-the-job training. The apprenticeship programs in those countries, however, have existed for many years. It may prove difficult, therefore, to adopt them quickly in the United States, at least on a large-scale basis.

In conclusion, reducing frictional unemployment will not be easy. Fortunately, frictional unemployment does not appear to be a major problem, because it is temporary and serves some useful social functions.

UNEMPLOYMENT IN EUROPE

Euro area– European countries that use the euro as their official currency.

Although unemployment is a problem in the United States, it has been an even greater problem in parts of Europe. As shown in Table 13.1, the unemployment rate for the European countries that use the euro, the **Euro Area**, was significantly higher than for the United States. Some of the largest European countries, including France, Germany, and Italy, are among the individual European countries with unemployment rates higher than in the United States.

Economists believe that unemployment rates are high in the Euro Area because of structural impediments that discourage employment. For convenience, we divide these impediments into two categories: (1) those that discourage firms from hiring more workers and (2) those that discourage unemployed persons from accepting jobs.

INFOTRAC College Edition

Keyword: *unemployment (Europe)*

Access InfoTrac at http://infotrac.cengage.com

Impediments to Hiring

As in the United States, European governments have set minimum wages that employers must pay. These minimum wages are higher in France and most European countries than in the United States. As noted, a minimum wage discourages firms from hiring people with minimal job skills and experience.

Labor unions in most European countries are more powerful than those in the United States. These unions have used the collective bargaining process to achieve relatively high wages for their members. Unfortunately, one of the effects of their success is to reduce the number of workers hired.

European firms must also pay relatively high social security taxes, unemployment taxes, and other payroll taxes. Additionally, government regulations often mandate lengthy vacations and other paid leaves. These taxes and paid leaves increase labor cost and reduce the number of workers hired.

In many European countries, it is both costly and time consuming to discharge workers. Often, firms must make large severance payments. In the United States, the typical discharged worker gets a week's severance pay for each year of service. In Germany, the average worker gets four times as much—one month's pay for each year of service. In addition, notification of dismissal must be given well in advance. In the United States, a discharged worker may get as much as a one-month notice, whereas in Germany, a

TABLE 13.1 STANDARDIZED UNEMPLOYMENT RATES FOR EURO AREA COUNTRIES AND THE UNITED STATES IN 2008

Ireland	4.6	Belgium	7.5
Netherlands	3.2	Italy	6.1
Austria	4.4	Finland	6.8
Luxemburg	4.2	Germany	8.4
Denmark	3.8	France	8.3
United States	**4.6**	Spain	8.3
Portugal	8.1	**Euro Area**	**7.5**

The unemployment rate for many European countries has been higher than for the United States. For the Euro Area (countries that have adopted the euro as their currency), it was more than 63 percent higher in 2007: 7.5 percent compared to 4.6 percent.

Source: Organization for Economic Cooperation and Development, Main Economic Indicators, February 2009.

discharged worker gets almost a seven-months notice. In some countries, firms must get government approval to discharge workers.

At first glance, it appears that these requirements regarding dismissal increase employment. As employees retire or quit, however, firms are reluctant to replace them because it is so costly to those that take their place.

Finally, in many European countries, government regulations and controls make it difficult for entrepreneurs to start new firms or expand existing ones. In the German state of North Rhine–Westphalia, a firm must obtain permission from almost 90 federal, state, and local government offices to open a new plant. In the United States, new firms are subject to fewer regulations. As a result, the growth of new firms has made an important contribution to the increase in employment in the United States.

Impediments to Accepting Employment

In both the United States and Europe, unemployed persons can draw unemployment benefits. Although these benefits serve a useful social purpose, they reduce the incentive to work. The disincentive effect of unemployment benefits is greater in Europe than it is in the United States because (1) benefits as a percentage of wages are higher in Europe and (2) unemployed Europeans can draw benefits for a longer period of time.

In addition, income tax rates are higher in many European countries than in the United States. High tax rates on income from work, combined with the loss of unemployment benefits when one goes to work, sharply reduce the incentive for unemployed Europeans to take jobs. Finally, unemployed persons in Europe have little or no incentive to work in order to obtain health insurance because it is usually provided by the state. In the United States, health insurance is usually provided by employers.

Summary

Unemployment is costly both to the unemployed individual and to society. The social cost of unemployment is the goods and services that could have been produced by the unemployed.

The unemployment rate is the percentage of the civilian labor force that is unemployed. Unemployment rates vary among demographic groups. Teenage, African-American, and Hispanic unemployment rates are well above the overall rate.

Economists recognize three types of unemployment: frictional, structural, and cyclical. Frictional unemployment is a minor policy concern because it is temporary. In contrast, the structurally unemployed face long-term unemployment unless they retrain, relocate, or obtain additional education. Structural unemployment is, therefore, a serious problem. Cyclical unemployment is also a serious problem.

Full employment is achieved when the economy is at the natural rate of unemployment. The natural rate of unemployment is the unemployment rate around which the unemployment rate fluctuates—about 6 percent. The natural rate of unemployment is higher than the lowest rate the economy can achieve—normally around 3.5 to 4.0 percent. The natural rate of unemployment consists primarily of frictional and structural unemployment. Part of the natural rate of unemployment is the unemployment created by the minimum wage.

The cyclical unemployment associated with a recession is typically caused by either adverse demand shocks or supply shocks, both of which can be illustrated with the model of aggregate supply–aggregate demand. Adverse supply shocks create both higher unemployment and inflation.

The cyclical unemployment rate can be reduced through either active macroeconomic policy or passive macroeconomic policy. The principal active macroeconomic policy approaches are expansionary fiscal and monetary policy. Although both approaches can reduce the cyclical unemployment rate, it is difficult to apply just the right amount of stimulus at just the right time.

Passive macroeconomic policy relies primarily on automatic stabilizers or market forces. Automatic stabilizers work quickly to reduce unemployment, but they can solve only about a third of the problem. The normal operation of the labor market will eventually reduce the cyclical unemployment rate as unemployed workers become willing to accept a lower wage. This approach works slowly, however.

Neither active nor passive macroeconomic policy can reduce structural unemployment. Government programs may be needed, especially those that retrain workers, subsidize firms to hire structurally unemployed workers and train them on the job, and help workers relocate to areas where jobs exist.

The unemployment rate in the Euro Area is higher than it is in the United States. The higher unemployment rate stems from structural impediments that reduce the incentives for firms to hire workers and for unemployed persons to take jobs. These impediments include high minimum wages, high payroll and income tax rates, high unemployment benefits, generous leave and termination policies, and government provision of health insurance.

Key Terms

Unemployment rate
Civilian labor force
Frictional unemployment
Structural unemployment
Cyclical unemployment
Full employment
Natural rate of unemployment
Recession
Demand shock
Supply shock
Maximum potential real GDP
Stagflation
Active macroeconomic policy
Passive macroeconomic policy
Expansionary fiscal policy
Expansionary monetary policy
Automatic stabilizers
Euro area

Review Questions

1. Briefly discuss both the economic and non-economic costs of unemployment to the individual and to society.
2. Suppose you are given the following information about the Simplistic economy:

Persons over 65 years not actively seeking employment	20,000
Homemakers	40,000
School-age children under 16 years	60,000
Military personnel	15,000
Persons 16 years and older working	85,000
Persons 16 years and older not working because of illness, labor disputes, vacation, bad weather, or personal reasons	5,000
Persons between 16 and 65 years actively seeking employment	6,000

   a. Calculate the number of persons in the civilian labor force.
   b. Calculate the number of persons who are unemployed.
   c. Calculate the unemployment rate.
3. "An increase in the unemployment rate is costly; however, this cost is not shared equally by all groups in society." Explain why this statement is true.
4. List the different types of unemployment. Should policy makers regard each type as equally detrimental to society? Explain.
5. Define full employment. Then illustrate an economy in equilibrium at full employment using an aggregate supply–aggregate demand diagram. Be careful to distinguish GDP at full employment from GDP at the economy's output ceiling (maximum potential real GDP).
6. Use the model of aggregate supply–aggregate demand to illustrate active monetary and fiscal policy to reduce unemployment. Identify the components of aggregate demand that are affected in each case and explain why.
7. Should government undertake stabilization policies if wage rates and other input prices are flexible? Suppose wage rates and other input prices are "sticky."
8. "If pursued vigorously, expansionary fiscal or monetary policies can be used to reduce unemployment caused by inadequate aggregate demand." If this statement is true, why do we still experience periods of cyclical unemployment?
9. What are automatic stabilizers and how do they work to reduce cyclical unemployment?
10. Can active macroeconomic policy reduce structural unemployment? Why or why not? If we cannot use stabilization policy, what—if

anything—can policymakers do to reduce structural unemployment?

11. Suppose the economy is at the output ceiling. In response to political pressure, Congress reduces taxes. What are the effects of this tax cut on GDP, the GDP deflator, and the unemployment rate? Illustrate and defend your answer.
12. Illustrate the impact of an increase in the minimum wage on the market for low-skill workers. Identify the increase in the wage rate for people who remain employed and the increase in unemployment created by this policy.
13. "Even though some low-skill workers are laid off as the minimum wage increases, the economic situation of the working poor is improved because those low-skill workers who retain their jobs are receiving a higher wage." Is this statement true or false? Defend your answer.
14. Identify the factors that account for a higher unemployment rate in the Euro Area than in the United States. Assess the effectiveness of active and passive macroeconomic policy in reducing Euro Area unemployment.

Web Sites

- ***Bureau of Labor Statistics, U.S. Department of Labor.***
  The site of choice for information about the United States labor market. Provides several on-line publications, including the *Monthly Labor Review*, and access to data on unemployment rates—**http://www.bls.gov**
- ***European Employment Observatory.***
  Provides information on European labor markets and labor market policy—**http://www. euemployment-observatory.net**
- ***International Labour Organization.***
  This United Nations agency promotes social justice and human rights with respect to labor—**http://www.ilo.org**

APPENDIX TO CHAPTER 13

The Labor Market

OUTLINE

As indicated by Figure 13.4 in the chapter, labor markets, like other markets in the economy, reflect the forces of supply and demand. The purpose of this appendix is to explain more fully the factors that determine how this market operates.

THE DEMAND FOR LABOR

The demand curve for labor indicates the maximum amount—or wage—that buyers of labor will pay for a unit of labor (the buyers' demand price). A downward-sloping demand curve for labor indicates that the amount that buyers are willing to pay falls as the quantity of labor purchased increases. To understand the circumstances in which this occurs, consider Table 13A.1.

Although the total output of cloth increases as the number of units of labor increases, column (3) indicates that each additional unit of labor makes a smaller contribution to total production. More formally, column (3) displays the marginal product of labor (MPL); namely, the change in the total output of cloth attributable to each additional unit of labor. Total output with no labor is zero and total output with one unit of labor is 100 yards of cloth; thus, the first unit of labor increases total output by 100 yards of cloth. Total output with 2 units of labor is 190 yards of cloth; thus, the second unit of labor adds 90 yards of cloth to total output. The third worker adds the difference between 270 yards and 190 yards, or 80 yards, and so on. Column (3) indicates that the production of cloth is subject to diminishing marginal product of labor.

Column (4) indicates that the buyers of labor can sell all the cloth produced at $10 a yard. Column (5) indicates the value to the buyer of the output produced by each additional unit of labor, the value of the marginal product of labor (VMPL). The first unit of labor produces 100 yards of cloth that can be sold for $10 per yard; thus, the VMPL of the first unit of labor is $1,000. The VMPL of the second unit of labor is $10 per yard times 90 yards of cloth, or $900, and so on. Formally,

$$\textbf{VMPL} = \textbf{Pc} \times \textbf{MPL}$$

Column (6) indicates the maximum amount that buyers are willing to pay for each unit of labor. Buyers are willing to pay no more than the value of each unit of labor's contribution to total output, or each unit's VMPL. If buyers were to pay more than

TABLE 13A.1 DETERMINATION OF BUYERS' DEMAND PRICE FOR LABOR

(1) TOTAL LABOR HIRED (L)	(2) TOTAL YARDS OF CLOTH PRODUCED (C)	(3) MARGINAL PRODUCT OF LABOR (MPL)	(4) SALES PRICE PER YARD OF CLOTH (PC)	(5) VALUE OF THE MARGINAL PROD-UCT OF LABOR (VMPL)	(6) BUYERS' DEMAND PRICE OR WAGE (W)
0	0				
1	100	100	$10	$1,000	$1,000
2	190	90	10	900	900
3	270	80	10	800	800
4	340	70	10	700	700
5	400	60	10	600	600
6	450	50	10	500	500
7	490	40	10	400	400
8	520	30	10	300	300
9	540	20	10	200	200
10	550	10	10	100	100
11	550	0	10	0	0

In this example, labor is combined with other resources to produce cloth. The relationship between the number of units of labor hired and cloth production (what economists call the production function) is expressed in columns (1) and (2). As expected, the amount of cloth produced increases as the number of workers hired increases.

this, they would suffer a loss from hiring that unit, a consequence that we assume rational buyers would want to avoid.

The demand curve for labor can be constructed by graphing the pairs of numbers in columns (1) and (6). This is illustrated in Figure 13A.1. As indicated in that diagram, the VMPL curve for labor is also the demand curve for labor.

THE SUPPLY OF LABOR

The supply curve of labor reflects the sellers' supply price; the minimum amount (wage) they must receive as compensation for leisure forgone. Those who place a relatively low (or high) value on leisure will require a relatively low (or high) wage to give up leisure and work instead. For the labor market as a whole, it is reasonable to assume that there is a range of values of leisure forgone. When these values are arrayed from low to high they form an upward-sloping supply curve of labor, S, as in Figure 13A.1.

MARKET EQUILIBRIUM

Given the demand and supply curves of Figure 134A.1, a competitive labor market would clear at a wage of $500 and 6 units of labor hired. The 6th unit of labor is paid a wage just equal to the value of its marginal product, or $500. Units of labor 1 through 5 are also paid the equilibrium VMPL of $500. This is less than buyers would be willing to pay for each of them, but more than the sellers of each unit require as compensation. Thus, both buyers

Figure 13A.1 A Competitive Labor Market
Equilibrium in the labor market is obtained where S = D, or S = VMPL. In equilibrium, all labor that is hired is paid the VMPL of the 6th, or last unit hired.

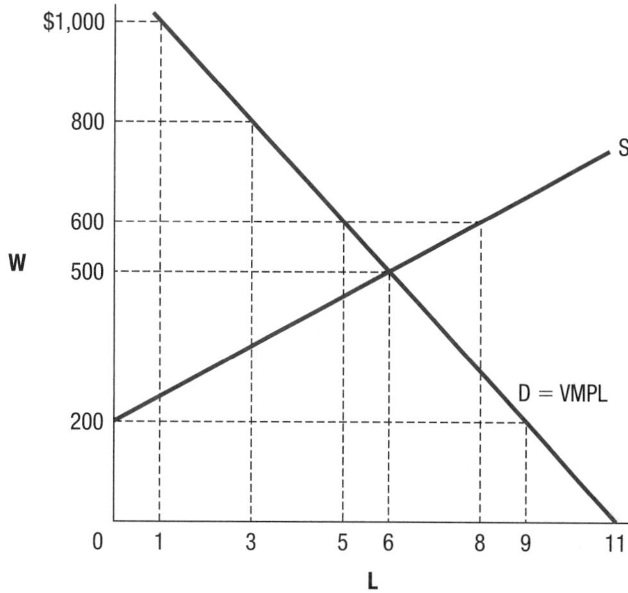

and sellers gain from buying and selling 6 units of labor at $500. Beyond 6 units, the amount that buyers are willing to pay (VMPL) is less than the amount that sellers must receive (the sellers' supply price, as indicated by the vertical distance to the supply curve). So, units 7 through 11 will not be bought or sold.

As a final application, suppose that the government establishes a minimum wage at $600. Buyers will no longer buy unit 6 because its VMPL ($500) is less than the minimum wage. Units 6, 7, and 8 will want to work at a wage of $600, however, so three units will be unemployed as a consequence of the minimum wage.

CHAPTER 14

Inflation: A Monetary Phenomenon

OUTLINE

During the expansion of the 1990s and the expansion that ended in December 2007, prices in the United States increased about 2.5 percent per year. Some prices, including college tuition, increased at a higher rate; others increased at a lower rate or, like desktop computers, even decreased. Although prices increased, they increased at a lower rate than the 3 percent rate of the 1980s and the approximately 7 percent rate of the 1970s. Currently, we may not think of inflation as a problem. But 25 to 30 years ago, inflation was a major economic problem. It had reached 10 percent for extended periods, a rate that causes prices to double every 7 years. Inflation at this rate causes major disruptions to the economy because it creates uncertainties about how much faster prices will rise and erodes the functioning of the price system.

In this chapter, we show that inflation helps some individuals and harms others. Among those who benefit are persons whose incomes rise more rapidly than prices. Those who are harmed include persons whose incomes rise less rapidly than prices. Although some people benefit from inflation, inflation—like unemployment—is costly to society. For that reason, policies to keep inflation low are important. To find such policies, we must determine the causes of inflation.

DEFINING INFLATION

Inflation–
A continuing rise in the price level.

Deflation–
A continuing fall in the price level.

Inflation is commonly defined as any increase in the price level. This definition fails to serve, though, because it includes both once-and-for-all increases in the price level and continuing increases. It is better to refer to a once-and-for-all increase in the price level as a *rise* in the price level and to refer to a continuing rise in the price level as **inflation.**

The distinction is important because once-and-for-all increases in the price level require no monetary policy action, but inflation does. Suppose, for instance, that an earthquake or a hurricane destroys part of the nation's capital stock. The decrease in capital stock reduces the aggregate supply of goods and services. As the aggregate supply curve shifts left, the price level rises. Once the economy adjusts to the lower capital stock, however, the price level stops rising. Consequently, policies to keep the price level from rising are unnecessary. On the other hand, if inflation occurs, the price level continues to rise until action is taken to stop it.

Deflation, the opposite of inflation, is a continuing fall in the price level. Deflations—usually associated with depressions—are now rare. The last deflation in the United States occurred during the Great Depression of the 1930s. Nevertheless, deflation reappeared in Japan in the 1990s and some analysts saw it as a threat to the German and U.S. economies in the early 2000s.

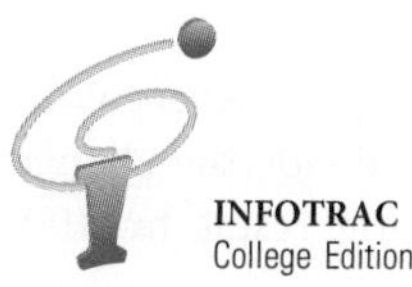

Keyword: *deflation*

Access InfoTrac at http://infotrac.cengage.com

MEASURING INFLATION

This section discusses two price indexes used to measure inflation.[1] They are (1) the implicit price deflator for GDP (the GDP deflator), and (2) the Consumer Price Index (CPI).

The GDP Deflator

As defined in Chapter 12, the GDP deflator is a weighted average of the prices of all final goods and services produced in the economy. It is, therefore, the broadest-based measure of the nation's price level. Price deflators are also available for the various components of GDP, such as consumption and investment. Like the GDP deflator, these deflators are available quarterly. Because of its comprehensiveness, most economists consider the GDP deflator to be the best measure of a nation's inflation rate.

The Consumer Price Index

Consumer price index (CPI)– A weighted average of the prices of goods and services purchased by a typical urban household.

The **Consumer Price Index (CPI)** is a weighted average of the prices of goods and services purchased by a typical urban household. It includes the prices of food, clothing, housing, transportation, medical care, and entertainment. The current market basket of goods and services was determined by a 1999–2000 survey of urban household purchases. In addition to the CPI, subindexes for such specific goods as food and energy are also compiled. Like the CPI, these subindexes are available monthly.

Although the GDP deflator is the best overall measure of inflation, the CPI is the most widely cited measure of inflation in the United States. The main reason for the CPI's popularity is that it measures the prices of goods and services purchased by households. The GDP deflator, in contrast, measures the prices of *all* final goods and services produced in the economy, including those purchased by firms and government.

Keywords: *measurement and inflation*

Access InfoTrac at http://infotrac.cengage.com

Because it is based on the prices of goods and services purchased by households, the CPI is widely regarded as a cost-of-living index. As a measure of the cost of living, however, it has several shortcomings. First, it is an index for the *typical* urban household. Consequently, we would not expect it to be accurate for the atypical household. For instance, suppose the typical urban household allocates 40 percent of its expenditures to housing. If the price of housing were to rise relatively rapidly, households allocating more than 40 percent of their expenditures to housing would find their cost of living rising more rapidly than the CPI. By the same token, households allocating less than 40 percent to housing would find their cost of living rising less rapidly.

Keywords: *inflation, cost, and standard of living*

Access InfoTrac at http://infotrac.cengage.com

Calculating the Inflation Rate

To determine the annual inflation rate (the percentage rate of increase in the price level) from one year to the next year, we apply the following formula:

$$\textbf{Inflation rate} = \frac{\textbf{Current year's price level} - \textbf{Previous year's price level}}{\textbf{Previous year's price level}} \times 100 \qquad (14.1)$$

First, we subtract the previous year's price level from the current year's price level to obtain the change in the price level from one year to the next. Then we divide the change in the price level by the previous year's price level and multiply the result by 100. (Multiplying by 100 expresses the inflation rate as a percentage.)

[1]In this context, the producer price indexes deserve mention. These indexes measure the prices received by domestic producers of commodities at various stages of production (finished goods, intermediate goods, and crude materials). These indexes are important because movements in them usually foreshadow movements in the CPI. For that reason, the indexes receive widespread attention when they are released each month.

ADDITIONAL INSIGHT

When Is an Increase in the CPI Not Inflation?

The Consumer Price Index (CPI) rose 0.5 percent in August and 1.2 percent in September 2005. On an annual basis, if prices were to rise at this rate, almost 2 percent every 2 months, prices would be up by more than 10 percent in a year. Based on the CPI for August and September 2005, can we conclude that inflation had again reached a double-digit rate? The answer is no because inflation requires a continuing increase in the price level. In November and December 2005 the CPI fell by 0.6 percent and then by 0.1 percent. If we were to experience the November-December rates for 12 months, it would yield more than a 4 percent reduction in the price level. What's going on?

The economy is reacting to energy price shocks caused by increases in energy prices in August, an uptick in a longer trend (see Chapter 5), and again in September because of Hurricanes Katrina and Rita in the Gulf of Mexico. In October energy prices stabilized and fell, followed by additional decreases in November and December. The steady increase in the relative price of energy and then the increases of the summer imparted an upward push to the CPI. But, as November and December show, that upward push reversed when energy prices fell.

These fluctuations in the CPI are one-time changes in the price level rather than continuing increases. They result when large unpredictable demand and supply changes affect fairly large sectors of the economy—energy and food, for example—for which quantity demanded and supplied are not very responsive to a change in price. Because of the volatility of energy and food prices, their effects are excluded in a measure of inflation called the core inflation rate. From August through December this core inflation rate increased between 0.1 and 0.2 percent a month, which would give an annual inflation rate of about 2 percent. Excluding food and energy prices, the CPI increased by about 2.2 percent for the entire year; including them, it was 3.4 percent.

Second, the CPI overstates the increase in the cost of living because it is based on a fixed market basket of goods and services. In actuality, when households find that some prices rise more rapidly than others, they substitute goods and services that have risen less in price for those that have risen more. The CPI does not take this substitution into account, and so it overstates the increase in the cost of living.

Third, the CPI also overstates the increase in the cost of living because it does not fully account for changes in quality. The quality of many goods and services (such as televisions, personal computers, and medical care) has improved over the years. If it took these changes fully into account, the CPI would increase less rapidly. Although the U.S. Bureau of Labor Statistics, the government bureau responsible for the CPI, does an excellent job in calculating it, the problems that we have mentioned and others are, in the end, unavoidable. For instance, when a new product comes on the market, it may not be represented in the index for several years. Most new products experience rapidly falling prices in their first years on the market. The CPI usually fails to capture these initial price decreases.

Despite its shortcomings as a measure of the cost of living, the CPI plays an important role in our economy. As the most common measure of inflation, it is often a basis for policy making. As a measure of the cost of living, it is a basis for labor negotiations. In addition, millions of workers have *cost-of-living adjustment (COLA)* clauses in their contracts. Under these clauses, wage rates increase automatically as the CPI rises. Similarly, tens of millions of retirees find that their social security benefits increase automatically as the CPI rises. Finally, the CPI is used to adjust the federal personal income tax system to eliminate the effects of inflation.

To illustrate, we can find the inflation rate for 2008. Taking 2000 as the base year, in 2008, the GDP deflator was 122.5 and the CPI was 125.0; in 2007, they were 119.8 and 120.4, respectively. Because the base year is the same, the different index numbers for the two price indices for the same year shows that they give different price level measures. Recall that the GDP deflator is a price index for all final goods and services, and that the CPI is a price index for consumer goods purchased by a typical urban consumer. Consequently, there is no reason for them to be the same. We substitute the GDP deflator numbers in the formula above to get the inflation rate. Inflation rate = [(122.5 − 119.8) ÷ 119.6] × 100, giving an inflation rate of 2.3 percent. If you calculate the inflation rate using the CPI, you will find it different from the rate based on the GDP deflator. How much different is it?

Recent Experience

Since 1940 inflation has been the norm in the United States. Before then, periods of continuing price increases were followed by periods of continuing price decreases. The price level rose during World War II and the immediate postwar period. It rose again during the Korean War. From 1953 to 1965, the price level increased at a moderate rate. Starting in 1966, it increased more rapidly, and inflation was high, by U.S. standards, throughout the 1970s.

As Figure 14.1 shows, the GDP deflator (measured on the left axis) has increased each year since 1979. Where this line (the large squares) is steeper, inflation is greater and vice-versa. The figure also directly shows the annual percentage change in the deflator (measured on the right axis) making it easier to see the ups and downs of the inflation rate. The figure shows that the annual inflation rate, peaked in 1981 at 9.4 percent. It decreased from 1981 to 1986 and then increased until 1990, peaking at 4.3 percent. Since the early 1990s, the inflation rate has been relatively low. In 1998 it was only 1.1 percent, the lowest rate since 1959. Even though the expansion continued until 2001 and resumed

Figure 14.1 The GDP Deflator and Its Annual Change: 1979–2008
The price level, as measured by the GDP deflator on the left axis, increased substantially from 1979 to 2008, by over 147 percent. It increased more rapidly in the 1980s than in the period after 1990. Graphing the inflation rate, the percentage rate of change of the price level, on the right axis, the inflation rate and its fluctuations are more easily seen. It reached 9 percent in 1980 and 1981 as it did in 1974 and 1975, illustrating the economic difficulties in that period. In contrast, the inflation rate was only about 1 percent at the beginning of the 1960s and about 2 percent at the end of the 1990s and into the 2000s.

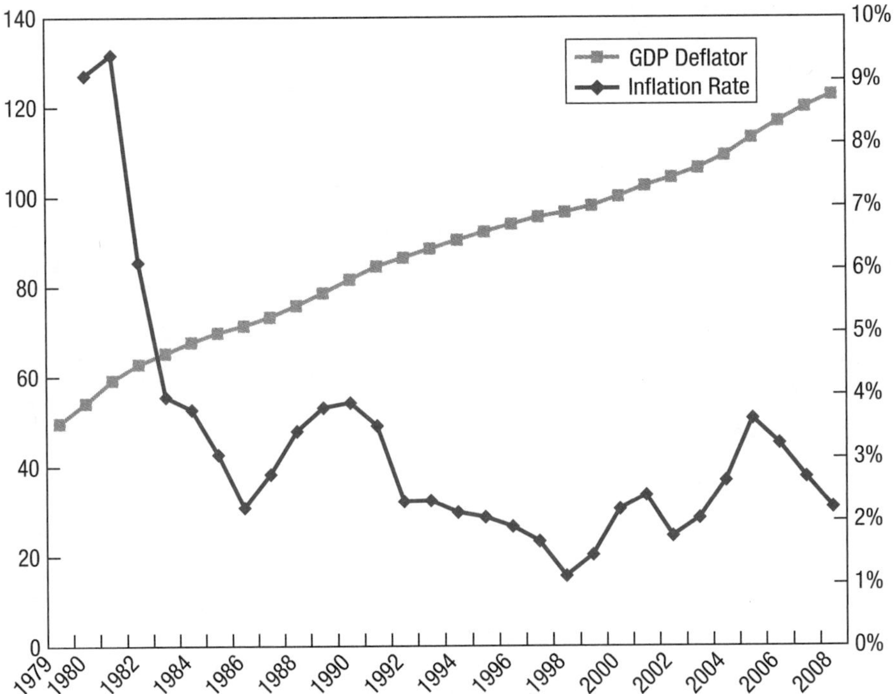

TABLE 14.1 INFLATION RATES FOR VARIOUS COUNTRIES: 1999–2007

	1999	2000	2001	2002	2003	2004	2005	2006	2007	AVERAGE
Turkey	55.6	49.9	54.8	44.1	22.5	9.9	5.4	11.5	9.2	29.2
Venezuela*	26.3	29.5	8	32.8	35.6	33.6	29.6	18.1	14	25.3
Indonesia	14.2	8.6	14.3	5.9	5.5	8.6	14.8	13.6	6.3	10.2
Mexico	15.1	12.1	5.9	7	8.6	7.4	5.5	4.5	2.7	7.6
South Africa	7.1	8.8	7.7	10.5	4.5	5.9	4.8	6.8	.	7.0
Philippines	7.4	4.9	8.1	3.5	4.5	6.2	6.5	5.3	.	5.8
Chile	2	4.6	3.6	4.2	6.1	7.5	7.6	12.4	4.9	5.9
Malaysia	0	9	−1.6	3.1	3.3	6	4.4	4	5.4	3.7
Israel	6.3	1.5	1.9	4.3	−0.5	−0.1	1	2.2	−1.4	1.7
China	−1.3	2.1	2.1	0.6	2.6	6.9	3.8	4.1	5.7	3.0
Thailand	−4	1.3	2.1	0.8	1.3	3.1	4.6	5	3.4	2.0
Australia	0.6	4	4	2.5	3.6	3.4	4.4	4.6	3.9	3.4
Korea	−0.1	0.8	3.5	2.8	2.7	2.7	−0.2	−0.5	1.2	1.4
United Kingdom	2.2	1.3	2.2	3.1	3.1	2.5	2.3	2.7	3.1	2.5
United States	1.4	2.2	2.4	1.7	2.1	2.9	3.2	3.2	2.7	2.4
Canada	1.7	4.2	1.2	1.1	3.3	3.2	3.4	2.4	3.2	2.6
New Zealand	0.4	2.5	4.2	1.2	1.4	3.7	1.9	2.4	4	2.4
Euro Area	1.5	1.3	2.4	2.6	2.1	1.9	1.9	1.9	2.2	2.0
Sweden	1.1	1.3	2	1.6	1.9	0.6	1.2	1.5	3.1	1.6
Switzerland	0.6	1.2	0.8	0.4	1	0.6	0.3	1.6	1.4	0.9
Singapore	−5.3	3.7	−1.6	−1.1	−0.8	4.3	0.7	0.6	4	0.5
Japan*	−1.3	−1.7	−1.3	−1.5	−1.6	−1.1	−1.2	−0.9	−0.8	−1.3

During the years 1999 to 2007, the U.S. inflation rate (as measured by the GDP deflator) averaged 2.4 percent. Some other countries, such as Turkey, Venezuela, and Indonesia, experienced double-digit inflation over these years. The Euro Zone had essentially the same rate as the United States, averaging 2 percent. Several countries experienced a year or so when the overall price level fell, but Japan has had deflation of about 1.3 percent per year.
*The arithmetic average.
Source: Federal Reserve Bank of St. Louis, *International Economic Trends* (February 2009), 6.

in 2002, the inflation rate has remained between 2 and 2.5 percent, except for 2005 when it exceeded 2.5 percent.

Table 14.1 shows recent inflation experience for the United States and selected other countries, with the final column giving the arithmetic average from 1999–2007. The inflation rate in the United States averaged 2.4 percent over this period. The United States experienced less inflation than most countries over that time. Some countries, including Turkey, Venezuela, and Indonesia, as shown in Table 14.1, had double-digit inflation. The Euro Zone had a lower inflation than the United States of 2 percent. One surprise in the table is the emergence of deflation in Japan and isolated incidences of it in other countries. Whether in the United States or abroad, inflation or deflation always has adverse effects.

Unanticipated inflation– Inflation that is unexpected or higher than expected.

Anticipated inflation– Inflation that is expected.

EFFECTS OF INFLATION

The effects of inflation (or deflation) depend largely on whether it is unanticipated or anticipated. **Unanticipated inflation** is inflation that is unexpected or higher than expected. For example, people might expect a 2 percent inflation rate and instead experience an actual inflation rate of 5 percent. **Anticipated inflation** is inflation that is expected. For instance, people might expect and experience inflation at a 2 percent rate.

The Redistribution of Income and Wealth

One effect of inflation is a redistribution of income and wealth—a substantial redistribution if the inflation is unanticipated. Some individuals gain because their wages and salaries rise more rapidly than the price level. Others lose because their wages, salaries, and pensions rise less rapidly than the price level. In this sense, real income is redistributed from some individuals to others. To illustrate, suppose workers in a particular industry, expecting no inflation, agree to a long-term contract calling for annual 4 percent wage increases. By most standards, 4 percent wage increases are very satisfactory, *if* no inflation is occurring. Suppose, however, that inflation occurs at an 8 percent rate. With wage rates rising less rapidly than prices, income is redistributed—in this case, from the workers to the owners of the firms in the industry.

In this example, workers received 4 percent wage increases that partially offset the 8 percent price increases. These wage increases partially offset the price increases, but inflation is a more serious problem for those living on fixed incomes. Consider someone who retired in 1990 on a fixed income. From 1990 to 2008, the CPI increased by about 65 percent or an average annual rate of 3.6 percent, which means that a retiree's fixed income in 2008 would buy only 60 percent of what it bought in 1990. This 40 perecnt reduction in the purchasing power of a fixed income occurred with inflation averaging 3.6 percent. If inflation had averaged 7 percent, as it did in the 1970s, the price level would more than double over the same 18 years, reducing the purchasing power of a fixed income by more than 50 percent.

High inflation rates, clearly, have a disastrous impact on persons living on fixed incomes. Fortunately, most retirees do not live on fixed incomes. Social Security benefits constitute the bulk of the typical retiree's income, and these benefits are **indexed**. That is, they are linked to the CPI so that they increase automatically as the CPI rises. If the CPI rises by, say, 5 percent, Social Security benefits increase by 5 percent. Consequently, the effects of inflation on retired persons are not as disastrous as one might think.

Indexing– Linking benefits to the CPI so that they increase automatically as the CPI rises.

Inflation also redistributes wealth. It causes some asset prices to rise by more than the price level and others by less. People whose assets appreciate more in price gain from the inflation; those whose assets appreciate less lose.

Creditor– A person to whom money is owed.

Debtor– A person who owes money.

One important type of redistribution is from creditors to debtors. A **creditor** is a person to whom money is owed. A **debtor** is a person who owes money. Suppose you borrow at a fixed interest rate to buy a home and that your monthly payment on the principal and interest is $800. Assume that the annual payment, $9,600, is one-third of your income. Then, over time, the price level doubles. The prices of the goods and services that you typically buy double, but, with the inflation, so does your income. Consequently, you can continue to buy the same amount of food, clothing, and so on. What about your mortgage payment? It remains the same. Because your income has doubled, your annual mortgage payment is only about 16 percent of your income; it's a lot easier to make your payments. To put it differently, the inflation means that you are able to repay the loan in dollars with substantially less purchasing power than those that you borrowed. You benefit from the inflation.

Just as debtors gain from inflation, creditors lose. They are repaid with dollars that have less purchasing power than the dollars that they lent. In the example, the institution from which you borrowed finds that the $800 monthly payment will buy only half as much as before because the price level has doubled.

Unanticipated inflation causes a substantial redistribution of income and wealth. With anticipated inflation, however, the redistribution is much less dramatic. When people anticipate inflation, they can take action to protect themselves. Consider once more the workers who agreed to a contract calling for 4 percent wage increases and then experienced

8 percent inflation. If the 8 percent inflation continues, these workers will expect the inflation rate to be 8 percent, and the inflation will become anticipated inflation. At the expiration of their contract, the workers will bargain for wage increases that take the anticipated inflation into account. A 12 percent per year increase would give the same real wage increase (4 percent) as a 4 percent increase gives in the absence of inflation.

With anticipated inflation, the redistribution of wealth from creditors to debtors is also less dramatic. When they expect no inflation, creditors are willing to lend money at relatively low interest rates. A lender might be willing to lend $100 for a year at a 4 percent interest rate, which means that the borrower must pay the lender $104 at the end of the year. If the price level rises by 8 percent during the year, the $104 that the lender receives at the end of the year will buy less than the $100 would have at the start of the year. Under these circumstances, the lender will no longer agree to lend at a 4 percent rate. Instead, the lender will insist on a rate that will compensate for the expected deterioration in the purchasing power of money. If the inflation rate is anticipated to be 8 percent, the lender will insist on a 12 percent rate. The additional 8 percent is to compensate for the anticipated inflation.

It is easy to see why the lender will insist on a higher interest rate when the anticipated inflation rate rises. It is perhaps less easy to see why borrowers will agree to it. To the typical borrower, however, a 12 percent interest rate with 8 percent inflation is no more burdensome than a 4 percent rate with no inflation. This is because, with 8 percent inflation, the typical wage earner can expect his or her income to rise 8 percent faster. Of course, not all wage earners will find their incomes rising 8 percent faster.

Thus, the switch from unanticipated to anticipated inflation causes market interest rates to rise. The rise in interest rates protects lenders so that no redistribution of wealth occurs between lenders and borrowers. (People who borrowed at relatively low interest rates before the increase in the inflation rate still benefit.)

Even with anticipated inflation, some redistribution of income and wealth occurs. Persons who retire often have part of their income that is fixed; for instance, they may have a pension that is fixed in nominal dollars, i.e., that it not indexed. Moreover, those who have lent money at a low interest rate can do little or nothing when they realize that the inflation rate has increased. Consequently, they are adversely affected by inflation. Others, however, gain at their expense, so that society as a whole is unaffected.

In one important case, society is adversely affected by an increase in the inflation rate. Inflation hurts people who hold money because it erodes purchasing power. Consequently, as the inflation rates rise, people attempt to reduce the amount of money that they hold. To the extent that they devote more time and effort to reducing their holdings of money, fewer resources are devoted to the production of goods and services. The reduced production represents a cost to society. Studies suggest that this cost is small at low inflation rates but increases as the inflation rate rises.

Inflation and Government

Inflation affects government in two important ways. First, the federal government is a huge debtor, with a national debt (see Chapter 15) of *$11 trillion (as of March 6, 2000)*. As a debtor, the federal government gains from inflation. Creditors, on the other hand, lose.

Second, under inflation the federal government gains additional real tax revenue at the expense of taxpayers because part of our nation's tax system is based on nominal income rather than real income. Before 1985, the federal personal income tax system had many tax brackets (for example, $20,000–$22,000). Moreover, as the taxpayer's income (and thus income tax bracket) increased, the tax rate on the incremental income also increased. Suppose the tax law levies a 10 percent tax on the first $20,000 of income and a 20 percent rate on the next $20,000. Now, if the price level doubles over some time span, the income of a typical household also doubles. Suppose Sara had income of $20,000 before the inflation and $40,000 afterward; so that her real before-tax income has not changed. She paid $2,000 in income tax before the inflation and she pays $6,000 after the inflation. The progressive income tax causes her tax payments to triple while her nominal income only doubles. To put it another way, after tax, her nominal income was $18,000 before and $34,000 after the inflation. Her real income after tax, however, fell from $18,000 to $17,000. This reduction in real income after tax occurred because the increase in *nominal* income moved Sara into a tax bracket with a higher tax rate, even though her real income had not changed. As a result, her real tax payment increased from $2,000 to $3,000.

The U.S. personal income tax before 1985 was such that inflation automatically raised tax rates on personal income, redistributing real income from taxpayers to government and, ultimately, to the beneficiaries of government spending. This redistribution may or may not have been desirable. With inflation automatically raising tax receipts, Congress did not have to raise tax rates to spend more. The increased tax rates were hidden; consequently, voters did not have an opportunity to vote for or against legislators who increased tax rates. Moreover, because inflation increases real tax revenue, Congress may have had less of an incentive to pursue anti-inflationary policies than it would otherwise have had.

To prevent the redistribution of income through the personal income tax system, Congress passed and President Reagan signed legislation in 1981 to index the personal income tax system, starting in 1985. The system is now adjusted each year to eliminate the effects of inflation on real tax revenue.

Although the federal personal income tax system is now indexed, the rest of the federal tax system is not. This is particularly important with regard to the federal corporate income tax system. When inflation occurs, corporations' real tax liability increases. The reduction in real after-tax profits makes it less profitable for them to invest in new plant and equipment. As a result, they reduce investment. Less investment means that the nation's capital stock increases less rapidly, which in turn means the nation's output and standard of living also increase less rapidly.

Inflation and Net Exports

Inflation also affects exports and imports. Suppose the United States is experiencing more inflation than the rest of the world. All other things equal, U.S. exports will become less competitive in world markets. Consequently, the United States will export less. This will have an adverse impact on output and employment in the economy's export-producing sector (such as the agricultural and airplane industries).

With prices rising more rapidly in the United States, imports become relatively less expensive. As a result, U.S. purchasers will buy fewer domestically produced goods and services and more imports. The increase in imports has an adverse impact on output and employment in the economy's import-competing sector (such as the automobile and steel industries).

Keywords: *inflation and economic aspects*

Access InfoTrac at http://infotrac.cengage.com

Thus, a higher inflation rate in the United States than in the rest of the world decreases U.S. exports and increases U.S. imports. (A lower inflation rate would have the opposite effect.) Over time, the dollar will depreciate (decrease) in value in terms of foreign currencies. The depreciation in the dollar will compensate for the higher inflation rate in the United States. Although it may take years, exports become more affordable to foreign purchasers and imports become less attractive to domestic purchasers. In the interim, both the export-producing and import-competing sectors of the U.S. economy will endure economic hardship.

Other Effects

As the inflation rate rises, it becomes more variable, making planning for the future more difficult. Under these circumstances, people use more resources to predict the inflation rate and to figure out ways to protect their real income and wealth. The opportunity cost of using more resources to deal with inflation is the value of the output of goods and services that must be given up.

A high and variable inflation rate also may lead to speculation in real estate, gold, antiques, and art. During periods of rising prices, these assets often appreciate significantly in value. While buying these assets may prove profitable, it does not increase the nation's capital stock. If saving is diverted from investment in plant and equipment to such assets as antiques and art, the nation's capital stock will grow less rapidly. As a result, the GDP growth rate will be reduced and the nation's standard of living will improve less rapidly.

Finally, if inflation becomes very high—hyperinflation—a nation's monetary system may disintegrate. With prices skyrocketing, the purchasing power of money collapses. As a result, people will hold little or no money. They also will insist on being paid often so that they can buy goods before they increase further in price. At some point, money will become worthless and people will exchange goods and services only for other goods and services. Barter is extremely inefficient because it takes much time and effort to find people who both have what you want and are willing to trade for what you have. The nation's output of goods and services will decline, and the economy may collapse.

History has provided many examples. The most famous involves Germany after World War I. In 1922, its inflation rate was over 5,000 percent. Prices increased almost continuously. Diners at restaurants found, for example, that they had to pay more for their meals than was listed on the menu when they ordered. Prices became astronomical, with meat and butter costing millions of marks per pound. Money became worthless or virtually so. It was used as kindling to start fires.

Hyperinflation– Extremely high inflation rates.

Although we could mention many examples of **hyperinflation**—extremely high inflation rates—inflation need not and typically does not reach such high proportions. The hyperinflation in post–World War I Germany was caused by the government's printing huge amounts of money. Most governments are much more prudent. One exception to this is Zimbabwe, whose government is printing money so rapidly that the rate of inflation in mid-November 2008 was 79,600,000,000 percent! With this kind of inflation, people simply abandon money and go to a barter system. The final result is total collapse of the economy.

MONEY AND THE MONEY SUPPLY

As just discussed, hyperinflations are caused by huge increases in the money supply. What about more moderate inflation rates? Are they also caused by increases in the money supply? This is a very important question. Before answering it, however, we must consider money's functions and the money supply.

Money's Functions

Money has three functions. Money serves as (1) a unit of account, (2) a medium of exchange, and (3) a store of value. With regard to money's *unit of account* function, we keep track of the value of things in terms of money. A pizza costs $5, a hamburger $2.50, a hot dog $1, and so on. By using a common measure, we can easily compare relative costs. A pizza costs twice as much as a hamburger and five times as much as a hot dog. This ease of comparison greatly aids decision making.

Medium of exchange– Anything used to purchase goods and services and pay debts.

Money's medium of exchange function is extremely important. A **medium of exchange** is something that can be used to purchase goods and services and pay debts. In ancient times, households were largely self-sufficient. They grew and cooked their own food, made their own clothes, built their own dwellings, and so on. Few goods and services were exchanged. Little need existed, therefore, for a medium of exchange. As time passed, however, households found it in their interest to specialize in relatively few activities and trade or barter the goods that they produced for other goods and services. As a result, a need for a medium of exchange developed. Money greatly simplified the exchange of goods and services. It would be almost impossible for a modern economy to function without a medium of exchange because the alternative—barter—is extremely inefficient.

With regard to its *store of value* function, money is a way for households to hold their savings. They may hold their savings in other forms, including bonds, common stock, and real estate. Although money is not unique as a store of value, it is convenient because it is easy to tap into. During periods of inflation, of course, money is an unsatisfactory store of value because rising prices erode its purchasing power. For this reason, households and firms reduce their holdings of money during periods of inflation.

The Money Supply

Money– Anything generally accepted as final payment for goods, services, and debt.

Currency (cash)– Paper money and coins.

Demand deposits– Checking accounts at commercial banks.

Money supply– Currency, traveler's checks, demand deposits, and other checkable deposits.

Because of the importance of the medium-of-exchange function, **money** usually is defined simply as anything generally accepted as final payment for goods, services, and debt. **Currency (cash)**—paper money and coins—is money because it is generally accepted as payment for goods, services, and debt. Similarly, **demand deposits**—checking accounts at commercial banks—are money because checks are generally accepted as payment for goods, services, and debt. The same is true of other checkable deposits, including those at savings and loan associations and credit unions. Based on this definition, however, savings and time deposits are not money because we cannot use them as final payment for goods, services, and debt. We must first convert them to currency or some other form of money. The same is true of other assets, such as bonds and stocks. Those assets are not generally accepted as final payment for goods, services, and debt.

With this definition of money, we can now define the nation's money supply. The **money supply** is currency, traveler's checks, demand deposits, and other checkable deposits. Like the other components of the money supply, traveler's checks are included in the money supply because they are generally accepted as final payment for goods, services, and debt. As shown in Table 14.2, they account for less than 1 percent of the nation's money supply. Currency accounts for 50.9 percent of the money supply, and demand and other checkable deposits account for the remaining 48.8 percent.

The money supply, as defined here, corresponds to one of the monetary aggregates published by the Federal Reserve. This aggregate is referred to as M1. The other aggregates—M2 and M3—are defined more broadly.

TABLE 14.2 THE MONEY SUPPLY AND ITS COMPONENTS: DECEMBER 2008

COMPONENT	AMOUNT (BILLIONS OF DOLLARS[a])	RELATIVE IMPORTANCE (PERCENT)
Currency	812.4	50.9
Traveler's checks	5.5	0.3
Demand deposits	465.7	29.2
Other checkable deposits	312.3	19.6
Totals	1,595.9	100.0

[a]Average of daily figures (seasonally adjusted).

Source: Board of Governors of the Federal Reserve System, *Federal Reserve Bulletin, Statistical Release,* Money Stock Measures, Table 3, March 5, 2009. http://www.federalreserve.gov/releases/

M2 includes the various components of M1. It also includes savings and (small-denomination) time deposits, money market deposit accounts, and money market mutual funds. Savings and time deposits are included because they are easily converted to cash or checkable deposits. Persons with money market deposit accounts or money market mutual funds can, within certain limits, write checks on these accounts. M2 is important because the Federal Reserve often emphasizes M2 in conducting monetary policy.

M3 is defined even more broadly. Many of its components, however, are not easily convertible to cash or checkable deposits. Consequently, it is not as important as the other measures, as suggested by the fact that the Federal Reserve places more emphasis on M1 and M2 than on M3 in conducting monetary policy.

ADDITIONAL INSIGHT

Currency Holdings and the Underground Economy

Although currency is convenient for small transactions, checkable deposits have many advantages as a medium of exchange. Currency can be lost, destroyed, or stolen. For large transactions, it is bulky. Checks can be made for any amount, large or small. They also provide a record of the transactions. Finally, checkable deposits are typically insured.

With these advantages, it is not surprising that checkable deposits account for almost half of the nation's money supply. Even so, both on a per capita basis and as a percentage of the money supply, currency is more important now than it was in 1960. Indeed, more than $2,400 in cash is in circulation for every person in the United States. For those of us who rarely have more than $20 or $30 in cash, this statistic is astounding.

What accounts for the large holdings of cash? Is it because we have more coin-operated machines and the like? Most experts believe that this explanation can account for only a small part of the increase in cash balances. Another possibility is that the increased proportion of immigrants in the U.S. population plays a role because immigrants, at least at first, tend to avoid banks and use cash. But this also could account for only a small increase in currency holdings. The two major sources of increased demand for U.S. currency are foreign holdings and the underground economy.

Much U.S. currency is held abroad because people in foreign countries often prefer dollars because they distrust their own currency. Large amounts of U.S. currency are held in Central and South America, Eastern Europe (particularly Russia), and the Middle and Far East. Although some U.S. currency has always been held abroad, the trend toward foreign ownership has become more pronounced in recent years. If we assume that 75 percent—the upper limit suggested by experts—of U.S. currency is held abroad, that still leaves about $600 per person, or $1,800 for a family of three. Moreover, about two-thirds of U.S. currency is in $100 bills, which suggests that the average person holds four $100 bills. We don't. Do you?

The underground economy is a part of the economy that uses $100 dollar bills because it is a cash economy. Convenience requires using big bills when you operate in a cash economy. People in the underground economy use cash because they don't want a paper trail to their illegal transactions—selling drugs, working off the books to escape taxes, or whatever. For example, years ago we knew some mechanics who specialized in working on old, bug-shaped foreign cars. These mechanics, who were countercultural in some dimensions, dealt only in cash. We never asked why.

It is significant that two-thirds of U.S. currency is held in its largest denomination, $100 bills, and that the largest euro note is 500 euros, worth about $600. It will be interesting to see the extent to which the euro replaces the dollar as an alternative currency in other countries and in the underground economy. A million dollars of currency is much easier to carry around in euros than in dollars.[a]

[a]See Kenneth S. Rogoff, "The Surprising Popularity of Paper Currency," *Finance and Development* 29, no. 1 (March 2002): 56–57.

The Federal Reserve

Central bank–
A government-established agency that controls the nation's money supply, conducts monetary policy, and supervises the monetary system.

The Federal Reserve, an independent agency of the federal government, is the United States' central bank. A **central bank** is a government-established agency that controls the nation's money supply, conducts monetary policy, and, in general, supervises the nation's monetary system. Because these functions are so important, countries typically have central banks. The United Kingdom's central bank is the Bank of England; the European Union's is the European Central Bank, and so on.

The Federal Reserve controls the nation's money supply. If policy makers at the Federal Reserve believe that the money supply should increase or decrease more rapidly, they can take the appropriate action. The Federal Reserve and the nation's monetary system are discussed in greater detail in the appendix to this chapter.

CAUSES OF INFLATION

After defining and discussing the nation's money supply, we now turn to the causes of inflation. Inflation is a continuing rise in the price level. In the absence of policies to reduce or eliminate it, inflation will continue indefinitely. Inflation, therefore, is a long-run phenomenon.

Quantity theory of money–
A theory emphasizing that the money supply is the principal determinant of nominal GDP.

Equation of exchange–
An equation showing the relationships among the money supply, the income velocity of money, the GDP deflator, and real GDP. ($M \times V = P \times GDP$).

Income velocity of money–
The number of times the money supply is used to purchase final goods and services during a year.

The Quantity Theory of Money

Inflation can best be explained in terms of the **quantity theory of money**. This theory emphasizes that the money supply is the principal determinant of nominal GDP. To present and understand the quantity theory of money, one starts with the equation of exchange. The **equation of exchange** shows the relationship among the money supply (M), the income velocity of money (V), the GDP deflator (P), and real GDP (GDP). It is

$$\mathbf{M \times V = P \times GDP} \tag{14.2}$$

(The money supply was defined earlier in this chapter; the GDP deflator and real GDP were defined in Chapter 12.) The **income velocity of money** is the number of times the money supply is used to purchase final goods and services during a year. It is calculated by dividing nominal GDP (P × GDP) by the money supply (M). Suppose that nominal GDP is $1 trillion and that the money supply is $100 billion. The income velocity of money is 10, obtained by dividing $1 trillion by $100 billion.

As the equation stands, it is a tautology—true by definition. This is so because the velocity of money is defined in terms of the other variables (V = nominal GDP/M). In the example, the money supply is $100 billion. If that much money is used to purchase $1 trillion worth of goods and services, it must be used 10 times. Another way to view it is to note that the left side of the equation of exchange (M × V) represents the amount spent on final goods and services, and the right side (P × GDP) represents the amount received for those final goods and services. These two amounts must be equal.

Keyword: *quantity theory of money*

Access InfoTrac at http://infotrac.cengage.com

The quantity theory of money assumes that the velocity of money is constant or approximately so. Although velocity varies to some extent from year to year, it shows greater stability in the long run. Because inflation is a long-run phenomenon, we shall assume initially that velocity is constant.

Chapter 12 shows that an increase in the money supply, through its impact on aggregate demand, results in an increase in nominal GDP. The same is true in the quantity theory. Moreover, the increase in nominal GDP is proportional to the increase in the money supply, provided that the velocity of money is constant. Suppose the money supply increases from $100 billion to $200 billion. If the velocity of money is constant at 10, nominal GDP must increase from $1 trillion to $2 trillion. If unemployment existed initially, both the GDP deflator and real GDP will rise. If full employment prevailed, only the GDP deflator will rise.

To determine the impact of an increase in the money supply on the inflation rate, we rewrite Equation 14.2 to obtain

$$\frac{\Delta M}{M} + \frac{\Delta V}{V} = \frac{\Delta P}{P} + \frac{\Delta(GDP)}{GDP}$$

In the equation, $\Delta M/M$ (the change in the money supply, ΔM, divided by the money supply, M) is the growth rate of the money supply; $\Delta V/V$ (the change in velocity, ΔV, divided by velocity, V) is the growth rate of velocity; $\Delta P/P$ (the change in the GDP deflator, ΔP, divided by the GDP deflator, P) is the inflation rate; and $\Delta(GDP)/GDP$ (the change in real GDP $\Delta(GDP)$ divided by real GDP) is the real growth rate of output. If the velocity of money is constant, ΔV and, therefore, $\Delta V/V$ equals zero, and we have

$$\frac{\Delta M}{M} = \frac{\Delta P}{P} + \frac{\Delta(GDP)}{GDP} \qquad (14.3)$$

Equation 14.3 states that the growth rate of the money supply equals the inflation rate plus the output growth rate. Rearranging terms gives

$$\frac{\Delta P}{P} = \frac{\Delta M}{M} - \frac{\Delta(GDP)}{GDP} \qquad (14.4)$$

Equation 14.4 states that the inflation rate equals the growth rate of the money supply less the output growth rate.

It is crucial to realize that the Federal Reserve determines the growth rate of the money supply, and thus that it has the major responsibility of controlling inflation. In the long run, the growth rate of output is determined by the growth rates of the nation's resources and by the rate of technological progress. Over the business cycle, the growth rate of real GDP varies. In the long run, however, aggregate supply and real GDP increase by about 3 percent per year.

The growth rate of the money supply that is consistent with a stable price level, or a zero inflation rate, can now be determined. To do so, substitute zero for the inflation rate and 3 percent for the output growth rate in Equation 14.4, and then solve for $\Delta M/M$. The solution is 3 percent, implying that the money supply can grow at a 3 percent rate and the price level will still remain constant.

The aggregate supply–aggregate demand framework can illustrate this result. Suppose that, in Figure 14.2, aggregate demand is AD_1 and aggregate supply is AS_1. (For convenience, the aggregate demand and supply curves are assumed to be linear.) The price level, given by the intersection of AD_1 and AS_1, is P_1. As the nation's capital stock and labor supply increase and technological progress occurs, aggregate supply increases. Suppose the new aggregate supply curve is AS_2. If aggregate demand increases at the same rate to AD_2, the price level, given by the intersection of AD_2 and AS_2, will be P_1, the same as the original price level. Should aggregate demand and supply continue to grow over time at the same rate, the price level will remain constant.

In the example, the money supply can grow at 3 percent without causing inflation. Suppose the money supply were to grow at, say, 8 percent. What would be the impact of the increased growth rate of the money supply on the inflation rate? Equation 14.4 gives the answer. With 8 percent growth in the money supply and 3 percent output growth, the inflation rate is 5 percent (8 percent – 3 percent).

Once again, the aggregate supply–aggregate demand framework can demonstrate this result. Suppose that, in Figure 14.3, aggregate demand is AD_1 and aggregate supply

Figure 14.2 Aggregate Demand, Aggregate Supply, And The Price Level
The price level is determined by aggregate demand and supply. The initial price level is P_1, given by the intersection of the initial aggregate demand curve AD_1 and aggregate supply curve AS_1. If aggregate demand and supply grow at the same rate—such as the shift from AD_1 to AD_2 and the shift from AS_1 to AS_2—the price level remains constant.

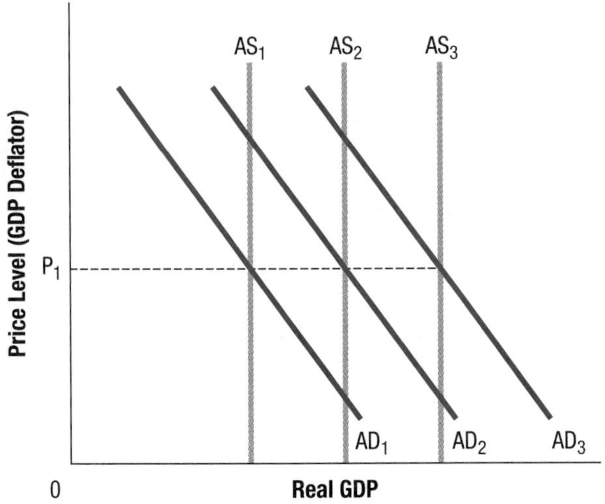

Figure 14.3 Aggregate Demand, Aggregate Supply, and Inflation
The price level is determined by aggregate demand and supply. The initial price level is P_1, given by the intersection of the initial aggregate demand curve AD_1 and aggregate supply curve AS_1. If aggregate demand grows more rapidly than aggregate supply—such as the shift from AD_1 to AD_2 compared to the larger shift from AS_1 to AS_2—the price level rises.

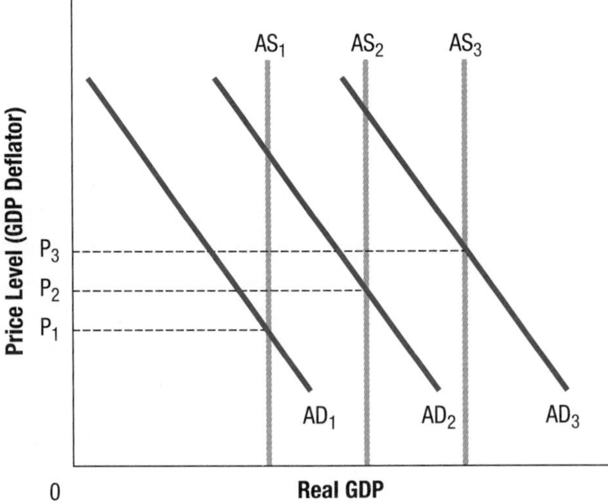

is AS_1. The price level, given by the intersection of AD_1 and AS_1, is P_1. As the nation's capital stock and labor supply increase and technological progress occurs, aggregate supply increases, say to AS_2. Previously, aggregate demand increased at the same rate as aggregate supply and the price level was constant. The money supply, however, is now increasing at an 8 percent rate rather than a 3 percent rate. With the velocity of money

INTERNATIONAL PERSPECTIVE

The Japanese Economy: "The Land of the Rising Price"

As we saw in Table 14.1, the Japanese economy experienced deflation from 1999 to 2007. In fact, the Japanese economy has stagnated since the beginning of the 1990s—when its stock market crashed—and its deflation has lasted 9 years. Its output growth has averaged less than 1 percent a year, while its unemployment rate is 4.5 percent. Although its current unemployment rate is below that of the European Union, the Japanese economy was accustomed to an unemployment rate of around 2 percent in the 1980s, a period when the annual output growth was about 4 percent per year.

The economic causes of Japan's lost decade and a half of economic growth or its decade and a half of stagnation are complex and not well understood by economists or other analysts. Its stock market crash at the beginning of this period is certainly part of the problem. This crash is sometimes referred to as a burst bubble. The analogy to a bubble is an attempt to explain a sudden collapse of a market or an economy after a period when investment in the stock market (financial investment), in plant and equipment (physical capital), and in new enterprises frenetically feeds upon itself. The burst dot-com bubble in the United States in the early 2000s provides another example of the excesses that sometimes occur in a market economy. It is associated with the collapse in U.S. investment—stock market, physical capital, and new enterprises—that led to the recession of 2001. Throughout 2005, many analysts were concerned that the housing market in many parts of the United States was a bubble and concerned that it might pop, leading to recession. As you read this, you may know whether these concerns were valid.

Although the Japanese economy grew at 1 percent from 1990 to 2005, its industrial production stagnated and fell by 15 percent in 2001. As a result, in 2002, 12 years after its stock market collapse, Japan's industrial production was about 10 percent below that at the beginning of the 1990s. In comparison, U.S. industrial production fell by much more than this after the stock market crash of 1929, but it returned to its precrash level in about 8 years. Thus, the Japanese industrial economy did not go as deeply into depression as the U.S. economy did in the Great Depression; Japan's overall loss in output, however, is comparable to the U.S. loss because its still ongoing economic collapse lasted much longer than the U.S. collapse.

Deflation has caused tremendous problems in the Japanese economy and has increased the difficulty of finding a solution. An unexpected deflation creates losses for debtors because they must repay their loans with money that is worth more than it was when they borrowed. With deflation, or lower-than-expected inflation, debtors find that their debts are much more burdensome. Some debtors have to sell physical assets to meet their obligations, increasing the downward pressure on asset prices. In addition to the downward pressure on asset prices, indebted consumers find it difficult to make their payments, which may decrease aggregate demand. Moreover, when consumers realize that prices are falling, they may postpone purchases in order to get a "better buy" later. It's like waiting for the price of a new generation of computers to fall before making the purchase. This adds to the downward pressure on aggregate demand. Firms, therefore, postpone investment because their sales are weak and also because they expect prices of capital equipment to fall. These decreases in aggregate demand intensify the deflation, creating a feedback effect that makes it difficult to halt a deflationary process.

No wonder *The Economist* could entitle an optimistic article about the Japanese economy "The Land of the Rising Price." The article anticipated that in December 2005 the Japanese economy would have a "cause for celebration" as it experiences a "momentous thing," "the return of inflation." Leaders of the Japanese government are concerned, however, that its central bank, which has been flooding the economy with money since 2001 in an attempt to pull the economy into a strong expansion, will turn off the monetary spigots too soon in an attempt to head off rapid inflation. The government leaders' concern is that the return of stable or slowly rising prices will be cut off by the central bank.[a]

---

[a]Suggested by various articles in *The Economist*, including "Terrible Twins? Economic Parallels Between America and Japan" (June 13, 2002); "Comparing Symptoms. The Risk of Deflation" (November 7, 2002); and "Land of the Rising Price" (December 17, 2005).

constant, aggregate demand also grows at 8 percent. Therefore, in period 2 the new aggregate demand curve has shifted farther to the right than has aggregate supply. Measured at the price level P_1, AD_2 is farther to the right than AS_2. The new price level P_2, given by the intersection of AD_2 and AS_2, is higher than the original price level, P_1.

With aggregate demand growing more rapidly than aggregate supply, the price level will continue to rise. With aggregate demand growing at an 8 percent rate and aggregate supply at a 3 percent rate, the price level will rise at a 5 percent rate.

Inflation Is a Monetary Phenomenon

In the above example, the inflation rate increases from 0 to 5 percent when the growth rate of the money supply increases from 3 percent to 8 percent. This demonstrates a very important proposition: In the long run, the greater the growth rate of the money supply, the greater the inflation rate. Excessive rates of growth of the money supply cause inflation; therefore, inflation is a monetary phenomenon. Figure 14.4 shows the relationship between the inflation rate and the money supply growth rate for 22 countries (Euro countries are grouped together) during the period 1994 to 2007. The average growth rates over the long time-period are used because inflation is a long-run phenomenon. Moving from left to right, countries have increasing inflation rates: from essentially zero for Japan, Singapore, and Switzerland to 20 percent or more for Indonesia, Venezuela, and Turkey. The second bar for each country gives the money supply growth rate. These bars generally increase, moving to the right, indicating that more inflation is associated with more money supply. The average inflation rate for the countries with inflation of 4 percent or less is about 2.1 percent per year; their money supply growth, about

Figure 14.4 The Long-Run Relation Between Inflation and Money Supply Growth: Cross-Country Data (1995–2008)

These data show the inflation rate for a country and money supply growth for 22 countries over the period 1995 to 2004. The countries are arranged from left to right according to their inflation rates, with the higher rates on the right. Notice that the higher inflation rate moving to the right is associated with a higher growth rate of the money supply. The highest inflation rate, for Turkey, is about 45 percent, and the associated money supply growth rate is about 60 percent. The second highest money supply growth rate is for Venezuela, about 38 percent, with an associated inflation rate of about 34 percent. The specific numbers and countries are not the point of the figure. The point is that there is a strong association between money supply growth and inflation, just as the quantity theory predicts.

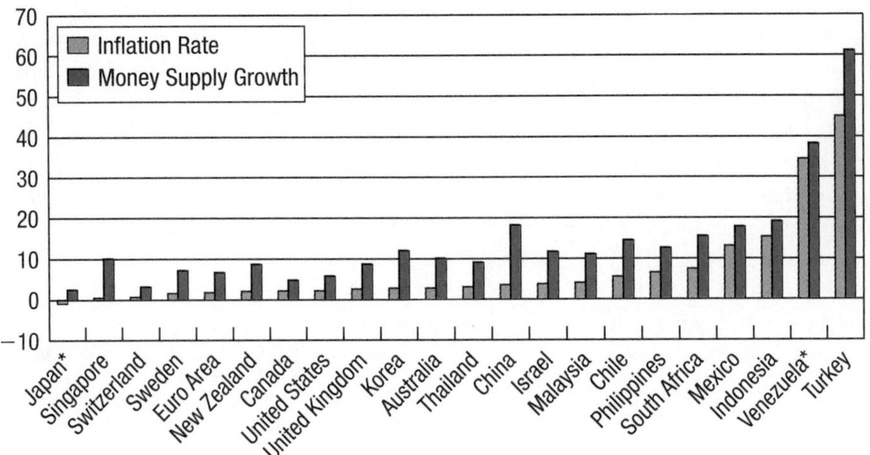

Source: Federal Reserve Bank of St. Louis, International Economic Trends (February 2009), 6.

8.5 percent per year. For the countries with inflation rates greater than 4 percent, the average inflation rate is 16.4 percent and the money supply growth rate about 23.8 percent. The fact that actual data trace out a positive relationship between the money supply and the inflation rate supports the quantity theory of money and the proposition that inflation is a monetary phenomenon. Before examining the policy implications of this explanation of inflation, we consider two qualifications.

Inflation as a Monetary Phenomenon: Two Qualifications

Based on Equation 14.4, an increase in the growth rate of the money supply causes the inflation rate to rise. This conclusion assumes that (1) the output growth rate is constant, and (2) the velocity of money is constant. If these assumptions are relaxed, the relationship between the growth rate of the money supply and the inflation rate is not as strong.

The Output Growth Rate. Previously, we assumed that real GDP grew at 3 percent. Although the output growth rate has averaged about 3 percent since 1929, the growth rate varies over the business cycle. Typically, it exceeds 3 percent during expansions (particularly during the early stages) and is less than 3 percent during contractions. Given this variation in growth rates, the inflation rate will vary over the business cycle even if the growth rate of the money supply is constant.

Suppose the economy is beginning to recover from a recession. During a recession, unemployment is high and firms have excess capacity. Because they have idle equipment and easily can hire more workers, firms can increase output relatively rapidly. Suppose the money supply is growing at 8 percent. If output grows at 3 percent—the long-run average—the inflation rate will be 5 percent. With excess capacity and high unemployment, output may grow at a higher rate, say 5 percent. With the money supply growing at 8 percent and output growing at 5 percent, the inflation rate is only 3 percent.

Output cannot grow at 5 percent indefinitely. Sooner or later, full employment will be achieved and output will grow less rapidly. If the money supply continues to grow at 8 percent and the output growth rate falls, the inflation rate will rise.

With variable output growth, the inflation rate varies even if the growth rate of the money supply is constant. Because the output growth rate varies in the short run, we find that the relationship between the growth rate of the money supply and the inflation rate is not as strong as originally stated. The long-run relationship, however, is clear. If the money supply grows faster than the long-run output growth rate, inflation will ensue. Thus, the short-run variation in the output growth rate does not modify the conclusion that inflation is a monetary phenomenon. Instead, it merely obscures the relationship between the growth rate of the money supply and the inflation rate.

The Velocity of Money. Just as the output growth rate varies in the short run, the velocity of money varies. Suppose the growth rate of the money supply increases. With velocity and the output growth rate constant, the inflation rate rises. If the velocity of money falls at the same time as the growth rate of the money supply increases, the inflation rate will rise, but by a smaller amount. In both situations, the increase in growth rate of the money supply is the same. In the second situation, the money supply circulates less rapidly and, therefore, has less of an impact on the inflation rate.

In the short run, the velocity of money may fall in response to an increase in the growth rate of the money supply. In the long run, however, the velocity of money is relatively constant. Consequently, the short-run variation in velocity does not alter the conclusion that inflation is a monetary phenomenon. Like the short-run variation in the output growth rate, it merely obscures the relationship between the growth rate of the money supply and the inflation rate.

Similarly, suppose government purchases increase while the money supply is constant. With the increase in government purchases, aggregate demand increases and the price level rises. With the money supply constant, the increase in the price level must stem from an increase in the velocity of money caused by the increase in government purchases.

Although factors other than the money supply (in this case, government purchases) affect the price level through variations in the velocity of money in the short run, these factors are much less important in the long run because of the relative constancy of the velocity of money in the long run. If the velocity of money is constant (or approximately so), it is the growth rate of the money supply that determines the growth rate of aggregate demand and, with a constant growth rate of aggregate supply, the inflation rate. Inflation is a monetary phenomenon.

Monopolies, Oil Markets, and Inflation

Economists generally agree that inflation is a monetary phenomenon. Some economists, however, argue that the exercise of monopoly power by firms, and particularly the Organization of Petroleum Exporting Countries (OPEC), can and has caused inflation. Firms are sometimes accused of causing inflation by exercising monopoly power. That is, firms are accused of raising prices even in the absence of increased demand or rising costs. This could not happen in a purely competitive economy. In a purely competitive economy, each product has many sellers. A single seller would be unable to raise prices above the market price and retain its customers. Moreover, because many sellers exist, it is impossible for them to collude. Thus, the argument that firms cause inflation cannot hold in an economy with substantial competition. Many economists believe that the U.S. economy is competitive enough that firms do not have enough pricing discretion to cause inflation.

Although part of the U.S. economy is best described as competitive, part of it is not. In industries characterized by imperfect competition, firms have discretion regarding the prices of their products. But these firms have no reason to engage in behavior that would be inflationary. Economic theory suggests that a monopolist (to take the simplest case) will set a price that maximizes profits. Once the monopolist sets the profit-maximizing price, however, management has no incentive to raise price further. (As explained in Chapter 5, a higher price would reduce profits.)

Monopolists are interested in charging "high" prices, but inflation is not about high prices. It is about rising prices. Although we would expect prices to be higher under monopoly or imperfect competition than under pure competition, we would *not* expect price to rise indefinitely under imperfect competition. Thus, we would not expect inflation to be a greater problem under imperfect competition than under pure competition.

Energy markets, and particularly petroleum markets, are perhaps another matter. We know from Chapter 5 that petroleum prices are subject to wide swings. For instance, from January 2005 to March 2009 we have experienced gasoline prices as low as $1.59 a gallon and as high as $4.05. During the same period the price of oil ranged from $30.28 to $145.31. On January 3, 2005 the price of oil was 42.16 and peaked in July 2008 at 145.31. Since then the price has fallen due to the worldwide recession that began December 2007. Increases in the prices of gasoline and oil cause increases in the cost of producing almost all goods and many services. Why would we not expect these price and cost increases to cause inflation? The simple answer is that these price increases are relative price increases. They are greater for goods and services that use a lot of energy—for example, gasoline—and less for goods and services that use relatively small amounts of energy—for instance, heart transplants. Some absolute prices, such as for electronics, fall. By definition, if the relative price of some goods increases, the relative price of other goods has to fall. In an economy where prices are flexible, these changing relative prices provide economic agents with the information and motivation necessary to economize in the new situation.

In terms of short-run aggregate demand and supply, this absolute price increase in energy shifts the short-run and long-run aggregate supply back. In the short run, the equilibrium price level increases, equilibrium output falls, and unemployment increases. This increase in the equilibrium price level is a once-and-for-all increase due to the short-run reduction in aggregate supply. If aggregate demand remains unchanged, the price level will not continue to increase. In fact, we can expect short-run aggregate supply eventually to increase, causing the price level and the unemployment rate to fall. In the Insight "When is an Increase in the CPI not Inflation?" this was the pattern of the price level changes associated with the hurricane disasters in the last half of 2005. (Changes in the unemployment rate also followed this pattern.)

INFLATION AND POLICY

Keywords: *monetary policy and inflation*

Access InfoTrac at http://infotrac.cengage.com

The appropriate cure for inflation depends upon its cause. Monetary policy, fiscal policy, supply-side policies, and incomes policy are proposed cures. We have argued that the inflation defined as a continuing increase in the overall price level is caused by continuing increases in aggregate demand. Monetary and fiscal policies are government actions that affect aggregate demand and, therefore, they are the appropriate policies to deal with inflation. In fact, many economists would agree that monetary policy is the appropriate policy to deal with inflation. Policy makers and some economists argue for *supply-side policies*, that is, government actions aimed at increasing aggregate supply, as a means of combating inflation. Others advocate *incomes policy*, which is government action, other than monetary and fiscal policies, to restrain or control wages and prices. These actions usually amount to imposing some type of price and wage ceilings.

Because monetary and fiscal policies are much more effective and important in dealing with inflation than supply-side policies and incomes policies, we limit the discussion of the latter to some brief comments. A reason that supply-side policies are ineffective against inflation is that it takes a 1 percentage point increase in the growth rate of GDP to reduce the inflation rate by 1 percentage point, other things being equal. (See Equation 14.4.) Suppose the inflation rate is 10 percent. Increasing the growth rate of GDP from 3 to 4 percent—a gigantic achievement—would only reduce the inflation rate to 9 percent. A reason that incomes policies are ineffective is that they create rigidities and shortages in the economy, just as any price ceiling does. As a result, people evade them, they have to be adjusted, and so on. History shows that they don't work.

Monetary Policy

Earlier, we concluded that inflation is a monetary phenomenon; that is, it is caused by excessive rates of growth of the money supply. To reduce the inflation rate, therefore, the growth rate of the money supply must be reduced. Reducing the growth rate of the money supply will cause aggregate demand to grow less rapidly. With aggregate supply growing at a constant rate in the long run, slower growth in aggregate demand will lower the inflation rate. We found earlier that an 8 percent growth rate in the money supply implies an inflation rate of 5 percent. If the money supply growth rate were reduced to 5 percent, the inflation rate would drop to 2 percent (see Equation 14.4).

Reducing the money supply growth rate reduces the inflation rate. Because the Federal Reserve controls the money supply, this would seem to be an easy matter. Unfortunately, two problems exist. One is that an unexpected reduction in the inflation rate causes a redistribution of income and wealth in much the same manner as an unexpected increase in the inflation rate. Firms that agreed to large wage increases in anticipation of continued inflation will find that the prices of their products increase less rapidly than expected if the inflation rate falls, making it more difficult for them to fulfill their contractual obligations. People who borrowed at high interest rates in anticipation of continued inflation and thus required to repay with dollars of greater-than-expected purchasing power also will find themselves worse off if the inflation rate falls. Because some firms and households will be adversely affected, they will resist policies aimed at reducing inflation.

Another problem is that the reduction in the inflation rate is likely to be accompanied by an increase in the unemployment rate in the short run. This is especially true if the inflation has continued for some time. One reason for the increase in unemployment is the contractual obligations of firms to pay higher wages. These contracts were presumably signed when it appeared that the inflation would continue. The reduction in the inflation rate means that firms will see the prices of their products increase less rapidly or not at all. Consequently, they may be forced to discharge workers in order to meet their contractual obligations to the remaining employees. Such reductions in employment cause the unemployment rate to rise.

Historically, reductions in inflation are often accompanied by increases in unemployment. This happened, for example, in the early 1980s. During President Carter's administration, the price level increased more rapidly each year. In 1979 and 1980, inflation (as measured by the CPI) reached double-digit levels. To reduce the inflation rate, the Federal Reserve sharply reduced the growth rate of the money supply. The inflation rate fell dramatically in 1982 and 1983. At the same time, the unemployment rate increased dramatically. As time passed, the unemployment rate returned to its full employment level.

During the transition period from a high inflation rate to a lower one, the unemployment rate tends to be above its full employment level. This increased unemployment, with its attendant hardships, is perhaps the most important reason why the Federal Reserve sometimes fails to take action to reduce the growth rate of the money supply to a level consistent with price stability.

Fiscal Policy

Because fiscal policy can alter aggregate demand, it is appropriate to examine its role in reducing inflation. In the short run, contractionary fiscal policy can hold the price level in check. As before, suppose the money supply, and hence aggregate demand, are growing at 8 percent. With aggregate supply growing at 3 percent, the inflation rate is 5 percent. To slow the rate of increase in aggregate demand, government spending may be reduced or taxes increased. If policy makers enact a contractionary fiscal policy, the effect of the growth of the money supply on aggregate demand will be at least partially offset. As a result, the price level will rise less rapidly. Unfortunately, so long as the money supply continues to grow, policy makers must continue to reduce government spending or raise taxes. Most government spending is for Social Security, national defense, interest on the national debt, and various programs to assist the poor. These programs cannot be cut indefinitely. Similarly, taxes cannot be raised indefinitely.

Thus, although contractionary fiscal policy may achieve temporary relief from increases in the price level, it cannot indefinitely offset the effects of the growth in the money supply on aggregate demand. Consequently, fiscal policy cannot be regarded as a serious alternative to monetary policy in fighting inflation. In the long run, contractionary monetary policy must be applied.

Monetary Policy in Action

The Federal Reserve, or Fed, has primary responsibility for achieving and maintaining a low inflation rate. When inflation threatens, the Fed significantly reduces the money supply growth rate and raises short-term interest rates. This is designed to reduce the growth rate of aggregate demand, thereby reducing the upward pressure on prices.

ADDITIONAL INSIGHT

Volcker and Greenspan: Architects of the "Long Boom"

Not many economists achieve "pop" status, but Alan Greenspan, in his 18 years as Chairman of the Board of Governors of the Federal Reserve System, did so. Greenspan is famous for his lack of clarity, as a bon vivant, and as a part of Ayn Rand's circle. Along with Bill Clinton and his successor Ben Bernanke, Greenspan is a saxophonist. His fame and popularity, however, are due mostly to the fact the he was the chief architect of monetary policy from 1987 to 2006. (Although the Chairman of the Board of Governors is in some ways the first among equals, every effective chairman has placed his mark on monetary policy.) The low rate of inflation over this period contrasts sharply with the high rates in the 1970s and early 1980s. Most of this period has also been a period of an expanding economy with falling unemployment rates.

An earlier—and not quite so popular—central banker stacked the deck for Greenspan by taming the inflation of the 1970s. President Jimmy Carter appointed Paul Volcker Chairman of the Board of Governors in summer of 1979. Volcker's position on inflation was clear. To control inflation, it would be necessary to reduce the growth rate of the money supply. President Carter's decision to appoint him was controversial because the prevailing opinion was that unwinding inflation in this way would have devastating effects on the economy in terms of recession and unemployment. Carter appointed him anyway, and Volcker's policies led to a recession in 1980 and a much deeper one in 1981–82. 1980 was an election year, and president Carter's chances of reelection were low due to his preceived mishandling of the economy and the Iran Hostage Crisis. In spite of this he was willing to appoint someone to fight inflation even though a recession could result. Following his defeat, President Reagan encouraged or at least did not dissuade Volcker from continuing his mission to fight inflation. Volcker displayed the determination, insight, and leadership necessary to reduce the inflation rate substantially without leading to the economic devastation that some feared. Because his policies were associated with a severe recession, Volcker's popularity is perhaps greater in retrospect, than it was when he was in office.

President Reagan appointed Alan Greenspan Chairman, and Presidents George H. W. Bush, Bill Clinton, and George W. Bush reappointed him. Greenspan began his term just in time to deal with the stock market crash of 1987; he then was faced with the Asian financial crisis, the pop of the dot-com bubble, and 9/11. Any and all of these extraordinary events could have been sufficient to damage the economy much more severely than they in fact did. Many people credit Greenspan's leadership and policies based on his detailed knowledge of and almost intuitive insights into the economy for the limited impact that these events had. In addition to this, over his long tenure the economy experienced only two short, mild recessions.

Ben Bernanke is the first academic economist to serve as Chairman of the Board of Governors. He has previously been Fed governor, but most of his career has been in academics. He is an expert on the Great Depression, and has clear ideas about how monetary policy should function. He is generally perceived as tough on inflation, but, as a student of the Great Depression, he is acutely aware of deflation's dangers. He has advocated that central banks set inflation targets so that economic agents know what to expect. Based on the current state of economic research Bernanke believes that credibly, effectively, and transparently pursuing a reasonable inflation target (2 to 3 percent) is the appropriate way to conduct monetary policy. If his pronouncements and testimonies are in fact transparent, he will differ greatly from Greenspan's mystique.[a] Bernanke follows two masters of monetary policy; events and his policies will tell us if he is a third.

---

[a]It may just be an urban legend, but it is said that after one of Greenspan's statements to Congress, the *Washington Post*'s headline reported "Greenspan Expects Slowdown: Interest Rates to Fall" and the *New York Times* headline read "Economy Improving: Inflation May Be a Danger — Greenspan." The story is too good to attempt to verify.

Except for the discount rate, the Federal Reserve has no direct control over interest rates.[2] The Fed, however, can alter the federal funds rate. *Federal funds* are loans between banks of their deposits at the Federal Reserve. The interest rate on these loans is called the *federal funds rate.* By increasing or decreasing bank reserves, the Fed can lower or raise the federal funds rate.

In 1994 and again in 1999 and 2000, the Fed raised interest rates to keep inflation from rising. In 1994, the Fed raised the federal funds rate on six occasions, for a total increase in the rate of 2.5 percentage points. In 1999 and 2000, the Fed again raised the federal funds rate six times, for a total of 1.75 percentage points. As the federal funds rate increased, other interest rates increased.

Critics of the Federal Reserve's actions note that the inflation rate did not rise substantially in either 1994 or 1999–2000. This, however, does not necessarily imply that the Fed's actions were unwarranted. Like an ocean liner, the U.S. economy has considerable momentum. If an ocean liner is headed toward a reef, the helmsman cannot wait until the last moment to turn the rudder. Because of the ship's momentum, the rudder must be turned well in advance. The same is true for the economy. If the Federal Reserve is to avoid a significant increase in the inflation rate, it must act before the inflation rate rises. Moreover, once the inflation rate rises, it is extraordinarily difficult to reduce it without causing a recession.

In January 2001, the Fed, suspecting that the economy was slowing, began a series of 13 cuts that totaled a decrease of 5 percentage points, reducing the federal funds rate to 1 percent. Although a recession began in March 2001, the Fed's actions may have reduced the length and severity of the recession. In June 2003, a year and a half after the first cut in 2001, the Fed cut the federal funds rate by another one-quarter percentage point, in an attempt to ensure economic recovery.

A year later, in June 2004, amidst increasing concerns about inflation and the economy developing too much steam, the Fed began a series of rate increases. The 13th 0.25 percent increase (December 2005) brought the federal funds rate to 4.25 percent. The Fed hoped that its policy of slowing monetary growth and increasing real short-term interests would lead the economy to a "soft landing." A soft landing occurs when the economy stabilizes with a low rate of inflation—less than 2 or 3 percent—and a low unemployment rate—5 percent or less. The policy was successful until the "housing bubble" burst and the resulting financial crisis and the economy entered a severe recession December 2007. In response, the Fed cut the Federal Funds Rate target rate to 0–0.25 percent in December 2008.

Summary

Inflation is a continuing rise in the price level, which means that it is a long-run phenomenon.

Although the GDP deflator is the most comprehensive of the various price indexes, the CPI usually receives more attention.

Unanticipated inflation causes a substantial redistribution of income and wealth. With anticipated inflation, the redistribution is less dramatic because people take action to protect themselves.

Inflation is costly to society because it results in fewer resources being devoted to the production of goods and services and reduces investment in new plant and equipment.

The nation's money supply—currency, travelers' checks, and checkable deposits—is controlled by the Federal Reserve.

With a constant income velocity of money, the inflation rate equals the growth rate of the money supply

[2]The discount rate is the interest rate at which banks and other depository institutions borrow from the Federal Reserve. It is discussed in the appendix to this chapter.

less the output growth rate. With the velocity of money and the output growth rate constant, the growth rate of the money supply determines the inflation rate. Inflation, therefore, is a monetary phenomenon.

In the short run, the velocity of money and the output growth rate vary, implying that the short-run relationship between the growth rate of the money supply and the inflation rate is not as strong as the long-run relationship.

To reduce the inflation rate, the growth rate of the money supply must be reduced. Reduced inflation is likely to be accompanied by increased unemployment in the short run.

Reducing government spending or raising taxes can keep the price level from rising in the short run. Because government spending cannot be cut or taxes raised indefinitely, fiscal policy cannot be regarded as a serious alternative to monetary policy in reducing inflation.

Since the early 1980s, the economy experienced a "long boom." Coming after the disastrous economic conditions of the 1970s with double-digit inflation and high unemployment, this long period of prosperity is remarkable. Many factors can account for this; our monetary policy discussion suggests that effective monetary policy has been one important factor. Unfortunately, the boom ended in December 2007, and it remains to be seen how effective monetary policy along with fiscal policy will be in ending this latest recession.

Key Terms

Inflation
Deflation
Consumer Price Index (CPI)
Unanticipated inflation
Anticipated inflation
Indexing
Creditor
Debtor
Hyperinflation
Medium of exchange
Money
Currency (cash)
Demand deposits
Money supply
Central bank
Quantity theory of money
Equation of exchange
Income velocity of money

Review Questions

1. What is the difference between an increase in the general price level and inflation? Why is it necessary to make this distinction?
2. Why is the CPI the most widely cited measure of inflation in the United States? Why is this index an imprecise measure of the cost of living?
3. "Inflation will always cause some economic agents to gain and others to lose." Is this statement true or false? Defend your answer.
4. How might unanticipated inflation result in a redistribution of income and wealth?
5. Inflation can be detrimental to the economy. Therefore, the proper role of government is to enact policies to deal with inflation. Why might government be reluctant to undertake anti-inflationary policies?
6. Aside from its effects on income, wealth, and the government, in what other ways might inflation affect the economy?
7. What is money? What basic functions does it perform?
8. "Inflation is a long-term phenomenon caused by too-rapid growth in the money supply." Is this statement true or false? Use the quantity theory of money in defense of your answer.
9. Use the aggregate demand–aggregate supply framework to demonstrate how increases in the money supply can result in inflation.
10. "If the growth rate of the money supply is constant, there will be no inflation." Is this statement true or false? Defend your answer.
11. Using the aggregate demand–aggregate supply model, explain how labor unions can cause inflation. Is such a scenario likely? Why or why not?
12. "A monopolist charges higher prices for its products than does a pure competitor; hence, an economy characterized by a large number of monopolies is more likely to experience inflation than an economy characterized by a large number of competitive firms." Is this statement true or false? Defend your answer.
13. Based on the discussion of oil markets and inflation, use an aggregate demand and supply diagram to describe the effects of an unexpected increase in the price of oil on the overall economy—price level, GDP, and, unemployment.

14. Explain and graphically show how monetary policy may be used to reduce inflation. Are any problems associated with the use of this policy?
15. In the long term, why can't fiscal policy reduce the inflation rate?
16. Go to http://www.swcollege.com/bef/econ_news.html—Economic News Online and choose either Employment, Unemployment, and Inflation or Monetary Policy under the macroeconomics category; then choose an EconNews story that interests you. Read the full summary, and answer the questions posed.

Web Sites

- *Million Dollar Babies.*
  Alan Kaim's site has photographs of some of the currency that has been printed during hyperinflations—**http://www.milliondollarbabies.com**
- *Board of Governors of the Federal Reserve System.*
  The official site of the Federal Reserve System's Board of Governors. Several parts of the site are of interest, including Testimony and Speeches, Monetary Policy, Economic Research and Data, and Publications and Education Resources. It also has links to each of the 12 Federal Reserve Banks, all of which have material of interest on their Web sites—**http://www.federalreserve.gov**
- *The European Central Bank.*
  Euros, European monetary policy, and more—**http://www.ecb.int/index.html**
- *Economic-Indicators.com.*
  R. Mark Rogers, author of the *Handbook of Key Economic Indicators*, 2nd ed. (McGraw-Hill, 1998) has developed a Web site that allows users to keep up to date on economic data—a one-stop shop—with links to numerous other policy and central bank sites—**http://www.economic-indicators.com**

APPENDIX TO CHAPTER 14
Money Creation and Monetary Policy

OUTLINE

This appendix first examines the money creation process and then considers the various ways in which the Federal Reserve can alter the money supply.

THE MONEY CREATION PROCESS

The actions of depository institutions and of the Federal Reserve are important in creating money. This section discusses both.

Depository Institutions

Depository institutions– Financial institutions that accept checkable and savings deposits.

Depository institutions are financial institutions that accept checkable and savings deposits. Commercial banks, savings and loan associations, mutual savings banks, and credit unions are depository institutions.

COMMERCIAL BANKS. Of these institutions, commercial banks are the second most numerous (after credit unions) and account for most of the deposits. There are about 10,000 commercial banks in the United States. Each bank is organized as a corporation and has a charter authorizing it to engage in banking. Banks offer a variety of services. For a start, they accept demand and time deposits, make business and consumer loans, and finance home mortgages. A commercial bank is either a national or a state bank. **National banks** are banks chartered by the federal government. **State banks** are those chartered by state governments. State banks outnumber national banks almost two to one, but national banks are typically larger.

National banks– Banks chartered by the federal government.

State banks– Banks chartered by state governments.

By law, national banks must belong to the Federal Reserve System. State banks may join if they meet the requirements. Most have elected not to do so. In fact, fewer than half of the nation's commercial banks are members of the Federal Reserve System. But these banks, called **member banks**, account for well over half of total deposits.

Member banks– Banks that are members of the Federal Reserve System.

Member banks are subject to the rules and regulations of the Federal Reserve System, including its reserve requirements. Member banks must hold a percentage of their deposits as cash and deposits at Federal Reserve Banks. Prior to the passage of the Depository Institutions Deregulation and Monetary Control Act of 1980, nonmember banks were required by state law to hold reserves, but the requirements were usually less restrictive than those of the Federal Reserve. Today, both member and nonmember banks are subject to the same reserve requirements.

Other Depository Institutions. Although commercial banks account for most deposits, the other depository institutions—savings and loan associations, mutual savings banks, and credit unions—are important. Savings and loan associations accept both checkable and savings deposits. Historically, they specialized in home mortgage lending, but they now make other types of loans as well. Like other depository institutions, mutual savings banks accept checkable and savings deposits and make loans. Geographically, they are concentrated in New York and New England. Credit unions differ from other depository institutions in that their depositors typically have the same employer or belong to the same labor union. Credit unions make loans, mostly consumer loans, but only to their depositors.

Since the 1970s, many of the distinctions among commercial banks, savings and loan associations, mutual savings banks, and credit unions have become blurred. Also, since the implementation of the Depository Institutions Deregulation and Monetary Control Act of 1980, the reserve requirements are the same for all depository institutions.

The Federal Reserve

After a long history of monetary crises in the United States, Congress created the Federal Reserve in 1913. The Federal Reserve is responsible for controlling the nation's money supply and conducting monetary policy.

A seven-person board of governors oversees the Federal Reserve. Members are appointed by the president (with Senate confirmation) to 14-year terms. The appointments are staggered so that one member is appointed every two years. The president also appoints a chairman of the board to a 4-year term. Historically, that person has commonly been referred to as the second most powerful person in the nation. Currently, Ben Bernanke is chairman of the Federal Reserve Board of Governors. He succeeded Alan Greenspan in 2006.

Rather than having a single central bank, as is common in other countries, the United States is divided into 12 Federal Reserve Districts, each with its own Federal Reserve Bank. Each of these district banks has its own board of directors. The district banks are located in Atlanta, Boston, Chicago, Cleveland, Dallas, Kansas City, Minneapolis, New York, Philadelphia, Richmond, St. Louis, and San Francisco. Some of these district banks have branch banks. The Federal Reserve Bank of Chicago, for example, has a branch bank in Detroit. For the most part, these Federal Reserve Banks—and their branch banks—do not deal directly with the general public. Instead, they provide services to commercial banks and other financial institutions.

Primary authority over control of the money supply rests with the Federal Open Market Committee (FOMC). The FOMC has 12 members. Each of the seven members of the Federal Reserve Board of Governors is a member of the FOMC. The other five members of the FOMC are presidents of Federal Reserve Banks. Because New York City is the nation's financial center, the president of the Federal Reserve Bank of New York is a permanent member. The presidents of the 11 other Federal Reserve Banks rotate.

In addition to controlling the money supply and conducting monetary policy, the Federal Reserve (1) assists in the check-clearing process, (2) supervises the operations of member banks, and (3) acts as the federal government's fiscal agent. Although these three functions are important, the Federal Reserve's role as manager of the nation's money supply is crucial if the nation is to achieve its economic goals.

The Federal Reserve and the Money Supply

Keywords: *Federal Reserve and money supply*

Access InfoTrac at http://infotrac.cengage.com

Vault cash– Cash held by banks and other depository institutions.

Required reserves– Reserves that depository institutions are required to hold.

Excess reserves– Reserves over and above required reserves.

Reserve requirement– The ratio of required reserves to deposits.

Open market operations– The purchase or sale of U.S. Treasury securities by the Federal Reserve.

As discussed previously, depository institutions must hold reserves against their deposits. Member banks, for example, hold their reserves in cash and deposits at their Federal Reserve Banks. (Cash held by banks and other depository institutions is usually referred to as **vault cash**. Because it is not actively circulating, vault cash is *not* counted as part of the nation's money supply.) **Required reserves** are reserves that depository institutions are required to hold. **Excess reserves** are reserves over and above those that are required. The **reserve requirement** is the ratio of required reserves to deposits.

Suppose Sunshine National Bank has demand deposits of \$5 million. If the reserve requirement is 20 percent, its required reserves are \$1 million (\$5 million × 20 percent). If its actual reserves against demand deposits are \$1.2 million, Sunshine Bank has required reserves of \$1 million and excess reserves of \$0.2 million (\$1.2 million − \$1 million). Because reserves earn no interest, depository institutions have a strong economic incentive to lend their excess reserves. (Like other firms, depository institutions are in business to make profits.)

Although the Federal Reserve can alter the money supply in several ways, it almost always uses open market operations to do so. **Open market operations** are the purchase or sale of U.S. Treasury securities. When the U.S. Treasury borrows, it issues Treasury securities. These securities are in effect IOUs indicating, in part, when the Treasury will repay the loan. The Treasury issues three types of securities: bills, notes, and bonds. Treasury bills mature in 1 year or less. Notes mature in 2 to 10 years. Bonds mature in 10 or more years.

The Creation of Money. We now consider the purchase of a U.S. Treasury security by the Federal Reserve and its impact on the money supply. In doing so, we have two purposes in mind. The first is to show that an open market purchase of Treasury securities results in an increase in the money supply. The second is to show that the purchase results in the creation of money by commercial banks or, more generally, depository institutions.[1] This money creation process results in an increase in the money supply that exceeds the initial increase.

Suppose the Federal Reserve buys a U.S. Treasury security from Melanie for \$10,000. It will pay for the security with a check drawn on a Federal Reserve Bank. If Melanie deposits this \$10,000 check in her checking account at Sunshine National Bank, Sunshine Bank's demand deposits increase by \$10,000. This increase in demand deposits constitutes an increase in the nation's money supply. (Recall that demand deposits are one component of the money supply.) This increase in the money supply, however, is only the beginning of the money creation process.

As the check that Melanie deposited at Sunshine Bank clears, the Federal Reserve credits Sunshine Bank's deposits at its Federal Reserve Bank. Consequently, Sunshine Bank's reserves increase by \$10,000. With an increase in demand deposits of \$10,000 and a reserve requirement of 20 percent, Sunshine Bank's required reserves increase by \$2,000 (\$10,000 × 0.20). Its excess reserves increase by \$8,000 (\$10,000 − \$2,000).

Sunshine Bank has excess reserves of \$8,000. Because reserves earn no interest, it has a strong incentive to lend these excess reserves. Suppose Sunshine Bank lends Joe the \$8,000 to pay for a car. If Joe's check is deposited in the car dealership's checking

---

[1]In describing the money creation process, we focus on the behavior of commercial banks because most people are more familiar with banks than with other types of depository institutions. Since all depository institutions are subject to the same reserve requirements, we would arrive at the same conclusions if both banks and other depository institutions were taken into account. Similarly, we focus on demand deposits. Because other checkable deposits are subject to the same reserve requirement as demand deposits, we would reach the same conclusions if both demand and other checkable deposits were considered.

account at Moonbeam National Bank, Moonbeam Bank's demand deposits increase by $8,000.

This increase in demand deposits at Moonbeam Bank represents an increase in the money supply. With an increase in demand deposits of $10,000 at Sunshine Bank and $8,000 at Moonbeam Bank, the total increase in the money supply is now $18,000 ($10,000 + $8,000). The money supply will continue to increase because, in addition to the increase in demand deposits, Moonbeam Bank experiences an increase in excess reserves. Sunshine Bank no longer has excess reserves. (It lent them to Joe.) Moonbeam Bank, however, has excess reserves. As the check that the car dealership deposited at Moonbeam Bank clears, the Federal Reserve credits Moonbeam Bank's deposits at its Federal Reserve Bank. With an $8,000 increase in both demand deposits and reserves and a reserve requirement of 20 percent, Moonbeam Bank's required reserves increase by $1,600 ($8,000 × 0.20) and its excess reserves increase by $6,400 ($8,000 − $1,600). Because reserves earn no interest, Moonbeam Bank has a strong incentive to lend these excess reserves.

Suppose Moonbeam Bank lends the $6,400 to Andrea and Greg to pay for remodeling their home. If Andrea and Greg's check is deposited in the builder's checking account at Starlight National Bank, Starlight Bank's demand deposits increase by $6,400.

This increase in demand deposits at Starlight Bank constitutes an increase in the money supply. With increases in demand deposits of $10,000 at Sunshine Bank, $8,000 at Moonbeam Bank, and $6,400 at Starlight Bank, the total increase in the money supply is now $24,400 ($10,000 + $8,000 + $6,400). The money supply will continue to increase, however, because in addition to the increase in demand deposits, Starlight Bank experiences an increase in excess reserves.

Although Sunshine and Moonbeam Banks no longer have excess reserves, Starlight Bank does. As the check that the builder deposited at Starlight Bank clears, the Federal Reserve credits Starlight Bank's deposits at its Federal Reserve Bank. With a $6,400 increase in both demand deposits and reserves and a reserve requirement of 20 percent, Starlight Bank's required reserves increase by $1,280 ($6,400 × 0.20) and its excess reserves increase by $5,120 ($6,400 − $1,280). Starlight Bank has a strong incentive to lend these excess reserves. And so it goes.

The Change in the Money Supply. Instead of following the money creation process indefinitely, we can derive an equation to determine the total increase in demand deposits and hence the money supply. Two simplifying assumptions are made. First, depository institutions do not hold excess reserves. Second, the public does not add to its holdings of cash.

In the illustration, demand deposits and reserves first increased by $10,000. This increase in demand deposits was followed by successive increases of $8,000 and $6,400. As demand deposits increased, more and more of the initial $10,000 increase in reserves was used as required reserves. Sunshine Bank's required reserves increased by $2,000 to support its $10,000 increase in demand deposits. Moonbeam Bank's required reserves increased by $1,600, and Starlight Bank's by $1,280. Given the assumptions, depository institutions will continue to make loans until all of the initial increase in reserves becomes required reserves. Thus, the initial change in reserves, denoted as ΔR, ultimately becomes a change in required reserves, denoted as ΔRR. In equation form,

$$\Delta \mathbf{R} = \Delta \mathbf{RR}$$

The change in required reserves, in turn, equals the ratio of required reserves to demand deposits (the reserve requirement) multiplied by the total change in demand deposits. If the ratio of required reserves to demand deposits is denoted as r and the total change in demand deposits as ΔDD, we have

$$\Delta R = \Delta RR = r\Delta DD$$

Dividing both sides of the equation by r and rearranging terms yields

$$\Delta DD = \frac{\Delta R}{r}$$

This equation indicates that the total change in demand deposits equals the initial change in reserves divided by the reserve requirement. In the illustration, the initial change in reserves is $10,000 and the reserve requirement is 20 percent. Consequently, the total change in demand deposits is calculated by dividing $10,000 by 0.20. Thus, the total change in demand deposits is $50,000. We know that this must be the case because with an initial increase in reserves of $10,000 and a 20 percent reserve requirement, demand deposits must ultimately increase by $50,000 for all of the increase in reserves to become required reserves.

The foregoing analysis indicates that the initial increase in reserves of $10,000 results in an increase in demand deposits of $50,000. Because demand deposits are a component of the nation's money supply, we find that the money supply also increases by $50,000. If the change in the money supply is denoted by ΔM, the relationship between the change in the money supply and the change in reserves is

$$\Delta M = \frac{\Delta R}{r} \qquad \textbf{(14.4)}$$

Equation 14A.1 indicates that a change in reserves, ΔR, results in a change in the money supply, ΔM, equal to the change in reserves divided by the reserve requirement, r.

Equation 14A.1 holds for both increases and decreases in the money supply. In our illustration, we showed that an open market purchase of U.S. Treasury securities by the Federal Reserve increases the money supply. Equation 14A.1 indicates that the total increase in the money supply is equal to the increase in reserves divided by the reserve requirement. By the same token, an open market sale of U.S. Treasury securities by the Federal Reserve decreases the money supply.

To illustrate, suppose the Federal Reserve sells a U.S. Treasury security to Tiffany for $10,000. Tiffany pays for the security with a check drawn on Boomtown National Bank. Boomtown Bank's demand deposits decrease by $10,000. As the check clears, Boomtown Bank's reserves also decrease by $10,000. The decrease in reserves will force Boomtown Bank to curtail its loans. This loss of reserves and curtailment of loans will lead to successive decreases in demand deposits and the money supply, just as an increase in reserves leads to successive increases in demand deposits and the money supply. (See Review Question 3 following this appendix.) Equation 14A.1 indicates that the total decrease in the money supply equals the decrease in reserves divided by the reserve requirement.

The Change in the Money Supply: Two Qualifications. The change in the money supply indicated by Equation 14A.1 is the maximum possible change. Again, the equation assumes that (1) depository institutions do not hold excess reserves, and (2) the public does not add to its holdings of cash. If these assumptions are met, the money supply will change by the amount indicated by Equation 14A.1. If the assumptions are not met, the change in the money supply will be less than the amount indicated by the equation.

To demonstrate that the change in the money supply indicated by Equation 14A.1 represents the maximum possible change, we now relax each of the assumptions. Previously, we assumed that depository institutions hold no excess reserves. Based on this assumption, institutions with excess reserves will lend them and the money creation process will be as described earlier. Suppose depository institutions lend only part of their excess reserves. If so, the corresponding increases in demand deposits will be smaller. As a result, the total increase in demand deposits and hence the money supply will be smaller, too.

Thus, if depository institutions hold excess reserves, the money supply increases in response to the purchase of U.S. Treasury securities by the Federal Reserve, but not by the maximum possible amount. The same is true if the public adds to its holdings of cash during the money creation process. If the public adds to its holdings of cash, depository institutions lose some of their reserves and so will not be able to increase their loans by as much as before. The corresponding increases in demand deposits will be smaller. As a result, the total increase in demand deposits and hence the money supply will be smaller.

In conclusion, we find that the money supply increases in response to an open market purchase. If the simplifying assumptions are met, the money supply increases by the maximum possible amount; if they are not met, the money supply increases by a smaller amount. We could develop an equation to determine the increase in the money supply when the assumptions are not met, but this is unnecessary for our purposes and beyond the scope of this text.

THE FEDERAL RESERVE AND CONTROL OF THE MONEY SUPPLY

The Federal Reserve can alter the money supply by (1) conducting open market operations, (2) changing reserve requirements, and (3) changing the discount rate.

Open Market Operations

As defined earlier, open market operations are the purchase or sale of U.S. Treasury securities. Suppose the Federal Reserve decides to increase the money supply by purchasing U.S. Treasury securities. It pays for these securities with checks drawn on Federal Reserve Banks. These checks will be deposited at various depository institutions. The Federal Reserve will credit these institutions' deposits at Federal Reserve Banks, and these increased deposits will constitute an increase in reserves. Banks and other depository institutions will respond by making new loans, and the money creation process will begin.

Keyword: *federal funds rate*

Access InfoTrac at http://infotrac.cengage.com

Just as the Federal Reserve increases the money supply by purchasing U.S. Treasury securities, it can reduce the money supply by selling Treasury securities. Those buying the securities pay for them with checks drawn on various depository institutions. During the check-clearing process, the Federal Reserve will reduce those institutions' deposits at Federal Reserve Banks. Banks and other depository institutions will respond to the decrease in reserves by curtailing their loans. Fewer loans will cause demand and other checkable deposits to decline. Because these deposits are part of the money supply, the nation's money supply will fall.

The ultimate authority regarding the conduct of open market operations rests with the Federal Open Market Committee. Once the committee decides on the appropriate course of action, it issues a directive to the appropriate person at the Federal Reserve Bank of New York. This person actually supervises the purchase and sale of the Treasury securities. The Federal Reserve almost *always* uses open market operations to control the nation's money supply.

Reserve Requirements

The Federal Reserve can also alter the money supply by changing the reserve requirements for depository institutions. If the Federal Reserve wants to increase the money supply, it can reduce reserve requirements, thereby creating excess reserves in the monetary system. As a result, depository institutions will make new loans, resulting in the creation of demand and other checkable deposits. The increase in these deposits constitutes an increase in the money supply.

In the illustration, it was assumed that depository institutions were required to have reserves equal to 20 percent of their deposits. Suppose that Sunshine Bank initially had $1 million in reserves and $5 million in deposits. As a result, it was not in a position to make new loans. Now suppose the reserve requirement was reduced to 10 percent. Sunshine Bank would be required to hold only $500,000 in reserves. It would be free to lend up to $500,000 (its excess reserves), and the money creation process would begin.

Just as the Federal Reserve can increase the money supply by reducing reserve requirements, it can decrease the money supply by raising them. By raising requirements, it can make depository institutions hold more reserves, forcing them to curtail loans. As fewer loans are made, demand deposits and, therefore, the nation's money supply fall. In the illustration, suppose the reserve requirement was raised from 20 to 30 percent. Sunshine Bank's required reserves would now be $1.5 million. With reserves of only $1 million, Sunshine Bank would have to curtail its loans. Fewer loans lead to fewer demand (and other checkable) deposits and, therefore, a smaller money supply.

Keywords: *Federal Reserve and interest rate*

Access InfoTrac at http://infotrac.cengage.com

Although changes in reserve requirements are a powerful means to alter the money supply, they are rarely used. For one thing, changing reserve requirements is a very blunt way to alter the nation's money supply. Even small changes in reserve requirements cause large changes in required reserves and the money supply. For another, changes in reserve requirements are not easily reversed. Suppose reserve requirements are lowered in order to increase the money supply. Should the increase in the money supply prove too large, the Federal Reserve could raise reserve requirements to reduce the money supply. But these new reserve requirements would be disruptive, especially for depository institutions not sufficiently liquid to meet them.

The Discount Rate

Keywords: *Federal Reserve and the discount rate*

Access InfoTrac at http://infotrac.cengage.com

In addition to using open market operations and altering reserve requirements, the Federal Reserve may alter the money supply by changing the discount rate. The **discount rate** is the interest rate at which depository institutions can borrow from Federal Reserve Banks. Each Federal Reserve Bank's rate is determined by that bank's board of directors. The rate must be approved, however, by the Federal Reserve Board of Governors.

If the Federal Reserve wishes to increase the money supply, it could reduce the discount rate, thus giving depository institutions a greater incentive to borrow. If the Federal Reserve does increase the money supply, their reserves increase, permitting an expansion in the money supply. If the Federal Reserve wishes to reduce the money supply, it could raise the discount rate, thereby discouraging depository institutions from borrowing. If they borrow less, their reserves decrease and the money supply falls.

Discount rate– The interest rate at which depository institutions can borrow from Federal Reserve Banks.

Although changing the discount rate is a means to alter the money supply, it is rarely altered for that purpose. Depository institutions are discouraged from borrowing from their Federal Reserve Banks except as a last resort. Consequently, the discount rate may change significantly without altering depository institution borrowing from the Federal Reserve.

Unlike reserve requirements, the discount rate is altered frequently. On most occasions, the intent is to bring it into line with other interest rates, not to alter the money supply. Consequently, when the discount rate is changed, we cannot be sure that the Federal Reserve is altering its monetary policy.

Summary

Depository institutions—financial institutions that accept checkable and savings deposits—include commercial banks, savings and loan associations, mutual savings banks, and credit unions. All depository institutions are subject to the same reserve requirements.

The Federal Reserve, an independent government agency, is the United States' central bank. It controls the nation's money supply, conducts monetary policy, and, in general, supervises the nation's monetary system.

A board of governors oversees the Federal Reserve. The Federal Open Market Committee, which includes the board of governors as members, has primary responsibility for the conduct of monetary policy.

Open market operations are the purchase or sale of U.S. Treasury securities by the Federal Reserve. If the Federal Reserve wishes to increase (or decrease) the nation's money supply, it can do so by buying (or selling) U.S. Treasury securities. By buying U.S. Treasury securities, the Federal Reserve adds to the reserves of the monetary system. The increase in reserves causes depository institutions to make new loans, increasing the nation's money supply.

The money creation process increases the money supply beyond the initial increase in reserves. The maximum possible increase in the money supply equals the initial increase in reserves divided by the reserve requirement.

The Federal Reserve can also alter the money supply by changing reserve requirements. If it wishes to increase (or decrease) the money supply, it can lower (or raise) the reserve requirement. Finally, the Federal Reserve can alter the money supply by changing the discount rate—the interest rate at which depository institutions can borrow from Federal Reserve Banks. If it wishes to increase (or decrease) the money supply, it can lower (or raise) the discount rate.

Key Terms

Depository institutions
National banks
State banks
Member banks
Vault cash
Required reserves
Excess reserves
Reserve requirement
Open market operations
Discount rate

Review Questions

1. Briefly discuss the structure of the Federal Reserve.
2. Suppose the required reserve ratio is 10 percent. Assume that the banking system has $20 million in deposits and $5 million in reserves. Find the required reserves, excess reserves, and the maximum amount by which demand deposits could expand.
3. Suppose the required reserve ratio is 25 percent. Assume that banks lend all of their excess reserves and the public does not add to its cash holdings. Briefly explain how the Federal Reserve's purchase of a $1,000 U.S. Treasury security will affect the money supply. Suppose the Federal Reserve had instead sold a $1,000 security. How would this action affect the money supply?
4. What factors could cause the increase in the money supply to be less than the maximum possible increase?
5. What actions can the Federal Reserve undertake if it wishes to increase the money supply?
6. "An increase in the discount rate means that the Federal Reserve is attempting to decrease the money supply." Is this statement true or false? Defend your answer.

CHAPTER 15
Sustained Budget Deficits: Is This Any Way to Run a Government?

OUTLINE

Budget– A statement of receipts (income) and outlays (expenditures) for a specific period of time (a year).

Unified budget– The federal budget with Social Security included.

The federal budget is on an unsustainable path. In the absence of significant policy changes, budget deficits could total over $6 trillion in the next decade, increasing the nation's public debt by a like amount. Thereafter, as the baby boomers exit the labor force, the deficit and debt are likely to grow even more rapidly. In fact, projected fiscal imbalances are so large that they pose a severe threat to the nation's economic health. In this chapter, we will examine the bases for these claims and the nature of the threat to the economy and to the reader, and suggest some things that might be done about it.

THE BUDGET, BUDGET BALANCES, AND DEBT

The Budget

The Federal **budget** is a statement of income (or receipts) and expenditures (or outlays) for a specific period of time (a year). The 2007 budget is recorded in Table 15.1. This is the **unified budget** of the federal government.

TABLE 15.1 FEDERAL GOVERNMENT UNIFIED BUDGET, 2007 (BILLIONS OF DOLLARS)

RECEIPTS		OUTLAYS	
Individual Income Taxes	**1,163**	**Discretionary**	**1,041**
		National Defense	447
Corporation Income Taxes	**370**	Domestic	417
		Homeland Security	30
Social Insurance Taxes	**870**	**Mandatory**	**1,451**
Social Security (OASDI)	635	Social Security (OASDI)	581
(OFF-BUDGET)	(635)	*(OFF-BUDGET)*	*(454)*[a]
Other Soc Ins Taxes	235	Medicare	436
		Medicaid	191
		Income Support Programs	202
		Other Retirement & Disabilit	161
		Other Mandatory	57
Other Receipts	**165**	**Net Interest**	**160**
Total Receipts	**2,568**	**Total Outlays**	**2,652**
Budget Balance (Receipts - Outlays)			
Unified Budget:	**2,568 − 2,652 = −84**		
Social Security (Off-Budget):	**635 − 454 = 181**		
Non-Soc Sec (On-Budget):	**(2,568 − 635) − (92,652 − 454) = −265**		

[a]Social Security Outlays Funded by Social Insurance Taxes.

Source: Congressional Budget Office, *The Budget and Economic Outlook: An Update*, September 2008.

Social Security– The federal program that provides retirement benefits, survivors' benefits, and disability benefits to people age 62 and over, and to their dependents.

Medicare– The federal government's principal health insurance program for people 65 years of age and older.

Discretionary outlay– A government outlay with a limit specified annually by Congress.

Mandatory outlay– A government expenditure that depends on criteria (such as age or income) that are not normally changed on an annual basis (also called "entitlements").

Budget balance– Total budget receipts minus total budget outlays.

Budget surplus– A positive budget balance; total receipts exceed total outlays.

Budget deficit– A negative budget balance: total outlays exceed total receipts.

Off-budget balance– Budget balance in the Social Security portion of the unified budget.

On-budget balance– Budget balance in the non–Social Security portion of the unified budget.

The left side of Table 15.1 displays the most important sources of federal revenue. The federal individual income tax is the most important of these, followed by social insurance taxes. The latter are receipts from the payroll tax for **Social Security** and **Medicare**.

The right side of Table 15.1 displays government outlays. Total outlays are divided into two types: discretionary and mandatory.

A **discretionary outlay** is one with a limit specified annually by Congress. A **mandatory outlay** is one that depends on criteria (such as age or income) that are not normally changed on an annual basis. Mandatory outlays are also referred to as "entitlements." The distinction between discretionary and mandatory is important because it indicates that Congress controls less than 35 percent of outlays through the normal appropriations process. In this environment, most of the debate over the budget normally revolves around relatively small annual changes in spending. And most of that attention is focused on what to do with the extra revenues produced by annual growth and not on a reallocation of funds committed to specific programs in the past.

Budget Balances

The "bottom line" of the budget is the **budget balance**—total receipts minus total outlays. If total receipts exceed total outlays, there is a positive balance, or **budget surplus**. If total receipts are less than total outlays, there is a negative balance, or **budget deficit**. If total receipts and total outlays are equal, the balance is zero and the budget is "balanced." Calculations displayed at the bottom of the table indicate that there was a deficit of $84 billion in the 2007 unified budget.

Table 15.1 contains two additional balances: (1) the balance in the Social Security portion of the budget, and (2) the balance in the non–Social Security portion of the budget. The Social Security portion of the budget had a surplus of $181 billion ($635 billion in Social Security receipts minus $454 billion in outlays for Social Security funded by social insurance taxes). This balance is also called the **off-budget balance**. The non–Social Security portion of the budget had a deficit of $265 billion in 2007. This balance is also called the **on-budget balance**. The unified budget balance is equal, then, to the sum of the on-budget (non–Social Security) balance and the off-budget (Social Security) balance. (Actually, the off-budget portion of the unified budget also includes receipts and outlays of the U.S. Postal Service, but the Postal Service balance is so small relative to the Social Security balance that it is not misleading to refer to the off-budget balance as the Social Security balance.)

Congress presumably distinguishes between on-budget and off-budget balances primarily to keep a separate account on Social Security. Some economists believe, however, that the *real* reason that Congress includes Social Security receipts and outlays financed by social insurance taxes in the unified budget is that currently their inclusion makes the budget deficit smaller than it would be if they were excluded ($84 billion in 2007 instead of $265 billion). This is likely to remain the case for the next 12 or 13 years. After that, annual Social Security outlays will exceed annual receipts, and it will be interesting to see if Congress *removes* Social Security from the budget at that time to continue to make the deficit look smaller.

Debt

If there is a deficit in the unified budget, the government normally must borrow money from the public (individuals and institutions, both foreign and domestic). The amount it

INFOTRAC College Edition

Keyword: *budget deficit*

Access InfoTrac at http://infotrac.cengage.com

borrows adds to the debt held by the public, or **public debt**. The public debt stood at $5,035 billion at the end of Fiscal 2007, primarily as a result of a long string of unified budget deficits.

The public debt should be distinguished from the gross federal debt, or **national debt**. The latter includes the public debt *and* the debt that federal agencies owe other federal agencies (also called intra-governmental holdings). In 2007, the Treasury borrowed $181 billion from Social Security (the 2007 surplus in Social Security), adding a like amount to the national debt (but not the public debt). The national debt was $11,077 billion as of March 2009. It consisted of a public debt of $5,088 billion and $5,989 billion in debt owed by federal agencies (such as the Treasury) to other federal agencies (such as Social Security).

Public debt– The portion of the national debt held by the public.

National debt– The debt of the federal government held by the public and by government agencies (also known as the "gross federal debt").

Intra-governmental debt– The portion of the national debt held by government agencies.

Economists and financial market participants pay close attention to the public debt rather than the national debt because the public debt has a more direct impact on the economy than the national debt. When the Department of the Treasury borrows from the public, it acquires resources that otherwise might be invested in the private sector. Thus, an increase in the public debt may affect the future course of the economy. By contrast, **intra-governmental debt** transactions have no effect on the private sector.

WHAT'S IN STORE?

The Deficit Over the Next Decade: Better … or Worse?

As noted, the 2007 budget deficit was $265 billion. It is important to know whether it is likely to shrink or expand in the future. Although this cannot be known for certain, the Congressional Budget Office (CBO) makes ten-year forecasts of the budget deficit that provide useful guidelines for policy makers. Unfortunately, there is considerable variation between forecasted outcomes. Which one is most plausible depends on the uncertain course of federal politics.

Baseline forecast– A forecast of the unified budget, reflecting the current law pertaining to receipts and expenditures, that the Congressional Budget Office is required to make each year.

The CBO's forecasts appear each year in its publication, *The Budget and Economic Outlook*. The latest available version is a September 2008 *Update*. The primary focus of this publication is the CBO's **baseline forecast**, a forecast that the CBO is required by law to make each year.

The baseline forecast is based on the assumption of *no change in the law* as it pertains to either the tax code or to the criteria that govern the disbursement of mandatory outlays. The baseline forecast also rests on an assumption about the rate at which discretionary outlays will grow (2 percent per year—the forecasted rate of inflation). As shown by the top line (Baseline Scenario) in Figure 15.1, under these circumstances the deficit is forecasted to increase significantly in 2008 and 2009. Then it will decline and stay at about the 2007 level through 2018. For the period 2009 through 2018 as a whole, the deficits are projected to total $3.8 trillion.

Some economists believe, however, that the law, especially as it relates to taxes, is likely to be changed. Some also believe that discretionary expenditures will grow faster than the CBO assumes in the baseline scenario. When these factors are incorporated in the forecast, the deficit outlook is even more pessimistic.

During the first George W. Bush administration, Congress made several changes in the tax code that reduced individual income taxes. Most of these provisions are scheduled by law to expire at the end of 2010. It is this factor that accounts for most of the sharp reduction in the baseline deficit in 2011–2015. The second George W. Bush administration has proposed changes in the law, however, that would make these provisions permanent. If this were to happen, projected receipts would decline relative to the baseline and the deficit would increase relative to the baseline deficit.

Figure 15.1 Unified Budget Deficit, 2007–2018: Baseline and Alternate Scenarios
This figure illustrates the course of the federal unified budget deficit according to the Congressional Budget Office Baseline Scenario and an alternate scenario constructed by the authors from CBO data.

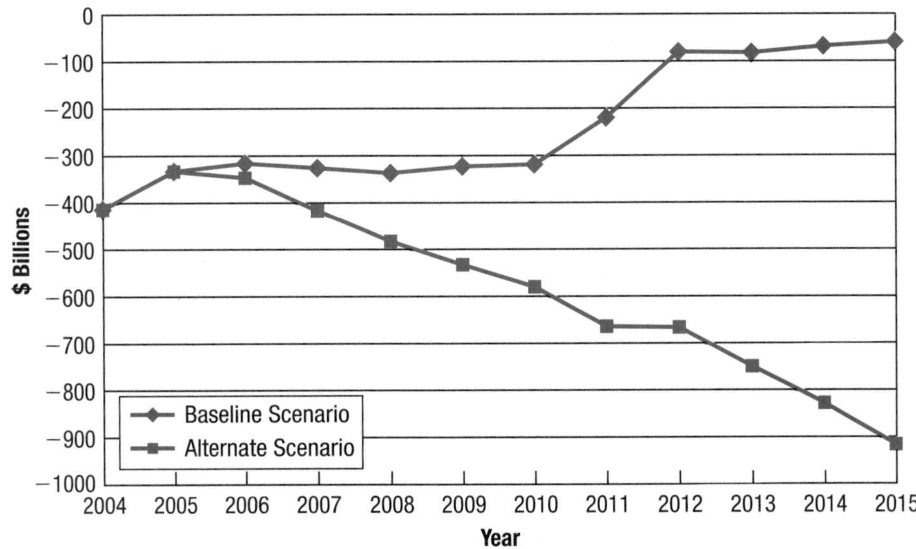

Source: Congressional Budget Office, Chapter 1, in *The Budget and Economic Outlook, An Update*, September 2008.

Alternative Minimum Tax (AMT)–
An extra tax that some people with higher taxable income have to pay on top of the regular income tax.

Another item at issue is a complex provision of the tax code known as the **Alternative Minimum Tax (AMT)**. The AMT is an extra tax some people have to pay on top of the regular income tax. The original impetus for adoption was to prevent taxpayers with very high incomes from using special deductions, exemptions, or credits to pay little or no tax. Approximately 19,000 taxpayers owed some AMT in 1970, but over 3 million people are paying it now. What happened? Blame it mostly on inflation. The AMT exemptions and brackets are not indexed for inflation, so many people whose income grows with the economy enter the AMT zone each year. Many of the people now subject to the AMT would not be considered rich, but their numbers will continue to grow unless Congress indexes the AMT for inflation. If Congress indexes the AMT for inflation—and many economists believe that it will—projected receipts would decline relative to the baseline, and the deficit would increase further relative to the baseline deficit.

As noted, the CBO assumes in the baseline that discretionary expenditures will grow at the projected rate of inflation (2 percent per year). They have grown historically, however, at about the rate at which the economy has grown. The CBO assumes that GDP will grow at 5.7 percent per year over the forecast period. If discretionary expenditures grow this fast also, outlays would grow relative to baseline outlays and the deficit would increase even further relative to the baseline deficit.

The alternate scenario in Figure 15.1 captures the effects of making the tax cuts from the first George W. Bush administration permanent, indexing the AMT for inflation, and reducing troop levels in Iraq. Figure 15.2 tells a similar tale in terms of the projected public debt. In the baseline scenario, the debt as a percent of GDP increases to over 41 percent of GDP to 2010 and then declines slightly to about 40 percent by 2018. The alternate scenario shows the public debt as a percent of GDP rising to just under 41 percent and then declining to under 36 percent by 2018.

Figure 15.2 **Public Debt as Percent of GDP: Baseline and Alternate Scenarios**
This figure illustrates the course of the public debt according to the Congressional Budget Office Baseline Scenario and an alternate scenario constructed by the authors from CBO data.

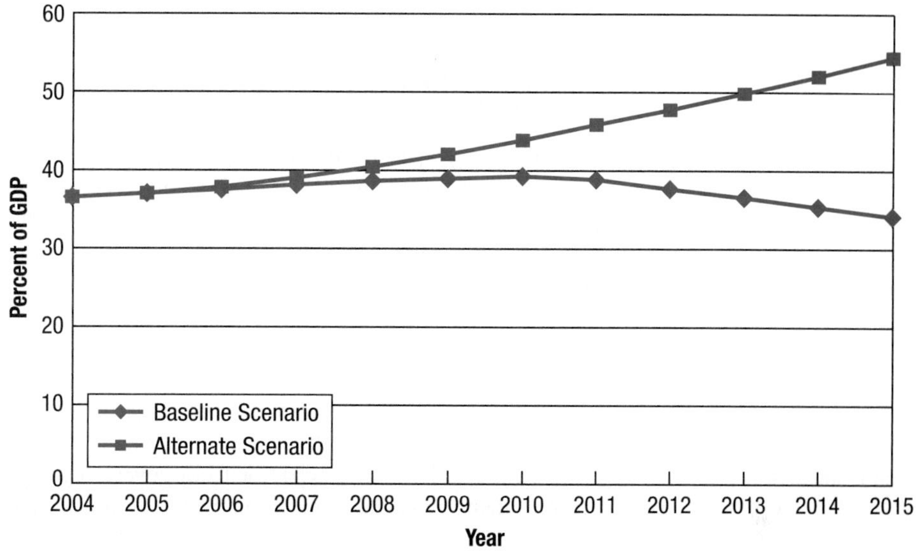

Source: Congressional Budget Office, Chapter 1, in *The Budget and Economic Outlook, An Update*, September 2008.

The Long-Run Deficit: Unsustainable

Although there is some uncertainty about whether the deficit will increase or decrease over the next decade, official projections indicate that the deficit will grow continuously after 2016. Table 15.2 presents the projection that appears in background material that

TABLE 15.2 PROJECTED UNIFIED FEDERAL BUDGET, 2010–2080 (PERCENT OF GDP)

YEAR	2010	2020	2030	2040	2060	2080
Receipts	**18.6**	**18.3**	**18.3**	**18.3**	**18.3**	**18.3**
Outlays:						
Discretionary	7.0	4.7	4.7	4.7	4.7	4.7
Mandatory						
Social Security	4.3	5.1	5.9	6.0	6.1	6.3
Medicare	2.7	3.1	4.1	4.8	5.3	5.3
Medicaid	1.5	1.9	2.3	2.7	3.2	3.9
Other	2.4	2.0	1.7	1.5	1.3	1.2
Subtotal: Mandatory	10.9	12.1	14.0	15.0	15.9	16.7
Net Interest	1.8	1.2	1.0	1.7	4.1	7.8
Total Outlays	19.7	18.0	19.7	21.4	24.7	29.2
Deficit	1.1	−0.3	1.4	3.1	6.4	10.9
Public Debt	38.4	24.3	28.1	52.4	140.0	283.4

Source: Office of the President, *Budget of the United States Government, Fiscal 2009, Analytical Perspectives*, p. 188.

accompanies the President's Budget for Fiscal 2009. According to this projection, both the deficit and public debt will increase dramatically relative to GDP, a point that is illustrated clearly in Figures 15.3 and 15.4. As the source notes, these trajectories are unsustainable.

The Long-Run Fiscal Imbalance: Now for Some Really Large Numbers

Keywords: *fiscal imbalance, fiscal gap*

Access InfoTrac at http://infotrac.cengage.com

Fiscal imbalance– A measure related to the budget that compares the present value of expected future outlays (PVFO) with the present value of expected future receipts (PVFR) and the current value of financial assets (CVFA)—also called a "fiscal gap."

Suppose that you were trying to make a large purchase, such as a house, and you approached your bank for a loan. In appraising your creditworthiness, they would compare an estimate of the future liability incurred via your loan (your monthly payments) with an estimate of your future ability to repay the loan (your monthly incomes). In estimating your financial liabilities they would also consider your other financial obligations (car payment, credit card debt, and so on). In estimating your ability to repay the loan they would consider your current financial assets (such as money in a savings account). They would lend you the money only if their estimate of your ability to repay the loan is larger than your monthly payments. If they did not subject your request to such scrutiny, you should put your money in a bank with sounder financial practices.

You should expect the same behavior from governments; namely, that when they are considering a major financial commitment they compare *expected future outlays for* ***all*** *obligations (including that commitment)* with *expected future income and current financial assets*. In fact, it is reasonable to expect the government to know at all times whether their expected future income and current assets are sufficient to cover their expected future outlays. To do this, they must determine whether they have a **fiscal imbalance**.

Fiscal imbalance (FI) is a measure that compares the present value of expected future outlays (PVFO) with the present value of expected future receipts (PVFR) and the current

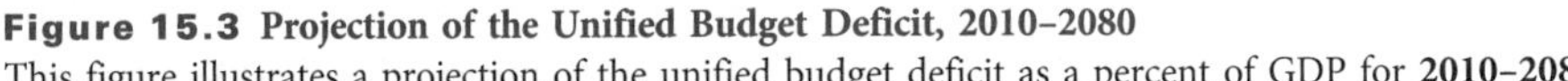

Figure 15.3 **Projection of the Unified Budget Deficit, 2010–2080**
This figure illustrates a projection of the unified budget deficit as a percent of GDP for **2010–2080**.

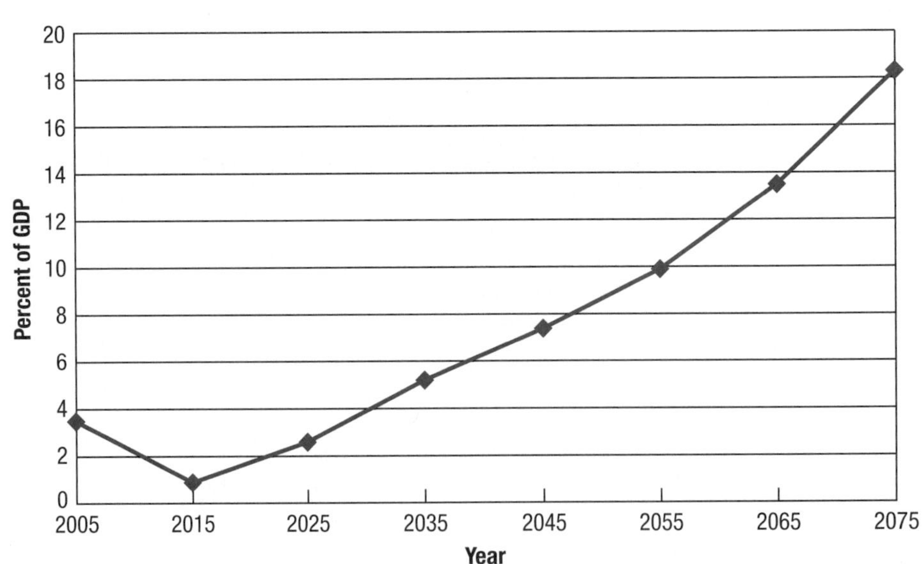

Source: Office of the President, *Budget of the United States Government, Fiscal Year 2009, Analytical Perspectives*, p. 188.

Keyword: *fiscal imbalance and economic growth, fiscal gap and economic growth*

Access InfoTrac at http://infotrac.cengage.com

Figure 15.4 Projection of the Public Debt, 2010–2080
This figure illustrates a projection of the public debt as a percent of GDP for **2010–2080**.

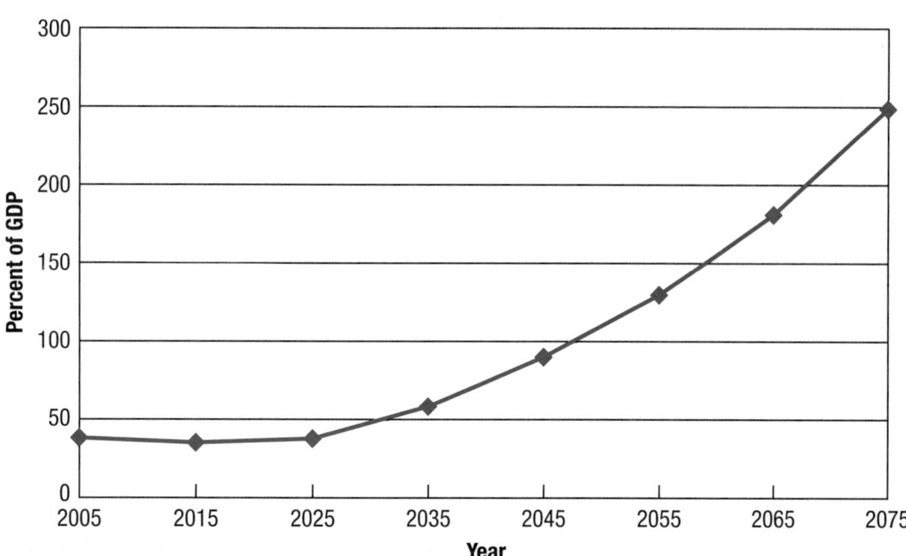

Source: Office of Management and Budget, *Analytical Perspectives, Budget of the United States Government, Fiscal Year 2009, Analytical Perspectives*, p. 188.

value of financial assets (CVFA). More formally:

$$FI_t = PVFO_t - PVFR_t - CVFA_t \quad (15.1)$$

where "t" represents specific years; for FI and CVFA, the year in which the estimate is being made, and for PVFO and PVFR, the future years over which outlays and receipts are projected. If the value of Equation (15.1) is positive, there is a fiscal imbalance (expected future outlays are greater than expected receipts and current assets).

For government, $CVFA_t$ is measured by the assets in various trust funds, such as the Social Security and Medicare trust funds. $PVFO_t$ is the *sum* of expected outlays, each of which is discounted by a rate of interest, and $PVFR_t$ is the *sum* of expected future receipts, each of which is also discounted by a rate of interest.

$PVFO_t$ is an estimate of the amount of money the government *needs today* at (t = 0) to meet its future obligations. To understand this, consider a simple case in which the government has an obligation of $1 billion one year from the present at (t = 1) and could earn an interest rate of 5 percent (i = .05) on its money. The amount of money it needs today to meet this obligation is determined by solving the following equation:

$$PVFO_0 = FO_1/(1+i)^1 \quad (15.2)$$

If the value of FO_1 is $1,000,000,000 and the value of "i" is 0.05, $PVFO_0$ is approximately $952,381,000 (= $1,000,000,000/$(1.05)^1$). Thus, if the government has $952,381,000 on hand, and it can earn 5 percent on this money, it will have the $1,000,000,000 it needs to meet its obligation one year from the present. That is: $952,381,000 (1.05) = $1,000,000,000.

ADDITIONAL INSIGHT

Didn't Anyone See This Coming?

Yes. The Congressional Budget Office did in 2002, although they envisioned a somewhat different trajectory from 2005 to 2025 than they do today. The Figure 15.5 shows both past (1950–2002) and projected future (2002–2075) balances in the unified budget as a percentage of GDP, as of 2002. They expected a budget surplus from 2006 through 2024, followed by a growing deficit for the remainder of the forecast period. In fact, the magnitude of the expected deficit in 2075 actually exceeds that of the Office of Management and Budget, reported in Table 15.2. They were not alone, by the way, in anticipating a surplus over the next two decades. That was the conventional wisdom before the tax cuts of the first George W. Bush administration, a recession in the economy, military engagements in Afghanistan and Iraq, increased funding for homeland security, and passage of the Medicare prescription drug bill.

$PVFR_t + CVFA_t$ is an estimate of the amount of money the government has ($CVFA_t$) and can expect to collect in today's dollars ($PVFR_t$). Continuing with the example, suppose that the government has $200,000,000 on hand ($CVFA_0$) and expects to collect taxes of $700,000,000 next year ($FR_1$). The present value of FR_1 is determined using the following equation:

$$\mathbf{PVFR_1 = FR_1/(1 + i)^1} \qquad \textbf{(15.3)}$$

If FR_1 is $700,000,000 and the value of "i" is 0.05, $PVFR_1$ is approximately $666,666,000. That is, $700,000,000 next year is equivalent to $666,666,000 today.

In this example, the present value of the government's future liability ($952,381,000) is greater than what the government can expect to have to cover this liability ($666,666,000 + $200,000,000, or $866,666,000). The difference between the two, $85,715,000, is the fiscal imbalance.

The fiscal imbalance can be determined for the entire unified budget or for specific components of the budget, such as Medicare and Social Security. Fiscal imbalances can also be determined for any length of time, or time horizon, or for any starting date (the year when $FI_t = FI_0$). We address the fiscal imbalance in Social Security in Chapter 16. Here we concentrate on the fiscal imbalances for the entire unified budget in 2004, for 75-year and permanent (infinite) time horizons.

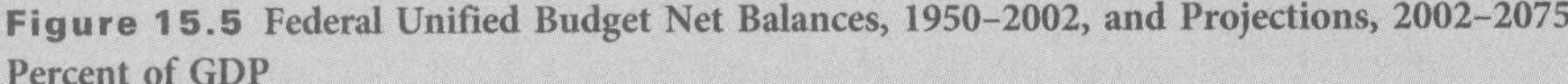

Figure 15.5 Federal Unified Budget Net Balances, 1950–2002, and Projections, 2002–2075
Percent of GDP

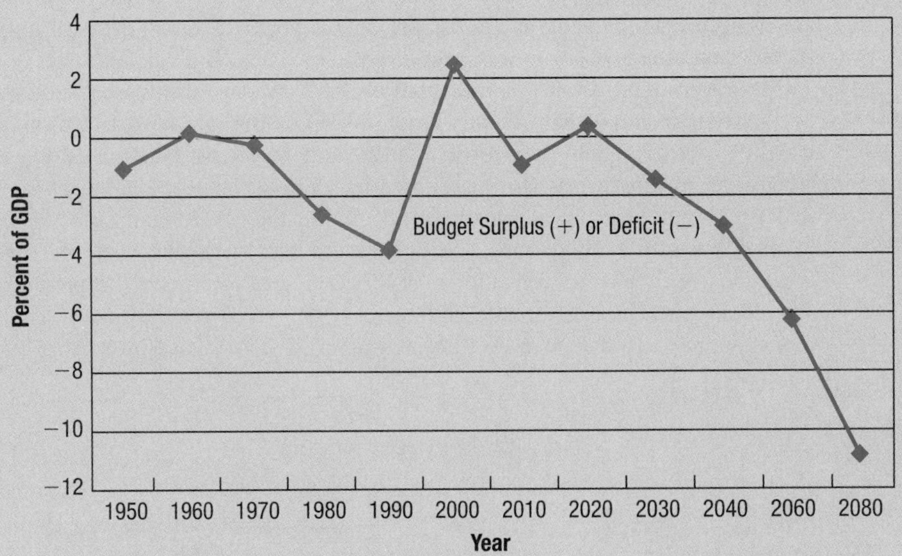

Source: Office of Management and Budget, *Analytical Perspectives, Budget of the United States Government, Fiscal Year 2009, Analytical Perspectives*, p. 188.

Auerbach, Gale, and Orszag have estimated that the 2004 fiscal imbalance (they call it the "fiscal gap") for the unified budget over the next 75 years is $23.1 trillion, when the forecasted budget is based on the CBO baseline. This means that the federal government needed another $23.1 trillion in the bank in 2004* in order to meet its future obligations. If the actual course of the budget is different than the CBO baseline, the fiscal imbalance is different, as well. If, for example, the tax cuts made in the first George W. Bush administration are made permanent for the forecast period, the AMT is indexed for inflation, and real discretionary spending per capita is held constant, the estimated 75-year 2004 fiscal imbalance is $36.3 trillion.

The fiscal imbalance is much greater if the time horizon is extended beyond 75 years because the budget is projected to be running substantial deficits after 75 years. If the time horizon is extended indefinitely, or in perpetuity, the 2004 fiscal imbalance increases to $63.2 trillion for the CBO baseline and to $85.2 trillion for the alternate baseline just described.

These are all huge numbers by any standards. Whether they are truly unsustainable, however, depends on their effects on the economy.

---

*Alan J. Auerbach, William G. Gale, and Peter R. Orszag. "Sources of the Long-Term Fiscal Gap," *Tax Notes*, May 24, 2004, pp. 1049–1059.

WAIT A MINUTE: CAN'T WE GROW OUR WAY OUT OF THE PROBLEM?

Keyword: *budget deficits and economic growth*

Access InfoTrac at http://infotrac.cengage.com

The rate of future productivity growth could have an important effect on the long-run budget outlook. Higher productivity growth has two effects on the budget, however; it increases the tax base, but it also increases outlays for programs with benefits that grow automatically as the economy grows, such as Social Security. How much higher productivity growth would reduce the deficit depends on how much it would increase the tax base relative to how much it would increase government outlays. Projections by the Office of Management and Budget have indicated that faster productivity growth would increase the tax base faster than it would increase future outlays, thus reducing the size of the fiscal imbalance.

The projection illustrated in Table 15.2 is based on an assumption that productivity will grow at 2.4 percent per year. If this rate of growth were to continue, would it solve

ADDITIONAL INSIGHT

So We're Deeply in Debt; What Would It Take To Pay It Off?

One way to fathom the size of our unfunded debt is to ask what it would take to pay it off by increasing taxes or reducing expenditures. Estimates made by Gokhale and Smetters, shown in the table below, indicate that significant sacrifices would be required.

Fiscal Imbalance as a Percent of Selected Taxes and Expenditures in 2005

Fiscal Imbalance As Percent Of:	Percent
Income Taxes	70.9
Payroll Taxes[a]	98.2
Discretionary Outlays	109.7
Social Security & Medicare Outlays	46.2
Non–Social Security & Medicare Outlays	57.3

[a]Also includes income taxes levied on Social Security Benefits.

Source: Gokhale, Jagdeesh, and Kent Smetters, *Fiscal and Generational Imbalances: New Budget Measures for New Budget Priorities*, Federal Reserve Bank of Cleveland, Policy Discussion Paper, 2003, p. 17.

the problem? *No.* According to the Government Accountability Office, eliminating the long-run fiscal imbalance would require productivity growth in the double-digit range every year for the next 75 years.[1] Maintaining a double-digit rate of growth is simply not possible.

These estimates indicate that income taxes would have had to be increased starting in 2005, and lasting forever, by 70.9 percent, if we were to rely on them alone to wipe out the fiscal imbalance. Sole reliance on payroll taxes (currently levied to fund Social Security and Medicare, but in this scenario used to fund other programs, as well) would have to be virtually doubled (98.2 percent increase) forever. Eliminating all discretionary expenditures forever would not be enough, by itself, to solve the problem. Social Security and Medicare benefits together would have to be cut by 46.2 percent if the cure fell exclusively on those programs, and it would take a cut of 57.3 percent in the rest of the budget if that were the strategy.

Although these estimates are bad enough, they undoubtedly understate the probable impact on the economy. Tax increases this large, for example, would have significant adverse effects on work effort, saving, and investment, the costs of which do not show up in this table.

HOW WILL THE ECONOMY BE AFFECTED?

In the Short-Run: Positively, If. . .

In the short-run—say, a year or two—deficits affect the economy positively if output is less than potential, or full employment, output. Assume that the budget is initially balanced and the economy enters a recession. Government expenditures will increase and tax revenues will decrease automatically. The budget will run a deficit as a consequence. Despite their impact on the budget, these changes will provide households with additional disposable income and enable them to maintain consumption at a higher level than they would be able to maintain otherwise, thereby moderating the recession. If this is a desirable outcome—and it normally is—government should not act to eliminate the deficit. In fact, a more appropriate fiscal policy may be to deliberately increase expenditures, reduce taxes, or do both. These changes would cause aggregate demand to increase, thereby increasing the nation's output and employment. The increase in government expenditures or decrease in tax revenue would help to restore prosperity despite a growing budget deficit.

In the Long Run: There Is No Silver Lining

Of course, this is not likely to be the kind of scenario that fits the 10-year horizon of the CBO or, even less so, the 80-year or infinite horizons. These periods may be punctuated occasionally by recessions, but they would not be dominated by cyclical downturns in the economy. Thus, the short-run positive influence of deficits doesn't count for much in the long run. Unfortunately, in the long run the deficits described above are quite likely to have significant negative effects on the economy. Among the possibilities are: (1) a lower future GDP, (2) a higher trade deficit, (3) a higher rate of inflation, and (4) a crisis of international confidence.

---

[1]David M. Walker, "A Look at Our Future: When Baby Boomers Retire," Government Accountability Office, May 16, 2005, p. 123.

Lower Future GDP To explain the long-run effects of government deficits on GDP, we begin with some national output and income accounting identities. From Chapter 12 we know that national output, or GDP, can be divided into four primary types of spending:

$$\mathbf{GDP = C + I_d + G + NX} \quad \mathbf{(15.4)}$$

National savings– The difference between national income produced in the United States (measured by GDP) and income spent on goods and services produced in the United States (measured by $C + I_g$). Also equal to the sum of private savings (household income minus taxes and consumption) and government savings (government receipts minus government outlays).

where C is private consumption (household purchases of goods and services), I_d is gross private *domestic* investment, G is government purchases of goods and services, and NX is net exports of goods and services (Exports – Imports).

Equation 15.4 is equivalent to

$$\mathbf{GDP - C - G = I_d + NX} \quad \mathbf{(15.5)}$$

The left-hand side of Equation 15.5 is also an expression for national savings. That is,

$$\mathbf{GDP - C - G = S} \quad \mathbf{(15.6)}$$

where "S" is **national savings**. To understand this expression, think of GDP also as a measure of total *income* produced in the United States (in national income accounting, every dollar spent is also a dollar of income to the recipient of the expenditure). Thus, the left-hand side of Equation 15.6 is equivalent to total income produced in the United States minus total expenditures by households and governments for goods and services produced in the United States, and the difference represents what is *not* spent, that is, what is saved.

Substituting S for (GDP – C – G) in Equation 15.5 yields

$$\mathbf{S = I_d + NX} \quad \mathbf{(15.7)}$$

or national savings is equal to the sum of domestic investment and net exports. Since national savings is the sum of private savings (PS) and government savings (GS), Equation 15.7 is equivalent to

Foreign investment in the United States– Annual purchases by foreign individuals and institutions of U.S. physical and financial assets (including any annual increase in U.S. dollars held in other countries).

United States' foreign investment– Annual purchases by U.S. citizens and institutions of physical and financial assets in other countries (including any increase in foreign currency held in the United States).

$$\mathbf{PS + GS = I_d + NX} \quad \mathbf{(15.8)}$$

For the last three decades, Net Exports (NX) has been negative; that is, exports of goods and services have been less than imports of goods and services. This means that the flow of dollars out of the United States to purchase foreign goods and services exceeds the flow of dollars into the United States to purchase domestic goods and services. Some of these excess foreign-held dollars are spent in the United States to purchase domestic physical (such as land, buildings, and factories) and financial (stocks and bonds) assets; those not spent are held primarily in foreign and domestic bank accounts. National income accountants refer to all of these uses of foreign-held dollars as **foreign investment in the United States**. (FIUS). Dollars are also spent by U.S. citizens and institutions to acquire foreign assets. This flow of spending constitutes **U.S. foreign investment** (USFI).

In international payments accounting, the flow of dollars into the United States must equal the flow of dollars out of the United States, or

$$\mathbf{X + FIUS = M + USFI} \quad \mathbf{(15.9)}$$

where X and M are exports and imports, respectively. The left-hand side of Equation 15.9 is a measure of dollars flowing into the United States and the right-hand side of this equation is a measure of dollars flowing out of the United States.

Rearranging terms yields

$$\mathbf{X - M = USFI - FIUS} \qquad (15.10)$$

or

$$\mathbf{NX = USFI - FIUS} \qquad (15.11)$$

Substituting USFI – FIUS for NX in Equation 15.8, and adding FIUS to both sides, gives us our final expression (finally):

$$\mathbf{PS + GS + FIUS = I_d + USFI} \qquad (15.12)$$

Sources of investment funds–
The three sources of investment funds are private savings, government savings, and foreign investment in the United States.

Uses of investment funds–
The two uses of investment funds are investment in the United States (private domestic investment) and investment in foreign countries.

To better understand Equation 15.12 it helps to think of the left hand-hand side as the **sources of investment funds** and the right-hand side as the **uses of investment funds**. That is, there are three sources of investment funds—private savings, government savings, and foreign investment in the United States, and two uses of those funds—investment in the United States and investment in foreign countries.

Now suppose that the government runs a deficit of \$400 billion in the unified budget; that is, outlays exceed receipts by \$400 billion. Government savings (GS) will be –\$400 billion. The conventional view is that this will create a fall in I_d, but that some of the decline in GS will be offset by increases in PS and FIUS and by a reduction in USFI. The usual reason given is that when the Treasury borrows the \$400 billion to finance the deficit, this will increase the demand for loanable funds relative to the supply of loanable funds, thereby increasing the interest rate for loanable funds. The increase in the interest rate will induce people to save more (increase PS) and it will also induce foreign investors to invest more in the United States (increase FIUS) and U.S. investors to invest less in foreign countries (decrease USIF).

In their review of the empirical literature, Gale and Orszag[2] conclude that an increase in the deficit will induce an increase in both PS and FIUS (but not affect USIF), with each induced increase offsetting about 25 percent of the fall in GS. Recording these changes in Equation 15.12 yields

$$\mathbf{\$100\ B - \$400\ B + \$100\ B = -\$200\ B + \$0}. \qquad (15.13)$$

Keyword: *long-run budget deficit, sustained budget deficits*

Access InfoTrac at http://infotrac.cengage.com

In other words, the \$400 billion deficit will decrease domestic investment (I_d) by \$200 billion.

Sustained annual budget deficits will produce sustained annual reductions in domestic investment. Sustained annual reductions in domestic investment will produce a smaller domestic capital stock. A smaller domestic capital stock will result in lower future output and income.

How bad could it get? In the presence of sustained budget deficits, the capital stock will decrease by one-half of the amount of the public debt (assuming the private saving and capital inflow offsets just discussed). According to the projections in Table 15.2, the public debt will be 2.83 times GDP in 2080. Thus, sustained budget deficits will reduce the capital stock by 1.515 times GDP.

Mankiw and Elmendorf[3] estimate that each dollar of capital produces \$0.095 of GDP. Given this estimate, the sustained budget deficit forecasted in Table 15.2 will reduce

[2]William G. Gale and Peter R. Orszag. "Economic Effects of Sustained Budget Deficits, *National Tax Journal*, 56, no. 3, (2003): 463–485.

[3]Douglas W. Elmendorf, and N. Gregory Mankiw, "Government Debt," in *Handbook of Macroeconomics*, vol. 1C, edited by John B. Taylor and Michael Woodford, (Amsterdam: Elsevier Science, 1999), 1615–1669.

GDP in 2080 by 0.095 times 1.515 GDP, or by 0.1439 times GDP (14.39 percent of GDP). This portends a substantial reduction in the future standard of living.

Higher Trade Deficit If, as argued above, an increase in the budget deficit induces an increase in foreign investment in the United States (FIUS), this will increase the demand for U.S. dollars. The increase in the demand for dollars will tend to increase the value of (appreciate) the dollar, provided that the U.S. dollar continues to be bought and sold in a flexible-rate currency market (see Chapter 18). An appreciation of the dollar will reduce exports and increase imports because it will raise the price of U.S. goods (require more foreign currency to buy a U.S. dollar) relative to the price of foreign goods, thereby increasing the trade deficit. An increase in the trade deficit will directly reduce the NX component of GDP (make it a larger negative number if NX is already negative—the usual case). It may also trigger policy actions that impose additional economic costs, as argued more fully in Chapter 17.

Keyword: *budget deficit and trade deficit, twin deficits*

Access InfoTrac at http://infotrac.cengage.com

Higher Rate of Inflation As noted, an increase in the budget deficit is likely to increase interest rates. In this event, the monetary authorities may be pressured to reduce interest rates (or keep them from rising) by increasing the nation's money supply (see the Appendix to Chapter 14 for a review of the methods that would be used). Such a strategy would increase the amount of borrowing in the economy, thereby increasing aggregate demand. If the economy is otherwise hovering at or near full employment, sustained use of this strategy is likely to increase the rate of inflation.

The size and duration of the projected debt increase the probability that the government will have an increasingly difficult time borrowing enough to finance budget deficits at reasonable interest rates. In this event, the monetary authorities may be tempted to raise the required revenue by increasing the money supply. The ensuing inflation is likely to increase the anticipated rate of inflation. Higher anticipated inflation will raise interest rates because lenders will increase rates enough to cover expected inflation—they have no desire to be paid back an amount with diminished purchasing power. Another increase in the money supply could ensue in an attempt to moderate now higher interest rates. But this could simply have the effect of increasing inflationary expectations and raising interest rates further. The economy would now be caught in the grip of an inflationary spiral that would not stop until the monetary authorities put the brakes on the growth of the money supply. This would most likely precipitate a significant downturn in the economy, as the monetary and economic history of the early 1980s teaches us.

Keyword: *budget deficits and inflation*

Access InfoTrac at http://infotrac.cengage.com

Crisis of International Confidence Any increase in U.S. prices reduces the real value of the government's debt—what can be purchased with interest income from the debt or from income received when the debt matures (some portion of it matures each year, requiring the Treasury to issue checks in the amount retired and to sell new securities to cover those checks). About 40 percent of the debt is held in foreign hands, and foreigners own a significant amount of other types of U.S. assets (both of these are part of the FIUS discussed above), as well. If they lose confidence in dollar-denominated assets, the capital inflow (the positive effect on FIUS) assumed in the calculations above would not materialize and the effect of sustained deficits on GDP would be even more pronounced.

HOW WILL THIS PROBLEM AFFECT YOU?

No one knows for sure, of course, but some outcomes seem more likely than others. At a minimum, the growing deficit will reduce the government's ability to fund programs you may care about, such as education, income support, and national defense.

In the longer run you will come to care increasingly about the future prospects for Social Security and Medicare, and it is clear from Table 15.2 that the long-run deficit problem cannot be fixed without fixing these programs. As will be explained in Chapter 16 on Social Security, this will most likely require an increase in taxes, or a reduction in benefits, or a dose of both. Given the probable effects of sustained deficits on GDP, you will most likely be paying your higher tax bill out of a paycheck that grows more slowly than it has in the past. You will also be faced with funding a larger share of your retirement income and old-age health care needs out of your own pocket. This means that you should start planning to save a lot on your own to cover these contingencies. Given the possibility of higher future rates of inflation, you will also have to be careful to invest part of your savings in assets that grow faster than inflation.

WHAT WOULD HELP?

Account for Long-Run Liabilities of Policy Choices

In case you haven't noticed, much of what you have read in this chapter about the long-run budget crisis is based on data from official government publications. The really bad news is hard to find (we had to dig deep into *Analytical Perspectives*, a companion volume to the president's budget), but there is reason to believe that the extent of, and dangers posed by, the nation's growing fiscal imbalance were slowly beginning to enter the consciousness of a growing number of policy makers. However, with the financial crisis and recession that began at the end of 2008, we are now talking about budget deficits in terms of trillions of dollars for the first time in our nation's history. In spite of the protests of a minority of members of congress, the concern about the fiscal imbalance seems to been put on the "back burner" for now. The problem appears to be nonpartisan as shown by the tax cuts of the first George W. Bush administration that "widened the fiscal gap by $11 trillion through 2080 and by $18 trillion over an infinite horizon."[4] Or the passage in 2003 of the Medicare prescription drug benefit that, according to the Medicare trustees, would add $8.7 trillion to the fiscal gap?[5]

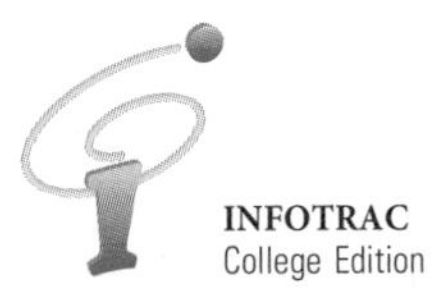

Keyword: *soft landing, hard landing*

Access InfoTrac at http://infotrac.cengage.com

Congress needs to have access to, and be guided by, information on the long-term costs of spending and tax proposals *before* they enact related laws. Commitments and obligations—such as those associated with Social Security and Medicare—are not adequately and consistently disclosed in the federal government's budget, and current federal financial reporting standards do not require such disclosure. Greater transparency about long-term costs would promote an intergenerational perspective in budget decision making. The CBO should make clear to policy makers whether a given legislative proposal would make the long-term fiscal outlook better or worse. One possibility would be to require the CBO to prepare a supplementary estimate in present value terms for the cost of major spending and tax proposals over a long time span—at least 75 years.

Hold the Line

Another thing that Congress could do is to actually validate the assumptions for taxes and spending that underlie the CBO 2007–2018 baseline. This would require that the tax cuts of 2001 and 2003 be allowed to expire as provided for under current law. It would also require that the AMT not be changed; specifically, that it not be indexed for inflation. It would also require Congress to reduce the share of the budget devoted to discretionary

[4]Auerbach, Gale, and Orszag, p. 1057. See also Web Sites.

[5]*2004 Annual Report of the Boards of Trustees of the Federal Hospital Insurance and Federal Supplementary Medical Insurance Trust Funds*, p. 108.

expenditures and then to hold them constant relative to GDP. These actions would not solve the long-run problem, but they would provide significant relief, eliminating 36 percent of the 75-year fiscal imbalance and 26 percent of the infinite horizon fiscal imbalance.

Fix Social Security, But Especially Medicare and Medicaid

Actually, the relief provided by holding the line is more important than what could be achieved by eliminating the fiscal imbalance for Social Security. Doing the latter would reduce the 75-year fiscal imbalance by only 5.5 percent and the infinite horizon fiscal imbalance by only 6.5 percent. Although fixing Social Security seems to command much of the policy debate spotlight, Congress clearly has more pressing problems to solve if it wants to move the budget toward fiscal solvency.

Medicaid– A joint federal/state program that pays for health care for low-income families and the disabled.

The stark truth is that, although reforming Social Security is important, the magnitude of the task pales in comparison to what must be done to eliminate the fiscal imbalances attributable to Medicare and **Medicaid**. If Congress manages to "hold the line," as suggested above, the Medicare fiscal imbalance is five times larger than the Social Security fiscal imbalance, and the Medicaid fiscal imbalance is three times larger than the Social Security fiscal imbalance.[6] Together, these programs account for 45 to 52 percent of the total fiscal imbalance.

Summary

The United States faces significant fiscal challenges. Official projections indicate sustained budget deficits for the next decade. These deficits will decline or expand, depending on what Congress does about the tax cuts of 2001 and 2003, the Alternative Minimum Tax, and the rate of growth of discretionary outlays. After the next decade, the fiscal picture worsens substantially, and the country faces sustained and growing budget deficits as far as the mind can perceive. This translates into enormous unfunded future liabilities, or fiscal imbalances, that cannot be materially reduced by growing the economy faster.

In the short run, budget deficits can have a positive effect on the economy, provided that output is below potential output. In the long run, sustained budget deficits will probably reduce potential GDP, increase the rate of inflation, increase the trade deficit, and precipitate a crisis of international confidence. They will also increase the likelihood of future tax hikes or benefit reductions, making it imperative that younger people save more, and in forms that provide some protection against inflation.

Congress can guard against making the situation worse by basing future tax and expenditure decisions on estimates of the future costs of current actions. It could reduce the fiscal imbalance significantly by holding the line; that is, by allowing the 2001 and 2003 tax cuts to sunset in 2010, leaving the Alternative Minimum Tax unchanged, and constraining the growth of discretionary expenditures. Eliminating the fiscal imbalance in Social Security would help, but not by as much as holding the line, and neither of these would be as effective as eliminating the fiscal imbalances for Medicare and Medicaid.

Key Terms

Social Security
Medicare
Budget
Unified budget
Discretionary outlay
Mandatory outlay
Budget balance
Budget surplus
Budget deficit
Off-budget balance
On-budget balance
Public debt
National debt
Intra-governmental debt
Baseline forecast
Alternative Minimum Tax (AMT)
Fiscal imbalance
National savings
Foreign investment in the United States
United States' foreign investment
Sources of investment funds
Uses of investment funds
Medicaid

[6] Auerbach, Gale, and Orszag, p. 1054. See also Web Sites.

Review Questions

1. Explain the differences between the unified budget and the non–Social Security budget.
2. How are a unified budget deficit, an on-budget deficit, and an off-budget surplus related?
3. Briefly describe what is in store for balances in the unified budget, the non–Social Security budget, and the public debt for the period 2005–2015, according to the CBO projection.
4. What are the principal assumptions that underlie the CBO projection? What happens to the projected deficits and debt if these assumptions are changed?
5. Distinguish between the national debt and the public debt. Which of the two concerns economists more? Why?
6. Briefly describe the trajectory of the unified budget deficit and the public debt after 2015. How large are they relative to GDP 75 years from now (2005)?
7. Define the fiscal imbalance. Suppose that the interest rate is 6 percent, that the government has current financial assets of $300 billion, that government receipts next year will be $2 trillion, and that government outlays next year will be $2.7 trillion. Calculate the one-year fiscal imbalance. Show your work.
8. "The 75-year fiscal imbalance is not a problem because we can grow our way out of it." Explain why you agree or disagree.
9. Suppose the economy is currently at less than full employment and the federal government's unified budget is balanced. Why would it be appropriate for the government to adopt policies that created a budget deficit? What if the economy were at full employment instead?
10. Use the accounting identity that relates the sources of investment funds to the uses of investment funds in an open economy (one with a foreign trade sector) to determine the effect of a $500 billion deficit in the unified budget on domestic investment. Assume the induced effects on private savings and foreign investment in the United States as explained in the chapter.
11. Suppose that sustained budget deficits increase the public debt to 100 percent of GDP and also assume that each dollar of capital produces $0.095 of GDP. Calculate the effect of these sustained budget deficits on GDP, expressed as a percentage of GDP.
12. Explain why sustained budget deficits might result in inflation.
13. Explain why sustained budget deficits might result in a trade deficit.
14. How might you have to change your financial planning in the face of sustained budget deficits?
15. What kind of information might help Congress avoid making fiscal imbalances worse as it changes the budget to meet changing circumstances?
16. When viewed in the context of fiscal imbalances, eliminating the Social Security imbalance is important, but not as important as other policy actions Congress could take. Explain.

Web Sites

- *Auerbach, Alan J., William G. Gale, and Peter R. Orszag, "Sources of the Long-Term Fiscal Gap,"* Tax Notes, *May 24, 2004, pp. 1049–1059.*
  In this source, the authors address the problem of allocating the long-term fiscal gap to specific government programs and policies. They show that Medicare, Medicaid, and the 2001–2003 tax cuts are more important sources of the fiscal gap than Social Security—**http://www.brookings.edu/views/articles/gale/20040524.pdf**
- *Congressional Budget Office,* The Budget and Economic Outlook, An Update, *September 2008.*
  Chapter 1 contains a summary of the CBO's projections of the unified budget and public debt for 2007–2018—**http://www.cbo.gov**
- *Gokhale, Jagdeesh, and Kent Smetters,* Fiscal and Generational Imbalances: New Budget Measures for New Budget Priorities, *Federal Reserve Bank of Cleveland, Policy Discussion Paper, 2003.*
  This study describes the deficiencies of the federal budget as a measure of the long-run effects of government programs and policies and develops estimates of two alternative measures: fiscal and generational imbalances—**http://www.clevelandfed.org/Research**

- *Kogan, Richard, and Robert Greenstein,* President Portrays Social Security Shortfall as Enormous, But His Tax Cuts and Drug Benefits will Cost at Least Five Times as Much, *Center for Budget and Policy Priorities, February 11, 2005.* This source underscores the point made at the end of this chapter that the long-run deficit in Social Security pales in comparison with other sources of the long-run deficit in the unified budget—**http://www.cbpp.org**
- *Office of Management and Budget,* Analytical Perspectives, Budget of the United States Government, Fiscal Year 2006
  This companion volume to *The Budget of the United States Government, Fiscal Year 2006* contains analyses of specific subjects related to the president's budget. Part III (pp. 208–219) contains projections and analyses of the 75-year and infinite budget horizons—**http://www.omb.gov**

CHAPTER 16
Social Security: Leading Issues and Approaches to Reform

OUTLINE

Growing old in America often brings a reduction in family income. The situation would be far worse, however, without Social Security. Social Security was established in 1935 to provide benefits to retired workers and their families. In addition to retirement benefits, Social Security also provides benefits to the survivors of deceased workers and to disabled workers and their families.

Social Security has been successful in providing a basic level of income support for its intended beneficiaries. All is not well with the program, however. It may reduce the nation's labor supply; it appears to reduce household savings; it may provide low individual rates of return on the money used to support retirement benefits; and it will be unable to pay all the retirement benefits promised after 2041. We will examine each of these problems in this chapter, but devote more than equal time to the prospects for funding retirement benefits in the long run.

PRINCIPAL FEATURES OF SOCIAL SECURITY

Social Security is the country's largest government expenditure program. In 2007, it paid total benefits of $585 billion to 34 million retired workers and their families, to 6 million survivors of deceased workers, and to 9 million disabled workers and their dependents. These benefits are financed primarily by a payroll tax levied on 96 percent of all workers (the principal exception—about 30 percent of state and local government employees). The Social Security payroll tax is levied on earnings up to an annually-indexed taxable maximum ($102,000 in 2008) at a rate of 12.4 percent, half of which is imposed on employers and half of which is deducted from employee paychecks. Self-employed individuals pay all 12.4 percent from their first $102,000 earned.

Social Security Trust Funds

The Social Security payroll tax is the second largest source of federal government revenue, exceeded only by the individual income tax. Revenues from the payroll tax are deposited in the Old-Age and Survivors Insurance (OASI) and Disability Insurance (DI) Trust Funds. Benefits and administrative costs are paid out of these trust funds. Balances remaining in the funds are invested in long-term U.S. Treasury bonds. At the end of 2007 the trust funds had balances totaling $2,238 billion, or enough to pay for about 3 years of estimated outlays. Although this may appear to be a large number, it is tiny relative to future benefit obligations. The expectation, however, is that the combination of trust fund balances *and* annual income will be sufficient to cover annual outlays until 2041.

Retirement Benefits

Social Security provides benefits to retirees based on a worker's lifetime earnings. Benefit determination begins with the record of annual earnings on which the Social Security payroll tax has been levied. Earnings realized before age 60 are adjusted or "indexed" to account for the change in the average national wage between the age at which the earnings were realized and age 60.

The indexing procedure uses equation 11.1:

$$\mathbf{IE_a = E_a\,(ANW_{60}/ANW_a)}, \qquad \mathbf{(11.1)}$$

where IE_a is the indexed value of earnings realized at age a (a < 60), E_a is earnings subject to the payroll tax at age a, ANW_{60} is the average national wage at age 60, and ANW_a is the average national wage at age a. ANW_{60}/ANW_a is the **wage indexing factor**—the ratio of the average national wage at age 60 to the average national wage at age a. To see how the equation works, consider an individual who earned $10,000 at age 40 (a = 40). Assume that the average national wage when the individual was age 60 is $39,800 and that the average national wage when the individual was 40 is $15,000. The value of the indexing factor is 2.653 ($39,800/$15,000) and the indexed value of these earnings is $26,530.

Wage indexing factor– The ratio of the average national wage at age 60 to the average national wage at age a (a < 60).

The earnings indexation procedure is intended to assure that Social Security retirement benefits reflect the general rise in the standard of living that occurred during *most* of an individual's working lifetime. Earnings after age 60 are not indexed; their actual value is used in the determination of benefits.

After indexed earnings are determined, Social Security adds the 35 years of highest earnings, chosen from the indexed earnings and earnings from age 60 to the age of retirement, which are not indexed. It divides this total by 420 (the number of months in 35 years) to determine the **average indexed monthly earnings** (AIME). It then applies a formula to the AIME to arrive at the **primary insurance amount** (PIA). The PIA is the base amount that a person would receive at the normal or full retirement age. The base amount is adjusted upward, however, for annual increases in the cost of living that occur between age 62 and the retirement age. The **normal retirement age** depends on when a person is born. It is currently (in 2007) 65 years and 10 months for individuals born in 1942. It will be 66 years for people born in 1943–1954. It will be 66 years and 2 months for people born in 1955, and increase 2 months for each of the next 5 birth years, reaching its current upper limit of 67 for people born in 1960 and later. The formula that applies for determining the PIA is the one specified for the year when a person turns age 62. For someone who will be 62 in 2008 the PIA formula is:

Average indexed monthly earnings (AIME)– Average monthly earnings for the highest 35 years of earnings, adjusted by the wage indexing factor.

Primary insurance amount (PIA)– The basic monthly Social Security benefit at the normal or full retirement age.

$$\begin{aligned} \text{PIA} = {} & 0.9\,(\text{First } \$711 \text{ AIME}) + 0.32\,(\$711 < \text{AIME} < \$4{,}288) \\ & + 0.15\,(\text{AIME over } \$4{,}288). \end{aligned}$$

Table 16.1 shows the results of calculations based on this formula for three hypothetical retirees who will be age 62 in 2008 and retire at age 66 in 2012. The cost of living is assumed to increase by 10 percent during this time.

Normal retirement age– The age at which an individual is eligible to receive full retirement benefits.

The first prospective retiree is a low-wage worker who earned $230,000 while working. Application of the wage indexing factor to actual earnings typically yields indexed earnings from 1.8 to 2.0 times higher than actual earnings. We assume in this case that total indexed earnings are $420,000, an amount that falls in the expected range. Division of earnings by 420 gives AIME of $1,000. Application of the PIA formula to this AIME yields $639 in the first bracket (0.9 × $711) and $92 in the second bracket (0.32 × ($1,000 – $711)). The third bracket does not apply in this case. The net result is a PIA of $731. When this person retires in 2012, his or her monthly benefit will be $731 plus

TABLE 16.1 DETERMINATION OF THE PRINCIPAL INSURANCE AMOUNT (PIA) FOR THREE INDIVIDUALS BORN IN 1946 WHO RETIRE AT THEIR NORMAL RETIREMENT AGE (66 YEARS)

ACTUAL EARNINGS	INDEXED EARNINGS	AIME	1ST BRACKET	2ND BRACKET	3RD BRACKET	PIA	PIA PLUS COLA	PIA/ AIME
$230,000	$420,000	$1,000	$639	$92	$0	$731	$804	0.80
$580,000	$1,050,000	$2,500	$639	$572	$0	$1211	$1332	0.53
$1,400,000	$2,100,000	$5,000	$639	$1145	$107	$1891	$2080	0.42

an adjustment of 10 percent for the assumed increase in the cost of living that occurred over the 4 years prior to retirement, or $804 = $731 + ($731 × 0.1).

The second and third workers have higher lifetime earnings, higher indexed earnings, higher AIME, and higher PIA. The *ratio* of PIA to AIME falls, however, as AIME increases. The behavior of the PIA/AIME ratio indicates that the Social Security PIA or benefit formula produces more generous benefits to lower- than to higher-income retirees.

The benefits we have just determined last for the remaining lifetime of the insured individual and beyond. Generally, surviving spouses and dependents of deceased retirees continue to receive from 50 to 100 percent of a retiree's benefits. Social Security retirement benefits are also indexed annually for inflation, using the Consumer Price Index (CPI). Thus, Social Security retirement benefits provide an inflation-protected annuity with guaranteed payments for the life of the retiree and the lives of surviving spouses and qualifying dependents.

Early retirement penalty– The amount by which Social Security benefits are reduced for people who retire before the normal retirement age.

Delayed retirement credit– The amount by which retirees' benefits are increased for each year that retirement is delayed beyond the normal retirement age, up to age 70.

The benefits noted in Table 16.1 are for single workers who will retire at their normal retirement age. They may retire as early as age 62, but if they retire before the normal retirement age, Social Security benefits are permanently reduced by an **early retirement penalty**. The early retirement penalty reduces the PIA (plus any cost of living adjustment) by approximately 0.5 percent per month for each month an individual retires before the normal retirement age.

Benefits are 50 percent larger for a retiree with a spouse, provided that the spouse does not qualify for a larger benefit on the basis of his or her own earnings record. Social Security retirees also receive additional benefits for dependents.

Workers who delay retirement beyond the normal retirement age receive extra Social Security benefits when they do retire. Future retirees will have their benefits increased by a **delayed retirement credit** of 8 percent for each year that retirement is delayed, up to age 70.

Income from Social Security receives more favorable treatment in the federal tax code than income from private retirement funds. Private retirement income is subject to federal income taxation. Only part of Social Security benefits is subject to taxation, however, and then only if earnings after retirement exceed tax-exempt levels. Finally, the contributions that employers make on behalf of workers (one-half of the Social Security payroll tax) are not included in income subject to taxation.

Keywords: *Social Security benefits, Social Security benefit formula*

Access InfoTrac at http://infotrac.cengage.com

LEADING ISSUES IN SOCIAL SECURITY

Is Social Security a Welfare Program?

Social Security benefits are an important source of income for most beneficiaries. In fact, they are an essential source of income for many. They provide more than half of total income for nearly two-thirds of beneficiaries over age 65, and 100 percent of income for nearly one-fifth of aged beneficiaries. Estimates indicate that more than 45 percent of the elderly would have incomes below the federal poverty line in the absence of Social Security. With Social Security, however, the poverty rate for the elderly has averaged about 2 percentage points less than the poverty rate for the population as a whole since 1982. Moreover, Social Security appears to be a welfare program because the benefit formula is designed so that the *ratio* of benefits to lifetime earnings falls as those earnings rise.

However, Social Security benefits increase as lifetime earnings increase. This makes them unlike welfare programs where program benefits decrease as earnings increase. That is, Social Security benefits are not income-conditioned. Although the Social Security benefit formula treats low earners more generously, the absence of income-conditioning results in only a small percentage of Social Security's expenditures going to reduce poverty among the elderly. In fact, June O'Neill estimates that less than 20 percent of Social Security benefits in 1999 were paid to aged households with income otherwise below the poverty line.[1]

Does Social Security Induce Early Retirement?

Keywords: *Social Security and early retirement*

Access InfoTrac at http://infotrac.cengage.com

History reveals a strong trend toward reduced labor force participation by older people. Since 1950, the labor force participation rate (the percentage of a certain population in the labor force) for men age 65 and older has fallen from 41.4 percent to less than 15 percent. Various factors have contributed to this trend: rising income, growth in private pensions, increased availability of government transfers, and changing lifestyles, to name a few. Social Security may have been a contributor, as well.

The most disturbing aspect of this trend is the large number of workers who retire early; nearly a third of Social Security beneficiaries leave the workforce before age 65. It is impossible to determine, on the basis of theory alone, if Social Security induces early retirement. On the one hand, the prospect of Social Security benefits encourages early retirement. On the other hand, Social Security discourages early retirement by exacting a penalty for early retirement, and it encourages later retirement by providing a delayed retirement credit. These penalties and rewards are currently designed to make the age of retirement an actuarially fair choice; that is, to make expected Social Security benefits the same regardless of age of retirement. Thus, most economists believe that Social Security, per se, will have little effect on age of retirement. If people continue to retire early in the face of the fair terms offered by Social Security other factors are apparently more important determinants of the date of retirement.

Does Social Security Reduce Household Savings?

Wealth substitution effect– The reduction in household savings caused by the substitution of Social Security wealth for other types of wealth.

Social Security wealth– The present value of Social Security benefits.

Induced retirement effect– The increase in household savings required to offset early retirement induced by the prospect of Social Security benefits.

The fact that many retirees depend so heavily on Social Security suggests to some economists that the prospect of Social Security benefits may induce people to save less of their pre-retirement income. If they do save less, private investment will fall, resulting ultimately in a smaller potential national output.

Social Security will reduce savings if workers believe that Social Security will provide them with enough retirement income that they can spend a larger share of their pre-retirement earnings. If this happens, economists say that Social Security has a **wealth substitution effect**—an effect that induces workers to substitute **Social Security wealth** (the present value of Social Security benefits) for other types of wealth, such as private pensions.

Economists also recognize, as already noted, that the prospect of Social Security benefits may induce workers to retire earlier. This **induced retirement effect** of Social

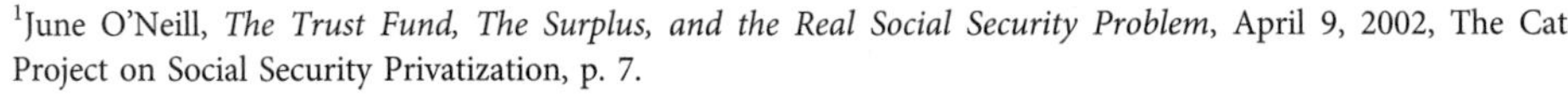

[1]June O'Neill, *The Trust Fund, The Surplus, and the Real Social Security Problem*, April 9, 2002, The Cato Project on Social Security Privatization, p. 7.

Security should increase savings; that is, workers will attempt to save more each year while working to make up for the years when they will not be working.

The net effect of Social Security on savings depends on the relative strength of these two effects, although the wealth substitution effect is expected to be the stronger of the two. Whether it is, however, requires empirical confirmation. Martin Feldstein is well known for his empirical studies of the relationship between Social Security and household savings. In the latest of several studies, Feldstein analyzed annual U.S. data from 1930 to 1992, and found that each dollar of Social Security wealth resulted in a decrease in household savings of $0.028.[2] This result indicates that the wealth substitution effect dominates the induced retirement effect, but not by much.

A slight edge, though, to the wealth substitution effect has important implications for national savings. For example, Social Security wealth was more than $9,000 billion in 1996 (Martin Feldstein and Andrew Samwick, "The Transition Path to Privatizing Social Security," National Bureau of Economic Research Working Paper no. 5761, September 1996). Multiplying this number by Feldstein's impact of 0.028 implies that Social Security wealth reduced household savings by $252 billion. This implies that investment and the nation's capital stock were $252 billion less than they would have been in the absence of Social Security. Because each dollar increase in the capital stock supports about a third of a dollar increase in potential output, Social Security may have reduced potential output in 1996 alone by as much as $84 billion, or about 1.0 percent of potential GDP. A similar effect would be expected for more recent years, and a cumulative effect of this size over many years would have a serious negative impact on the standard of living.

Feldstein's estimate may be correct; however, other studies have produced different results. Munnell, for instance, found a negative effect of Social Security on savings, but only about one-sixth as large as Feldstein's.[3] Leimer and Lesnoy found that Social Security wealth may actually *increase* savings, depending on how it is estimated.[4] More recently, Bernheim and Levin, using new measures of expected Social Security benefits, found that expected Social Security wealth reduced the savings of single individuals by $1.21 for each dollar of Social Security wealth, but that it had no effect on the saving behavior of couples.[5]

Given the mixed results of the empirical research, we cannot be certain how much Social Security affects household savings. It seems premature, however, to rule out the possibility of a negative impact.

Keywords: *Social Security and saving*

Access InfoTrac at http://infotrac.cengage.com

Does Social Security Provide Low Individual Rates of Return?

Social Security benefits, like most good things in life, are not free. The typical retiree pays Social Security taxes over a working lifetime of 40 to 50 years and receives 15 to 20 years of retirement benefits. This elicits considerable interest in comparing benefits received with taxes paid or "contributions" made. Actual comparisons vary by individual, but calculations for "representative" individuals sufficiently convey the general results.

Let us examine the prospects for a typical college graduate. Our subject is a person born in 1982 who entered college in fall 2000 at age 18, graduated in 2004, and faces the real (inflation-adjusted) wage profile illustrated in Figure 16.1. This is the same

---

[2]Martin Feldstein, "Social Security and Saving: New Time-Series Evidence," *National Tax Journal* 49 No 2 (June 1996): 151–64.

[3]Alicia H. Munnell, *The Future of Social Security* (Washington, D.C.: Brookings Institution, 1977).

[4]Dean R. Leimer and Selig D. Lesnoy, "Social Security and Private Saving: New Time Series Evidence," *Journal of Political Economy* 90 (June 1982): 606–29.

[5]B. Douglas Bernheim and Lawrence Levin, "Social Security and Personal Saving: An Analysis of Expectations," *American Economic Review* 79 (May 1989): 97–102.

Figure 16.1 Projected Real Wages of a Typical College Graduate, 2000–2049 (in 2002 dollars)
This figure illustrates how the real wages of a typical college graduate increase immediately following graduation (Year 5) and continue to grow throughout much of the individual's working lifetime.

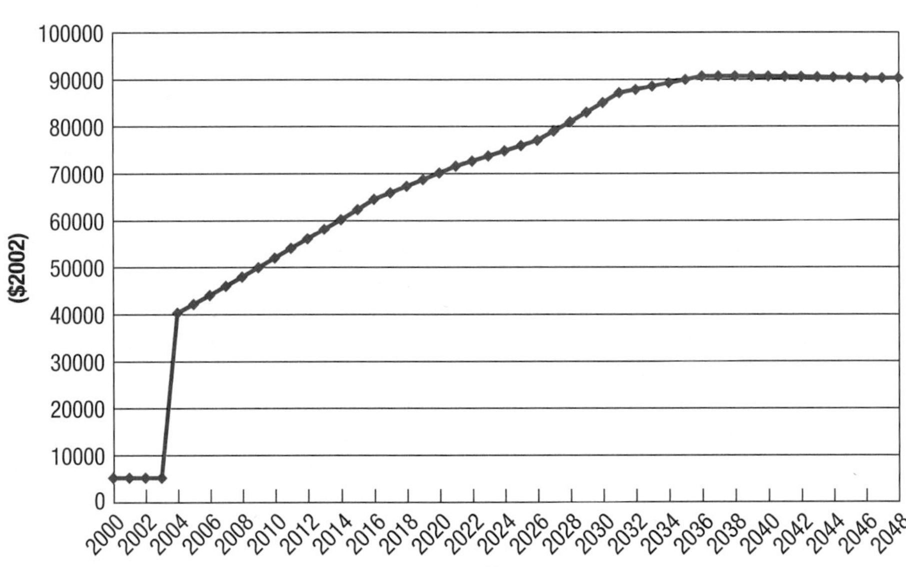

wage profile for college graduates used in Chapter 9 to determine the rate of return from investing in a college education.

During college, our student worked part time, earning $5,200 per year. The first job after graduation provides a wage of $40,261, the average real wage (in 2002 dollars) paid a new college graduate in 2005. If the lifetime wage profile in the future is the same as in the past, the real wage for our college graduate is projected to rise rapidly for 33 years, reaching a peak of $90,601 at age 55. It will then fall slightly to $90,163 by age 64. Given this wage profile, the typical college graduate is projected to earn real wages of $3,167,100 from ages 23 through 66.

Our graduate will pay Social Security taxes based on these wages. The wages, per se, constitute the projected tax base. Projected taxes are equal to the tax base times the payroll tax rate. Since we are interested in determining the rate of return from investing in Social Security retirement benefits, the appropriate tax rate is the portion of the payroll tax rate earmarked for retirement benefits only. Unfortunately, data on this tax rate are not available. The closest we can come is the tax rate levied to finance the retirement *and* survivors' benefits of Social Security. Use of this tax rate will overstate taxes to some unknown, but probably small, degree. On the other hand, our projected retirement benefits do not include a deduction of income taxes paid on those benefits. This causes us to overstate benefits to some unknown, but probably small, degree. In the absence of better information, we assume that these two errors offset each other.

This chain of reasoning still does not resolve the issue of taxes paid on expected wages, however. We know that our graduate will have a payroll tax deduction of 5.3 percent of wages for retirement and survivors' insurance. We also know that our graduate's employer will pay a matching rate of 5.3 percent. Our graduate could pay anywhere from 5.3 percent to 10.6 percent, however, depending on the portion of the employer's share that is shifted to the employee in the form of a lower pretax wage. For reasons examined below in the section "Who Pays the Social Security Payroll Tax?" we believe that all of the employer's share of the tax will be shifted to employees. Thus, the appropriate tax rate is 10.6 percent.

Following retirement, our graduate will receive real Social Security benefits of $24,300 (in 2002 dollars) per year for 20 years (the assumed remaining lifetime at age 67). Figure 16.2 illustrates the profile of projected taxes and benefits, assuming that all of the burden of the payroll tax falls on workers. Total taxes (the area between the horizontal axis and the taxes line) are $353,966, and total benefits (the area between the horizontal axis and the benefits line) are $485,998.

Based on this projection, it appears that an investment in Social Security is worth it. The reader who has studied Chapter 9, however, knows that the tax payments and benefits must be adjusted for date of occurrence by discounting them at an appropriate rate of interest. For the latter, we use the 3 percent real rate of interest that the Social Security actuaries assume will be earned on government bonds in the future. Figure 16.3 shows the dramatic effect that discounting has, especially on projected benefits. According to our calculations, the sum of the present value of taxes is $164,072 and the sum of the present value of benefits is only $87,488. Thus, the real rate of return is less than the discount rate; in this case, it is only 1.02 percent. If the worker's best alternative is the assumed 3 percent real rate of return expected on long-term government bonds, the investment made in Social Security is not worth it.

INFOTRAC College Edition

Keywords: *Social Security and financial returns, Social Security and rate of return*

Access InfoTrac at http://infotrac.cengage.com

Table 16.2 summarizes the estimates we have made for the typical college graduate.

Are expected rates of return this low for everyone? No. Individuals with lower lifetime earnings can expect to earn higher rates of return because the PIA formula provides higher retirement benefits relative to taxes paid. But the sad truth is that the expected *average* real rate of return *for all individuals* born in 1982 is less than 2 percent. Moreover, individuals born after 1982 can expect to do no better than the 1982 cohort.

The reader is also advised that the rates of return likely to be realized may be even lower than these. The reason is that, as explained below, either future taxes may have to be increased or future benefits may have to be reduced in order to eliminate a long-run deficit in Social Security. Either of these adjustments would reduce the real rate of return from Social Security retirement benefits.

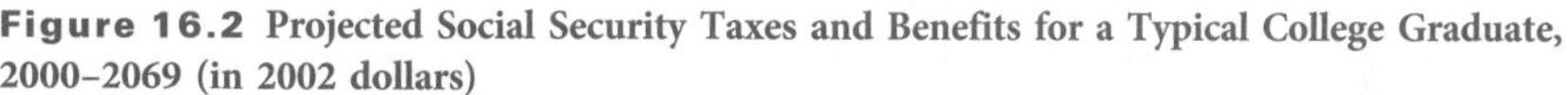

Figure 16.2 Projected Social Security Taxes and Benefits for a Typical College Graduate, 2000–2069 (in 2002 dollars)

This figure illustrates projected real Social Security taxes (–) and benefits (+) for a typical college graduate. Taxes are collected for the 4 years the student is in school and the 44 years while the graduate is in the workforce. Benefits are received for 20 years following retirement at age 67.

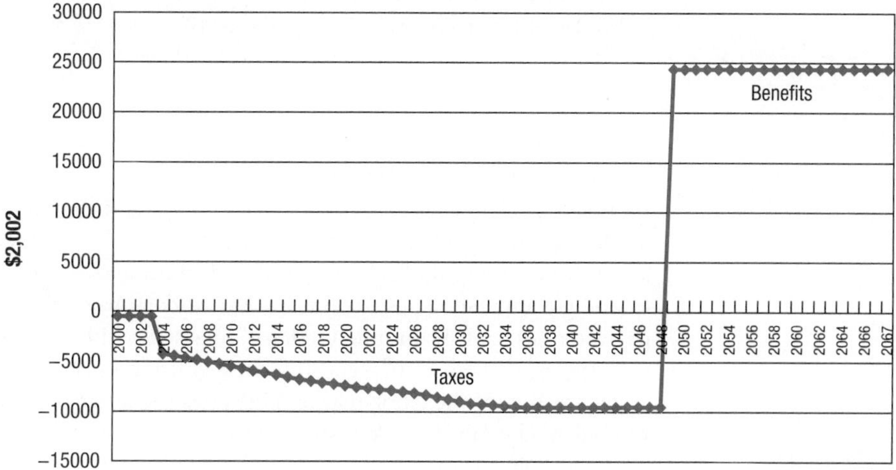

Figure 16.3 Effect of Discounting on Value of Social Security Taxes and Benefits (in 2002 dollars)

This figure shows the effects on taxes and benefits from discounting both at 3 percent per year.

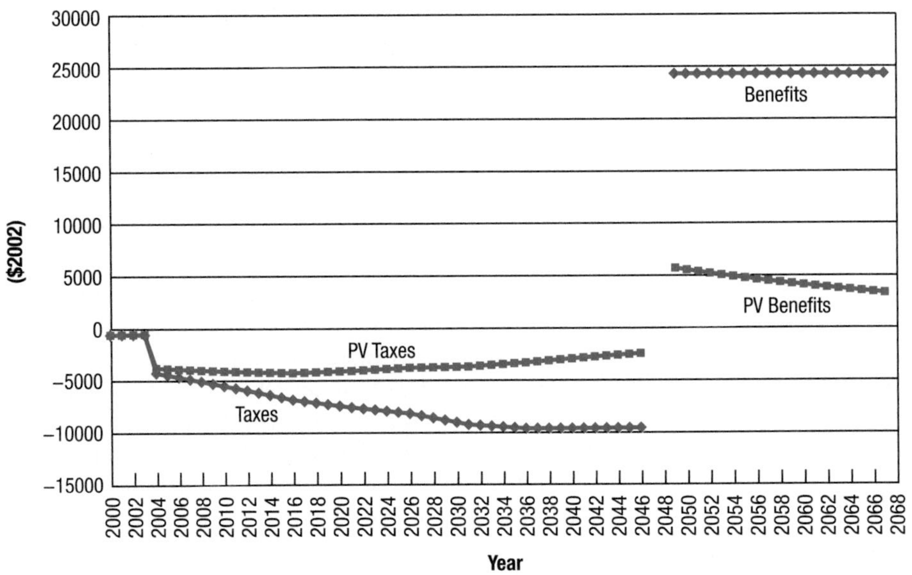

TABLE 16.2 ESTIMATES OF REAL SOCIAL SECURITY TAXES AND BENEFITS AND REAL RATE OF RETURN FOR A TYPICAL COLLEGE GRADUATE

Sum of Earnings Subject to Tax	$3,167,001
Sum of Taxes Paid	$353,966
Sum of Benefits Received	$485,998
Sum of Benefits Minus Taxes	$132,032
Sum of Present Value of Taxes Paid	$164,072
Sum of Present Value of Benefits Received	$87,488
Sum of Present Value of Benefits Minus Taxes	–$76,584
Real Rate of Return (Percent)	1.02

Who Pays the Social Security Tax?

As noted, Social Security retirement, survivors' and disability benefits are financed primarily by a 12.4 percent tax levied on taxable payroll. The law requires employers to collect half of the tax through a payroll deduction and to remit twice that amount to the federal government. Thus, it appears that workers pay half of the tax and that employers pay the other half. Economic theory is consistent with this view, but it is also consistent with the case where employers shift their entire portion of the tax to workers.

Figure 16.4 of the labor market illustrates the latter possibility. Wage rates and hours worked in the labor market are determined by the supply of, and demand for, labor. Although the vertical supply curve indicates that changes in the wage rate do not affect

Figure 16.4 Effect of the Social Security Payroll Tax on Hours Worked with a Vertical Labor Supply Curve

The payroll tax lowers the demand for labor from D_1 to D_2. The imposition of the tax does not change the number of hours worked, and workers pay all of the tax in the form of a reduced wage ($W_1 - W_2$).

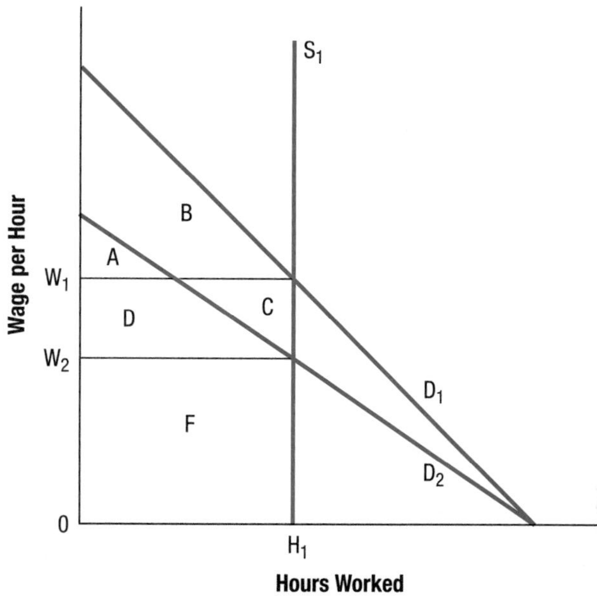

Substitution effect of a wage decrease– The decrease in hours worked because of a fall in the wage rate.

Income effect of a wage decrease– The increase in hours worked to replace the decrease in income resulting from a wage rate reduction.

hours worked, the wage rate actually has two potential effects on hours worked. On the one hand, reductions in the hourly wage, or hourly reward from working, induce individuals to work fewer hours. This **substitution effect of a wage decrease** causes workers to substitute leisure for work. On the other hand, a reduction in the hourly wage will reduce the size of the employees' paychecks, which may induce them to work more hours to make up the reduction in the hourly wage. If it does, there is an **income effect of a wage decrease.** The net effect of a change in the wage rate on hours worked depends on the relative strengths of the two effects. In this case, there is no net effect on hours worked. This could be either because the two effects offset each other, or because both of them are unimportant.

The demand curve for labor indicates the value of the output produced by each hour of work. In the absence of the payroll tax, the demand for labor is D_1, the supply of labor is S_1, and the equilibrium wage rate and hours worked are W_1 and H_1, respectively. The total value of output produced is the sum of the values produced by each hour of labor, or the area under the demand curve, A + B + C + D + F. Workers receive earnings equal to the wage rate times the number of hours worked, or the area C + D + F. Employers claim area A + B—the remaining value of output produced—in the form of rent, interest, and profits.

The payroll tax is imposed on employers; that is, they must make the total tax payment to the federal government. From their perspective, therefore, the tax reduces the maximum amount they are willing to pay for each hour of labor. The maximum amount they are willing to pay for labor in the absence of the tax is the value produced by each hour of labor. This is the amount indicated by the height of the demand curve at each hour of labor. Imposition of the Social Security payroll tax for retirement and survivors' benefits reduces the amount employers are willing to pay by 0.124 of that height. This effect is indicated in Figure 16.4 by comparing D_1 (willingness to pay without the tax) and D_2 (willingness to pay with the tax). The height of D_2 is everywhere 0.876 times the height of D_1.

After the tax is imposed, a new equilibrium forms at W_2 and H_1. No change occurs in the number of labor hours, but the wage rate falls by the same percentage as the payroll tax rate. Labor's earnings fall to area F only. Employers' income, A + B, remains the same as before the tax, and the government collects tax revenues equal to C + D, which just happens to be the amount by which labor's earnings fall. Thus, the full burden of the tax falls on labor.

Keywords: *Social Security payroll tax and incidence, Social Security payroll tax and who pays*

Access InfoTrac at http://infotrac.cengage.com

Another possibility is illustrated in Figure 16.5. The labor supply curve in this figure is positively sloped, indicating that the substitution effect of a reduction in the wage rate is stronger than the income effect. The pretax equilibrium is at W_1 and H_1, as in Figure 16.4. Imposition of the tax changes the equilibrium to W_2 and H_2; the tax decreases the wage rate realized by workers and reduces the number of labor hours. Total taxes collected are equal to the product of the tax per hour of labor, $W_3 - W_2$, and the number of hours of labor, H_2, or the area A′ + B′ + C′ + D′. Employees pay half of the tax, or C′ + D′, and employers pay the other half, or A′ + B′. This case is probably what Congress assumed would happen when they wrote the law requiring only half of the payroll tax to be deducted from worker's wages.

It is important to determine which view is correct. If the labor supply curve is vertical, the payroll tax has no effect on hours worked, but it places a large burden on workers. This significantly reduces the rate of return they will realize from Social Security. If the labor supply curve is upward-sloping, the payroll tax reduces hours worked and, places a smaller tax burden on workers. Consequently, they will realize higher rates of return from Social Security than in the vertical supply curve case. We believe that the weight of the evidence indicates that the supply curve of labor is vertical, or nearly so, and

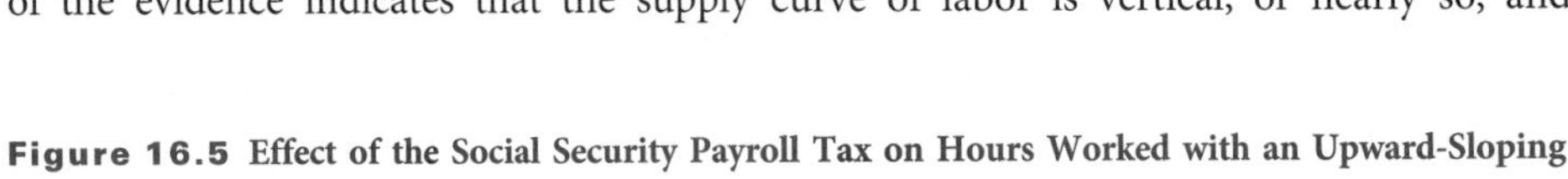

Figure 16.5 Effect of the Social Security Payroll Tax on Hours Worked with an Upward-Sloping Labor Supply Curve

The payroll tax lowers the demand for labor from D_1 to D_2. The imposition of the tax reduces the number of hours worked ($H_1 - H_2$) and workers pay some ($W_1 - W_2$) of the tax ($W_3 - W_2$) in the form of a reduced wage. Employers pay the remainder ($W_3 - W_1$) of the tax.

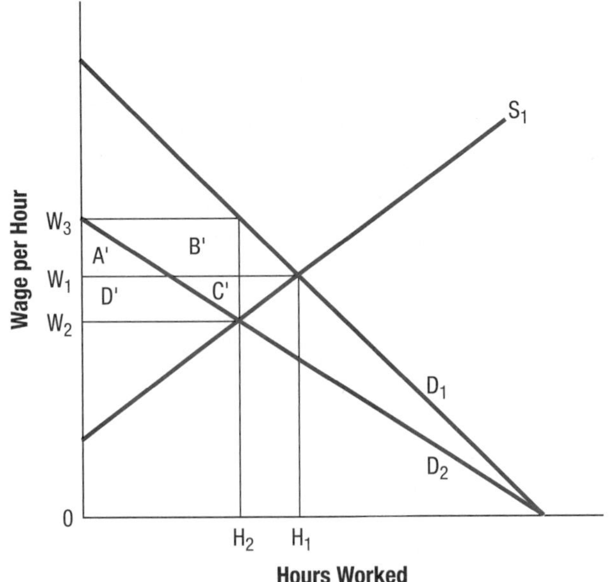

that the primary effect of the payroll tax, therefore, shows up as significantly lower individual rates of return on Social Security.[6]

Can Social Security Fulfill Its Long-Run Obligations?

The question most often raised about Social Security is whether it will be able to provide future generations the benefits they have been promised. The general answer is "No; not under the current provisions of the law," but the magnitude of the problem grows as the time horizon is extended. The financial prospects for Social Security are described in the *2008 Annual Report of the Board of Trustees of the Federal Old-Age and Survivors Insurance Trust Funds* for a 75-year horizon. Since much of what we describe below comes from that source, we will make the same distinction.

75-Year Horizon (2008–2082). In determining prospects for Social Security over the next 75 years, the Social Security trustees rely on projections of income and expenditures prepared by Social Security actuaries. Because the future cannot be predicted with certainty, they project Alternatives I, II, and III. The assumptions underlying Alternative I produce the most optimistic projection of trust fund surpluses; those underlying Alternative III produce the most pessimistic projection. Most observers rely, however, on Alternative II, the "best estimate" projection, as the guide for long-run planning.

Keywords: *Social Security trust fund, Social Security projections*

Access InfoTrac at http://infotrac.cengage.com

According to Alternative II's 75-year projections in the 2008 annual report, the future for Social Security looks promising for a few years and then becomes increasingly bleak. The promising aspect is that the OASI and DI trust funds (hereafter referred to as the "trust fund") will have an annual surplus through 2016. After that, however, annual expenditures will exceed annual tax receipts. Annual tax receipts *plus* interest earnings on accumulated balances will be sufficient to keep trust fund balances growing until 2027. Starting in 2027, the balances in the trust fund will shrink rapidly as the U.S. Treasury securities in the fund are redeemed and the proceeds are used to cover annual outlays in excess of annual receipts. Finally, in 2041, all the securities owned by the trust fund will have been redeemed and the trust fund will be exhausted (see Figure 16.6).

Payroll taxes and other tax income will continue to flow into Social Security after 2041, but they will be insufficient to pay all promised benefits and expenses. Initially, they will cover about 78 percent of promised benefits. At the end of the projection period, annual income will cover only 75 percent of promised benefits. Thus, although Social Security can provide benefits to future generations, without significant changes it will fall short of providing all the benefits it currently promises over the next 75 years.

Cost rate– The ratio of annual Social Security benefits and administrative costs to taxable payroll.

Income rate– The ratio of annual Social Security income to taxable payroll.

The fact that there will still be a substantial revenue flow dedicated to Social Security after the trust funds are exhausted is illustrated in Figure 16.7. The curve labeled **"cost rate"** indicates the projected outlays from 2005 through 2080 for benefits and administrative costs as a share of taxable payroll. The curve labeled **"income rate"** indicates projected tax revenue for the same time period. From 2005 through 2016, the income rate exceeds the cost rate. Starting in 2017, Social Security has a growing cash flow problem; the cost rate exceeds the income rate by a percentage that grows slowly each year. The amount by which the cost rate exceeds the income rate after 2041 is a measure of the degree to which Social Security will be unable to pay promised benefits in the absence of changes in the law. For example, in 2085, the cost and income rates are 17.63 and 13.30 percent of taxable payroll, respectively. The difference between the two, 4.33 percent, is 25 percent of the cost rate. This is a measure of the percentage of promised benefits that cannot be paid at that time unless the law changes.

[6]James J. Heckman, "What Has Been Learned about Labor Supply in the United States in the Past Twenty Years?" *American Economic Review* 83 (May 1993): 116–21.

Figure 16.6 **Old Age and Survivors and Disability Insurance Trust Funds, 2005–2041**
The combined OASI and DI Trust Funds had a balance of $2.24 trillion at the end of 2007. The balance will grow to until 2027 and then decline rapidly. The funds will become exhausted in 2041.

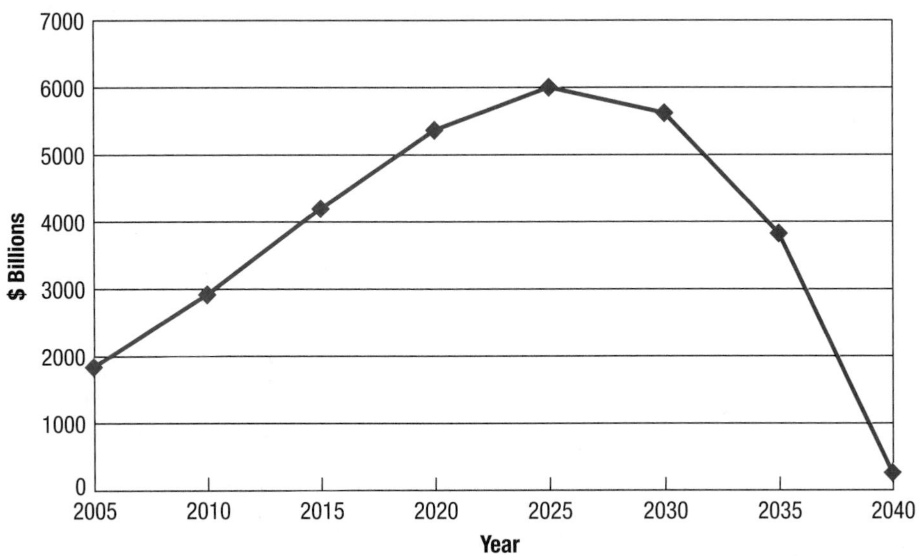

Figure 16.7 **Projected Cost and Income Rates, 2005–2085**
Income as a share of taxable payroll is projected to exceed costs as a share of taxable payroll through 2016. Starting in 2017, annual cost exceeds annual income until the end of the projection period, at which time the two series are still diverging.

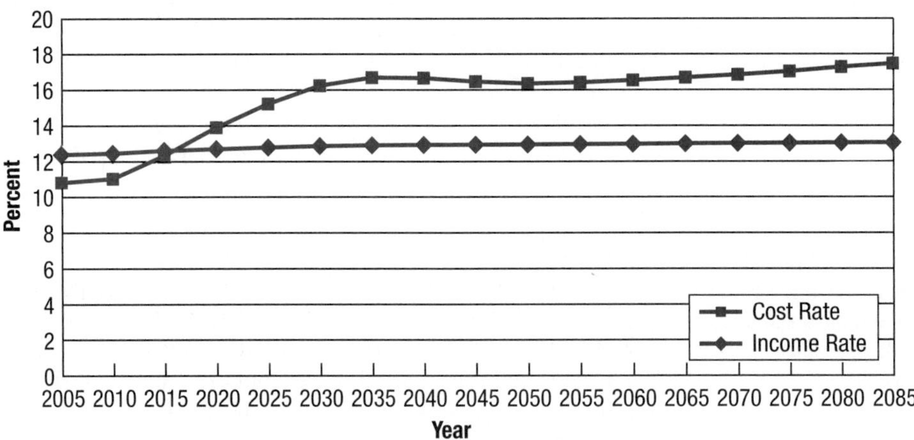

A useful way to summarize the 75-year shortfall of income relative to costs is the size of the increase in the Social Security payroll tax rate that would be required to close the 75-year gap. If the payroll tax were increased by 1.92 percentage points in 2008 (increased from 12.4 percent to 14.32 percent) and maintained at that level through 2085, the trust fund balances would be positive for the entire 75-year period. Alternatively, a cut in Social Security benefits of 12.8 percent for each of the next 75 years would also close the 75-year funding gap.

What lies behind the 75-year funding gap? It can be explained in a variety of ways, but two factors are particularly important: (1) retirement of the Baby Boom generation, and (2) the legacy debt.

Baby Boom Generation– The cohort of individuals born from 1946 through 1964.

Legacy debt– Total Social Security benefits, minus Social Security taxes plus interest, for cohorts born before 1936.

Baby Boomers. The 75-year funding problem is often attributed to the large increase in the number of retired individuals that takes place after the **Baby Boom Generation** (individuals born in the period 1946–1964) starts to retire. In fact, the swelling of the ranks of retirees is an important source of the increase in the cost rate that occurs between 2010 and 2050. Most of the Baby Boomers will retire between 2010 and 2030. Assuming an average period of 20 years over which Social Security benefits will be paid, the Boomers will increase projected benefit outlays from 2010 through 2050.

We can't blame it all on the Baby Boomers, however. Other factors are at work while they are alive, and it is clear from Figure 16.7 that the long-run financing problem does not go away after the Boomers are dead. In fact, it grows worse after they are gone.

Legacy Debt. We have illustrated and argued above that future retirees can expect the present value of their Social Security retirement benefits to be less than the present value of their Social Security payroll taxes. This is not the general case. In fact, cohorts of Social Security retirees born before 1936 have received, or will receive, retirement benefits that exceed payroll taxes plus interest (or, what is the same thing, present value of benefits greater than present value of taxes). This situation has created a large **legacy debt**—benefits received by past and present retirees in excess of the taxes they have paid plus interest compounded on those tax payments.

The legacy debt of a cohort of retirees is paid by current workers. When these workers become retirees any legacy debt they are responsible for is paid by then current workers. So every successive cohort is paid back for what it lent to each preceding cohort. It may appear from this scheme of inter-cohort sharing that no one bears a cost because of the legacy debt. Not so, if there is a legacy debt, part of each successive cohort's taxes must be used to pay the legacy debt of each preceding cohort of retirees. Thus, each successive cohort receives smaller retirement benefits of its own for a given tax contribution. Alternatively, because of the legacy debt, taxes paid by each successive cohort must increase to keep benefits received at a given level over time. This required increase in taxes to cover the legacy debt of successive cohorts helps to explain the increasing cost rate illustrated in Figure 16.7.

INTERNATIONAL PERSPECTIVE

Public Pension Plans in Trouble: The U.S. Is Not Unique

The combination of an aging population and a maturing pension scheme spell long-run difficulty for the U.S. Social Security system. The United States has lots of company, however, and in some ways is even better off than other developed countries, at least according to the numbers in the following table.

In 1990, the present value of Social Security pension promises in the United States amounted to about 90 percent of GDP, or nearly $5 trillion. As you know from reading the text, receipts from the payroll tax and other sources will not accumulate fast enough at currently legislated rates to pay all these obligations. Other countries appear in worse shape, however; Canada, Germany, Japan, and the United Kingdom owed more than 100 percent of GDP in 1990 to current and future retirees, and in France and Italy the obligation exceeded 200 percent.

In order to meet these obligations in the future, each of these countries must find additional revenues, reduce benefits, or both. One revenue possibility is the adoption of a once-and-for-all increase in taxes. Had these countries done this in 1990, the increase required to avoid a long-run deficit would have ranged from 1.1 percent of GDP in the United States to 5.3 percent of GDP in Italy. One benefit-reduction possibility would be to adopt an increase in the normal retirement age. Had these countries used this policy in 1990, the increase required to avoid a long-run deficit would have ranged from 4 years in the United States to a whopping 16 years in Canada.

Means of Financing Pension Liabilities

Country	Tax Increase (as % of GDP)	Increase in Retirement Age (years)
Canada	4.4	16
France	4.0	8
Germany	3.6	11
Italy	5.3	10
Japan	4.3	9
United Kingdom	3.5	12
United States	1.1	4

These options do not exhaust the possibilities for these countries to deal with the long-run deficit in public pension plans, of course, but they do illustrate some of the tough choices to be made. Americans who lament this fact may feel fortunate to know that the task may be easier for the United States than for other countries.

Source: World Bank, *Averting the Old Age Crisis* (New York: Oxford University Press, 1994), 159.

APPROACHES TO SOCIAL SECURITY REFORM

Reforming Social Security is on virtually everyone's federal policy agenda. In reforming Social Security, the logical place to start is to state clearly what the proposed reform should accomplish. There are a potentially large number of goals, but three reform goals appear to command widespread agreement: (1) the long-run fiscal imbalance should be eliminated, (2) national savings should be increased, and (3) individuals should receive a higher rate of return. Ideally, these goals would be accomplished while Social Security still provides guaranteed inflation-protected annuities, more generous benefits to low lifetime income earners, and benefits to survivors and disabled individuals and their families.

There are two general approaches to Social Security reform: (1) fixing the current system by changing the amount of taxes paid and/or benefits received; and (2) investing in private securities. We argue that it is possible to eliminate the long-run fiscal imbalance by changing the amount of taxes paid and/or benefits received, but that it is not possible to increase the individual rate of return using this approach. We also argue that it is possible to increase the individual rate of return and eliminate the long-run fiscal imbalance by using some portion of Social Security payroll tax revenues to establish individual accounts containing investments in private securities. To ensure that national savings also increase, however, individual accounts must be funded by an increase in taxes.

Fixing the Current System

In the broadest sense, eliminating the long-run fiscal imbalance in Social Security requires either reduced benefits or increased revenues, or some of both. There is no shortage of suggestions regarding how this might be done. A good model, however, is the one developed by Peter Diamond and Peter Orszag.

The reforms suggested by Diamond and Orszag are adjustments for what the authors identify as the principal sources of Social Security's long-run fiscal imbalance: increasing life expectancy, increased earnings inequality, and the legacy debt. They focus on two dimensions of increasing life expectancy: a gradual increase in life expectancy of 4 years for individuals who survive to age 65 over the next 75 years, and an increase in the percentage of the population age 62 that will survive for an additional 20 years or more. They credit the increase in earnings inequality in the United States over the last two decades with increasing the share of taxable payroll above the maximum taxable payroll cap,

TABLE 16.3 CONGRESSIONAL BUDGET OFFICE SIMULATION OF THE DIAMOND AND ORSZAG SOCIAL SECURITY REFORM PROPOSAL (TAX AND BENEFIT CHANGES AS A PERCENT OF TAXABLE PAYROLL)

	YEAR					
	2005	2025	2045	2065	2085	2105
Tax Increases						
Extend coverage to new state and local workers	0.00	0.20	0.27	0.17	0.16	0.19
Raise maximum taxable payroll	0.00	0.31	0.58	0.66	0.66	0.63
Increase taxes for increasing life expectancy	0.00	0.17	0.41	0.61	0.83	0.99
Impose legacy tax above maximum taxable payroll	0.62	0.60	0.70	0.80	0.84	0.85
Impose legacy tax below maximum taxable payroll	0.00	0.10	0.73	1.41	1.98	2.00
Total Increase in Taxes	0.62	1.37	2.69	3.65	4.46	4.66
Benefit Reductions and Increases						
Reduce top PIA bend rate	0.00	0.07	0.20	0.27	0.36	0.33
Reduce benefits for increasing life expectancy	0.00	0.06	0.29	0.62	0.96	1.22
Reduce benefits for legacy cost	0.00	0.02	0.53	1.44	2.34	2.80
Increase Benefits for Disadvantaged*	−0.01	−0.44	−0.92	−1.11	−1.18	−1.16
Total Net Reduction in Benefits	−0.01	−0.30	0.11	1.21	2.48	3.18
Interactions Among Reforms	0.02	−0.09	−0.10	0.04	−0.20	−0.22
Total Effect of All Reforms	0.63	0.98	2.70	4.90	6.74	7.62

*Disabled, low lifetime earners, widows.
Source: Congressional Budget Office, based on Social Security trustees' 2004 intermediate demographic assumptions and CBO's August 2004 economic assumptions.

or what is the same thing, with reducing the percentage of taxable payroll subject to the Social Security payroll tax.[7]

Diamond and Orszag submitted their proposals to the Congressional Budget Office for analysis. The CBO has provided the results of their analysis on its Web site. Table 16.3 summarizes their findings.

The CBO reported their results as a percent of taxable payroll, with a *positive* number indicating *both* tax *increases* and benefit *reductions.* As indicated, Diamond and Orszag proposed a series of tax changes that would ultimately increase taxes by 4.66 percent of taxable payroll. They also proposed several benefit changes: three benefit reductions that would ultimately reduce benefits by 4.35 percent of taxable payroll, and benefits increases for disabled workers, low lifetime earners and widows that would ultimately increase benefits by 1.16 percent of taxable payroll.

Diamond and Orszag actually propose tax increases and benefit cuts that eventually total 9 percent of taxable payroll. Tax increases and benefit cuts designed to pay for the legacy debt are 5.75 percent of taxable payroll in 2105, or 64 percent of the total. Adjustments for increases in life expectancy account for 2.21 percent of taxable payroll, or

[7]Peter A. Diamond and Peter R. Orszag, *Saving Social Security: A Balanced Approach* (Washington, D. C.: Brookings Institution Press, 2004).

25 percent of the 2105 total increase in taxes and benefit reductions. Tax collections from newly hired state and local workers and raising the cap on the maximum taxable payroll account for most of the remainder.

Figure 16.8 shows how the reforms proposed by Diamond and Orszag change the income and cost rates over the next 100 years (unlike Figure 16.7 where the time horizon is only 75 years). As noted in the legend to the figure, the Diamond and Orszag proposals produce an income rate (IRDO) that exceeds the cost rate (CRDO) after 2045. Although the figure does not show this directly, the excess of the projected IRDO over CRDO is sufficiently large to eliminate the Social Security fiscal imbalance for 100 years. The figure also suggests that the Diamond and Orszag reforms would continue to ensure fiscal solvency beyond 100 years.

What About the Individual Rate of Return? As long as each successive cohort has to pay for the legacy debt it inherits, eliminating the fiscal imbalance by fixing the current system cannot produce an increase in the rate of return. It will be permanently stuck at less than 3 percent.

What About National Savings? National savings is the sum of government and private savings. Government savings will increase if reducing the Social Security deficit induces Congress to decrease planned unified budget deficits or increase planned unified budget surpluses. Private savings will increase if achieving long-run solvency induces households to save more and business firms to increase their contributions to private pensions.

We are skeptical that any of these effects would occur. Social Security, per se, will likely run surpluses for a longer period of time than under current law. In such circumstances, Congress will be tempted to run a larger deficit in the non–Social Security portion of the budget. If so, there will be no net effect on planned deficits or surpluses in the unified budget.

Figure 16.8 Effect of Diamond and Orszag Reform Plan on Income Rate and Cost Rate, 2005–2105

In this diagram, CRCL is the cost rate under the current law, IRCL is the income rate under the current law, CRDO is the cost rate with the Diamond and Orszag proposals in place, and IRDO is the income rate with the Diamond and Orszag proposals in place. Under the current law, income and cost rates are diverging at the end of the 100-year horizon. With the Diamond and Orszag proposals in place, the income rate exceeds the cost rate after 2045.

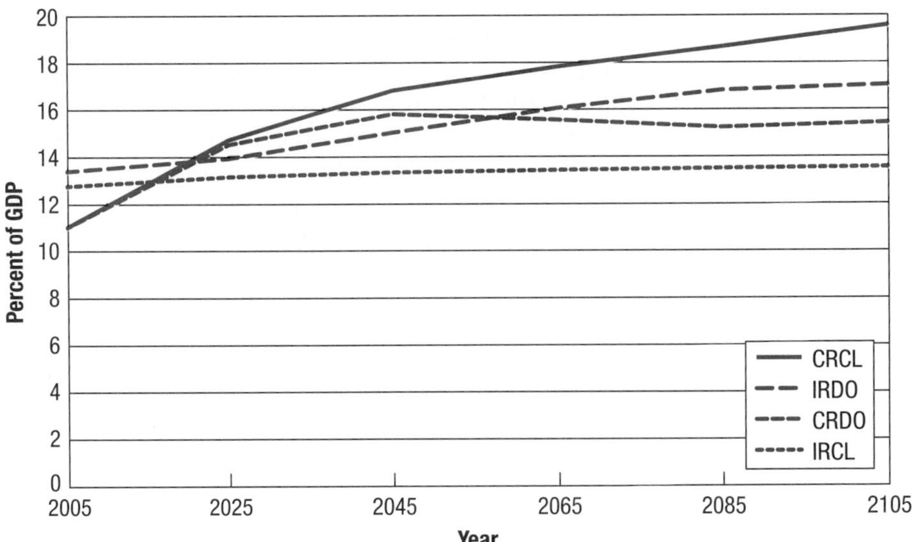

In the household sector, the most likely effect of eliminating the long-run deficit is to increase the certainty of Social Security benefits. This should increase the effect of the wealth substitution effect, thereby reducing household savings. The business sector is also likely to perceive that Social Security benefits have been made more certain. This perception may induce them to decrease their contributions to private pensions.

Investing in Private Securities

There are two general approaches to investing in private securities: (1) investing the Social Security trust fund in equities (stocks); and (2) establishing individual accounts. Both of these approaches are capable of increasing the rate of return for individuals. Investing the Social Security trust fund in equities is unlikely to eliminate the long-run Social Security deficit or increase national savings. Whether the establishment of individual accounts would achieve fiscal solvency and increase national savings depends on how they are financed.

Investing the Trust Fund in Equities. Under current law, balances in the Social Security trust fund must be invested in U.S. Treasury bonds. Over the period 1871–2004, the geometric average real rate of return on these securities was 2.7 percent. Over the same period, stocks yielded 6.8 percent. Several proposals have been made to take advantage of this differential by investing some of the trust fund balances in equities. Long-run simulations of the distribution of returns on equities indicate that investing in stocks could lengthen the remaining life of the trust fund (produce a later date of trust fund exhaustion). Investing even a large share of the balances in equities, however, would be unlikely to eliminate the long-run deficit entirely.

Critics of such an approach worry about the increased risk of price declines associated with equities, and severe critics do not hesitate to raise the specter of major stock market crashes. Proponents argue, however, that Social Security has the ability to spread this risk across lengthy periods of time, thereby reducing the probability that such risk would impair the long-run balances in the trust fund.

Critics also observe that such a practice would reduce the money available to finance the public debt, thus driving up the cost of borrowing to the government and exacerbating the negative effects of federal budget deficits. Critics also express concern that, since stock purchases convey corporate ownership, the government will vote its shares to achieve purposes inconsistent with increasing private wealth. Proponents counter that private capital markets are so large that investing even as much as 30 percent of the trust fund in equities would have little impact on either interest rates or corporate policies.

What About the Individual Rate of Return? Assuming that Social Security could earn the historical rates of return on equities (6.8 percent) and government bonds (2.7 percent), and the equity/bond split was 30/70, the weighted rate of return would be a little over 3.9 percent, or nearly 50 percent higher than the rate on government bonds alone. Such an increase would be associated, of course, with additional risk.

What About National Savings? The arguments made about the probable impact of fixing Social Security with benefit cuts and tax increases on national savings are also pertinent to this approach. Given that the long-run deficit is not eliminated under this approach, however, there may be a smaller probability in this case that national savings will decline.

Establishing Individual Accounts. There have been several proposals to supplement Social Security with individual accounts. George W. Bush established the President's Commission on Strengthening Social Security (PCSSS) partly for this purpose. Their final report, *Strengthening Social Security and Creating Personal Wealth for All Americans*, issued in December 2001, contains the essence of a plan that subsequently provided the blueprint for the President's proposal for Social Security Reform in his State of the Union address in February, 2005. The plan at issue is "Plan 2" of the PCSSS.

Plan 2 would allow for the establishment of individual accounts and switch from wage indexing of initial benefits to price indexing of benefits. To ease the pain for low lifetime earners, the plan would provide a new minimum benefit for workers with low lifetime earnings. It would also increase the survivor benefit for some widows and widowers. If Social Security experienced a shortfall during a phase-in period, general revenue funds would be transferred to the Social Security trust fund.

In Plan 2, workers could have up to 4 percentage points of their payroll taxes (with a limit of $1,000, indexed to the average wage) diverted to their own individual accounts, which would be invested in a mix of stock and bond mutual funds. Participation in individual accounts would be voluntary, but there would be a strong incentive for individuals to participate.

The principal and interest in the personal accounts would be converted to annuities that would supplement Social Security benefits at retirement, or be distributed to workers' heirs if they died before retiring. Social Security would reduce Social Security retirement benefits of a participant by the amount diverted to the individual account plus 2 percent interest compounded annually. Thus, the individual accounts would be, in effect, financed by a loan costing 2 percent per year.

The Congressional Budget Office released its *Long-Term Analysis of Plan 2 of the President's Commission to Strengthen Social Security* in July 2004. Table 16.4 summarizes the effects of Plan 2 in terms of percent of taxable payroll over a 100-year horizon. Three of the factors listed—adding individual accounts financed by diverting payroll tax revenues, increasing the minimum benefit, and raising benefits for widows and widowers—would add to Social Security's fiscal imbalance, so they are prefaced by a minus sign. The other factor—price indexing of benefits—would reduce Social Security's fiscal imbalance, so this item is treated as a positive element. It is clear from Table 16.4 that Plan 2 has a large positive effect on long-run Social Security balances.

Figure 16.9 illustrates the income and cost rates under current law (IRCL and CRCL) and compares them to the income and cost rates under Plan 2 (IRP2 and CRP2). Current law refers to benefits scheduled under current law; the reduction in benefits that would be necessary after the trust fund becomes exhausted is not illustrated. Under Plan 2 the income rate eventually falls substantially below the cost rate, ensuring fiscal

TABLE 16.4 CONGRESSIONAL BUDGET OFFICE SIMULATION OF THE PRESIDENTIAL COMMISSION REFORM PLAN 2 (TAX AND BENEFIT CHANGES AS A PERCENT OF TAXABLE PAYROLL)

	2005	2025	2045	2065	2085	2105
Add individual accounts	0.00	−1.73	−0.58	0.28	0.48	0.61
Increase the minimum benefit	0.00	−0.28	−0.74	−0.85	−0.94	−0.87
Raise benefit for widow(er)s	0.00	−0.04	−0.06	0.00	−0.03	−0.08
Price indexing of benefits	0.00	1.00	3.44	6.32	8.85	11.17
Interactions across provisions	0.00	0.02	0.05	0.28	0.47	0.52
Total Effect	0.00	−1.03	2.11	6.03	8.83	11.35

Source: Congressional Budget Office, based on Social Security trustees' 2004 intermediate demographic assumptions and CBO's January 2004 economic assumptions.

Figure 16.9 **Effect of Presidential Commission Reform Plan 2 on Income and Cost Rate, 2005–2105**
In this diagram, CRCL is the cost rate under the current law, IRCL is the income rate under the current law, IRP2 is the income rate under Plan 2 and CRP2 is the cost rate under Plan 2. With Plan 2 in place, the income rate eventually exceeds the cost rate.

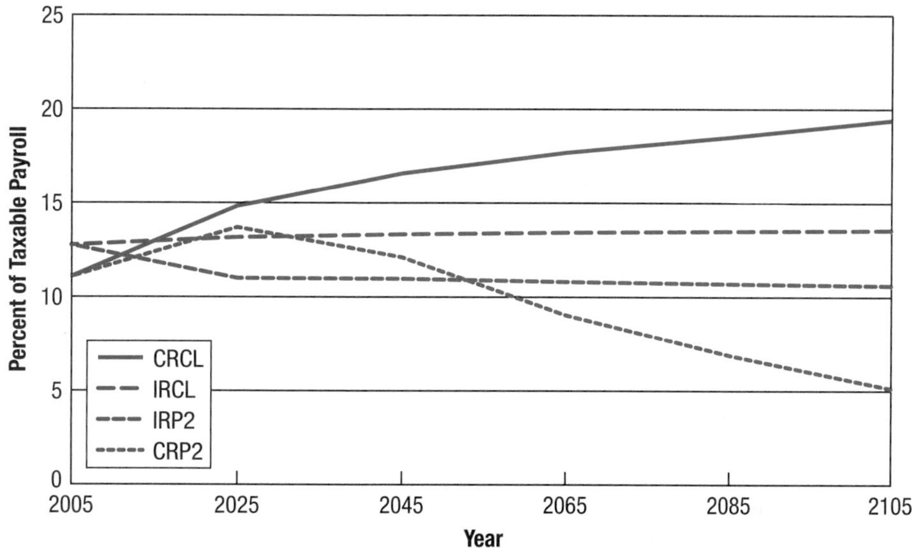

solvency over the 100-year horizon. In fact, the fall in the cost rate is greater than the decrease needed to ensure fiscal solvency.

The CBO assumed that the money in the individual accounts would be invested as follows: (1) 20 percent in treasury bonds that would earn 3.3 percent per year; (2) 30 percent in corporate bonds that would earn 3.8 percent per year; and (3) 50 percent in equities that would earn 6.8 percent per year. Each of these rates was reduced by 0.3 percent in CBO's analysis to account for administrative costs.

All these rates are higher than the cost of the loan, so participants would realize increased retirement benefits if these rates were certain. But they are not. They are subject to market risk. That is, historical rates have varied both above and below each of these rates, with the greatest variation associated with equities. To account for the effect of market risk on expected returns, the CBO ran 500 random simulations of projected outcomes. The results of these simulations are illustrated in Figure 16.10.

This figure displays projected benefits as a percent of GDP. The benefits from Plan 2 are designated as IA90 and IA10. They consist of the combined benefits from the individual accounts and Social Security retirement benefits (reduced to pay back the participants' loans). Eighty percent of the CBO's simulations of Plan 2 yield benefits that fall in the range between IA90 and IA10.

Projections of Social Security retirement benefits are also based on economic and demographic factors that are subject to risk. So the CBO also performed 500 simulations of the Social Security retirement benefits that could be funded by trust fund balances and annual income (that is, they allowed for the exhaustion of the trust funds and assumed that benefits after that date would be reduced to equal annual income). The results of these simulations are indicated in Figure 16.10 by TF90 and TF10. Eighty percent of the CBO's simulations of trust-fund-financed benefits fall in the range between TF90 and TF10.

These simulations indicate that Plan 2 is likely to produce significantly higher benefits, but that it could produce slightly smaller benefits. Higher benefits are likely under Plan 2, but they are not guaranteed.

Figure 16.10 **Trust Fund-Financed and Plan 2 Benefits, 2005–2105**
The difference between the top line (IA90) and the bottom line (IA10) indicates the range within which benefits from Plan 2 will be realized 80 percent of the time. The difference between the middle two lines (TF90 and TF10) indicates the range within which benefits from trust fund-financed benefits will be realized 80 percent of the time. Both higher and lower benefits are possible under Plan 2.

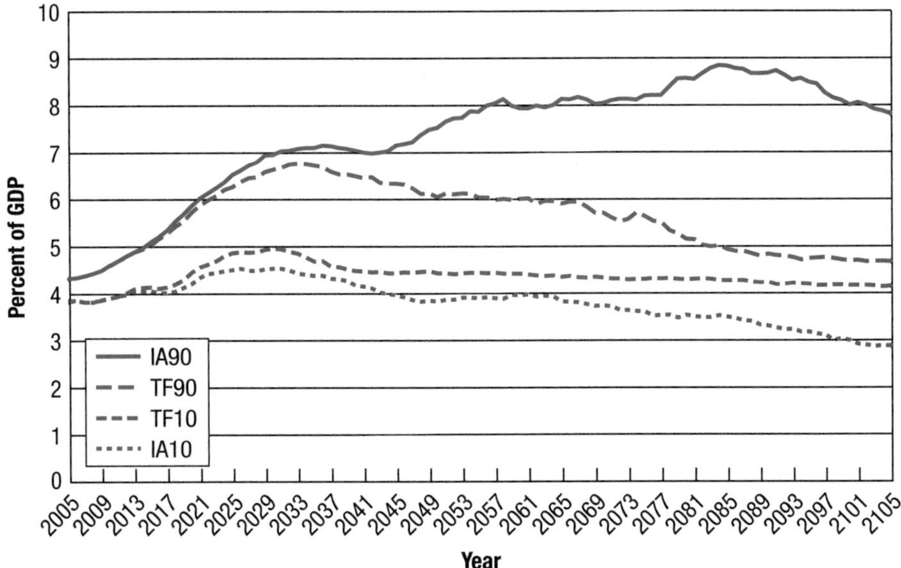

What About the Individual Rate of Return? The CBO did not estimate the rates of return from Plan 2. Estimates of the rate of return from the president's plan are available, however, and the two plans are quite similar. In fact, the only substantial difference is in the method used to recapture the loan to establish individual accounts; the president's plan would reduce benefits more for higher-income retirees than for lower-income retirees through "progressive price indexing." The effect of a 50/50 split between stocks and bonds on the rate of return from the president's plan has been simulated by Robert Shiller of Yale University.[8] He found that the total return on this portfolio, plus the benefits provided by Social Security after the loan is repaid with interest, exceeds the total return from the Social Security benefits that can be funded in the absence of reform. The expected rate of return on the president's plan is 4 percent. However, Shiller also found that there could be net losses from the president's plan with this portfolio allocation 20 percent of the time.

What About National Savings? We are aware of no estimates of the probable effects of Plan 2 on national savings. It seems possible that participants will perceive that they are saving more under Plan 2 than they would have been under current law, and save less in other forms. Probably the only sure way to get an increase in national savings while eliminating the long-run fiscal imbalance is to finance individual accounts with an increase in taxes. Several plans of that type have been proposed, but their analysis is beyond the scope of this chapter.[9]

---

[8]Robert J. Shiller, "The Life-Cycle Personal Accounts Proposal for Social Security: An Evaluation," Yale University: Cowles Foundation Discussion Paper No. 1504, April 2005.

[9]See, especially, Sylvester J. Scheiber and John B. Shoven, *The Real Deal*, New Haven, CT: Yale University Press, 1999, 386–408; also Martin Feldstein and Andrew Samwick, "The Transition Path in Privatizing Social Security," in Martin Feldstein, ed., *Privatizing Social Security*, Chicago: Chicago University Press, 1998, 215–260.

Summary

In this chapter, the term "Social Security" refers to the federal Old-Age and Survivors' Insurance (OASI) and Disability Insurance (DI) programs that provide benefits to retired workers and to their survivors and to disabled workers and their families.

Social Security is financed by payroll taxes that are deposited in the OASI and DI trust funds. Money is disbursed from the funds to pay benefits. Retirement benefits are based on the 35 years of highest indexed earnings. Indexed earnings are actual earnings adjusted by a wage index. Initial benefits are based on a formula that relates the amount paid to indexed earnings. This formula is progressive in the sense that it provides more generous benefits to lower lifetime earners than to higher lifetime earners.

Social Security retirement benefits are subject to an early retirement penalty and a reward for working beyond the normal retirement age. Benefits received by retirees are indexed each year for inflation. Benefits last for the lifetime of the recipient. Spouses of retirees receive benefits at least as large as one-half of the benefits of the principal earner.

Social Security makes a major contribution to reducing poverty among elderly Americans, but it is not a welfare program.

Social Security may not induce workers to retire early because the actuarial value of Social Security benefits does not vary with the age at retirement.

Social Security probably reduces household savings, due to the accumulation of Social Security wealth. Although the effect of Social Security wealth on household savings is small, the level of Social Security wealth is large enough that Social Security probably has a significant negative effect on the capital stock and GDP.

Individual real rates of return from investing in Social Security are low. They are likely to be only about 1 percent for college graduates. They are less than 3 percent on average for all cohorts of individuals born after 1936.

The Social Security payroll tax appears to be borne entirely by workers, which is not what Congress intended.

The latest 75-year projections indicate that the trust fund will run annual surpluses until 2016, but that balances will fall thereafter and become exhausted in 2041, after which Social Security will be able to pay only 75 to 78 percent of the benefits promised by current law.

The cost rate not only exceeds the income rate after 2016, but it continues to grow faster, producing a growing divergence between the two rates at the end of the 75-year projection period. The problems associated with Social Security have spurred the development of reform plans. Generally, the goals of such reform are: (1) eliminate the long-run fiscal imbalance; (2) increase the individual rate of return; and (3) increase national savings.

Two approaches to Social Security reform have dominated the policy agenda: (1) fixing the current system; and (2) investing in private securities.

Diamond and Orszag have proposed a plan with a number of individual provisions to address increases in life expectancy, increasing income inequality, and the legacy debt. Their plan appears to eliminate the fiscal imbalance for at least 100 years, but it will not increase the rate of return or national savings.

Trustees could invest some portion of trust fund balances in private securities and increase the rate of return for individuals, but these extra returns would not be sufficient to eliminate long-run fiscal imbalances. Such a plan is also unlikely to increase national savings.

The President's Commission on Strengthening Social Security has proposed three reform plans. Its Plan 2 would divert a portion of payroll tax revenues to individual accounts. The money in these accounts would be invested in a mix of stocks and bonds. The balances in these accounts would be annuitized at retirement. Participants would receive these annuities and lifetime benefits from Social Security (reduced by the taxes diverted to individual accounts and a 2 percent annual interest rate on those taxes). Initial Social Security retirement benefits would be indexed to prices instead of the current indexation by wages.

Plan 2 would eliminate the fiscal imbalance for at least 100 years. It offers the prospect of higher benefits, but benefits could be lower. It may increase the rate of return, but participants could suffer losses as much as 20 percent of the time. It is doubtful that Plan 2 would increase national savings.

Key Terms

Wage indexing factor
Average indexed monthly earnings (AIME)
Primary insurance amount (PIA)
Normal retirement age
Early retirement penalty
Delayed retirement credit
Wealth substitution effect
Social Security wealth

Induced retirement effect
Substitution effect of a wage decrease
Income effect of a wage decrease
Cost rate
Income rate
Baby Boom Generation
Legacy debt

Review Questions

1. Explain how and why earnings are indexed to determine Social Security retirement benefits.
2. Explain how Social Security provides more generous returns to the poor than to the rich, using the concepts of the PIA and AIME.
3. In theory, Social Security may or may not induce people to save less. Explain.
4. In theory, Social Security may or may not induce people to retire early. Explain.
5. If Social Security does induce people to save less, it only reduces savings by less than 3 cents for each dollar of Social Security wealth. Surely, this is a negligible effect. Do you agree or disagree? Explain.
6. Given benefits and costs that can be measured in dollars, Social Security benefits exceed costs by a large margin. However, Social Security pays only a 1 to 2 percent real rate of return for the typical college graduate. Explain.
7. "The Social Security payroll tax appears to be paid largely by workers, not by both workers and employers as Congress intended." Explain how this can be, using a diagram to illustrate your answer.
8. Social Security faces a long-run fiscal imbalance, according to three measures introduced in this chapter. What are these measures and how large is the imbalance according to each of them?
9. It is often said that the long-run deficit in Social Security can be eliminated at relatively low cost if the problem is addressed right away. Explain.
10. What are the principal problems addressed by the Diamond-Orszag reform plan?
11. What are the principal elements of the Diamond-Orszag reform plan?
12. Assess the probable success of the Diamond-Orszag reform plan in terms of (1) eliminating the long-run fiscal imbalance; (2) increasing the rate of return; and (3) increasing national savings.
13. What are the principal problems addressed by Plan 2?
14. What are the principal elements of Plan 2?
15. Assess the probable success of Plan 2 in terms of (1) eliminating the long-run fiscal imbalance; (2) increasing the rate of return; and (3) increasing national savings.

Web Sites

- The 2008 Social Security Trustees Report is available at—**http://www.ssa.gov/OACT/TR/TR08/trTOC.html**
- CBO's analyses of Social Security are available at—**http://www.cbo.gov/publications/bysubject.cfm?cat=11**

CHAPTER 17

International Trade: Beneficial, but Controversial

OUTLINE

The foreign trade sector is an important part of the U.S. economy. Exports accounted for 12 percent of GDP in 2007, 2 percentage points higher than 2004 (see Figure 17.1). As measured by imports, however, foreign trade accounted for over 17 percent of GDP in 2007, up from 15 percent in 2004. The export sector was 50 percent bigger than the durable goods sector and slightly bigger than the nonresidential construction sector of the U.S. economy. The import sector was only slightly bigger than gross private domestic investment.

No one questions whether the levels of activity in durable goods, nonresidential construction, and gross private domestic investment are important to the overall health of the economy. Not so foreign trade. There are many critics of foreign trade. Especially vocal are those who equate the excess of imports relative to exports with an excess of jobs lost relative to jobs gained. Economic theory recognizes that there are losses as a consequence of foreign trade, but also that there are gains and, more importantly, that gains exceed losses. To understand this, it helps to start with the reasons why trade occurs.

Figure 17.1 U.S. Imports and Exports as percent of GDP, 1980–2007

U.S. imports have increased relative to GDP over the past 28 years, reaching over 17 percent of GDP in 2007. During the same time period, U.S. exports increased to 12 percent of GDP and international trade has assumed a larger role in the U.S. economy.

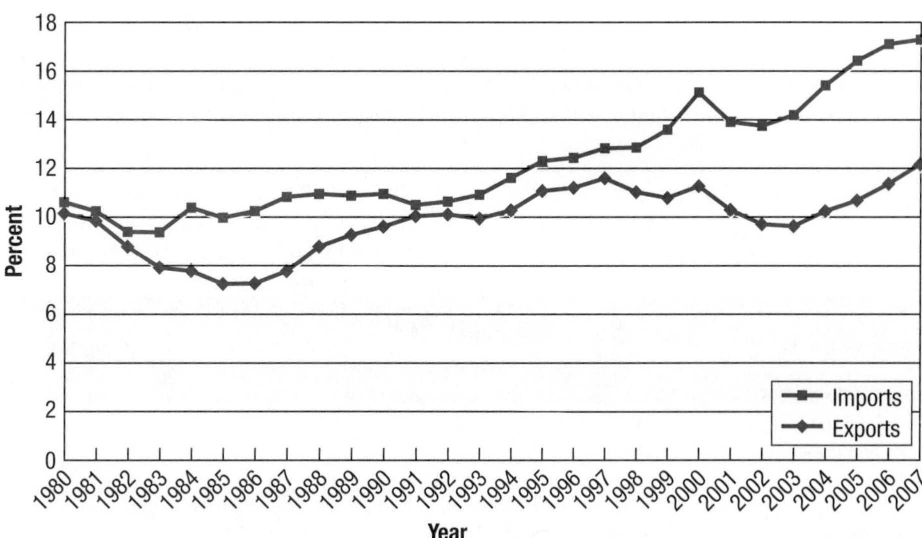

Source: Authors' calculations based on data for gross domestic product from the U.S. Bureau of Economic Analysis Web site (http://www.bea.gov).

COMPARATIVE ADVANTAGE: THE BASIS FOR TRADE

Comparative advantage– The advantage a country has if it produces a good or service at a lower opportunity cost than its trading partner.

Comparative disadvantage– The disadvantage a country has if it produces a good or service at a higher opportunity cost than its trading partner.

Absolute advantage– The advantage a country has if it can produce more of a good or service with the same inputs as its trading partner.

Absolute disadvantage– The disadvantage a country has if it produces less of a good or service with the same inputs as its trading partner.

Trade among nations is based on comparative advantage. A country has a **comparative advantage** (or a **comparative disadvantage**) in a good or service if it can produce the good or service at a lower (higher) opportunity cost than its trading partner. Countries gain by producing goods and services for which they have a comparative advantage and exchanging them for goods and services for which they have a comparative disadvantage.

The principle of comparative advantage was developed early in the nineteenth century by David Ricardo, a famous English economist. Following Ricardo, we construct a simple example of trade based on comparative advantage. The example assumes two countries, the United States and the United Kingdom; two goods, wheat and cloth; and one factor of production, labor. Although the volume of international trade depends on transportation costs, they do not alter the principle of comparative advantage, so they are ignored in this example.

Table 17.1 indicates that a U.S. worker can produce either 6 bushels of wheat or 6 yards of cloth per day. In contrast, a U.K. worker can produce either 1 bushel of wheat or 4 yards of cloth. Because U.S. workers can produce a larger amount of both goods, the United States has an **absolute advantage** in the production of both wheat and cloth. Correspondingly, the United Kingdom has an **absolute disadvantage** in the production of both goods.

It may appear that no basis for mutually advantageous trade exists. After all, output per worker is higher in the United States for both goods. But trade is *not* based on absolute advantage; it is based on comparative advantage. As noted, a country has a comparative advantage in producing a good if it can produce it at a lower opportunity cost than its trading partner.

Table 17.1 notes the opportunity costs of producing wheat and cloth in the two countries. In the United States, it is necessary to give up 1 yard of cloth to obtain 1 bushel of wheat. Thus, the opportunity cost of 1 bushel of wheat is 1 yard of cloth. In the United Kingdom, the opportunity cost of 1 bushel of wheat is 4 yards of cloth. Thus, the U.S. has a comparative advantage in producing wheat. The United Kingdom has an opportunity cost of one-fourth bushel of wheat compared to an opportunity cost of 1 bushel of wheat in the U.S. for producing a yard of cloth. Consequently, the United Kingdom has a comparative advantage in producing cloth.

Trade occurs between two countries only if each is better off as a result. The United States will be better off by trading only if it can get *more than 1 yard of cloth* in exchange

TABLE 17.1 OUTPUT PER WORKER AND OPPORTUNITY COST IN THE UNITED STATES AND THE UNITED KINGDOM (UNITS PER DAY)

COUNTRY	WHEAT (BUSHELS)	CLOTH (YARDS)	OPPORTUNITY COST OF WHEAT (YARDS OF CLOTH PER BUSHEL)	OPPORTUNITY COST OF CLOTH (BUSHELS OF WHEAT PER YARD)
United States	6	6	1	1
United Kingdom	1	4	4	¼

Because output per worker is higher for both wheat and cloth in the United States, it has an absolute advantage in the production of those goods and the United Kingdom has an absolute disadvantage. Because the opportunity cost of wheat is lower in the United States, it has a comparative advantage in producing wheat. The opportunity cost of producing cloth is lower in the United Kingdom, so it has a comparative advantage in producing cloth.

for 1 bushel of wheat (because it can get 1 yard of cloth for one bushel of wheat without trade by shifting workers from wheat production to cloth production). The United Kingdom will be better off by trading only if it can get 1 bushel of wheat for *less than 4 yards of cloth* (because it can get one bushel of wheat for 4 yards of cloth without trade by shifting workers from cloth production to wheat production).

Suppose that the U.S. offers to trade 1 bushel of wheat for 2 yards of cloth. This offer is likely to be accepted because both countries would be better off as a result. The United States would be better off because it could get 2 yards of cloth by giving up 1 bushel of wheat. Domestically, it can get only 1 yard of cloth by giving up 1 bushel of wheat. The United Kingdom would also be better off because it could get 1 bushel of wheat by giving up 2 yards of cloth. Domestically, it must give up 4 yards of cloth to get 1 bushel of wheat.

This example shows that countries gain from international trade by producing goods in which they have a comparative advantage and exchanging them for goods in which their trading partners also have a comparative advantage. We can demonstrate this result in a slightly different manner, one that shows that international trade results in a higher level of consumption for both countries.

Suppose that the United States has a workforce of 400 workers and that the United Kingdom has a workforce of 200. As illustrated in Figure 17.2, with full employment the United States can produce 2,400 bushels of wheat and zero yards of cloth or zero wheat and 2,400 yards of cloth, or one of the combinations in between. All of these combinations lie on the U.S. production possibilities curve.

With full employment, the United Kingdom can produce 200 bushels of wheat and zero cloth or 800 yards of cloth and zero wheat, or any of the other combinations of wheat and cloth on the U.K. production possibilities curve in Figure 17.3.

Figure 17.2 **Trade with the United Kingdom Increases Consumption of Cloth in the United States**

The United States initially produces combination A. It exports 150 bushels of wheat to the United Kingdom, moving it to point B. It receives imports of 300 yards of cloth, moving it to point D. At D, it has more cloth than it could produce itself by shifting domestic production from wheat to cloth (point C).

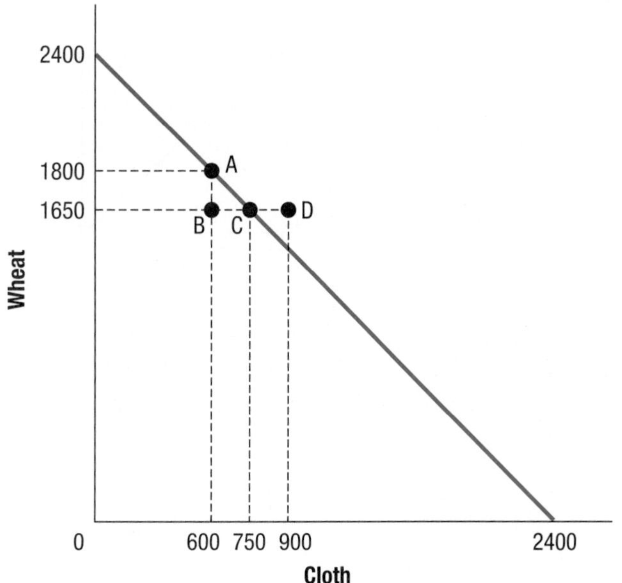

Suppose that without international trade, the United States produces and consumes 1,800 bushels of wheat and 600 yards of cloth (point A in Figure 17.2) and that the United Kingdom produces and consumes 50 bushels of wheat and 600 yards of cloth (point A in Figure 17.3). Now suppose that the United States offers to trade 150 bushels of wheat for 300 yards of cloth. Since these are the same exchange terms as above, they will be accepted by the United Kingdom.

After this trade takes place, the United States will move from point A to point D (Figure 17.2) and the United Kingdom will also move from point A to point D (Figure 17.3). To see why, it helps to refer to intermediate point B in both diagrams. The move from A to B in Figure 17.2 reflects the number of bushels of wheat that the U.S. exports to the United Kingdom, leaving it with 1,650 bushels of wheat and 600 yards of cloth *before the imports of cloth are recorded.* The move from A to B in Figure 17.3 reflects the number of yards of cloth that the United Kingdom exports to the United States, leaving it with 300 yards of cloth and 50 bushels of wheat *before the imports of wheat are recorded.*

In the United States, 300 yards of cloth are imported from the United Kingdom, moving it to 1,650 bushels of wheat and 900 yards of cloth at point D. In the United Kingdom 150 bushels of wheat are imported from the United States, leaving it with 300 yards of cloth and 200 bushels of wheat at point D. In the absence of trade, the United States could have consumed only 1,650 bushels of wheat and 750 yards of cloth (point C in Figure 17.2); that is, what it could have produced without trade. In the absence of trade, the United Kingdom could have consumed only 300 yards of cloth and 125 bushels of wheat (point C in Figure 17.3); that is, what it could have produced without trade. Trade enables both countries to consume more than they could produce domestically.

Figure 17.3 Trade with the United States Increases Consumption of Wheat in the United Kingdom

The United Kingdom initially produces combination A. It exports 300 yards of cloth to the United States, moving it to point B. It receives imports of 150 bushels of wheat, moving it to point D. At D, it has more wheat than it could produce itself by shifting domestic production from cloth to wheat (point C).

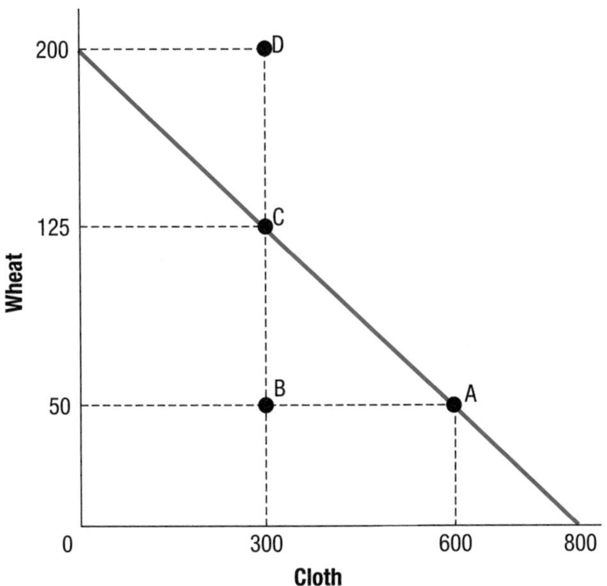

The additional consumption makes both countries better off. In this example and in general, international trade is advantageous. It allows countries to specialize in the production of goods in which they have a comparative advantage and exchange those goods for goods in which its trading partners have a comparative advantage. In this way, all countries that trade achieve higher levels of consumption than they could achieve by relying solely on their own resources.

NET WELFARE GAINS FROM FREE TRADE OF EXISTING PRODUCTS

But what about textile (cloth) producers and workers in textile firms? We know that the United States can produce cloth, so if textiles are imported, U.S. textile producers will suffer from losses in sales and some textile workers will lose their jobs. This is true, as far as it goes, but it is only part of the story. Textiles will not be imported in the real world unless U.S. consumers value them more highly relative to their price than domestically produced textiles. So, although textile imports create losses for workers and producers, they also create gains for consumers. It turns out, moreover, that gains to consumers exceed losses to workers and producers.

And what about wheat consumers? If wheat is exported, U.S. consumers of wheat, or of products incorporating wheat, will suffer from reduced availability of wheat. Again, this is true as far as it goes, but although exports create losses for consumers, they also create gains for workers and producers that exceed those losses.

We will demonstrate these results using supply and demand analysis and some of the measures related to that analysis that we have used previously (especially in Chapter 4). To simplify the analysis, we assume that both the cloth and wheat markets are highly competitive. We also assume that consumers are rational in the sense that they will buy products of comparable quality at the lowest price that they can pay, and that producers are rational in the sense that they will sell their products at the highest price that they can get.

Consumers' surplus– The difference between the price that consumers are willing to pay (their demand price) and the price that they must pay.

Producers' surplus– The difference between the price that producers receive and the price that they must receive (their supply price).

Net welfare gain– From imports: a gain in consumers' surplus that exceeds the loss in producers' surplus; from exports: a gain in producers' surplus that exceeds the loss in consumers' surplus.

Net Welfare Gains from Imports

Figure 17.4 shows the domestic market for cloth. In the absence of supplies from other countries, the market would clear at Q_b (the quantity before international trade) and P_b (the price before international trade). U.S. consumers will buy cloth from other countries, however, if some is available at a price less than P_b. Suppose that is the case; that there is an unlimited supply available at price P_a. Given the lower world price, U.S. consumers will buy Q_d from domestic producers, some of whom are more efficient than their rest-of-world counterparts. They will consume Q_c, however, importing $Q_c - Q_d$ from lower-cost producers outside the United States.

Before imported cloth is available, consumers reap net benefits in this market equal to the difference between what they are *willing to pay* for the cloth they buy, their demand price, and the price they *must* pay, P_b, summed over all the units they buy. Their net benefit, or **consumers' surplus**, is equal to area A. Before imported cloth is available, U.S. producers enjoy net benefits equal to the difference between the price they *receive*, P_b, and the price they *must receive* to cover costs, their supply price, summed over all units that they provide. Their net benefit, or **producers' surplus**, is equal to area B + C.

With the fall in price to P_a there is a gain in consumers' surplus of B + D + E and a loss in producers' surplus of B. The gain in consumers' surplus is larger than the loss in producers' surplus by the area D + E. Thus, area D + E represents the **net welfare gain** from trade for cloth.

Figure 17.4 The U.S. Market for Cloth, with Imports
With no imports, the market would clear at Q_b and P_b, producing net gains to consumers (consumers' surplus) equal to area A and net gains to producers (producers' surplus) equal to area B + C. With trade, the price will fall to P_a, and consumers will buy Q_a; Q_c from domestic producers and $Q_a - Q_c$ from the rest of the world. Trade will increase the net gains of consumers by the area B + D + E and reduce the net gains of producers by area B, leaving a net gain from trade of area D + E.

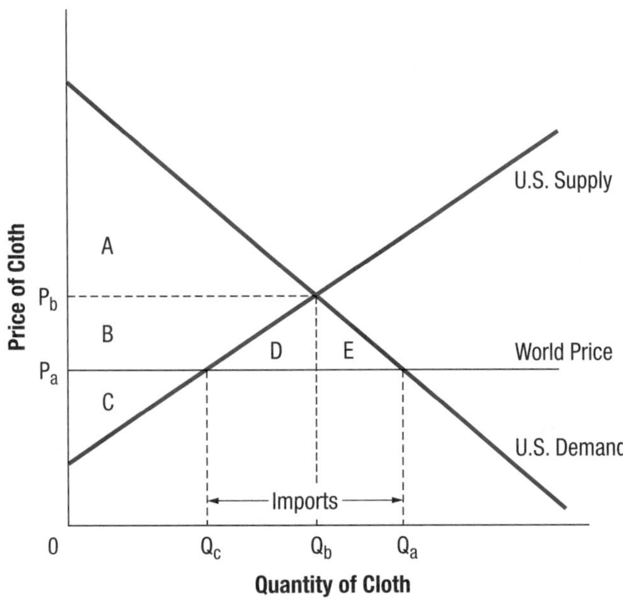

U.S. production will fall from Q_b to Q_c. Because of this, some U.S. workers will lose their jobs. There is a net loss to workers, however, only to the degree that they are unable to find alternative employment. Under normal conditions, an economy at or close to full employment, many of them may find other jobs and net losses to workers may be small.

Net Welfare Gains from Exports

Figure 17.5 shows the domestic market for wheat. In the absence of demand from the rest of the world, the market would clear at Q_b (the quantity before international trade) and P_b (the price before international trade). U.S. producers will export some of their harvest, however, if they can sell it for more on the world market. Suppose that buyers in the rest of the world are willing to pay P_a for unlimited quantities of wheat. This will raise the market price to P_a. At that price, U.S. producers will supply Q_a, U.S. consumers will buy Q_c at that price, and $Q_a - Q_c$ will be exported.

Keyword: *gains from trade*

Access InfoTrac at http://infotrac.cengage.com

Before the price increase, consumers' surplus is A + B + D. It is only area A after the price increase. Thus, U.S. consumers suffer losses equal to B + D. Before the price increase, producers' surplus is C + E. After the price increase producers' surplus is C + E + B + D + F. The loss in consumers' surplus, B + D, is offset by part of the gain in producers' surplus. There is net gain from international trade, however, equal to area F. The increase in U.S. production, $Q_a - Q_c$, also creates additional jobs in the export sector of the U.S. economy.

Figure 17.5 The U.S. Market for Wheat, with Exports
With no exports, the market would clear at Q_b and P_b, producing net gains to consumers (consumers' surplus) equal to area A + B + D and net gains to producers (producers' surplus) equal to area C + E. With trade, the price will increase to P_a, U.S. consumers will buy Q_c and U.K. consumers will buy $Q_a - Q_c$. Trade will reduce the net gains of consumers by the area B + D and increase the net gains of producers by area B + D + F, leaving a net gain from trade of area F.

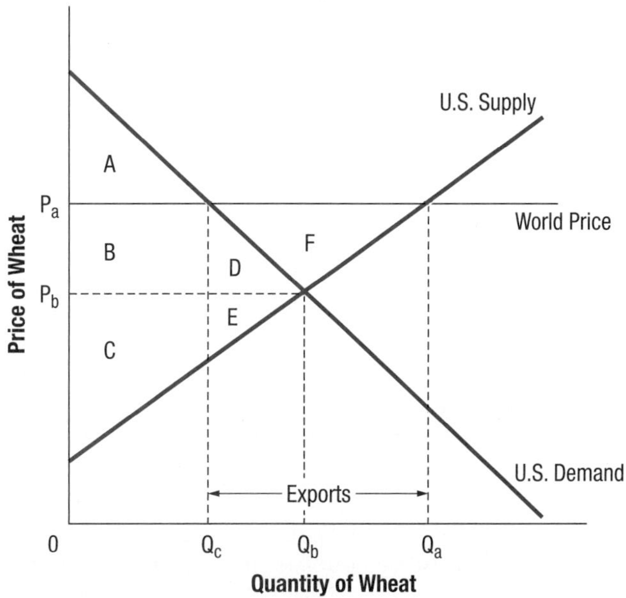

WELFARE GAINS FROM FREE TRADE OF NEW VARIETIES OF EXISTING PRODUCTS

The preceding examples illustrate that countries benefit from free trade by allowing consumers to take advantage of lower world prices and by allowing producers to take advantage of higher world prices. Countries also benefit from trade because trade provides consumers with access to a greater variety of goods than they would have in the absence of trade.

Elasticity of substitution between varieties of a good– The degree to which one variety of a good is substitutable for (just as good as) another variety of the good.

In this context, the gains from trade depend largely on three variables: the elasticity of substitution, product quality, and product importance. The **elasticity of substitution between varieties of a good** is a measure of the degree to which consumers consider varieties of the same type of good substitutable for one another. The higher the elasticity of substitution, the more consumers view one variety to be "as good as another." Thus, increased availability of varieties of a good with a high elasticity of substitution adds little to consumer welfare. Such is the case for goods like gasoline. Alternatively, the increased availability of varieties with a low elasticity of substitution, such as French and American wine or Japanese and American automobiles, can add greatly to consumer welfare.

Gains from trade are also realized from differences in quality across varieties. Consumers value access to varieties perceived to be of higher quality. For example, many Americans presumably value the opportunity to buy what they perceive to be Japanese automobiles of higher quality than American automobiles.

The gain from greater variety in available products depends on the degree of importance of a good in consumers' budgets. Consumers will place a higher value on increased availability of new varieties in products that command a larger share of their budgets. For example, greater variety in automobiles counts for more than greater variety in shoes.

Economists at the Federal Reserve Bank of New York have reported on estimated welfare gains from the greater variety of goods provided U.S. consumers through international trade over the last 30 years.[1] They find that increased variety in available goods has reduced import prices by 1.2 percentage points per year. This translates into a value to consumers of $260 billion in 2001, or about 3 percent of GDP. According to this estimate, U.S. consumers view increased variety in goods as an important benefit of international trade.

DECREASING COSTS

In some industries, the average cost of production falls as output increases. Large-scale production may, for example, facilitate more efficient use of machinery, resulting in decreasing average costs. Decreasing average costs can be passed along to consumers in the form of lower prices.

In the absence of international trade, an industry's market may be too small for firms to achieve the lowest possible average cost. With international trade, these firms may be able to increase production and sell the extra output abroad, resulting in lower average costs and prices. Domestic producers would realize welfare gains with no welfare losses to domestic consumers. If domestic demand for the traded product increases, domestic consumers would also realize welfare gains.

Although markets in the United States are typically large, international markets for U.S. products enable some industries to produce more, thus lowering average costs and prices. The commercial aircraft industry is an example. If that industry's sales were confined to the United States, the average cost and price of aircraft would be higher than they are today. The possibility of increasing output and selling the extra output abroad is important, even for a large country like the United States. It is even more important for smaller countries with limited domestic markets.

INCREASED COMPETITION

As discussed in Chapter 5, the lack of effective competition among firms results in higher prices and lower output. The same analysis applies to the lack of effective competition between domestic and foreign firms.

Domestically, a few firms may dominate an industry. A case in point is the U.S. automobile industry. For all practical purposes, the domestic auto industry consists of only three firms (General Motors, Ford, and Chrysler). If foreign competition did not exist, these firms would be able to restrict output and raise prices.

Domestic producers, however, are subject to considerable competition from foreign automobile manufacturers, especially firms from Japan and Western Europe. This competition forces domestic producers to charge lower prices. International trade in

[1] Christian Boda and David Weinstein, "Are We Underestimating the Gains from Globalization for the United States?" *Current Issues in Economics and Finance* 11, no. 4 (Federal Reserve Bank of New York, April 2005).

automobiles also provides consumers with some of the benefits of greater variety discussed above.

IF FREE TRADE IS SO BENEFICIAL, WHAT ABOUT...?

We observed at the beginning of this chapter that free trade is often criticized. So far, however, we have concentrated on the beneficial aspects of free international trade. Here we consider some of the primary sources of dissatisfaction with free trade.

U.S. Jobs Lost

As noted, imports reduce the level of output and employment in import-competing firms in the United States. Critics of free trade argue that this problem has gotten much worse as the level of imports has risen (see Figure 17.1). In fact, between 1983 and 2003, the number of jobs embodied in imports doubled, from 5.5 million to 11 million.[2] To some, this outsourcing, or offshoring, of American jobs is a sufficient reason to limit the volume of international trade.

One source of concern is that rising imports raise the *unemployment rate* by shifting jobs overseas. This concern is contrary to both economic theory and history. Macroeconomic forces, including monetary policy, ensure that over time employment losses attributable to imports are offset by employment gains elsewhere in the economy, so that the natural rate of unemployment prevails on average. Between 1980 and 2007, imports rose from about 10 percent of GDP to 17 percent (see Figure 17.1), yet the economy was at full employment in 2007 and private employment had grown by more than 34 million jobs over the same time period.

Some critics are unmoved by such averages and stress instead the difficulty that workers displaced by rising imports have in finding new jobs. One study indicated that only about two-thirds of workers displaced for any reason found another job within three years, and that earnings on new jobs were about 8 percent lower than earnings on previous jobs.[3] Another study found that displaced workers in industries facing heavy import competition had a more difficult time finding alternative jobs, and suffered greater earnings losses than displaced workers in industries facing less import competition.[4] A case can be made, then, for policies that promise to reduce the duration of unemployment and enhance the earnings potential of workers displaced by imports.

A third concern is that import competition shifts the employment mix from high-quality jobs to low-quality jobs. For example, some critics of free trade contend that it pushes workers out of manufacturing jobs and into less desirable service sector jobs. Such an effect would be consistent with the experience of displaced workers, but we are aware of no conclusive evidence on this point.

A balanced view of the effect of international trade on jobs would not focus exclusively on job losses, but would also recognize that international trade creates new

---

[2]Erica L. Groshen, Bart Hobijn, and Margaret M. McConnell, "U.S. Jobs Gained and Lost Through Trade: A Net Measure," *Current Issues in Economics and Finance* 11, no. 8 (Federal Reserve Bank of New York, August 2005).

[3]Henry Farber, "Job Loss in the United States, 1981–2001," Industrial Relations Section Working Paper 471 (Princeton: Princeton University Press, 2003).

[4]Lori G. Kletzer, *Job Loss from Imports: Measuring the Costs* (Washington, D.C.: Institute for International Economics, 2001).

Keyword: *outsourcing of American jobs*

Access InfoTrac at http://infotrac.cengage.com

jobs through increased exports. In fact, during the same period (1983–2003) when jobs embodied in imports grew by 5.5 million, jobs embodied in exports grew by about 3 million.[5] Thus, the net job loss over this period was only 2.6 million jobs, or about 130,000 per year. This was an average of less than 0.2 percent of all jobs in the U.S. economy.

Critics moved by the plight of displaced workers will probably dismiss this observation as irrelevant and argue that the relevant issue is that of doing something to ease the pain of those displaced for prolonged periods of time. As noted above, this may be a number close to one-third of the workers displaced by imports, or about 90,000 per year (one-third of the 5.5 million increase in jobs embodied in imports from 1983–2003, divided by 20). This is not a trivial number, but it is a manageable problem. The solution, however, is not to limit international trade by the imposition of devices like tariffs or quotas. The preferred choice is between fiscal and monetary policy or job training and relocation assistance, depending upon whether the unemployment at issue has the characteristics of cyclical unemployment (use monetary or fiscal policy) or structural unemployment (use job training and relocation assistance).

Cheap Foreign Labor

Some critics of foreign trade claim that the United States has a competitive disadvantage because wages are much higher in the United States than in foreign countries. Therefore, barriers to trade—such as tariffs or quotas—must be erected to protect those industries.

High wages do not necessarily imply high costs, however. Wages in the United States are high because labor productivity is high. (See the Appendix to Chapter 13, where we show that workers in competitive labor markets are paid according to their marginal product.) Workers in the United States are well trained and work with relatively large amounts of capital. It is not surprising, therefore, that they are very productive and earn high wages.

Given high productivity, high wages don't necessarily mean that the United States is a high-cost producer. To understand this, consider the following expression for average labor cost (AC), where W is the wage per worker, N is the number of workers, and Q is the quantity of output:

$$AC = (W \times N)/Q, \quad \text{or} \qquad (17.1)$$

$$AC = W \times (N/Q) \qquad (17.2)$$

Productivity– Quantity of output per unit of input.

The term (N/Q), number of workers per unit of output, is the inverse of (Q/N). (Q/N) is a conventional measure of **productivity**, or output per unit of labor input. Larger values of (Q/N) mean greater labor productivity. A larger value for (Q/N) is equivalent, then, to a smaller value for (N/Q), so a smaller value for (N/Q) means higher productivity. Inspection of (17.2) indicates that high wages do not necessarily mean a high value for AC; high wages can be offset by low values of (N/Q) or, what is the same thing, high productivity. In many real-world cases, higher U.S. productivity makes it possible for U.S. producers to compete successfully with foreign producers paying lower wages.

The other side of the "cheap foreign labor" coin is the charge that U.S. imports exploit foreign labor. Excluding coercion, foreign workers gain from exports to the United States just as U.S. workers gained from exporting wheat to the United Kingdom in the earlier example. (see Figure 17.5 and the attendant discussion).

---

[5]Groshen, Hobijn, and McConnell, "U.S. Jobs Gained and Lost."

National Defense

Some people argue that industries producing goods important to national security should be protected from international competition. They claim, for example, that industries producing steel, petroleum, scarce minerals, and military hardware are crucial for national defense and so should be protected. Proponents of this argument may recognize that protectionist measures raise the prices of these products. They believe, however, that the benefits of assured military preparedness outweigh the welfare losses associated with higher prices.

Even if we concede the validity of this argument, interfering with free trade in strategic and critical materials is not appropriate. If increased national security is a benefit, it is a benefit shared by society as a whole. Thus, the appropriate measure is to impose a general tax and then use the tax proceeds to buy and stockpile strategic and critical materials from other countries.

Infant Industries

Some people argue that new, or infant, industries should be protected from international competition while in their formative stages. They claim that such industries will eventually have a comparative advantage. Initially, however, they will be unable to compete with industries already established in other countries. According to this argument, protection would only be temporary. It would be eliminated as the industry becomes competitive in world markets.

Although this view may have some relevance for currently less-developed countries—and it had some relevance when the United States was relatively underdeveloped—it is not particularly relevant for the present-day U.S. economy. In the United States, mature industries (such as the steel and automobile industries) typically request protection. These industries often claim that they need time to modernize in order to become more competitive, and that protection will provide them that time. Once the modernization is complete, they claim, the protection can be removed.

Industries may use that time to modernize. On the other hand, protection reduces or eliminates the incentive to modernize. Indeed, experience suggests that little modernization occurs unless competition forces it. So, even if new industries need help in establishing themselves, protective measures such as tariffs and quotas are not the best means to that end. Economists agree that direct government subsidies would be a better approach. With subsidies, prices remain low to consumers. Subsidies also make it clear which industries are being helped and to what extent.

Trade Deficits

Trade deficit– A negative net balance in the international trade account; imports greater than exports.

It is fashionable among critics of foreign trade to point to the large and growing **trade deficit** (imports greater than exports) as evidence that free trade has gotten the country into trouble. As Figure 17.6 indicates, the United States *does* have a large and growing trade deficit. In fact, it reached an all-time high in 2006, both in absolute dollars and as a percent of GDP. Free trade per se has little to do, however, with the burgeoning trade deficit.

The recent trend in the trade deficit began in the last third of the 1990s as a result of a substantial acceleration in productivity growth in the United States. Rising productivity growth was reflected in rising rates of return from investing in the United States. Rising rates of return attracted foreign investment to the United States. Foreigners had to acquire U.S. dollars to buy American assets. This drove up the price of the dollar on the foreign exchange market (the dollar appreciated). The appreciation, or increased international purchasing power of the dollar, led to an increase in U.S. imports. As the dollar increased in value relative to other currencies, these currencies depreciated in value

Figure 17.6 U.S. Trade Deficit, 1980–2007
The U.S. trade deficit has grown almost steadily since 1998, reaching a record level over $757 billion (over 5.7 percent of GDP) in 2007.

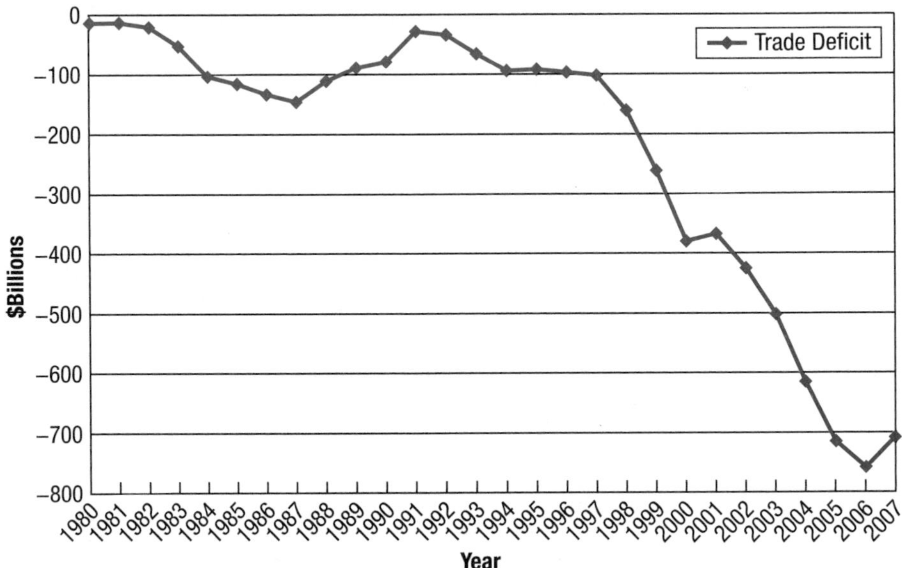

relative to the dollar. This made U.S. goods relatively more expensive, depressing demand for U.S. exports. The net result was an increasing trade deficit.

The investment boom stopped with the 2001 recession. Just as domestic investment was falling, however, the federal government began to run large budget deficits. This led to an increase in the supply of U.S. Treasury securities to finance these deficits. These securities were snapped up by foreign investors seeking a safe harbor for investment funds and by foreign central banks seeking to keep the dollar from depreciating. The result was continued upward pressure on the value of the dollar, downward pressure on the prices of imports, and upward pressure on the prices of exports.

The bottom line of this story is that the rising trade deficit was not caused by free trade, but by inadequate domestic saving. In the latter half of the 1990s, the private sector did not save enough to finance desired investment in the United States, leaving much of the task to foreign investors. More recently, the large decrease in U.S. government saving (a budget deficit constitutes negative saving by the government)—coupled with a continued decline in U.S. private saving—provided a fertile ground for both foreign private investors and foreign central banks. During both time periods, free trade had little, if anything, to do with the trade deficit.

TRADE POLICY

The principle of comparative advantage suggests that unrestricted, or free, international trade is beneficial to the economy. Our examination of the relative size of gains and losses from international trade in cloth and wheat indicates that unrestricted trade will generate positive net gains, whether a country is an importer or exporter. Free international trade also provides benefits from greater variety in available goods and services, lower costs from increased competition, and lower prices and larger output from reduced market power of domestic firms.

As noted, free trade also means job losses for some U.S. workers and impaired profits for some domestic firms. They do not suffer losses silently, and they do not hesitate to appeal to Congress for protection or relief from competition. Congress sometimes listens and enacts or assists the establishment of restraints on trade. When doing so, Congress reduces economic welfare and often provides protection at very high cost in terms of jobs or businesses saved. To illustrate this claim, we will consider the most frequently used methods of protection, namely tariffs, quotas, and voluntary export restraints.

Tariffs

Tariff–
A tax levied on a good when it crosses a nation's border.

A **tariff** is a tax levied on a good when it crosses a nation's borders. The United States has tariffs on many imported goods, including chemicals, softwood lumber, textiles, apparel, and footwear. Historically, the United States has had high tariffs. With the passage of the Smoot-Hawley Act in 1930, the average tariff on imported goods reached 60 percent. Since then, tariffs have been significantly reduced. Today, the average tariff on imports into the United States is only about 5 percent. Some goods, however, are still subject to higher tariffs.

Smaller tariffs mean smaller losses to the U.S. economy, but any tariff that effectively raises the price of imported goods to consumers is a source of net welfare losses. This point can be understood with the aid of Figure 17.7, which illustrates a tariff on cloth imports (this is Figure 17.4 modified to illustrate a tariff).

The market for cloth clears at price, P_b, and quantity, Q_b, before the tariff is imposed. After the tariff is imposed, the price rises to P_t and the quantity demanded falls to Q_t.

Figure 17.7 Net Welfare Loss from a Tariff
Imposition of a tariff on imports of cloth produces a loss in consumers' surplus of area B + D + E + F. Area B is offset by a gain in producers' surplus and area E (tariff revenue) is offset by government expenditure of tariff revenues, leaving a net welfare loss of area D + F.

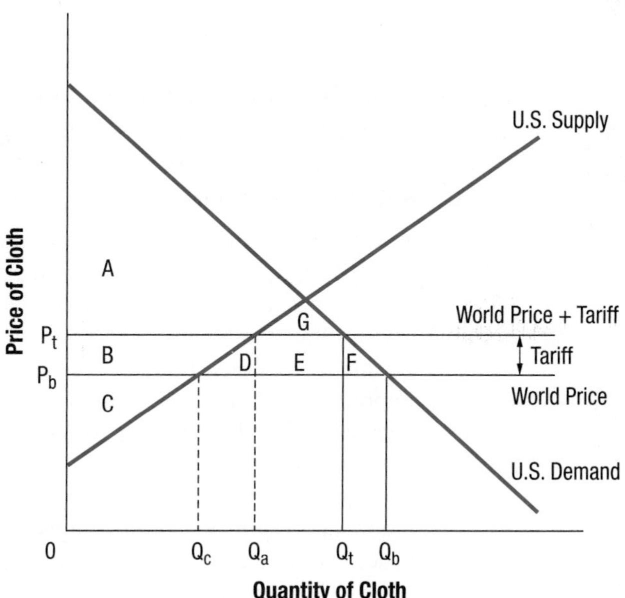

The quantity imported before the tariff is $Q_b - Q_c$ and the quantity imported after the tariff is $Q_t - Q_a$. Thus, the tariff increases the price to consumers, reduces the total quantity consumed, and reduces the total quantity imported.

Before the tariff, U.S. consumers enjoyed a consumers' surplus of A + B + D + E + F + G. After the tariff, consumers' surplus is only A + G. Thus, consumers lose B + D + E + F. Producers' surplus before the tariff is C; after the tariff it is C + B. Thus, producers gain B. So far it appears that there is a net loss to society of D + E + F—the difference between the loss of B + D + E + F to consumers and the gain of B to producers. Area E, however, represents the revenues that will be collected from imposing the tariff. Although this is a loss to consumers, it becomes a gain to other citizens when the government spends these revenues on public programs and projects. (This assumes, of course, that the benefits from this spending are at least as large as the costs of the programs and projects.) Thus, the net loss to society is D + F. In other words, society is worse off on two accounts. There is an uncompensated welfare loss to consumers (area F), resulting from a smaller quantity consumed. There is also an uncompensated loss to consumers (area D) who must pay the increased cost of producing $Q_a - Q_c$ from relatively inefficient domestic suppliers.

Quotas

Import quota– An upper limit on the amount of a good that may be imported during any time period.

An **import quota** specifies the maximum amount of a good that may be imported during some time period. Although tariffs are more common than quotas, the United States has set quotas for various goods, including steel, textiles, sugar, and beef.

By limiting the amount that can be imported, a quota—like a tariff—results in a higher price for the product. Indeed, the price may be higher with a quota than with a tariff. With a tariff, imports can increase in response to an increase in demand. With a quota, it is not possible to import more. The potential for importing more with a tariff than with a quota results in a lower price increase with a tariff for a given increase in demand (rightward shift in the demand curve). Thus, in a growing economy, the uncompensated losses to consumers from consuming a smaller quantity (area F in Figure 17.7) and from paying for the increased costs of producing additional quantities from relatively inefficient domestic producers (area D in Figure 17.7) are likely to be larger with a quota than with a tariff. Area E is also likely to be larger with a quota than with a tariff. In the case of a quota, however, this loss to consumers is offset by a gain to holders of import licenses, for whom area E reflects increased profits.

Voluntary export restraints (VERs)– Agreement whereby exporting nations limit the amounts of goods that they ship to importing nations.

Voluntary Export Restraints

Voluntary export restraints (VERs) are agreements whereby exporting nations agree to limit the quantities that they ship to importing nations. The United States negotiated a VER with Japan on automobiles in the early 1980s. Under this agreement, the Japanese "volunteered" to limit the number of automobiles that they would export to the United States. (As with most VERs, the Japanese agreed because they feared that even more stringent import restrictions might be imposed.) The United States has negotiated VERs on steel, machine tools, televisions, VCRs, and lumber with various countries, thus limiting U.S. imports of those products.

Keywords: *restraints on trade, tariffs, trade quotas*

Access InfoTrac at http://infotrac.cengage.com

VERs are more likely to be substitutes for quotas than for tariffs. Thus, the effects of VERs on economic welfare are similar to those of quotas. Like quotas, they shift resources from industries that have a comparative advantage to those that have a comparative disadvantage and reduce consumer welfare.

Trade Agreements

Trade policy is not necessarily welfare-reducing. In fact, since World War II, barriers to international trade have been reduced significantly by the adoption of trade agreements.

ADDITIONAL INSIGHT

If You Think That the Costs of Protection Are Small, Consider This

Saving jobs by imposing trade restrictions imposes high costs on U.S. consumers. Economists at the Federal Reserve Bank of Dallas have examined the cost to U.S. consumers of saving a job in various industries. The table below illustrates their findings for the 20 most costly industries. Annual cost per job saved ranges from $132,870 for costume jewelry to $1,376,435 for benzenoid chemicals (used in suntan lotion and other products). And that's not all. When protection raises prices in an industry there is a further series of price increases, as the higher prices are passed along to consumers of products that incorporate the protected commodities. For example, the protection of softwood lumber raises the price of new homes. Incorporation of these secondary effects raises the total cost of protection to nearly $100 billion dollars per year.

It would be much cheaper, in all the industries illustrated, to simply provide a subsidy equal to a significant portion of their previous wage to each displaced worker after some period of searching without success for another job.

The High Cost of Protection

Protected Industry	Jobs Saved	Total Cost ($ million)	Annual Cost per Job Saved
Benzenoid chemicals	216	$297	$1,376,435
Luggage	226	290	1,285,078
Softwood lumber	605	632	1,044,271
Sugar	2,261	1,868	826,104
Polyethylene resins	298	242	812,928
Dairy products	2,378	1,630	685,323
Frozen concentrated orange juice	609	387	635,103
Ball bearings	146	88	603,368
Maritime services	4,411	2,522	571,668
Ceramic tiles	347	191	551,367
Machine tools	1,556	746	479,452
Ceramic articles	418	140	335,876
Women's handbags	773	204	263,535
Canned tuna	390	100	257,640
Glassware	1,477	366	247,889
Apparel and textiles	168,786	33,629	199,241
Peanuts	397	74	187,223
Rubber footwear	1,701	286	168,312
Women's nonathletic footwear	3,702	518	139,800
Costume jewelry	1,067	142	132,870
Total	191,764	$44,352	
Average (weighted by jobs saved)			$231,289

Source: Federal Reserve Bank of Dallas, *Annual Report 2002*, p. 19.

In reducing trade barriers, countries have taken two approaches: (1) trade negotiations on a global basis; and (2) the formation of regional trading blocs.

General Agreement on Tariffs and Trade (GATT)– An international organization founded in 1947 to establish rules of conduct for international trade.

World Trade Organization (WTO)– Successor organization to GATT, founded in 1995.

Embargo– The prohibition of trade in a product.

GATT AND WTO. Since World War II, eight rounds of international trade negotiations have been conducted under the auspices of the **General Agreement on Tariffs and Trade (GATT)**, an international organization founded in 1947 to establish rules of conduct for international trade. Each of these rounds resulted in reductions in tariffs.

The Uruguay Round—so called because discussions were held in Punta del Este, Uruguay—was the eighth, and last, round of GATT negotiations. The negotiations were both long and difficult. They began in 1986, and agreement was not reached until December 1993.

The 1993 agreement was more comprehensive than past agreements. It covered trade in services as well as trade in goods. It also covered trade-related intellectual property rights (such as patents and copyrights) and trade-related investment. Finally, it created the **World Trade Organization (WTO)**, which monitors trade among the 148 countries that have now signed the agreement.

Under the agreement, many tariffs and nontariff barriers (quotas, VERs, and so forth) are to be reduced or eliminated. Although the agreement took effect on January 1, 1995, the reductions in trade barriers will require negotiations for many years. New agreements are hammered out at WTO Ministerial Conferences, held every two years. The fifth Ministerial Conference was held in Cancun, Mexico in September 2003. The sixth Ministerial Conference took place in Hong Kong in December 2005.

INTERNATIONAL PERSPECTIVE

The WTO: An International Conspiracy?

In 1995, the World Trade Organization (WTO) was formed as a successor to the General Agreement on Tariffs and Trade (GATT). Currently 148 nations, including the United States, belong to the WTO. Member nations account for most of the world's trade. Like GATT, the WTO provides a framework for multilateral trade negotiations, issues ground rules for the conduct of international trade, and helps resolve trade disputes.

With regard to international trade, the WTO has an important role. Even so, some people are critical of the WTO. In many cases, this criticism dates back to the GATT. Environmentalists were particularly upset with GATT's ruling regarding tuna imported from Mexico. In 1976, Congress passed and the president signed the Marine Mammal Protection Act. In part, the act outlawed the practice of catching tuna with large nets that also snared dolphins that were feeding on the tuna. (Most of the dolphins failed to escape from the nets and died.) U.S. fishing fleets had to abide by the law; foreign fleets did not. Subsequently, the United States imposed an **embargo** (a prohibition on trade in a product) on tuna caught by foreign fishing fleets that did not follow the U.S. practice.

Mexico protested the embargo, and in 1991 GATT ruled against the United States. Under GATT rules, it is the *product* (in this case, tuna) that is relevant, not the *process* by which it is produced. (Under GATT rules, the only time that the process becomes relevant is when the good is produced by prison labor.) Mexico also protested on other grounds, noting, for example, that dolphins are not an endangered species.

In 1998, environmentalists were again upset when the WTO ruled against U.S. restrictions on imports of shrimp caught in nets without adequate means to exclude sea turtles, an endangered species. The WTO conceded that measures to protect endangered species were consistent with WTO rules, but ruled that the U.S. approach was implemented in a discriminatory and arbitrary fashion.

Although the WTO has disappointed environmentalists and other groups in the United States from time to time, no evidence indicates an international conspiracy against the United States. The WTO has ruled in favor of the United States in various disputes, including several with the European Union. The WTO, for the most part, continues to perform the same functions as GATT, including provision of a framework for trade negotiations and resolution of trade disputes. In resolving disputes, it is rarely possible to please everyone.

Keywords: *GATT, World Trade Organization*

Access InfoTrac at http://infotrac.cengage.com

North American Free Trade Agreement (NAFTA)– An agreement by the United States, Canada, and Mexico to eliminate trade barriers among the three countries.

Rather than relying entirely on the global approach to trade agreements, many countries have formed regional trading blocs. That is, they have agreed to reduce or eliminate trade barriers among themselves while maintaining barriers against countries outside the bloc.

The North American Free Trade Area. In 1988, the United States and Canada ratified an agreement to gradually eliminate trade barriers between the two countries beginning January 1, 1989. Following the agreement between the United States and Canada, the two countries began talks with Mexico regarding the formation of a free trade area to include Mexico. President George H. W. Bush announced in August 1992 that the leaders of the three nations had reached an agreement—the **North American Free Trade Agreement (NAFTA)**. The agreement was later approved by Congress and the other countries' legislative bodies and took effect January 1, 1994. At its inception, the free trade area encompassed 362 million people and had a combined GDP that was 25 percent greater than that of the European Union.

The agreement called for the elimination of tariffs over a 15-year period, although many tariffs were scheduled to be eliminated much sooner than that. It also called for the elimination of quotas and other trade barriers. While eliminating trade barriers within the free trade area, each country was to remain free to maintain trade barriers against nonmember countries. Finally, the agreement called for opening investment opportunities within each country to member countries.

ADDITIONAL INSIGHT

Trade Negotiations, Labor, and the Environment

Multilateral trade negotiations are complex and time-consuming. It takes years or even decades to reach an agreement to reduce tariffs and other trade barriers. In the future, these negotiations promise to become even more complex as some parties attempt to link the negotiations to labor and environmental standards.

Individuals favoring a linkage argue that many countries—particularly those that are less developed—have labor and environmental standards less stringent than those in the United States. To them, trade agreements offer an opportunity to raise those standards. True, working conditions are worse in most countries than in the United States. In those countries, the workplace is often unpleasant and unsafe, the workweek is long, wages are low, and retirement and fringe benefits are minimal or nonexistent. However, many of these countries are at the same stage of development now as the United States was 100 years ago. To impose the United States' current labor standards on those countries, even if it were possible, could have a devastating effect on their development. Raising the cost of employing workers would reduce employment, causing further impoverishment or even starvation. Indeed, policy makers in less-developed countries overwhelmingly believe that linking trade negotiations to labor standards serves only to keep their citizens among the downtrodden.

With regard to environmental standards, some individuals claim that without safeguards, policy makers will allow environmental standards in their countries to deteriorate in order to entice multinational corporations to locate plants there. The evidence, however, is that many of these corporations use environment-friendly technologies. In addition, evidence indicates that as a country's income per capita rises, more of its resources go to reducing pollution. This has been the case in the United States and elsewhere. Because lowering barriers to international trade helps countries develop, emphasis should be placed on reducing those barriers.

Finally, to the extent that labor and environmental standards diverge among countries in an unsatisfactory manner, international institutions already exist that monitor and advocate higher standards. These include the International Labor Organization and the United Nations Environmental Protection Agency. Rather than linking trade negotiations to labor and environmental standards, it may be better to rely on the expertise of these organizations.

European Union (EU)– An agreement by nations in Europe to eliminate trade barriers among member countries.

Keywords: *NAFTA, EU*

Access InfoTrac at http://infotrac.cengage.com

Trade adjustment assistance– Assistance provided by the federal government to workers displaced and businesses harmed by free trade.

Keywords: *trade adjustment assistance for workers, trade adjustment assistance for firms, trade adjustment assistance for farmers and fishermen*

Access InfoTrac at http://infotrac.cengage.com

THE EUROPEAN UNION. The **European Union (EU)** is another important trading bloc. It was founded in 1957 with six members: Belgium, France, Italy, Luxembourg, the Netherlands, and West Germany. Nine other countries—Austria, Denmark, Finland, Greece, Ireland, Portugal, Spain, Sweden, and the United Kingdom—joined later. The EU has eliminated most trade barriers between member countries. As a result, trade within the EU has increased tremendously. The EU, however, still maintains trade barriers against nonmember nations.

Trade Adjustment Assistance

Rather than give up the benefits of free trade, proponents of free trade often argue for more compensation for the losers from free trade. The Trade Act of 1974 created a program of **trade adjustment assistance** (TAA) to provide reemployment services and benefits to workers who lose their jobs or whose hours of work and wages are reduced as a result of increased imports. TAA offers a variety of benefits and reemployment services to assist unemployed workers to prepare for and obtain suitable employment. Workers may be eligible for training, job search and relocation allowances, income support, and other reemployment services.

The Trade Act of 1974 also provides for financial assistance to manufacturers adversely affected by import competition. This cost-sharing federal assistance program pays for half the cost of consultants or industry-specific experts for projects that improve a manufacturer's competitiveness. Twelve Trade Adjustment Assistance Centers (TAACs) have been established under the auspices of the Trade Act, which cover the 50 states and the District of Columbia. The TAACs sign cooperative agreements with business firms whereby they agree to help them achieve international quality certifications and otherwise provide them with trade adjustment assistance. Assistance is provided in market research, quality assurance, management information systems, and in developing new manufacturing machines and procedures, new technologies, new exporting opportunities, and product diversification.

Finally, amendments to the 1974 Trade Act in 2002 extended TAA benefits to farmers and fishermen who experience significant price declines as a result of increased imports.

Economists generally endorse the principle of trade adjustment assistance on the grounds that, because the welfare gains from trade exceed the welfare losses from trade, the losers could be compensated for their losses out of the gains that are realized, and society could still reap a net gain. Whether the kind or scope of assistance provided by the current version of trade adjustment assistance is consistent with this principle is a matter beyond the scope of this brief examination.

Summary

U.S. participation in world trade has been increasing, as measured by imports as a share of GDP. The foreign trade sector is large enough to have a significant, but controversial, impact on the economy.

Trade among nations is based on the principle of comparative advantage, whereby countries produce and export goods and services in which they have a comparative advantage and import goods and services in which they have a comparative disadvantage. A country has a comparative advantage in goods and services for which its opportunity cost is lower than that of its trading partners. Trade based on the principle of comparative advantage makes all trading partners better off.

Not everyone gains from international trade. In the case of imports, domestic consumers reap welfare gains, and domestic producers and workers suffer welfare losses. The gains to consumers outweigh the losses to producers and workers, however. In the case of exports, domestic consumers suffer welfare losses, but domestic producers and workers reap welfare gains. Here, too, the gains exceed the losses.

Free international trade also provides welfare gains to consumers by providing them with a wider variety of goods and services from which to choose; lower costs of production and prices induced by the threat of foreign competition; and lower prices and greater output by reducing market power in domestic markets otherwise supplied by a few dominant firms.

Although free trade confers significant benefits to U.S. consumers and producers, it is a source of concern and controversy. Critics emphasize jobs lost through imports but often do not acknowledge the jobs gained through exports. In any event, annual net losses are small enough that they could be managed through monetary and fiscal policy or job training and relocation assistance.

Critics also express concern about the use of cheap foreign labor to produce U.S. imports. Exports from other countries confer the same gains to foreign workers, however, as those conferred on U.S. workers by U.S. exports. Other countries may be able to offer their goods in the U.S. market at relatively low prices because their wage rates are lower than wage rates in the U.S. Lower wage rates do not necessarily translate into lower costs per unit and lower prices, however. This depends on the relationship between wage rates and labor productivity.

Some critics argue that allowing free trade in strategic and critical materials may impair U.S. national defense capabilities. This may be true, but using the tax system to acquire the resources to purchase and stockpile these materials makes more sense than restraining free trade.

A case can be made for protecting infant industries from foreign competition in their early stages of development. The number of such cases is probably much larger in a developing country, however, than in a mature economy like that of the United States. Here, the protection afforded specific industries has often resulted in a failure of those industries to become more competitive on their own in international markets.

Perhaps the number one criticism of free trade currently is that it has led to record trade deficits in the United States. The trade deficits of the last decade, however, cannot be attributed to free trade; rather, they are due to a falling rate of private saving and rising negative savings (rising budget deficits) by the federal government.

Most countries—including the United States—restrict trade in various ways. Among other measures, they impose tariffs, quotas, and voluntary export restraints.

These protectionist measures raise domestic prices by restricting imports. As a result, consumers are worse off. Domestic producers, however, receive higher prices and are better off. Society as a whole is worse off, however, because the losses to consumers are greater than the gains to producers. In a growing economy, quotas are likely to impose greater net welfare losses than tariffs.

Since World War II, countries have significantly reduced barriers to international trade. In reducing these barriers, countries have followed both global and regional approaches.

Finally, trade adjustment assistance is available in the United States for workers, business firms, farmers, and fishermen. Such assistance may be viewed as just compensation from the welfare gains from free trade.

Key Terms

Comparative advantage
Comparative disadvantage
Absolute advantage
Absolute disadvantage
Consumers' surplus
Producers' surplus
Net welfare gain
Elasticity of substitution between varieties of a good
Productivity
Trade deficit
Tariff
Import quota
Voluntary export restraints (VERs)
General Agreement on Tariffs and Trade (GATT)
World Trade Organization (WTO)
Embargo
North American Free Trade Agreement (NAFTA)
European Union (EU)
Trade adjustment assistance

Review Questions

1. Describe the relationship between U.S. exports and imports since 1980. How important is international trade to the U.S. economy?
2. Distinguish between absolute advantage and comparative advantage.

3. Suppose that a worker in the United States is able to produce more beef and more steel than a worker in Japan. Does this mean that Japan will be unable to trade with the United States? Defend your answer.
4. Use the information in this table to answer parts a, b, and c.

Country	Car Production per Day	Wine Production per Day
United States	6	2
France	1	1

   a. Which country has the absolute advantage in cars? In wine? Explain.
   b. Which country has the comparative advantage in cars? In wine? Explain.
   c. Is there a basis for trade between the two countries? Explain in detail why or why not.
5. The United Kingdom can produce 8 loaves of bread and zero quarts of milk, or zero loaves of bread and 32 quarts of milk, or any linear combination of bread and milk between these two combinations. The United States can produce 24 loaves of bread and zero quarts of milk, or zero loaves of bread and 48 quarts of milk, or any linear combination of bread and milk between these two combinations. Suppose that each country specializes in the product in which it has a comparative advantage (that is, produces only that product) and trades some of that product for the one in which it has a comparative disadvantage. Illustrate a trade that will make consumers in both countries better off.
6. International trade affects consumers, producers, and workers. Illustrate and explain why economists normally conclude that free international trade is a good thing for society, on balance, referring to the effects of international trade on each of these parties.
7. "If we allow free trade in the automobile industry, some automobile workers will lose their jobs. This unemployment will make society worse off." What advantages of free trade does this argument overlook? How might the unemployment be alleviated at lower cost than the cost imposed by a tariff?
8. Use the example illustrated in Figure 17.5 to explain why free trade is unlikely to result in the exploitation of cheap foreign labor.
9. Suppose that wages in the United States and Mexico are $20 per hour and $5 per hour, respectively, and that labor productivity in the United States and Mexico are 10 units per hour and 2 units per hour, respectively. Which country has the lower average cost? Show the calculations you used to get your answer.
10. What should the United States do to ensure the availability of strategic materials in which it has a comparative disadvantage? Why?
11. What is the infant-industry argument? Is it likely to be valid for a mature economy like that of the United States? If it is valid, what would be a better solution than imposing trade restrictions?
12. Free trade does not create trade deficits; they can be attributed to inadequate U.S. savings. Explain.
13. How is each of the following affected by a tariff? Illustrate the effects and show that the losses to consumers exceed the gains to producers.
   a. consumers
   b. domestic producers
14. It may be cheaper to pay a worker displaced by imports his or her salary than to impose a tariff or quota on imported goods in order to save his or her job. Explain, using examples.
15. Despite the fact that society is generally better off with free trade, governments often impose trade barriers. Why might a government take such action?
16. Compare and contrast the global and regional approaches to reducing barriers to international trade.
17. What is the World Trade Organization (WTO)? Why are environmentalists disappointed in the WTO?
18. Trade negotiations are complex and lengthy. Explain why they may be even more complex and time-consuming in the future.
19. What is trade adjustment assistance? Why do economists favor such assistance in principle?

CHAPTER 18

Financing Trade and the Trade Deficit

OUTLINE

In the previous chapter, we focused on trade in the global economy. In modern economies, trade involves transactions of goods and services in exchange for money. Sellers ultimately want to be paid in their own currency. (In some cases, foreign sellers will gladly accept U.S. dollars, but this is not the case for most of the trade that takes place.) So U.S. buyers must first exchange U.S. dollars for the currency of the seller's country and then exchange that currency for the goods and services they want to buy. They do this in the market for foreign currency. In this chapter, we initially examine how the foreign currency market works to determine the price that citizens of one country have to pay for the currency of another.

In the previous chapter, we examined the chronic and growing U.S. trade deficit. Here we show how the trade deficit is financed by an inflow of capital from other countries, as reflected in the balance of payments. We also examine how its chronic trade deficit has made the United States the world's largest debtor nation and explore what this might mean for the U.S. economy.

Finally, where we examined tariffs and quotas in the previous chapter as means of reducing the trade deficit, in this chapter we ask if it makes much sense to reduce the trade deficit by government regulation of exchange rates or capital flows.

PRICING THE MEDIUM OF EXCHANGE: CURRENCY MARKETS

In international trade, the sellers of goods and services ultimately want payment in their own currency. So buyers must first exchange their country's currency for the currency of the seller's country. Buyers do that in the currency market that supplies the seller's currency. Next, buyers exchange that currency for the goods and services they want to buy.

The market forces will determine the *price* of a currency; the amount of one currency that must be given up to get a unit of another currency. The price established in a currency market is called the **exchange rate.** So an exchange rate is the number of units of one currency required in exchange for a unit of another currency. If 100 Japanese yen are required in exchange for a dollar, the exchange rate is 100 yen per dollar. Similarly, if 10 Mexican pesos are required in exchange for a dollar, the exchange rate is 10 pesos per dollar. If 100 yen exchange for a dollar and 10 pesos for a dollar, the exchange rate between the Japanese and Mexican currencies is 100 yen for 10 pesos, or 10 yen per peso.

Exchange rate– The number of units of one currency required in exchange for one unit of another.

Exchange rates are important; they help determine the cost of internationally traded goods, services, and assets. Suppose you are going to Mexico for spring break vacation. If the vacation costs 6,000 Mexican pesos and the exchange rate is 10 Mexican pesos per

American dollar, you will pay 600 American dollars. If the exchange rate is only 9 Mexican pesos per American dollar, the same vacation will cost you about 667 American dollars. Thus, seemingly small changes in exchange rates can significantly alter the cost of foreign goods and services.

Exchange rates are determined in two general types of currency markets: flexible-rate currency markets and fixed-rate currency markets.

Flexible-Rate Currency Market

Flexible-rate currency market– A market in which exchange rates are determined by the demand for and supply of currency.

In a **flexible-rate currency market**, exchange rates are determined by the demand for and supply of currency. To illustrate, consider two countries, the United States and Japan. The Japanese have a demand for dollars in terms of their price in yen, as shown in Figure 18.1. The demand for dollars is based on the demand by Japanese consumers, business firms, and governments for goods and services produced in the United States, and for U.S. assets, such as stocks, bonds, and real property. As the exchange rate (the number of yen necessary to purchase one dollar) rises, the quantity of dollars demanded decreases (like all demand curves). If the exchange rate in Figure 18.1 increased from 100 yen per dollar to 110 yen per dollar, the quantity of dollars demanded would decrease from $180 billion to $160 billion.

The supply of dollars is based on American demand for Japanese goods and services and Japanese assets. As the exchange rate rises, the quantity of dollars supplied increases (like all supply curves). If the exchange rate increased in Figure 18.1 from 100 yen per dollar to 110 yen, the quantity of dollars supplied would increase from $180 billion to $200 billion.

In Figure 18.1, the equilibrium exchange rate is 100 yen per dollar. At that exchange rate, the quantity of dollars demanded by the Japanese, $180 billion, equals the quantity of dollars supplied to them, also $180 billion. Because the quantity demanded equals the quantity supplied, no tendency exists for the exchange rate to change. Suppose, however, that the exchange rate was temporarily at 110 yen per dollar. At that exchange rate, the

Figure 18.1 Flexible-Rate Currency Market
In a flexible-rate currency market, exchange rates are determined by demand and supply. In this figure, the equilibrium exchange rate—given by the intersection of the demand and supply curves—is 100 yen per dollar.

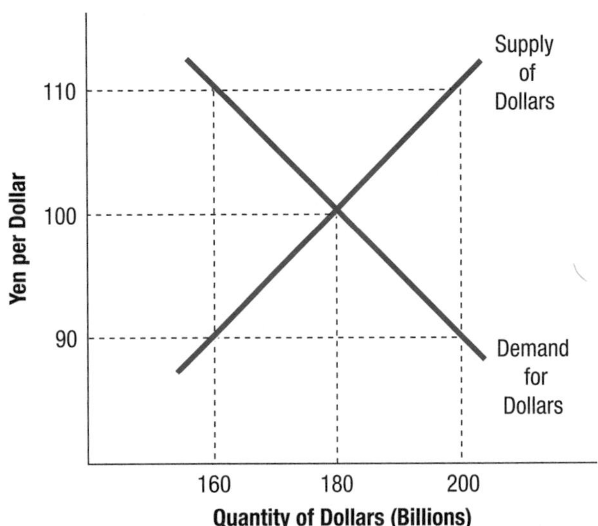

quantity of dollars demanded is only $160 billion and the quantity supplied is $200 billion. Given the excess supply of dollars, the exchange rate would fall. As the exchange rate fell, U.S. goods, services, and assets would become less expensive to the Japanese. If the exchange rate were 110 yen per dollar, 110 yen would buy a dollar's worth of U.S. goods. If the exchange rate fell to 100 yen per dollar, the same goods would cost only 100 yen. Because U.S. goods, services, and assets would be cheaper to the Japanese, they would increase the quantity of dollars demanded with a view to buying more American goods.

Just as the quantity of dollars demanded by the Japanese increases as the exchange rate falls, the quantity of dollars supplied to them decreases. As the exchange rate falls, Japanese goods, services, and assets become more expensive to Americans. If the exchange rate is 110 yen per dollar, a dollar will buy 110 yen worth of Japanese goods. If the exchange rate fell to 100 yen per dollar, a dollar would buy only 100 yen worth of Japanese goods. Because Japanese goods, services, and assets would become more expensive to Americans, they would buy less of them and the quantity of dollars supplied to the Japanese would decrease.

As long as the quantity of dollars supplied exceeds the quantity of dollars demanded, the yen–dollar exchange rate will fall. In Figure 18.1, it will fall to 100 yen per dollar. At that rate, the quantity supplied equals the quantity demanded, and the exchange rate is in equilibrium.

Suppose the exchange rate were 90 yen to the dollar. At that price, the quantity of dollars demanded would be $200 billion and the quantity supplied would be only $160 billion. Given the excess demand for dollars, the exchange rate would rise. As the exchange rate increased, U.S. goods, services, and assets would become more expensive to the Japanese. Therefore, they would have an incentive to buy fewer of them and the quantity of dollars demanded by the Japanese would decrease. At the same time, the quantity of dollars supplied to the Japanese would increase. As the exchange rate increased, Japanese goods, services, and assets would become less expensive to Americans. If they were less expensive, Americans would buy more of them, thereby increasing the quantity of dollars supplied.

When the yen–dollar exchange rate falls in a flexible-rate currency market, the yen will **appreciate** in value because it now takes fewer yen to purchase a dollar. The dollar, on the other hand, will **depreciate** because it now takes more dollars to buy the same quantity of yen. When the yen–dollar exchange rate rises in a flexible-rate currency market, the yen depreciates because it takes more yen to purchase a dollar. The dollar appreciates because it takes fewer dollars to buy the same quantity of yen.

Appreciation–
A rise in the value of one currency relative to another *in a flexible-rate currency market.*

Depreciation–
A fall in the value of one currency relative to another *in a flexible-rate currency market.*

The Impact of an Increase in U.S. Output. As noted, in a flexible-rate currency market, the yen–dollar exchange rate is determined by Japanese demand for dollars and the supply of dollars to them. The exchange rate, therefore, will change if either the demand for or supply of dollars changes. Suppose GDP in the United States rises while GDP in Japan remains constant. As U.S. GDP rises, domestic households and firms buy more from abroad. Consequently, the United States will import more from Japan, causing the supply of dollars to the Japanese to increase.

In Figure 18.2, the initial dollar demand and supply curves are D_0 and S_0, respectively. The exchange rate, therefore, is e_0. If U.S. households and firms buy more Japanese goods and services, the supply of dollars to the Japanese increases to S_1. With the increase in the supply of dollars, the yen–dollar exchange rate would fall to e_1. Because it now takes more dollars to buy the same quantity of yen, the dollar would depreciate. The yen, in turn, would appreciate.

The Impact of an Increase in U.S. Interest Rates. Suppose that interest rates rise in the United States relative to interest rates in Japan. This would provide an

Figure 18.2 Effect of an Increase in Real GDP on the Exchange Rate
An increase in real GDP causes the United States to import more from Japan. As a result, the supply of dollars to Japan increases. The shift in the supply curve from S_0 to S_1 causes the exchange rate to fall from e_0 to e_1, and the dollar to depreciate.

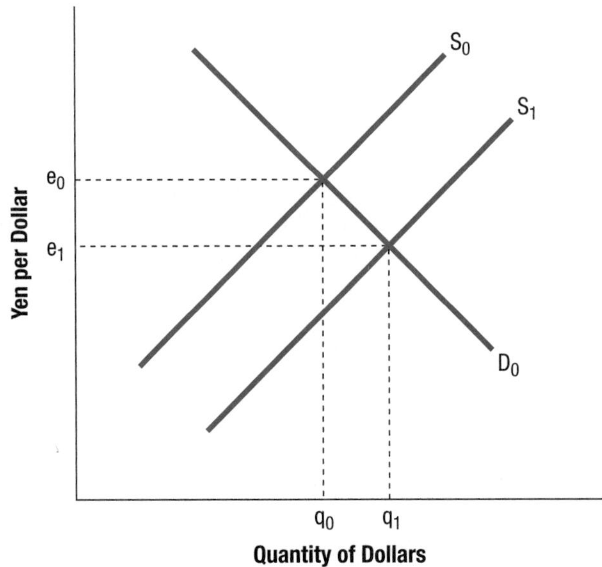

incentive for the Japanese to buy U.S. Treasury securities and other dollar-denominated assets. Therefore, the Japanese demand for dollars would increase. Similarly, with interest rates relatively higher in the United States, Americans have less incentive to buy yen-denominated assets. Therefore, the supply of dollars to the Japanese would decrease.

In Figure 18.3, the initial demand and supply curves are D_0 and S_0, respectively; the exchange rate, therefore, is e_0. With the increase in the demand for dollars and the decrease in supply, the new demand and supply curves would be D_1 and S_1, respectively. As a result, the new exchange rate would be e_1. With the rise in the exchange rate, the yen would depreciate and the dollar would appreciate.

If the yen depreciated, U.S. goods and services would be more expensive to the Japanese, whereas Japanese goods and services would be cheaper to Americans. As a result, the United States would export less to Japan and import more from Japan. Output and employment, therefore, would fall in both the U.S. export and import-competing sectors.

In 1981 and 1982, interest rates in the United States increased relative to those in most of the world's major trading nations, as a result of expansionary fiscal policies and contractionary monetary policies pursued by the United States. With higher interest rates, the dollar appreciated against most major currencies. The appreciation depressed U.S. exports and stimulated U.S. imports, resulting in large current account deficits in the early and mid-1980s, and a downturn in the export and import-competing sectors of the economy.

Fixed-rate currency market–
A market in which central banks intervene to keep exchange rates constant.

Fixed-Rate Currency Markets

In a flexible-rate currency market, exchange rates are determined by the demand for and supply of currencies. If demand or supply changes, then exchange rates will also change. In a **fixed-rate currency market,** this will not occur. In such a market, central banks will intervene to keep exchange rates constant.

Figure 18.3 Effect of a Higher Interest Rate on the Exchange Rate
If interest rates in the United States rose relative to those in Japan, the Japanese would invest more heavily in the United States and Americans would invest less heavily in Japan. Consequently, the Japanese demand for dollars would increase and the supply of dollars to Japan would decrease. The shifts in the demand and supply curves to D_1 and S_1, respectively, would cause the exchange rate to rise from e_0 to e_1 and the dollar to appreciate.

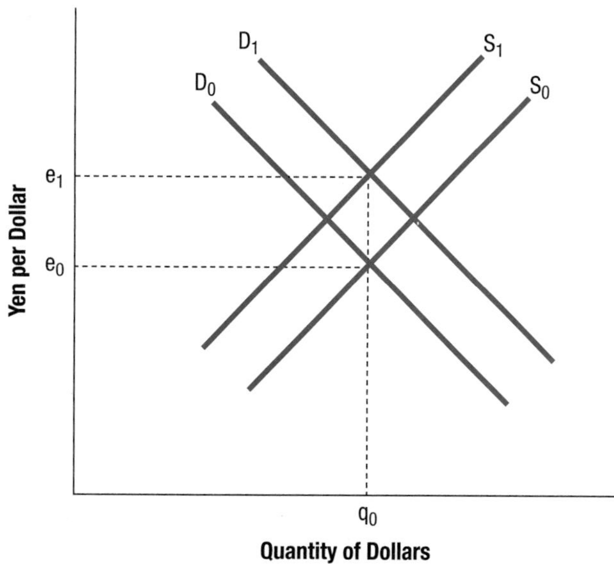

In Figure 18.4, we illustrate a fixed-rate currency market. Suppose that the U.S. government wants to maintain the exchange rate at 110 yen per dollar when the equilibrium exchange rate is 100 yen per dollar. At 110 yen per dollar there is an excess supply of dollars. Thus, the exchange rate would tend to fall. The Federal Reserve would have to intervene to keep it from falling. To keep the exchange rate at 110 yen per dollar, the Federal Reserve would have to buy, or increase the demand for, dollars. In this case, it would have to use 4.4 trillion Japanese yen to buy $40 billion in foreign exchange markets.

Devaluation–
A fall in the value of one currency relative to another *in a fixed-rate currency market.*

Balance of payments deficit–
The amount by which the home country's purchases of foreign goods, services, and assets exceed the rest of the world's purchases from it *at a given exchange rate.*

A supply of dollars greater than the demand for dollars indicates that U.S. consumers and investors want to supply more dollars to buy Japanese goods, services, and assets than Japanese consumers and investors want to acquire to buy U.S. goods, services, and assets. If this situation persisted, the Federal Reserve would eventually exhaust its holdings of yen. At that point, it would probably allow the exchange rate to fall, and a **devaluation** of the dollar would occur. This would reduce the price of U.S. goods, services, and assets to Japanese buyers and increase the price of Japanese goods, services, and assets to U.S. buyers. U.S. exports of goods and services to Japan would increase relative to U.S. imports of Japanese goods and services. Japanese investment in the United States would also increase relative to U.S. investment in Japan. Eventually, the **balance of payments deficit** would disappear.

Suppose, alternatively, that the desired exchange rate is 90 yen per dollar and that the U.S. government is committed to keeping it at that level. If the equilibrium exchange rate were 100 yen per dollar, there would be an excess demand for dollars. The exchange rate would tend to rise and the Federal Reserve would have to intervene to keep it from rising. To keep the exchange rate at 90 yen per dollar, the Federal Reserve would have to sell, or increase the supply of, dollars. In this case, it would have to supply $40 billion to buy $3.6 trillion yen in foreign exchange markets.

Figure 18.4 **Fixed Exchange Rates**
In a fixed-rate currency market, central banks buy and sell foreign currencies to keep exchange rates constant. If the exchange rate were 110 yen per dollar, the Federal Reserve would have to use its holdings of yen to buy dollars to keep the dollar from depreciating. If the exchange rate were 90 yen per dollar, it would have to use its holdings of dollars to buy yen to keep the dollar from appreciating.

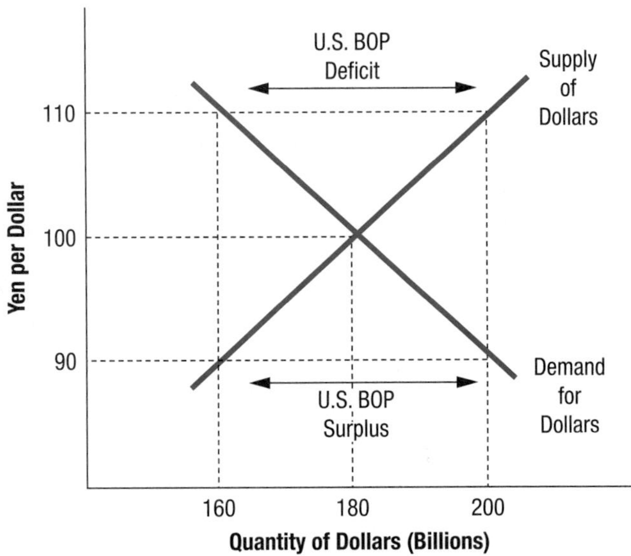

A demand for dollars greater than the supply of dollars would indicate that Japanese consumers and investors want to supply more yen to buy U.S. goods, services, and assets than U.S. consumers and investors want to acquire in order to buy Japanese goods, services, and assets. If this situation persisted, the Federal Reserve would have to continue to buy yen. While the Federal Reserve can use dollars to buy yen more or less indefinitely, it may become reluctant to do so because that action also increases the money supply. Alternatively, the Japanese may become reluctant to accumulate more dollars. At that point, the Federal Reserve would probably allow the exchange rate to rise and a **revaluation** of the dollar would occur. This would increase the price of U.S. goods, services, and assets to Japanese buyers and reduce the price of Japanese goods, services, and assets to U.S. buyers. U.S. imports of goods and services from Japan would increase relative to U.S. exports of goods and services to Japan. U.S. investment in Japan would also increase relative to Japanese investment in the United States. Eventually, the **balance of payments surplus** would disappear.

Revaluation–
A rise in the value of one currency relative to another *in a fixed-rate currency market.*

Balance of payments surplus–
The amount by which the rest of the world's purchases of the home country's goods, services, and assets exceed its purchases from the rest of the world *at a given exchange rate.*

FINANCING THE TRADE DEFICIT

For the last three decades, U.S. net exports (NX) have been negative; that is, exports of goods and services have been less than imports of goods and services. Thus, the flow of dollars out of the United States to purchase foreign goods and services exceeds the flow of dollars into the United States to purchase domestic goods and services. The excess outflow is exactly offset by a capital inflow. Part of this capital inflow consists of dollars spent by foreigners to invest in financial assets, such as U.S. stocks and bonds. Another part consists of dollars spent by foreigners to acquire real property. The remainder consists of dollars held by foreigners as balances in U.S. banks and dollars held by foreigners in the form of U.S. currency. These four types of assets are normally lumped together and referred to simply as foreign investment in the United States. Given this terminology, it follows that the trade deficit is financed by foreign investment in the United States. This money represents an investment from the foreign perspective, but it represents borrowing from the U.S. perspective. Thus, it is often said that the trade deficit is financed by borrowing from foreigners. One can also say that the United States is selling off its assets such as land, real estate, mineral rights, and the like.

The Balance of Payments

Balance of payments– A summary of all economic transactions between the residents of one country and those of all other countries during a given period of time.

The relationship between dollars out and dollars in is reflected in the nation's balance of payments. The **balance of payments** is a summary of all financial transactions between the residents of one country and those of all other countries during a given period of time. These transactions include exports, imports, and various capital flows. Table 18.1 summarizes the U.S. balance of payments in 2007.

The transactions in Table 18.1 are divided into two categories: those that give rise to dollar in-payments and those resulting in dollar out-payments. In-payments are recorded as plus (credit) items; out-payments as minus (debit) items. Exports of goods and services (line 1) are recorded as a plus item because they provide dollar in-payments; imports of goods and services (line 2) are entered as a minus item because they require dollar out-payments.

In 2007, exports were $1,646 billion while imports were $2,346 billion. Imports, therefore, exceeded exports by $700 billion. Net income receipts and payments (line 3) include interest, dividend, and other income payments received from foreign investments as well as those made to foreigners. Unilateral transfers (line 4) include foreign aid as well as private monetary gifts to residents of foreign countries. In 2007, net unilateral transfers were −$113 billion.

The balance on current account (line 5) is obtained by adding exports (line 1), imports (line 2), net income receipts/payments (line 3), and net unilateral transfers (line 4). In 2007, this balance was −$731 billion.

TABLE 18.1 U.S. BALANCE OF PAYMENTS, 2007 (BILLIONS OF DOLLARS)

Current Account	
1. Exports of goods and services	+$1,646
2. Imports of goods and services	−2,346
3. Income receipts/payments, net	+82
4. Unilateral transfers, net	−113
5. Balance on current account (1 + 2 + 3 + 4)	−731
Capital and Financial Account	
6. U.S. purchase of foreign assets	−1,291
7. Foreign purchase of U.S. assets	+1,647
8. Official capital flows	+411
9. Statistical discrepancy and financial derivatives, net	−36
10. Balance on capital and financial account	−731*
11. Overall balance (5 + 10)	0

In 2007, the United States' current account deficit was $731 billion. This deficit, due primarily to an excess of imports over exports, was offset by a financial account surplus of $731 billion. The overall balance, therefore, was $0. (+ indicates dollars in; − indicates dollars out)
Source: Bureau of Economic Analysis, *U.S. International Transactions Accounts Data*, Table 1, 17 June 2008.

We now turn from the current account (lines 1 through 4) to the capital and financial account (lines 6 through 9). U.S. purchases of foreign assets were $1,291 billion in 2007 (line 6). They include direct private investment abroad by U.S. corporations (such as the establishment of foreign subsidiaries) and purchases of foreign securities (such as stocks and bonds) by U.S. citizens. Foreign purchase of U.S. assets (line 7) were $1,647 billion. They also include direct private investment in the United States by foreign corporations and purchases of U.S. securities by foreigners. In 2007, these capital flows totaled +$356 billion, indicating that more capital was flowing from other countries to the United States than from the United States to other countries.

Official capital flows (line 8) reveals that foreign official assets in the United States significantly increased. Official capital flows include the purchase and sale of dollars, dollar-denominated assets (such as U.S. Treasury securities), and foreign currencies by the United States and foreign governments. The statistical discrepancy and net financial derivatives (line 9) complete the capital and financial account. The statistical discrepancy itself is an adjustment for errors and omissions in the data. It is included in the capital account because most of the errors and omissions relate to capital flows.

The balance on capital and financial account, the +$732 billion shown in line 10, is obtained by summing lines 6 through 9 (the number exceeds $731 billion because of rounding). The overall balance is given in line 11. It is obtained by summing lines 5 and 10. Note that this balance is 0. It is always zero because the balance of payments must always balance; all international transactions must be financed in some way.

The current account deficit in 2007 was due largely to that year's trade deficit. The trade deficit is the sum of lines 1 and 2, or −$700 billion. It accounted for 96 percent of the current account deficit. The United States has had deficits in its current account every year since 1981, with the single exception of 1991 when it had a very small surplus. Throughout that time, most of the current account deficit has occurred because the United States has imported more than it has exported.

HAVE WE ACCUMULATED TOO MUCH DEBT?

Cumulative deficits mean growing debt. By the end of 2007, the foreign and international portion of U.S. public debt reached $2.4 trillion or nearly 26 percent of total public debt. It will continue rising as long as the country has a current account deficit and a capital account surplus.

It is not surprising that foreign households, firms, and governments wish to invest in the United States (that is, lend money to U.S. borrowers). The United States is the largest market in the world. Moreover, its market for goods and services is growing rapidly. The United States is also a safe place to invest. Its government is stable and the inflation rate is normally low relative to the inflation rate in many other countries.

The magnitude of the debt raises some concerns, however. As long as creditors believe that the United States is capable of servicing this debt, they will continue to invest here.

Thus, the United States could potentially be the world's largest debtor more or less indefinitely.

The ability of a country to service its debt is often judged on the basis of its ratio of international indebtedness to GDP. The higher this ratio, the greater the likelihood that the country will have problems in paying the interest on this debt and paying the principal as it falls due. In 2007, the United States' net indebtedness was nearly 26 percent of its GDP. Although this percentage continues to rise, other countries—including Canada and Australia—have much higher ratios of net foreign indebtedness to GDP and continue to prosper. Based on the experience of these countries, the United States may be in no imminent danger.

If foreign creditors eventually believed that the United States was not capable of servicing its international debt the inflow of foreign capital would decrease. According to those who do not view a large international debt as a serious problem, this is not a cause for alarm. They argue that the problem is largely self-correcting. With a reduced capital inflow, the demand for dollars and dollar-denominated assets would decrease, causing the dollar to depreciate. As a consequence, U.S. exports would rise as U.S. goods and services became less expensive to foreigners. Similarly, U.S. imports would fall as foreign goods and services became more expensive to U.S. households and firms. The end result would be a smaller current account deficit and a smaller international debt.

Not every economist holds such an optimistic view, however. Some believe that chronic and large-scale borrowing portends serious costs for the U.S. economy. They argue that these costs have been hidden in recent years because the United States has had historically low interest rates, resulting from the Federal Reserve's attempts to spur economic recovery after the 2001 recession and from a downturn in domestic investment. They believe that this fortunate scenario will not persist indefinitely. They argue that interest rates will inevitably rise, and that the costs of U.S. borrowing will have serious economic consequences if the past trajectory of the current account deficit is maintained. In this scenario, the costs of servicing the international debt would constitute a large loss by American households of claims to future income. The longer the debt is allowed to grow, the more significant would be the loss of future income claims.

More ominously, in this scenario, foreign investors may come to doubt the ability of the United States to service its debt. *Private foreign investors* are unlikely to be willing to continue to finance record U.S. deficits at current low interest rates as the risk grows that interest rates will rise. Already, this risk implies large capital losses for holders of low-yielding, dollar-denominated securities. The willingness of *government foreign investors* to continue to accumulate U.S. assets is also likely to weaken. Asian central banks, in particular, have been willing to finance U.S. deficits despite the risk of future capital losses in order to support their own export-led growth. However, the scale of financing required from them to sustain U.S. current account deficits will eventually exceed their capacity to accumulate U.S. dollars.

The very fact that private and government foreign investors have been willing to finance U.S. current account deficits at low cost may prove to be a mixed blessing. The dollar's privileged position may well lead to excessive U.S. debt. This would let the United States delay needed adjustments, but increase the cost of these adjustments when they finally occur.

Reducing the underlying trade deficit will require an increase in national savings (in order to reduce dependence on foreign investment in the United States). This means that either, or both, private consumption spending and the U.S. budget deficit will have to fall as a share of income. The only way this can happen without a slowdown in U.S. growth is if exports grow relative to imports. The only way that can happen is if the rest of the world—especially the dynamic Asian economies—increases its imports of U.S. goods and services relative to their exports to the United States. In other words, current trade patterns need to be reversed.

Accomplishing this would not be easy. U.S. private saving rates have been falling for so many years that a major adjustment in household behavior appears to be necessary. For reasons outlined in Chapter 15, the prospects are bleak for increasing U.S. government savings (reducing the budget deficit). It is even harder to imagine that governments in economies with export-led growth will be able to easily change patterns of trade that have proved to be so beneficial. Economists who believe this happy coincidence of

INTERNATIONAL PERSPECTIVE

The Euro

The 11 countries of the European Economic and Monetary Union (EMU) formally introduced the euro on January 1, 1999. A single currency was intended to ease the problems of traveling from one country to another and to make trade much easier.

The initial transition period ran from January 1, 1999, to December 31, 2001. During this period, the euro did not circulate as a currency. For cash transactions, each EMU country used its own currency. To buy something with euros, however, a person could write a check or use a credit card or travelers' check. Bank accounts, credit cards, and travelers' checks denominated in euros have been available since January 1, 1999.

Starting January 1, 2002, each EMU country's currency and coins were withdrawn from circulation. They were replaced with euro notes and coins. The replacement process was completed by March 1, 2002.

Why did these countries adopt a single currency and form a monetary union? As previously stated, it is more convenient to use one currency when traveling from one country to another or conducting business with parties in other countries. (Think of how inconvenient it would be if each of the 50 U.S. states had a separate currency!)

In addition to reducing transactions costs, a single currency eliminates risk associated with fluctuations in exchange rates. Less risk should encourage increased trade among member countries.

Although the move to a single currency will lead to significant benefits, costs will also occur. With a single currency and common monetary policy, individual countries will be unable to conduct an independent monetary policy. Suppose a shock occurs that affects some countries more than others. The countries more adversely affected will be unable to respond with an independent monetary policy.

In addition, individual countries will be unable to alter exchange rates vis-à-vis other EMU countries. This eliminates another policy that could be used to stimulate output and employment. By eliminating independent monetary and exchange rate policy, individual countries must rely on fiscal policy, which may prove a slender reed.

Given limited migration among EMU countries and inflexible European labor markets, unemployment could increase. (See Chapter 13 for a fuller discussion of the unemployment problem in Europe.) If it does, relations among the EMU countries will be strained.

adjustments is unlikely to happen smoothly see a future of rising U.S. interest rates and declining U.S. growth rates.

INFOTRAC College Edition

Keywords: *European Union, euro*

Access InfoTrac at http://infotrac.cengage.com

SHOULD COUNTRIES HAVE FLEXIBLE OR FIXED CURRENCY EXCHANGE RATES?

The question of whether the United States has too much international debt may be the most important current issue raised by sustained trade deficits. The most *persistent* issue, however, is whether the United States should have flexible or fixed exchange rates. There are legitimate arguments for each. We start with arguments for **flexible exchange rates**.

Flexible exchange rate– An exchange rate determined by demand and supply.

The Case for Flexible-Rate Currency Markets

Proponents argue that flexible exchange rates result in greater economic stability. Suppose that the United States' major trading partners experience a recession. As a consequence, the demand for U.S. exports falls. If exchange rates are free to adjust, the dollar will depreciate, making American goods and services less expensive to foreigners. As a result, they will buy more U.S. goods and services, at least partially offsetting the initial decrease in U.S. exports.

Fixed exchange rate--An exchange rate kept constant through central bank purchases and sales of foreign currencies.

In contrast, suppose that the United States had **fixed exchange rates.** Despite the decrease in exports, exchange rates would remain constant. The dollar would not depreciate. Consequently, American goods and services would not become less expensive to foreigners, and no offsetting increase in exports would occur. As a result, the U.S. export and import-substitution sectors, and the economy as a whole, would suffer a loss in jobs and income.

Keyword: *flexible exchange rates*

Access InfoTrac at http://infotrac.cengage.com

Another argument for flexible exchange rates has to do with monetary policy. In fixed-rate currency markets, central banks must buy or sell their own nations' currencies to keep exchange rates constant. To keep a country's currency from depreciating, its central bank must use foreign currencies to buy the domestic currency. When it does this, it reduces the nation's currency in circulation—a principal component of its money supply. This effect on the money supply may be the opposite of what the central bank would like to have to reduce unemployment.

In a flexible-rate currency market, central banks have no commitment to keep exchange rates constant. As discussed in Chapter 14, they can alter the domestic money supply to achieve or maintain full employment and price stability.

The Case for Fixed-Rate Currency Markets

Proponents of fixed exchange rates argue that less risk and uncertainty exist under that system. In a flexible-rate currency market, rates can and do change day to day. These fluctuations can result in too-frequent reallocations of domestic resources between export- and import-competing sectors of the economy. They may also lead to less international trade and investment.

Proponents of flexible exchange rates concede that exchange rates do fluctuate under that system. They note, however, that firms can take action to protect themselves against unforeseen changes in exchange rates. They also note that central banks in many countries have acted successfully to moderate exchange rate fluctuations and that there is little reason to doubt their ability to do so in the future.

Proponents of fixed exchange rates argue that flexible exchange rates may lead to destabilizing speculation. Suppose a currency is depreciating. If speculators believe that it will depreciate further, they will sell the currency, causing it to depreciate even more. To the extent that destabilizing speculation does occur, exchange rates in flexible-rate currency markets will fluctuate even more.

Keyword: *fixed exchange rates*

Access InfoTrac at http://infotrac.cengage.com

Opponents of fixed exchange rates argue that destabilizing speculation is less likely to occur when exchange rates adjust continuously than when a country is forced to devalue because of a balance of payments deficit. If a country has a balance of payments deficit and meager foreign currency holdings to defend the domestic currency, speculators may sell the domestic currency, perhaps forcing a devaluation or a larger devaluation than otherwise would take place.

Finally, proponents of fixed exchange rates assert that fixed exchange rates provide a discipline to central banks. With fixed exchange rates, central banks must act to keep exchange rates constant. This prevents them from increasing the money supply rapidly, which would cause inflation.

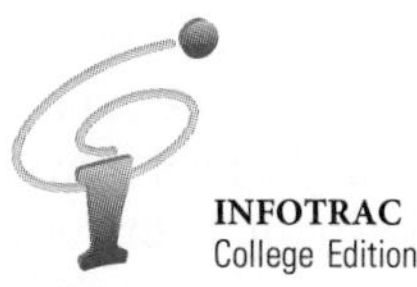

Keyword: *Peso crisis*

Access InfoTrac at http://infotrac.cengage.com

Opponents of fixed exchange rates concede that the flexible exchange rate system can be more inflationary than a fixed exchange rate system. Even so, they argue that central banks should not be committed to keeping exchange rates constant. Instead, they should be free to pursue whatever policies are necessary for full employment. Flexible exchange rates allow central banks this freedom.

As we have seen, strong arguments exist both for and against flexible exchange rates. Even so, many countries have switched from fixed to flexible exchange rates in recent years.

INTERNATIONAL PERSPECTIVE

The Mexican Peso Crisis

When the North American Free Trade Agreement (NAFTA) went into effect on January 1, 1994, it was widely anticipated that trade between the United States and Mexico would grow rapidly. In 1994, trade did grow rapidly. In December 1994, however, the peso depreciated vis-à-vis the dollar, depressing U.S. exports to Mexico and stimulating U.S. imports from Mexico.

In 1994, Mexican authorities were maintaining an approximately constant exchange rate between the peso and dollar by buying and selling pesos in foreign exchange markets. At the same time, Mexico was experiencing a current account deficit that was largely financed by foreign investment in Mexico. As time passed, the deficit became larger. Moreover, events within Mexico —including a rebellion in Chiapas Province and the assassination of the ruling party's presidential candidate, Luis Donaldo Colosio—caused concern abroad. As a result, the peso began to depreciate. To keep the peso from depreciating further, Mexican authorities used their international reserves (including dollars) to buy pesos in foreign exchange markets. By December 1994, Mexico's holdings of international reserves were low.

On December 20, the Mexican peso was devalued by 20 percent. This devaluation proved insufficient, and by December 27 the exchange rate was 5.7 pesos per dollar, a decline of nearly 40 percent since just before the initial devaluation. With the assistance of a direct loan package that included $20 billion from the United States, the situation eventually stabilized, but not before interest rates soared and the Mexican economy experienced a severe recession.

The depreciation of the peso made Mexican goods and services much cheaper to Americans. It also made American goods and services much more expensive to Mexicans. Consequently, U.S. imports from Mexico increased in 1995 while its exports to Mexico decreased. In addition to the depreciation of the peso, the recession in Mexico contributed to the decrease in imports from the United States.

For the United States, the net effect of these changes was to go from a trade surplus with Mexico, averaging about $4 billion from 1991 through the third quarter of 1994, to a trade deficit of about $15 billion. Even so, output in the United States continued to rise and the unemployment rate continued to fall. In 1994, the U.S. unemployment rate was 6.1 percent. In 1995, it was only 5.6 percent.

With the Mexican economy now expanding, U.S. exports to Mexico attained record levels and are expected to continue to grow in the future. Indeed, in the absence of another peso crisis, the growth in trade between the United States and Mexico that was anticipated with the signing of the North American Free Trade Agreement is likely to occur.

SHOULD CAPITAL FLOWS BE CONTROLLED?

In addition to foreign exchange markets, the allocation of resources across countries depends heavily on the global capital market, the market that facilitates the flow of funds for the purchase and sale of financial and real assets. Historically, economists have favored free international capital movements. Various countries, however, limited or banned capital flows during World Wars I and II. Following World War II, many of these countries dropped their controls. With the advent of the Mexican and Asian financial crises (both of which are described as International Perspectives in this chapter), policy makers and economists began reconsidering the desirability of limiting capital flows.

Controls may be applied to either capital outflows or capital inflows (or both). An increase in net capital outflows causes a balance of payments deficit. In a country with a fixed exchange rate, the central bank must use its holdings of foreign currencies to buy the domestic currency to keep exchange rates from rising. If the central bank's holdings of currencies are meager, the country may be forced to devalue its currency. Similarly, if the country's exchange rates are flexible and capital starts flowing from the country, the domestic currency will depreciate. To prevent a devaluation or depreciation of its currency, a country may impose controls to reduce the capital outflow.

If capital starts flowing to a country with fixed exchange rates, the demand for its currency increases, causing a balance of payments surplus. The country's central bank must use its holdings of domestic currency to buy foreign currencies to keep exchange rates constant. This increases the domestic money supply, causing prices to rise. An increase in the price level makes the country's goods and services less competitive in world markets, thereby decreasing exports. The rise in the price level also makes foreign goods and services relatively cheaper, thereby increasing imports.

Rather than buying foreign currencies to keep exchange rates constant, the country's central bank could revalue its currency. The revaluation, however, would make its goods and services more expensive to foreigners and foreign goods and services less expensive to its citizens. Consequently, the country's exports would fall and its imports would rise, imposing hardships on its export- and import-competing sectors.

If capital starts flowing to a country with flexible exchange rates, the demand for its currency increases, causing an appreciation of the currency. As before, the appreciation would make its goods and services more expensive to foreigners and foreign goods and services less expensive to its citizens. Consequently, the country's exports would fall and its imports would rise, imposing hardships on its export- and import-competing sectors.

To prevent prices from rising or a revaluation of its currency, a country with fixed exchange rates may elect to impose controls to limit or prevent capital inflows. To keep its currency from appreciating, a country with flexible exchange rates may decide to impose controls on capital inflows. Finally, a country may impose controls on capital inflows because of the volatility of these flows or because the government prefers local ownership of its assets.

Capital controls vary considerably; they range from taxing capital transactions to an outright ban. Perhaps the best-known tax approach is the Tobin plan, named after James Tobin, a Nobel Prize winner in economics, who proposed it in 1972. To reduce the short-term volatility of capital flows, he proposed that a tax be applied to foreign currency transactions.

Should countries impose capital controls? Strong arguments exist on both sides of the debate. The traditional view is that capital should be free to flow from countries offering low prospective returns to countries offering higher prospective returns. Barring distortions caused by tax systems and the like, this will ensure an efficient global allocation of resources. Critics of the traditional view note, however, that distortions do exist. They also claim that investors and speculators exhibit herdlike behavior, giving rise to greater volatility of capital flows than warranted.

Keywords: *international capital flows*

Access InfoTrac at http://infotrac.cengage.com

Proponents of the traditional view also claim that capital controls are ineffective. In today's high-tech world, many ways exist for households and firms to evade controls. Witness the flow of drug money from the United States to Colombia. Moreover, controls invite corruption among government officials and disrespect for the law. Critics, on the other hand, claim that controls are effective. The debate over their effectiveness continues with no resolution in sight.

Proponents of controls claim that unimpeded capital flows can result in large changes in prices and exchange rates that destabilize the economy. Capital flows have undoubtedly contributed to the instability of some economies. For countries with sound banking systems and well-developed financial markets, however, capital flows have been less of a problem.

Keywords: *Asian crisis, Asian financial crisis*

Access InfoTrac at http://infotrac.cengage.com

Proponents of controls also argue that capital controls allow time for countries to initiate new policies and undertake fundamental reforms in their banking systems and financial markets. The evidence on this point is mixed. Some countries have used this time wisely to initiate new policies. Others have simply procrastinated.

INTERNATIONAL PERSPECTIVE

The Asian Financial Crisis

The importance of a sound banking system is illustrated clearly by the Asian financial crisis of 1997–1999. Throughout most of the 1970s, 1980s, and 1990s, the economies of Thailand, Malaysia, Indonesia, South Korea, and the Philippines were the envy of the rest of the world. They were growing rapidly. Unemployment was low and inflation was moderate. In general, they enjoyed government budget surpluses and moderate current account deficits.

Their apparent successes masked some underlying financial weaknesses, however. The ratio of short-term foreign debt to foreign exchange reserves in most of the countries was high, and banks had engaged in large-scale foreign lending. Many of these loans were risky, with a high proportion in real estate, rather than in ventures that increased productive capacity.

In 1997, several events occurred that triggered a financial crisis. In Korea, two large conglomerates failed and Kia, Korea's third largest automaker, was in great difficulty. In Thailand, nonbank financial companies experienced difficulty because of bad real estate loans. In May, Thailand's largest finance company failed.

In July, the Bank of Thailand announced that it would no longer maintain a fixed exchange rate, and the Thai currency, the baht, would be allowed to float. As a result, the baht depreciated significantly. Speculators attacked other currencies, including the Philippine peso, the Malaysian ringgit, the Indonesian rupiah, and the Korean won. The values of these currencies plummeted as speculators sold them and capital flowed from the countries. By January 1998, the rupiah, for example, lost 80 percent of its value against the dollar. The crisis spread to stock markets, and stock prices dropped dramatically.

As time passed, the various economies turned downward. What had started primarily as a financial crisis spread to the real economy. Output decreased and unemployment increased. By 1999, the worst of the crisis appeared to have passed. Although still shaky, the East Asian economies began to grow once more.

In conclusion, capital controls may benefit some countries, particularly in the short run, but they are no substitute for appropriate economic policies, a sound banking system, and smoothly functioning financial markets.

Summary

An exchange rate is the number of units of one currency exchangeable for a unit of another. Exchange rates are important because they help to determine the relative cost of internationally traded goods, services, and assets.

In a flexible-rate currency market, exchange rates are determined by demand and supply. The United States has flexible-rate currency markets, but the Federal Reserve does intervene occasionally to dampen fluctuations in exchange rates.

In a fixed-rate currency market, central banks intervene to keep exchange rates constant. If a currency trading in such a market was depreciating, the central bank of that country would use its holdings of foreign currencies to buy their own currency, thereby keeping it from depreciating. Conversely, if the currency of that country was appreciating, the central bank would use the currency of its country to buy foreign currencies, thus keeping its own currency from appreciating.

Since the early 1980s, the United States has experienced large current account deficits, caused primarily by an excess of imports over exports. The deficits have been financed by foreign investment in this country. As these deficits have occurred, the United States' foreign indebtedness has risen, making the United States the world's largest debtor nation. Whether this situation is sustainable is one of the most important unanswered questions in international finance, and one on which economists disagree.

A perennial issue in international finance is whether it is better for a country to embrace fixed-rate or flexible-rate currency markets. Here, too, economists do not agree. Even so, a growing number of countries are relying on flexible-rate currency markets.

Another important issue is whether capital should be allowed to flow freely from one nation to another. As a result of the Mexican, East Asian, and other financial crises, various economists have questioned the wisdom of allowing unrestricted capital flows. It is clear, however, that capital controls are no substitute for appropriate economic policies, a sound banking system, and smoothly functioning financial markets.

Key Terms

Exchange rate
Flexible-rate currency market
Appreciation
Depreciation
Fixed-rate currency market
Devaluation
Balance of payments deficit
Revaluation
Balance of payments surplus
Balance of payments
Flexible exchange rate
Fixed exchange rate

Review Questions

1. If the yen–dollar exchange rate is 100 yen per dollar, what is the dollar–yen exchange rate?
2. Explain how exchange rates are determined in:
   a. flexible-rate currency markets.
   b. fixed-rate currency markets.
3. Suppose the British pound for U.S. dollar exchange rate falls. Does the dollar appreciate or depreciate? Defend your answer.
4. Suppose the U.S. dollar appreciates relative to the Japanese yen. How will the exports and imports of the two countries be affected?
5. Assuming flexible-rate currency markets, how will each of the following affect the exchange rate—from the perspectives of both the buying and selling countries?
   a. an increase in real GDP abroad
   b. an increase in the home country's inflation rate
   c. an increase in foreign interest rates
   d. renewed confidence in the home country's economy
6. What is the euro? Why should Americans be interested in it?
7. Briefly explain why the balance of payments must balance.
8. Even though the United States has a large current account deficit, it has an overall balance of payments of zero. Why, then, is there concern about the large current account deficit? How does the United States finance a current account deficit? Is the concern warranted?
9. Summarize the advantages and disadvantages of flexible-rate and fixed-rate currency markets.
10. Suppose a country suddenly experiences a capital outflow. Describe the impact on the country assuming:
    a. flexible-rate currency markets.
    b. fixed-rate currency markets.
11. What are capital controls? Why might a country wish to impose them?
12. Critically evaluate the following statement: "The Asian financial crisis was all about financial transactions; the countries involved continued to grow."
13. What impact did the Asian financial crisis have on U.S. exports to that region? Defend your answer.

Glossary

Absolute advantage The advantage a country has if it can produce more of a good or service with the same inputs as its trading partner; also the advantage that an individual has if he can produce a good at lower cost than another individual.

Absolute disadvantage The disadvantage a country has if it produces less of a good or service with the same inputs as its trading partner.

Acid rain A solution of sulfuric acid and precipitation.

Active macroeconomic policy The deliberate use of expansionary monetary or fiscal policy to reduce cyclical unemployment (also called **stabilization policy**).

Adverse selection Self-selection that results in a pool of insured individuals dominated by high-risk, high-cost individuals.

Aggregate demand curve A curve showing the quantity of final goods and services (real GDP) that will be purchased at each price level (GDP deflator).

Aggregate supply curve A curve showing the quantity of final goods and services (real GDP) that will be produced at each price level (the GDP deflator).

Allocative efficiency loss (deadweight loss) Maximum total net benefit minus actual total net benefit.

Alternative Minimum Tax (AMT) An extra tax that some people with higher taxable income have to pay on top of the regular income tax.

Ambient concentrations Concentrations of pollutants in the atmosphere.

Anticipated inflation Inflation that is expected.

Appreciation A rise in the value of one currency relative to another *in a flexible-rate currency market.*

Automatic stabilizers Features of government taxes and expenditures that automatically increase aggregate demand in a recession.

Average indexed monthly earnings (AIME) Average monthly earnings for the highest 35 years of earnings, adjusted by the wage indexing factor.

Baby Boom Generation The cohort of individuals born from 1946 through 1964.

Balance of payments A summary of all economic transactions between the residents of one country and those of all other countries during a given period of time.

Balance of payments deficit The amount by which the home country's purchases of foreign goods, services, and assets exceed the rest of the world's purchases from it *at a given exchange rate.*

Balance of payments surplus The amount by which the rest of the world's purchases of the home country's goods, services, and assets exceed its purchases from the rest of the world *at a given exchange rate.*

Barrier to entry Any condition that prevents new firms from entering an industry with the same cost conditions as existing firms.

Baseline forecast A forecast of the unified budget, reflecting the current law pertaining to receipts and expenditures, that the Congressional Budget Office is required to make each year.

Basic benefit (BB) Maximum benefit paid by an income-tested transfer program; normally when gross income of the beneficiary is less than or equal to the deductible.

Benefit (B) Amount received by a beneficiary from an income-tested transfer program.

Benefit reduction rate (BRR) Ratio of the change in the benefit to the change in gross income in an income-tested transfer program.

Best technology The technology that requires the fewest resources to produce a given combination of goods and services.

Break-even gross income (BEGI) The gross income at which benefits become zero in an income-tested transfer program.

Budget A statement of receipts (income) and outlays (expenditures) for a specific period of time (a year).

Budget balance Total budget receipts minus total budget outlays.

Budget deficit A negative budget balance: total outlays exceed total receipts.

Budget surplus A positive budget balance; total receipts exceed total outlays.

Business cycles Recurring fluctuations in the general level of economic activity.

Capital gain The market price of an asset minus the purchase price of that asset.

Capital intensity The ratio of capital to labor in production, or units of capital per unit of labor.

Capital stock The nation's accumulated stock of structures, producers' durable equipment, and business inventories.

Cartel An organized group of producers who manage their output and pricing as if they were a monopoly.

Cash transfer A transfer in the form of cash.

Central bank A government-established agency that controls the nation's money supply, conducts monetary policy, and supervises the monetary system.

Civilian labor force The number of people 16 years of age or older who are employed plus the number of people not employed but looking for work.

Coase's theorem The thesis that the assignment and enforcement of property rights can lead to the efficient level of pollution.

Coefficient of the price elasticity of demand The percentage change in quantity demanded divided by the percentage change in price; it is a measure of the responsiveness of consumers to price changes.

Common property resource A resource that is the property of all.

Commutative justice A norm for a market economy based on voluntary exchange. Voluntary exchange means exchange of equal market value.

Comparative advantage The advantage a country has if it produces a good or service at a lower opportunity cost than its trading partner.

Comparative advantage The advantage that an individual has if she can produce a good at lower opportunity cost than another individual.

Comparative disadvantage The disadvantage a country has if it produces a good or service at a higher opportunity cost than its trading partner.

Competitive market For this issues-oriented analysis, the two most important conditions are that a market is competitive if the market has (1) many buyers and sellers so that both buyers and sellers are price takers and (2) easy entry of new producers so that new firms enter in response to economic profit and compete that profit away. More theory-oriented approaches add two conditions, namely that (1) firms in the industry produce the same or very similar products, and (2) both buyers and sellers have good information about market conditions.

Complement A good used with another good. An increase in the price of one good results in a decrease in demand for its complement.

Consumer price index (CPI) A weighted average of the prices of goods and services purchased by a typical urban household.

Consumers' surplus The difference between the price that consumers are willing to pay (their demand price) and the price that they must pay.

Contraction phase The phase of the business cycle during which real GDP, employment, productive capacity use, and profits decrease while unemployment rises.

Cost rate The ratio of annual Social Security benefits and administrative costs to taxable payroll.

Creative destruction Economic progress where the introduction of new technologies forces old ones out.

Creditor A person to whom money is owed.

Criteria pollutants Pollutants that are subject to the National Ambient Air Quality Standards (NAAQS).

Currency (cash) Paper money and coins.

Cyclical unemployment Unemployment resulting from the business cycle.

Debtor A person who owes money.

Decrease in demand A situation in which, at each price, consumers plan to purchase less of a good; it is depicted by a leftward shift of the demand curve. It may also be interpreted as a reduction in the value of an additional unit of the good, which emphasizes the downward shift of the curve.

Decrease in supply A situation in which, at each price, producers plan to sell less of a good; it is depicted by a leftward shift of the supply curve. It may also be interpreted as an increase in the supply price for each quantity of the good, which emphasizes the upward shift of the curve.

Deductible (D) An allowance for essential needs that is disregarded in determining benefits from a transfer program (also called the *disregard*).

Defensive medicine Medical procedures or diagnostic tests performed to reduce the risk of a lawsuit.

Deflation A continuing fall in the price level.

Delayed retirement credit The amount by which retirees' benefits are increased for each year that retirement is delayed beyond the normal retirement age, up to age 70.

Demand curve A curve (line) showing the quantity demanded of a good for each possible price, holding constant other factors that affect demand.

Demand deposits Checking accounts at commercial banks.

Demand price The price at which consumers will just buy the exact quantity on the market. It is the maximum price that anyone will pay for the last unit.

Demand shock A contraction in aggregate demand large enough to cause a recession.

Depository institutions Financial institutions that accept checkable and savings deposits.

Depreciation A fall in the value of one currency relative to another *in a flexible-rate currency market.*

Devaluation A fall in the value of one currency relative to another *in a fixed-rate currency market.*

Discount factor The value of the divisor $(1 + i)^t$ used to discount a future value.

Discount rate The interest rate at which depository institutions can borrow from Federal Reserve Banks.

Discretionary outlay A government outlay with a limit specified annually by Congress.

Distributive justice Equality among people, providing a norm of equal opportunity, with the hope that equal opportunity combined with commutative justice will move people toward equality.

Dynamic allocative efficiency An efficient allocation of resources in the long run.

Early retirement penalty The amount by which Social Security benefits are reduced for people who retire before the normal retirement age.

Economic approach to organization An approach that mimics the market in designing a profit or nonprofit organization. In particular, it assigns decision rights to people who have relevant specific knowledge, evaluates those decisions in relation to the organization's objective, and rewards decisions that advance the objective.

Economic profit A rate of earning in excess of the minimum necessary to attract economic resources into a particular use.

Economic rent seeking Attempt by people to gain an economic advantage through production of new or better products or through production of products at a lower cost.

Efficiency improvement A change from less than the best to the best technology, which allows more output to be produced with the same resources.

Efficiency in resource allocation (allocative efficiency) An allocation of resources that satisfies wants as fully as possible.

Efficiency loss from pollution Marginal social cost (MSC) minus marginal benefit (MB), summed over all units produced for which MSC > MB.

Efficient output The output where marginal social benefit equals marginal social cost.

Elasticity of substitution between varieties of a good The degree to which one variety of a good is substitutable for (just as good as) another variety of the good.

Embargo The prohibition of trade in a product.

Emissions reduction credit A credit for reducing emissions more than required by regulations.

Emissions tax A tax charged polluters for each unit of pollutants emitted.

Entrepreneurship The ability to see how other resources might be combined in producing a profitable good or service and the willingness to risk organizing a business to do so.

Equation of exchange An equation showing the relationships among the money supply, the income velocity of money, the GDP deflator, and real GDP. ($M \times V = P \times GDP$).

Equilibrium A state of rest for the economy or market. Market equilibrium occurs at the price at which quantity demanded equals quantity supplied—the equilibrium quantity exchanged.

Euro area European countries that use the euro as their official currency.

European Union (EU) An agreement by nations in Europe to eliminate trade barriers among member countries.

Excess burden of taxation (deadweight loss from taxation) Net benefit not realized because of taxation.

Excess demand (shortage) A situation in which quantity demanded exceeds quantity supplied at a given price.

Excess reserves Reserves over and above required reserves.

Excess supply (surplus) A situation in which quantity supplied exceeds quantity demanded at a given price.

Exchange rate The number of units of one currency required in exchange for one unit of another.

Expansion phase The business cycle phase during which real GDP, employment, productive capacity use, and profits increase while unemployment falls.

Expansionary fiscal policy Fiscal policy to reduce unemployment that increases the difference between government expenditures and tax collections.

Expansionary monetary policy Monetary policy to reduce unemployment that normally involves an increase in the money supply.

Exports Goods and services produced in this country and purchased by foreigners.

External benefit A benefit created by a market that is realized by individuals other than the buyers and sellers.

External costs Costs created by producers or consumers, but paid by others.

Final goods Goods purchased (or available to be purchased) for final use.

Fiscal imbalance A measure related to the budget that compares the present value of expected future outlays (PVFO) with the present value of expected future receipts (PVFR) and the current value of financial assets (CVFA)—also called a "fiscal gap."

Fiscal policy Use of government purchases and taxes to achieve full employment and other economic goals.

Fixed exchange rate An exchange rate kept constant through central bank purchases and sales of foreign currencies.

Fixed-rate currency market A market in which central banks intervene to keep exchange rates constant.

Flexible exchange rate An exchange rate determined by demand and supply.

Flexible-rate currency market A market in which exchange rates are determined by the demand for and supply of currency.

Foreign investment in the United States Annual purchases by foreign individuals and institutions of U.S. physical and financial assets (including any annual increase in U.S. dollars held in other countries).

Foreign trade effect The change in net exports caused by a change in the price level that causes a change in the relative desirability of domestic and foreign goods and services.

Free rider An individual who uses goods or services provided by others without paying for them.

Frictional unemployment Temporary unemployment arising from the normal job-search process.

Full employment The state of the economy where the rate of unemployment equals the natural rate of unemployment.

Future value (FV) The value at a future date of a current amount of money.

GDP deflator A weighted average of the prices of all final goods and services produced in the economy.

General Agreement on Tariffs and Trade (GATT) An international organization founded in 1947 to establish rules of conduct for international trade.

General knowledge Knowledge that is easy to transfer to another person, including people in another part of the organization or the economy.

Government failure Allocative inefficiency resulting from government activities.

Government purchases of goods and services The purchases of federal, state, and local governments.

Greenhouse gas A gas that helps the Earth retain heat from the sun.

Gross domestic product (GDP) The market value of all final goods and services produced in the economy over the relevant time span, usually one year.

Gross income (GI) Income that serves as the basis for determining the benefits from transfer programs; usually income from earnings and nonincome-tested cash transfers, such as Social Security benefits.

Gross private domestic investment Firms' purchases of new equipment, purchases of all newly produced structures, and changes in business inventories.

High-stakes testing Focuses on achievement testing, with demonstration of achievement important for completing high school and for subsequent employment opportunities and college admission.

Human capital The knowledge and skills embodied in people, as used in the production process.

Hyperinflation Extremely high inflation rates.

Import quota An upper limit on the amount of a good that may be imported during any time period.

Imports Goods and services produced abroad and bought by persons in this country.

Income effect of a wage decrease The increase in hours worked to replace the decrease in income resulting from a wage rate reduction.

Income rate The ratio of annual Social Security income to taxable payroll.

Income velocity of money The number of times the money supply is used to purchase final goods and services during a year.

Income-tested transfer A transfer, the amount of which falls as a beneficiary's income increases (also called a means-tested transfer).

Increase in demand A situation in which, at each price, consumers plan to purchase more of a good, depicted by a rightward shift of the demand curve. It may also be interpreted as an increase in the demand price, which emphasizes the upward shift of the curve.

Increase in supply A situation in which, at each price, producers plan to sell more of a good; it is depicted by a rightward shift of the supply curve. It may also be interpreted as a reduction in supply price for each quantity of the good, which emphasizes the downward shift of the curve.

Indexing Linking benefits to the CPI so that they increase automatically as the CPI rises.

Induced retirement effect The increase in household savings required to offset early retirement induced by the prospect of Social Security benefits.

Inferior good A good that consumers purchase less of when their income rises.

Inflation A continuing rise in the price level.

Interest rate effect The change in consumption and investment caused by a change in the price level that ultimately causes interest rates to change.

Intermediate goods Goods purchased for resale or for use in producing other goods.

Intra-governmental debt The portion of the national debt held by government agencies.

Labor All physical and mental abilities used by people in production.

Land Resources found in nature, such as land, water, forests, mineral deposits, and air.

Law of demand As the price of some good changes with other factors constant, the quantity demanded for that good changes in the opposite direction.

Law of supply As the price of some good changes with other factors constant, the quantity supplied for that good changes in the same direction.

Legacy debt Total Social Security benefits, minus Social Security taxes plus interest, for cohorts born before 1936.

Managed care Health care that is reviewed by someone other than the patient or provider to determine whether the right services are being provided and whether the cost of provision is minimized.

Mandatory outlay A government expenditure that depends on criteria (such as age or income) that are not normally changed on an annual basis (also called "entitlements").

Marginal abatement cost The cost of abating or eliminating an additional unit of pollutants.

Marginal benefit The satisfaction value received from consumption of an additional unit of a good or service.

Marginal benefit curve (demand curve) A curve that depicts the benefits from each additional, or marginal, unit.

Marginal cost The opportunity cost of producing an additional unit of a good.

Marginal cost curve (supply curve) A curve that depicts the costs of providing each additional, or marginal, unit.

Marginal external benefit External benefit on the additional, or marginal, unit.

Marginal external costs (MEC) External costs attributable to each additional unit of production.

Marginal principle To maximize profits, the producer should choose the output that equates marginal revenue and marginal cost.

Marginal revenue The change in total revenue associated with a one-unit change in the output sold by a producer.

Marginal social benefit The sum of the marginal benefit and the marginal external benefit.

Marginal social costs (MSC) The sum of marginal costs and marginal external costs.

Market failure A situation in which a market fails to achieve allocative efficiency.

Market power A situation in which a firm or a few firms can affect the price received for their product, and new firms do not enter the industry in response to economic profit.

Marketable pollution permit A permit that can be bought and sold that allows a polluter to emit a specified quantity of a pollutant or pollutants.

Maximum potential real GDP The largest output the economy can produce; the vertical portion of the aggregate supply curve.

Medicaid A joint federal/state program that pays for health care for low-income families and the disabled.

Medicare Federal health insurance program for people 65 and over.

Medium of exchange Anything used to purchase goods and services and pay debts.

Member banks Banks that are members of the Federal Reserve System.

Monetary benefits and costs Benefits and costs valued in dollars.

Monetary policy Use of the money supply to achieve full employment and other economic goals.

Money Anything generally accepted as final payment for goods, services, and debt.

Money income Measure of income used to determine the official poverty rate; includes earnings (before taxes), interest, dividends, and private and government cash transfers, such as alimony and child support payments, Social Security benefits, unemployment benefits, and payments from the Temporary Assistance to Needy Families program.

Money supply Currency (including coins), traveler's checks, demand deposits, and other checkable deposits.

Monopoly An industry with a single producer of a good that has no close substitutes.

Moral hazard The risk that insurance for an event will increase the probability of the event occurring.

National banks Banks chartered by the federal government.

National debt The debt of the federal government held by the public and government agencies (also known as the "gross federal debt").

National savings The difference between national income produced in the United States (measured by GDP) and income spent on goods and services produced in the United States (measured by $C + I_g$). Also equal to the sum of private savings (household income minus taxes and consumption) and government savings (government receipts minus government outlays).

Natural monopolies Monopolies that exist if demand and cost conditions are such that only one firm can survive in an industry.

Natural rate of unemployment The normal rate of unemployment around which the unemployment rate fluctuates.

Net exports of goods and services The amount by which foreign spending on domestically produced goods and services is greater (or less) than domestic spending on goods and services produced abroad.

Net welfare gain From imports: a gain in consumers' surplus that exceeds the loss in producers' surplus; from exports: a gain in producers' surplus that exceeds the loss in consumers' surplus.

Nominal GDP GDP measured on the basis of current, or nominal, prices.

Noncash transfer A transfer in the form of goods or services.

Nonexcludable good A good that is impossible or extremely difficult to exclude nonpayers from consuming.

Nonmonetary benefits and costs Benefits and costs not valued in dollars.

Nonrival good A good that one person can consume without reducing the amount available for others to consume, such as a feeling of security in a safe city.

Nonstudent benefits Benefits of a college education to nonstudents.

Nonstudent costs Costs of a college education paid by nonstudents.

Normal good A good that consumers purchase more of when their income rises.

Normal retirement age The age at which an individual is eligible to receive full retirement benefits.

North American Free Trade Agreement (NAFTA) An agreement by the United States, Canada, and Mexico to eliminate trade barriers among the three countries.

Off-budget balance Budget balance in the Social Security portion of the unified budget.

Official poverty threshold The annual cost of a nutritionally adequate diet multiplied by three.

Oligopoly An industry with only a few producers or sellers of a good.

On-budget balance Budget balance in the non–Social Security portion of the unified budget.

Open market operations The purchase or sale of U.S. Treasury securities by the Federal Reserve.

Opportunity cost The value of the best alternative sacrificed when a choice is made.

Passive macroeconomic policy The intentional reliance on market forces or automatic stabilizers to reduce cyclical unemployment.

Peak The highest point in the business cycle, during which real GDP is at a maximum and employment, profits, and productive capacity use are high.

Personal consumption expenditures Household purchases of durable and nondurable goods and services.

Physical capital Man-made, durable items used in the production process, such as factories, equipment, dams, and transportation systems.

Physician-induced demand Ineffective health care prescribed by physicians to increase their own wealth.

Political rent seeking The attempt to gain economic advantage through government action.

Poor person A person who lives in a family with money income below the poverty threshold.

Poverty rate The number of poor people divided by the U.S. population.

Pre-transfer poverty rate An estimate of the poverty rate without the income provided by government cash transfers.

Present value (PV) The current value of a future amount of money.

Present value decision rule A rule used to determine if an investment is financially sound; an investment is financially sound according to this rule if the sum of the present value of benefits is equal to or greater than the sum of the present value of costs.

Price elastic Demand is price elastic if the elasticity coefficient is greater than 1.0.

Price floor A minimum price set by government, below which the market price is not allowed to go.

Price index A measure of the price level for a given period relative to the base period.

Price inelastic Demand is price inelastic if the elasticity coefficient is less than 1.0.

Primary insurance amount (PIA) The basic monthly Social Security benefit at the normal or full retirement age.

Producers' surplus The difference between the price that producers receive and the price that they must receive (their supply price).

Production possibilities curve A curve showing the maximum combinations of two goods or services that can be produced by an economy when resources are fully used and the best technology is applied.

Productivity Quantity of output per unit of input.

Profit Total revenue minus total cost.

Property right A legally defined and enforceable right to use property for specific purposes.

Public debt The portion of the national debt held by the public.

Public good A good that provides benefits from which no one can be excluded.

Quantity demanded The quantity of a good that consumers plan to buy at each possible price, holding constant other factors that affect demand.

Quantity supplied The quantity of a good that producers will plan to sell at each possible price, holding constant other factors that affect supply.

Quantity theory of money A theory emphasizing that the money supply is the principal determinant of nominal GDP.

Rate of return (ROR) The discount rate, r, at which the sum of the present value of costs is equal to the sum of the present value of benefits.

Rate of return decision rule A rule used to determine if an investment is financially sound; an investment is financially sound according to this rule if the rate of return on the investment is equal to or greater than the rate of return on the best alternative use of funds.

Ration To allocate a limited supply of goods and services to people.

Real balance effect The change in consumption caused by a change in the price level that changes the real value of financial assets that have fixed dollar values.

Real GDP per capita Gross domestic product adjusted for inflation and population growth.

Real GDP GDP measured on the basis of constant prices; reflects only changes in quantities.

Real national health care expenditures per capita National health care expenditures adjusted for inflation and population growth.

Recession A decline in real GDP for two or more consecutive quarters.

Relative price The price of one good in terms of another good. It measures what must be given up to obtain a good.

Required reserves Reserves that depository institutions are required to hold.

Reserve requirement The ratio of required reserves to deposits.

Revaluation A rise in the value of one currency relative to another *in a fixed-rate currency market.*

Scarcity The common situation for all economies, in which aggregate wants exceed the economy's ability to meet them because of limited resources.

Social benefits Benefits that accrue to all individuals; applied to college education, benefits to students and nonstudents.

Social costs Costs paid by all individuals; applied to college education, costs to students and nonstudents.

Social rate of return (ROR) Rate of return realized by students and nonstudents from investing in a college education; the discount rate at which the sum of the present value of social benefits is equal to the sum of the present value of social costs.

Social Security The federal program that provides retirement benefits, survivors' benefits, and disability benefits to people age 62 and over, and to their dependents.

Social Security wealth The present value of Social Security benefits.

Sources of investment funds The three sources of investment funds are private savings, government savings, and foreign investment in the United States.

Specific knowledge Knowledge that is costly to transfer to another person and is particularly costly to transfer to someone in another part of the organization or the economy.

Stagflation Simultaneous stagnation (a reduction in real GDP) and inflation (an increase in the GDP deflator) created by a supply shock.

State banks Banks chartered by state governments.

Static allocative efficiency An efficient allocation of resources in the short run.

Structural unemployment Unemployment caused by structural changes in the economy that eliminate jobs.

Student benefits Benefits of a college education to students.

Student costs Costs of a college education paid by students.

Student rate of return (ROR) Rate of return realized by students from investing in a college education; the discount rate at which the sum of the present value of student benefits is equal to the sum of the present value of student costs.

Student rate of return without government support The student rate of return from investing in a college education when government pays none of the costs.

Substitute A good used in place of another good. An increase in the price of one good results in an increase in demand for the substitute good.

Substitution effect of a wage decrease The decrease in hours worked because of a fall in the wage rate.

Supply curve A curve (line) showing the quantity supplied of a good for each possible price, holding constant other factors that affect supply.

Supply price The price at which sellers will just put a specific quantity of a good or service on the market. It is the minimum price that a seller will accept in return for selling one more unit of a good or service.

Supply shock A contraction in aggregate supply large enough to cause a recession.

Target efficiency The degree to which transfer program benefits are confined to the poor.

Target price A guaranteed price for a product. The product is sold at the market price and the government pays the producer the difference between it and the guaranteed price.

Tariff A tax levied on a good when it crosses a nation's border.

Technical progress Technological and efficiency improvements combined.

Technological improvement An improvement in best technology that allows more output with a given amount of resources.

Third-party payment A payment made directly to the provider of a good or service by a party other than the buyer.

Total benefit The sum of marginal benefits; also the area under the marginal benefit or demand curve.

Total cost The sum of marginal costs; also the area under the marginal cost or supply curve.

Total net benefit Total benefit minus total cost; also the area between the demand and supply curves.

Total revenue The price per unit times the quantity sold (the rectangle under the demand curve, where the height of the rectangle is the price per unit and the base of the rectangle is the quantity sold).

Trade adjustment assistance Assistance provided by the federal government to workers displaced and businesses harmed by free trade.

Trade deficit A negative net balance in the international trade account; imports greater than exports.

Transactions costs The costs of finding willing buyers and sellers and negotiating a mutually acceptable price.

Transfer Cash, goods, or services paid for by taxpayers and provided to beneficiaries of government programs free of charge.

Trough The lowest point of the business cycle, during which real GDP is at a minimum and employment, profits, and productive capacity use are low.

Unanticipated inflation Inflation that is unexpected or higher than expected.

Unemployment rate The percentage of the civilian labor force that is unemployed.

Unified budget The federal budget with Social Security included.

Unit elastic Demand is unit elastic if the elasticity coefficient equals 1.0.

United States' foreign investment Annual purchases by U.S. citizens and institutions of physical and financial assets in other countries (including any increase in foreign currency held in the United States).

Uses of investment funds The two uses of investment funds are investment in the United States (private domestic investment) and investment in foreign countries.

Utilization review A process used to determine if the medical care prescribed by a physician is appropriate.

Value of a life The value people put on their own lives, inferred from what they must be paid to incur small but predictable increases in the risk of dying.

Vault cash Cash held by banks and other depository institutions.

Voluntary export restraints (VERs) Agreement whereby exporting nations limit the amounts of goods that they ship to importing nations.

Voucher A coupon that can be used to pay for something, such as health care or health insurance.

Wage indexing factor The ratio of the average national wage at age 60 to the average national wage at age a ($a < 60$).

Wage subsidy Subsidy paid to an employer equal to a percentage of the difference between a designated maximum wage and a worker's wage.

Wasteful spending Spending that provides benefits that are less than costs.

Wealth substitution effect The reduction in household savings caused by the substitution of Social Security wealth for other types of wealth.

World Trade Organization (WTO) Successor organization to GATT, founded in 1995.

Index

Note: Page numbers in italic type refer to figures or tables.

F

I

N

O

P

Q

R

U

V